ISBN 978-2-84707-139-9
«Formula 1 Yearbook 2007-08» is also published
in French language under the title «L'Année Formule 1 2007-08» (ISBN 978-2-84707-133-7)

© December 2007, Chronosports S.A.

Le Vergnolet Parc, CH-1070 Puidoux, Suisse. Tel. : (+41 21) 694 24 44. Fax : (+41 21) 694 24 46.

E-mail: info@chronosports.com   Internet: www.chronosports.com

Printed in France by Imprimerie Clerc s.a.s., Rue de la Brasserie, F-18206 St-Amand Montrond.
Bound by Reliures Brun, F-45331 Malesherbes Cedex.
Clerc s.a.s. & Reliures Brun both are Qualibris companies.

Mario Renzi thanks for their technical support Carré Couleur, Nikon France, Picto Lyon, as well as Fuji Film France.
Special thanks Robert Rui, Jean-Philippe Lavergne, Nicolas Brunet, Bruno Paré and all the Clerc team.

FORMULA 1 YEARBOOK
2007-08

Photos
Mario Renzi
Laurent Charniaux / XPB Agency
Lukas T. Gorys
Darren Heath
Steve Domenjoz
WRI Agency

Editor
Luc Domenjoz

Page Layout
Loraine Lequint & Cyril Davillerd

Results and statistics
Cyril Davillerd

Drawings
Pierre Ménard

Gaps and lap charts
Michele Merlino

Translated by
Anthony Peacock

CHRONOSPORTS
EDITEUR

Photos (double pages):

Mario Renzi: 10-11; 20-21; 100-101; 118-119; 126-127; 158-159; 166-167; 182-183.

Laurent Charniaux: 84-85; 88-89; 96-97; 114-115; 142-143; 206-207.

XPB: 130-131.

Lukas T. Gorys: 150-151; 196-197.

Darren Heath: 44-45; 64-65; 76-77; 78-79; 92-93; 104-105; 110-111; 122-123; 146-147; 154-155; 162-163; 170-171; 174-175; 178-179; 188-189; 192-193; 200-201.

Steve Domenjoz: 136-137 & all the helicopter shots.

CONTENT

Foreword

" *T*here is no better way to celebrate Ferrari's 60th anniversary than to win both Formula 1 titles. Kimi Raikkonen's conquest of the drivers' championship and the Scuderia's victory in the constructors' championship has enriched what is already an exceptional record of achievement for Ferrari. Now we are up to 30 titles, divided equally amongst both drivers' and constructors' championships.

The 2007 season will stick in our memories as a year that was rich in emotions, with the action on the track being every bit as intense as the events off it. We started the year with a new management structure and of course a new driver. When Michael Schumacher decided to retire at the end of the 2006 season, and other key people with whom we had enjoyed a lot of success also decided to stand down, many people asked if we would be able to remain competitive.

Now we have the answer. Leaving aside the two world titles, we actually did better than last year - as the raw statistics show.

On the track, this season was marked out by a fierce duel against some very strong competitors. Yet obviously it was also affected by an act of disloyalty that left a bitter taste in our mouths. Thankfully the truth eventually came out, so there is no need to say anything more on the subject.

The final Grand Prix of the season in Brazil was the culmination of all the emotions we had experienced throughout the season. We scored a fantastic one-two there, which was born out of concerted teamwork and the two exceptional drivers we have in Kimi and Felipe.

Of course our result would not have been enough had our rivals not hit problems, but that was out of our hands. From our point of view, our mission was accomplished like clockwork.

We made a few mistakes with regard to reliability throughout the season, but we will analyse those problems over the winter in order to be perfectly competitive in 2008.

Each year shows us just how tough it is to stay at the top. The fact that Ferrari is fighting down to the final Grand Prix for the championship titles practically every year - with the exception of 2005 - only underlines what an extraordinary period we are privileged to experience at the moment, which will remain unique in Ferrari's history. "

Jean Todt
November 28, 2007

SEASON ANALYSIS

The winter tests pointed to Kimi Raikkonen as favourite. While the Finn eventually claimed the title, it was far from a walk in the park. We analyse the myriad twists and turns of the 2007 season..

A story of ups and downs...and a flat floor

At the start of the Australian Grand Prix, nobody could have predicted - even in their wildest fantasies - just what an extraordinary sequence of events would have unfolded throughout the 2007 season: a championship that would not be definitively concluded until a month after its final round.

Following the winter tests, Kimi Raikkonen seemed to be the odds on favourite for the championship. Ferrari was the only one of the big teams to have intimate knowledge of the Bridgestone tyre range, as Bridgestone - which Ferrari had worked with for years - now became Formula 1's exclusive tyre supplier.

At the time, only the real motor racing aficionados had heard the name Lewis Hamilton, McLaren's new young driver who had yet to contest his first Grand Prix. Many people found Ron Dennis's decision to hand over one of his cars to a complete rookie unusual, as McLaren is traditionally a team that has favoured experience. Of course Hamilton had just won the GP2 championship the year before - but that did not usually qualify a driver for a top-line drive with one of the leading teams.

It was clear that Lewis Hamilton was hiding something special - there's no way that Ron Dennis would have given him the drive otherwise - but how was he going to face up to the talents of Fernando Alonso, who was reputed (along with Kimi Raikkonen) to be one of the two best drivers in the

world? Lewis Hamilton would no doubt be very much in the shadow of Alonso all year. That's at least what Alonso believed, Ron Dennis reckoned and what Hamilton himself feared. Hamilton knew that he was in the role of race driver at the last minute, and only because there was nobody better available following Kimi Raikkonen's move to Ferrari at the end of 2006.

Back then, it was incomprehensible to think that Lewis Hamilton might be second in the World Championship at the end of 2007 in front of Alonso. While the two cars actually ended up equal on points, it was Hamilton who is classified in front of Alonso by virtue of his better results.

At the time as well it was impossible to imagine the sinister spy story that would rip apart Ferrari and McLaren and squat over the entire season like a malignant presence. The scandal reached epic proportions, threatening the very existence of one of the richest teams in Formula 1 and providing a soap opera that was discussed at nearly every workplace in Europe and beyond.

Nobody would have thought too that Fernando Alonso would end up in such a bitter divorce from his McLaren team, following an incredible series of exchanges and conflicts with Lewis Hamilton. As soon as Hamilton realised that he had the talent to do it, he was unwilling to wait for his first F1 title: a fact that must have displeased his two-time champion team mate.

By the time Alonso realised the danger, it was already too late. As a newcomer into McLaren himself, he had to fight somebody who was already part of the family. When Alonso realised that Hamilton was like a son to Ron Dennis, he felt betrayed and trapped: caught in a golden cage into which he had locked himself until 2009. There was confusion too: this was never how it was meant to be for him. And yet...

> Lewis Hamilton finished his first World Championship in second place, just one point behind Kimi Raikkonen. This was an achievement in itself, but the young Englishman broke several records en route - including that of the highest number of consecutive podiums for a rookie.

(->>>)

Back to Australia. After a five-month break over the winter the small world of Formula 1 reconvened in the Melbourne paddock; buoyed, as always at the start of the year, with enthusiasm.

By Sunday night, Lewis Hamilton had underlined his first achievement by finishing on the podium of his maiden Grand Prix and being faster than Fernando Alonso on occasions.

It was an agreeable diversion for the F1 community, but he certainly did not usurp Kimi Raikkonen from the role of title favourite. Raikkonen stamped his authority on the opening race, claiming pole position and victory with no apparent problems.

The Italian team's configuration made the car more sensitive to exactly the right set-up.

For the Finn though, it would be the end of the honeymoon period. His times in winter testing and his performance in Australia may have made him look unbeatable, but behind the scenes he was struggling. His sublime talent masked the difficulties in Melbourne but the truth was that he was finding it difficult to adapt himself to the Ferrari chassis.

His natural driving style based around oversteer clashed with Ferrari's long-wheelbase car, which had a tendency to understeer. As Jean Todt, the boss of the Scuderia acknowledged at the end of the year, the Italian team took several weeks to work out how exactly to give the Finn the sort of car that he really needed.

Worse was to follow though: at the end of the Australian Grand Prix McLaren asked the FIA for a rule clarification. In their opinion, the flat floor of the Ferrari was illegal (along with that of several other teams). Without wishing to spark off a string of

disqualifications at the very first race, the British team thought it best to simply notify the sport's governing body of their suspicions.

It would emerge later, of course, that McLaren knew exactly what they were doing. They were entirely aware of how Ferrari's flat floor worked thanks to information furnished to them by Nigel Stepney: a Ferrari employee turned traitor after he was promoted internally to a job he did not like.

Before the second round of the season - the Malaysian Grand Prix - the FIA published the clarification that McLaren requested. This meant that a number of engineers had to hurriedly re-design their cars: luckily there was a three-week break between the two opening rounds of the season that allowed them to do this. Sure enough, the teams turned up at Sepang with modified cars.

Of all the teams, it was Ferrari that seemed to suffer most from the change. Over the course of the winter, the F2007's designers had decided to stretch the wheelbase (the distance between the front and the rear axle). It was a bold move as most of the other designers from rival teams had gone in a completely different direction, opting to instead decrease the wheelbase.

The Italian team's configuration made the car more sensitive to exactly the right set-up. In order to work perfectly, the F2007 had to be as stable as possible through every corner and bump in the road. That was precisely the function of the flat floor, which somehow managed to even out the pitch and yaw movements during braking, acceleration and turn-in.

Suddenly, it seemed that these rule changes (or clarifications) had a profound effect on the competitiveness of the Ferrari chassis. Interesting too is the fact that Ferrari would probably have walked all over the championship had these modifications to the rules not been made.

McLaren was aware that asking for the clarification would have damaged Ferrari's chances, but they would have harboured little doubt that Ferrari would soon fight back. This was just a breathing space.

Throughout the year, the pendulum seems to swing

quite drastically from Ferrari to McLaren and back again. Often it would happen quite brutally from race to race, with seemingly no rhyme or reason to it. In actual fact this was again down to the flat floor (or its absence) on the Ferrari, which now struggled to adapt itself to circuits that were bumpy and uneven.

Monaco is a prime example, being a surface with several bumps where the surface changes frequently. That's the case throughout the lap and the red cars

(->>>)

∧
Having made a magnificent start to the season, Felipe Massa was completely dominated by Kimi Raikkonen from the French Grand Prix onwards - apart from Turkey. He finished fourth in the championship, 16 points behind his team mate.

<
It was a difficult championship for Fernando Alonso, who finished in third place - just one point behind the winner. As the season went on, the Spaniard became more and more isolated within the team. Conversely, McLaren became increasingly suspicious of a driver intent on betraying them. It was an impossible situation that could only lead to a bitter divorce between the two parties.

CHAMPIONSHIPS 2007

Drivers

1. Kimi Räikkönen	Ferrari	110
2. Lewis Hamilton	McLaren Mercedes	109
3. Fernando Alonso	McLaren Mercedes	109
4. Felipe Massa	Ferrari	94
5. Nick Heidfeld	BMW	61
6. Robert Kubica	BMW	39
7. Heikki Kovalainen	Renault	30
8. Giancarlo Fisichella	Renault	21
9. Nico Rosberg	Williams Toyota	20
10. David Coulthard	Red Bull Renault	14
11. Alexander Wurz	Williams Toyota	13
12. Mark Webber	Red Bull Renault	10
13. Jarno Trulli	Toyota	8
14. Sebastian Vettel	BMW 1 /// STR Ferrari	6
15. Jenson Button	Honda	6
16. Ralf Schumacher	Toyota	5
17. Takuma Sato	Super Aguri Honda	4
18. Vitantonio Liuzzi	STR Ferrari	3
19. Adrian Sutil	Spyker Ferrari	1
20. Rubens Barrichello	Honda	0
21. Scott Speed	STR Ferrari	0
22. Kazuki Nakajima	Williams Toyota	0
23. Anthony Davidson	Super Aguri Honda	0
24. Sakon Yamamoto	Spyker Ferrari	0
25. Christijan Albers	Spyker Ferrari	0
Markus Winkelhock	Spyker Ferrari	

Constructors

1. Scuderia Ferrari Marlboro		204
2. BMW Sauber F1 Team		101
3. ING Renault F1 Team		51
4. AT&T Williams		33
5. Red Bull Racing		24
6. Panasonic Toyota Racing		13
7. Scuderia Toro Rosso		8
8. Honda Racing F1 Team		6
9. Super Aguri F1 Team		4
10. Etihad Aldar Spyker F1 Team		1
11. Vodafone McLaren Mercedes		203

(<<<-)

> Jarno Trulli on the limit at the Sao Paulo circuit. Toyota's 2007 season was not up to the Japanese company's expectations. The team principal, Tomita-san, had aimed for victories before the season start - but in the end Toyota finished the championship sixth (or seventh if you count McLaren). Not only were there no wins, but there was not even a podium. Toyota has undoubtedly sealed the unenviable record of the most money spent per championship point in the history of Formula 1 !

The duel between Ferrari and McLaren was so intense that it was easy to forget that emotions ran just as high further down the field. Takuma Sato was overjoyed to finish the Spanish Grand Prix in eighth place and score a World Championship point. A month later in Canada the Super Aguri driver would do even better with a sixth place.
v

were absolutely nowhere. Another example was Montreal, with exactly the same situation and exactly the same problem for the Maranello squad. Not to mention Budapest or Monza.

On the flip side, on surfaces where the asphalt was as smooth and flat as a billiard table, the Ferraris were untouchable to the extent that the most common view of an F2007 was its rear wing disappearing into the distance. This was the case at Magny-Cours, Silverstone, Belgium and Interlagos - where the track had just been entirely resurfaced.

In any case, by the time he got to Sepang, the advantage held by Kimi Raikkonen in Australia had completely disappeared. He had struggled to get to grips with the chassis before at the best of times, but now with its redesigned floor he found it a real handful. Ever the professional, Kimi managed to limit the damage in Malaysia - but he wasn't happy. In practice Raikkonen was beaten by his team mate Felipe Massa, using his previous experience of Ferrari to good effect.

The diminutive Brazilian kept the upper hand over Kimi Raikkonen in Bahrain and Barcelona, where he took back-to-back pole positions and race wins. It only underlined just how much Raikkonen was in trouble with the car, as most observers (apart from a few Brazilians) rate him as a significantly bigger talent than Massa.

While Felipe Massa was racking up the points, Kimi Raikkonen was working away behind the scenes - particularly in private testing - in order to try to understand how to get the best out of his recalcitrant Ferrari F2007.

Kimi is determined, and step by step it started to come together. In June the Scuderia's development programme had a setback due to a windtunnel breakdown that stopped all aerodynamic development work for two weeks. That's an eternity in the world of Formula 1, where the teams use their wind tunnels 24 hours a day and seven days a week, alternating teams of aerodynamicists so that the work is non-stop...

July is when Kimi Raikkonen began to turn his season round. It was about time. After the United States Grand Prix (and another Lewis Hamilton victory), the Finn had a 26-point deficit to the World Championship leader. At this points in the season though, the Ferrari driver was beginning to lose all hope of winning the championship, with McLaren having emerged from three consecutive wins. At Magny Cours and Silverstone the Finn turned round the situation to his advantage and brought home two

emphatic victories. Even so, on both occasions pole position eluded him. Massa took the pole in France whereas it was Lewis Hamilton's turn in Britain in front of his home crowd. Finally though the package of Raikkonen and Ferrari was beginning to gel.

He did not always have it his own way though. At the Nurburgring he qualified on pole position, underlining his new found competitiveness. In the race the sudden rain storm drowned his chances of victory. Having been caught out by the amount of water he missed the pit lane entrance and went off a few hundred metres down the road. He would later

retire from the Grand Prix with a hydraulic problem. Hungary, a high-downforce circuit, did not suit the Ferraris. In Turkey Raikkonen finished just behind his team mate: everything was decided in qualifying when Massa took pole position. In Italy the Ferraris once more had to face a circuit that did not suit them, with its ancient asphalt and big curves. The Ferraris could only limit the damage and Kimi finished on the podium, in third place behind Lewis Hamilton. In Japan Raikkonen was not able to take advantage of the rain in order to make up ground on Hamilton. He finished third behind his compatriot Heikki Kovalainen, whom he

(->>>)

Spies like us…

The spy scandal between McLaren and Ferrari this year took on gargantuan proportions. It characterised all of the summer months providing yet another intriguing backdrop to the deterioration of the relationship between Fernando Alonso and Lewis Hamilton (see pages 18-19).

Nonetheless this is not the first spy scandal to hit motor racing. Back in 1914 the German driver Christian Lautenschlager, who had just won the French Grand Prix, found himself in England when the First World War broke out. The British government took advantage of the occasion to seize his Mercedes and send it to the workshops of Rolls Royce, where British engineers dissected the engine to draw inspiration for aircraft powerplants.

The most serious spying affair dates from 1977. At the time an American called Don Nicholls - who also happened to be a CIA agent - was in charge of the Shadow team. The team's engineer at the time, Tony Southgate, resigned in order to set up his own team, Arrows. Having only a few days before the start of the 1978 season Southgate had taken with him the drawings of the new Shadow DN9 in order to copy them. This became the Arrows A1. Don Nicholls did not take very kindly to this and filed a case at the High Court in London. The Court found in his favour and outlawed the Arrows A1.

The 1978 season ended up being dominated by the Lotus 79, the first F1 car with ground effect. It was a car that mystified most of the paddock and caused a few jealousies. One night before the Swedish Grand Prix a Lotus mechanic returned to the garage as he had forgotten something. As well as the missing item he found Maurice Philippe, Tyrrell's technical director, on all fours having a good look at the car !

A year later the Williams FW07 was unbeatable. In order to understand its secrets Lotus boss Colin Chapman sent his sporting director Peter Collins to measure the rear wing and suspension travel of the Williams.

When he received these instructions, Collins thought it was a joke at first - until Chapman barked: *"And if you don't*

come back with the information don't bother coming into work on Monday !"

Unfortunately just as Collins had found the Williams FW07, he was surprised by a Williams mechanic at the point when he was about to start measuring. At the time these situations were rarely brought out into the open. The Williams team didn't issue any formal complaint but at the next Grand Prix they presented Collins with a wooden ruler in front of the whole paddock. On it was inscribed: *"To be used in case of emergency but don't get caught….."*

Ferrari themselves have been implicated in fraud. At the 1980 German Grand Prix there technical director at the time, Harvey Postlethwaite, organised a late night raid on the Williams garage, which wasn't guarded. The Italian engineers spent all night taking photos and measuring the FW07B from all angles.

At the time this sort of gamesmanship was just the sort of thing that went on all the time in Formula 1. Nobody had really thought about the idea of intellectual property.

All that changed quite a long time ago and security is now a dominant feature of the paddock. These days every team has a small army of security guards that protect the cars and equipment all day and all night. Espionage is now limited to photographs and observation of the cars on the grid. This is one of the few times when the cars are revealed away from the safety of their pit garages and rival technical directors get the chance to see them at close quarters. A lot of useful information can be gleaned from just a casual look.

Teams often pay photographers to supply them with material that is interesting. At the 1997 Brazilian Grand Prix the British photographer Darren Heath put his camera into the footwell of the McLaren that David Coulthard had just retired by the side of the track. His photo, published by all the major magazines, revealed a third secret pedal on the McLaren for lateral braking. This allowed the driver to limit the braking on one side of the car in order to achieve a better turn-in to corners.

<
The BMW Sauber team put in a solid but discreet performance, finishing twice on the podium but never managing a win. Nonetheless they were there or thereabouts most of the time, finishing in the points with the regularity of a Swiss watch. At the end of the year, the Hinwil-based team scored 101 points and was runner-up in the championship (third if you count McLaren). The hardest part will be doing better next year.

(<<<-)
caught up just at the end of the race.

The Japanese Grand Prix was a disaster for Ferrari after the Scuderia made the wrong tyre choice. The team took the start on intermediate tyres whereas the rain did not stop and the wet tyres would have been the best choice.

The Scuderia Ferrari had made a camel fit through the eye of a needle.

By the end of the Japanese Grand Prix Lewis Hamilton's latest victory had virtually guaranteed him the championship title. With a 17 point deficit and two races left to run it was practically all over for Kimi Raikkonen. Hauling back those 17 points in two races would necessitate a win and a second place at minimum, but the McLarens were looking stronger and stronger. In order to stand any chance Raikkonen would have to hope that Lewis Hamilton scored next to no points. This looked unlikely considering that the McLaren driver had never been out of the top five all year (apart from at the Nurburgring when he was caught out by rain).

And yet the improbable became true. Lewis Hamilton became stuck in the gravel on his way into the pits in China while Kimi Raikkonen went on to win the race. The Englishman was unlucky in the extreme: Shanghai is the only circuit out of all 17 races held this year where there is a gravel trap on the way into the pits. In fact, many people asked why the gravel trap was there in the first place given that speeds there are so low.

So it was simply a pit full of sand that cost Lewis Hamilton the world championship. His team paid the price of pride, wanting to win the race at all costs when just a few points would have sufficed.

With Fernando Alonso having finished second in Shanghai, three drivers would go into the finale at Sao Paulo with a chance of winning the title. Lewis Hamilton was still favourite with a four point margin over Fernando Alonso, and a seven point margin over Kimi Raikkonen.

Hamilton's chances got even better when he qualified on the front row while his two rivals were on the second row. But once more, the young Briton was hit by bad luck. A gearbox problem but also an off-road excursion and an eccentric pit stop strategy meant that he only finished seventh: an unusual set of circumstances given his near faultless season up to that point.

When it came to it, Lewis and his team cracked under the pressure. Kimi Raikkonen made the most of it to take an imperious victory while his team mate Felipe Massa kept Fernando Alonso at bay. The Scuderia Ferrari had made a camel fit through the eye of a needle. Kimi Raikkonen would win the world title with 110 points against the 109 points of the McLaren drivers, after what was probably the most tense and extraordinary Grand Prix of the last decade. As Norbert Haug, Mercedes's competitions boss pointed out at the end of the Grand Prix: *"We've got two cars on 109 points each but that still doesn't make 110."*

In Formula 1 time never stands still. Drivers always think of the future. As soon as he had crossed the line and drunk the champagne Kimi Raikkonen would have already been thinking about 2008. The Finn knew he could do better in the future. Having grown accustomed to the ways of the Scuderia with

<
The whole world heard about Robert Kubica following his terrible accident at the Canadian Grand Prix. Thankfully he emerged unscathed, a deliverance for which he thanks the picture of Pope John Paul II placed inside his helmet. Popes do indeed have their uses.

a car that is now to his liking he should be a formidable competitor next year. The competition should also be a little easier in 2008. With Fernando Alonso having left McLaren he is unlikely to be in a car that is competitive. Now that his bad luck has finally deserted him Kimi Raikkonen can hope for more wins and titles in the future.

<
Flavio Briatore in deep discussion with Mario Thiessen. As well as the action on the track, there was plenty of activity on the sidelines as the teams discussed the renewal of the famous 'Concorde Agreement', which divides up the commercial revenue from Formula 1. Despite several meetings, no agreement was reached before the end of the season.

<
Tyres were a focal point of discussion in 2006, but the subject went quiet in 2007. A single supplier meant that all the teams had the same equipment, although Bridgestone decided that every car would have to run both the hard and the soft option tyre during the course of a race.
To tell the difference, a white band is drawn across the soft tyre - by hand with a special pen !

<<
"I reckon it's left after the swimming pool..."
For a team coming off the back of two World Championships, Renault's 2007 season was very disappointing. There were no wins to speak of and just one lucky podium.

> British Grand Prix. It's Kimi Raikkonen's second consecutive win and the real start of his title fight. Heading into the United States Grand Prix, the Finn was fourth in the championship with a 26-point gap to Lewis Hamilton

> v

On the podium in Brazil. Jean Todt's smile tells you just how much he thinks of his new World Champion, after an incredible race at Interlagos.
> v

It's the smile of a World Champion - which is a bit wider than his usual - from Kimi Raikkonen in Brazil. Next to him is his race engineer Chris Dyer, who used to be Michael Schumacher's engineer up until the end of last season.
v

Kimi Raikkonen: a worthy flying Finn

There are Formula 1 drivers - each as astonishing, temperamental and egotistical as each other. Then there's Kimi Raikkonen: a man who doesn't complain, who wields his steering wheel like an artist, but about whom we know very little.

The fact that he comes from Finland already says something though. The talent of Finnish rally drivers is well known. At the beginning of the 1980s Keijo (known as 'Keke') Rosberg was the first Finn to make it to the top in single-seaters and win the Formula 1 World Championship. After him, Mika Hakkinen pulled off the same feat on two occasions. Will Kimi Raikkonen do even better? From the outside, he seems even more focussed on his driving than either

of him. Keke Rosberg was a fantastic driver, good company but sometimes irritable, Mika Hakkinen was a lot let less loquacious as he got older, but Kimi? He takes reserve to a new extreme. Few drivers have succeeded in keeping themselves to themselves in the same way as Kimi Raikkonen.

The Finn's anodyne outward character compared to his prodigious turn of speed has made him something of an enigma. *"When I saw him drive for the first time in private testing, I knew straight away that I was looking at a World Champion,"* said Michael Schumacher in 2001 - before Raikkonen had even contested his first Grand Prix. It was a sign. With his speed and unnatural ability to find the best set-up, the Finn was the perfect driver. The only thing he was lacking was the ability to converse. Raikkonen's comments on most subjects rarely pass his self-imposed 10-second limit.

Whether he wins, loses or breaks down in sight of the chequered flag, Kimi retains his usual implacable expression - untouched by either a smile or a frown. In the paddock, his stoical isolation continues to astonish. Many people wondered what his reaction would be when he claimed the world title: his ultimate goal. The response came in Sao Paulo: a slightly wider smile than usual, if you looked carefully (see photo opposite). As Kimi Raikkonen

himself said when he stepped down from the podium, it wasn't going to change his life.

Penetrating his inner being is impossible to even his close friends. *"Kimi never says anything, that's true,"* said his father Matti at his son's first Grand Prix in 2001. *"Even when we're having dinner at home he tends to be silent!"*

Like most drivers, Kimi owes everything to the financial efforts of his parents, Matti and Paula. He was born in Espoo, a small town north of Helsinki. His father was a mechanic and made a small motorbike for Rami, his eldest son, and Kimi, the younger. Kimi was on that bike when he was aged just five and he soon progressed to karting. It rapidly became clear that the Finn had enormous talent and it wasn't long before he had moved onto Formula Renault. He drove the Renault Championship while he was doing military service, and the Finnish army was willing to give him leave provided he kept on winning races. One second place and he was back to barracks! Unsurprisingly, this system gave him ample motivation and worked brilliantly: he won the championship that year with seven wins out of 10 races.

Then Peter Sauber agreed to give Kimi a test in his F1 car. That was followed by another test, mainly thanks to the smooth talking of Kimi's manager.

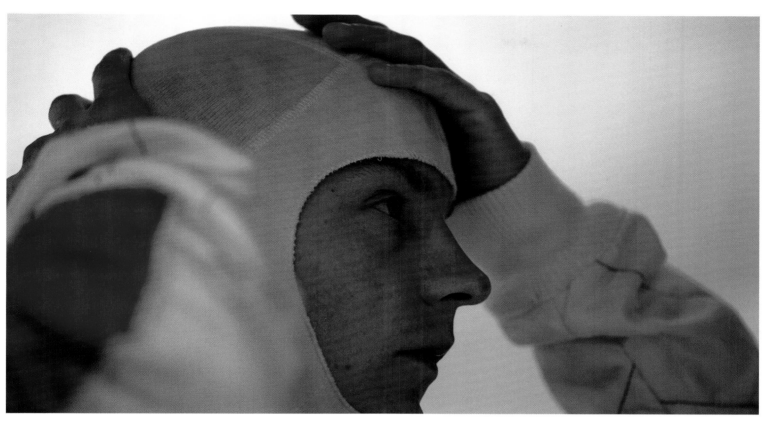

By now Sauber was convinced of Kimi's talent and he applied to the FIA for a special waiver to grant the young Finn a superlicence, which was needed to race in F1. The FIA were reluctant to do so, but in the end they agreed to a probationary period of four Grands Prix. It was a lot to ask: Kimi had only taken part in 12 single-seater races before his first F1 Grand Prix. Any mistakes in the first four races and his career would be over before it had even begun.

Luckily for him, he finished his first Grand Prix for Sauber with a sixth-place finish in the points. It was at Melbourne, a circuit he did not know, as he had never previously even been out of Europe before. Kimi took the Formula 1 world by storm. In September Ron Dennis signed him up to McLaren, paying Peter Sauber 35 million dollars for his contract.

In 2007, after five years at McLaren, Kimi Raikkonen moved to Ferrari. Following an early victory in Australia, Kimi then struggled to get on the pace of his team mate. In fact, it took him far longer to get used to his new team than he had bargained for.

"At the beginning, Kimi didn't like the car very much," said Ferrari team principal Jean Todt at the end of the season. *"The problem was that we didn't have enough history together to really know what would suit him."*

In any case, the problem was eventually solved. Having fought back from a deficit of 26 points to Lewis Hamilton before the United States Grand Prix in June, he finally managed to beat the Englishman to the title by one point after Brazil.

Kimi is married to Jenni - who was Miss Scandinavia in 2000 - and lives in Pfaffikon close to Zurich. That also says a lot about him. *"I like it there because Pfaffikon is just full of old people,"* he says. *"That makes life easy as nobody recognises me when I go to the shops."*

"I don't believe in luck. You only fail when you haven't worked hard enough to succeed."

Up until this year, Kimi Raikkonen had been the victim of spectacular misfortune. In 2003 and 2005 he had everything that was needed to win the world title with McLaren, but he failed on each occasion due to a succession of disastrous mechanical breakdowns.

In the last two Grands Prix of this year - particularly Brazil - Kimi's guardian angel seemed to be making up for lost time. Having started the Brazilian Grand Prix as the least favourite amongst the title protagonists, he finally captured the Holy Grail he had been searching for since the start of his career.

"I don't believe in luck," he said. *"You only fail when you haven't worked hard enough to succeed. I don't know if we call what happened today 'luck'. But whatever it's called, I'm going to take it!"*

The title won't change his personality though, as Kimi confirmed in his own inimitable style.

"Whether I'm champion or not won't change anything for me. Lots of people will probably write all sorts of shit about me, but I really don't care. In the past, criticism used to bother me but now it makes no difference. I'm not a sensitive person."

Nobody has ever seen Kimi angry - the man himself says he is incapable of getting wound up - but several people have seen him merry. Behind the ice man mask lurks the sort of party animal that is rapidly becoming an endangered species in F1. This is the man, don't forget, who was found dancing on a table in a London club displaying his assets. He is also one to haunt his hotel bar at the end of the season, dressed only a dressing gown and throwing bottles across the room in a stupor.

Ron Dennis, his boss at the time, took offence at this sort of behaviour and demanded that Kimi should behave himself. Jean Todt, his new boss at Ferrari, laughs at the attempts to discipline him.

"The Finns are drinkers, everyone knows that," he says. *"It doesn't stop them from winning Grands Prix."*

That's probably why Kimi is ultimately now happier at Ferrari than he was at McLaren. *"I feel a lot better this season,"* said the Finn. *"Ferrari is a very impressive family; I prefer to win the World Championship with them than with any other team."*

Now that he has shifted the weight of expectation off his shoulders and is as comfortable with the team as Michael Schumacher was in his day, Kimi Raikkonen can look forward to some more titles with serenity. That's his style anyway.

< Kimi with his wife Jenni. The Finn shares a stunning house near Zurich in Switzerland with the equally stunning former Miss Scandinavia. *"I can go out and do my shopping with no problems as nobody recognises me there,"* he says.

< Even in Japan, Kimi has his fans. He may be one of the more taciturn drivers but he is still incredibly popular with the spectating public. A lot of that is down to the fact that he drives a red car with a prancing horse on it…

> United States Grand Prix. Just as he had done a week earlier in Canada, Lewis Hamilton finishes in front of Fernando Alonso - claiming the upper hand within the McLaren team.

McLaren's annus horribilis

Nobody could quite remember the last time that there was such a poisonous atmosphere in the paddock. Between McLaren and Ferrari, the war was not just limited to the track. The conflict spilled over onto the sidelines as well. As summer came and the 'spygate' scandal hit the headlines, both McLaren and Ferrari personnel retreated to their respective motorhomes. McLaren did their best to cut their drivers off from the rest of the world: they were only allowed to speak to drivers in the presence of a team PR representative, and they even managed to wriggle out of the official press conferences to which they were invited.

The 'spygate' subject seemed to dominate every conversation, and the on-track action between Lewis Hamilton, Fernando Alonso, Felipe Massa and Kimi Raikkonen was almost relegated to a sideshow.

The whole thing of course could have been avoided if Ferrari had not decided last year to promote their chief mechanic Nigel Stepney to a role overseeing the test team. It was a function that took him away from the races and led to his dissatisfaction.

In fact, he was so upset that he was already looking for work elsewhere - and that is why he first got in touch with his old friend and colleague Mike Coughlan, a designer at McLaren.

In March, just before the season got underway, Stepney sent Coughlan the infamous e-mail setting out two elements of the Ferrari that he felt did not conform to the rules.

Mike Coughlan then informed McLaren's management, who then asked the FIA for clarification about the rules during the Australian Grand Prix. A few days later the FIA published the clarification requested, asking Ferrari (amongst other teams) to modify their flat floor in time for the next Grand Prix.

According to Ferrari McLaren therefore benefited from confidential information, without which it would not have gone to the FIA. This, maintained the Italian team, was a breach of the international sporting code - where article 151c forbids "any fraudulent conduct or any act prejudicial to the interests of any competition or to the interests of motor sport generally".

> Curiously, neither of the two protagonists were summoned by the FIA court or ordered to give evidence.

The story didn't stop there either. As the FIA judgement revealed (see pages 184 and 185), Nigel Stepney and Mike Coughlan has a long-running dialogue, with a constant flow of e-mails and text messages.

And that's where it gets complicated. According to Ron Dennis, Coughlan kept the dossier to himself "for his personal archive". He only showed some of the drawings to two McLaren employees who "did not pay them much attention".

On the face of it, it seems Dennis was lying. The Ferrari drawings were like a gift from God for the team: why pretend otherwise?

For Ferrari, it was incredibly bad news. The information now in McLaren's possession detailed how Ferrari calculated their race strategy - meaning that McLaren would easily be able to counter it.

Ultimately that is why the FIA imposed such a heavy penalty on the British team - and for a while it had seemed as if McLaren was about to be thrown out of the 2008 Championship as well. By deciding not to appeal, Ron Dennis's squad tacitly admitted its guilt.

Nonetheless, the whole affair could actually be a lot more complex than the mere facts that are detailed below. Because if McLaren benefited from Ferrari's confidential information then the opposite is likely to be true, say McLaren - Coughlan was probably passing information about McLaren's strategies to Stepney as well. Curiously, neither of the two protagonists at the heart of the scandal - Stepney and Coughlan - were summoned by the FIA court or ordered to give evidence. And like in all good stories, the presumed culprit Nigel Stepney hid himself away in Spain and declared his innocence as soon as the dirt started flying.

"The whole thing is a set-up against me," said Stepney through his lawyer. "It wasn't me who sent the dossier to Coughlan."

There are several grey areas. But you did not need to be Sherlock Holmes to work out that there was considerably more to this whole sordid affair than first met the eye. Spying has been part of everyday life in Formula 1 since the sport was invented.

> French Grand Prix. It's clearly every man for himself during the drivers' parade, a few hours before the race.

Ron Dennis, the McLaren team principal, says that the weeks between the eruption of the 'spygate' scandal on 3 July and the FIA World Council judgement on 13 September were the worst times of his life. It was very nearly the end of McLaren.
∨

Chronology

1. At the end of February, disgruntled Ferrari employee Nigel Stepney betrays his team and sends an e-mail to Mike Coughlan - McLaren's designer - with the drawings of the Ferrari F2007's flat floor.
2. Thanks to this information, McLaren obtains an immediate rule clarification from the FIA that penalizes Ferrari.
3. At the end of April, Stepney sends Coughlan a 780 page dossier detailing the settings of the Ferrari F2007 as well as some internal Ferrari procedures.
4. On 27 June, Mike Coughlan's wife Trudy takes the dossier to a photocopying shop in Woking. On the same day, the shop employee calls Ferrari to alert them to the fraud using a number he has found in the report.
5. On 3 July, Ferrari instigates legal action against Mike Coughlan. A search of his home uncovers the dossier.
6. On 5 July at Silverstone Ron Dennis promises that nobody at McLaren apart from Mike Coughlan was aware of the dossier.
7. The FIA gets involved. On 26 July, the World Council meeting decides that McLaren has breached article 151c of the sporting code, which governs the integrity of the sport. No punishment is given though due to lack of evidence. McLaren is warned that if new evidence emerges, they could be thrown out of not only the 2007 championship but also the 2008 series.
8. On 31 July, the Italian Automobile Club writes to Max

Mosley to express their outrage at the leniency of the verdict. They ask Mosley to put the case before the FIA Appeal Court so that Ferrari's arguments can be heard as well. Moseley agrees and sets the date of the appeal hearing for 13 September.
9. On 30 August, the new evidence brought by Ferrari convinces Mosley to cancel the judgement of 26 July and to start the procedure all over again. The new elements consist of an e-mail exchange between Pedro de la Rosa, McLaren's third driver, Mike Coughlan and Fernando Alonso.
10. On 13 September, the FIA sentences McLaren to a 100 million dollar fine and the loss of all constructor points earned during the 2007 season. Exceptionally, the drivers are allowed to keep their driver points.
11. A week later, at the appeal deadline, McLaren announces that it will not be appealing against the judgment.
12. McLaren emerges from the 2007 championship with zero points. Under normal circumstances it would have scored 203 points and lost the constructors' title by one point from Ferrari. Taking away the Hungarian Grand Prix penalty (where the team was not allowed to score the 15 points that it would otherwise have earned), McLaren would have scored 218 points at the end of the year and won the constructors' title.

Fernando Alonso's nightmare

It's strange how things can turn round so quickly. Before the first Grand Prix of 2007, nobody would have bet a thing on Lewis Hamilton finishing in front of Fernando Alonso at the end of the championship. After all, the Spaniard had been decorated with two world titles while the Englishman was a total rookie and just hoping to finish on the podium at least once during the year.

And yet... It didn't take Fernando Alonso too long to figure out that he had quite a task on his hands. As Lewis Hamilton hit his winning streak, Alonso felt himself becoming increasingly isolated within his own team. The antagonism reached the point where Alonso felt compelled to betray his team to the FIA - which cost McLaren all its points and 100 million dollars.

By the end of the season Alonso was almost a broken man, pushed to the sidelines. He knew that the team favoured Hamilton even though they refused to admit it and despite the fact that there was a special FIA scrutineer appointed during the Brazilian Grand Prix to ensure equal treatment. *"I don't think it's a secret that there's a difficult atmosphere in the team,"* said Alonso at Interlagos. *"I've heard that the team bosses think that I'm an enemy of the team and that's not very nice."*

The Spaniard's initial contract with McLaren ran to the end of 2009. However, experience has already shown that it is impossible and ill-advised to make a driver drive for a team against his will. A few days after the season was over, it was announced that McLaren and Alonso would go their separate ways. Alonso was at pains to emphasise that he did not have to pay any compensation in order to leave his contract early. This was despite the displeasure of McLaren's partners - especially Vodafone, Madrilena, and Santander - who had all come aboard knowing that a Spanish two-time champion was joining the team.

It was a sad end to a partnership that had promised so much at the beginning of the season. Before the typhoon called Lewis Hamilton had rushed in and knocked Alonso off his feet.

The Spaniard's problems essentially stemmed from having such a talented young Englishman alongside him in an English team - which he could never have guessed at when he originally signed his contract.

The fact is that Fernando Alonso will struggle to find a car as competitive as the McLaren. As well as hurting his feelings, the unfortunate 2007 season could well turn out to have hurt his Formula 1 career.

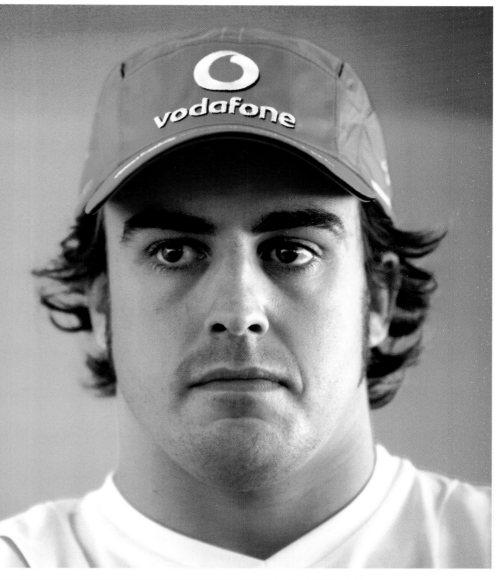

<
(left)
European Grand Prix. Fernando Alonso's last victory for McLaren during the time that he and Ron Dennis were still on good terms. Even though Alonso turned his back on Dennis on the podium.

(opposite)
As soon as things started to go wrong, in Monaco, Fernando Alonso was considering other options for 2008.

<
(left)
The two-time World Champion was full of enthusiasm before the first race of the season in Melbourne. And he carefully chose the books that he was going to autograph…

(opposite)
Raquel del Rosario, Fernando's wife, tried to support her husband during his miserable season. Alonso, however, has always refused to confirm their marriage.

THE ACTORS

These days, most of the big teams employ nearly a thousand people, all of whom are focussed on getting their two cars as high up the grid as possible at every Grand Prix. The drivers are just the tip of the iceberg - but they are in the eye of the storm. We meet the principal actors.

McLaren Mercedes

1 | Fernando ALONSO

DRIVER PROFILE

- Name — ALONSO DÍAZ
- Firstname — Fernando
- Nationality — Spanish
- Date of birth — 29ᵗʰ July 1981
- Place of birth — Oviedo (E)
- Lives in — Mont-sur-Rolle (CH) & Oxford (GB)
- Marital status — married to Raquel del Rosario
- Kids — -
- Hobbies — sports on tv, movies, computers
- Favorite music — Spanish groups
- Favorite meal — pasta
- Favorite drinks — mineral water
- Height — 171 cm
- Weight — 68 kg
- Web — www.fernandoalonso.com

STATISTICS

Grands Prix	105	Podiums	49
Starts	104	GP in the lead	48
Wins	19	Laps in the lead	1159
Pole positions	17	Km in the lead	5548
Fastest laps	11	Points scored	490

CAREER

2007	F1 McLaren-Mercedes, 109 pts, 3ʳᵈ
2006	F1 Renault, 134 pts, *World Champion*
2005	F1 Renault, 133 pts, *World Champion*
2004	F1 Renault, 59 pts, 4ᵗʰ
2003	F1 Renault, 55 pts, 6ᵗʰ
2002	F1 Renault, test driver
2001	F1 Minardi-European, 0 pt, 23ʳᵈ
2000	F3000 4ᵗʰ • F1 Minardi test driver
1999	F. Nissan Euro Series Champion
1998	Karting (E) Champion Inter-A
1997	Karting (E & I) Champion Inter-A
1996	Karting (E & World) Champion Jr.
1993-95	Karting (E) Champion Jr.
1984-92	Karting (E) Asturian Champion kids category

2 | Lewis HAMILTON

DRIVER PROFILE

- Name — HAMILTON
- Firstname — Lewis Carl
- Nationality — British
- Date of birth — 7ᵗʰ January 1985
- Place of birth — Stevenage (GB)
- Lives in — Geneva (CH)
- Marital status — single
- Kids — -
- Hobbies — playing guitar, remote-controlled machines
- Favorite music — R&B, Reggae, Hip-Hop
- Favorite meal — italian and chinese food
- Favorite drinks — orange juice
- Height — 174 cm
- Weight — 68 kg
- Web — www.lewishamilton.com

STATISTICS

Grands Prix	17	Podiums	12
Starts	17	GP in the lead	12
Wins	4	Laps in the lead	321
Pole positions	6	Km in the lead	1448
Fastest laps	2	Points scored	109

CAREER

2007	F1 McLaren-Mercedes, 109 pts, 2ⁿᵈ
2006	GP2 Series Champion
2005	F3 Euroseries Champion; F3 Masters Winner Zandvoort Pau & Monaco GP
2004	F3 Euroseries 5ᵗʰ; F3 Bahrain Superprix Winner
2003	F. Renault (GB) Champion
2002	F. Renault (GB) 3ʳᵈ; F. Renault EuroCup, 5ᵗʰ
2001	F. Renault Winter Series (GB), 5ᵗʰ
2000	Karting (EUR) Champion Formule A; World Cup, Champion; Elf Masters Bercy Winner
1999	Karting (I) Champion Intercontinental A; (EUR) Junior ICA, 2ᵗʰ
1998	Karting (EUR) Junior ICA
1997	Karting (GB) Junior Yamaha, Champion Super One
1996	Karting (GB) Cadet, Champion Sky TV Kart Masters & Champion 5 Nations
1995	Karting (GB) Cadet, Champion Super One & Champion STP

It was all supposed to be so easy for the double world champion. He was joining McLaren at just the right time, as the team came good and he would stroll to a trio of titles, handsomely helped by his able and charming young assistant, Lewis Hamilton. But McLaren bless 'em have always insisted on equality among its drivers and there was no Divine Right to number one status for the Spaniard. He was seriously rattled by the fact he was immediately outpaced by Hamilton and, by the time he had regained his composure on the driving front, the press kept lighting fires under his sense of security. He still drove very well at times, taking the same number of wins, four, as Hamilton, but on balance, the Englishman had the edge. At the time of writing, we do not know where Alonso will be next year. Wherever it is, he will be older, wiser and hopefully, ready to accept that he can be beaten by his team-mate. As for his recent boss, Dennis must be wondering why he ever told the media that he knew how to handle difficult driver pairings.

Simply amazing! Do we really need to go through all the superlatives that apply to Lewis Hamilton's rookie performance this year? Just look at the start of his first ever F1 race when he drove around the outside of Alonso at the first corner. Where does that sort of ability come from? His detractors say that never has a driver been so well prepared for F1 over a period of around a decade. But the boy still had to get the job done, even if he was in the best car. He was never off the podium for the first eight races, including his first win in Montreal. But in the end, he lost the title that was in his grasp through his own mistakes, especially in the final races. By the closing stages of the year he was coming under huge pressure from the media both at home and abroad, so it's not surprising something had to give. The sad side of the story is that he is moving to Switzerland, because he cannot deal with the demands of the public at home in England. It all seems slightly cynical as it is impossible to watch an evening of television in the UK without seeing Lewis on some show or other and now there are stories that one will be able to buy shares in the boy wonder, as well as being able to buy his autobiography. It is all a bit too much too soon.

Ron Dennis

Norbert Haug

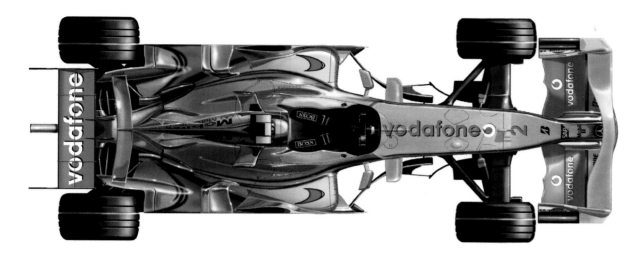

McLAREN MP4-22-MERCEDES
LEWIS HAMILTON
CANADIAN GRAND PRIX

SPECIFICATIONS

- Chassis — McLaren MP4-22
- Type — Monocoque moulded carbon fibre/aluminium honeycomb composite
- Suspensions (Front & rear) — inboard torsion bar/damper system operated by pushrod and bell crank with a double wishbone arrangement
- Shock absobers — Koni
- Transmission — McLaren longitudinal, sequential semi-automatic, with electronic control 7 speeds + reverse
- Clutch — Hand-operated
- Electronic ignition — McLaren Electronic Sytems
- Spark plugs / battery — NGK / GS Yuasa Corporation
- Engine — Mercedes-Benz FO 108T V8 (90°) of 95 kg
- Displacement — 2400 cm³
- Power — about 740 bhp
- Maximum revs — 19,000 rpm
- Valves — 32 valves pneumatic distribution
- Fuel / oil — Mobil unleaded / Mobil 1 products
- Brakes (discs) — Hitco ventilated carbon-fibre disc brakes
- Brakes (calipers) — Akebono
- Tyres — Bridgestone Potenza
- Wheels dimensions — 13"
- Wheels — Enkei ES-071
- Wheel base — not revelated
- Total lenght — not revelated
- Total width — not revelated
- Total height — not revelated
- Front track — not revelated
- Rear track — not revelated
- Weight — 605 kg, driver + camera + ballast

TEAM PROFILE

- Address — McLaren Technology Centre Cherstey Road, Woking, Surrey GU21 5JY Great Britain
- Telephone — +44 (0) 1483 711 117
- Fax — +44 (0) 1483 711 119
- Web — www.mclaren.com
- Founded in — 1963
- First Grand Prix — Monaco 1966
- Official name — Vodafone McLaren Mercedes
- Team Principal, Chairman et CEO, McLaren Group — Ron Dennis (GB)
- Chief Operating Officer, McLaren Group — Martin Whitmarsh (GB)
- General Director — Jonathan Neale
- Vice President, Mercedes-Benz Motorsport — Norbert Haug
- Managing Director, Mercedes-Benz — Ola Källenius
- Engineering Director — Paddy Lowe
- Design & Developpment Director — Neil Oatley
- Chief Designer — Mike Coughlan
- Head of Aerodynamics — Simon Lacey
- Chief Engineer MP4-22 — Pat Fry
- Chief Engineer MP4-23 — Tim Goss
- Head of Vehicle Engineering — Mark Williams
- Race Team Manager — Dave Ryan
- Operations Director — Simon Roberts
- Chief Mechanic — Steve Giles
- Race Engineer (1) — Mark Slade
- Race Engineer (2) — Phil Prew
- Press Officers — Ellen Kolby, Claire Barratt
- Number of employees — 540
- Partners Mercedes-Benz, Vodafone • (technologic) Exxon Mobil Corporation, Mobil 1, Bridgestone, BAE Systems, SAP • (corporate) Johnnie Walker, Aigo, Hugo Boss, Santander, Hilton, Schüco, TAG Heuer, Mutua Madrileña • (associate) Steinmetz • (official suppliers) Henkel Technologies, Nescafé XPress, FedEx, Kenwood, Sonax, Advanced Composites Group, Enkei, Akebono, Kangaroo TV, GS Yuasa, Mazak, BELTE, Sports Marketing Surveys, Sparco, SGI, Koni, Charmilles

STATISTICS

- Grands Prix — 630
- Wins — 156
- Pole positions — 133
- Fastest laps — 134
- Podiums — 418
- One-two — 44
- GP in the lead — 270
- Laps in the lead — 9217
- Km in the lead — 43358
- Points scored — 3148,5 (3159,5)

- Constructors' World titles — 8 (1974, 1984, 1985, 1988, 1989, 1990, 1991 & 1998)
- Drivers' World titles — 11 (1974: Emerson Fittipaldi, 1976: James Hunt, 1984: Niki Lauda, 1985, 86 & 89: Alain Prost, 1988, 90 & 91: Ayrton Senna, 1998 & 99: Mika Häkkinen)

POSITION IN CHAMPIONSHIP

1966	9th, 2 + ¹ pts	1977	3rd, 60 pts	1988	1st, 199 pts	1999	2nd, 124 pts
1967	10th, 3 pts	1978	8th, 15 pts	1989	1st, 141 pts	2000	2nd, 152 pts
1968	2nd, 49 +¹pts	1979	7th, 15 pts	1990	1st, 121 pts	2001	2nd, 102 pts
1969	4th, 38 (40)pts	1980	7th-, 11 pts	1991	1st, 139 pts	2002	3rd, 65 pts
1970	4th-, 35 pts	1981	6th, 28 pts	1992	2nd, 99 pts	2003	3rd, 142 pts
1971	6th, 10 pts	1982	2nd, 69 pts	1993	2nd, 84 pts	2004	5th, 69 pts
1972	3rd, 47 (49) pts	1983	5th, 34 pts	1994	4th, 42 pts	2005	2nd, 182 pts
1973	3rd, 58 pts	1984	1st, 143,5 pts	1995	4th, 30 pts	2006	3rd, 110 pts
1974	1st, 73 (76) pts	1985	1st, 90 pts	1996	4th, 49 pts	2007	Excluded
1975	3rd, 53 pts	1986	2nd, 96 pts	1997	4th, 63 pts		(203 pts)
1976	2nd, 74 (75) pts	1987	2nd, 76 pts	1998	1st, 156 pts		

2007 TEST DRIVERS

- Pedro DE LA ROSA (E)
- Gary PAFFETT (GB)

SUCCESSION OF DRIVERS 2007

- Fernando ALONSO (E) — the 17 Grands Prix
- Lewis HAMILTON (GB) — the 17 Grands Prix

What credibility can there be in a sport where, because of an intense dislike between two people, a team boss and a member of the sport's ruling body, a team can be fined one hundred million dollars and be wiped off the Constructors' classification? Without going into the rights and wrongs of the whole "Stepneygate" spy scandal, the incident has left a nasty taste in the mouth, when this year's racing was some of the best we have seen for years. And that was down to the season-long battle between Ferrari and McLaren. If the silver cars looked like winning everything it was because they had brilliant reliability, much improved on the past, especially on the engine side. McLaren also had an edge in qualifying, as its shorter (than Ferrari) car meant it could get those tyres working quicker. The MP4-22 was also great over the kerbs and on tight tracks, handing the advantage to its red rivals on tracks with longer corners. Therefore technically, there was little to stop them winning. But then came the politics and the team imploded. Ron Dennis tied himself in verbal knots trying to explain to the media how he was treating both his drivers equally, when he should have been keeping all this soul searching in house. Trying to deny that Alonso and Hamilton were at one another's throats was an act of crass stupidity, which left the team nowhere to go with the media. In the end, they lost the Drivers' crown because of stupid mistakes like leaving Hamilton out on tyres down to their canvas in China. If the relationship had been better the team could have got one driver to help the other take the crown, but in the end they divided and failed, allowing Raikkonen to sail through the middle. The team's general arrogance meant it got little sympathy from within the paddock. In fact, it was hard for people to stop laughing at the thought of the championship order in the paddock next year, when the gigantic Brand Centre "motorhome" will be wedged down the poor end of the paddock. And don't even begin to look at the facilities McLaren will have to deal with in Brazil!

Renault

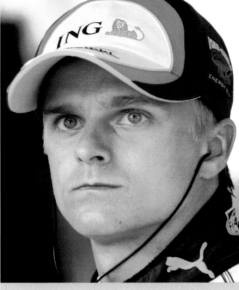

3 | Giancarlo FISICHELLA

DRIVER PROFILE

- Name — *FISICHELLA*
- Firstname — *Giancarlo*
- Nationality — *Italian*
- Date of birth — *14th January 1973*
- Place of birth — *Roma (I)*
- Lives in — *Roma (I) and Monaco (MC)*
- Marital status — *married to Luna*
- Kids — *daughter (Carlotta) & son (Christopher)*
- Hobbies — *football, tennis, stream fishing, pool*
- Favorite music — *Elton John, Madonna, Robbie Williams*
- Favorite meal — *pasta "bucatini alla matriciana"*
- Favorite drinks — *Coca-Cola and orange juice*
- Height — *172 cm*
- Weight — *66 kg*
- Web — *www.giancarlofisichella.com*

STATISTICS

• Grands Prix	196	• Podiums	18
• Starts	194	• GP in the lead	14
• Wins	3	• Laps in the lead	210
• Pole positions	3	• Km in the lead	1093
• Fastest laps	2	• Points scored	267

CAREER

2007 F1 *Renault, 21 pts, 8th*
2006 F1 *Renault, 72 pts, 4th*
2005 F1 *Renault, 58 pts, 5th*
2004 F1 *Sauber-Petronas, 22 pts, 11th*
2003 F1 *Jordan-Ford, 12 pts, 12th*
2002 F1 *Jordan-Honda, 7 pts, 11th*
2001 F1 *Benetton-Renault, 8 pts, 11th*
2000 F1 *Benetton-Supertec, 18 pts, 6th*
1999 F1 *Benetton-Supertec, 13 pts, 9th*
1998 F1 *Benetton-Mecachrome, 16 pts, 9th*
1997 F1 *Jordan-Peugeot, 20 pts, 8th*
1996 F1 *Minardi-Ford, 0 pt, 19th* • ITC *6th* • F1 *Ferrari tests*
1995 DTM *15°* • ITC *10°* • F1 *Minardi tests*
1994 F3 *(I) Champion; GP Macau Winner*
1993 F3 *(I) 2nd* • Karting *(EUR) 3rd*
1992 F3 *(I) 8th*
1991 Karting *(EUR) 2nd* • F. Alfa Boxer
1990 Karting *(World) 2nd*
1989 Karting *(EUR) 2nd; (World) 4th*
1984-88 Karting *(I) Minikart 60cc > Juniors 100cc > KIC 100cc*

4 | Heikki KOVALAINEN

DRIVER PROFILE

- Name — *KOVALAINEN*
- Firstname — *Heikki*
- Nationality — *Finnish*
- Date of birth — *19th October 1981*
- Place of birth — *Suomussalmi (FIN)*
- Lives in — *Oxford (GB)*
- Marital status — *single*
- Kids — *-*
- Hobbies — *skiing, cyclism, golf, viedo games*
- Favorite music — *Nightwish, rock*
- Favorite meal — *tomato pasta*
- Favorite drinks — *mineral water*
- Height — *172 cm*
- Weight — *66 kg*
- Web — *www.heikkikovalainen.net*

STATISTICS

• Grands Prix	17	• Podiums	1
• Starts	17	• GP in the lead	3
• Best result	1 x 2nd	• Laps in the lead	9
• Best qualif.	2 x 6th	• Km in the lead	40
• Fastest laps	0	• Points scored	30

CAREER

2007 F1 *Renault, 30 pts, 7th*
2006 F1 *Renault third driver*
2005 GP2 Series *2nd* • F1 *Renault tests*
2004 World Series by Nissan *Champion* • F1 *Renault tests* • *"Race of Champions" Winner*
2003 World Series by Nissan *2nd* • F1 *Renault & Minardi tests*
2002 F3 *(GB) 3rd*; GP Macau, *2nd*; F3 Masters, *4th*
2001 F. Renault *(GB) 4th*; F3 GP Macau, *8th*
2000 Karting *(FIN) FA, 2nd*; *(Scandinavia), FA Champion; (World) Formula Super A, 3rd*; *Elf Masters Bercy Winner*
1999 Karting *(FIN) FA, 2nd*; *(World) FA, 17th*
1991-98 Karting

Flavio Briatore

Pat Symonds

Alan Permane

Denis Chevrier

With Alonso defecting to McLaren and a rookie in the other car, "Fisico" was supposed to take on the mantle of Number 1 driver at Renault this year, but it was never going to happen. While he can show a finesse and style behind the wheel that is hard to match, the Italian could never be described as a leader of men. But while some might point at this attitude and say it reflects a lack of commitment, that is far from the truth. Fisichella tried his best and if the team occasionally managed to harness its experience to overcome poor performance, then Giancarlo could usually be relied on to bring the car home in the points. In Monaco, where the track demands a high level of skill combined with plenty of experience, we saw some of the old-style Fisi, as he qualified on the second row and brought the car home just shy of the podium in fourth place. It definitely did not help Giancarlo's cause that later in the year, his team-mate began to outshine him and on top of that, rumours that Alonso would, like the Prodigal Son, be welcomed back to the bosom of his Renault family in 2008 must have unnerved the likeable Roman.

Hard to believe now, but over the winter months before the season started for real, one topic for journalists bored with the endless hanging around of test sessions at the Spanish tracks was whether or not Heikki Kovalainen could be the new world champion! No, don't laugh. The Finn was driving for the team that had taken the title for the past two years, he had a blistering turn of speed and was reckoned to be a bright, intelligent and hard working lad. On top of that, unlike his famous Finnish compatriots such as Hakkinen and Raikkonen, Heikki actually liked to talk and was not averse to smiling. In a matter of months, the question was not about world titles but job titles: in other words, would he still have a job or would he be replaced before the end of the season by tester, Nelson Piquet Junior? Some disastrous early races could be put down mainly to the problems with the R27 which was behaving more unpredictably than a bunch of F1 Stewards. Gradually, both car and driver got better, until the rookie began to out-perform his team-mate. He first showed signs of what might be possible, driving from the back to fourth place in Canada. Finally, a podium appeared on the horizon, although actually it was impossible to see it through the bad weather. At the rain lashed Fuji circuit, a much more confident Kovalainen had a great dice with fellow Finn Raikkonen to take second place.

RENAULT R27
HEIKKI KOVALAINEN
ITALIAN GRAND PRIX

SPECIFICATIONS

• Chassis	Renault R27
• Type	Monocoque moulded carbon fibre/aluminium honeycomb composite
• Suspensions front	Carbon fibre top and bottom wishbones, inboard rocker/pushrod system, torsion bar and damper units
• Suspensions rear	Carbon fibre top and bottom wishbones vertically-mounted, torsion bars and horizontally-mounted damper on the top of the gearbox casing
• Shock absobers	Renault F1
• Transmission	seven-speed semi-automatic titanium gearbox + reverse gear, instantaneous gearchange system
• Clutch	not revelated
• Electronic ignition	Magneti Marelli Step 11
• Spark plugs / battery	Champion / Renault F1 Team
• Radiators	Secan / Marston
• Engine	Renault RS27 V8 (90°) of 95 kg
• Displacement	2400 cm³
• Power	more than 700 bhp
• Maximum revs	19,000 rpm
• Valves	32 valves pneumatic distribution
• Fuel / oil	Elf / Elf
• Brakes (discs)	Hitco ventilated carbon-fibre
• Brakes (calipers)	AP Racing
• Tyres	Bridgestone Potenza
• Wheels dimensions	13"
• Wheels	O.Z. Racing
• Wheel base	3100 mm
• Total lenght	4800 mm
• Total width	1800 mm
• Total height	950 mm
• Front track	1450 mm
• Rear track	1400 mm
• Weight	605 kg, driver + camera + ballast

TEAM PROFILE

• Address	Renault F1 UK	Renault F1 France
	Whiteways Technical Centre,	1-15, avenue du Pdt Kennedy
	Enstone, Chipping Norton,	91177 Viry-Châtillon
	Oxon OX7 4EE	France
	Great Britain	
• Telephone	+44 (0) 1608 678 000	+33 (0)1 69 12 58 00
• Fax	+44 (0) 1608 678 609	+33 (0)1 69 12 58 17
• Web		www.ing-renaultf1.com
• Founded in	1973	
• First Grand Prix	Great Britain 1977	
• Official name	ING Renault F1 Team	
• Renault F1 President	Alain Dassas > Bernard Rey	
• Managing Director	Flavio Briatore	
• Chassis Technical Director	Bob Bell	
• Executive Director of Engineering	Pat Symonds	

• Deputy Managing Director Technical (Engine) Rob White
• Deputy Managing Director Support Operations André Lainé

• Head of Engine Track Operations	Denis Chevrier
• Chief Race Engineer	Alan Permane
• Chief Designer	Tim Densham
• Assistant Chief Designer	Martin Tolliday
• Engine Project Managers	Léon Taillieu, Axel Plasse
• Sporting Manager	Steve Nielsen
• Chief Mechanic	Gavin Hudson
• Engineering Coordinator	Paul Seaby
• Race Engineer (3)	David Greenwood, Ricardo Penteado
• Race Engineer (4)	Adam Carter, Rémi Taffin
• Head of Communications	Jean-François Caubet
• Communications Manager	Patrizia Spinelli
• Number of employees	470 (GB) / 280 (F)

• Title Sponsor ING • Partners Elf, Hanjin Shipping, Bridgestone, Chronotech • Official suppliers 3D Systems, Altran, CD-adapco, Champion, Charmilles, DMG, Elysium, Eutelsat, Lancel, Lombardi, Magneti-Marelli, Network Appliance, OZ Racing, Processia Solutions, Puma, Tecnomatix, Vistagy, Xansa • iPartner Stellent Inc. • Technologic Phantom Works

STATISTICS

• Grands Prix	227
• Wins	33
• Pole positions	50
• Fastest laps	27
• Podiums	90
• One-two	2
• GP in the lead	82
• Laps in the lead	2424
• Km in the lead	11723
• Points scored	976

• Constructors' World titles	2
	(2005 & 2006)
• Drivers' World titles	2
	(2005 & 2006: Fernando Alonso)

POSITION IN CHAMPIONSHIP

1977 non classé	1982 3rd, 62 pts	2003 4th, 88 pts
1978 12th, 3 pts	1983 2nd, 79 pts	2004 3rd, 105 pts
1979 6th, 26 pts	1984 5th, 34 pts	2005 1st, 191 pts
1980 4th, 38 pts	1985 7th, 16 pts	2006 1st, 206 pts
1981 3rd, 54 pts	2002 4th, 23 pts	2007 3rd, 51 pts

2007 TEST DRIVERS

• Nelson PIQUET Jr. (BR)
• Ricardo ZONTA (BR)

SUCCESSION OF DRIVERS 2007

• Giancarlo FISICHELLA (I)	the 17 Grands Prix
• Heikki KOVALAINEN (FIN)	the 17 Grands Prix

It takes a really strong and well organised team to finish third in the Formula 1 World Championship and that is especially true if your car is, to put it bluntly, a dog. It was hard to understand just why the R27, which seemed so similar to its title-winning predecessor, was struggling to run in the midfield. If you had any aesthetic sensibilities, you would probably claim the team was being punished by the Gods for the car's revolting new paint scheme, which went with its new title sponsor, ING. This unfortunate name led to the Anglo Saxons in the paddock referring to it as that F***ING awful Renault! Would you believe, some of the performance shortfall was blamed on the Bridgestones (of course) but there was an element of truth in this. The problem was eventually traced to wrong aerodynamic data, most of it relating to the front of the car, which is exactly where more downforce was needed to make the Bridgestone work properly. You would have to say that losing their double world champion, Alonso and their tyre supplier, Michelin was also going to make life tough. The fact that the Anglo-French team simply does not have the huge resources enjoyed by Ferrari and McLaren did not help matters either. But, Renault is one of the best organised and run organisations in the paddock and the top men had seen it all before. This meant there never seemed to be much sense of panic, even in their darkest moments and the guys worked through the difficulties and, now that they know what went wrong, we can expect a real return to form in 2008, although at the time of writing, it is not yet known if their Spanish talisman, Fernando Alonso, will be back to lead them into battle.

Ferrari

5 | Felipe MASSA

DRIVER PROFILE

- Name — MASSA
- Firstname — Felipe
- Nationality — brasilian
- Date of birth — 25th April 1981
- Place of birth — São Paulo (BR)
- Lives in — Monaco (MC)
- Marital status — married to Rafaela
- Kids — -
- Hobbies — nautical skiing, football, cinema, music
- Favorite music — all, black music, hits
- Favorite meal — pasta, brasilian food, churrascaria
- Favorite drinks — champain of the podiums!
- Height — 166 cm
- Weight — 59 kg
- Web — www.felipemassa.com

STATISTICS

• Grands Prix	88	• Podiums	17
• Starts	87	• GP in the lead	14
• Wins	5	• Laps in the lead	456
• Pole positions	9	• Km in the lead	2201
• Fastest laps	8	• Points scored	201

CAREER

2007	F1	Ferrari, 94 pts, 4th
2006	F1	Ferrari, 80 pts, 3rd
2005	F1	Sauber-Petronas, 11 pts, 13th
2004	F1	Sauber-Petronas, 12 pts, 12th
2003	F1	Ferrari, test driver
2002	F1	Sauber-Petronas, 4 pts, 13th
2001		Euro F3000 Champion •
		F1 Sauber tests • FIA ETC • 24H Sicilia 2nd
2000		F. Renault (I) Champion • F. Renault Eurocup Champion
1999		F. Chevrolet (BR) Champion
1998		F. Chevrolet (BR) 5th
1990-97		Karting national and international level

6 | Kimi RÄIKKÖNEN

DRIVER PROFILE

- Name — RÄIKKÖNEN
- Firstname — Kimi Matias
- Nationality — Finnish
- Date of birth — 17th October 1979
- Place of birth — Espoo (FIN)
- Lives in — Pfäffikon (CH), Espoo (FIN)
- Marital status — married to Jenni
- Kids — -
- Hobbies — snowboard, skateboard, jogging
- Favorite music — U2, Darude, Bomfunk Mc, Eminem
- Favorite meal — mushrooms pasta, chicken
- Favorite drinks — pineapple juice, water and milk
- Height — 175 cm
- Weight — 71 kg
- Web — www.kimiraikkonen.com

STATISTICS

• Grands Prix	122	• Podiums	48
• Starts	121	• GP in the lead	44
• Wins	15	• Laps in the lead	850
• Pole positions	14	• Km in the lead	4207
• Fastest laps	25	• Points scored	456

CAREER

2007	F1	Ferrari, 110 pts, *World Champion*
2006	F1	McLaren-Mercedes, 65 pts, 5th
2005	F1	McLaren-Mercedes, 112 pts, 2nd
2004	F1	McLaren-Mercedes, 45 pts, 7th
2003	F1	McLaren-Mercedes, 91 pts, 2nd
2002	F1	McLaren-Mercedes, 24 pts, 6th
2001	F1	Sauber-Petronas, 9 pts, 10th
2000		F. Renault (GB) Champion; (EUR) • F1 tests Sauber
1999		F. Renault 3rd; "Winter Series" Winner
		Karting (FIN) FA, 2nd; (World) F. Super A, 10th
1998		Karting (FIN) FA, Champion; (Nordic) Champion;
		Super A (EUR) 2nd; Monaco Cup Super A, 3rd; (World) F. Super A
1997		Karting (FIN) Class Intercontinental A, Champion;
		(Nordic) Class Intercontinental A, 4th • KWC
1996		Karting (European Series, World, Nordic & FIN); FA, 4th
1995		Karting FA
1994-93		Karting (National) Class Raket, Finnish Cup
1988-92		Karting (National) Class A, B, C, Mini, Raket Jr.

The Boy From Brazil is a grown-up now and he was still in the title fight until just three races from the end of the season. Whereas Raikkonen never had much to say when asked about Michael Schumacher's current role with the Reds, Massa admitted that his former team-mate had been very helpful and he was usually keen to repeat this at press conferences just after he had beaten Raikkonen and those two McLaren lads. Charming, funny and occasionally outspoken, Felipe clearly felt at home with the Scuderia and equally clearly had plans to show Kimi whose team this was. And that feeling was not dented when the Finn won the first race of the year. However, of the two Ferrari's it was Felipe's that seemed to have the most mechanical problems and he also suffered the fiasco of not being refuelled during qualifying at the Hungaroring. It seemed at times, that once he had settled his tyre problems, Kimi had the slight edge in terms of speed, but the two men got on well and let's not forget that Raikkonen's final win in Brazil was given to him by Massa, who must have felt more willing to do so after he had signed a new long term contract with the Scuderia just a week or so earlier.

If four drivers were in the running for the crown this season, for most of the time, it looked like a two way scrap between the two team-hates at McLaren. But within sight of the Finnish line, the man who had said the least, but eventually won the most races, won the title. The Kimster did it and he deserved it. If people thought he would not fit in at all at Ferrari, after irritating the hell out of Ron Dennis, those people were missing one important fact. Jean Todt had a life before F1 and much of it was spent sitting next to very fast and very mad Finns in rally cars. The Ferrari boss knows all there is to know about getting the most out of Scandinavians and most of the time that means letting them do what they like when they are outside the car. This year we saw a relaxed, smiling and happy Kimi, even if he still didn't exactly have anything interesting to say. But you have to realise that an introverted Finn stares at his shoes while he talks to you and an extrovert Finn stares at your shoes. After winning the opening round in Melbourne, Raikkonen struggled a bit getting to grips with the Bridgestone, but he came back strongly in the second half of the season with Spa his most convincing demonstration. Anyone who enters snowmobile races under the name of James Hunt and turns up to take part in a boat race wearing a gorilla suit, is surely a truly worthy World Champion.

Jean Todt

Mario Almondo

Stefano Domenicali

Gilles Simon

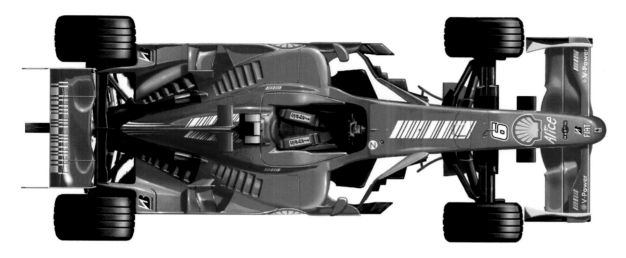

FERRARI F2007
KIMI RAIKKONEN
BRITISH GRAND PRIX

SPECIFICATIONS

- Chassis — *Ferrari F2007*
- Type — *Monocoque moulded carbon fibre/aluminium honeycomb composite*
- Suspensions (Front & rear) — *Independent suspension, push-rod activated torsion springs*
- Shock absobers — *Sachs*
- Transmission — *Semi-automatic sequential electronically controlled gearbox / quick shift 7 speeds + reverse*
- Clutch — *not revelated*
- Electronic ignition — *Magneti Marelli*
- Spark plugs / battery — *NGK / not revelated*
- Engine — *Ferrari Type 056 V8 (90°) of 95 kg*
- Displacement — *2398 cm³*
- Power — *more than 700 bhp*
- Maximum revs — *19,000 rpm*
- Valves — *32 valves pneumatic distribution*
- Fuel / oil — *Shell V-Power ULG 62 / Shell SL-0977*
- Brakes (discs) — *Brembo ventilated carbon-fibre*
- Brakes (calipers) — *Brembo*
- Tyres — *Bridgestone Potenza*
- Wheels dimensions — *13"*
- Wheels — *BBS*
- Wheel base — *3135 mm*
- Total lenght — *4545 mm*
- Total width — *1796 mm*
- Total height — *959 mm*
- Front track — *1470 mm*
- Rear track — *1405 mm*
- Weight — *605 kg, driver + camera + ballast*

TEAM PROFILE

- Address — *Ferrari SpA, Via A. Ascari 55-57, 41053 Maranello (MO), Italia*
- Telephone — *+ 39 (0)536 949 450*
- Fax — *+ 39 (0)536 949 049*
- Web — *www.ferrariworld.com*
- Founded in — *1929*
- First Grand Prix — *Monaco 1950*
- Official name — *Scuderia Ferrari Marlboro*
- President — *Luca Cordero di Montezemolo*
- Chief Executive Officer — *Jean Todt*
- Technical Director — *Mario Almondo*
- Sporting Director — *Stefano Domenicali*
- Race Technical Manager — *Nigel Stepney*
- Head of Chassis Design — *Aldo Costa*
- Engine Technical Director — *Gilles Simon*
- Technical Director - Trackside Operations — *Luca Baldisserri*
- Chief Designer — *Nikolas Tombazis*
- Engineering Consultant — *Rory Byrne*
- Head of Technical Dept — *Tiziano Battistini*
- Head of R&D — *Simone Resta*
- Head of Aerodynamics — *John Iley*
- Race Engineer (5) — *Rob Smedley*
- Race Engineer (6) — *Chris Dyer*
- Engine Manager (race) / (test) — *Mattia Binotto / Noël Cavey*
- Operations Manager (practice) — *Luigi Mazzola*
- Operations Director (race) — *David Lloyd*
- Press Officer — *Luca Colajanni*
- Number of employees — *900*
- Main Sponsor — *Philip Morris (Marlboro)*
- Partners *Fiat, Shell, Telecom Italia (Alice), Bridgestone, AMD, Martini, Acer, Mubadala* • Official suppliers *Brembo, Magneti Marelli, Mahle, OMR, Puma, SKF, Europcar, Finmeccanica, Infineon, Iveco, NGK, Sanbittèr, Tata Consultancy Services* • Suppliers *BBS, Microsoft, Sabelt, Selex Communications, Technogym, TRW*

STATISTICS

- Grands Prix — 758
- Wins — 201
- Pole positions — 195
- Fastest laps — 205
- Podiums — 603
- One-two — 76
- GP in the lead — 357
- Laps in the lead — 12490
- Km in the lead — 65166
- Points scored — 3804,5 (3851,5)

- Constructors' World titles — 15 (1961, 64, 75, 76, 77, 79, 82, 83, 99, 2000, 2001, 2002, 2003, 2004 et 2007)
- Drivers' World titles — 15 (1952 & 1953: Alberto Ascari, 1956: Juan Manuel Fangio, 1958: Mike Hawthorn, 1961: Phil Hill, 1964: John Surtees, 1975 & 1977: Niki Lauda, 1979: Jody Scheckter, 2000, 2001, 2002, 2003 & 2004: Michael Schumacher & 2007: Kimi Räikkönen)

POSITION IN CHAMPIONSHIP

Year	Pos	Year	Pos	Year	Pos	Year	Pos
1958	2nd, 40 (57) pts	1971	3rd , 33 pts	1984	2nd, 57,5 pts	1997	2nd, 102 pts
1959	2nd, 32 (38) pts	1972	4th, 33 pts	1985	2nd, 82 pts	1998	2nd, 133 pts
1960	3rd, 26 (27) pts	1973	6th, 12 pts	1986	4th, 37 pts	1999	1st, 128 pts
1961	1st, 40 (52) pts	1974	2nd, 65 pts	1987	4th, 53 pts	2000	1st, 170 pts
1962	5th *, 18 pts	1975	1st, 72,5 pts	1988	2nd, 65 pts	2001	1st, 179 pts
1963	4th, 26 pts	1976	1st, 83 pts	1989	3rd, 59 pts	2002	1st, 221 pts
1964	1st, 45 (49) pts	1977	1st, 95 (97) pts	1990	2nd, 110 pts	2003	1st, 158 pts
1965	4th, 26 (27) pts	1978	2nd, 58 pts	1991	3rd, 55,5 pts	2004	1st, 262 pts
1966	2nd, 31 (32) pts	1979	1st, 113 pts	1992	4th, 21 pts	2005	3rd, 100 pts
1967	4th *, 20 pts	1980	10th, 8 pts	1993	4th, 28 pts	2006	2nd, 201 pts
1968	4th, 32 pts	1981	5th, 34 pts	1994	3rd, 71 pts	2007	1st, 204 pts
1969	5th *, 7 pts	1982	1st, 74 pts	1995	3rd, 73 pts		
1970	2nd, 52 (55) pts	1983	1st, 89 pts	1996	2nd, 70 pts		

2007 TEST DRIVERS

- Luca BADOER (I)
- Marc GENÉ (E)

SUCCESSION OF DRIVERS 2007

- Felipe MASSA (BR) — the 17 Grands Prix
- Kimi RÄIKKÖNEN (FIN) — the 17 Grands Prix

It was bound to go wrong: after Martinelli and Byrne had moved on from engine and car design the year before, 2007 started with further disaster as Ross Brawn was taking a sabbatical, for a year or longer and horror of horrors, Michael Schumacher had retired, to be replaced by an indolent Finn. So that would explain why, for the first time in three years, the Scuderia won nine races and took nine poles on its way to winning the Constructors' and Drivers' titles, even if the former was handed to them before the end of the year. The only reason the Drivers' crown wasn't decided until the final race was the lack of reliability of the F2007, which let Massa down particularly badly. Apart from that, the guessed at advantage of being the only team to have previously used Bridgestones, who ran a monopoly on supply this year, did not materialise. In fact, the long wheelbase of the F2007 meant the red cars actually suffered more than most when it came to warming up the front tyres for that all important quick single lap in qualifying. Did the absence of Brawn and, whisper it, Nigel Stepney in the garage, have any effect? Well maybe, because there were a few more errors in the garage and the pit lane, but in the end, the team's tenacity, driven forward by Jean Todt, the last of the "old brigade" still standing, produced the result they wanted in Brazil. Involved in the spy scandal, the Scuderia drivers and race team seemed far more isolated from all this political nonsense than their opposite numbers at McLaren and ultimately that had to be a contributory factor to their success.

Honda

7 | Jenson BUTTON

DRIVER PROFILE

- Name   BUTTON
- Firstname   Jenson
- Nationality   British
- Date of birth   19th January 1980
- Place of birth   Frome, Somerset (GB)
- Lives in   Monaco (MC)
- Marital status   engaged to Florence
- Kids   -
- Hobbies   web surfing, video games, shopping
- Favorite music   Jamiroquai, Kool And The Gang, the 70'
- Favorite meal   curry, fish and pasta
- Favorite drinks   water and orange juice
- Height   183 cm
- Weight   68,5 kg
- Web   www.jensonbutton.com

STATISTICS

• Grands Prix	139	• Podiums	15
• Starts	135	• GP in the lead	13
• Wins	1	• Laps in the lead	104
• Pole positions	3	• Km in the lead	522
• Fastest laps	0	• Points scored	229

CAREER

2007	F1 *Honda, 6 pts, 15th*
2006	F1 *Honda, 56 pts, 6th*
2005	F1 *B·A·R-Honda, 37 pts, 9th*
2004	F1 *B·A·R-Honda, 85 pts, 3rd*
2003	F1 *B·A·R-Honda, 17 pts, 9th*
2002	F1 *Renault, 14 pts, 7th*
2001	F1 *Benetton-Renault, 2 pts, 17th*
2000	F1 *Williams-BMW, 12 pts, 8th*
1999	F3 *(GB) 3rd ; GP Macau, 2nd*
1998	F. Ford *(GB) Champion; F. Ford (EUR) 2nd;*
	F. Ford Festival Winner
1997	Karting *(EUR) Super A, Champion; Winter Cup, 2nd;*
	A. Senna Memorial Cup Winner-Suzuka
1996	Karting *(EUR) FA, 5th; (AMER.) 3rd; Coupe du Monde, 3rd*
1995	Karting *(I) Senior ICA, Champion; (Monde) FA, 3rd*
1994	Karting *(GB) Jr. TKM, 4th; (EUR+ITA) Intercontinental A Jr.*
1990-93	Karting *(GB) Open, 3x Champion; Jr. TKM, Champion;*
	(GB) Junior, 2x Champion
1989	Karting *(GB) Super Prix Winner*

8 | Rubens BARRICHELLO

DRIVER PROFILE

- Name   BARRICHELLO
- Firstname   Rubens Gonçalves
- Nationality   Brasilian
- Date of birth   23rd May 1972
- Place of birth   São Paulo (BR)
- Lives in   Monaco (MC)
- Marital status   married to Silvana
- Kids   two sons (Eduardo and Fernando)
- Hobbies   golf, karting, bowling
- Favorite music   pop, rock, Biagio Antonacci
- Favorite meal   pasta
- Favorite drinks   Red Bull
- Height   172 cm
- Weight   70 kg
- Web   www.barrichello.com.br

STATISTICS

• Grands Prix	253	• Podiums	61
• Starts	250	• GP in the lead	44
• Wins	9	• Laps in the lead	722
• Pole positions	13	• Km in the lead	3487
• Fastest laps	15	• Points scored	519

CAREER

2007	F1 *Honda, 0 pt, 20th*
2006	F1 *Honda, 30 pts, 7th*
2005	F1 *Ferrari, 38 pts, 8th*
2004	F1 *Ferrari, 114 pts, 2nd*
2003	F1 *Ferrari, 65 pts, 4th*
2002	F1 *Ferrari, 77 pts, 2nd*
2001	F1 *Ferrari, 56 pts, 3rd*
2000	F1 *Ferrari, 62 pts, 4th*
1999	F1 *Stewart-Ford, 21 pts, 7th*
1998	F1 *Stewart-Ford, 4 pts, 14th*
1997	F1 *Stewart-Ford, 6 pts, 14th*
1996	F1 *Jordan-Peugeot, 14 pts, 8th*
1995	F1 *Jordan-Peugeot, 11 pts, 11th*
1994	F1 *Jordan-Hart, 19 pts, 6th*
1993	F1 *Jordan-Hart, 2 pts, 17th*
1992	F3000 *3rd*
1991	F3 *(GB) Champion*
1990	GM Lotus series *Champion* • F. Vauxhall Lotus *11th*
1989	F. Ford 1600 *(BR) 4th*
1981-88	Karting *(BR) 5x Champion*

"What do you think of Lewis Hamilton?" Like all the other British drivers, this was the question Button was asked the most in 2007. How he remained polite in front of his inquisitors is a mystery. Maybe it had something to do with the large sums of money Honda is committed to putting in his bank account for the next few years. However, the Englishman's reputation remains intact as, every time it rained and car performance was less of an issue, he shone at the wheel. It will be interesting to see what his talent and Ross Brawn's skills can do in the new no-traction control era. Just remember the wet Nurburgring when he went from the back to ninth place in just one lap or Fuji where he got up to fourth place before colliding with Heidfeld in the zero visibility conditions. You can make up your answer to what Button, with eight years of disappointment under his belt, really thinks about Lewis Hamilton's first F1 season!

When Rubens lined up on the grid for the Brazilian GP, he was taking part in his 250th Grand Prix and this was going to be his last chance of 2007 to put his miserable statistic in the dustbin. Every year since his 1993 F1 debut, the Paulista has scored some points, but with none coming in Interlagos this year, he ended 2007 with a great big zero. This is man who has won nine grands prix and almost won a world title. Given that Barrichello has presumably not forgotten how to drive, it is clear that he just did not have the equipment to do anything. Towards the end of the year, he clearly had enough and when the Fuji Stewards investigated a possible overtaking move in practice under yellow flags, the Brazilian jokingly asked to be banned until the end of the season, adding that his team-mate, although not present, would agree to the same!

Yasuhiro Wada

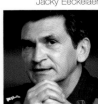

Nick Fry

Shuhei Nakamoto

Jacky Eeckelaert

HONDA RA107
JENSON BUTTON
FRENCH GRAND PRIX

SPECIFICATIONS

- **Chassis** — Honda RA107
- **Type** — Moulded carbon fibre and honeycomb composite structure
- **Suspensions (Front & rear)** — Wishbone and pushrod-activated torsion springs and rockers, mechanical anti-roll bar
- **Shock absorbers** — Showa
- **Transmission** — Honda F1 sequential, semi-automatic, hydraulic activation 7-speed + reverse, Honda internals
- **Clutch** — Alcon
- **Electronic ignition** — Honda PGM-IG / Honda PGM-FI
- **Spark plugs / battery** — NGK / 3Ah lead acid
- **Engine** — Honda RA807E V8 (90°) of 95 kg
- **Displacement** — 2400 cm³
- **Power** — more than 700 bhp
- **Maximum revs** — 19,000 rpm
- **Valves** — 32 valves pneumatic distribution
- **Fuel / oil** — ENEOS / ENEOS
- **Brakes (discs)** — Alcon ventilated carbon-fibre
- **Brakes (calipers)** — not revelated
- **Tyres** — Bridgestone Potenza
- **Wheels dimensions** — 13"
- **Wheels** — BBS
- **Wheel base** — not revelated
- **Total lenght** — 4700 mm
- **Total width** — 1800 mm
- **Total height** — 950 mm
- **Front track** — not revelated
- **Rear track** — not revelated
- **Weight** — 605 kg, driver + camera + ballast

TEAM PROFILE

- **Address** — Honda Racing F1 Team, F1 Team Operations Centre, Brackley, Northants NN13 7BD, Great Britain
- **Telephone** — +44 (0)1280 84 40 00
- **Fax** — +44 (0)1280 84 40 01
- **Web** — www.hondaracingf1.com
- **Founded in** — 1964
- **First Grand Prix** — Germany 1964
- **Official name** — Honda Racing F1 Team
- **Chairman, Honda Racing F1 Team** — Yasuhiro Wada
- **General Manager, Honda Motor Motorsports Division**
- **CEO, Honda Racing F1 Team** — Nick Fry
- **President, Honda Racing Development, Ltd.** — Hiroshi Abe
- **Senior Technical Director** — Shuhei Nakamoto
- **Technical Director Assistant** — Jörg Zander
- **Sporting Director** — Gil de Ferran
- **Race Team Manager** — Ron Meadows
- **Director of Strategy and Business Planning** — Otmar Szafnauer
- **Head of Aerodynamics** — Loïc Bigois
- **Chief Aerodynamic** — Mariano Alperin-Bruvera
- **Engineering Director** — Jacky Eeckelaert
- **Chief Race Engineer** — Craig Wilson
- **Senior Race Engineer (7)** — Andrew Shovlin
- **Senior Race Engineer (8)** — Jock Clear
- **Chief Mechanic** — Alistair Gibson
- **Press Officers** — Nicola Armstrong, Tracy Novak
- **Number of employees** — 360 (GB) / 370 (J)
- **Partners** Bridgestone, Celerant Consulting, ENEOS, Fila, Gatorade, NGK, NTN, Ray-Ban, Seiko, Universal Music Group
- **Technical partners** Alcon, Avaya, Haas Automation, Showa, Showa Denko Group, PerkinElmer, TÜV SÜD Automotive
- **Suppliers** +GF+ AgieCharmilles, Autoglym, Barco, Cablefree Solutions Ltd, CIBER UK, CYTEC, DAF Trucks, Endless Advance Ltd, Glasurit Automotive Refinish, HPC, IBM, Instron, Kyowa Electronic Instruments, Laverstoke Park, Lincoln Electric, MTS Systems, Matrix Communications, NCE, Oliver Sweeney, Pipex, Sandvik Coromant, STL Communications Ltd, Takata, Tripp Luggage • **Charity Partner** Helen & Douglas House

STATISTICS

- **Grands Prix** — 70
- **Wins** — 3
- **Pole positions** — 2
- **Fastest laps** — 2
- **Podiums** — 8
- **One-two** — 0
- **GP in the lead** — 10
- **Laps in the lead** — 104
- **Km in the lead** — 592
- **Points scored** — 140

- **Best classification in constructors' championship** — 4ᵗʰ (1967 & 2006)
- **Best classification in drivers' championship** — 4ᵗʰ (1967: John Surtees)

POSITION IN CHAMPIONSHIP

1964 9ᵗʰ, 0 pt	2006 4ᵗʰ, 86 pts
1965 6ᵗʰ, 11 pts	2007 8ᵗʰ, 6 pts
1966 8ᵗʰ, 3 pts	
1967 4ᵗʰ, 20 pts	
1968 6ᵗʰ, 14 pts	

2007 TEST DRIVERS

- Christian KLIEN (A)
- Mike CONWAY (GB)
- James ROSSITER (GB)

SUCCESSION OF DRIVERS 2007

- Jenson BUTTON (GB) — the 17 Grands Prix
- Rubens BARRICHELLO (BR) — the 17 Grands Prix

"It's the end of the world." "Jenson and Rubens have got the whole world on their shoulders." "My world just went up in smoke." "My world is spinning." These are just some of the awful puns that came out during the year, based on the fact Honda had decided to go all "green" on us, with a map of the world on their car, but forgot to build a chassis that could go round a race track. After coming on strong in 2006, giving Jenson Button his long-awaited maiden F1 victory, this was supposed to be a year of challenging for the title. Instead, it turned into probably one of the worst seasons any major player has ever had in the sport and it was a complete disgrace, which has put a deep and lasting stain on Honda's more than impressive past record in the sport as an engine supplier. We could give you all the technical reasons why the car was rubbish - the aero results were wrong as the wind tunnel was incorrectly calibrated, the engineers did not take note of what was happening on their computer screens or the test track, the car did not suit the Bridgestones, the entire aero package was flawed (Button did not even notice he'd lost the front wing after knocking it off in Japan!) and probably the sandwiches in the factory canteen were no good either. Truth is, the team was badly run, probably due to the departure of technical director Geoff Willis. Possible salvation came mid-November, when former Ferrari technical director Ross Brawn was appointed Team Principal.

BMW Sauber

9 | Nick HEIDFELD

DRIVER PROFILE

- Name — *HEIDFELD*
- Firstname — *Nick*
- Nationality — *German*
- Date of birth — *10th May 1977*
- Place of birth — *Moenchengladbach Rheydt (D)*
- Lives in — *Staefa (CH)*
- Marital status — *engaged to Patricia*
- Kids — *a daughter (Juni) & and a son (Joda)*
- Hobbies — *tennis, golf, motorcycle, music, cinema*
- Favorite music — *hits, Outkast*
- Favorite meal — *pasta, appetizers*
- Favorite drinks — *orange juice with sparkling water*
- Height — *165 cm*
- Weight — *59 kg*
- Web — *www.adrivo.com/nickheidfeld/*

STATISTICS

• Grands Prix	135	• Podiums	7
• Starts	132	• GP in the lead	3
• Best result	3 x 2nd	• Laps in the lead	4
• Pole positions	1	• Km in the lead	20
• Fastest laps	0	• Points scored	140

CAREER

2007 F1 *BMW, 61 pts, 5th*
2006 F1 *BMW, 23 pts, 9th*
2005 F1 *Williams-BMW, 28 pts, 11th*
2004 F1 *Jordan-Ford, 3 pts, 18th*
2003 F1 *Sauber-Petronas, 6 pts, 14th*
2002 F1 *Sauber-Petronas, 7 pts, 10th*
2001 F1 *Sauber-Petronas, 12 pts, 8th*
2000 F1 *Prost-Peugeot, 0 pt, 20th*
1999 F3000 *Champion* • F1 *McLaren tests*
1998 F3000 *2nd* • F1 *McLaren tests*
1997 F3 *(D) Champion; GP Monaco Winner* •
          F1 *McLaren tests*
1996 F3 *(D) 3rd; GP Macau, 6th; Masters Zandvoort, 3rd*
1995 F. Ford 1800 Inter *Champion* • F. Ford *(D) 2nd*
1994 F. Ford 1600 *(D) Champion*
1993 F. A Laval *(F)*
1992 Karting *(D) Junior, 5th*
1991 Karting ADAC Jr. Kart Trophy, *3rd;*
          World and European Championship
1986-90 Karting *(D)*

10 | Robert KUBICA

DRIVER PROFILE

- Name — *KUBICA*
- Firstname — *Robert*
- Nationality — *Polish*
- Date of birth — *7th December 1984*
- Place of birth — *Cracovia (PL)*
- Lives in — *Cracovia (PL)*
- Marital status — *single*
- Kids — *-*
- Hobbies — *karting, bowling, video games*
- Favorite music — *pop/rock*
- Favorite meal — *italian food*
- Favorite drinks — *orange juice*
- Height — *184 cm*
- Weight — *73 kg*
- Web — *www.kubica.pl*

STATISTICS

• Grands Prix	22	• Podiums	1
• Starts	22	• GP in the lead	2
• Best result	1 x 3rd	• Laps in the lead	6
• Best qualif.	1 x 4th	• Km in the lead	34
• Fastest laps	0	• Points scored	45

CAREER

2007 F1 *BMW, 39 pts, 6th*
2006 F1 *BMW, 6 pts, 16th*
2005 World Series by Renault *Champion* • F3 *GP Macau, 2nd*
2004 F3 Euro Series *7th*; F3 *GP Macau, 2nd*
2003 F3 Euro Series *12th*; F3 *Masters Sardaigne Winner*
2002 F. Renault 2000 *(I), 2nd*
2001 F. Renault 2000 *(I)*
2000 Karting *(EUR) Formule A, 4th; (Monde) Formule A, 4th*
1999 Karting *(I & D) Champion Junior ;*
          Monaco Trophy Winner
1998 Karting *(I) Champion Junior; (EUR) Junior, 2nd*
          Monaco Trophy Winner
1995-97 Karting *(PL) Champion Junior*

10 | Sebastian VETTEL

> SEE TORO ROSSO FERRARI

Mario Theissen

Willy Rampf

Beat Zehnder

Peter Sauber

Best of the rest? You betcha! Eight years in Formula 1 and the man known for having the silliest walk in the paddock, diverted attention from his legs this year, by consistently being the man whose name appeared fifth on the timing sheets after the quartet of McLaren and Ferrari drivers. He also diverted attention from his walk by growing the sort of beard that any American Redneck would be proud of! And at the end of the year, he was fifth in the title rankings, having visited the podium twice for a second place in Montreal and a third in Budapest. One gets the impression that little Nick might not be the most naturally gifted man on the grid, but he definitely works at his craft and he is not afraid of going wheel to wheel when it matters, although unfortunately in Sepang and Nurburgring the two BMW drivers went wheel to wheel a bit too harshly with one another. Consistency was what it was all about and throughout the year, the German lad only finished outside the points area on three occasions. If BMW continue to improve technically then 2008 could see Nick become a race winner at last.

While most people in the paddock were still arguing over how to pronounce his name - the sport's first Polish racer was busy making sure that, whatever the correct pronunciation, he was getting his name in the headlines. If you read this section of the book from beginning to end, you will get bored with the statement that such and such a driver, having come from Michelins in '06, found it hard to adapt to the Bridgestones this year. It was certainly true of Kubica, as the aggression at the wheel that suited the French rubber, did not sit well with the Japanese product. This meant that Heidfeld usually had the upper hand between the two of them and it is also fair to say that Lady Luck seemed to prefer the German driver to the Polish one. He always seemed to bounce back stronger than before. Bounce could be a poor choice of words, given how much of the Montreal scenery he bounced off. It was a straightforward misunderstanding that saw him collide with Trulli and then triggered the biggest crash that any driver has survived in the modern era of the sport. Kubica emerged with a sprained ankle. A week later, asked if had seen the accident on TV, he replied he had seen it twice, the first time "live!" A real character and still not that experienced, so we have not yet seen the best of him.

BMW SAUBER F1.07
NICK HEIDFELD
CANADIAN GRAND PRIX

SPECIFICATIONS

• Chassis	BMW Sauber F1.07
• Type	Carbon-fibre monocoque and honeycomb composite structure
• Suspensions (Front & rear)	Upper and lower wishbones, inboard springs and dampers, actuated by pushrods
• Shock absobers	Sachs
• Transmission	7-speed quick shift gearbox + reverse, longitudinally mounted, carbon-fibre clutch
• Clutch	AP Racing
• Electronic ignition	BMW
• Spark plugs / battery	NGK / not revelated
• Engine	BMW P86/7 V8 (90°) of 95 kg
• Displacement	2400 cm³
• Power	more than 700 bhp
• Maximum revs	19,000 rpm
• Valves	4 valves per cylinder pneumatic distribution
• Fuel / oil	Petronas / Petronas
• Brakes (discs)	Brembo ventilated carbon-fibre
• Brakes (calipers)	Brembo
• Tyres	Bridgestone Potenza
• Wheels dimensions	13"
• Wheels	O.Z. Racing
• Wheel base	3110 mm
• Total lenght	4580 mm
• Total width	1800 mm
• Total height	1000 mm
• Front track	1470 mm
• Rear track	1410 mm
• Weight	605 kg, driver + camera + ballast

TEAM PROFILE

• Address	BMW Motorsport - Sauber Wildbachstrasse 9 CH - 8340 Hinwil Switzerland
• Telephone	+41 (0)19 37 90 00
• Fax	+41 (0)19 37 90 01
• Web	www.bmw-sauber-f1.com
• Founded in	1970 (Sauber); 2006 (BMW)
• First Grand Prix	Bahrain 2006
• Official name	BMW Sauber F1 Team
• BMW Motorsport Director	Mario Theissen
• Technical Director	Willy Rampf
• Technical Director Powertrain	Markus Duessman
• Head of Track Engineering	Michael Krack
• Head of Aerodynamics	Willem Toet
• Cheef Designer	Jörg Zander (> Honda)
• Team Manager	Beat Zehnder
• Consultant	Peter Sauber
• Chief Mechanic	Urs Kuratle
• Race Engineer (9)	Andy Borme
• Race Engineer (10)	Giampaolo Dall'Ara
• Test Team Engineer	Ossi Oikarinen
• Number of employees	650
• Title Partner	Petronas
• Officials Partners	Intel, Credit Suisse, Dell, Puma
• Technicals Partners	Bridgestone
• Officials Suppliers	Ansys Fluent, Certina, Dalco, Dräxlmaier, DuPont, MAN, NGK, Walter Meier, Würth, ZF Sachs AG
• Promoting Suppliers	AS Elevators, Brütsch/Rüegger, W.L. Gore, Klauke Industries, Lista, Mitsubishi, MTS, Oerlikon Balzers

STATISTICS

• Grands Prix	35	
• Best result	1 x 2nd	
• Best qualification	1 x 2nd	
• Fastest laps	0	
• Podiums	4	
• One-two	0	
• GP in the lead	4	
• Laps in the lead	9	
• Km in the lead	49	
• Points scored	137	

• Best classification in constructors' championship
2nd (2007)

• Best classification in drivers' championship
5th (2007: Nick Heidfeld)

POSITION IN CHAMPIONSHIP

2006 5th, 36 pts
2007 2nd, 101 pts

2007 TEST DRIVERS

• Sebastian VETTEL (D)
• Timo GLOCK (D)

SUCCESSION OF DRIVERS 2007

• Nick HEIDFELD (D)	the 17 Grands Prix
• Robert KUBICA (PL)	16 Grands Prix (all except USA)
• Sebastian VETTEL (D)	1 Grand Prix (USA)

In the early days of Sauber, the Swiss team was often overlooked and forgotten, as it did not seem to fit into F1 very well and its performances were certainly nothing much to write home about. And to some extent, BMW-Sauber, the 2007 version, could also be forgotten, but this time, for all the right reasons. While other teams and their bosses seemed more intent on playing politics and trying to manipulate the media, Dr. "Super Mario" Theissen, simply gave his thin smile behind his thin-framed spectacles and got on with the job of running a team that continues to get better and better. It might not have been able to match McLaren and Ferrari, although it did get its white cars ahead of the Reds in Canada, but it was head and shoulders above the rest of the pack. The predominantly white livery on the F1 07 was very neat and simple and those two adjectives perfectly describe the way this team went about its business. The car might have lacked the sophistication of the top two teams but it was a good straightforward package for the engineers and drivers to work with and it even pioneered some aero ideas, being the first team to run the two and a half plane front wing. A total of 101 points is less than half what Ferrari scored, but this was a truly impressive team performance and there is no reason to think German-Swiss tandem won't be a serious threat in 2008. To say the team is sometimes forgotten is not entirely true, because one of the great attractions of their paddock area is the fact that their catering girls are dressed like nurses out of a 1970s soft-porn film!

Toyota

11 | Ralf SCHUMACHER

DRIVER PROFILE

- Name — *SCHUMACHER*
- Firstname — *Ralf*
- Nationality — *German*
- Date of birth — *30th June 1975*
- Place of birth — *Hürth-Hermühlheim (D)*
- Lives in — *Hallwang (Salzburg) (A)*
- Marital status — *married to Cora*
- Kids — *a son (David)*
- Hobbies — *karting, tennis, horsing, backgammon*
- Favorite music — *soft rock*
- Favorite meal — *pasta and Austrian food*
- Favorite drinks — *Apfel Schorler*
- Height — *178 cm*
- Weight — *73 kg*
- Web — *www.ralf-schumacher.de*

STATISTICS

• Grands Prix	182	• Podiums	27
• Starts	180	• GP in the lead	21
• Wins	6	• Laps in the lead	401
• Pole positions	6	• Km in the lead	1937
• Fastest laps	8	• Points scored	329

CAREER

2007 F1 *Toyota, 5 pts, 16th*
2006 F1 *Toyota, 20 pts, 10th*
2005 F1 *Toyota, 45 pts, 6th*
2004 F1 *Williams-BMW, 24 pts, 9th*
2003 F1 *Williams-BMW, 58 pts, 5th*
2002 F1 *Williams-BMW, 42 pts, 4th*
2001 F1 *Williams-BMW, 49 pts, 4th*
2000 F1 *Williams-BMW, 24 pts, 5th*
1999 F1 *Williams-Supertec, 35 pts, 6th*
1998 F1 *Jordan-Mugen Honda, 14 pts, 10th*
1997 F1 *Jordan-Peugeot, 13 pts, 11th*
1996 F3000 *(J) Champion* • GT *(J) 3rd* • *F1 McLaren tests*
1995 F3 *(D) 2nd*; *GP Macau Winner*
1994 F3 *(D) 3rd*
1993 F. BMW ADAC Jr. *2nd* • *F3*
1992 Karting *(D) 2nd* • F. BMW ADAC Jr.
1991 Karting *(D) Champion Jr.*; *NRW Cup Winner;*
Gold Cup Winner

12 | Jarno TRULLI

DRIVER PROFILE

- Name — *TRULLI*
- Firstname — *Jarno*
- Nationality — *Italian*
- Date of birth — *13th July 1974*
- Place of birth — *Pescara (I)*
- Lives in — *St Moritz (CH) & Pescara (I)*
- Marital status — *married to Barbara*
- Kids — *two sons (Enzo et Marco)*
- Hobbies — *musicc, cinema, karting, computers*
- Favorite music — *pop, rock, jazz, blues*
- Favorite meal — *pizza*
- Favorite drinks — *Coca-Cola, Fanta*
- Height — *173 cm*
- Weight — *60 kg*
- Web — *www.jarnotrulli.com*

STATISTICS

• Grands Prix	184	• Podiums	7
• Starts	181	• GP in the lead	10
• Wins	1	• Laps in the lead	147
• Pole positions	3	• Km in the lead	605
• Fastest laps	0	• Points scored	183

CAREER

2007 F1 *Toyota, 8 pts, 13th*
2006 F1 *Toyota, 15 pts, 12th*
2005 F1 *Toyota, 43 pts, 7th*
2004 F1 *Renault & Toyota, 46 pts, 6th*
2003 F1 *Renault, 33 pts, 8th*
2002 F1 *Renault, 9 pts, 8th*
2001 F1 *Jordan-Honda, 12 pts, 9th*
2000 F1 *Jordan-Mugen Honda, 6 pts, 10th*
1999 F1 *Prost-Peugeot, 7 pts, 11th*
1998 F1 *Prost-Peugeot, 1 pt, 15th*
1997 F1 *Minardi-Hart & Prost-Mugen Honda, 3 pts, 15th*
1996 F3 *(D) Champion*
1995 F3 *(D) 4th* • Karting *(I) Champion 100 FSA;*
"Ayrton Senna" World Cup Winner 100 FSA
1994 Karting *(World) Champion 125 FC;*
(EUR & North USA) Champion 100 FSA;
"Ayrton Senna" World Cup Winner 100 FSA
1993 Karting *(Monde) 100 SA, 2nd...*
1992 Karting *(Monde) 125 FC, 2nd*
1991 Karting *(Monde) Champion 100 FK*
1988-90 Karting *(I) Champion 100 National Class*
1987 Karting *Gold medal "Youth Games" Junior class 100*
1983-86 Mini-Kart

Tsutomu Tomita

John Howett

Pascal Vasselon

Richard Cregan

The last Schumacher standing was looking a bit wobbly on his feet in terms of F1 career prospects come the winter, as he did not so much wave goodbye to Toyota, but rather eased his way unnoticed out the door. Ralf knows how to win races, he has done it six times in total, but that all seems in the past now and his best finish of the year was a sixth place in Hungary. Of course, being in a Toyota doesn't help matters, but Ralf's driving style made matters worse as his high speed entry into corners did not suit the Bridgestones - thank goodness that in 2008, no one will be able to blame their tyres anymore! At the time of writing, the only Schumi in town reckons he will be racing in F1 next year, but there has already been controversy over a potential move to Force India, or whatever the old Jordan team is called today, because technical director, Mike Gascoyne, who worked with the German at Toyota, has threatened to resign if Ralf sits in one of his cars. What a great vote of confidence! However, Schumacher insists he enjoys racing and wants to continue. But as a driver who only seems to try his best when producing is going smoothly, will he find a team boss prepared to take a gamble or will he be racing in the DTM?

Poor Jarno. Ten years, a whole decade in Formula 1 and the Italian has so little to show for it. But is it really all a case of being in the wrong place at the wrong time? Because it is generally accepted that Jarno can be quick, especially in qualifying. It used to be said that while he could qualify, he could not race, but this no longer applies. It's just that he drives for Toyota, which means his car is most likely to be in shot on TV as he is being passed by a better package. He tended to out-perform his team mate in 2007, because at least he had the intelligence to make his driving style suit the way the car worked on its tyres. The Italian seems to cope well enough with his lack of success. No doubt the pay cheque, a loving family and a successful wine producing business all help to ease the pain of never having quite made it. The other side of the argument is that a truly great driver motivates his team and drives them along to push themselves harder to get results. This is something that Trulli cannot do and to be honest, not since Michael Schumacher has any driver seemed to exert that real level of power over a team that used to be commonplace in the days of Senna, Prost, Mansell and so on.

TOYOTA TF107
JARNO TRULLI
UNITED STATES GRAND PRIX

SPECIFICATIONS

• Chassis	Toyota TF107
• Type	Carbon-fibre monocoque and honeycomb composite structure
• Suspensions (Front & rear)	Carbon fibre double wishbone arrangement, with carbon fibre trackrod and pushrod
• Shock absorbers	Penske
• Transmission	Toyota/Williams F1 sequential, longitudinally mounted, semi-automatic /seamless 7-speed + reverse
• Clutch	not revelated
• Electronic ignition	Toyota / Magneti Marelli
• Spark plugs / battery	DENSO / not revelated
• Engine	Toyota RVX-07 V8 (90°) of 95 kg
• Displacement	2398 cm³
• Power	about 740 bhp
• Maximum revs	19,000 rpm
• Valves	4 valves per cylinder pneumatic distribution
• Fuel / oil	Esso / Esso
• Brakes (discs)	Hitco ventilated carbon-fibre
• Brakes (calipers)	Brembo
• Tyres	Bridgestone Potenza
• Wheels dimensions	13"
• Wheels	BBS Magnesium
• Wheel base	3090 mm
• Total lenght	4530 mm
• Total width	1800 mm
• Total height	950 mm
• Front track	not revelated
• Rear track	not revelated
• Weight	605 kg, driver + camera + ballast

TEAM PROFILE

• Address	Toyota Motorsport GmbH Toyota-Allee 7 50858 Köln-Marsdorf Deutschland
• Telephone	+49 (0) 223 418 23 444
• Fax	+49 (0) 223 418 23 37
• Web	www.toyota-f1.com
• Founded in	1999
• First Grand Prix	Australia 2002
• Official name	Panasonic Toyota Racing
• Chairman & Team Principal TMG	Tsutomu Tomita > Tadashi Yamashima
• President TMG	John Howett
• Executive Vice-President TMG	Yoshiaki Kinoshita
• Executive Vice-President TMC	Kazuo Okamoto
• Managing Officer TMC	Masayuki Nakai, Hisayuki Inoue
• Director Technical Co-ordination	Noritoshi Arai
• Senior General Manager Chassis	Pascal Vasselon
• Senior General Manager Engine	Luca Marmorini
• Team Manager	Richard Cregan
• Projects Managers	John Litjens, Mark Tatham
• Chef aérodynamicien	Mark Gillan
• Chief Engineer Race & Test	Dieter Gass
• Consultant	Frank Dernie
• Race Engineer (11)	Francesco Nenci
• Race Engineer (12)	Giancula Pisanello
• Chief Mechanic	Gerard Lecoq
• Number of employees	600
• Title Partner	Panasonic
• Partners	DENSO, BMC Software, Bridgestone, Dassault Systems, Ebbon-Dacs, EMC, KDDI, Kingfisher Airlines, Magneti Marelli, Time Inc., Alpinestars, DanTrim, Esprit, KTC, MAN, Nautilus Inc., Takata

STATISTICS

• Grands Prix	104
• Best result	2 x 2nd
• Pole positions	2
• Fastest laps	1
• Podiums	6
• One-two	0
• GP in the lead	5
• Laps in the lead	37
• Km in the lead	197
• Points scored	163

• Best classification in constructors' championship
        4th (2005)
• Best classification in drivers' championship
        6th (2005: Ralf Schumacher)

POSITION IN CHAMPIONSHIP

2002	10th, 2 pts	2005	4th, 88 pts
2003	8th, 16 pts	2006	6th, 35 pts
2004	8th, 9 pts	2007	6th, 13 pts

2007 TEST DRIVERS

• Franck MONTAGNY (F)
• Kohei HIRATE (J)
• Kamui KOBAYASHI (J)

SUCCESSION OF DRIVERS 2007

• Ralf SCHUMACHER (D)	the 17 Grands Prix
• Jarno TRULLI (I)	the 17 Grands Prix

Every year it's the same argument with the Publisher. He wants a review of the teams and drivers competing in Formula 1 and therefore I don't understand why I have to write about Toyota. Six years in the sport, the biggest budget, possibly the biggest team and no wins. If memory serves correctly, it became apparent several years ago now that the Communist way doesn't work anymore, but Toyota continue to insist on the "everyone is equal" theory, with design and decision making all done by committee. It might have worked seventy years ago for building tractors in the Ukraine, but it really is not the way forward when building Toyotas in Cologne. It is not the staff that is the problem, as engineering and management talent is there, it's just they are all working under the dark cloud of Toyota Japan. This year's TF107 was not that different to the previous year's car and suffered pretty much the same problems, such as lack of aerodynamic efficiency from its old fashioned design concept. The one thing that could be said is that, if all the F1 cars were painted the same colour, they would be very hard to tell apart, apart from the Toyota which looks like it was designed a generation ago, from its wishbone arrangements to its old style side pods.

Red Bull Renault

14 | David COULTHARD

DRIVER PROFILE

- Name   COULTHARD
- Firstname   David
- Nationality   British (Scotish)
- Date of birth   27th March 1971
- Place of birth   Twynholm (Scotland, GB)
- Lives in   Monaco (MC)
- Marital status   engaged to Karine Minier
- Kids   -
- Hobbies   Golf, swimming, cyclism, cinema
- Favorite music   Maroon 5, Scissor Sisters
- Favorite meal   pasta, thai food
- Favorite drinks   tea and mineral water
- Height   183 cm
- Weight   72,5 kg
- Web   www.davidcoulthard.co.uk

STATISTICS

• Grands Prix	229	• Podiums	61
• Starts	228	• GP in the lead	61
• Wins	13	• Laps in the lead	896
• Pole positions	12	• Km in the lead	4206
• Fastest laps	18	• Points scored	527

CAREER

2007   F1 Red Bull-Renault, 14 pts, 10th
2006   F1 RBR-Ferrari, 14 pts, 13th
2005   F1 RBR-Cosworth, 24 pts, 12th
2004   F1 McLaren-Mercedes, 24 pts, 10th
2003   F1 McLaren-Mercedes, 51 pts, 7th
2002   F1 McLaren-Mercedes, 41 pts, 5th
2001   F1 McLaren-Mercedes, 65 pts, 2nd
2000   F1 McLaren-Mercedes, 73 pts, 3rd
1999   F1 McLaren-Mercedes, 45 pts, 4th
1998   F1 McLaren-Mercedes, 56 pts, 3rd
1997   F1 McLaren-Mercedes, 36 pts, 3rd
1996   F1 McLaren-Mercedes, 18 pts, 7th
1995   F1 Williams-Renault, 49 pts, 3rd
1994   F1 Williams-Renault, 14 pts, 8th • F3000 9th
1993   F3000 3rd • F1 Williams tests • 24H du Mans Winner GT
1992   F3000 9th • F1 Benetton tests
1991   F3 (GB) 2nd; GP Macau & Marlboro Masters Zandvoort Winner
1990   F. Vauxhall-Lotus (GB) 4th • GM Lotus Euroseries 5th
1989   F. Ford 1600 (GB) Champion; F. Ford Festival 3rd
1986-88 Karting (Ecosse) Open Kart, 3x Champion;
         (GB) Super Kart 1, 2x Champion
1983-85 Karting (Ecosse) Junior, 3x Champion

15 | Mark WEBBER

DRIVER PROFILE

- Name   WEBBER
- Firstname   Mark Alan
- Nationality   Australian
- Date of birth   27th August 1976
- Place of birth   Queanbeyan (NSW-AUS)
- Lives in   Buckinghamshire (GB)
- Marital status   engaged to Ann
- Kids   -
- Hobbies   VTT, guided planes, PS2
- Favorite music   INXS, U2, "Red Hot", Pink, Oasis...
- Favorite meal   pasta, pizza, chocolate, ice cream & desserts
- Favorite drinks   apple juice, limonade & sparkling water
- Height   184 cm
- Weight   74 kg
- Web   www.markwebber.com

STATISTICS

• Grands Prix	105	• Podiums	2
• Starts	104	• GP in the lead	4
• Best result	2 x 3rd	• Laps in the lead	10
• Best qualif.	3 x 2nd	• Km in the lead	45
• Fastest laps	0	• Points scored	79

CAREER

2007   F1 Red Bull-Renault, 10 pts, 12th
2006   F1 Williams-Cosworth, 7 pts, 14th
2005   F1 Williams-BMW, 36 pts, 10th
2004   F1 Jaguar, 7 pts, 13th
2003   F1 Jaguar, 17 pts, 10th
2002   F1 Minardi-Asiatech, 2 pts, 16th
2001   F3000 2nd • F1 Benetton tests
2000   F3000 3rd • F1 Arrows & Benetton tests
1999   24H du Mans • F1 Arrows tests
1998   FIA-GT 2nd
1997   F3 (GB) 4th;Marlboro Masters Zandvoort, 3rd;GP Macau, 4th
1996   F3 (GB) 2nd • F. Ford Festival Winner; F. Ford Cup (EUR), 3rd
1995   F. Ford (AUS) 4th; F. Ford Festival, 3rd
1994   F. Ford (AUS) 14th
1993   Karting "King of Karting Clubman" Winner;
         Coupe Canberra Winner
1992   Karting (AUS) NSW & ACT Champion
1991   Karting (AUS) Junior

Shhh...Whisper it, but with the departure of Schumi, "DC" is now the oldest guy on the grid and he doesn't like the fact that people go on about it quite a bit, usually adding that it's strange he is driving for the team that is supposed to be getting down and dirty wid da kids! But the old boy still loves driving a grand prix car and he proved on several occasions that he deserves his place on the grid: in Bahrain he charged through the field from the back, in Spain he fought a car that had a gear or two missing and, as usual, he was fast in his "home" race, Monaco, although he had to deal with a grid penalty for getting in the way of Kovalainen. His best finish of the year came in Japan where he finished fourth while the less experienced boys threw themselves at the scenery in the atrocious conditions. He produced an autobiography this year, a sure sign that retirement cannot be too far away. The revelation from his book that seemed to cause the most interest was the fact that, as a lad, he suffered from Bulimia. Until then, the narrow minded F1 media had probably thought Bulimia was a country in Eastern Europe.

Joining Red Bull Racing after two frustrating years with Williams, the sport's only Aussie driver looked set for the good times at last. Most pundits reckoned he would thrash his teammate and given that his car would be powered by world champions Renault and designed by top techie Adrian Newey, there was plenty to be optimistic about. Unfortunately, this prognosis didn't take into account Webber's attraction to bad luck and the car's lack of reliability, which saw him retire seven times. Yes, he easily out-qualified Coulthard most of the time, but in the races, it was hard to tell which man did the best job. In fact, it was hard to tell which man was which, given that they could well pass themselves off as twins in terms of height, build and chiselled jaws. Webber drove a mature race in the rain affected European GP to take his and the team's best result when he finished third and in the typhoon conditions in Fuji he looked to be heading for a certain second place and maybe even the win, until Vettel crashed into him, ending both their races. To make matters worse, some of Japan's more exotic food options had made Mark so ill, he had to be sick in his helmet during the race! What the Australians call "talking down the porcelain telephone!"

Christian Horner

Adrian Newey

Geoff Willis

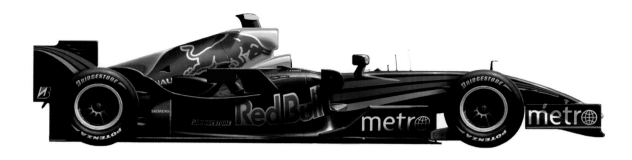

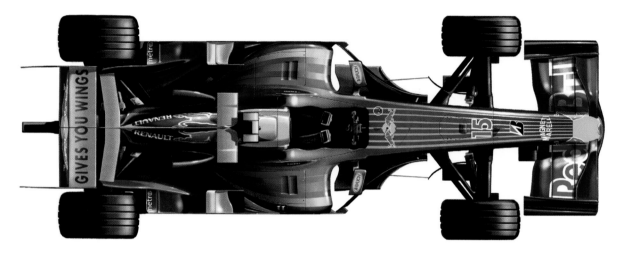

RED BULL RB3-RENAULT
MARK WEBBER
EUROPEAN GRAND PRIX

SPECIFICATIONS

• Chassis	Red Bull RB3
• Type	Carbon-fibre monocoque and honeycomb composite structure
• Suspensions (Front & rear)	Aluminium alloy uprights, upper and lower carbon wishbones and pushrods, torsion bar springs and anti-roll bars, multimatic dampers
• Shock absobers	Multimatic
• Transmission	Seven-speed gearbox, longitudinally mounted with hydraulic system for power shift and clutch operation
• Clutch	AP Racing
• Electronic ignition	Magneti Marelli & Pi
• Spark plugs / battery	Champion / Renault F1 Team
• Engine	Renault RS27 V8 (90°) of 95 kg
• Displacement	2400 cm³
• Power	more than 700 bhp
• Maximum revs	19,000 rpm
• Valves	32 valves pneumatic distribution
• Fuel / oil	Elf / Elf
• Brakes (discs)	Hitco ventilated carbon-fibre
• Brakes (calipers)	Brembo
• Tyres	Bridgestone Potenza
• Wheels dimensions	12.7"-13 (AV) / 13.4"-13 (AR)
• Wheels	AVUS Racing
• Wheel base	not revelated
• Total lenght	not revelated
• Total width	not revelated
• Total height	not revelated
• Front track	not revelated
• Rear track	not revelated
• Weight	605 kg, driver + camera + ballast

TEAM PROFILE

• Address	Red Bull Racing Bradbourne Drive, Tilbrook, Milton Keynes, MK7 8BJ Great Britain
• Telephone	+44 (0)1908 279 700
• Fax	+44 (0)1908 279 711
• Web	www.redbullf1.com
• Founded in	2005
• First Grand Prix	Australia 2005
• Official name	Red Bull Racing
• PDG Red Bull	Dietrich Mateschitz
• General Director	Helmut Marko
• Team Principal Red Bull Racing	Christian Horner
• Chief Technical Officer,	Adrian Newey
• Technical Chief Dept, RBT	Keith Saunt
• Technical Director, RBT	Geoff Willis
• Team Manager course, RBR	Jonathan Wheatley
• Head of R&D, Red Bull Technology	Andrew Green
• Head of Race and Test Engineering	Paul Monaghan
• Chief Aerodynamicist, RBT	Peter Prodromou
• Chief Designer, Red Bull Technology	Rob Marshall
• Aerodynamicist	Ben Agathangelou
• Race Engineer (14)	Guillaume Rocquelin
• Race Engineer (15)	Kieran Pilbeam
• Chief Mechanic	Kenny Handkammer
• Head of Communication	Eric Silbermann
• Press Officers	Katie Tweedle, Britta Roeske
• Number of employees	300
• Partners	Hangar-7, Renault, Quehenberger, Bridgestone, Metro, Mac Tools, Magneti Marelli, Siemens, Platform, MSC Software, Leica Geosystems

STATISTICS

• Grands Prix	53	• Best classification in
• Best result	1 x 3ʳᵈ	constructors' championship
• Best qualification	1 x 4ᵗʰ	5ᵗʰ (2007)
• Fastest laps	0	• Best classification in
• Podiums	2	drivers' championship
• One-two	0	10ᵗʰ (2007: David Coulthard)
• GP in the lead	4	
• Laps in the lead	8	
• Km in the lead	39	
• Points scored	74	

POSITION IN CHAMPIONSHIP

2005 7ᵗʰ, 34 pts
2006 7ᵗʰ, 16 pts
2007 5ᵗʰ, 24 pts

2007 TEST DRIVERS

• Robert DOORNBOS (NL)
• Michael AMMERMULLER (D)

SUCCESSION OF DRIVERS 2007

• David COULTHARD (GB)	the 17 Grands Prix
• Mark WEBBER (AUS)	the 17 Grands Prix

"Okay, you've had your fun, now show us what you can do." That phrase pretty much sums up the attitude of the world of F1 to the fizzy drink funsters. For the past two years, Red Bull had shaken up the sleepy F1 giant with its huge paddock hospitality area, its pretty girls, its irreverent Red Bulletin magazine and generally laid back approach. Old hands compared the impression it made to the early days of Benetton, a team which put aside the fun to start winning world titles. On paper, Red Bull should be capable of doing the same, requiring an outsize hat-rack in the factory cloakroom to accommodate the headwear of such large brained genii of the sport as Adrian Newey and Geoff Willis. While there were signs of improvement, there were definitely no championships nor even race wins, although Mark Webber came close in Japan until he was punted off the track by Toro Rosso's Sebastian Vettel. It was the Australian who scored the team's best result of the year, taking his first podium in the European GP. Poor reliability was the problem in the first part of the season, when the arrival of the team's press officer in the media centre would invariably be greeted with a chorus of "hydraulics?" Newey's aggressive aero-focussed packaging put a strain on cooling and this also affected the gearbox. Early in the year, Newey became suspicious about data coming out of the wind tunnel and his doubts were confirmed. This led to a swift re-design and much improved performance in the last third of the season. The Renault engine did the job, allowing them to outperform the "real" Renault team very often, although the engine supply deal was done so late in the winter, that packaging problems reared their head in the early stages. Expect a step forward in 2008.

Williams Toyota

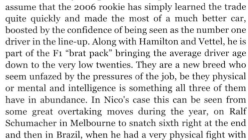

16 | Nico ROSBERG

DRIVER PROFILE

• Name	ROSBERG
• Firstname	Nico
• Nationality	German
• Date of birth	27th June 1985
• Place of birth	Wiesbaden (D)
• Lives in	Monaco (MC)
• Marital status	single
• Kids	-
• Hobbies	football, snowboarding, jet-ski
• Favorite music	3 Doors Down
• Favorite meal	vegetable pasta, chocolate cake
• Favorite drinks	Apfel Schorler
• Height	178 cm
• Weight	69 kg
• Web	www.nicorosberg.com

STATISTICS

• Grands Prix	35	• Podiums	0
• Starts	35	• GP in the lead	0
• Best result	1 x 4th	• Laps in the lead	0
• Best qualif.	1 x 3rd	• Km in the lead	0
• Fastest laps	0	• Points scored	24

CAREER

2007	**F1** Williams-Toyota, 20 pts, 9th
2006	**F1** Williams-Cosworth, 4 pts, 17th
2005	GP2 Series Champion • F1 Williams tests
2004	F3 Euro Series 4th • F1 Williams tests
2003	F3 Euro Series 8th • F1 Williams tests
2002	F. BMW ADAC (D) Champion • F1 Williams tests
2001	Karting (Monde) Super A
2000	Karting (EUR) FA, 2nd
1999	Karting (I) ICA Jr., 2nd; (EUR) ICA Jr., 4th
1998	Karting (North USA) Champion ICA Jr.
1997	Mini-Kart (F) Champion
1996	Mini-Kart (F) Champion Regional "Côte d'Azur"

17 | Alex WURZ

DRIVER PROFILE

• Name	WURZ
• Firstname	Alexander
• Nationality	Austrian
• Date of birth	15th February 1974
• Place of birth	Waidhofen Thaya (A)
• Lives in	Monaco (MC)
• Marital status	married to Julia
• Kids	three sons (Felix, Charlie & Oscar)
• Hobbies	VTT, Kitesurfing, climbing, skiing, canyoning
• Favorite music	Foo Fighters, Moby, Red Hot Chili Peppers
• Favorite meal	italian food
• Favorite drinks	Apfel Schorler
• Height	187 cm
• Weight	79 kg
• Web	www.alexwurz.com

STATISTICS

• Grands Prix	69	• Podiums	3
• Starts	69	• GP in the lead	0
• Best result	3 x 3rd	• Laps in the lead	0
• Best qualif.	4 x 5th	• Km in the lead	0
• Fastest laps	1	• Points scored	45

CAREER

2007	**F1** Williams-Toyota, 13 pts, 11th
2006	F1 Williams-Cosworth, third pilote
2005	**F1** McLaren-Mercedes, 6 pts, 17th
2001-2004	F1 McLaren-Mercedes, third pilote
2000	**F1** Benetton-Playlife, 2 pts, 15th
1999	**F1** Benetton-Playlife, 3 pts, 13th
1998	**F1** Benetton-Playlife, 17 pts, 7th
1997	**F1** Benetton-Renault, 4 pts, 14th • FIA GT
1996	24H du Mans Winner• FIA ITC 16th
1995	F3 (D) 6th
1994	F3 (D) 2nd
1993	F3 (A) Champion; (D) 13th
1992	F. Ford (D) Champion; International Cup Winner F. Ford; F. Ford 1600 (A) Champion
1991	F. Ford 1600 Jr. (A) 4th; F. Ford (A) 2nd; International Cup F. Ford, 2nd
1989-90	Karting (A) 2nd; (Middle East) 4th
1986	BMX World Champion

The young Rosberg apparently takes some notice of what the old Rosberg has to say, but Keke reckons he knows better than to try and give out driving advice. So, we must assume that the 2006 rookie has simply learned the trade quite quickly and made the most of a much better car, boosted by the confidence of being seen as the number one driver in the line-up. Along with Hamilton and Vettel, he is part of the F1 "brat pack" bringing the average driver age down to the very low twenties. They are a new breed who seem unfazed by the pressures of the job, be they physical or mental and intelligence is something all three of them have in abundance. In Nico's case this can be seen from some great overtaking moves during the year, on Ralf Schumacher in Melbourne to snatch sixth right at the end and then in Brazil, when he had a very physical fight with both BMWs to eventually come home in a fine fourth place, his best result of the year. Now, if only he could stop looking like a male model in a shampoo commercial, we might be able to take him more seriously next season, but rest assured he is still near the top of several teams' shopping lists for the future.

You've got to hand it to the Austrian and admire his determination to be a grand prix driver: three races in 1997, then full seasons in '98, '99 and 2000 and only one race in 2005, before landing the Williams seat for this season. Equally, one should admire his common sense in realising the time had come to hang up his helmet just before the final round. So, if even the man himself reckoned it was time to stop, how come he scored 13 points and finished on the podium in third spot in Canada? Always an analytical sort of guy, Alex realised that maybe he just did not have the pace anymore and his points and his podium this season came mainly from using eleven years experience to make the most of unusual situations. On top of that, he became a father for the third time just before the Chinese GP and wants to spend more time with his young family. Mind you, a few sleepless nights getting up for "baby" and he might be back on the job market soon!

Sir Frank Williams

Sam Michael

Rod Nelson

17 | Kazuki NAKAJIMA

DRIVER PROFILE

• Name	NAKAJIMA
• Firstname	Kazuki
• Nationality	japonaise
• Date of birth	11th January 1985
• Place of birth	Aichi (J)
• Marital status	single
• Hobbies	foot soccer, music
• Height	175 cm
• Weight	62 kg
• Web	www.kazuki-nakajima.com

STATISTICS

• Grands Prix	1	• Fastest laps	0
• Starts	1	• Podiums	0
• Best result	1 x 10th	• GP in the lead	0
• Best qualif.	1 x 19th	• Points scored	0

CAREER

2007	**F1** Williams-Toyota, 0 pt, 22nd • GP2 Series 5th
2006	F3 Euro Series 7th
2005	F3 (J) 2nd; GP Macau. 5th • Super GT GT300 Class 11th
2004	F3 (J) 5th
2003	F. Toyota Champion
1996-2000	Karting

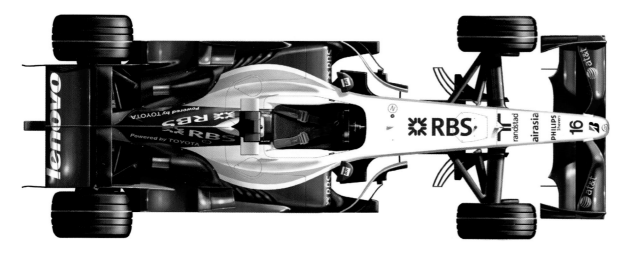

WILLIAMS FW29-TOYOTA
NICO ROSBERG
SPANISH GRAND PRIX

SPECIFICATIONS

• Chassis	Williams FW29
• Type	Carbon-fibre & aramide epoxy monocoque, honeycomb composite structure
• Suspensions (Front & rear)	Carbon fibre double wishbone arrangement, with composite toelink and pushrod activated torsion springs
• Shock absorbers	Williams F1
• Transmission	Williams F1 LG11 longitudinal, semi-automatic selection electro-hydraulically actuated "seamless" 7 speeds + reverse
• Clutch	not revealed
• Electronic ignition	Williams F1 & Toyota / Magneti Marelli
• Spark plugs / battery	DENSO / not revealed
• Engine	Toyota RVX-07 V8 (90°) of 95 kg
• Displacement	2398 cm³
• Power	about 740 bhp
• Maximum revs	19,000 rpm
• Valves	32 valves pneumatic distribution
• Fuel / oil	Petrobras / Petrobras
• Brakes (discs)	Carbon Industry
• Brakes (calipers)	AP Racing
• Tyres	Bridgestone Potenza
• Wheels dimensions	13", 350 mm (AV) / 375 mm (AR)
• Wheels	Rays Wheels magnesium
• Wheel base	3100 mm
• Total lenght	4500 mm
• Total width	950 mm
• Total height	1800 mm
• Front track	not revelated
• Rear track	not revelated
• Weight	605 kg, driver + camera + ballast

TEAM PROFILE

• Address	Williams F1 Team Grove, Wantage, Oxfordshire, OX12 0DQ - Great Britain
• Telephone	+44 (0)1235 777 700
• Fax	+44 (0)1235 777 739
• Web	www.williamsf1.com
• Founded in	1969
• First Grand Prix	Argentina 1975
• Official name	AT&T Williams
• President Director General	Sir Frank Williams
• CEO, Williams F1 Team	Adam Parr
• Director of Engineering	Patrick Head
• Technical Director	Sam Michael
• Chief Designer	Ed Wood
• Head of Aerodynamics	Jon Tomlinson
• Chief of Aerodynamics	Loïc Bigois (> Honda)
• Chief Operations Enginee	Rod Nelson
• Race Team Manager	Tim Newton
• Test Team Manager	Mike Condliffe
• Operating Manager	Alex Burns
• Marketing Manager	Scott Garrett
• Engineering Senior	John Russell
• Chief Mechanic	Carl Gaden
• Race Engineer (16)	Tony Ross
• Race Engineer (17)	Xevi Pujolar
• Press Officers	Liam Clogger, Claire Williams, Silvia Hoffer
• Number of employees	450
• Partners	AT&T, RBS, Lenovo, Philips, Petrobras, Accenture, AirAsia, Allianz, Bridgestone, Hamleys, ORIS, Randstad, Reuters, Battery, DeWALT, MAN, PPG, Puma, QinetiQ, Rays, SKF

STATISTICS

• Grands Prix	511	• Constructors' World titles	9
• Wins	113		(1980, 1981, 1986, 1987, 1992,
• Pole positions	125		1993, 1994, 1995, 1996 & 1997)
• Fastest laps	129	• Drivers World titles	7
• Podiums	294		(1980: Alan Jones,
• One-two	33		1982: Keke Rosberg,
• GP in the lead	216		1987: Nelson Piquet,
• Laps in the lead	7466	1992: Nigel Mansell, 1993: Alain Prost,
• Km in the lead	34637		1996: Damon Hill &
• Points scored	2539,5		1997: Jacques Villeneuve)

POSITION IN CHAMPIONSHIP

1975	9ᵗʰ, 6 pts	1984	6ᵗʰ, 25,5 pts	1993	1ˢᵗ, 168 pts	2002	2ⁿᵈ, 92 pts
1976	n.c., 0 pt	1985	3ʳᵈ, 71 pts	1994	1ˢᵗ, 118 pts	2003	2ⁿᵈ, 144 pts
1977	n.c., 0 pt	1986	1ˢᵗ, 141 pts	1995	2ⁿᵈ, 112 pts	2004	4ᵗʰ, 88 pts
1978	9ᵗʰ, 11 pts	1987	1ˢᵗ, 137 pts	1996	1ˢᵗ, 175 pts	2005	5ᵗʰ, 66 pts
1979	2ⁿᵈ, 75 pts	1988	7ᵗʰ, 20 pts	1997	1ˢᵗ, 123 pts	2006	8ᵗʰ, 11 pts
1980	1ˢᵗ, 120 pts	1989	2ⁿᵈ, 77 pts	1998	3ʳᵈ, 38 pts	2007	4ᵗʰ, 33 pts
1981	1ˢᵗ, 95 pts	1990	4ᵗʰ, 57 pts	1999	5ᵗʰ, 35 pts	
1982	4ᵗʰ, 58 pts	1991	2ⁿᵈ, 125 pts	2000	3ʳᵈ, 36 pts	
1983	4ᵗʰ, 36 pts	1992	1ˢᵗ, 164 pts	2001	3ʳᵈ, 80 pts	

2007 TEST DRIVERS

• Kazuki NAKAJIMA (J)
• Narain KARTHIKEYAN (IND)

SUCCESSION OF DRIVERS 2007

• Nico ROSBERG (D)	the 17 Grands Prix
• Alex WURZ (A)	16 Grands Prix (AUS > PRC)
• Kazuki NAKAJIMA (J)	1 Grand Prix (BR)

To finish first, first you have to finish, is one of the oldest racing sayings, but it is as true as ever today. Okay, so Williams never actually finished first, but then, unless it said Ferrari or McLaren on your car, third was the best you could hope for in a grand prix. But after an embarrassingly bad 2006 for what is the third most successful team in the sport, there were signs of the old Williams poking through the gloom this year. And much of that was down to the fact they had finally found some reliability again. Technical Director Sam Michael, with the backing of Patrick Head introduced some major changes on the personnel front to ensure that whatever the designers came up with in terms of a package, it would be run with maximum efficiency and reliability. The plan seems to have worked. One key element was the arrival of the Toyota engine and, how embarrassing, the customer team did much better than the factory team. But then that's not saying much, as my Granny's cat could run a tighter operation than Toyota. But at least they gave Williams an engine to play with nice and early so there was plenty of time to marry it to the chassis and get it running reliably. In fact, the year only saw three non-finishes for mechanical reasons.

Toro Rosso Ferrari

18 | Vitantonio LIUZZI

DRIVER PROFILE

- Name — LIUZZI
- Firstname — Vitantonio "Tonio"
- Nationality — Italian
- Date of birth — 6th August 1981
- Place of birth — Locorotondo (BA) (I)
- Lives in — Pescara (I)
- Marital status — single
- Kids — -
- Hobbies — girls, music, foot soccer, karting, fashion
- Favorite music — Rythm'n Blues, pop
- Favorite meal — pizza & pasta
- Favorite drinks — Coca-Cola, Red Bull
- Height — 178 cm
- Weight — 68 kg
- Web — www.liuzzi.com

STATISTICS

Grands Prix	39	Podiums	0
Starts	39	GP in the lead	0
Best result	1 x 6th	Laps in the lead	0
Best qualif.	2 x 11th	Km in the lead	0
Fastest laps	0	Points scored	5

CAREER

2007 F1 STR-Ferrari, 3 pts, 18th
2006 F1 STR-Cosworth, 1 pt, 19th
2005 F1 RBR-Cosworth, 1 pt, 24th
2004 F3000 Champion
2003 F3000 4th
2002 F3 (D) 9th; Inter. F3 • F3000 test drivers •
     F1 Williams test drivers
2001 Karting FIA-CIK, Champion • F. Renault (D) 3rd
2000 Karting (World) 6th; World Cup, 2nd;
     (World) 125cc, 3rd • F3 test drivers
1999 Karting (EUR); A. Senna Memorial Trophy Winner •
     F. Palmer Audi test drivers
1998 Karting (EUR) 3rd; (World).7th; F. Super A
1997 Karting (I) 2nd; (World) 7th; Brazilian Karting Prix Winner
1996 Karting (I) Champion
1995 Karting (I) 2nd; (EUR) 5th; (World) 2nd
1994 Karting (I) 2nd
1993 Karting (I) Champion
1991-92 Karting

The stylish Italian was reckoned to be "the next big thing" when he came into F1, but he has yet to show his true potential. It did not help that he realised early on that the team wanted to get rid of him and it probably did not help that his team-mate had a destabilising influence on the team. However, the arrival of the highly rated Vettel meant the Italian had someone to compare himself to and in this case there was not much between them and clearly, Liuzzi raised his game against the German, partly because that's the way life goes and partly because his professional F1 career was at stake. His best result was sixth in China, where he was on a less effective strategy than his team-mate. The sport needs colourful characters to add some light amid all the bland corporate drivers on the grid, so it will be a shame if Tonio does not find a seat for 2008.

19 | Scott SPEED

DRIVER PROFILE

- Name — SPEED
- Firstname — Scott Andrew
- Nationality — American
- Date of birth — 24th January 1983
- Place of birth — Manteca, CA (USA)
- Lives in — Scottsdale, AZ (USA)
- Marital status — single
- Kids — -
- Hobbies — cyclism, golf, skiing, climbing
- Favorite music — U2
- Favorite meal — jelly sandwich, peanuts butter
- Favorite drinks — Red Bull
- Height — 177 cm
- Weight — 67 kg
- Web — www.scottspeed.com

STATISTICS

Grands Prix	28	Podiums	0
Starts	28	GP in the lead	0
Best result	2 x 9th	Laps in the lead	0
Best qualif.	1 x 11th	Km in the lead	0
Fastest laps	0	Points scored	0

CAREER

2007 F1 STR-Ferrari, 0 pt, 21st
2006 F1 STR-Cosworth, 0 pt, 20th
2005 GP2 Series 3rd • F1 test drivers RBR
2004 F. Renault (D) Champion •
     F. Renault 2000 Eurocup Champion • IRL tests
2003 F3 (GB) 23rd
2002 F. Mazda (USA) • F. Barber Dodge (USA)
2001 F. Russell (USA) Champion
1993-2000 Karting (USA) several titles of Champion

The American racer was not as bad or as rude as people said he was. Hey, he's just American okay, that's the way they are. He had very strong opinions, knew exactly what he wanted from his car and thought he knew how to get it. However, even pre-season he had upset his team bosses and they might have sacked him even if he had won a race. His best result was a well judged drive to ninth on the driver's circuit that is Monaco. But he's gone now, this is F1, so let's move on.

19 | Sebastian VETTEL

DRIVER PROFILE

- Name — VETTEL
- Firstname — Sebastian
- Nationality — German
- Date of birth — 3rd July 1987
- Place of birth — Heppenheim (D)
- Lives in — Heppenheim (D)
- Marital status — single
- Kids — -
- Hobbies — VTT, swimming, snowboarding, fitness
- Favorite music — all
- Favorite meal — pasta
- Favorite drinks — Red Bull
- Height — 174 cm
- Weight — 64 kg
- Web — www.sebastianvettel.de

STATISTICS

Grands Prix	8	Podiums	0
Starts	8	GP in the lead	1
Best result	1 x 4th	Laps in the lead	3
Best qualif.	1 x 7th	Km in the lead	14
Fastest laps	0	Points scored	6

CAREER

2007 F1 BMW & STR-Ferrari, 6 pts, 14th •
     World Series by Renault 3rd
2006 F3 Euro Series 2nd; F3 Masters 6th • World Series by
     Renault 15th • F1 BMW. Sauber test driver
2005 F3 Euro Series 5th; F3 (E) 15th; F3 Masters 11th
2004 F. BMW ADAC (D) Champion
2003 F. BMW ADAC (D) 2nd
2002 Karting (EUR) ICA, 6th; (D) 10th
2001 Karting (EUR) Champion ICA Jr.; (D) Champion Jr.;
     Monaco Junior Cup & Paris-Bercy Winner
2000 Karting (D) Junior, 5th;
1995 Karting

This was a rollercoaster year for the German youngster who does not look old enough to drive and does not seem to have big enough muscles to lift up his crash helmet. However, there is no doubting his talent and he scored a point on his debut race, when he stood in for Kubica in the BMW-Sauber in Indianapolis. "This is certainly no BMW," commented Seb when he first drove the STR2 in Hungary, where he made another debut, this time his first drive with the Italian team. After Speed's aggressive manner in terms of working with the team, young Seb was regarded as a breath of fresh air and there was a definite sense of calm in the garage after his arrival. Once the car made some progress after the Spa test, he began to show why he is highly rated. He was heading for a fantastic podium in the hell of Fuji until he had that accident, running into the back of Webber. For about an hour, the young lad cried like a baby that he almost is, but after a few days in Tokyo he pulled himself together and took a genuine fourth place in China. The battle between the two Sebs - he is joined in 2008 by Sebastian Bourdais - should be a fascinating contest.

Dietrich Mateschitz

Gerhard Berger

Franz Tost

TORO ROSSO STR2-FERRARI
VITANTONIO LIUZZI
JAPANESE GRAND PRIX

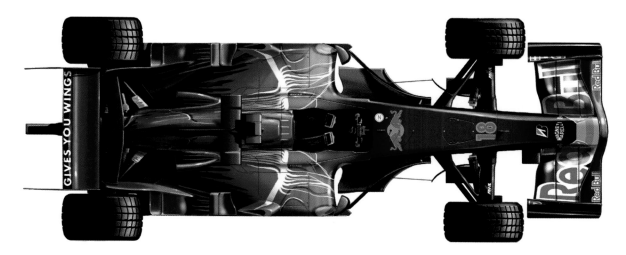

SPECIFICATIONS

• Chassis	Toro Rosso STR2
• Type	Carbon-fibre monocoque and honeycomb composite structure
• Suspensions (Front & rear)	Aluminium alloy uprights, upper and lower carbon wishbones and pushrods, torsion bar springs and anti-roll bars, multimatic dampers
• Shock absobers	Sachs
• Transmission	Semi-automatic sequential, longitudinally mounted, semi-automatic "seamless" hydraulic system, 7 speeds + reverse
• Clutch	AP Racing
• Electronic ignition	Magneti Marelli & Pi
• Spark plugs / battery	not revelated
• Engine	Ferrari Type 056 V8 (90°) of 95 kg
• Displacement	2398 cm³
• Power	more than 700 bhp
• Maximum revs	19,000 rpm
• Valves	32 valves pneumatic distribution
• Fuel / oil	Castrol / Castrol
• Brakes (discs)	Hitco ventilated carbon-fibre
• Brakes (calipers)	Brembo
• Tyres	Bridgestone Potenza
• Wheels dimensions	12.7"-13 (AV) / 13.4"-13 (AR)
• Wheels	AVUS Racing
• Wheel base	not revelated
• Total lenght	not revelated
• Total width	not revelated
• Total height	not revelated
• Front track	not revelated
• Rear track	not revelated
• Weight	605 kg, driver + camera + ballast

TEAM PROFILE

• Address	Scuderia Toro Rosso
	Via Spallanzani, 21
	48018 Faenza (RA)
	Italia
• Telephone	+39 (0)546 696 111
• Fax	+39 (0)546 620 998
• Web	www.scuderiatororosso.com
• Founded in	2006
• First Grand Prix	Bahrain 2006
• Official name	Scuderia Toro Rosso
• PDG Red Bull	Dietrich Mateschitz
• Co-owner	Gerhard Berger
• Team Principal	Franz Tost
• Technical Director	Alex Hitzinger
• General Director	Gianfranco Fantuzzi
• Engineer	Giorgio Ascanelli
• Chief Designer	Robert Taylor
• Team manager	Massimo Rivola
• Chief Engineer	Laurent Mekies
• Race Engineer (18)	Riccardo Adami
• Race Engineer (19)	John McGill, Graziano Michelacci
• Test Engineer	Stefano Sordo
• Head of Communication	Eric Silbermann
• Press Officer	Fabiana Valenti
• Number of employees	170
• Partners	Hangar-7, Amik Italia, Bridgestone, VolksWagen, USAG, Avus Wheels, Magneti Marelli

STATISTICS

• Grands Prix	35	• Best classification in constructors' championship	
• Best result	1 x 4th		7th (2007)
• Best qualification	1 x 8th		
• Fastest laps	0	• Best classification in drivers' championship	
• Podiums	0		14th (2007: Sebastian Vettel)
• One-two	0		
• GP in the lead	1		
• Laps in the lead	3		
• Km in the lead	14		
• Points scored	9		

POSITION IN CHAMPIONSHIP

2006   9th, 1 pt
2007   7th, 8 pts

2007 TEST DRIVER

• None

SUCCESSION OF DRIVERS 2007

• Vitantonio LIUZZI (I)	the 17 Grands Prix
• Scott SPEED (USA)	10 Grands Prix (AUS > EUR)
• Sebastian VETTEL (D)	7 Grands Prix (H > BR)

It was not looking good Scuderia Toro Rosso for much of the season with a possible fourth place for Tonio Liuzzi in Montreal ending in the "champions' wall" at the last corner with a handful of laps to go. There was acrimony and bitterness in the camp, as it was clear right from the start of the year that team bosses Gerhard Berger and Franz Tost wanted to get rid of both their drivers, Liuzzi and Scott Speed. After those two gentlemen shared a gravel trap on the opening lap of the European GP, a heated row between Tost and Speed ended with the two men nearly coming to blows in the garage. Tost ended up with the nickname "Cassius Clay" and Speed lost his drive, eventually landing a Red Bull drive in NASCAR. However, the arrival of the delightfully outspoken Giorgio Ascanelli as technical director - he had once been Berger's race engineer - signalled the start of some change for good. Heading into the final races it was clear the Ferrari-powered STR2 had found some pace and the arrival of Sebastian Vettel seemed to galvanise the team and spur on his team-mate, who by then knew his future lay elsewhere. In the floods of Fuji, Vettel was actually lying third with a few laps to go, but then, while running behind the Safety Car and thanks to some dubious moves from leader Hamilton, he ran into the back of the second placed man...who happened to be Webber from sister team Red Bull. A disaster! But it meant Liuzzi was now promoted to eighth and took a point, except he was found guilty of overtaking under yellow flags and lost it. Seven days later in Shanghai...salvation! Vettel fourth and Liuzzi sixth

Spyker Ferrari

20 | Adrian SUTIL

DRIVER PROFILE

- Name — *SUTIL*
- Firstname — *Adrian*
- Nationality — *German*
- Date of birth — *11ʰ janvier 1983*
- Place of birth — *Gräfelfing (D)*
- Lives in — *Munich (D)*
- Marital status — *single*
- Kids — *-*
- Hobbies — *piano, billiards rock, pop, Phil Collins*
- Favorite music
- Favorite meal — *italian food*
- Favorite drinks — *Coca-Cola*
- Height — *183 cm*
- Weight — *75 kg*
- Web — *www.adriansutil.com*

STATISTICS

- Grands Prix — 17 • Podiums — 0
- Starts — 17 • GP in the lead — 0
- Best result — 1x8ʰ • Laps in the lead — 0
- Best qualif. — 3x19ʰ • Km in the lead — 0
- Fastest laps — 0 • Points scored — 1

CAREER

2007 F1 *Spyker-Ferrari, 1 pt, 19ʰ*
2006 F3 *(J) Champion; GP Macau, 3ʳᵈ •*
 F1 Midland tests drivers
2005 F3 *Euroseries 2ⁿᵈ; Marlboro Masters*
 Zandvoort, 2ⁿᵈ • A1GP 15ʰ
2004 F3 *Euroseries 17ʰ*
2003 F. *ADAC BMW (D), 6ʰ*
2002 F. *Ford 1800 (CH) Champion*
2001 *Karting (EUR)*
2000 *Karting (D) ICA, 3ʳᵈ*

Colin Kolles

Michiel Mol

The young German scored one point this year, or rather he won it in the courts when Liuzzi was disqualified from eighth place in the Japanese Grand Prix. Many experts reckon it is the first of many points Lewis Hamilton's best mate in the paddock will score in Formula 1 in the future. Spa is always a good test of a driver and in Belgium, Sutil went from 19th to 12th on the opening lap, admittedly with the benefit of running the softer tyres, but nevertheless it was impressive and he had been fighting hard with Liuzzi before getting that eighth place in Fuji. How good could he be? Well, apparently, McLaren had even considered hiring him to replace the departed Alonso.

Mike Gascoyne

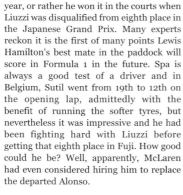

21 | Christijan ALBERS

DRIVER PROFILE

- Name — *ALBERS*
- Firstname — *Christijan*
- Nationality — *Dutch*
- Date of birth — *16ʰ April 1979*
- Place of birth — *Eindhoven (NL)*
- Lives in — *Laaren (NL)*
- Marital status — *married*
- Kids — *-*
- Hobbies — *walking, karting, squash*
- Favorite music — *hits radio*
- Favorite meal — *pizza, steak french fries*
- Favorite drinks — *Coca-Cola light*
- Height — *176 cm*
- Weight — *68 kg*
- Web — *www.albersf1.com*

STATISTICS

- Grands Prix — 46 • Podiums — 0
- Starts — 46 • GP in the lead — 0
- Best result — 1x5ʰ • Laps in the lead — 0
- Best qualif. — 1x13ʰ • Km in the lead — 0
- Fastest laps — 0 • Points scored — 4

CAREER

2007 F1 *Spyker-Ferrari, 0 pt, 25ʰ*
2006 F1 *Midland-Toyota, 0 pt, 22ⁿᵈ*
2005 F1 *Minardi-Cosworth, 4 pts, 19ʰ*
2004 DTM *3ʳᵈ • F1 Minardi tests driver &*
 tests Jordan
2003 DTM *2ⁿᵈ*
2002 DTM *12ʰ • F1 tests driver Minardi*
2001 DTM *14ʰ • F1 3ʳᵈ Minardi driver*
2000 *F3000*
1999 F3 *(D) Champion; F3 Masters, 4ʰ*
1998 F3 *(D) 5ʰ*
1997 *Karting (NL) ICA 100cc, Champion •*
 F. Ford 1800 (NL & B) Champion;
 Renault Megane Marlboro Masters
 Champion

If the Dutchman was as good as he thought he was, he would be brilliant. Sadly, this was not the case. He tended to irritate the team, he was not as quick as Sutil and he was not bringing in too much money, therefore he was shown the door following the British Grand Prix. Unless another Dutch team enters the sport, it is unlikely that he will find his way back in the near future.

Markus WINKELHOCK

DRIVER PROFILE

- Name — *WINKELHOCK*
- Firstname — *Markus*
- Nationality — *German*
- Date of birth — *13ʰ June 1980*
- Place of birth — *Stuttgart Bad Cannstatt (D)*
- Lives in — *Berglen, Steinach (D)*
- Marital status — *single*
- Kids — *-*
- Hobbies — *music, karting*
- Favorite music — *rock, pop*
- Favorite meal — *pasta*
- Favorite drinks — *Coca-Cola*
- Height — *175 cm*
- Weight — *65 kg*
- Web — *www.m-winkelhock.de*

STATISTICS

- Grands Prix — 1 • Podiums — 0
- Starts — 1 • GP in the lead — 1
- Best result — - • Laps in the lead — 6
- Best qualif. — 1x22ⁿᵈ • Km in the lead — 31
- Fastest laps — 0 • Points scored — 0

CAREER

2007 F1 *Spyker-Ferrari, 0 pt, not classified*
 • DTM
2006 *Porsche Supercup •*
 F1 Midland tests driver
2005 *World Series by Renault 3ʳᵈ •*
 F1 tests driver Midland
2004 *DTM*
2003 F3 *Euro Series 4ʰ; F3 Masters, 6ʰ*
2002 F3 *(D) 7ʰ*
2001 F3 *(D) 5ʰ*
2000 F. *Renault 2000 Eurocup 6ʰ;*
 F. Renault 2000 (I) 21ˢᵗ
1999 F. *Renault (D) 4ʰ*
1998 F. *König (D) 2ⁿᵈ*

The late Manfred Winkelhock is usually remembered as a friendly and likeable person, who knew there was more to life than F1 and his son Markus seems to share his father's easy charm and also an attitude that does not regard Formula 1 as the only thing that matters in life. He got one chance to show what he could this year, replacing Albers for his home race at the Nurburgring. It was certainly a debut to remember. With rain clouds gathering at the start, the team brought him in on the parade lap and fitted him with rain tyres. He went from pit lane to lead the race three laps later!

Sakon YAMAMOTO

DRIVER PROFILE

- Name — *YAMAMOTO*
- Firstname — *Sakon*
- Nationality — *Japanese*
- Date of birth — *9ʰ July 1982*
- Place of birth — *Toyohashi (J)*
- Lives in — *Barcelona (E)*
- Marital status — *single*
- Kids — *-*
- Hobbies — *music, foot soccer indoor*
- Favorite music — *rock, pop*
- Favorite meal — *pasta*
- Favorite drinks — *Coca-Cola*
- Height — *172 cm*
- Weight — *63 kg*
- Web — *www.sakon-yamamoto.com*

STATISTICS

- Grands Prix — 14 • Podiums — 0
- Starts — 14 • GP in the lead — 0
- Best result — 1x12ʰ • Laps in the lead — 0
- Best qualif. — 1x19ʰ • Km in the lead — 0
- Fastest laps — 0 • Points scored — 0

CAREER

2007 F1 *Spyker-Ferrari, 0 pt, 24ʰ;*
 pilote d'essais Super Aguri •
 GP2 Series 30ʰ
2006 F1 *Super Aguri-Honda, 0 pt, 26ʰ •*
 F. Nippon *(J) 11ʰ • Super GT Japan GT500 (J) 21ˢᵗ*
2005 F. Nippon *(J) 10ʰ • Super GT Japan*
 GT500 (J) 13ʰ • F1 Jordan tests driver
2004 F3 *(J) 7ʰ*
2003 F3 *Euro Series*
2002 F3 *(D & I)*
2001 F3 *(GB), (J) 4ʰ*
2000 *Karting (J) FSA, 3ʳᵈ*
1999 *Karting (World) FA, 10ʰ*
1994-98 *Karting (J)*

For someone dismissed as a "pay driver," Sakon Yamamoto did a workmanlike job when he took over from Winkelhock for the final seven races of the season. He had obviously learnt something in the seven races he drove for Super Aguri the previous year, but of course the main benefit he brought to the team was a bag of much needed gold. He saved his best performance for his home race, splashing through the deluge to bring his orange car across the line in twelfth place at Fuji.

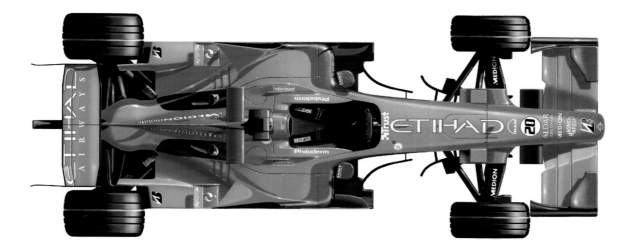

SPYKER F8-VII-FERRARI
ADRIAN SUTIL
MONACO GRAND PRIX

SPECIFICATIONS

- Chassis — *Spyker F8-VII*
- Type — *Carbon-fibre monocoque and honeycomb composite structure*
- Suspensions (Front & rear) — *Aluminium alloy uprights, upper and lower carbon wishbones and pushrods, torsion bar springs and anti-roll bars, multimatic dampers*
- Shock absorbers — *not revelated*
- Transmission — *In-house Spyker design. 7-speed + reverse longitudinal gearbox with electrohydraulic sequential gear change*
- Clutch — *AP Racing*
- Electronic ignition — *Magneti Marelli et Pi*
- Spark plugs / battery — *NGK / not revelated*
- Engine — *Ferrari Type 056H V8 (90°) of 95 kg*
- Displacement — *2398 cm³*
- Power — *more than 700 bhp*
- Maximum revs — *19,000 rpm*
- Valves — *32 valves pneumatic distribution*
- Fuel / oil — *Elf / Liqui Moly*
- Brakes (discs) — *not revelated*
- Brakes (calipers) — *not revelated*
- Tyres — *Bridgestone Potenza*
- Wheels dimensions — *13"*
- Wheels — *BBS*
- Wheel base — *+3000 mm*
- Total lenght — *5000 mm*
- Total width — *1800 mm*
- Total height — *950 mm*
- Front track — *1480 mm*
- Rear track — *1418 mm*
- Weight — *605 kg, driver + camera + ballast*

TEAM PROFILE

- Address — *Spyker F1 Team Ltd., Dadford Road, Silverstone, Northamptonshire, NN12 8TJ Great Britain*
- Telephone — *+44 (0)1327 850 800*
- Fax — *+44 (0)1327 850 866*
- Web — *www.spykerf1.com*
- Founded in — *2006*
- First Grand Prix — *Italia 2006*
- Official name — *Etihad Aldar Spyker F1 Team*
- Managing Director & Team Principal — *Colin Kolles*
- Director of Formula 1 — *Michiel Mol*
- CEO, Spyker Cars — *Victor Muller*
- Chief Technical Officer — *Mike Gascoyne*
- Chief Operational Officer — *Patrick Missling*
- Technical Director — *James Key*
- Team Manager — *Andy Stevenson*
- Chief Designer — *John McQuilliam*
- Head of Electronics — *Mike Wroe*
- Head of Production — *Simon Shinkins*
- Head of Aerodynamics — *Simon Phillips*
- Chief Race and Test Engineer — *Dominic Harlow*
- Race Engineer (20) — *Bradley Joyce*
- Race Engineer (21) — *Jody Egginton*
- Chief Mechanic — *Andy Deeming*
- Press Officer — *Lucy Nell*
- Number of employees — *200*
- Title Sponsor — *Etihad Airways, Aldar Abu Dhabi*
- Sponsors *Twins Investments BV, LeasePlan, MAN, Rhino's, Superfund, GPupdate.net, Bridgestone, RotoZip, McGregor Fashion, Quick, 4net, Philoderm, Trust, Exact, Medion, Dremel, Dream7, Navteq, Kemppi, AD Sportwereld, MaxCredible* • Suppliers *Laurent-Perrier, Scientio, Supergenco, Touchpaper, UPS direct, Vandenberg, Arqiva, CMG, Samsung, gr8, Metris, Sparco, TAG, STL, DDS Catia, Weigl, Rocket Bikes, McGregor Fashion, Exact, Medion Mobile, Carrera, Amalgam, AVG*

STATISTICS

- Grands Prix disputés — 20
- Best result — 1 x 8th
- Best qualification — 1 x 16th
- Fastest laps — 0
- Podiums — 0
- Doublés — 0
- GP in the lead — 1
- Laps in the lead — 6
- Km in the lead — 31
- Points scored — 1
- Best classification in constructors' championship — 10th (2006 & 2007)
- Best classification in drivers' championship — 19th (2007: Adrian Sutil)

POSITION IN CHAMPIONSHIP

2006 10th, 0 pt
2007 10th, 1 pt

2007 TEST DRIVERS

- Fairuz FAUZY (MAL)
- Giedo VAN DER GARDE (NL)
- Adrian VALLES (E)
- Markus WINKELHOCK (D)

SUCCESSION OF DRIVERS 2007

- Adrian SUTIL (D) — *the 17 Grands Prix*
- Christijan ALBERS (NL) — *9 Grands Prix (AUS > GB)*
- Markus WINKELHOCK (D) — *1 Grand Prix (EUR)*
- Sakon YAMAMOTO (J) — *7 Grands Prix (H > BR)*

Whatever else you can say about them, the folk at Spyker must be really good at two things at least: removing paint from bodywork to cope with the changes of livery from Jordan to Midland to Spyker and now for 2008 to Force India. The other talent is sewing driver name badges on fire suits as they got through four drivers this year. This year's car, in the orange colours of Dutch sportscar builder, Spyker was basically the previous year's Midland with the big difference that, instead of Toyota power, it had a Ferrari V8 pushing it along. (With no less than three teams running their engines, the Prancing Horse engine specialists were certainly not short of data to analyse.) Like all teams running on a tiny budget, they suffered most from a lack of aero development. That meant their life was spent battling at the back of the grid. There was enough in the Piggy Bank to produce a "B" specification car in time for the Italian GP and that did lead to some improvement. The team itself is sound in terms of its personnel, many of whom have been there since the early Jordan days. On top of that they benefit from the very obvious management skills of "The Rottweiler" also known as Technical Director Mike Gascoyne. Vijay Mallya, the man who has now bought the team, attended several races in the latter half of the year: if he only sold the jewellery he was wearing himself at the track, he could probably run the team for a year! So, with a sound team and better financing, 2008 could see India becoming a force to be reckoned with in F1.

Super Aguri Honda

22 | Takuma SATO

DRIVER PROFILE

- Name — SATO
- Firstname — Takuma
- Nationality — Japanese
- Date of birth — 28th January 1977
- Place of birth — Tokyo (J)
- Lives in — Monaco (MC)
- Marital status — single
- Kids — -
- Hobbies — cyclism, walking, staying with friends
- Favorite music — pop, some japanese groups
- Favorite meal — japanese food
- Favorite drinks — fresh fruits juices
- Height — 164 cm
- Weight — 59 kg
- Web — www.takumasato.com

STATISTICS

• Grands Prix	90	• Podiums	1
• Starts	89	• GP in the lead	1
• Best result	1 x 3rd	• Laps in the lead	2
• Best qualif.	1 x 2nd	• Km in the lead	10
• Fastest laps	0	• Points scored	44

CAREER

2007	F1 Super Aguri-Honda, 4 pts, 17th
2006	F1 Super Aguri-Honda, 0 pt, 23rd
2005	F1 B·A·R-Honda, 1 pt, 23rd
2004	F1 B·A·R-Honda, 34 pts, 8th
2003	F1 B·A·R-Honda, 3 pts, 18th
2002	F1 Jordan-Honda, 2 pts, 15th
2001	F3 (GB) Champion; F3 International Invitation Challenge √ Winner; F3 Masters Zandvoort Winner; F3 GP Macau Winner; F3 Elf Masters, 3rd • F1 B·A·R tests driver
2000	F3 (GB) 3rd
1999	F. Opel Euroseries (GB) 6th • F3 (GB) 4th
1998	F. Vauxhall Jr.
1997	Karting (J) Champion • Driving school Honda
1996	Karting (J) Champion

23 | Anthony DAVIDSON

DRIVER PROFILE

- Name — DAVIDSON
- Firstname — Anthony
- Nationality — British
- Date of birth — 18th April 1979
- Place of birth — Hemel Hempstead (GB)
- Lives in — Northamptonshire (GB)
- Marital status — married to Carrie
- Kids — -
- Hobbies — informatic, photography, music
- Favorite music — Trance
- Favorite meal — thaï food
- Favorite drinks — no in particular
- Height — 165 cm
- Weight — 56 kg
- Web — www.anthonydavidson.com

STATISTICS

• Grands Prix	20	• Podiums	0
• Starts	20	• GP in the lead	0
• Best result	3 x 11th	• Laps in the lead	0
• Best qualif.	2 x 11th	• Km in the lead	0
• Fastest laps	0	• Points scored	0

CAREER

2007	F1 Super Aguri-Honda, 0 pt, 23rd
2006	F1 Honda third driver
2005	F1 B·A·R-Honda, 0 pt, not classified
2004	F1 B·A·R third driver
2003	F1 B·A·R tests driver • 12H Sebring 2nd • 24H du Mans • "Petit Le Mans" 2nd
2002	F1 Minardi-Asiatech, 0 pt, not classified; B·A·R-Honda third driver
2001	F1 B·A·R-Honda tests driver • F3 (GB) 2nd; F3 European Cup Champion; GP Pau and Spa Elf Masters Winner
2000	F. Ford Zetec (GB) 2nd; F. Ford Festival World Cup Winner
1999	F. Ford Zetec (GB) Champion • Karting (EUR) FSA, 20th
1998	Karting (North America) WKA/FMK, 3rd
1997	Karting (Oceania) CIK
1996	Karting (EUR) CIK; Formule A, 2nd
1995	Karting (GB) JICA, RAC/MSA Jr., Champion
1994	Karting (GB) JICA, RAC/MSA Jr., Champion
1992-93	Karting (GB) Junior, Champion Open
1987-91	Karting (GB) Cadet, Multiple 60cc Winner

For the opening race of the season in Melbourne, Takuma Sato drove to the track every day in a bright red London-style taxi. His passengers did not always look that comfortable as they got out to accompany their driver into the paddock. Maybe that was because Taku-san has a reputation for being the last of the late brakers. Like so many of his Nippon predecessors in the sport, his driving style could also be described as fearless. His skill and last year's Honda first scored a point in Spain, but it was the Canadian chaos that allowed Sato to take a sixth place in great style, as his drive included amazing passing moves down the outside of Schumacher and Alonso going into the dreaded last corner at the Montreal track. Another chaotic race, the Nurburgring, also looked as though points might be on the cards as he overtook half a dozen cars on the first lap and was up to tenth before a hydraulic failure meant he had to park it.

While Sato is officially 17th in the championship on 4 points, Anthony Davidson is twenty third with no points at all. The figures do not give an honest picture of the tiny Englishman's first full season as a Grand Prix driver, after a career as Honda test driver. Generally, in terms of pure pace, he was quicker than his team-mate, out-qualifying him ten to seven. However, all the team's bad luck seemed to gravitate towards his side of the garage. He had qualified eleventh in the season opener but then had to be lifted out of the cockpit in great pain at the end of the race after a collision with Albers. In Montreal, a fifth place beckoned until a suicidal groundhog took a stroll in front of his car and in Brazil, Sutil's spinning Spyker pushed him out of the race. Before the season started, Anthony stated he was happy that all the British media attention was focussed on Lewis Hamilton, but seventeen races later, no points on the board and his team's future in doubt, maybe he wished he could eat his words.

Aguri Suzuki

Daniel Audetto

Mark Preston

SUPER AGURI SA07-HONDA
TAKUMA SATO
SPANISH GRAND PRIX

SPECIFICATIONS

- Chassis — Super Aguri SA07
- Type — Moulded carbon fibre and honeycomb composite. Integral roll protection structures.
- Suspensions (Front & rear) — Double wishbones, pushrod operated torsion bars and dampers. Mechanical anti-roll bar.
- Shock absobers — Showa
- Transmission — SAF1 Honda carbon composite maincase. 7 speed + reverse sequential "quick shift" electro hydraulically controlled
- Clutch — Sachs
- Electronic ignition — Honda PGM-IG / Honda PGM-FI
- Spark plugs / battery — NGK / 2.5 Ah au plomb
- Engine — Honda RA807E V8 (90°) of 95 kg
- Displacement — 2400 cm³
- Power — more than 700 bhp
- Maximum revs — 19,000 rpm
- Valves — 32 valves pneumatic distribution
- Fuel / oil — ENEOS / ENEOS
- Brakes (discs) — AP Racing ventilated carbon-fibre
- Brakes (calipers) — Hitco
- Tyres — Bridgestone Potenza
- Wheels dimensions — 13"
- Wheels — BBS
- Wheel base — 3135 mm
- Total lenght — 4680 mm
- Total width — 1800 mm
- Total height — 950 mm
- Front track — 1460 mm
- Rear track — 1420 mm
- Weight — 605 kg, driver + camera + ballast

TEAM PROFILE

- Address — Super Aguri F1 Limited Leafield Technical Centre Langley, Witney, Oxfordshire OX29 9EF Great Britain
- Telephone — +44 (0)1993 87 1600
- Fax — +44 (0)1993 87 1702
- Web — www.saf1.co.jp
- Founded in — 2006
- First Grand Prix — Bahrain 2006
- Official name — Super Aguri F1 Team
- Team principal — Aguri Suzuki
- Managing Director — Daniel Audetto
- Head of operations — Kevin Lee
- Technical Director — Mark Preston
- Sporting Director — Graham Taylor
- Chief Designer — Peter McCool
- Engineering Director — Mark Ellis
- Head of Research and Developpment — Gerry Hughes
- Chief of Aerodynamics — Ben Wood
- Team manager — Michael Ainsley-Cowlishaw
- Race Engineer (22) — Richard Connell
- Race Engineer (23) — Antonio Cuquerella
- Chief Mechanic — Phil Spencer
- Head of Communication — Emma Bearpark
- Number of employees — 150
- Partners — SS United Group Oil&Gas, Honda, Metris, Bridgestone, Rodac, Autobacs, Speakerbus, Seiko, Takata, Samantha Thavasa Japan Limited, Nippon Oil Corporation (ENEOS), Four Leaf, NGK, Pioneer, Kinotrope, Nexsan Technologies

STATISTICS

- Grands Prix — 35
- Best result — 1 x 6th
- Best qualification — 1 x 10th
- Fastest laps — 0
- Podiums — 0
- One-two — 0
- GP in the lead — 0
- Laps in the lead — 0
- Km in the lead — 0
- Points scored — 4

- Best classification in constructors' championship — 9th (2007)
- Best classification in drivers' championship — 17th (2007: Takuma Sato)

POSITION IN CHAMPIONSHIP

2006 11th, 0 pt
2007 9th, 4 pts

2007 TEST DRIVERS

- Sakon YAMAMOTO (J)
- James ROSSITER (GB)

SUCCESSION OF DRIVERS 2007

- Takuma SATO (J) — the 17 Grands Prix
- Anthony DAVIDSON (GB) — the 17 Grands Prix

You have got a young cousin. He hasn't got much money, but he wants to compete in the same running races that you have been taking part in for several years now. He asks if you can let him have some running shoes you no longer need. You think, what harm can it do, and give him those old shoes you used in 2006, now that you have a shiny new pair for the 2007 races. But then your fit young cousin starts doing a bit better than you in the races, so you get in a sulky bad mood and when he asks for new shoe laces and studs once the season is in full swing, you say no.

You get the idea don't you. In 2006, the new Super Aguri team was set up by Honda pretty much as a vehicle for Takuma Sato and it used old and under funded Arrows chassis. For this year, Honda handed over their own 2006 car, the one that took the Mothership team to the upper reaches of the championship. It was still a good car this year and immediately, Super Aguri began to out-perform Honda. Obviously, Honda had to keep quiet when Aguri and Toro Rosso's status in the sport came under fire for being "customer teams" but secretly, the Tokyo boys probably agreed with the sentiment that this was bad for the sport. Inevitably, as the season moved on, the lack of budget, made worse by a sponsor who failed to pay up, began to take its toll and, despite a few changes to the aero package from the tiny staff of 200, Takuma Sato and Anthony Davidson inevitably began to slide down the grid.

SPOTLIGHTS

The title fight was what grabbed all the attention throughout the season, but there were several other interesting sideshows. We examine some of the other events that characterised the season, and look back at the history of the magnificent Spa circuit on its return to the F1 calendar.

^
Angel face, pleasing smile: not only Lewis Hamilton has an uncommon talent, but on top of that is he a perfect driver from a marketing point of view.

A fairy tale called Lewis Hamilton

Who said that fairy tales only existed in children's books? At barely 22 years old, Lewis Hamilton was living his dream. This year, he became a top driver in one of Formula 1's top teams, and he missed out on the championship by just two points in his first year. Along the way he beat his two-time World Champion team mate Fernando Alonso in the same car. His exploits are unique in the history of the sport.

Lewis Hamilton is not the same as the others. Unlike many drivers, there's not a shred of arrogance to him. Even when he is bombarded by autograph requests, or hounded by paparazzi at home, he manages to stay calm and smiling. No wonder that he has now chosen Geneva as a bolthole from the Lewis-mania that he finds in England.

It's fair to say that the British have gone mad for their new hero. Everything he says or does seems to end up in the newspapers, and his story is an astonishing one.

It all started when Lewis's grandfather decided to leave his native Trinidad and Tobago in order to look for work in London. Eventually, he became an underground train driver. Lewis's father, Anthony, set out on the same career path, becoming a train driver. He then went on to hold down three different jobs, in order to give his family the best start in life.

Lewis's parents were divorced when the youngster was only two. He started off under the care of his mother, but he then went to live with his father, his stepmother Linda and his half-brother Nicholas when he was 10. Still today, just prior to his move to Geneva, Lewis lives with his family close to Luton: an unprepossessing area to the north of London. Family is very important to all the

Hamiltons. *"My best friend is my brother Nicholas,"* Lewis says frequently. He plays on the Playstation as often as he can with his brother; unsurprisingly they mostly play driving games. Nicholas also comes to support Lewis at most of the Grands Prix, despite his cerebral palsy.

It's a family that would have simply resembled thousands of others, had Lewis not been exceptionally gifted behind a steering wheel. He started karting when he was aged just seven, and it wasn't long before he was beating adults in a BBC television programme. Aged 10, he won the

British Cadet Karting Championship.

He was invited to the Autosport Awards, a prestigious annual awards ceremony, to collect his prize from Jacques Villeneuve - shortly before the Canadian made his Formula 1 debut. During the dinner, Lewis was wandering around collecting autographs for his autograph book. When he got to Ron Dennis, he asked the McLaren boss for an autograph and also whether or not he could have a go in a McLaren F1 car one day. An amused Ron Dennis wrote his mobile phone number next to his autograph and

asked Lewis to call him if he won the karting championship next year too.

Lewis duly won the championship again, and Ron kept his word. In 1998, Lewis entered McLaren's young driver programme. It was a wise decision from the team as Lewis won every championship he contested: from Formula Renault, to Formula 3, to GP2. Such a stunning record of achievement is extremely rare in motorsport.

When he showed up for his first Formula 1 race in Melbourne 2007, he said that he would be delighted if he could finish on the podium once in his first season. He did infinitely better than that, winning four Grands Prix and just missing out on the World Championship title at his first attempt.

He is philosophical about it, knowing that there will be other opportunities. One of Lewis's greatest strengths is that he has not become bigheaded despite his success. "I just like staying at home and I'm not into flash toys," he explains. "When I'm at home I do my own washing and ironing, which is no big deal. We've not got a cleaning lady so there's no choice!"

Having recently split up with his Chinese girlfriend he has no official partner for the moment, even though he has been seen out with the daughter of Mansour Ojjeh, McLaren's co-owner. "I'm devoting myself entirely to Formula 1," he told the German newspaper Bild am Sonntag at the end of the year. "At the moment I've not got the time to think about

relationships." Lewis knows how to have a good time too. On the evening of the Brazilian Grand Prix, having lost the championship a few hours earlier, he stood in for the DJ at a Sao Paulo nightclub where all the McLaren team had agreed to meet.

His father had always been very firm with him: "Don't smoke, don't drink and don't go out with girls," he used to say. "Otherwise you'll have to look for another job!" After all, everything in a fairy tale has to be perfect - including the hero.

∧
British Grand Prix: Lewis Hamilton takes pole position in front of his home crowd, but is not able to capitalise upon it on Sunday afternoon.

"Every time I close my visor, I can't help smiling!"

- *What surprised you most during the course of this season?*

LH: Everything! As a rookie, I had it all to learn. I needed to understand how people worked in F1 and how the team functioned. The most incredible thing about F1 though is all the stuff that goes on outside the car. The trickiest thing is knowing how to manage your time. For me it was all new: the paddock intrigue, the non-stop politics, the hundreds of journalists, the situations like the one I had in China on Friday. I arrived there all happy after winning in Japan and then suddenly I was told that I needed to go and see the stewards. From my point of view I thought it was unfair because I had done nothing wrong. Because I'm a pessimist like my dad, I was convinced that I would get a penalty of some sort but luckily I didn't. F1 can be like that. But even though experiences like that are tricky I try to find the positive side always, which was that I learnt something. Now, I'm going to make sure that nothing like that ever happens to me again by not putting myself in the same situation.

- *You were under a lot of pressure this first year. How did you resist it?*

LH: I only have pressure when I talk to journalists! When I'm driving the car I don't think about anything other than what I'm doing. Everything's clear in my mind then; I'm happy and relaxed. If I'm thinking about something else then I can't put good laps in. You have to focus.

- *But this season, there was definitely more pressure than you has been used to in the past...*

LH: That's not quite true actually. In all the time I've been under contract to McLaren, for the last 10 years, the team has always put pressure on me. I wouldn't have been able to continue with them had I not won each of the junior championships. Last year in GP2, Ron Dennis told me that if I won the championship he would give me a test in the Formula 1 car. Isn't that pressure as well? So the team prepared me well for my first season in Formula 1 I think. Before my first

Grand Prix, they explained everything to me for a few weeks beforehand: the rules, the starting procedures and so on.

- *Do you still enjoy driving the car?*

LH: For me, driving an F1 car - which furthermore is a McLaren - is a dream come true every day. Every time I put down my visor and select first gear to drive out of the garage I can't stop smiling. It's too good a feeling for words.

- *Have you been able to take in what is happening yet?*

LH: Not at all. Still today [at the Chinese Grand Prix] I'm convinced that one day I'm going to wake up, that none of this is real. It's just incredible. I've wanted to be a Formula 1 driver ever since I started karting 15 years ago. Today, I'm just enjoying every hour that passes.

- *Did you believe that you could win the world title in your first season?*

LH: Never in a million years. Of course I believe in myself, but not to that extent. For me it's a big surprise to find myself in this situation. But of course I'm very, very happy about it.

- *You seem to be very close to Ron Dennis, your boss. How much has he helped you?*

LH: When I met him for the first time, when I was 10 years old, I wasn't really aware of what I was doing. I even asked him for his phone number and he told me to call him back next year, to see if I had won again. That's exactly what I did. Now, I'd say that he's more like a second father to me. He's always believed in me, and always told me to pay no attention to my background. The most important thing for him is that I win races...

<
Lewis Hamilton missed out on the world title by just two points. Those two points went missing on numerous occasions. There was the gravel trap near the pits at the Chinese Grand Prix of course, which ironically was the only race of the year with a gravel trap at the pit lane entrance! Then there was the puncture in Turkey, and also the European Grand Prix where he slithered off on the first corner. He got going again, but it was another opportunity missed...

Lewis Hamilton:
programmed to succeed

By finishing seventh at the Brazilian Grand Prix, Lewis Hamilton just missed out on winning the 2007 Formula 1 Championship by two points. He ended up with second place in the standings, held jointly with his teammate Fernando Alonso. But on countback - bearing individual results in mind - the Briton did better than the Spaniard over the course of the season and so officially became the championship runner-up in his first F1 season.

It was a fantastic and at the same time almost surreal performance. A few months earlier, nobody would have bet even a Euro on his chances. Before starting his first Grand Prix, in Australia, even Hamilton himself said that he would be delighted to "finish on the podium at least once this season."

Since then, he has manage to consign Michael Schumacher to history.

After all, how many people were still talking about the retired seven-time World Champion at the end of the 2007 season?

The arrival of Lewis Hamilton shook up the established order of Formula 1. Up until this year, it seemed to be a given that experience was one of the most important factors that enabled any driver to climb to the top of the tree. Hamilton proved the exact opposite, given that he had never even sat in an F1 car until the end of the 2006 season.

That only came about because McLaren team principal Ron Dennis promised him a test in the Formula 1 car only if he won the GP2 championship, which young Lewis was contesting throughout the 2006 season.

Just one year after that first Formula 1 test at Silverstone, Lewis Hamilton claimed second place in the Formula 1 World Championship - aged barely 22 and in his first season.

It's true that Lewis Hamilton was driving a McLaren-Mercedes, one of the two best cars in the field. Not many rookies are delivered that golden opportunity. And of course he arrived in Formula 1 under the best possible circumstances - having been groomed and nurtured by the McLaren team for 10 years. As the years went on, he became the darling of the team: Ron Dennis looked after him like a son. Lewis had been preparing for this moment ever since he wandered over to Ron Dennis aged 10, autograph book in hand, and asked him if he could drive one of his cars. Before the first Grand Prix of the season, the former three-time World Champion Jackie Stewart described

Hamilton as: *"The best-prepared rookie in the history of Formula 1."*

Lewis's talent was witnessed by the fact that he won all of the championships in which he participated, from karting to GP2, via Formula Renault and Formula 3. On each of the stop-off points on his journey to Formula 1, Lewis was considered to be an exceptional driver. Interestingly, he was perhaps never the quickest over one lap but he demonstrated an easy mastery of what was needed to become a complete racing driver. He had the mechanical sympathy not to wear out tyres and burn out brakes; he could see the bigger picture of a race while still pulling off some astonishing manoeuvres.

He also had a very clear understanding of the technological science behind racing, getting to grips with the black art of aerodynamics swiftly. His driving style is all about braking hard and making a committed entry into corners. He somehow manages to combine the style of Ayrton Senna, the analytical approach of Alain Prost, and the ability of Michael Schumacher to build a team around himself.

It's hard to find fault with him, and that is the reason why he is not the most popular person amongst his fellow drivers - who are all to some extent envious of his rapid rise to the top. Lewis Hamilton makes very few mistakes, knows how to seize upon the ghost of a chance and does not let himself be intimidated on the track - to the extent of occasionally treading on the verge of what is allowed. But the Briton has not just distinguished himself through all the records he has broken this year. He has marked himself out as the first in-house, homegrown racing driver to make it to the top within his team.

Up until now, every World Champion was his own man: a strong-willed individualist utterly convinced of his own superiority. They were on the whole self-trained, their characters forged on the rocky climb up through the junior formulae before arriving in Formula 1.

Lewis Hamilton is the exact opposite: he is the carefully-honed product of 10 years of training within the team - and the biggest success story of McLaren's young driver programme.

In Formula 1, drivers are ultimately the disposable final piece piece of the jigsaw. No other sport in the world is characterised by teams that are quite so complex and composed of so many hundreds of people. Every single time that Kimi Raikkonen faced Fernando Alonso on the track this year, he was supported by the 850 employees of the Ferrari race team. Alonso had 600 people working for McLaren behind him, as well as 400 Mercedes employees tasked with developing and maintaining the V8 engine.

<
Lewis Hamilton in deep discussion with one of his engineers. The young Briton spends hours debriefing the set-up of his car, and his team maintains that he has an excellent sense of technical analysis.

Teamwork is what it's all about, and at the heart of every team there's a strong sense of belonging. Team kit is worn by all the team members all the time - even on the aeroplane - and most people who work in Formula 1 spend more time with their colleagues than they do at home. For many people, Formula 1 is their family.

It's a family in which the drivers rarely belong. With their favourable treatment, multi-million dollar salaries and private planes, they are often considered as hired mercenaries, selling their services to the highest bidder.

Many have little sense of loyalty, passing from one team to the next with impunity.

Maybe that is the difference between Lewis Hamilton and those who have preceded him to the top of Formula 1. Far from being a gun for hire, Lewis Hamilton is as much a part of the McLaren family as any of the mechanics. Lewis lives and breathes McLaren, he knows everyone that works there and he feels comfortable amongst them. Having signed a long-term deal with McLaren 10 years ago, he simply feels at home. He spends plenty of time at the factory, talking to everyone from the chef to the technical director.

Maybe it's this new approach to racing that has allowed him to finish second in the World Championship in only his first season. At 22 years of age Lewis is still very young, and only the paternal protection offered by McLaren has

allowed him to focus exclusively on his driving and achieve all the results that he has managed to do so far. It's this family feeling that has enabled him to defeat the mighty Fernando Alonso in the same car. As the season wore on, Lewis became progressively closer to his team while Fernando became increasingly estranged.

On Saturday night before the Brazilian Grand Prix, the McLaren team assembled at the "Fogo de Chao" churrascaria for a final meal before the decisive race, at 9pm. There was Dennis, his wife Lisa and one of their daughters. Also present was Mansour Ojjeh (McLaren's co-owner), his wife and their daughter - who was holding Lewis Hamilton's hand. As well as Lewis, his brother Nicholas and father Anthony came along. It was a proper family dinner where Fernando Alonso was notable by his absence. This, of course, was the man whom Ron Dennis had described as McLaren's worst enemy.

One day, when he is older, it's not impossible that Lewis Hamilton might sever his umbilical cord to McLaren. In the meantime, he seems on the verge of extending his contract with the Woking-based team for another five years. That should give him enough time to seal the World Championship he so narrowly missed out on this year. The talent is all there.

< (opposite)
Ron Dennis found him, trained him and treats him like a son. The two men only had one cross word this season, in qualifying for the Hungarian Grand Prix where Lewis disobeyed the orders of his boss...

<< (opposite page)
Lewis Hamilton is an excellent marketing machine: an enormous poster of his adorns the TAG Heuer shop in Tokyo's trendy Harajuku district.

^
At Silverstone, on the occasion of Renault's 30th anniversary in Formula 1, the team painted one of its 2007 cars in the original 1977 race colours. A trip down memory lane for many fans.

Thirty years ago, Renault unleashed its unprecedented Formula 1 car

14 July 1977 - 14 July 2007. There are a few wrinkles now around his eyes, but the face of the man under the crash helmet is still instantly recognisable. On July 14 1977, Jean-Pierre Jabouille took to the circuit at Silverstone in the new Renault RS01. For the French manufacturer, it was the first few kilometres of an adventure that would lead them to one of the most comprehensive records of achievement in Formula 1 30 years later.

It was bright but cold at Silverstone on the morning of that Thursday 14 July 1977, when the first day of practice for the British Grand Prix started (1). At Renault Sport, the dawning of that summer day marked the beginning of a whole new era. After months of testing and preparation, the small team from that giant corporation that was still called 'la Regie' at the time, embarked on their Formula 1 adventure.

The word 'adventure' was no exaggeration. Renault had decided to go down a very different route to the rest of the F1 world. The team would make its debut with a turbocharged car, an idea that seemed ridiculous to many people - including several who worked for Renault.
Nonetheless, the team would win its massive gamble. Jean-Pierre Jabouille, the driver who took charge of all the engine development from day one would win his first Grand Prix two years later at the Dijon-Prenois circuit. Turbo technology would go on to become the norm in Formula 1 before it was banned. After a few sabbatical years, the famous Renault badge is back with its own Formula 1 team in today's modern era. The results, at the end of the 2007 season, include 154 pole positions, 113 victories, and eight constructors' titles. Thirty years after that initial outing, Jean-Pierre Jabouille remembers everything about the British Grand Prix in vivid detail. The Frenchman opens up his box of memories for "L'Equipe" magazine, recalling an era when everything was different, simpler, and maybe just a bit more fun than it is now.

- Why did you decide to throw yourselves into making a turbo car? The rules at the time made it almost impossible... (2)
-Jean-Pierre Jabouille: I knew that Renault wanted to come into Formula 1 with something that was 'different'. The company didn't want to just copy Ford, which was selling F1 engines to everybody. The problem we had was one that was the opposite of the situation we see today: apart from Ferrari, there were no big manufacturers in Formula 1. Consequently, everything was regarded with a bit of suspicion. So far, with a reasonably small team, we had managed to win every formula we attempted. Naturally, the next step was to have a go at Formula 1. There were three of us pushing in this direction: Jean Terramorsi (Renault's competitions manager at the time), Francois Guiter from Elf, and me. Without Guiter's support, it's certain that Renault would never have come to F1. In order to force the hand of the management, it was Guiter who ordered two 1500cc turbo engines from Renault in February 1975 and paid for them, officially to carry out some performance testing. The engines cost Elf about 500,000 Francs at the time (just over 76,000 Euros).

- The first tests must have been quite hair-raising...
J-P J: Quite! The first time I tested the engine we had mounted it on a prototype chassis as used for Le Mans, in order to try and keep everything secret. The idea was for nobody to know that we were actually testing a Formula 1 engine. I remember that the unions were all against it, saying that Formula 1 was too expensive. The first test was basically a disaster. It

was at Paul Ricard, and the turbo only really kicked in down the long straight. The power just arrived in one go, a bit like a fighter plane. Basically the car was impossible to drive, even on the straight. I did a lap, came in and said: "I honestly think we should forget this whole idea. It will never work!" But then Bernard Dudot, the man responsible for the engine, asked me to test the car again - this time with a smaller turbo. Suddenly the engine was about 50% more usable, but with less power. At that point I thought that if we can make such good progress just by changing one part, maybe the idea is worth pursuing and we might just get there!

- But the car wasn't a single-seater yet?
J-P J: Exactly. We had built a prototype called the A500 that was the same size as Formula 1 car. We used to go to all the circuits the day after the Grand Prix to see if our cars were anywhere near the ballpark in terms of lap times. We were miles away! It was hard going, as the engine used to break after three or four laps. Despite having so little running time, I was meant to give some opinions about the engine, chassis and tyres in order to map out the future development. The tyre part was very important, as we were pioneering radial tyres with Michelin as well. I remember that whenever temperatures became hotter, the response from the turbo was painful.

- How did the green light to go to Formula 1 come about?
J-P J: We went testing again at Paul Ricard. The Renault management said that the F1 project would

go ahead if we managed to get under a certain lap time that we had fixed as our objective. I think it was 1m07s. Anyway, we did it! We were on qualifying tyres of course and we had played around with the car a bit, but we still did it. At the time, the engine cover interfered with the downforce on the rear wing. So I asked them to move the rear wing by 15 centimetres in order to make it work better. Of course we were way outside the regulations but it allowed us to set the time we needed! So Bernard Hanon, who was the boss of Renault back then, gave us the green light to go to Formula 1.

- Why was the debut at Silverstone?
J-P J: Beforehand, we weren't really ready. Making our debut in France two weeks earlier would have put on too much pressure. But I remember that we were massively impatient to get going! We'd been testing for months and we really wanted to see how we measured up to everyone else in competition. We were also keen to see if we could finish a race, as we had never managed to get through the 300 kilometres of a Grand Prix - except one time at Paul Ricard when it was cold. At Silverstone we retired after 16 laps, which at least gave the English something to laugh about.

- What do you remember of that famous first day: 14 July 1977?
J-P J: I remember mostly what the journalists reported at the time: Ken Tyrrell burst out laughing when he saw us arriving in the paddock. It was him who came out with the "yellow teapot" nickname for the RS01. Like most drivers, I was quite proud back then and I didn't find it funny. "Go ahead, laugh," I told him. "One day you won't be laughing anymore." I've always believed that in France, we can be just as good as any other nation. But this was England and people regarded us as extraterrestrials. Silverstone was quite excruciating. We really didn't know a lot about the car at all. For example, when it was cold - as was the case that day - we couldn't start the engine. We got round the problem by appointing a mechanic to get up at 5am to empty the oil and warm it up separately before we got going!

- You were clearly deeply involved in the development of the project. It's not like today's drivers, who are hardly ever to be seen in the factory, is it?
J-P J: (laughs) It's true: I spent an awful lot of time at Renault. I used to go to the Viry-Chatillon factory every day. In fact, I reckon they were always delighted to see the back of me. I used to break their balls, try to speed things up and basically stress them out. When Alain [Prost] replaced me, they said to him: 'You're not going to be like Jabouille and hang round the factory all the time, are you?' I used to spend hours on end in the wind tunnel. That was the key to going quickly, although there were some people like Ken Tyrrell who maintained that it was useless.

- Was it an enriching experience - in every sense of the word?
J-P J: Are you kidding? I hardly earned anything for all that work. If there's one person who practically earned nothing out of Formula 1, then that's me. When I started at Alpine Renault, I earned 1000 Francs a month [150 Euros]. And when I was a Formula 1 driver, I earned 700,000 Francs a year [106,000 Euros]. So you see? Formula 1 didn't make me rich.

- Any regrets?
J-P J: None whatsoever. I've only got good memories, despite the aftermath of my accident. I think that in 1980 I should have won the championship. I really thought that we could do it. I was on the front row several times and I had a good feeling with the circuits. But the team boss [Gerard Larousse] made some bad decisions. He was stubborn, that pissed me off and in September I decided to join Ligier for 1981. Immediately afterwards, I had my accident. (3)

- You came to Silverstone for the 2007 British Grand Prix. How do you think Formula 1 has changed in the last 30 years?
J-P J: Fundamentally, the cars have stayed the same. Of course there has been a lot of progress, but the biggest changes have been the appearance of electronics and carbon fibre-based materials. If you hit a guardrail at 100kph in my day, you would be guaranteed to smash both legs up if you were lucky - and that's exactly what happened to me. Now the risk of injury is a lot less, as we saw from Robert Kubica's crash in Canada. Personally, I've never seen such a terrifying accident. But the following day the lad is up on his feet and there's nothing wrong with him: I find that incredible. In that respect, the rate of progress has been phenomenal. Not too much else has changed although the teams are a lot richer now. Back in the old days, there used to be 20 of us at the racetrack and about 60 back at the factory. Nowadays, there are 100 people at the circuit and 1000 back at the factory. At the end of the day though suspension is still suspension, and a gearbox is still a collection of cogs.

Notes :

(1) At the time, qualifying took place in two sessions, during the two days before the Grand Prix. In England, the Grand Prix used to take place on the Saturday in order to give local residents some rest on Sunday. So qualifying was on Thursday and Friday.

(2) From 1966, the engine rules in Formula 1 allowed two different types of units: conventional (or 'atmospheric') motors of 3000cc or blown motors of 1500cc.
This strict ratio led many manufacturers with previous experience of turbocharging, such as Porsche and BMW, to believe that turbos would never be competitive in Formula 1. Nonetheless, turbocharged engines were gradually adopted by all the manufacturers before they were banned from 1989.

(3) Jean-Pierre Jabouille had a terrible accident at the 1980 Canadian Grand Prix, when his Renault RS10 slammed into the tyre barrier on lap 26. Both the Frenchman's legs were shattered.

The formidable 1500cc turbocharged engine that would revolutionise Formula 1.
∨

> McLaren launched its sumptuous 'brand centre' at Silverstone. There are three floors of cutting-edge luxury. Below: the lounge on the third floor
∨

> The interior of the 'brand centre': an oasis of stylish calm. It's hard to believe that we are in the middle of an F1 paddock and not in a first class airport lounge.

Red Bull has the biggest motorhome in the paddock, as it serves both the Red Bull team and Toro Rosso. This leviathan is 32 metres long....
>
∨

Ferrari's new three-storey motorhome introduced in Barcelona.
∨

Motorhomes, a reflection of every team's ego.

As nobody has worked out exactly what to call them yet, they are still referred to as 'motorhomes'. Maybe it's as much out of nostalgia as paucity of vocabulary. Nonetheless, the glass and aluminium palaces that adorn the paddock these days have very little in common with the caravans from the old days.

The problem, however, hardly justifies the statuesque solutions that are a hallmark of modern Formula 1. Each team brings nearly 100 people to each Grand Prix (engineers, mechanics, marketing teams and so forth). They also invite several clients, friends and celebrities. In order to give everyone somewhere to relax, get some food, and meet each team brings a portable structure to every race - as well as an army of cooks and waiters.

When motor sport first began, everything was quite simple. A hurried sandwich in the corner of the garage was the only real option, and the mechanics - their hands stained with oil and grease - demanded nothing else. At the beginning of the 1960s the first guests started turning up to the paddock. Their hands were clean, and they demanded something a little more elaborate. In 1964 tyre firm Goodyear bought a bus with an awning, under which all their guests were invited to have a drink and something to eat from a nearby barbeque.

Following on from their example, motorhomes became commonplace. Most of them were large caravans, around which the teams would drape a tent. This system worked well for years, until McLaren decided to graduate to a two-storey motorhome at the end of the 1990s, in order to benefit from some extra space. On the ground floor, an ultra-modern kitchen with a dumb waiter allowed the staff to send cold drinks up to the second floor, where there was a meeting room with a giant screen next to the boss's oval office. In order for the motorhome to drive down the motorway, the top floor would be lowered thanks to an ingenious hydraulic system. The total cost: three million Euros per motorhome.

War was declared. Three years later, Renault introduced the 'Taj Mahal'. Instead of having motorhomes linked by tents, Renault had them linked with a false floor. The net result was that there was more room to accommodate guests.

McLaren had no intention of being left behind. The following year the British team inaugurated its 'communication centre'" a collection of offices and meeting rooms in aluminium and glass that the team erected at each circuit and then took down. It was truly a fortress of a motorhome and it cost nearly 12 million Euros.

The next shot came from Red Bull. In 2006, the energy drink firm took advantage of its purchase of Minardi to cover the space reserved for two teams with a single structure somewhat bombastically called the Energy Station. This monolith measures 32 metres by 14, needing 25 lorries to haul it around and three days to put up. The structure can accommodate up to 500 people and it regularly plays host to the paddock.

This year, it invited the best-known chefs from each country to come and cook. On Thursday the chefs charmed any passing guests with their creations, which were mostly tiny but delicious. The soundtrack came from a DJ flown in from Ibiza. Everything, naturally, was free - in the finest traditions of paddock hospitality.

So what is this monumental effort and expense all in aid of? Nothing, obviously. It just goes to enrich the scenery in the very closed and exclusive club that is the inner world of Formula 1.

Up to now though, there were two teams that had steadfastly refused to get sucked into this particular arms race. The first was Sauber - up until 2005 Peter Sauber made do with his two old canopy motorhomes, which dated back to the days when his team used to contest the Le Mans 24 Hours. Following the takeover by BMW, his team has now followed the corporate trend and now has a quirky two-storey structure in the shape of a sail.

Ferrari, perhaps surprisingly, was the other dissenter. Maranello's philosophy was never to spend money that could instead be invested in the cars. It was a theory that worked well up until Spain, where the Scuderia introduced a huge three-storey tower that dwarfs everything else in the paddock.

"We wanted to create an efficient, integral structure," explained its creator Jon Williams. "The ground floor is for the journalists, press conferences and the bar. The second and third floors are for our guests."

The structure consists of pre-fabricated blocks weighing eight tonnes each and it can be build in a day thanks to a crane specifically designed for the job.

McLaren, naturally, was quick to stay ahead of this hedonistic championship in itself. In England it rolled out the new 'brand centre' - more expensive, more beautiful and more incredible than anything previously seen in an F1 paddock.

The ego of men always leads to the absurd. And there is never a better illustration than Formula 1.

The BMW-Sauber F1.07

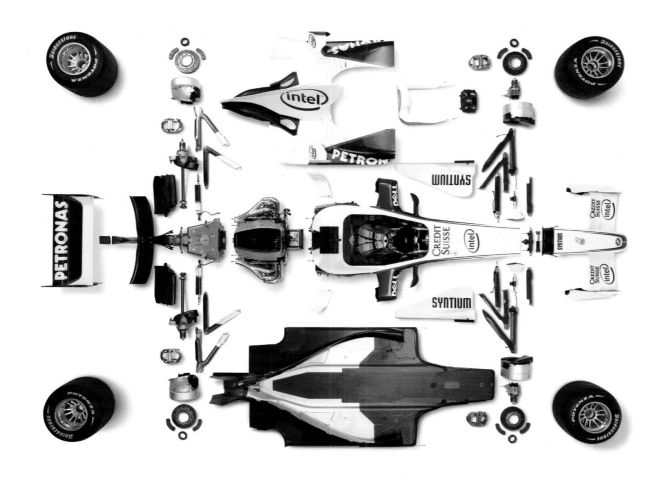

<
A Formula 1 car consists of about 5000 components, leaving aside the engine that is made of 3000 components by itself. On this photo are the most important elements of the BMW Sauber F1.07.

"Monaco" version

"Monza" version

<
Formula 1 cars tend to change at each Grand Prix. This is not just because the teams are constantly improving them: it is also because they are adapted for the specific demands of each circuit.
Here, for example, are the two BMW Sauber cars used in Monaco and in Monza.
Monaco is the slowest circuit all year, and for this race the teams utilise the biggest wing angles, in order to generate maximum downforce despite the slow speeds. By contrast, Monza is the quickest circuit. In Italy, downforce serves only to slow the car down on the long straights, and that is why the wing elements are almost flat. The drawings clearly show the differences.

"Mr E" is still the Formula 1 ringmaster

Aged 76, he still rules over the F1 paddock with an iron fist. A good number of team bosses and race organisers have lost a lot of sleep because of him.

Charles Bernard Ecclestone, known simply as 'Bernie' or 'Mr E' normally greets you with a beaming smile and always says something amusing. But behind his British humour, there's a hard-nosed negotiator and a brilliant businessmen. As soon as you meet him, you realise that it is far better to have him as a friend than an enemy.

At the end of 2005 Bernie sold parts of his family business, Bambino Holdings, to an investment firm, CVC Capital. Bambino Holdings holds SLEC Holdings (standing for Slavica Ecclestone Holdings), which in turn owns FOM (Formula One Management, responsible for organising all the Grands Prix, right down to providing the official timing) and ASM (All Sport Management SA, which is based in Geneva and looks after the paddock club, the commercial areas of the circuit and Grand Prix advertising).

So now it is CVC Capital who holds the commercial rights to Formula 1 up until 2099. Bernie's role is now effectively that of their agent, but his power, brio and ability to make quick decisions remains unaffected.

He's still the boss. It's said that at Grands Prix Bernie and God decide the weather. But nobody knows in which order. We meet the first one to find out:

- *You've sold all your parts of the business that controls the commercial rights to Formula 1. Now it seems that you are intent on increasing the number of Grands Prix every year. Why is this? To increase the return for your investors?*

- No, that's not the idea at all. We just want the championship to be a little more interesting and international. We want it to be a real world championship.

- *Formula 1 has changed a lot over the last 30 years. All the drivers and team bosses have become millionaires. And the atmosphere is not the same as it once was...*

- That's true enough, the atmosphere has changed a lot with time. The paddock is less friendly and there were more girls back in the day! It was more relaxed back then. But there's nothing I can really do about that, it's just natural evolution.

- *What are your plans to improve the spectacle?*

- Well, what would you do in my place?

- (totally caught out) *Hmm...try and encourage a bit more overtaking?*

- But we've never stopped trying to do that. The problem is, you see, that I was a sort of dictator when I took over Formula 1: I did exactly what I liked. Now that we're trying to run it as more of a democracy, it's not so easy. You need to convince the world to agree with you about everything, and it takes ages to accomplish things that are nonetheless obvious and will end up happening anyway. We've still got plenty more ideas about how to improve the show.

- *It seems that street circuits are in vogue at the moment. The projects for races at Singapore, Valencia and Abu Dhabi seem to go against the agenda of safety established by the FIA. There's obviously a lot less room for error at street circuits than at purpose-built facilities.*

- Do you think so? We've been racing at Monaco for 65 years now and it's really not all that dangerous.

- *But that's not what the drivers say. Some of them say that the Armco is much too close.*

- Well, those of them who say that would be better off looking for a different job.

- *The new projects for Grands Prix seem all well and good, but are you ignoring the American market?*

- (thinks) It's true that we've ended our contract with Indianapolis this year. But the Americans don't work in the same way to the rest of the world. Over there, they have no help from the government or regional councils. The Grand Prix has to be subsidised by private money, and all these private firms want guarantees that they won't lose money. They're not willing to take any risks at all and that's odd. The Americans are ambitious in a lot of ways but not when it comes to Formula 1. I've not quite understood how they work yet, or how their television rights system is organised. It's all coming out of my ears a bit.

- *And Canada? It's no secret that the facilities at the Gilles Villeneuve circuit are becoming a bit dated now...*

- I sincerely hope that the city of Montreal will make it a priority to start modernising the circuit, step by step. When I was the organiser of that race, I got the current grandstands built at the end of the rowing lake. When was that exactly? I don't remember any more, but it would have to be a good 20 years ago. Since then, there's been a lick of paint from time to time but nobody has really taken charge of it. I still think that the circuit acts as an ambassador for Canada and certainly for the city of Montreal. They ought to reflect on that and do something, because during the Grand Prix things like the pitlane building symbolise the country for hundreds of millions of TV viewers all across the world...

- *So if Montreal does nothing is their Grand Prix under threat, a bit like the French Grand Prix?*

- The basic problem is that I travel all over the world to meet candidates who are interested in hosting a new Grand Prix. I bring out a load of photos and plans, show them the circuits at Bahrain and Shanghai and tell them: *"this is what we want, this is what you have to do."* Then they come back to me and say: *"but look at Canada! Or Silverstone."*

> "We're not just a mafia. We're the mafia!" FIA President and Bernie Ecclestone enjoy a joke at their own expense. Between them, they control all the legislative and commercial aspects of Formula 1.

(->>>)

From Las Vegas to Indianapolis, Formula 1's American dream

"If it doesn't work this time, then I think it's the end for Formula 1 in the USA." The phrase was uttered by Bernie Ecclestone at the 2000 Monaco Grand Prix, on the occasion of a small reception to celebrate a five-year deal with IMS: the famous 'Indianapolis Motor Speedway'.

This cradle of American motorsport would host the United States Grand Prix, hopefully bringing success where others had failed.

But a series of tribulations that characterised the history of Formula 1 in the United States cast some doubts over the success of this latest contract. Even though this time the circumstances seemed to be different. For Indianapolis, Bernie Ecclestone seemed to have done everything to ensure that the race would be a success. In the past, most American Grands Prix had been last-minute affairs, organised at hastily convened street circuits and even, in the case of Las Vegas, in the car park of a hotel. Indianapolis by contrast was a permanent venue with decent facilities. The paddock and pits were entirely rebuilt for the Grand Prix, while a new infield circuit was built to accommodate the bulk of the action. Formula 1 cars would use just one turn of the famous oval, run the opposite way to how it is normally.

Above all, the mythical Indianapolis Motor Speedway benefited from a real history in motorsport, as the famous Indy 500 has taken place on it every year since 1909. Along with the Le Mans 24 Hours, this is probably the most famous race in the world.

Motorsport ran through the veins of Indianapolis, and it was a venue that was assailed by fans every year for the Indy 500. There was no reason, or so the theory went, why those fans should not equally turn up to see one of those Grands Prix that was so loved by all those folks back in Europe.

The first year, 2000, was a resounding success. When the opening free practice sessions started on Friday, the grandstands were already packed. The enthusiastic crowd gave a standing ovation to the very first Formula 1 cars venturing out onto the oval - which as it happened were the Minardis.

Afterwards, the initial fever soon died down. Not even the most hard-bitten residents of Indianapolis were really interested in Grand Prix racing. In the last few years, more than half the crowd were tourists. Most of them were South Americans but there were also a fair number of Europeans, who were having a holiday in the United States at the same time as watching the Grand Prix.

The Indy 500, in May, attracts around 400,000 spectators around the speedway. Formula 1 had to be content with about a fifth of that figure.

Spectator attendance certainly wasn't helped by the fiasco of the 2005 US Grand Prix. This was the year when Michelin were unable to run at the circuit, meaning that all the teams apart from Ferrari, Jordan and Minardi came into the pits after the parade lap and took no further part in the action.

On that day, the few Americans who still believed in Formula 1 were massively discouraged. In 2006 the organisers offered more than 20,000 free tickets - paid for by Michelin - in order to make up for the disappointment of the previous years and try and get the fans back to Indianapolis. This incentive didn't work though: in 2007 there were actually even fewer spectators than there had been in 2006.

At the heart of it there is a fundamental problem with Formula 1 in America. Whether it's at Long Beach, Las Vegas, Detroit, Dallas or Phoenix, F1 simply doesn't interest American fans.

Americans look for a good spectacle above everything else. They do not think that Grands Prix have enough rhythm, contrast and above all action (i.e. accidents) to keep them watching.

Worse still, they believe that Grands Prix are too technical and do not allow enough overtaking. They're used to a good but undemanding day out, driving to the circuits with their families and a cool box full of beer.

Oval racing - whether it's Nascar or Champ Car - is in many ways the polar opposite to Formula 1. On a speedway, you often need to wait for the final 10 laps to find out who is going to win. Fuel stops, yellow flags and overtaking are constantly mixing up the action. When European technology met American spectacle at Indianapolis, two cultures collided.

"Formula 1 is a bit like football," was how Bernie Ecclestone described the dilemma of the American Grand Prix. *"Sometimes a match will end up as a 0-0 draw. But people prefer basketball where the scores are more often in the region of 60 to 80."*

The final contract signed with the Indianapolis Motor Speedway brought Formula 1 Stateside to a close in 2007. Many people expected Bernie Ecclestone to announce a new deal until 2012 during the weekend of the race but he failed to reach an agreement with the local organisers, who were asking for a discount that was just too big.

Suddenly, Formula has lost its foothold in the States. This came as a big disappointment to the teams - particularly to Honda, which has called for two or three races in the USA. Under pressure from the manufacturers, Bernie Ecclestone has promised to look at ways of returning to the USA in 2009. Nobody is holding their breath.

(<<<-)

And they have a point; I don't know what to say to that. These circuits set a bad example. Furthermore they've got plenty of space in Montreal: there is every opportunity to do something really good.

- *But why did you decide that Magny-Cours was no longer suitable before putting it back on the calendar?*

- Nobody wanted to go there anymore. There are no hotels, no airport, no historical interest, nothing. No reason to stay.

- *Fair point. But doesn't Spa have the same problem?*

- (slightly put out) No. People like Spa. It's a fantastic track with a long history behind it. And personally, I like going there.

- *The teams and sponsors need the American market. Don't they carry any weight in the decision-making process as to which circuits form the calendar?*

- No, the teams have nothing to do with it. It's just me who decides.

- *There aren't many friendships in Formula 1. But you seem to get on very well with Flavio Briatore. In Monaco you spent a lot of time on his yacht. What do two millionaires talk about in their spare time?*

- (laughs) Well, we talk about everything and nothing, just like the rest of the world. Nothing special. Back in the days when the team used to belong to the Benetton family, it was about to stop in Formula 1 because there was nobody to manage the team. Then Benetton remembered this character in New York who was looking after their American business. They asked me to help him get started in Formula 1 and we've remained good friends since.

- *You're 76 years old. People in the paddock often wonder what will happen when you're not there any more...*

- I don't think anyone will take my place. I imagine that my responsibilities will be

divided up amongst lots of different companies and consequently lots of different directors. And I imagine they may well do a better job than me - why not?

< A less than cordial handshake between Bernie Ecclestone and Mrs Hulmann, the owner of the Indianapolis Motor Speedway. Formula 1's relationship with Indianapolis was over after the 2007 USA Grand Prix. But can it truly consider itself to be a 'world' championship without visiting the biggest economic power of the planet?

^
In 2007 Honda launched a new marketing concept. There were no sponsors on the car, but instead a big map of the world - backed up by the myearthdream.com website. The Japanese team made the search for more environmental motoring technologies its key message this year.

According to the FIA, Formula 1 is greener than athletics

Deep within the Maranello factory, there is a 'secret' department within Ferrari. One of the people locked within it is Gerald Brussoz. He doesn't come to races any more and he's not allowed to talk to his old friends in the paddock. The Frenchman joined Ferrari in 2005 and since the winter of 2006 he has been working on the Scuderia's most secret and strategic project: the KERS (Kinetic Energy Recovery System). It's a project that will determine the success or failure of Ferrari from the 2009 season onwards.

First of all, some background. At the beginning of the 2007 season global warming created a storm - not just in the weather but also in the minds of politicians. This was extremely bad news for motorsport, a fundamentally useless and polluting activity, which some more extreme governments had talked about banning with immediate effect. It had even been discussed in the corridors of power in Brussels.

In order to quell this risk the FIA - the governing body of world motorsport - decided to take the initiative by declaring Formula 1 to be a pioneering test bed for 'green' technologies.

The FIA's idea is to get manufacturers to use their huge budgets to carry out research in a few months that would have taken years without the constant pace of competition. It's a laudable projects with good intentions, but it has met with fierce resistance from Formula 1's engineers (see page opposite). Engineers tend to be purists, and the idea of slowing down the cars or changing the fundamental method of propulsion is anathema to them. Undeterred, FIA President Max Mosley set out a new vision of the future.

"Up until now in Formula 1, the power of an engine has been limited by its cubic capacity. From now on it will be limited by the amount of energy it can provide. This is intended to encourage research into how to get the maximum energy out of the fuel available." The real revolution will come in 2011 though. *"The engines will be a lot smaller, turbocharged, and with a limited amount of energy going in,"* said Max Mosley. *"But we'll already introduce the KERS from 2009."*

When braking from 320 to 80 kph, a Formula 1 car sheds energy equivalent to 2500 horsepower.

The system will work by recovering the kinetic energy dissipated under braking in order to re-launch the cars when they accelerate again. The figures show that it's a worthwhile exercise, an F1 car sheds energy equivalent to 2500 horsepower when braking from 320 to 80kph. The team that does the best job in harnessing that energy and returning it to the driving wheels will obviously have a major advantage when it comes to winning Grands Prix.

The problem is that in research terms, 2009 is already tomorrow. Most teams begin work on the following year's car in January of the current year.

Some hybrid road cars manage to recover kinetic energy already, but the truth is that they do not recover very much of it. To research this field in Formula 1 requires an enormous step forwards. Which is exactly why Max Mosley has taken the line that Formula 1 is more useful to the environment than other sports.

Mosley has also decided to offset all the carbon produced by Formula 1. A complex calculation has allowed the FIA to determine how much pollution the 22 cars generate over the course of the season, as well as by transport used by the teams during the year.

The FIA has also been discreetly involved in a scheme to plant trees in Mexico for the past 11 years. *"All these things together mean that Formula 1 is actually a lot more ecological than athletics, for example, which does nothing to compensate for its movements all around the world,"* says Mosley.

It's the travel around the world that is the real issue. During a Grand Prix weekend, a two-car team will use about 750 litres of fuel. That's not an insignificant figure, but it's still only enough to power a Boeing 747-400 for about three and a half minutes.

By contrast, a team of 100 people and its equipment (which generally weighs about 40 tonnes) uses 51 tonnes of fuel to get to Melbourne for the first race of the year. Put this way, the fuel used by the two cars in the race is just 1.5% of the total fuel consumption of the team during the Australian Grand Prix.

This is why the carbon-offset programme has been put in place by the FIA: to compensate for all those flights that do the real damage. So far, however, the scheme has not been expanded to take into account the movements of journalists and spectators.

Max Mosley is hoping that his arguments in favour of Formula 1's carbon neutral status, as well as its usefulness for 'green' research, will convince the politicians to leave it alone.

These new rule changes will undoubtedly change the face of Formula 1. Unless the teams manage to persuade Max Mosley to change his mind, the 2009 championship risks being dominated by the KERS system. The winner will undoubtedly be the team whose engineers have worked best in this completely unknown area. Gerald Brussoz and his colleagues still have several sleepless nights ahead of them...

<
Rubens Barrichello on the limit at Interlagos. Honda's earth dream certainly didn't help the Brazilian during the 2007 season, which he finished without scoring a single point for the first time in his long career.

Nobody wants KERS - apart from Honda

<
A wheel hub is carefully cleaned between two qualifying sessions. In 2009, the KERS system is set to revolutionise the way Formula 1 cars are powered.

A number of technical problems related to the rule changes characterised the discussions over the summer (see page 172).

While the ECU problem seemed to be the most urgent one to solve, the engineers were even more vehemently opposed to another, more revolutionary, item on the FIA's wish list: the KERS system. This new technology for 2009, designed to harness kinetic energy lost under braking, was the stuff of nightmares for the engineers.

It's technology that will feature heavily in the car of tomorrow. For the moment though it is still in its infancy and it seems hard to understand how the system could work on today's precisely engineered F1. *"It's a bit like putting a wooden spring in a luxury watch,"* was how Rob Whyte - responsible for Renault's engine division - described it. By the time this summer came round Renault, like most teams, were deeply concerned about their lack of progress on the KERS system. Adding to their woes was the fact that they had not even started their tests with the standard ECU yet.

"I think it's a bit crazy to start using road car systems for Formula 1 cars," added Whyte. *"On the road, the engine is flat-out for maybe 2% of the time. In F1, it's more like 75% of the time. It's night and day. These two types of car have nothing to do with each other. Absolutely nothing."*

Max Mosley's motives are defensible though: by insisting on the KERS system for 2009 he is trying to protect Formula 1 from the ecological craze engulfing Europe.

"Max's agenda is solely political," added Whyte. *"He wants to safeguard the long-term future of the sport by proving that F1 is neither polluting nor useless."* Strictly speaking Formula 1 is not polluting any more, as the FIA has been offsetting carbon emissions since 1997 (see opposite). It's also fair to say that F1 would be less useless if the engineers focussed on technology that could eventually be applied to everyday cars.

"It's a worthy objective, but a ridiculous way to go about it," said Rob Whyte. *"In 2009, the cars will carry two enormous batteries. It's just nonsense. There's everything still to do in that area, as the 2009 cars are already being looked at in our design offices. It will never work..."*

Time is running out for the teams, who are hoping to form a united front in order to get the new KERS legislation pushed back. Only Honda believes that it is worth pushing forward with the new plan, at any cost. Interestingly, the unanimous agreement of all the teams is needed to change the technical rules. So it could be that Honda alone determines the face of the 2009 Formula 1 World Championship. Watch this space.

F1 returns to Spa:
a tradition of motor sport

Jacques Vassal
is a journalist, writer and translator. Since the 80s he has written for the main French motor sporting magazines: Le Fanauto, Auto-Passion, Automobile Historique, Rétroviseur, Gentlemen Drivers plus the British magazine Octane. He is the co-author with Pierre Ménard of the Formula 1 Legends Collection published by Chronosport. In 2006, he wrote the "Livre d'Or" for the FFSA covering the French Grands Prix for the Centenary. He is also well know for his writings on popular, folk and country and blues music as well as on French and world blues and songs (in magazines from Rock & Folk to Chorus).

The Belgian Grand Prix has been cancelled from the F1 calendar several times in its long history, to the consternation of drivers, teams, journalists and fans alike. It was welcomed back enthusiastically for 2007 because even in its reworked and modernised form, Spa-Francorchamps remains one of the greatest circuits in the world - and one of the very last to follow the natural contours of the surrounding countryside. Here is how the legend of this great motor sport venue was written.

Immediately after its foundation in 1896, the Royal Automobile Club of Belgium organised a first, twelve-kilometre race at Spa. In 1913, the small town in the Ardennes held its own "Grand Prix". But the country had no permanent circuit, and it was only in 1920 that suitable land was found amidst the valleys, forests and rivers surrounding Spa. Indeed, the thermal waters from which the town takes its name are still conjured up by corners such as La Source ("the source") and Eau Rouge ("red water" after the iron-rich water of the region) on the modern circuit.

The hazards of the Ardennes
The first circuit, composed of the roads linking Spa, Malmedy and Stavelot, measured 14.914 km in total. A series of modifications at Stavelot were to shorten it to 14.856 km in 1935, 14.5 km in 1939, 14.120 km in 1950 and finally to 14.100 km in 1960. "The steep elevation changes created a series of hazards for drivers and cars alike: at Eau Rouge, which was created in 1939 to eliminate the corner at Ancienne Douane (the old customs house); the downhill stretch at Burnenville; the downhill stretch and kink at Masta; the climb towards Blanchimont; and the hairpin at La Source, the only heavy braking point on the whole circuit. For many years, Spa counted alongside the Nurburgring's Nordschleife as one of the most dangerous circuits in the world."
The circuit opened with a motorbike race in 1921, and Spa held its first four-wheeled Grand Prix for sports cars on 12 August 1923. The 24 Hour Race began in 1924, imitating the event at Le Mans. And then, in

1925, the Grand Prix proper began. To the great displeasure of the organisers, only seven cars entered: three from Alfa Romeo, and four from Delage. Other marques such as Bugatti and Sunbeam scratched. Antonio Ascari won the race ahead of Giuseppe Campari in their P2 Alfa Romeos, and both made a lengthy pit stop to eat lunch after the Delage contingent had retired! The spectators jeered and hissed the drivers, but it was hard to know where to cast the blame. Following this fiasco, Spa held only the 24 Hour Race but after the circuit was fully paved in 1928, the Grand Prix returned in 1930 (with Louis Chiron taking victory in his Bugatti). From this point onwards, the race would become a true 'Grande Epreuve'. The legend began with victories for drivers such as Nuvolari (1933, Maserati), Dreyfus (1934, Bugatti), Caracciola (1935, Mercedes) and Hasse (Auto Union, 1937), and battles between the great teams from Italy, Germany and France. Alas, on 25 June 1939, Briton Richard 'Dick' Seaman lost control of his Mercedes at Club House, the fast left-hander preceding La Source, and left the road. The car hit a tree and caught fire. The unfortunate driver died from his injuries and burns several hours later in hospital.

One of Spa's notorious hazards was that races were often run in the wet; grip and visibility could change in the space of just a single lap. The hazard that claimed Seaman would do the same to others after the war: in 1958, Scot Archie Scott-Brown perished at the wheel of his Lister-Jaguar in a sports car race. Battling with American Masten Gregory (also aboard a Lister-Jaguar), he crashed at the same corner as Seaman (the corner had been renamed after the pre-war driver) and hit a marshalling post. His car immediately caught fire, and he would die two days later from serious burns. Young Formula 1 hopefuls Chris Bristow (Cooper-Climax) and Alan Stacey (Lotus-Climax) were both killed during the 1960 Grand Prix, the first at Burnenville and the second at Malmedy. During official practice, Stirling Moss had crashed on the downhill section before Burnenville after his Lotus-Climax lost a wheel; he suffered

multiple injuries and could not race for several weeks. Several years later, in 1966, the first lap of the Grand Prix brought torrential rain and a sequence of accidents. At the start line, the circuit was dry when the race began, although the skies looked threatening. Without the benefit of a reconnaissance lap, the drivers had reached the highest point of the circuit when the rain began to fall. Swede Joachim Bonnier (Cooper-Maserati), on dry tyres, crashed at Burnenville; Briton Mike Spence (Lotus-BRM) did the same trying to avoid Bonnier; then Swiss Joseph Siffert (Cooper-Maserati), braking hard to avoid the other two cars, collected the Brabham of Denis Hulme. Four cars were immediately out of the race, and one of them (Bonnier's Cooper) was to remain balancing on a small stone wall for the rest of the race; fortunately, none of the drivers was injured. Next, future triple World Champion Jackie Stewart skidded and left the track at high speed in his BRM. The car crashed heavily, trapping the Scot. Minutes passed, during which Stewart could feel fuel dripping onto his shoulders and injured neck. Eventually, his teammate Graham Hill freed him, assisted by American Bob Bondurant - but only after they had switched off the ignition. This accident was the catalyst for Jackie Stewart's long campaign to improve car and circuit safety.

A Milanese March
Spa has been made better and safer in the intervening years, but it remains a circuit that is respected and adored in equal measures. And with good reason, for it has seen some epic battles. In 1947, three years before the beginning of the World Championship for Drivers, the Ardennes welcomed the new Formula 1 cars for the first true post-war Belgian Grand Prix (the 1946 edition was held for sports cars, in Brussels). On 29 June, the 35-lap race (a total of 507 km) was contested by eighteen cars, including four works Alfetta 158's, Talbot and Maserati. Frenchman Jean-Pierre Wimille, team leader for the Milanese marque, was head and shoulders above the rest: he set fastest

lap, and won the race by a lap from Achille Varzi and Count Trossi, who ensured Alfa filled the first three positions. Only Frenchman Raymond Sommer, who put in a valiant performance at the wheel of his Maserati, was able to offer any resistance to the Alfettas' dominance. After a one-year break, Formula 1 returned to Spa in 1949. Alfa Romeo did not attend, after the Milanese factory withdrew from competition for the entire year. Although only fourteen cars entered, the race proved hard-fought: it marked the debut of the Ferrari 125C (featuring a 1500cc turbocharged V12) driven by Ascari and Villoresi, while Maserati also faced competition from the 4.5 litre unblown Talbot-Lago, driven by Chiron, Rosier, Etancelin and Levegh. This was to be the day when the Talbot-Lago of Louis Rosier would beat the more powerful Ferraris of Ascari and Villoresi. Thanks to better fuel consumption, the French cars were able to make one stop less than their Italian rivals. Ferrari and his chief engineer Aurelio Lampredi would remember the lesson, for they subsequently began a new avenue of F1 development, producing large capacity, normally aspirated engines: the 275 F (3.3l) made its debut at Spa in 1950. It was soon followed by the 340 F 1 (4.1l), and finally the last in the line, the 375 F 1 (4.5l). In spite of these developments, though, the Alfetta (1.5l turbocharged straight eight) dominated at Spa in 1950 and 1951. 1950 brought

victory for a future world champion, the great Argentine Juan Manuel Fangio. After battling tooth and nail with team-mate Nino Farina as they chased Sommer's Talbot, Fangio gained the upper hand decisively when the Frenchman retired with mechanical failure, followed by Farina being forced to slow with transmission problems (he eventually

finished fourth after being passed by Rosier's Talbot). Fangio, though, preserved his car and won from veteran teammate Luigi Fagioli. In 1951, though, this time aboard the Alfetta 159, Fangio was unable to repeat his win after another duel with teammate Farina. The Argentine set a lap record, at an average speed of 193.940 kph, but the Italian was nonetheless leading. On lap 14, Farina stopped to refuel; Fangio did the same the next lap. However, he lost a quarter of an hour when the mechanics were unable to remove a stuck rear wheel. He eventually restarted, but all hope of the win - or even points - had gone. Farina won ahead of the Ferraris of Ascari and Villoresi, while Fangio could only take a meagre ninth place. It is worth remarking that the Alfetta 159 was hitting 330 kph at the bottom of the downhill stretch to Masta, close to the maximum speed of a modern F1 car, but that the drivers had to brake around four hundred metres before Stavelot, all the while fighting to control the car with the large, wood-rimmed steering wheel.

The coronation of Ascari

For 1952 and 53, the International Sporting Commission decreed that only Formula 2 cars would be eligible for the world championships. Many feared the spectacle would be cheapened: the best of the normally-aspirated, two litre F2 engines were only developing 170 bhp in 1952, compared to nearly double for the F1 cars of the previous year (380 bhp for the Ferrari 375 F 1, over 400 for the Alfetta 159). But the F2 cars were lighter, could brake later, cornered faster and had better fuel consumption. All of that helped to partially compensate the reduced power and speed. On the teams' front, Alfa Romeo and Talbot-Lago had departed, leaving Ferrari and Maserati to be joined by Gordini, Cooper-Bristol and HWM in order to fill the grids. When it came to drivers, the old guard such as Farina, Villoresi and Taruffi - perhaps even Fangio and Ascari - were being challenged by a new young breed, including Frenchmen Maurice Trintignant, Robert Manzon and Jean Behra, and Britons Stirling Moss, Peter Collins and Mike Hawthorn. Thanks to this, the two Grands Prix run to F2 rules at Spa remain long in the memory, in spite of the dominance of the Ferrari 500 F 2 and its driver Alberto Ascari throughout the period. In 1952, the only challenge to the Ferraris came in the early stages from Behra's Gordini; subsequently, the pace was slowed by rain. Ascari took an almost easy win, at an average of nearly 166 kph with a best lap at 172.6 kph. By 1953, the four-cylinder Ferrari 500 F 2 engine was developing 185 bhp, against the 190 bhp of the Maserati's six cylinder - which came at the price of thirstier fuel consumption. Maserati had developed the more-powerful, lighter and better-handling A6/SSG to

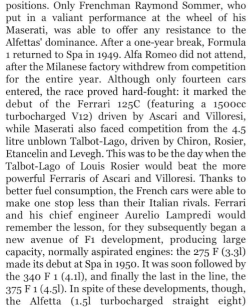

> 19/06/60 : Jack Brabham won the Belgian Grand Prix from Bruce McLaren and Olivier Gendebien. The podium was monopolised by Cooper-Climaxes : F1 had entered the rear-engine era. Phil Hill's Ferrari Dino 246 F1 - with the engine at the front - could only manage fourth, a lap down on the winner.

> 13/06/65 : Pushing hard through the Eau Rouge complex, Graham Hill (BRM) leads Jim Clark (Lotus 33), Jackie Stewart (BRM) and Richie Ginther (Honda). Clark was to win from his young compatriot Jackie Stewart - who was only in his first season of Formula 1.

replace the ageing A6 GCM. Furthermore, the Modenese marque had bolstered its driver line-up: Fangio returned in imperious form to lead the team, after sitting out much of the 1952 season following a serious accident at Monza; and he was joined by two other Argentines, Froilan Gonzalez and the young Onofre Marimon. All three were ready to take the fight to Ferrari. The 1953 Belgian Grand Prix was run in fine weather, and the cars were even faster than the previous year, with Gonzalez setting the lap record at 185.518 kph. The Maseratis of Gonzalez and Fangio led the opening ten laps, with Ascari struggling to keep pace. Then both faltered: on lap 11, Gonzalez retired with a broken throttle pedal - no doubt after the "Pampas Bull" had pressed too hard! Three laps

later, Fangio's engine failed; Juan Manuel subsequently took over the car of Belgian John Claes, and began a sensational climb through the field to third position, somewhat helped by the retirements for the Ferraris of Farina (engine) and Hawthorn (fuel flow). However, his efforts came to naught when, on the final lap, he crashed violently following a spin at Stavelot. Nothing more stood in the way of another Ferrari-Ascari victory, and he took the win at an average of nearly 181 kph ahead of his teammate and mentor Villoresi.

The Fangio years
Fangio was to get his revenge the following year, which was the first season of the CSI's new 2.5 litre

Formula 1. The Ferrari 625 F 1 and the Maserati 250 F differed little from their respective predecessors, the 500 F 2 and A6/SSG, while their 2.5 litre engines developed around 240 bhp. However, Ferrari had chosen to develop two cars: alongside the 625 F 1, he entered two examples of the 555 "Squalo": it featured a shorter-stroke, Lampredi-designed engine which developed 10 horsepower more and a shorter-wheelbase chassis. The ensemble was almost guaranteed to be faster, but what of reliability? Elsewhere, Gordini had developed a six-cylinder engine, while HWM and Cooper-Bristol had departed. The two great innovations of the era were the Mercedes W 196 and the Lancia D 50. To the disappointment of the spectators, though, neither was ready for 20 June: the Mercedes made its debut at Reims, in the French Grand Prix on 4 July; while the Lancia was only to appear at the end of the year in Spain. This meant Ascari and Villoresi, both Lancia drivers, were unable to compete at Spa. Fangio had been altogether more cunning, signing with Mercedes while ensuring he could compete in a Maserati at the start of the year. He thus won the Argentine GP on 17 January in a brand new 250 F, and arrived at Spa leading the world championship ahead of Farina on Ferrari. As soon as practice had begun, the performance gains were clear for all to see: Fangio took pole in 4:22.1 (compared to his 4:30 aboard the A6/SSG a year earlier). In the race, the Argentine prudently allowed the fiery Farina (Ferrari Squalo) into the lead at the start, and even left Mike Hawthorn (625 F1) to close on the Italian. He only attacked on lap 3: Farina fought back and re-passed, but Fangio soon asserted himself and appeared to be leading comfortably. However, anything can happen in motor racing - and it usually does. On lap 8, Fangio lost his goggles, and a brief pit stop to collect a new pair saw him lose the lead to Farina. Once more, as he had done twelve months previously, the Argentine began a momentous charge through the field; on lap 14, at Malmedy, he passed Farina - who immediately reclaimed the position! These two drivers, both world

<
12/06/66 : Coming round
Les Combes, John
Surtees (Ferrari 312)
would go on to beat
Jochen Rindt (Cooper-
Maserati) after a Grand
Prix characterised by
incidents and accidents.
One of them was Jackie
Stewart's crash, which
would have grave
consequences for the
future of the circuit.

The next years were to be known as the 'Clark era'. The Scottish champion had made his first visit to Spa in 1958, driving a Lister-Jaguar in the same race where his countryman Archie Scott-Brown met his death. This memory contributed to Clark's visceral loathing of the circuit, but his talent allied to his professionalism meant he achieved extraordinary feats in the Ardennes. In his first Grand Prix there in 1960, driving a 2.5 litre Climax engined Lotus 18, he finished 5th. Then, at the wheel of the 1.5 litre V8 Lotus-Climax cars, firstly the Type 25 then the Type 33, he took four consecutive victories. The first came under sunny skies in 1962, and Clark battled hard from 5th on the grid to head the field at the end. In 1963 and 1965, when both races were run in wet and stormy weather, the Scot demonstrated uncanny expertise in the difficult conditions, as Senna would several generations later. But it is the 1964 race, run in dry, sunny weather, that truly deserves commemoration: it was a Grand Prix rich in incident, and a day when Lady Luck played her part in helping Jim Clark to victory. Once again, he had missed out on pole position in practice (Clark would start 6th): that honour fell to Gurney (Brabham-Climax), whose lap of 3:50.9 put him ahead of Hill and Brabham. Initially, the race appeared to be a battle between Gurney and Surtees (Ferrari 158), but 'Big John' retired on lap 5 following engine failure. Gurney took the lead, with a lead of nearly thirty seconds over Hill and Clark; the extreme heat meant Clark had to pit to refill his radiator, while Gurney's spirited driving took his Brabham to lap record after lap 20, breaking the 220 kph benchmark (3:49.2, 221.465 kph). Alas, on lap 30, the American pitted from a comfortable lead to take on fuel. However, the mechanics were not expecting him, and a furious Gurney accelerated away, certain in the knowledge he would run out of fuel - which duly occurred. It was a victory gone begging. Graham Hill was the next potential winner, but the fuel pump on his BRM failed on lap 31. Bruce McLaren took the lead, but his alternator belt failed on the final lap, just before La Source hairpin. He coasted to within sight of the finish line, at which moment Clark - who had driven like a man possessed after his unscheduled pit stop - swept through to victory! A little later, Jim ran out of fuel himself, and only learned of his win from Gurney, who had stopped at the opposite end of the circuit.

07/06/70 : Jochen Rindt
(Lotus 49C), Jean-Pierre
Beltoise (Matra MS120)
and Jack Brabham
(Brabham-Ford) hunt
down the March-Ford
cars of Jackie Stewart
and Chris Amon.
However, it was Pedro
Rodriguez (BRM) who
would go on to win the
final Belgian Grand Prix
held on the 14-kilometre
circuit.
v

champions, at the wheel of the two best cars in the field, were engaged in a battle royal. Fangio eventually emerged victorious; having once again passed Farina at Malmedy, and in doing so had set the lap record at 4:25.5 (191.5 average). Farina retired (engine), while Hawthorn was delayed by a broken exhaust, meaning Fangio eventually won a breathtaking race by over a minute from Trintignant (Ferrari), who had battled for much of the race against Behra's Gordini. It also marked the first podium for Stirling Moss in a privately entered Maserati 250 F.

Fangio's domination grew the next year. In the meantime, he had taken his second world title with Mercedes, and the Argentine returned to the Ardennes in 1955 with Karl Kling and Stirling Moss as teammates. Fangio was shadowed throughout by Moss, forming the famous 'train' from start to finish of the Grand Prix. Impressive the demonstration may have been (with Fangio taking fastest lap at an average of 195 kph), but many observers found it a little one-sided. After a moving rearguard action from Eugenia Castellotti aboard his Lancia D 50 - as if he were paying tribute to the recently deceased Alberto Ascari - the Mercedes drivers were never troubled.

For 1956, Fangio turned to the Scuderia. Ferrari raced with V8-engined cars, based on the Lancia D 50. Driving this 'Lancia-Ferrari', Fangio was joined by Briton Peter Collins, the two young Italians Eugenio Castellotti and Luigi Musso, and occasionally by Spaniard Alfonso de Portago. After once again winning in Argentina (sharing a car with Musso), and an unusual poor race at Monaco, Fangio was determined to get back to winning ways at Spa. He took pole in 4:09 but fluffed his start, allowing Moss (Maserati 250 F) and his teammates to get away in front. For the third successive year, though, Fangio thrilled onlookers with one of his characteristic attacking drives. He set lap record after lap record, shouldered arms against Collins and Moss, and took the lead. Alas, his transmission failed on lap 24, allowing Collins to take the win. Moss set the lap record in 4:14.7, an average of 199.575 kph. The symbolic barrier of the 200 kph lap had been passed in practice. Spa was now rivalling Reims and Monza as the fastest circuit in Europe.

The Clark era

After a sabbatical in 1957, F1 cars - minus Fangio, on the eve of his retirement - returned to Spa on 15 June 1958. Speeds had increased significantly, notably thanks to the Vanwalls with their aerodynamic bodywork. The race was fought between Ferrari (Musso, Hawthorn) and Vanwall (Moss, Brooks, Lewis-Evans). Tony Brooks, ever brilliant and intelligent on the most demanding circuits, took the win ahead of Hawthorn, who set the fastest lap at an average of 213 kph. From that point on, mid-engined cars were to seize the

initiative in F1: in 1960, Cooper-Climax took the first three positions at Spa, with double world champion Jack Brabham ahead of New Zealander Bruce McLaren, and Belgian Olivier Gendebien. The race also saw a unique exploit: the race lap record was set by Brabham at 217.960 kph (3:51.9) then equalled by two other drivers, American Phil Hill (Ferrari) and Scot Innes Ireland (Lotus-Climax).

1961 ushered in a new era of 1.5 litre power, replacing the outgoing 2.5 litre engines, with a 450 kg minimum weight limit. It was the cue for Ferrari to switch to the mid-engined layout, and the attractive, competitive 156 dominated proceedings. At the Belgian Grand Prix, the Italian constructor annexed the first four positions, in the order of P. Hill, Von Trips, Ginther and Gendebien at the wheel of a yellow 156, painted in the colours of its entrant, the Equipe Nationale Belge. Californian Richie Ginther set the fastest lap in 3:59.8 (an average of 211.676 kph), barely eight seconds slower than the 2.5 litre cars.

province, sports cars continued to write their chapter of the Spa legend. The ultimate lap record is held in perpetuity by Henri Pescarolo at the wheel of a Matra 670 prototype (powered by a three litre V12), who set the final mark at 3:13.4 in 1973, an average of 262.461 kph. What's more, the Frenchman was clocked at 360 kph near the Masta Kink! Indeed, a new chicane was tested at this very point, but the idea was abandoned.

A long interlude followed. The years between 1979 and 1983 saw the construction of a shorter, modern circuit of 6.949 km. The new section of track turned sharply right at Les Combes, and included a steep descent and a series of difficult corners, notably at Pouhon. This section of permanent circuit, which rises gently before falling dramatically from Les Combes to Stavelot, remains a prime example of how a circuit can be integrated into the natural terrain. To the joy of drivers and spectators alike, landmarks such as the hairpin at La Source and the sweeping climb of Eau Rouge were retained, helping to retain the identity of the true Spa. The section through Eau Rouge remains a formidable challenge: whether it be drivers from F1, GT and Touring Cars, or competitors in the Prototype categories of the 1000 km, all know the feeling of extreme compression as the car bottoms out on its suspension, just at the moment when the road sweeps towards the sky; and the opposite when, over the crest, they must fight against the feeling of weightlessness as the car generates 'negative g'. All the while, they must judge the perfect line for the series of corners, which dictate a car's speed along the straight all the way to Les Combes; a mistake at the bottom will almost certainly lead to an accident at the top. Ironically, it was the supposedly safe circuit of Zolder that saw Gilles Villeneuve perish in 1982 after an accident in his Ferrari 126 C. The Grand Prix eventually returned to Spa in 1983, and another golden era had begun. Brand new pit buildings had been erected before La Source, with the start and finish line was now located at this point. The track remained a true test of man and machine, and although modern TV cameras tend to flatten the gradients, anybody who has visited or, better still, driven the circuit, knows exactly how much it swoops and soars.

From Prost/Senna to Schumacher

Among all the great battles in Formula1 history, that between Frenchman Alain Prost and Brazilian Ayrton Senna during the 80s and 90s was one of the very best. Prost took his first victory at Spa in 1983, at the wheel of a Renault, ahead of countryman Patrick Tambay driving for Ferrari. Senna only made his F1 debut in 1984 (for Toleman-Hart) and the Belgian GP was run at Zolder

---

^
15/09/85 : Ayrton Senna (Lotus-Renault 97T), seen flying through the complex, was renowned for his mastery of wet conditions. Having started second on the grid, he only managed to set fifth-fastest race lap. But he went on to win by 28 seconds from Mansell (Williams-Honda) and 55 seconds from Prost (McLaren-TAG Porsche).

The old and the new

The 1.5 litre era ended in 1965; for 1966, it was the 'return to power' as three litre engines graced Spa, bringing with them the accidents mentioned earlier - and a well-deserved win for John Surtees (Ferrari 312) ahead of Jochen Rindt (Cooper-Maserati). The grand old circuit still had a few tricks up its sleeve, though, and the next two years brought triumph for two great drivers of this remarkable decade: Dan Gurney and Bruce McLaren. What's more, both had become constructors, and each won at Spa with a car of their own creation. The elegant Eagle-Weslake V12, with its beautiful soundtrack, took the chequers with the Californian at the wheel in 1967; just a week earlier, he had won the Le Mans 24 Hours, sharing a Ford Mk IV with A. J. Foyt. In 1968, New Zealander McLaren, master of all he surveyed at the time in CanAm, took the first in a long-running series of wins for the marque, driving his McLaren-Cosworth M 7 A. For Gurney and the Eagle, though, this was to be their one and only win.

In spite of the addition of run-off areas and a brand new surface, Spa remained a dangerous place in light of the speeds the cars were reaching: McLaren's average in 1968 was 236.797 kph (over 28 laps, totalling 394.8 km), while John Surtees' fastest lap (in the Honda RA 301 V12) was in 3:30.5, or 241.140 kph. Of greater concern, though, was the number of immovable objects (houses, bridges, kilometre markers) in the event of an accident: it is worth remembering that at this time, the circuit - one of the last remaining 'natural' venues - was still made up of a series of main roads, which were simply closed off and marshalled for practice and the race. In the late 1960s, the GPDA (Grand Prix Drivers Association), with Jackie Stewart in the vanguard, sought to ban the circuit definitively. The 1969 race was

cancelled; and in 1970, F1 cars raced for the final time on this grand circuit, but with a chicane at Malmedy breaking up the long downhill section from Burnenville to Stavelot. Appropriately, the win went to the BRM of Pedro Rodriguez, a true racer's racer, who just three weeks earlier had amazed spectators at the wheel of his Porsche 917, during a thrilling duel with Gulf-Wyer team-mate Jo Siffert in the 1000 km race. And while the Grand Prix was consigned to the insipid wasteland of Nivelles near Brussels, then Zolder in Limburg

---

>
25/08/91 : This time Senna's McLaren-Honda (pictured in front of Prost's Ferrari) took a resounding pole. His fifth and last victory at Spa was claimed by just 1.9 seconds from his team mate Gerhard Berger. Once again, Senna set only the fifth-fastest race lap.

that year, so his first taste of the Ardennes in an F1 car came in 1985. In the meantime, he had signed for Lotus, whose turbocharged Renault engines pumped out more than 800 bhp. Senna had taken the first of his 41 wins earlier in the season, in monsoon conditions at Estoril, Portugal, putting in the kind of assured driver that led observers to recall Clark in similar circumstances. The date of the Belgian race was postponed until 15 September, at the request of the drivers after the track had broken up earlier in the year, and Senna arrived at Spa looking to boost his tally of wins. In a dry qualifying session, he was beaten to pole by Prost (McLaren-TAG Porsche). But as Sunday came, so did the rains, and Senna once again took full advantage; the Brazilian overtook Prost at the start, as the Frenchman took a minimum-risk approach with one eye on the championship, so much so that he was also passed by Nigel Mansell (Williams-Honda). Senna proceeded to put in an exemplary performance, taking his first win at Spa - and the second of his career - with a 28.4 second margin over Mansell (who would win the following year ahead of Senna's Lotus-Renault) and a 55 second advantage on Prost!

The Frenchman got his revenge in 1987, but the following year saw his nemesis join him at McLaren. With Honda power, the two men dominated the season, with the Brazilian often getting the upper hand over his French team-mate. This was certainly the case at Spa, where Senna took pole in 1:53.718 (average of 219.701 kph) ahead of Prost. The Professor made the better start, but on the Kemel straight, Senna made a sumptuous pass, having taken some downforce off his rear wing to improve his straightline speed. He then proceeded to drive away from his team-mate, inexorably increasing his advantage until he had built a thirty second lead, which he held to the flag. Senna would take three more wins in the Ardennes at the wheel of the 3.5 litre McLaren-Honda, initially with V10 then later V12

<
30/06/92 : Spa-Francorchamps was also the scene of Michael Schumacher's first F1 victory. His Benetton-Ford is pictured at La Source in front of Nigel Mansell (Williams-Renault), who would finish some 36 seconds behind him.

power. In 1991, he equalled Clark's record of four consecutive wins at the circuit (and took his fifth win in total, putting him ahead of the Scot), but the race also saw the debut of a young German with a comparable level of ambition: Michael Schumacher. Driving a Jordan for this one race, he was soon at the wheel of a Benetton, replacing Nelson Piquet as team leader the following season. It was at Spa in 1992 that Schumacher took his first Grand Prix win ahead of some of the sport's great names, including Senna (hampered that day by a poor tyre choice) and the dominant Williams-Renaults of Mansell and Patrese. Already giving signs of his special talent, Schumacher

had carefully managed his tyres and chosen to pit at exactly the right moment. As the outright holder of nearly every one of the sport's records, it is only appropriate that the German has won most races at Spa, with a total of six.

Fangio, Ascari, Brabham, Clark, Prost, Senna, Schumacher, Hakkinen (the author of a legendary pass on Schumacher and Ricardo Zonta in 2000) and Raikkonen have all triumphed in the Ardennes. Each has successfully conjured the perfect blend of skill and application that, at Spa more than any other circuit, allows a true champion to shine.

<
27/08/2000 : Mika Hakkinen (McLaren-Mercedes) passes Michael Schumacher (Ferrari) with a particularly brave move. Against all expectations, the Finn would go on to win an extremely memorable Belgian Grand Prix.

ATMOSPHERE

According to the proverb, a picture is worth a thousand words. How could Red Bull's joy at Mark Webber's podium finish at the Nurburgring be better expressed ? We bring you some of the most striking and fascinating images to illustrate an extraordinary season of Formula 1. Starting, of course, with those unforgettable F1 girls…

The fairer sex

It's hard to escape the truth : Formula 1 is a man's world.
The drivers, team bosses and technical directors are all male ; as are the majority of the fans. There aren't so many ladies present at the circuit, but those who make it light up the paddock with their beauty - whether they are models or journalists.

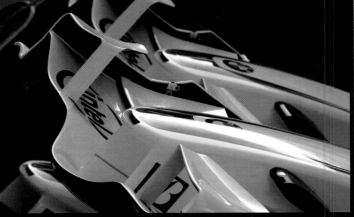

In the shadow of giants

The duel between Ferrari and McLaren monopolised attention to the extent that it was sometimes hard to remember that there were nine other teams out there as well. The best of the rest, BMW-Sauber, deserve a double page to themselves. How long before the first victory ?

In colour

A Formula 1 season is a multitude of places, people, action, shapes and colours. Here are some examples, chosen at random from the 50,000 photos looked at during the making of the
2007 «Formula 1 Yearbook»

ww.GP-Jpdate.net

The look of a champion

The perfect moment that every driver prefers is when he closes his visor, selects first gear, and takes to the track : they all say so. Within their helmets they feel cocooned in their world, far from the stress and intrigue of the paddock. Equally, they are harder to identify. Which is which ?

From left to right, top to bottom : David Coulthard, Kimi Räikkönen, Giancarlo Fisichella, Christijan Albers, Nico Rosberg, Ralf Schumacher, Fernando Alonso, Felipe Massa, Nick Heidfeld, Scott Speed, Heikki Kovalainen, Anthony Davidson, Vitantonio Liuzzi, Jenson Button et Rubens

Nuts and bolts

Formula 1 cars are characterised by beautifully sculpted bodywork, but their decoration is down to the individual team. Under the skin, the delicate forms of carbon suspension arms, gearbox cogs, and wing elements are equally to be admired. A Formula 1 car is art in motion, from top to bottom.

THE 17 GRANDS PRIX

From Australia to Brazil, there was never a dull moment throughout the 2007 season. Seven fascinating months, 17 memorable races, and an inestimable number of memories. Lights, camera, action !

KIMI'S FIRST WIN IN FRONT OF THE MCLARENS: A SIGN OF THINGS TO COME?

Having led from start to finish - minus a short period of about six laps in the middle of the race - Kimi Raikkonen underlined his status as 2007 season favourite: a privilege that had been accorded to him during pre-season testing, where he set several fastest times.Behind him, the opposition were also making their point. McLaren went for a completely different technical solution to Ferrari - using a shorter wheelbase than they had in 2006 - whereas the Italian squad controversially went for a wheelbase that was eight centimetres longer. Nonetheless, there was not a huge amount to choose between the two. Fernando Alonso may have been the quickest McLaren driver on the day, but the debut of his teammate Lewis Hamilton - who exhibited an almost unnaturally calm and composed mastery of the conditions - surprised everybody. At Melbourne, we saw the start of an exciting future in Formula 1.

> Three teams, three hopes of victory in 2007. BMW Sauber, Honda and Toyota all hoped to end up on the top step of the podium this year.

The season start: a field of dreams

Melbourne is a perfect place to start any World Championship. The state capital of Victoria hosted its 12th Australian Grand Prix with unaltered enthusiasm - at least from the outside. From the inside, the tale is slightly more worrying as the race is losing more and more money every year.

By the time the sums for the 2007 Australian Grand Prix were added up, in November, it turned out that this year's event had lost 30 million Australian dollars, compared to a turnover of 71 million Australian dollars. A reduction in advertising and the number of spectators were blamed for the slump but as ever the Australian government put a brave face on it, saying that it managed to recoup a lost of the money lost through extra tax revenue that the Grand Prix brings: such as sales tax on food and hotel accommodation.

The actual circuit may not be the most interesting one that the championship visits, but just like Montreal's circuit on the Ile Notre Dame, it has the advantage of being just a few minutes from the city centre and easily accessible by public transport, thanks to an efficient tram network.

The inhabitants of Melbourne love F1, and the feelings are mutual. Proof of this is the good mood that reigns in the paddock. It's the simple pleasure of being in a sunny and welcoming city, but it's also down to the optimism that radiates from all of the championship protagonists.

The first Grand Prix of the season is always F1's field of dreams: everyone arrives with high aspirations, and the hope that the motor sport gods will smile upon their ambitions.

After spending two years in the shadow of Renault in the constructors' championship, Ferrari started with the firm objective of regaining the coveted number one - and the winter test sessions gave their ambitions plenty of substance. McLaren were only just behind them. Thanks to the arrival of double World Champion Fernando Alonso, the 'silver arrows' were proudly able to display the number one and number two on their nose cones. This was despite the fact that 2006 was the first season in 10 years that McLaren had failed to win a Grand Prix, which was largely down to woeful reliability.

Leaving aside the 'big three' championship challengers (Ferrari, McLaren and Renault), there were others who claimed to have victory in their sights. Amongst them was Honda. In 2006, the Japanese team won the Hungarian Grand Prix by pure chance. This year, according to the company's top management, more victories would follow. Also amongst the potential winners was Toyota, which entered its sixth season of F1 still hoping for the elusive first win. Toyota's biggest boss promised that it would come in 2007. A surprise also seemed to be in store from Red Bull, which benefited not just from the services of David Coulthard and Mark Webber, but also from the talented engineer Adrian Newey (who proved his worth at McLaren and Williams) to head up its technical team. The problems they encountered in 2006 should have been behind them, thanks to a powerful and reliable Renault engine. There were so many hopes as the season started. Which turned into as many disappointments when the season-closing Brazilian Grand Prix was over.

Changing a winning team at Ferrari

All good things one day have to come to an end. And so Ferrari found themselves without Michael Schumacher, without technical director Ross Brawn, and without engine guru Paolo Martinelli.

The fabled Scuderia had lost three essential people within its organisations; three musketeers who had worked hand in hand for 11 years - following the arrival of Michael Schumacher and Ross Brawn at Ferrari in 1996.

Team principal Jean Todt stepped up to a bigger role within Ferrari's management and so had less of a hands-on presence. He consequently asked Michael Schumacher to give him a hand, but the seven-time world champion's exact role remained vague even as the season started in March.

How would Maranello cope with these revolutions? One of the team's engineers confided: *"It's true that Michael had this ability to build the team around him. We just need to hope that Kimi has the same sort of skills. It's far from a foregone conclusion. As for Ross (Brawn), he was the one who provided direction in all our technical meetings. When he wasn't there the discussions were all over the place, in true Italian style..."*

Without Ross Brawn, and without Schumacher, the Ferrari team was just going to have to motivate itself. There was no way that they could count on the charisma of Kimi Raikkonen, well known as the iceman, to hold all the mechanics' hands.

Finally, there was the intriguing prospect of a rivalry between the two drivers. With the undisputed number one, Michael Schumacher, having taken his leave Felipe Massa was keen to demonstrate that he could be world champion too. The fact that his illustrious teammate was paid twice as much as him (Raikkonen supposedly collected 30 million Euros this year) would only have increased the diminutive Brazilian's will to win.

> Everyone in Formula 1 loves Australia. Because of the sunshine, the friendly atmosphere in Melbourne's bars, the laid-back atmosphere… and the undeniable charms of the natives.

> Rubens Barrichello reflects. About to start his first Grand Prix of the year, the Brazilian would never have dreamt that he would end the season without scoring a single championship point - which has never happened to him since his Formula 1 debut in 1993.

Dreams

^
The glorious setting for the Albert Park circuit, right in Melbourne's southern suburbs. The sea is not too far away and neither is the city centre. It's a magical atmosphere.

Pole position: The Raikkonen-Alonso duel begins

After some rain in the morning, the sun was back for the first qualifying session of the season. In 2007 qualifying would follow the same three-way format as it had the previous year, with two 15-minute knockout sessions designed to eliminate six cars each time, before the final showdown.

There were some upsets from the very beginning: while the pair of Super Aguris went through into qualifying two with their 2006 Honda chassis, Rubens Barrichello was knocked out in the new car. In the second 15 minutes, the people taking an unexpectedly early bath included Felipe Massa, who was unlucky in

his Ferrari, Heikki Kovalainen in the reigning World Champion Renault, and both Williams drivers.
Pole position finally went to Kimi Raikkonen (surprisingly, this was only the second pole of his career) in front of Fernando Alonso's McLaren.
The front row delivered a clear message that the World Championship fight would be between the Ferraris and the McLarens. Having said that, nobody quite expected Nick Heidfeld to be third in the BMW-Sauber. "Quick Nick" also managed to get in front of Lewis Hamilton, Fernando Alonso's young teammate. Of course, the secrets of the race remained to be revealed, with several different strategies in play during qualifying. On a street circuit passing is always risky. The importance of starting towards the front would have led many drivers to opt for a light fuel load at the beginning.

IN BRIEF

+ Most drivers tested both tyre compounds supplied by Bridgestone in free practice, which according to the new rules both had to be used during the race. The conclusion drawn was that the hard and the soft tyres were virtually interchangeable. In the interests of safety, the Japanese tyre manufacturer had brought in tyres that were so tough that they could last the distance of several Grands Prix. In order to know which tyre was being used at any given moment, Bridgestone decided to distinguish the soft tyres with a white circle.

+ The Dutch Spyker team had added to their budget thanks to two sponsorship deals with companies based in the United Arab Emirates, including Abu Dhabi's national airline Etihad Airways. Spyker also managed to shave eight kilos off the total weight of their car, by reducing the paintwork from three layers to just one. Each layer of paint adds four kilos to the total.

+ The 2007 rules - as opposed to those that will be in force in 2008 - did not allow third cars to run during Fridays. Nonetheless, teams were allowed to replace

one of the regular drivers with the third driver. Along with many others, Toyota's reserve driver Frank Montagny was hoping to use this possibility in order to run at race weekends this years. He said: « I've already done 8000 kilometres of private testing this year. And here, the car is ready with my set-up. » In the end though, the teams chose to stick with their regular race drivers. On the first Friday of the season, only Sebastian Vettel in the BMW-Sauber and Kazuki Nakajima (the son of Satoru) in the Williams-Toyota drove in the morning session.

+ The teams didn't stop during the off-season: the new McLaren MP4-22s carried out more than 13,200 kilometres of private testing - or the equivalent of more than 40 Grands Prix. Renault went slightly better by racking up 13,300 kilometres of testing.

+ Bernie Ecclestone turned up late in Melbourne, having spent all of Thursday in Singapore to sign the country's 2008 Grand Prix contract. This race is scheduled to take place at night, with the circuit lit up by floodlights.

<
Australia's Toyota importer put all their weight behind the event - decorating the city's trams in the colours of the team and its sponsors.

STARTING GRID

Driver	Time	No.
* F. MASSA penalty for an engine exchange (-10 pos.)		
C. ALBERS starts from the pit lane.		
C. ALBERS*	1:31.932	21
V. LIUZZI	1:29.267	19
S. SPEED	1:28.305	17
A. WURZ	1:27.393	15
H. KOVALAINEN	1:26.964	13
A. DAVIDSON	1:26.909	11
R. SCHUMACHER	1:28.692	9
M. WEBBER	1:27.934	7
R. KUBICA	1:27.347	5
N. HEIDFELD	1:26.556	3
K. RÄIKKÖNEN	1:26.072 (221.800 km/h)	1
F. MASSA*	1:29.339	22
A. SUTIL	1:29.339	20
D. COULTHARD	1:28.579	18
R. BARRICHELLO	1:27.679	16
J. BUTTON	1:27.264	14
N. ROSBERG	1:26.914	12
T. SATO	1:28.871	10
J. TRULLI	1:28.404	8
G. FISICHELLA	1:27.634	6
L. HAMILTON	1:26.755	4
F. ALONSO	1:26.493	2

Kimi Raikkonen wins. But who can beat Ferrari?

Victory! Kimi Raikkonen drives into parc ferme, triumphantly greeted by his new team.

Another win - of sorts. Takuma Sato qualified 12th and finished the race in 12th place. For Super Aguri, that's like a victory.

There was a lot of shuffling of feet and gazing at the ground. Shortly after arriving at the paddock in Melbourne for the Australian Grand Prix, most people realised just how much work still lay ahead to try and crack Ferrari's superiority.

At McLaren, Martin Whitmarsh kept a realistic perspective. *"We've worked very hard over the winter, but the development process is far from over,"* he said. *"The car we have here is still evolving: we will be modifying it entirely between now and the Spanish Grand Prix in six weeks time."*

The first improvements for the MP4-22 were expected already for the following weekend at Sepang, following a week of tests just before the Malaysian Grand Prix. *"I'm worried,"* admitted Fernando Alonso. *"We've got no choice: we need to push more, work hard, and make better progress. There was no chance of winning today, but luckily I've managed to limit the damage as far as the championship is concerned."*

The two-time World Champion was second in his McLaren, just over seven seconds behind Kimi Raikkonen's Ferrari. It was a minimal gap that did not reflect the real difference between the F2007 and the MP4-22. In Melbourne, for the first time since his arrival at Ferrari in 1993, Jean Todt called upon Aldo Costa - the

creator of the F2007 - to meet the press after the race. *" We've got a very busy test and development programme this year,"* said Ferrari's engineer. *"The car will be improved for every race."*

Kimi Raikkonen is never one for false modesty, and he explained that he knew his car was superior from the start. *"The car was just perfect here,"* he said. *"We knew that already, but until the race gets underway you can never be 100% sure about the way things are going to go. So I wasn't pushing too hard: there was still plenty left in reserve."* It was a perfect race for the iceman, apart from one small off-road excursion (*"my fault: I wasn't looking where I was going,"* he admitted with characteristic candour).

Had Raikkonen pushed to the limit, and had Massa in the other car not been forced to start from the back, Ferrari would have dominated the race with a frightening margin over its rivals. The dust had barely settled on the first race before people were asking just what needed to be done to beat Ferrari this year.

The five moments of the Australian Grand Prix

The moment of anger

Flavio Briatore was not happy - not happy at all. The Renault boss gave his new recruit Heikki Kovalainen an ear bashing just as he started his Grand Prix career. The young Finn finally ended up 10th in his first Formula 1 race, having made several mistakes along the way including two excursions onto the grass that cost him several places. "*I really don't know what got into him today,*" fumed Briatore. "*Maybe it was his brother driving. His race was pitiful. He didn't just make mistakes: he made massive mistakes. It's his first race so on this one occasion I will let him off. But there are no second chances. I believe that it was Lewis Hamilton's first race too, and I didn't notice many mistakes from him...*"

The telephone moment

Kimi Raikkonen is a long way from being as demonstrative as Michael Schumacher was at Ferrari. As soon as Raikkonen stepped from his winning F2007 in parc ferme, team principal Jean Todt tried to embrace him but the Finn was having none of it. Then, when Todt handed his driver a mobile phone, Raikkonen just gave it straight back to him. Raikkonen explained: "*I think it was Michael on the phone. But it was a very bad line so I could hardly hear.*" In fact, there seems to be very little love lost between Schumacher and his replacement. Raikkonen freely admitted: "*Michael? I reckon I've only seen him twice. Once at the launch of the car and then at a test session. But he was arriving as I was leaving, so we just missed each other.*"

The moment of bad luck

Robert Kubica was holding a solid fourth place in his BMW Sauber when he was forced to retire on lap 37, with his transmission stuck in fifth gear. "*It was

a shame,*" said the Pole. "*My strategy meant that my final stint would be the quickest, so I was hoping to gain another place.*" Nick Heidfeld underlined the pace of the BMW Sauber by finishing fourth himself.

The face-saving moment

It was a terrible weekend for Honda, which was dominated by none other than the Super Aguris. These cars were, after all, just last season's Honda chassis attached to 2007-specification engines. So how could a privately run outfit with an old chassis beat a full factory team with a 2007 chassis? It was

only at the end of the race that Takuma Sato's Super Aguri lost some ground and eventually finished 12th - just behind the Honda of Rubens Barrichello. Honour was salvaged - for the time being.

The moment that never was

The Spyker team lodged an appeal against Super Aguri, accusing the Japanese squad of using a chassis that they had not designed themselves. The rules do indeed state that each team has to own the intellectual property of their cars. However, the complaint was rejected because it had not been lodged within the correct time stipulated.

Λ
Lewis Hamilton in front of Fernando Alonso: this was the order for the first 42 laps until Hamilton pitted for the second time, which allowed the Spaniard to pass him and finish runner-up.

<
Refuelling at Renault. While Giancarlo Fisichella came out of the first Grand Prix quite well by finishing fifth, Heikki Kovalainen was totally eclipsed by his team mate and could only manage 10th.

FALSE START

In spite of the encouragement from Kylie Minogue - who came to see him on the grid before the start of the race - Webber finished his home Grand Prix in a lowly 13th place. *"I don't know what happened, but it all went pear-shaped today,"* said the Australian. *"That's part of the whole game: some days are just like that…"*

Lewis Hamilton, first podium, first surprise

> ^
> The young Lewis Hamilton put in an excellent performance on what was his first official day at work on Friday. The Briton set third-fastest time in his McLaren-Mercedes, just ahead of his teammate Fernando Alonso. « It's been a fantastic day for me! » he beamed. « To come out of the garage, drive down the pit lane for the first time and take to the track: I was living my dream. Today was a really memorable day. » In fact, it was the start of an incredible story.

The Fleet Street journalists from London could hardly believe their luck. For years they had just had to put up with following Jenson Button and hoping for impossible victories that never came. For them, it was as if McLaren's new boy Lewis Hamilton was a gift from God. Here he was: black, talented, good-looking, kind, unpretentious and with a strong sense of family values - he was constantly looking after his younger brother Nicholas, who has cerebral palsy.

It was a classic rags to riches tale, with all the

Alonso: *"I won't be missing Michael!"*

Fernando Alonso was getting to grips with a new life at McLaren. Having been seduced by the English team, he already saw himself adding to his collection of titles - while Ferrari was in a potentially weaker position in the absence of Michael Schumacher. Fernando Alonso hoped so anyway - and he certainly wasn't shedding any tears over the German's departure.

"I don't think I'm going to miss him very much!" said Alonso with a big smile at Melbourne. It takes time to heal a rivalry - as Fernando himself would find out.

hallmarks of a fairytale. It was also all that was needed to send the rabid British tabloid press into overdrive. They pounced upon Lewis Hamilton and his family as the ideal fodder for their starving media machine: and not all of the coverage was respectful. On Saturday, the Daily Mirror - one of Britain's most salacious newspapers - put a private conversation between Lewis Hamilton and his girlfriend on their website: a banal story about a satellite navigation system that didn't work. That provoked the wrath of Lewis's father, Anthony Hamilton, who banned the British press from his son's entourage - for the time being, anyway.

Nonetheless, it seemed difficult to criticise the young Englishman. At Melbourne, he pulled off the achievement of finishing his first Grand Prix on the podium, exactly as Jacques Villeneuve had done when he made his Grand Prix debut for Williams in 1996.

It was a worthy parallel that seems to promise a bright future for Lewis Hamilton. When he stepped off the podium, the Englishman felt both a lot of emotion and a great deal of joy. He still hadn't really taken it all in. *"It's an amazing, incredibly powerful, feeling"* he said. *"I'm just delighted to be here. To be on the podium in my first Grand Prix is*

beyond my wildest dreams. I've worked so hard for so many years to get here, and now it's all paying off."

It was clear that at the start of the year, the McLaren MP4-22 was one of the two best cars of the field. Lewis Hamilton's biggest achievement was not so much to have finished third but to have stayed in front of his highly regarded teammate, Fernando Alonso, for so long. It was only on the 43rd lap, during the second round of pit stops, that Fernando was able to have the upper hand. *"Fernando was very quick,"* said Lewis. *"I was going as quickly as I could, but I lost a lot of time with the backmarkers that allowed him to close up to me. It's not easy to stay in front of a two-time World Champion. Then I lost at least five seconds behind a Super Aguri, which finished off my chances. But I still knew that I had done a reasonable job in my first race."*

Everybody admired Hamilton's composure and modesty after the podium ceremony. He was feted by his team and bombarded with compliments, but he remained calm and smiling throughout. Only later did it become clear that he was capable of following in Jacques Villeneuve's footsteps all the way to the championship title.

> >
> 49th lap: David Coulthard tries to pass Alexander Wurz under braking for the third corner. Despite his experience, the Scot brakes too late and piles into the Austrian, taking off spectacularly over the Williams. « It was entirely my fault, » said Coulthard after the race. « I was far too optimistic there. » He went over to apologise to Wurz afterwards.

> >>
> The remarkable «Melbourne Central» shopping centre, symbolised by the city's old bullet factory that has been left intact under a new glass roof. Melbourne's extensive and varied shopping facilities mean that there is something for everyone.

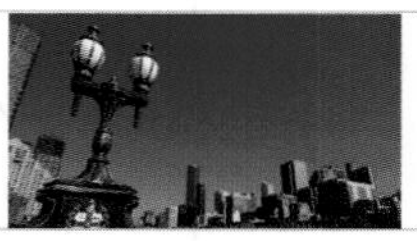

PRACTICE

Date	Weather (AM)	Air temperature	Track temperature	Weather (PM)	Air temperature	Track temperature
Friday March 16, 2007	Overcast, wet track	20-23°c	22-24°c	Cloudy, drizzle	21-20°c	27-25°c
Saturday March 17, 2007	Overcast	21-24°c	23-28°c	Sunny	22-23°c	35-38°c

All the time trials

N° Driver	Nat.	N° Chassis- Engine [Nbr. GP]	Pos. Free 1 Friday 10:00-11:30	Laps	Pos. Free 2 Friday 14:00-15:30	Laps	Pos. Free 3 Saturday 11:00-12:00	Laps	Pos. Q1 Saturday 14:00-14:15	Laps	Pos. Q2 Saturday 14:22-14:37	Laps	Pos. Q3 Saturday 14:45-15:00	Laps
1. Fernando Alonso	E	McLaren MP4-22 03 - Mercedes [1]	1. 1:29.214	23	7. 1:28.040	25	7. 1:26.786	10	4. 1:26.697	3	1. 1:25.326	6	2. **1:26.493**	10
2. Lewis Hamilton	GB	McLaren MP4-22 04 - Mercedes [1]	4. 1:30.878	14	3. 1:27.829	29	3. 1:26.467	12	2. 1:26.674	3	3. 1:25.577	3	4. **1:26.755**	10
3. Giancarlo Fisichella	I	Renault R27-02 [1]	12. 1:32.011	14	4. 1:27.941	33	2. 1:26.454	18	10. 1:27.270	4	6. 1:25.944	6	6. **1:27.634**	11
4. Heikki Kovalainen	FIN	Renault R27-03 [1]	8. 1:31.571	20	18. 1:30.097	10	8. 1:26.937	13	14. 1:27.529	4	13. **1:26.964**	6		
5. Felipe Massa	BR	Ferrari F2007 261 [1] -> [1]	2. 1:30.707	7	1. 1:27.353	32	5. 1:26.547	14	5. 1:26.712	3	16. **DNF**	3		
6. Kimi Räikkönen	FIN	Ferrari F2007 260 [1]	19. 1:39.242	7	2. 1:27.750	33	1. 1:26.064	14	1. 1:26.644	3	4. 1:25.644	3	1. **1:26.072**	11
7. Jenson Button	GB	Honda RA107-04 [1]	5. 1:31.162	15	14. 1:29.066	30	17. 1:28.119	21	15. 1:27.540	8	14. **1:27.264**	6		
8. Rubens Barrichello	BR	Honda RA107-02 [1]	10. 1:31.737	12	15. 1:29.542	12	15. 1:28.039	16	17. **1:27.679**	9				
9. Nick Heidfeld	D	BMW Sauber F1.07-05 [1]	17. 1:37.249	12	5. 1:27.970	27	6. 1:26.753	18	6. 1:26.895	4	2. 1:25.358	6	3. **1:26.556**	11
10. Robert Kubica	PL	BMW Sauber F1.07-04 [1]			9. 1:28.281	26	12. 1:27.753	19	3. 1:26.696	3	5. 1:25.882	6	5. **1:27.347**	10
11. Ralf Schumacher	D	Toyota TF107/03 [1]	20. 1:39.550	9	16. 1:29.574	26	13. 1:27.887	13	11. 1:27.328	7	9. 1:26.739	4	9. **1:28.692**	11
12. Jarno Trulli	I	Toyota TF107/04 [1]	22. 1:44.130	11	12. 1:28.921	33	14. 1:27.897	16	9. 1:27.014	6	8. 1:26.688	6	8. **1:28.404**	11
14. David Coulthard	GB	Red Bull RB3 1 - Renault [1]	7. 1:31.528	9	10. 1:28.495	23	18. 1:28.208	12	19. **1:28.579**	6				
15. Mark Webber	AUS	Red Bull RB3 2 - Renault [1]	9. 1:31.661	16	17. 1:29.801	11	11. 1:27.390	13	7. 1:26.978	6	7. 1:26.623	6	7. **1:27.934**	11
16. Nico Rosberg	D	Williams FW29-03 - Toyota [1]			8. 1:28.055	29	16. 1:28.061	5	16. 1:27.596	7	12. **1:26.914**	6		
17. Alexander Wurz	AUT	Williams FW29-04 - Toyota [1]	13. 1:32.194	18	6. 1:27.981	31	10. 1:27.322	9	13. 1:27.479	7	15. **1:27.393**	6		
18. Vitantonio Liuzzi	I	Toro Rosso STR2 - Ferrari [1]	15. 1:34.627	8	22. 1:31.693	16	19. 1:28.332	15	20. **1:29.267**	6				
19. Scott Speed	USA	Toro Rosso STR2 - Ferrari [1]	21. 1:41.763	9	19. 1:30.383	28	20. 1:28.485	9	18. **1:28.305**	7				
20. Adrian Sutil	D	Spyker F8-VII/03 - Ferrari [1]	14. 1:34.043	26	20. 1:31.108	35	21. 1:28.678	19	21. **1:29.339**	6				
21. Christijan Albers	NL	Spyker F8-VII/01 - Ferrari [1]	16. 1:35.055	10	21. 1:31.175	32	22. 1:30.547	7	22. **1:31.932**	7				
22. Takuma Sato	J	Super Aguri SA07-04 - Honda [1]	11. 1:31.782	7	13. 1:29.009	23	9. 1:27.266	12	12. 1:27.365	6	10. 1:26.758	6	10. **1:28.871**	11
23. Anthony Davidson	GB	Super Aguri SA07-03 - Honda [1]	18. 1:39.221	6	11. 1:28.727	28	4. 1:26.491	17	8. 1:26.986	6	11. **1:26.909**	6		
35. Sebastian Vettel	D	BMW Sauber F1.07-03	3. 1:30.857	22										
38. Kazuki Nakajima	J	Williams FW29-01 - Toyota	6. 1:31.401	21										

Fastest lap overall
F. Alonso 1:25.326 (223,739 km/h)

Maximum speed

N° Driver	S1 Qualifs	Pos.	S1 Race	Pos.	S2 Qualifs	Pos.	S2 Race	Pos.	Finish Qualifs	Pos.	Finish Race	Pos.	Radar Qualifs	Pos.	Radar Race	Pos.
1. F. Alonso	283,4	2	285,9	2	292,9	1	296,7	7	293,8	3	294,6	4	304,3	13	305,9	10
2. L. Hamilton	286,3	1	283,1	4	287,9	15	297,0	5	294,2	2	295,4	2	304,4	12	306,6	8
3. G. Fisichella	282,7	4	283,3	3	292,1	3	297,1	3	293,5	5	292,0	9	305,3	8	304,8	11
4. H. Kovalainen	282,2	6	279,7	12	292,0	4	297,1	2	293,5	4	292,2	8	304,9	10	304,3	12
5. F. Massa	281,3	9	282,5	5	289,5	8	297,1	4	292,5	7	297,9	1	306,9	2	307,6	5
6. K. Räikkönen	283,4	3	285,9	1	290,4	6	296,8	6	295,0	1	295,4	3	308,3	1	307,7	4
7. J. Button	280,0	12	276,2	19	288,0	14	289,9	19	289,6	15	288,0	19	302,8	17	302,5	19
8. R. Barrichello	281,5	8	280,9	7	290,4	5	298,1	1	291,7	10	291,8	10	306,0	6	307,2	6
9. N. Heidfeld	279,8	13	280,1	10	285,2	20	293,8	13	289,6	14	290,2	14	302,4	19	304,2	13
10. R. Kubica	282,2	5	280,9	6	285,3	18	291,8	17	289,0	20	289,5	15	302,1	20	302,0	20
11. R. Schumacher	276,2	19	276,8	18	287,4	16	289,3	20	289,3	18	287,6	20	303,7	15	302,5	18
12. J. Trulli	281,1	10	279,3	14	288,6	12	290,2	18	290,8	12	289,0	17	303,8	14	304,1	14
14. D. Coulthard	277,4	18	280,0	11	285,3	19	295,1	9	289,2	19	291,0	12	304,8	11	307,7	3
15. M. Webber	281,7	7	279,1	15	289,6	7	293,1	16	291,0	11	288,5	18	306,6	3	306,3	9
16. N. Rosberg	279,0	16	280,3	9	292,5	2	294,9	10	292,0	8	293,1	5	305,3	9	308,8	2
17. A. Wurz	279,5	15	279,5	13	288,7	10	295,8	8	291,8	9	293,0	6	306,5	4	309,4	1
18. V. Liuzzi	279,6	14	280,5	8	288,6	11	294,5	11	289,3	17	289,0	16	305,7	7	307,0	7
19. S. Speed	273,9	20	276,1	20	287,1	17	293,5	15	289,4	16	290,3	13	306,3	5	303,7	16
20. A. Sutil	273,3	21	274,6	21	282,6	21	287,3	21	285,5	21	286,3	21	301,0	21	296,9	21
21. C. Albers	272,7	22	273,3	22	280,6	22	283,0	22	282,5	22	282,5	22	298,4	22	296,6	22
22. T. Sato	281,0	11	277,2	17	289,3	9	293,8	12	293,1	6	291,1	11	302,9	16	303,9	15
23. A. Davidson	278,8	17	278,4	16	288,2	13	293,7	14	290,2	13	292,5	7	302,6	18	303,7	17

Best sector times

Qualifs	**S1** F. Alonso	28.371	**S2** N. Heidfeld	22.704	**S3** K. Räikkönen	34.002	= 1:25.077
Race	**S1** K. Räikkönen	28.461	**S2** K. Räikkönen	22.843	**S3** F. Alonso	33.920	= 1:25.224

RACE

Date	Weather	Air temperature	Track temperature	Humidity	Wind speed
Sunday March 18, 2007 (14:00)	Sunny and warm	21-22°c	38-42°c	49%	1.2 m/s

Classification & retirements

Pos.	Driver	Constructor	Tyres	Laps	Time	Km/h
1.	K. Räikkönen	Ferrari	MMS	58	1:25:28.770	215,893
2.	F. Alonso	McLaren Mercedes	MMS	58	+ 7.242	215,588
3.	L. Hamilton	McLaren Mercedes	MMS	58	+ 18.595	215,113
4.	N. Heidfeld	BMW	SMM	58	+ 38.763	214,273
5.	G. Fisichella	Renault	MMS	58	+ 1:06.469	213,130
6.	F. Massa	Ferrari	SM	58	+ 1:06.805	213,117
7.	N. Rosberg	Williams Toyota	MMS	57	1 tour	212,027
8.	R. Schumacher	Toyota	MMS	57	1 tour	211,051
9.	J. Trulli	Toyota	MMS	57	1 tour	210,737
10.	H. Kovalainen	Renault	MMS	57	1 tour	210,718
11.	R. Barrichello	Honda	SMM	57	1 tour	210,682
12.	T. Sato	Super Aguri Honda	MMS	57	1 tour	210,498
13.	M. Webber	Red Bull Renault	MMS	57	1 tour	209,288
14.	V. Liuzzi	STR Ferrari	MMS	57	1 tour	209,008
15.	J. Button	Honda	MSM	57	1 tour	208,951
16.	A. Davidson	Super Aguri Honda	MMS	56	2 tours	208,332
17.	A. Sutil	Spyker Ferrari	MMS	56	2 tours	205,437

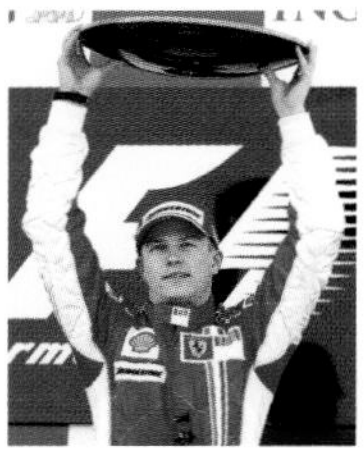

Driver	Constructor	Tyres	Laps	Reason
A. Wurz	Williams Toyota	MS	48	Hit by Coulthard
D. Coulthard	Red Bull Renault	MMS	48	Accident following collision with Wurz
R. Kubica	BMW	MM	36	Gearbox stuck in fifth gear
S. Speed	STR Ferrari	MM	28	Slow front puncture
C. Albers	Spyker Ferrari (T-Car)	M	10	Went off

Tyres M: Medium & S: Soft

Fastest laps

	Driver	Time	Lap	Km/h
1.	K. Räikkönen	1:25.235	41	223,978
2.	F. Alonso	1:26.314	20	221,178
3.	L. Hamilton	1:26.351	20	221,083
4.	R. Kubica	1:26.642	19	220,341
5.	N. Rosberg	1:26.721	40	220,140
6.	N. Heidfeld	1:26.722	37	220,137
7.	G. Fisichella	1:26.892	18	219,707
8.	F. Massa	1:27.044	28	219,323
9.	M. Webber	1:27.501	21	218,178
10.	H. Kovalainen	1:27.592	44	217,951
11.	D. Coulthard	1:27.706	44	217,668
12.	R. Schumacher	1:27.796	42	217,444
13.	J. Trulli	1:28.034	45	216,857
14.	R. Barrichello	1:28.098	17	216,699
15.	V. Liuzzi	1:28.282	44	216,247
16.	A. Wurz	1:28.303	24	216,196
17.	J. Button	1:28.387	42	215,991
18.	T. Sato	1:28.487	20	215,746
19.	A. Davidson	1:28.489	41	215,742
20.	A. Sutil	1:28.687	40	215,260
21.	S. Speed	1:28.953	22	214,616
22.	C. Albers	1:30.899	9	210,022

Pit stops

	Driver	Lap	Duration	Stop	Total
1.	N. Heidfeld	14	26.633	1	26.633
2.	K. Räikkönen	19	24.905	1	24.905
3.	R. Barrichello	19	25.170	1	25.170
4.	G. Fisichella	20	24.426	1	24.426
5.	R. Kubica	21	24.065	1	24.065
6.	F. Alonso	22	24.412	1	24.412
7.	M. Webber	22	33.832	1	33.832
8.	L. Hamilton	23	24.025	1	24.025
9.	A. Sutil	22	24.856	1	24.856
10.	V. Liuzzi	23	24.634	1	24.634
11.	A. Sutil	•23•	12.672	2	37.528
12.	R. Schumacher	24	23.548	1	23.548
13.	T. Sato	24	24.708	1	24.708
14.	J. Trulli	25	23.699	1	23.699
15.	A. Sutil	•24•	12.673	3	50.201
16.	S. Speed	25	25.051	1	25.051
17.	H. Kovalainen	27	23.296	1	23.296
18.	N. Rosberg	27	22.297	1	22.297
19.	J. Button	27	22.818	1	22.818
20.	D. Coulthard	28	24.717	1	24.717
21.	F. Massa	29	27.970	1	27.970
22.	A. Davidson	29	22.281	1	22.281
23.	J. Button	30	12.841	2	35.659
24.	A. Wurz	32	26.136	1	26.136
25.	N. Heidfeld	38	23.625	2	50.258
26.	R. Barrichello	39	22.954	2	48.124
27.	N. Rosberg	41	23.328	2	45.625
28.	K. Räikkönen	42	22.685	2	47.590
29.	T. Sato	42	29.317	2	54.025
30.	L. Hamilton	43	23.352	2	47.377
31.	M. Webber	42	32.145	2	1:05.977
32.	A. Sutil	41	24.718	4	1:14.919
33.	J. Button	43	22.908	3	58.567
34.	G. Fisichella	44	21.704	2	46.130
35.	F. Alonso	45	21.509	2	45.921
36.	R. Schumacher	45	24.116	2	47.664
37.	V. Liuzzi	45	22.510	2	47.144
38.	A. Davidson	45	22.309	2	44.590
39.	H. Kovalainen	46	21.809	2	45.105
40.	J. Trulli	46	22.794	2	46.493
41.	D. Coulthard	47	20.963	2	45.680

•• Drive-through penalty: Sutil.
- Ignoring blue flags in favour of L. Hamilton
- Crossing white line on pit lane exit

Race leader

Driver	Laps in the lead	Nbr de Laps
K. Räikkönen	1 > 18	18
L. Hamilton	19 > 22	4
K. Räikkönen	23 > 42	20
F. Alonso	43 > 44	2
K. Räikkönen	45 > 58	14

Driver	Nbr. de Laps	Kilometers
K. Räikkönen	52	275,756 km
L. Hamilton	4	21,212 km
F. Alonso	2	10,606 km

Lap chart

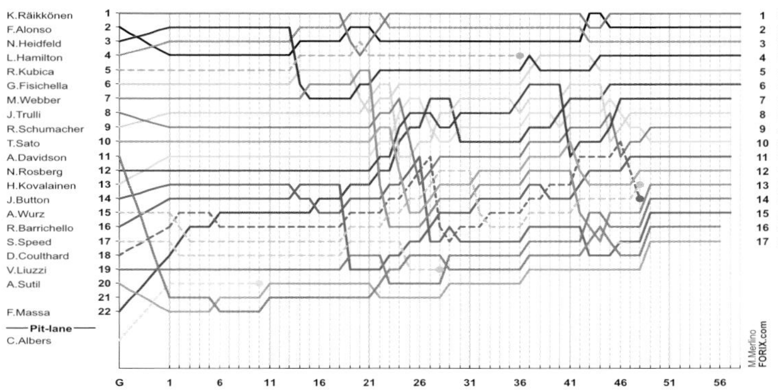

Gaps on the lead board

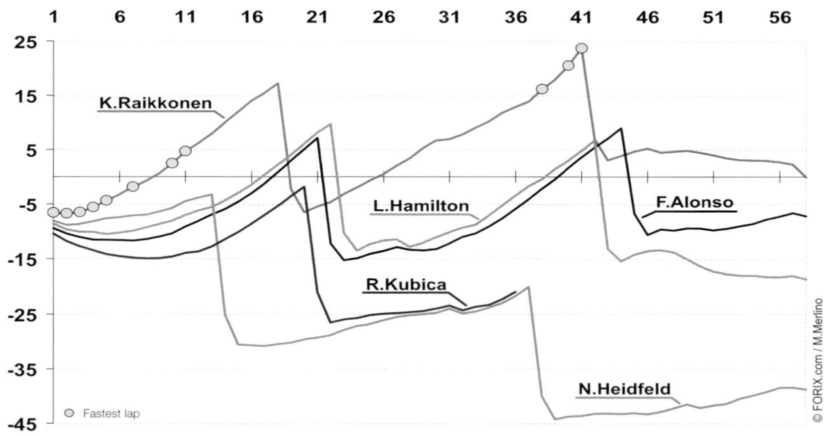

The table "Leading Gaps" is base on the lap by lap information, but only for some selected drivers (for ease of understanding). It adds-in the gaps between these drivers. The line marked "0" represents the winner's average speed. In general, this starts at a slower speed than its eventual average speed, because of the weight of fuel carried on board the car. Then, it goes above the average, before dropping again during the refueling pit stops. This graph therefore allows one to see at any given time the number of seconds (vertically) seperating the drivers on every lap (horizontally).

CHAMPIONSHIPS 1/17

Drivers

	Driver	Team	Wins	Points
1.	K. Räikkönen	Ferrari	1🏆	10
2.	F. Alonso	McLaren Mercedes		8
3.	L. Hamilton	McLaren Mercedes		6
4.	N. Heidfeld	BMW		5
5.	G. Fisichella	Renault		4
6.	F. Massa	Ferrari		3
7.	N. Rosberg	Williams Toyota		2
8.	R. Schumacher	Toyota		1
9.	J. Trulli	Toyota		0
10.	H. Kovalainen	Renault		0
11.	R. Barrichello	Honda		0
12.	T. Sato	Super Aguri Honda		0
13.	M. Webber	Red Bull Renault		0
14.	V. Liuzzi	STR Ferrari		0
15.	J. Button	Honda		0
16.	A. Davidson	Super Aguri Honda		0
17.	A. Sutil	Spyker Ferrari		0
	A. Wurz	Williams Toyota		-
	D. Coulthard	Red Bull Renault		-
	R. Kubica	BMW		-
	S. Speed	STR Ferrari		-
	C. Albers	Spyker Ferrari		-

Constructors

	Constructor	Wins	Points
1.	Vodafone McLaren Mercedes		14
2.	Scuderia Ferrari Marlboro	1🏆	13
3.	BMW Sauber F1 Team		5
4.	ING Renault F1 Team		4
5.	AT&T Williams		2
6.	Panasonic Toyota Racing		1
7.	Honda Racing F1 Team		0
8.	Super Aguri F1 Team		0
9.	Red Bull Racing		0
10.	Scuderia Toro Rosso		0
11.	Etihad Aldar Spyker F1 Team		0

THE CIRCUIT

Name	Albert Park Grand Prix Circuit; Melbourne	**Latitude**	37°51'00.00"S
Lenght	5303 m	**Longitude**	144°58'08.00"E
Distance	58 laps, 307,574 km		

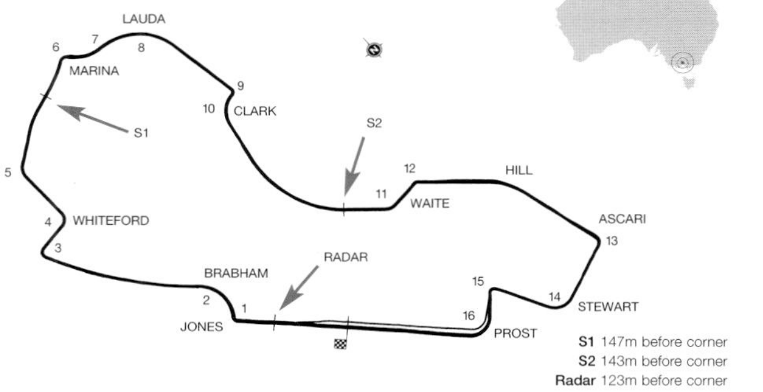

S1 147m before corner
S2 143m before corner
Radar 123m before corner

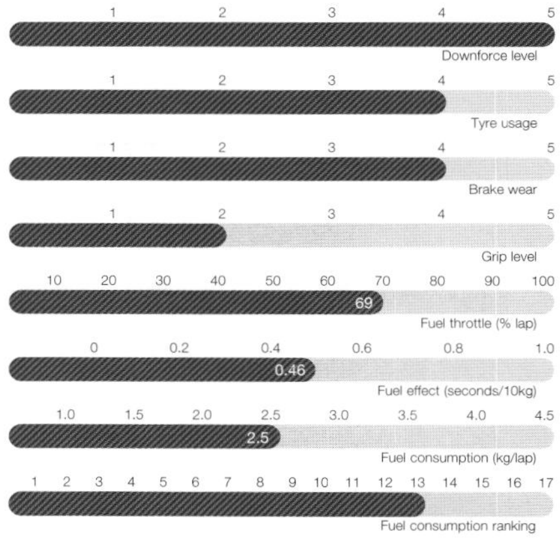

A ONE-TWO
WITH TEAM SPIRIT

The Ferraris came to Sepang as the big
favourites. And yet they weren't quite able to
match the McLarens in terms of race pace. As
it would turn out later, this was all down to a
request for clarification about the legality of the
Ferrari's floor, which had been filed by
McLaren on the evening of the Australian
Grand Prix. McLaren knew all about it because
of the Coughlan affair - which would only blow
up properly three months later. In any case, the
FIA duly issued a rule clarification, which
forced Ferrari to urgently change the design of
their floor and no doubt compromised their
performance. From this race onwards, the
pendulum would swing in either Ferrari's or
McLaren's favour depending on the circuit
layout and characteristics - whether the track
was fast or narrow, slow or bumpy.
In the meantime, Lewis Hamilton and Fernando
Alonso got on with the job of sealing the first
of four one-twos that they would claim over the
course of the season - and the only one after
which their relationship was good enough to
pose together for the cameras after the
chequered flag.

Felipe Massa makes his mark

> It was the fourth pole position of Felipe Massa's career, whose fiancee Raffaela Bassi had come to Kuala Lumpur. And Felipe only had eyes for her…

The duel between the Ferraris and the McLarens that had been seen at the first Grand Prix of the season at Melbourne seemed to be finally underway. In Saturday's qualifying session, the quickest time went to Felipe Massa's Ferrari - with Fernando Alonso's McLaren less than three-tenths of a second behind him. This implied that the Silver Arrows were considerably closer than they had been to the Scuderia in Australia three weeks earlier. Fernando Alonso said: *"We've got to be realistic and admit that our pace - particularly over long stints - isn't at Ferrari's level yet. We've improved the car greatly since Melbourne and we should be a lot closer, but victory is still out of our reach…"*

As for Ferrari, they could see that they faced some tough competition from the two McLarens - but they also faced internal competition between their own two drivers. Team orders, for the moment, were out of the question. It was every man for himself between Ferrari's two drivers.

In Australia, Massa had started from the back of the grid following an engine change. He got back up to sixth place, but could do nothing to stop his teammate's seemingly effortless victory. The same story would not be the case in Malaysia, according to Massa, and the Brazilian's pole position - which he hoped to convert to a victory - served notice of his intent.

Kimi Raikkonen, on the contrary, wasn't able to fight for pole position as he was worried about his engine. *"I think that the engine will manage to hold on, but I am having to look after it,"* he said. *"Also, I haven't found a very good set-up this weekend."*

The intense heat that is a constant feature of the Sepang circuit could clearly become a deciding factor in the race. *"It's a bit like driving in a sauna,"* said Felipe Massa. *"It's going to be important to drink a lot tonight* in order to be ready to lose a lot of fluid in sweat during the race. Of course I just mean drink water : nothing else !"* It was an innocent little joke aimed specifically at Kimi Raikkonen sat next to him, whose well-known fondness for alcoholic refreshment has excited a lot of tabloid interest.

Fernando Alonso fits into the McLaren mould. For now…

Fernando Alonso embarked on a whole new existence at the start of the 2007 season. He had a new team (McLaren), new house (close to Lausanne in Switzerland) and a new marital status (rumour had it that he was secretly married a few weeks earlier). Aged 25, with two World Championship titles already behind him, the Spaniard had the confident look of someone who had turned a corner that was more difficult than most of those found on the world's racing circuits.

McLaren, for him, was a whole world away from Renault. The French team worked on efficiency and discretion, with a just a few sober and functional buildings forming the team's premises. McLaren-Mercedes, by contrast, was a behemoth. Its Woking factory - bombastically christened 'Paragon' - with its two underground wind tunnels, private lake and award-winning architecture, cost 750 million Euros. Even the smallest detail in the British team has millions spent on it.

McLaren is Formula 1 pushed to the limit. Fernando Alonso himself remembers that he was impressed. *"It's true that when they come and get you from the airport and you see the factory for the first time, it takes your breath away,"* he says. *"It's not fair to compare Renault to McLaren, but I can say that here I found some very motivated people who want to be the best at any price. Everything at McLaren is super* professional. These are people who are just focussed on winning, and who have a huge number of sponsors behind them. With the support of a team like this, I should be able to win more World Championships."*

With his new red baseball cap on his head, and his corporate white t-shirt, Alonso appeared to have been successfully inserted with the McLaren microchip. He certainly seemed happy enough to have left Renault. *"Renault was a team that I grew up with so there was* obviously a special relationship with the engineers there. They didn't always listen to me, but we understood each other without having to speak. I'm starting at McLaren with two titles under my belt and suddenly people are taking me seriously. People listen to me and pay attention to what I am saying."* It was a supreme irony that the adventure ended so acrimoniously on November 2, less than seven months later…

> Who said that McLaren lacked humour ? At the post-race family photo, a happy prankster tripped up Fernando Alonso. Even when he's about to fall over, he still has style…

STARTING GRID

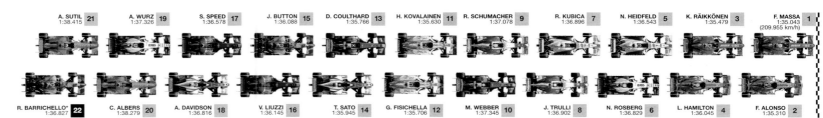

* R. BARRICHELLO penalty for an engine exchange (-10 pos.) Starts from the pit lane.	A. SUTIL 21 1:38.415	A. WURZ 19 1:37.326	S. SPEED 17 1:36.578	J. BUTTON 15 1:36.088	D. COULTHARD 13 1:35.766	H. KOVALAINEN 11 1:35.630	R. SCHUMACHER 9 1:37.078	R. KUBICA 7 1:36.896	N. HEIDFELD 5 1:36.543	K. RÄIKKÖNEN 3 1:35.479	F. MASSA 1 1:35.043 (209.955 km/h)

| R. BARRICHELLO* 22 1:36.827 | C. ALBERS 20 1:38.279 | A. DAVIDSON 18 1:36.816 | V. LIUZZI 16 1:36.145 | T. SATO 14 1:35.945 | G. FISICHELLA 12 1:35.706 | M. WEBBER 10 1:37.345 | J. TRULLI 8 1:36.902 | N. ROSBERG 6 1:36.829 | L. HAMILTON 4 1:36.045 | F. ALONSO 2 1:35.310 |

Alonso – Raikkonen : a constant duel

In the Sepang paddock on Saturday night, you would have been quite hard pushed to find someone prepared to bet even a Euro on McLaren's chances in the Malaysian Grand Prix. Ferrari had dominated practically every practice session, and both cars would start from the 'clean' side of the track. It was also worth noting that Ferrari had dominated the Australian Grand Prix with such consummate ease that it seemed difficult for anybody else to get in the way of a repeat triumph in Sepang. *"We're not able to win races at the moment,"* said Fernando Alonso as he landed in Malaysia on Thursday. *"We can try to reduce the gap a bit, but there are no quick fixes : the Ferraris will be in front".*

How wrong could he be ? When the chequered flag fell the Ferraris were not only behind but quite a long way behind. Kimi Raikkonen managed to save face by finishing third, but Felipe Massa - who had started from pole position - was fifth, behind the BMW Sauber of Nick Heidfeld.

The Malaysian Grand Prix turned out to be the scene of one of those upsets that leaves engineers perplexed. *"We were quick today, but not quite quick enough to get past the McLarens,"* admitted Kimi Raikkonen.

Everything was won and lost at the start. Despite qualifying on the dirty side of the track, the two McLarens came out of the first chicane in first and second places. From there, it was virtually all over. Lewis Hamilton held back the Ferraris while his team mate Fernando Alonso managed to make a clean getaway. *"We knew that we had a chance to do something special at the start,"* said Alonso afterwards. *"But if it hadn't have worked, and the Ferraris had started in front of us, then I'm sure we wouldn't have been able to keep on their pace."*

This meant that Ferrari remained the favourite, despite their hiccup in Malaysia. Round three between Kimi Raikkonen and Fernando Alonso the following weekend in Bahrain looked like being a good one.

Ron Dennis struggles to take it in

What a party ! To celebrate Fernando Alonso and Lewis Hamilton's one-two, everyone wore a florescent orange t-shirt. With a glass of champagne in his hand, Ron Dennis had a smile on his face again : just like the old days. After all, it had been two years since McLaren had won a Grand Prix. *"That's true enough,"* he said. *"I read in the press sometimes that we didn't have the passion any more, and that we weren't motivated enough. And yet I can tell you that we worked really hard to get back on top. It's not just down to a driver or an engineer that we're back here : it's down to everyone. The whole team has made progress."*

It was a one-two that gave the impression of having been trouble-free, but this was far from the case. *"We had a radio communications breakdown for about 15 minutes,"* said Ron Dennis. *"It was just when Fernando was about to come in to stop for fuel again. We were concerned that he might run out of*

fuel, so we put out a pit board with a big yellow arrow telling him that he should come in. It was a big relief when I finally saw him come into the pit lane !"

In order to win the Grand Prix, as Fernando Alonso explained, it was important to make a good start. And as Ron Dennis continued : *"To make a good start, you need good traction : there's no mystery to it. We've been working very hard in this area over several months. It's a lot easier to talk about it than it is to actually do it. But I think that this time our engineers have come up with some clever solutions. The hard thing now is going to be keeping up this level of performance."*

IN BRIEF

+ *"It was tough : very tough,"* said Fernando Alonso. *"My drinks bottle had heated up to at least 60 degrees : it was like drinking tea !"* The ambient temperature on Sunday reached 36 degrees.

+ There was quite a crowd at Sepang : 115,000 spectators. The queues on the motorway were so long that thousands of people missed the race.

+ Lewis Hamilton finished on the podium for a second time at his second Grand Prix. The last person to achieve this was Peter Arundell in 1964.

ʌ
"Take that !" The two McLaren-Mercedes drivers got on well… at the beginning of the season.

<
At the start of the race, Felipe Massa did everything he could to get past Lewis Hamilton, who had surprised him at the first corner. The duel saw the Brazilian pass the McLaren twice, but on each occasion he lost his advantage a few metres down the road. *"It was definitely the toughest battle of my career,"* commented Lewis Hamilton. *"I knew that Felipe was quicker on the straights and that he would be pushing there. I braked as late as I could but he braked even later. Then I knew that he would end up in the grass !"*

MIXED FORTUNES

The start of the season did not go according to plan for Renault, which had hoped to challenge once more for the championship. While Giancarlo Fisichella (pictured) managed to bring home seven points in two races, Heikki Kovalainen only just managed to claim eighth in Sepang.

> Nick Heidfeld finished fourth for the second consecutive time in his BMW Sauber, which he had qualified in fifth place

Drivers unhappy about being kept in the dark…

Behind the scenes in Sepang, one subject was being constantly talked about : how the next Malaysian Grand Prix would take place at night, illuminated by giant floodlights. It's an idea that has already been tried out in the United States with some success, and a pet project of Bernie Ecclestone.

In fairness, it should give an extra twist to the spectacle and allow Asian races to take place at more suitable times for the European viewing public. Some uninformed people also believe that it would mean Asian races could run without the furnace-like heat that has characterised the events so far.

Bernie Ecclestone's idea of night races is designed to please the sport's commercial partners, who have been disappointed by the low television audiences often produced by the Asian events.

Equally, the scheme masks another more self-interested purpose. Since selling his portfolio of businesses to the CVC Capital investment group, the Englishman's priority was to convince the teams to accept more Grands Prix every year - which is the sole way for him to reap maximum benefit. Ecclestone would like to increase the number of races to 20 per year , and he has projects pending in Mexico, Singapore, South Africa, Moscow, Korea and India. Unfortunately, the teams are not of the same opinion. *"I would never accept more than 18 Grands Prix per season,"* said Ron Dennis. *"Life would just be too hard for our personnel. At the start of the year, some people were away from home for more than five weeks. With 20 races, I would need two parallel race teams. It's out of the question."* Really ? In F1, it's normally Bernie who gets his way…

The Sepang circuit is built entirely within a palm grove, on land belonging to Kuala Lumpur's international airport (KLIA), seen in the background.
∨

SNAPSHOTS OF THE WEEKEND

+ 62,000 litres : that's the amount of water the Formula 1 paddock drank during the Malaysian Grand Prix weekend, largely down to roasting temperatures that fluctuated between 35 and 36 degrees centigrade.

+ Kimi Raikkonen arrived in Malaysia sporting a spectacular tattoo on his right arm, which he had treated himself to during his holidays in Australia. Jean Todt remained impervious. *"I couldn't care less if he had a tattoo or not,"* said Todt. *"If he wants to put a tattoo all over his face, that's fine by me. If a sponsor were to complain, I would rather change the sponsor and keep Kimi happy."*

+ *"We need to make a huge, massive amount of progress,"* said Giancarlo Fisichella emphatically,

after Renault's disappointing performance during Saturday's qualifying session. Both cars were knocked out during the second phase of qualifying - and this meant that neither of the yellow cars would make the top 10 on the grid.

+ *"think night racing is an impossible idea. A Grand Prix isn't like a football match. What would happen if there was a power cut ?"* It's fair to say that Fernando Alonso isn't a fan of making the 2008 Malaysian Grand Prix a night race.

+ *"At the end of the Australian Grand Prix, it's true that Michael - I mean Kimi - had a problem with a water leak."* Jean Todt seemed to have difficulty in remembering the identity of his star driver on Thursday…

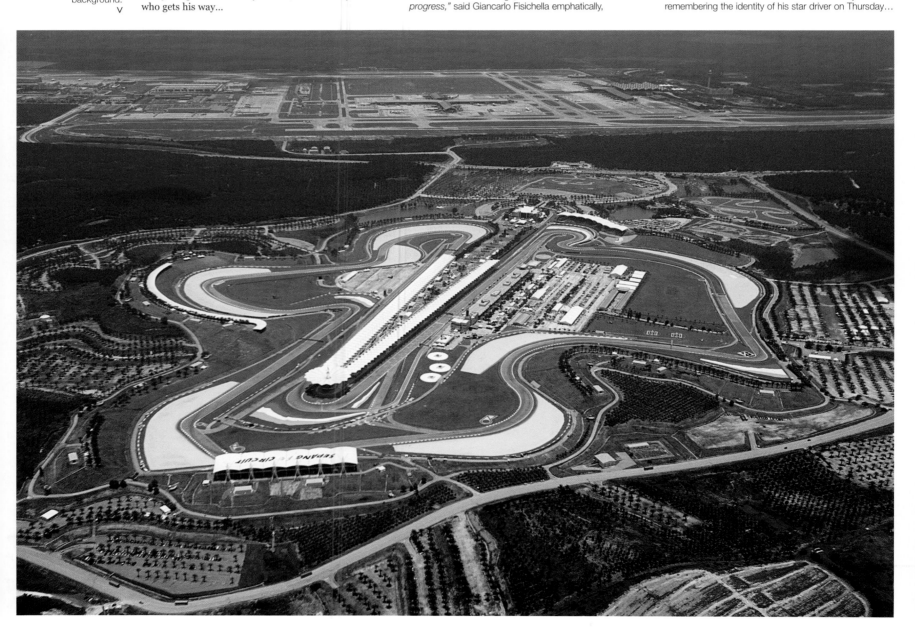

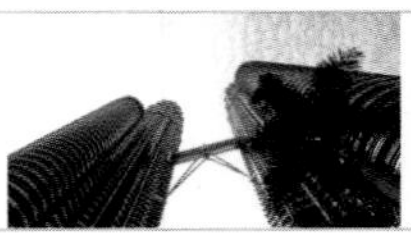

PRACTICE

Date	Weather (AM)	Air temperature	Track temperature	Weather (PM)	Air temperature	Track temperature
Friday April 6, 2007	Sunny and warm	30-32°c	33-50°c	Scattered clouds	34-35°c	48-50°c
Saturday April 7, 2007	Sunny and warm	32-34°c	44-47°c	Cloudy	34-35°c	49-45°c

All the time trials

N° Driver	Nat.	N° Chassis- Engine [Nbr. GP]	Pos. Free 1 Friday 10:00-11:30	Laps Tr.	Pos. Free 2 Friday 14:00-15:30	Laps Tr.	Pos. Free 3 Saturday 11:00-12:00	Laps Tr.	Pos. Q1 Saturday 14:00-14:15	Laps Tr.	Pos. Q2 Saturday 14:22-14:37	Laps Tr.	Pos. Q3 Saturday 14:45-15:00	Nb. Tr.
1. Fernando Alonso	E	McLaren MP4-22 01 - Mercedes [2]	2. 1:35.220	24	12. 1:37.041	26	3. 1:35.311	11	1. 1:34.942	3	1. 1:34.057	3	2. **1:35.310**	10
2. Lewis Hamilton	GB	McLaren MP4-22 05 - Mercedes [2]	3. 1:35.712	22	9. 1:36.797	30	1. 1:34.811	14	2. 1:35.028	3	3. 1:34.650	3	4. **1:36.045**	10
3. Giancarlo Fisichella	I	Renault R27-04 [2]	15. 1:38.300	26	2. 1:35.910	36	13. 1:36.434	15	12. 1:35.879	6	12. **1:35.706**	6		
4. Heikki Kovalainen	FIN	Renault R27-01 [2]	14. 1:38.143	24	3. 1:36.106	37	18. 1:36.876	6	14. 1:36.902	6	11. **1:35.630**	6		
5. Felipe Massa	BR	Ferrari F2007 260 [2]	1. 1:34.972	17	1. 1:35.780	34	2. 1:34.953	15	5. 1:35.340	3	2. 1:34.454	3	1. **1:35.043**	10
6. Kimi Räikkönen	FIN	Ferrari F2007 261 [2]	4. 1:35.779	20	4. 1:36.160	33	5. 1:35.498	7	3. 1:35.138	3	4. 1:34.687	3	3. **1:35.479**	10
7. Jenson Button	GB	Honda RA107-04 [2]	20. 1:39.331	17	15. 1:37.578	29	17. 1:36.658	20	13. 1:35.913	9	15. **1:36.088**	6		
8. Rubens Barrichello	BR	Honda RA107-02 [2]->[1]	19. 1:39.234	21	21. 1:38.713	20	19. 1:36.972	19	19. **1:36.827**	7				
9. Nick Heidfeld	D	BMW Sauber F1.07-05 [2]			10. 1:36.862	25	7. 1:36.160	20	6. 1:35.617	3	6. 1:35.203	6	5. **1:36.543**	10
10. Robert Kubica	PL	BMW Sauber F1.07-04 [2]	10. 1:37.121	12	7. 1:36.717	18	4. 1:35.385	16	4. 1:35.294	3	5. 1:34.739	3	7. **1:36.896**	8
11. Ralf Schumacher	D	Toyota TF107/03 [2]	9. 1:37.052	22	8. 1:36.760	28	9. 1:36.245	20	10. 1:35.736	6	10. 1:35.595	6	9. **1:37.078**	10
12. Jarno Trulli	I	Toyota TF107/04 [2]	7. 1:36.597	25	16. 1:37.712	34	20. 1:37.473	16	7. 1:35.666	7	7. 1:35.255	6	8. **1:36.902**	10
14. David Coulthard	GB	Red Bull RB3 3 - Renault [1]	11. 1:37.484	7	13. 1:37.203	25	11. 1:36.273	13	9. 1:35.730	6	13. **1:35.766**	6		
15. Mark Webber	AUS	Red Bull RB3 2 - Renault [2]	6. 1:36.522	20	11. 1:36.906	18	10. 1:36.257	17	8. 1:35.727	6	9. 1:35.579	6	10. **1:37.345**	9
16. Nico Rosberg	D	Williams FW29-03 - Toyota [2]	5. 1:36.308	21	5. 1:36.523	31	6. 1:35.770	16	11. 1:35.755	6	8. 1:35.380	6	6. **1:36.829**	10
17. Alexander Wurz	AUT	Williams FW29-04 - Toyota [2]			6. 1:36.621	21	14. 1:36.473	16	20. **1:37.326**	5				
18. Vitantonio Liuzzi	I	Toro Rosso STR2 - Ferrari [2]	13. 1:37.882	20	17. 1:37.855	26	12. 1:36.297	18	15. 1:36.140	6	16. **1:36.145**	6		
19. Scott Speed	USA	Toro Rosso STR2 - Ferrari [2]	18. 1:39.130	9	20. 1:38.650	20	15. 1:36.501	14	17. **1:36.578**	6				
20. Adrian Sutil	D	Spyker F8-VII/03 - Ferrari [2]	16. 1:38.720	29	19. 1:38.419	28	21. 1:38.018	20	22. **1:38.415**	6				
21. Christijan Albers	NL	Spyker F8-VII/01 - Ferrari [2]	22. 1:40.074	25	22. 1:39.807	23	22. 1:38.225	20	21. **1:38.279**	6				
22. Takuma Sato	J	Super Aguri SA07-04 - Honda [2]	17. 1:38.966	10	14. 1:37.282	30	16. 1:36.545	18	16. 1:36.430	7	14. **1:35.945**	5		
23. Anthony Davidson	GB	Super Aguri SA07-02 - Honda [2]	21. 1:39.357	9	18. 1:38.334	27	8. 1:36.195	19	18. **1:36.816**	6				
35. Sebastian Vettel	D	BMW Sauber F1.07-03	12. 1:37.837	39										
38. Kazuki Nakajima	J	Williams FW29-03 - Toyota	8. 1:36.885	15										

Fastest lap overall
F. Alonso 1:34.057 (212,156 km/h)

Maximum speed

N° Driver	S1 Qualifs	Pos.	S1 Race	Pos.	S2 Qualifs	Pos.	S2 Race	Pos.	Finish Qualifs	Pos.	Finish Race	Pos.	Radar Qualifs	Pos.	Radar Race	Pos.
1. F. Alonso	285,7	14	289,9	10	155,3	3	152,9	3	267,1	3	263,9	6	294,5	13	296,4	14
2. L. Hamilton	286,7	8	290,1	6	152,9	12	151,7	8	267,7	1	264,3	4	297,6	5	296,5	13
3. G. Fisichella	286,6	9	288,6	15	154,9	5	154,4	2	266,9	4	263,5	7	296,8	7	297,7	7
4. H. Kovalainen	288,0	4	288,6	14	153,9	6	150,9	13	265,4	9	263,5	8	299,2	2	296,7	12
5. F. Massa	286,3	10	294,9	1	156,5	2	154,6	1	266,8	5	267,9	1	297,1	6	302,3	1
6. K. Räikkönen	290,0	1	291,5	2	157,9	1	152,8	4	267,1	2	263,4	9	299,8	1	301,2	3
7. J. Button	283,3	20	290,7	3	153,3	9	149,1	18	262,9	19	261,2	15	293,0	17	297,0	10
8. R. Barrichello	283,4	19	289,0	13	153,3	8	151,8	7	262,2	20	262,6	11	292,8	18	297,0	9
9. N. Heidfeld	286,7	7	290,4	5	155,2	4	151,3	11	266,1	7	264,0	5	296,6	8	297,9	6
10. R. Kubica	287,0	6	289,3	12	151,1	18	150,3	15	265,0	10	263,4	10	296,4	9	295,8	16
11. R. Schumacher	285,9	13	288,0	17	153,1	11	150,5	14	264,2	14	261,4	13	292,5	19	294,4	18
12. J. Trulli	284,3	17	286,9	19	148,3	22	147,6	20	263,3	18	260,3	16	292,1	20	294,7	17
14. D. Coulthard	286,1	11	284,8	20	153,3	10	151,1	12	263,8	16	258,6	20	295,4	11	292,5	20
15. M. Webber	283,9	18	287,8	18	152,1	15	152,0	5	264,7	11	259,3	18	293,7	16	293,2	19
16. N. Rosberg	289,1	2	290,0	7	153,5	7	152,0	6	266,4	6	267,7	2	298,0	4	299,2	4
17. A. Wurz	285,4	15	289,9	8	150,1	19	151,5	10	264,0	15	266,9	3	293,9	15	301,6	2
18. V. Liuzzi	286,1	12	288,2	16	152,5	13	151,7	9	264,2	13	260,3	17	295,7	10	297,1	8
19. S. Speed	285,2	16	289,9	9	152,3	14	149,9	16	263,4	17	259,1	19	294,1	14	296,2	15
20. A. Sutil	278,7	22	277,7	22	150,0	21			257,3	22			285,9	22		
21. C. Albers	279,2	21	281,3	21	150,0	20	147,0	21	258,6	21	253,2	21	287,1	21	285,9	21
22. T. Sato	288,2	3	290,7	4	151,4	16	149,8	17	265,8	8	262,6	12	295,0	12	296,8	11
23. A. Davidson	287,1	5	289,4	11	151,3	17	148,1	19	264,7	12	261,4	14	299,0	3	299,0	5

Best sector times

	S1		S2		S3		
Qualifs	**S1** R. Kubica	24.767	**S2** F. Alonso	30.873	**S3** F. Alonso	38.383	= 1:34.023
Race	**S1** L. Hamilton	25.197	**S2** F. Alonso	31.695	**S3** F. Alonso	39.199	= 1:36.091

RACE

Date	Weather	Air temperature	Track temperature	Humidity	Wind speed
Sunday April 8, 2007 (15:00)	Sunny and warm	34-35°c	50-56°c	58%	1.3 m/s

Classification & retirements

Pos.	Driver	Constructor	Tyres	Laps	Time	Km/h
1.	F. Alonso	McLaren Mercedes	MMH	56	1:32:14.930	201,893
2.	L. Hamilton	McLaren Mercedes	MMH	56	+ 17.557	201,255
3.	K. Räikkönen	Ferrari	MMH	56	+ 18.339	201,227
4.	N. Heidfeld	BMW	MMH	56	+ 33.777	200,669
5.	F. Massa	Ferrari	MMH	56	+ 36.705	200,563
6.	G. Fisichella	Renault	MMH	56	+ 1:05.638	199,527
7.	J. Trulli	Toyota	HMM	56	+ 1:10.132	199,367
8.	H. Kovalainen	Renault (T-Car)	MMH	56	+ 1:12.015	199,300
9.	A. Wurz	Williams Toyota	MMH	56	+ 1:29.924	198,666
10.	M. Webber	Red Bull Renault	HHM	56	+ 1:33.556	198,538
11.	R. Barrichello	Honda	MMH	55	1 lap	197,240
12.	J. Button	Honda	HMM	55	1 lap	197,215
13.	T. Sato	Super Aguri Honda	MMH	55	1 lap	196,908
14.	S. Speed	STR Ferrari	MMH	55	1 lap	196,691
15.	R. Schumacher	Toyota	MMH	55	1 lap	196,304
16.	A. Davidson	Super Aguri Honda	MMH	55	1 lap	196,084
17.	V. Liuzzi	STR Ferrari	MMMH	55	1 lap	196,045
18.	R. Kubica	BMW	MMH	55	1 lap	196,010

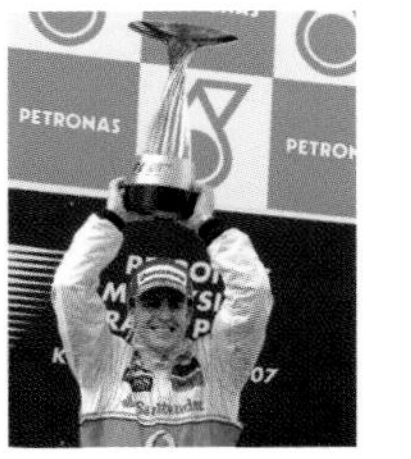

Driver	Constructor	Tyres	Laps	Reason
N. Rosberg	Williams Toyota	MMH	42	Overheating engine following water leak
D. Coulthard	Red Bull Renault	HM	36	Brake pedal blockage due to contact with steering column
C. Albers	Spyker Ferrari	M	7	Gearbox stuck in first gear, leading to overheating
A. Sutil	Spyker Ferrari	M	0	Damaged rear suspension, contact with Button and into gravel trap

Tyres H: Hard & M: Medium

Fastest laps

	Driver	Time	Lap	Km/h
1.	L. Hamilton	1:36.701	22	206,355
2.	F. Alonso	1:36.861	42	206,014
3.	F. Massa	1:37.199	42	205,298
4.	K. Räikkönen	1:37.228	40	205,237
5.	N. Heidfeld	1:37.417	55	204,838
6.	N. Rosberg	1:37.704	18	204,237
7.	H. Kovalainen	1:37.810	41	204,015
8.	A. Wurz	1:37.864	19	203,903
9.	G. Fisichella	1:37.879	44	203,872
10.	J. Trulli	1:38.016	40	203,587
11.	D. Coulthard	1:38.098	28	203,416
12.	V. Liuzzi	1:38.447	21	202,695
13.	T. Sato	1:38.496	37	202,595
14.	M. Webber	1:38.540	55	202,504
15.	R. Barrichello	1:38.566	32	202,451
16.	J. Button	1:38.658	54	202,262
17.	R. Kubica	1:38.874	53	201,820
18.	S. Speed	1:39.098	54	201,364
19.	R. Schumacher	1:39.243	52	201,070
20.	A. Davidson	1:39.566	32	200,417
21.	C. Albers	1:41.495	5	196,608

Pit stops

	Driver	Lap	Duration	Stop	Total
1.	V. Liuzzi	2	37.684	1	37.684
2.	R. Kubica	11	35.953	1	35.953
3.	R. Barrichello	12	29.725	1	29.725
4.	F. Massa	17	31.178	1	31.178
5.	A. Wurz	17	30.767	1	30.767
6.	S. Speed	17	30.072	1	30.072
7.	T. Sato	17	28.996	1	28.996
8.	F. Alonso	18	30.566	1	30.566
9.	K. Räikkönen	18	31.472	1	31.472
10.	J. Trulli	18	29.933	1	29.933
11.	A. Davidson	18	30.189	1	30.189
12.	N. Rosberg	19	29.579	1	29.579
13.	R. Schumacher	19	29.718	1	29.718
14.	V. Liuzzi	19	29.083	2	1:06.767
15.	L. Hamilton	20	29.073	1	29.073
16.	M. Webber	21	30.949	1	30.949
17.	J. Button	21	29.018	1	29.018
18.	N. Heidfeld	22	30.129	1	30.129
19.	H. Kovalainen	22	28.260	1	28.260
20.	G. Fisichella	23	28.813	1	28.813
21.	D. Coulthard	26	29.718	1	29.718
22.	R. Kubica	27	31.454	2	1:07.407
23.	R. Schumacher	28	28.991	2	58.709
24.	A. Wurz	34	31.872	2	1:02.639
25.	R. Barrichello	34	30.320	2	1:00.045
26.	S. Speed	34	31.202	2	1:01.274
27.	A. Davidson	34	29.495	2	59.684
28.	V. Liuzzi	36	30.083	3	1:36.850
29.	J. Button	37	29.359	2	58.377
30.	L. Hamilton	38	28.984	2	58.057
31.	N. Rosberg	38	30.969	2	1:00.548
32.	J. Trulli	38	29.380	2	59.313
33.	H. Kovalainen	39	28.437	2	56.697
34.	F. Alonso	40	28.864	2	59.430
35.	T. Sato	39	35.358	2	1:04.354
36.	F. Massa	40	29.107	2	1:00.285
37.	K. Räikkönen	41	28.169	2	59.641
38.	N. Heidfeld	42	27.692	2	57.821
39.	G. Fisichella	42	27.760	2	56.573
40.	M. Webber	42	28.828	2	59.777

Race leader

Driver	Laps in the lead	Nbr of Laps
F. Alonso	1 > 18	18
L. Hamilton	19 > 20	2
N. Heidfeld	21	1
F. Alonso	22 > 40	19
K. Räikkönen	41	1
F. Alonso	42 > 56	15

Driver	Nbr of laps	Kilometers
F. Alonso	52	288,236 km
L. Hamilton	2	11,086 km
N. Heidfeld	1	5,543 km
K. Räikkönen	1	5,543 km

Lap chart

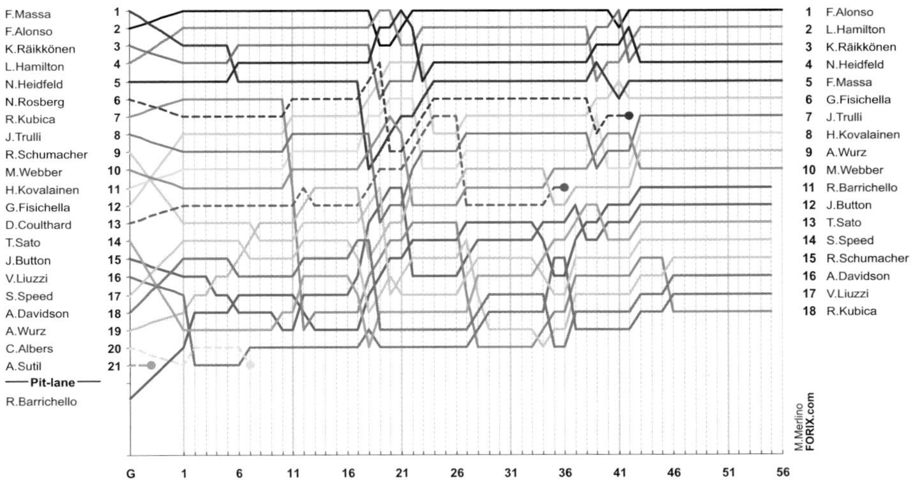
F.Massa
F.Alonso
K.Räikkönen
L.Hamilton
N.Heidfeld
N.Rosberg
R.Kubica
J.Trulli
R.Schumacher
M.Webber
H.Kovalainen
G.Fisichella
D.Coulthard
T.Sato
J.Button
V.Liuzzi
S.Speed
A.Davidson
A.Wurz
C.Albers
A.Sutil
Pit-lane
R.Barrichello
G 1 6 11 16 21 26 31 36 41 46 51 56
1 F.Alonso
2 L.Hamilton
3 K.Räikkönen
4 N.Heidfeld
5 F.Massa
6 G.Fisichella
7 J.Trulli
8 H.Kovalainen
9 A.Wurz
10 M.Webber
11 R.Barrichello
12 J.Button
13 T.Sato
14 S.Speed
15 R.Schumacher
16 A.Davidson
17 V.Liuzzi
18 R.Kubica
M.Merlino FORIX.com

Gaps on the lead board

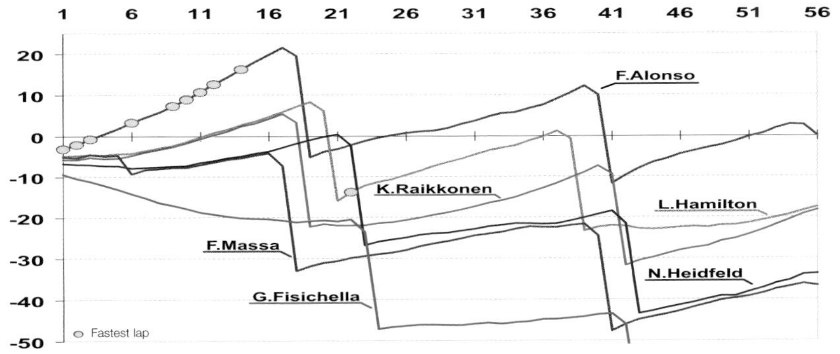
1 6 11 16 21 26 31 36 41 46 51 56
20
10
0
-10
-20
-30
-40
-50
F.Alonso
K.Raikkonen
L.Hamilton
F.Massa
N.Heidfeld
G.Fisichella
Fastest lap

CHAMPIONSHIPS 2/17

Drivers

	Driver	Team	Wins	Points
1.	F. Alonso	McLaren Mercedes	1🏆	18
2.	K. Räikkönen	Ferrari	1🏆	16
3.	L. Hamilton	McLaren Mercedes		14
4.	N. Heidfeld	BMW		10
5.	G. Fisichella	Renault		7
6.	F. Massa	Ferrari		7
7.	J. Trulli	Toyota		2
8.	N. Rosberg	Williams Toyota		2
9.	H. Kovalainen	Renault		1
10.	R. Schumacher	Toyota		1
11.	A. Wurz	Williams Toyota		0
12.	M. Webber	Red Bull Renault		0
13.	R. Barrichello	Honda		0
14.	T. Sato	Super Aguri Honda		0
15.	J. Button	Honda		0
16.	V. Liuzzi	STR Ferrari		0
17.	S. Speed	STR Ferrari		0
18.	A. Davidson	Super Aguri Honda		0
19.	A. Sutil	Spyker Ferrari		0
20.	R. Kubica	BMW		0
	D. Coulthard	Red Bull Renault		-
	C. Albers	Spyker Ferrari		-

Constructors

	Constructor	Wins	Points
1.	Vodafone McLaren Mercedes	1🏆	32
2.	Scuderia Ferrari Marlboro	1🏆	23
3.	BMW Sauber F1 Team		10
4.	ING Renault F1 Team		8
5.	Panasonic Toyota Racing		3
6.	AT&T Williams		2
7.	Red Bull Racing		0
8.	Honda Racing F1 Team		0
9.	Super Aguri F1 Team		0
10.	Scuderia Toro Rosso		0
11.	Etihad Aldar Spyker F1 Team		0

THE CIRCUIT

Name Sepang Circuit; Kuala Lumpur
Lenght 5543 m
Distance 56 laps, 310,408 km
Latitude 2°45'38.55"N
Longitude 101°44'18.00"E

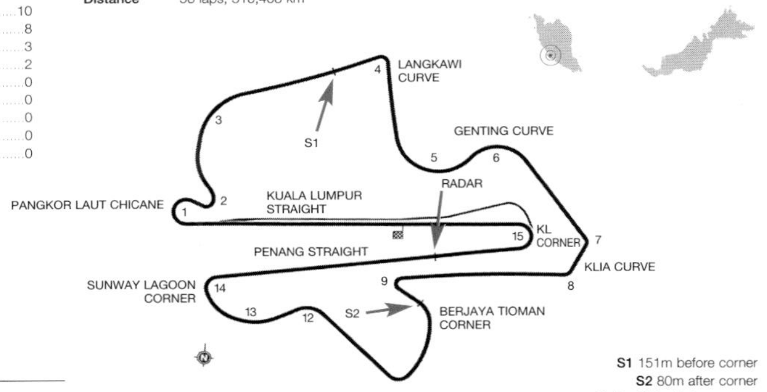
LANGKAWI CURVE
GENTING CURVE
RADAR
KUALA LUMPUR STRAIGHT
PANGKOR LAUT CHICANE
PENANG STRAIGHT
KL CORNER
KLIA CURVE
SUNWAY LAGOON CORNER
BERJAYA TIOMAN CORNER
S1
S2
1
2
3
4
5
6
7
8
9
12
13
14
15

S1 151m before corner
S2 80m after corner
Radar 270m before corner

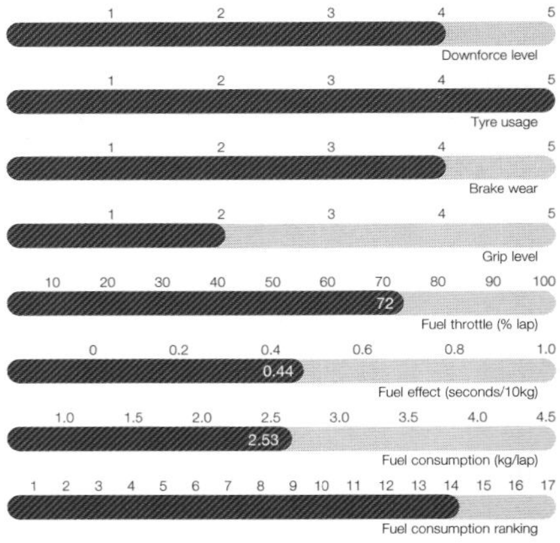
Downforce level
Tyre usage
Brake wear
Grip level
Fuel throttle (% lap)
72
Fuel effect (seconds/10kg)
0.44
Fuel consumption (kg/lap)
2.53
Fuel consumption ranking

POLE, VICTORY AND FASTEST LAP FOR FELIPE MASSA - THE STARRING ROLE FOR LEWIS HAMILTON.

On paper, it seemed that the Bahrain Grand Prix was Felipe Massa's race of the year - after he obtained the 'grand slam' of pole, win and the fastest lap. But in actual fact, the hero of the race was none other than Lewis Hamilton. With a second-place finish, the young Englishman entered the history books by becoming the only driver to end up on the podium in his first three races. Three drivers now held the joint lead of the championship on 22 points each : Fernando Alonso, Kimi Raikkonen and Hamilton.

> He qualified in pole position at Sepang and had the quickest car of the lot. But in a race that should have been a walk in the park for him, Felipe Massa somehow managed to get caught out and finished the Malaysian Grand Prix only in fifth place. It was a troubled start to the season that nevertheless failed to disturb the Brazilian's unruffled optimism. *"On that occasion, I was really unlucky,"* he said. *"I don't know what the problem is, but that little bit extra is still standing between me and the results I want. In Malaysia, it all went wrong at the start. I saw Fernando's car getting bigger and bigger in my mirrors as we headed down to the first corner. At the braking point he was beside me, on the inside of the corner. So what could I do ? The worst part was that I found myself on the slippery side of the corner and Lewis was able to take advantage of that to get in front of me as well. My only chance was to get back past Lewis as quickly as possible so as not to let Fernando get away. So I tried it, and it didn't work. But I've got no regrets. I had a call from Michael (Schumacher) on the phone. I won't tell you what he said, but I've got a real feeling that my season starts here…"*

Felipe Massa takes another pole, Lewis Hamilton alongside him

Having finished third in Australia and second in Malaysia, logic dictated that Lewis Hamilton would be aiming for victory in Bahrain. He had every possibility to do so : during practice the young Briton topped the time sheets for the very first time in his fledgling F1 career.

His ambitions did not stop there : he wanted to win. On Saturday, he was once again in front of his World Champion teammate Fernando Alonso, who could only manage fourth on the grid.

"The car's still not exactly perfect," said Lewis Hamilton. *"But let's just say that we've made a lot of* progress since last week and now we seem to be a lot closer to Ferrari than we were. In fact, I reckon we're a bit quicker towards the end of the longer stints now."* The most important thing, according to Lewis Hamilton, would be to get the start right. By starting second, he would get going from the 'dirty' side of the grid. Felipe Massa, sitting in pole position explained : *"In Malaysia, it wasn't particularly a factor. But here, with the sand constantly blowing onto the circuit, it's always better to start from the clean line."*

Massa was also in pole position the previous weekend at Sepang, but he was caught out by the two McLarens at the first corner and he was determined not to make the same mistake again. *"I'm definitely going to be more aggressive,"* he vowed before the start. It was a threat that didn't scare Lewis Hamilton though. *"I know that Felipe is trying to play on my nerves,"* said Hamilton. *"But it makes no difference to me. I'm just going to be a bit careful : games like that can be dangerous."*

IN BRIEF

+ In Bahrain, a deal between Ferrari and the Aldar real estate company was signed to build a theme park based around Ferrari. Work has already begun on the site, located on the exclusive Yas island in Abu Dhabi - which is already a Ferrari shareholder. The park will cover 250,000 metres, with 24 different attractions for all ages and a driving school, at the circuit that will host the forthcoming Abu Dhabi Grand Prix, scheduled for 2009.

+ Heikki Kovalainen was given a stern talking -to by his team boss Flavio Briatore after only finishing 10th in the Australia Grand Prix, being threatened with the sack unless his performances improved. The Finn didn't make things easier for himself in Bahrain by qualifying outside the top 10, managing only 12th. *"I'm disappointed but I feel that I got* the most possible out of my car and that it was difficult to do better"*, he said.

+ Lewis Hamilton was 23rd on the grid when he drove the Bahrain circuit for the first time, in Formula 3. From this position right at the back he was able to fight his way up and win the race ! *"I was lucky, but it will be a lot more difficult in F1,"* he said. *"It's a different ballpark at this level…"*

> Fernando Alonso and Ron Dennis share a relaxing moment together : a rare photograph that is now virtually a collectors' item !

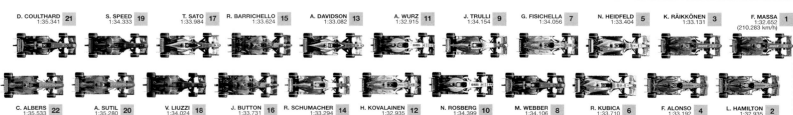

D. COULTHARD 21 1:35.341	S. SPEED 19 1:34.333	T. SATO 17 1:33.984	R. BARRICHELLO 15 1:33.624	A. DAVIDSON 13 1:33.082	A. WURZ 11 1:32.915	J. TRULLI 9 1:34.154	G. FISICHELLA 7 1:33.404	N. HEIDFELD 5 1:33.404	K. RÄIKKÖNEN 3 1:33.131	F. MASSA 1 1:32.652 (210.283 km/h)
C. ALBERS 22 1:35.533	A. SUTIL 20 1:35.280	V. LIUZZI 18 1:34.024	J. BUTTON 16 1:33.731	R. SCHUMACHER 14 1:33.294	H. KOVALAINEN 12 1:32.935	N. ROSBERG 10 1:34.399	M. WEBBER 8 1:34.106	R. KUBICA 6 1:33.710	F. ALONSO 4 1:33.192	L. HAMILTON 2 1:32.935

All on 22 points : a three-way fight for the title

No rookie had ever managed to finish his first three races on the podium in the history of Formula 1. Nonetheless, this unique feat was accomplished by Lewis Hamilton, McLaren-Mercedes' remarkable prodigy.

Happiness clearly comes in twos : not only did Hamilton claim second place in the race, but he also took second place in the championship, equalling his team mate Fernando Alonso as well as Kimi Raikkonen. Technically speaking, both Alonso and Raikkonen were ahead of him as they had each won a Grand Prix - but who's counting ? Felipe Massa, just five points further behind, completed the leading championship group with everything to play for.

The 2007 title would undoubtedly go to one of those four drivers - but which one ? The first three races demonstrated just how far the pendulum could swing from team to team. A driver who dominated one race could find himself nowhere in the next one. This was exactly the case for Fernando Alonso, who won in Malaysia but was a long way back in Bahrain, after brake problems dropped him to fifth behind the BMW Sauber of Nick Heidfeld. As for Kimi Raikkonen - the

winner in Australia - he was never really in a position to fight for the lead, having been stuck behind Fernando Alonso from the first lap. *"It was quite a difficult weekend,"* said Raikkonen. *"We're not exactly up there in terms in terms of handling, and I hope we'll find out why in the next few weeks. I know that some new parts are coming that should give us a solution."*

Following the cancellation of the San Marino Grand Prix, there would be a four week gap until the next race at Barcelona : enough time for the teams to resolve any problems on their cars. Denis Chevrier, Renault's operations director, explained : *"We're not pretending that things are suddenly going to be better next time, but we will have a car that is slightly redesigned in Spain. That could shake things up a bit. You always start the season with a car that is fresh out of winter testing, whereas later you prepare a car that will be good until July"*

Renault would not be the only ones with a revised and corrected car for Barcelona : this would be the case for practically all of the teams. A brand new championship was getting ready to kick off in Spain.

Nothing scares Lewis Hamilton

No driver has ever made a such a scintillating entrance into Formula 1 as Lewis Hamilton : he was third in Australia, then second in Malaysia, before showing himself to be considerably quicker than Fernando Alonso in Bahrain, where he finished just behind the winner.

The young Englishmen felt that victory had been within his grasp. *"I reckon I could have won,"* he said at the finish. *"We were very quick this weekend, apart from maybe the second stint on used tyres. But I think I would have been on pole if Felipe Massa had not managed to put in a perfect lap. If I could have been in front of him, then I reckon I could have pulled away. I was definitely quicker than him..."*

By finishing his third Grand Prix on the podium for the third time, Lewis Hamilton entered motor sport's history books, becoming the only driver ever to have pulled off such an achievement. *"I'm proud to have scored those three podiums : it's good,"* he said. *"My family and I have worked very hard over the last 13 years to get here, and it's what we deserve now. I don't really know what it's like to have fans or a fan club : I'm looking forward to the British Grand Prix to find out. But I hope I'll still be able to walk the streets without a problem ! At the moment I'm just looking forward to going home : I've been away for nine weeks now..."*

He goes there leading the championship, which he is understandably pleased about. *"It's fantastic to have the same number of points as Fernando and Kimi, but*

when it comes to it I'm basically third - because of their wins so far this year. Having said that, I see no reason why I can't fight for the championship title as well. I've got the same car as Fernando and I seem to be as quick as he is. I feel a bit more confident now that we have shown ourselves to be capable of winning races..."

^
"I dedicate this victory to my fiancee. That was a dreadful week, and she has been very patient with me", said Felipe Massa.

<< (on the left)
Lewis Hamilton managed to hold off Kimi Raikkonen perfectly, who was just behind him.

< (opposite)
Retirement for Jenson Button...after just three corners. *"I got off to quite a good start, but at the second corner Takuma (Sato) boxed me in and I had nowhere to go. It had to be the gravel trap. When I got back onto the track in turn three, David (Coulthard) cut me up and I had nowhere to go again ! We touched and I spun. My anti-stall system didn't work, so that was my day's work over !"*

THE SOLITUDE OF SAND

You won't find too many traffic jams on the way to the Sakhir circuit. The small number of spectators are only to be found on the start-finish straight. The rest of the track is just desert. It is truly a circuit in the middle of nowhere.

> *"I like you Mario, but you really need to stay off the sunbed !"* Nick Heidfeld and Mario Thiessen joked with each other as they celebrated yet another fourth place finish for the German driver - his fourth on the trot. The Zurich-based team confirmed their position just behind the Ferraris and the McLarens. In fact, Nick Heidfeld managed to overtake Fernando Alonso at Bahrain to finish less than three seconds off the podium. *"I wouldn't have believed that I could get past Fernando, particularly as his top speed was quicker than mine. Luckily he made a mistake at turn 13."* With sixth place for Robert Kubica, the team collected eight points in total in order to be sure of third in the constructors' championship.

Honda: a real disaster!

In February, when they launched their 'earth car' (devoid of any sponsorship but decorated with a map of the world) Honda had little idea of the disaster that awaited them.

In Bahrain, after finishing two Grands Prix a long way off the points, Jenson Button reckoned that the livery was *"the only positive point about the whole car"*. Apart from that, nothing really worked. *"It's quite hard to point the finger at one specific thing,"* said the Englishman. *"We're dealing with a lot of instability under braking, particularly from the back. The car finds it hard to hit the apexes of the corners, and then coming out of them there's no traction. Our traction control doesn't seem to work either. The car is so difficult to drive that it's virtually impossible to take the same corner twice in the same way. Then when I put a bit of wing on to improve the stability, we're nowhere in terms of top speed."* Apart from that, things are obviously looking good...

Various theories are flying about the Anglo-Japanese team as to why their car is so problematical. *"Bits of it work : I don't think the gearbox is a problem,"* said team boss Nick Fry. In fact he was quite right : the gearbox and the rear suspension were the only parts to remain unaltered in the coming weeks.

As for the rest, the team was working non-stop on a B-spec for the troublesome RA107 chassis. *"Unfortunately, the car's got no grip,"* added Nick Fry. *"So we're going to introduce some big changes, especially in terms of aerodynamics, at Barcelona, Canada and Magny-Cours."*

It was already too late for Honda to be in the top three of the constructors' championship, the target announced at the start of the season. In fact, Honda's hopes of victory did not last long at all.

> Jarno Trulli finished seventh and scored two points. *"It was like a win, because I really had to fight to stay ahead of the others"* he said. *"It's hard to push and stop others passing you at the same time, particularly given that my top speed was not as quick as everybody else's."*

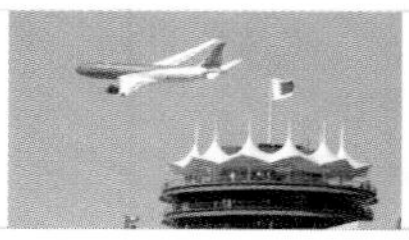

PRACTICE

Date	Weather (AM)	Air temperature	Track temperature	Weather (PM)	Air temperature	Track temperature
Friday April 13, 2007	Sunny	30-32°c	36-42°c	Sunny	32°c	43°c
Saturday April 14, 2007	Sunny	30-31°c	35-37°c	Sunny, some clouds	32-35°c	42-45°c

All the time trials

N° Driver	Nat.	N° Chassis- Engine [Nbr. GP]	Pos.	Free 1 Friday 10:00-11:30	Laps Tr.	Pos.	Free 2 Friday 14:00-15:30	Laps Tr.	Pos.	Free 3 Saturday 11:00-12:00	Laps Tr.	Pos.	Q1 Saturday 14:00-14:15	Laps Tr.	Pos.	Q2 Saturday 14:22-14:37	Laps Tr.	Pos.	Q3 Saturday 14:45-15:00	Nb. Tr.
1. Fernando Alonso	E	McLaren MP4-22 01 - Mercedes [1]	4.	1:34.161	15	5.	1:33.784	30	7.	1:33.235	11	3.	1:33.049	3	5.	1:32.214	3	4.	**1:33.192**	10
2. Lewis Hamilton	GB	McLaren MP4-22 05 - Mercedes [1]	3.	1:34.110	17	2.	1:33.540	33	1.	1:32.543	12	2.	1:32.580	3	2.	1:31.732	3	2.	**1:32.935**	10
3. Giancarlo Fisichella	I	Renault R27-04 [1]	14.	1:35.697	17	15.	1:34.796	34	9.	1:33.602	17	12.	1:33.556	6	10.	1:32.889	6	7.	**1:34.056**	10
4. Heikki Kovalainen	FIN	Renault R27-01 [1]	12.	1:35.474	21	12.	1:34.585	33	10.	1:33.605	21	10.	1:33.467	6	12.	**1:32.935**	6			
5. Felipe Massa	BR	Ferrari F2007 260 [1]	2.	1:33.679	17	4.	1:33.772	28	6.	1:32.950	12	1.	1:32.443	3	1.	1:31.359	3	1.	**1:32.652**	10
6. Kimi Räikkönen	FIN	Ferrari F2007 261 [1]	1.	1:33.162	21	1.	1:33.527	33	2.	1:32.549	16	4.	1:33.161	3	3.	1:31.812	3	3.	**1:33.131**	10
7. Jenson Button	GB	Honda RA107-04 [1]	11.	1:35.445	24	22.	1:36.079	19	16.	1:34.023	20	16.	1:33.967	8	16.	**1:33.731**	6			
8. Rubens Barrichello	BR	Honda RA107-02 [2]	17.	1:35.911	20	11.	1:34.391	28	18.	1:34.397	17	14.	1:33.776	6	15.	**1:33.624**	6			
9. Nick Heidfeld	D	BMW Sauber F1.07-05 [1]	6.	1:35.076	30	7.	1:34.076	34	3.	1:32.652	15	5.	1:33.164	3	4.	1:32.154	4	5.	**1:33.404**	10
10. Robert Kubica	PL	BMW Sauber F1.07-04 & 03 [1]	7.	1:35.248	24	3.	1:33.732	37	4.	1:32.755	15	8.	1:33.348	4	6.	1:32.292	3	6.	**1:33.710**	10
11. Ralf Schumacher	D	Toyota TF107/03 [1]	13.	1:35.573	24	18.	1:35.427	29	20.	1:35.144	11	15.	1:33.923	7	14.	**1:33.294**	6			
12. Jarno Trulli	I	Toyota TF107/04 [1]	5.	1:34.896	26	10.	1:34.366	33	14.	1:33.724	22	6.	1:33.218	6	7.	1:32.429	6	9.	**1:34.154**	10
14. David Coulthard	GB	Red Bull RB3 3 - Renault [2]	20.	1:36.513	7	9.	1:34.359	32	15.	1:33.826	13	21.	**1:35.341**	4						
15. Mark Webber	AUS	Red Bull RB3 2 - Renault [1]	19.	1:36.483	18	14.	1:34.677	24	8.	1:33.399	14	11.	1:33.496	6	8.	1:32.808	6	8.	**1:34.106**	10
16. Nico Rosberg	D	Williams FW29-03 - Toyota [1]	9.	1:35.375	19	8.	1:34.189	34	11.	1:33.614	14	9.	1:33.349	6	9.	1:32.815	6	10.	**1:34.399**	10
17. Alexander Wurz	AUT	Williams FW29-04 - Toyota [1]	10.	1:35.398	20	6.	1:33.973	26	12.	1:33.658	17	13.	1:33.759	6	11.	**1:32.915**	6			
18. Vitantonio Liuzzi	I	Toro Rosso STR2 - Ferrari [1]	8.	1:35.292	23	17.	1:35.268	38	13.	1:33.700	18	18.	**1:34.024**	6						
19. Scott Speed	USA	Toro Rosso STR2 - Ferrari [1]	15.	1:35.726	22	20.	1:35.687	34	19.	1:34.791	11	19.	**1:34.333**	6						
20. Adrian Sutil	D	Spyker F8-VII/03 - Ferrari [1]	21.	1:37.084	27	19.	1:35.582	31	22.	1:35.436	18	20.	**1:35.280**	8						
21. Christijan Albers	NL	Spyker F8-VII/01 - Ferrari [1]	22.	1:38.258	29	21.	1:35.835	30	21.	1:35.395	22	22.	**1:35.533**	7						
22. Takuma Sato	J	Super Aguri SA07-04 - Honda [1]	16.	1:35.856	15	16.	1:35.001	35	17.	1:34.082	21	17.	**1:33.984**	6						
23. Anthony Davidson	GB	Super Aguri SA07-03 - Honda [1]	18.	1:36.243	6	13.	1:34.595	29	5.	1:32.900	20	7.	1:33.299	6	13.	**1:33.082**	6			

Fastest lap overall

F. Massa 1:31.359 (213,259 km/h)

Maximum speed

N° Driver	S1 Qualifs	Pos.	S1 Race	Pos.	S2 Qualifs	Pos.	S2 Race	Pos.	Finish Qualifs	Pos.	Finish Race	Pos.	Radar Qualifs	Pos.	Radar Race	Pos.
1. F. Alonso	244,0	1	246,7	1	278,3	1	276,8	1	286,3	3	287,0	1	309,6	11	311,9	4
2. L. Hamilton	243,0	2	245,6	3	277,8	2	276,3	2	286,3	5	286,1	4	307,8	12	310,2	7
3. G. Fisichella	240,8	9	243,2	8	274,8	11	273,4	7	283,3	11	282,7	10	307,5	15	306,6	11
4. H. Kovalainen	241,8	5	244,5	6	274,9	10	272,7	9	283,0	13	281,4	14	307,0	17	306,9	10
5. F. Massa	242,8	3	245,2	4	275,5	8	272,5	11	286,3	4	286,7	3	311,7	4	305,4	15
6. K. Räikkönen	241,6	7	244,9	5	276,6	5	274,3	4	285,9	6	285,4	6	314,7	1	312,2	2
7. J. Button	236,4	20			271,4	16			281,5	17			306,6	19	251,6	21
8. R. Barrichello	236,6	19	239,5	18	271,2	17	268,5	16	282,1	15	277,4	18	306,8	18	303,0	18
9. N. Heidfeld	240,4	10	243,6	7	276,7	3	275,1	3	285,4	7	284,5	7	311,7	3	312,2	3
10. R. Kubica	240,3	11	242,8	10	276,1	7	272,7	10	284,2	10	281,9	13	310,5	8	304,9	16
11. R. Schumacher	238,3	16	241,6	13	271,0	18	268,3	17	281,8	16	283,8	8	307,1	16	307,4	9
12. J. Trulli	239,2	13	240,8	14	273,2	13	264,7	20	283,0	12	281,0	16	307,7	13	305,6	14
14. D. Coulthard	236,7	18	241,7	11	265,2	22	273,6	6	281,1	19	283,6	9	310,0	9	310,4	6
15. M. Webber	239,8	12	240,6	17	275,5	9	273,8	5	284,8	8	282,6	11	310,7	6	309,5	8
16. N. Rosberg	242,4	4	245,8	2	276,2	6	273,0	8	286,9	1	285,4	5	313,6	2	311,8	5
17. A. Wurz	241,2	8	242,9	9	276,7	4	271,5	13	286,4	2	286,7	2	311,6	5	313,5	1
18. V. Liuzzi	237,8	17	240,7	16	270,9	19	269,4	15	282,7	14	281,3	15	310,6	7	306,0	13
19. S. Speed	238,9	15			272,4	15			280,8	20			309,8	10	227,5	22
20. A. Sutil	231,7	22	236,9	19	268,1	20	267,1	18	275,2	22	277,4	19	298,0	22	297,5	19
21. C. Albers	234,0	21	236,1	20	266,5	21	266,1	19	276,2	21	274,6	20	299,8	21	296,7	20
22. T. Sato	239,0	14	240,8	15	272,7	14	270,0	14	281,3	18	280,8	17	304,3	20	304,0	17
23. A. Davidson	241,7	6	241,7	12	274,2	12	271,9	12	284,7	9	282,5	12	307,7	14	306,1	12

Best sector times

	S1		S2		S3		
Qualifs	**S1** F. Massa	29.315	**S2** F. Massa	39.154	**S3** L. Hamilton	22.832	= 1:31.301
Race	**S1** F. Massa	30.091	**S2** N. Heidfeld	40.595	**S3** L. Hamilton	23.280	= 1:33.966

RACE

Date	Weather	Air temperature	Track temperature	Humidity	Wind speed
Sunday April, 2007 (14:30)	Sunny and warm	28-30°c	32-39°c	24%	3.8 m/s

Classification & retirements

Pos.	Driver	Constructor	Tyres	Laps	Time	Km/h	
1.	F. Massa	Ferrari	MMH	57	1:33:27.515	197,887	
2.	L. Hamilton	McLaren Mercedes	MMH	57	+ 2.360	197,804	
3.	K. Räikkönen	Ferrari	MMH	57	+ 10.839	197,505	
4.	N. Heidfeld	BMW	MMH	57	+ 13.831	197,400	
5.	F. Alonso	McLaren Mercedes	MMH	57	+ 14.426	197,379	
6.	R. Kubica	BMW	MMH	57	+ 45.529	196,293	
7.	J. Trulli	Toyota	MMH	57	+ 1:21.371	195,056	
8.	G. Fisichella	Renault	MMH	57	+ 1:21.701	195,045	
9.	H. Kovalainen	Renault	MMH	57	+ 1:29.411	194,781	
10.	N. Rosberg	Williams Toyota	MMH	57	+ 1:29.916	194,764	
11.	A. Wurz	Williams Toyota	MMH	56	1 tour	194,018	
12.	R. Schumacher	Toyota	MMH	56	1 tour	193,705	
13.	R. Barrichello	Honda	MMH	56	1 tour	193,084	
14.	C. Albers	Spyker Ferrari	MMH	55	2 tours	190,418	
15.	A. Sutil	Spyker Ferrari	MHMM	55	2 tours	183,479	
16.	A. Davidson	Super Aguri Honda	MMH	51	6 tours	193,333	Engine oil leak

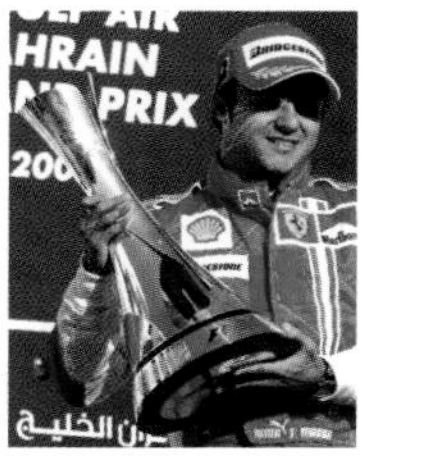

Driver	Constructor	Tyres	Laps	Reason
M. Webber	Red Bull Renault	MMH	41	Gearbox problem
D. Coulthard	Red Bull Renault	MM	36	Broken right-rear driveshaft
T. Sato	Super Aguri Honda	MM	34	Engine failure
V. Liuzzi	STR Ferrari	HMM	26	Hydraulic problems
J. Button	Honda	M	0	Contact with Coulthard and spin
S. Speed	STR Ferrari	MM	0	Crash with Sutil and spin

Tyres H: Hard & M: Medium

Fastest laps

	Driver	Time	Lap	Km/h
1.	F. Massa	1:34.067	42	207,120
2.	L. Hamilton	1:34.270	18	206,674
3.	K. Räikkönen	1:34.357	39	206,483
4.	F. Alonso	1:34.420	46	206,346
5.	N. Heidfeld	1:34.470	38	206,236
6.	R. Kubica	1:34.819	46	205,477
7.	J. Trulli	1:35.153	40	204,756
8.	G. Fisichella	1:35.200	51	204,655
9.	D. Coulthard	1:35.384	34	204,260
10.	H. Kovalainen	1:35.475	27	204,065
11.	N. Rosberg	1:35.556	51	203,893
12.	M. Webber	1:35.705	37	203,575
13.	V. Liuzzi	1:35.723	23	203,537
14.	R. Barrichello	1:35.842	50	203,284
15.	R. Schumacher	1:35.845	37	203,278
16.	A. Wurz	1:35.992	27	202,966
17.	A. Davidson	1:36.111	27	202,715
18.	T. Sato	1:36.359	23	202,193
19.	A. Sutil	1:36.772	45	201,330
20.	C. Albers	1:37.184	40	200,477

Pit stops

	Driver	Lap	Duration	Stop	Total
1.	A. Sutil	1	5:08.638	1	5:08.638
2.	V. Liuzzi	2	30.216	1	30.216
3.	V. Liuzzi	•9•	18.997	2	49.213
4.	D. Coulthard	17	30.164	1	30.164
5.	A. Wurz	17	30.964	1	30.964
6.	R. Schumacher	17	30.002	1	30.002
7.	M. Webber	18	33.345	1	33.345
8.	L. Hamilton	19	31.744	1	31.744
9.	G. Fisichella	19	32.711	1	32.711
10.	T. Sato	20	31.360	1	31.360
11.	C. Albers	20	31.647	1	31.647
12.	F. Massa	21	30.216	1	30.216
13.	J. Trulli	21	30.170	1	30.170
14.	V. Liuzzi	21	2:31.479	3	3:20.692
15.	A. Sutil	19	41.185	2	5:49.823
16.	F. Alonso	22	30.382	1	30.382
17.	N. Rosberg	22	29.446	1	29.446
18.	K. Räikkönen	23	30.141	1	30.141
19.	N. Heidfeld	23	29.990	1	29.990
20.	R. Kubica	23	29.525	1	29.525
21.	H. Kovalainen	25	29.193	1	29.193
22.	R. Barrichello	26	30.772	1	30.772
23.	A. Davidson	28	28.441	1	28.441
24.	A. Wurz	34	30.812	2	1:01.776
25.	D. Coulthard	35	30.805	2	1:00.969
26.	M. Webber	38	29.771	2	1:03.116
27.	R. Schumacher	38	29.425	2	59.427
28.	N. Rosberg	39	29.579	2	59.025
29.	A. Davidson	39	29.747	2	58.188
30.	F. Massa	40	30.034	2	1:00.250
31.	A. Sutil	37	30.326	3	6:20.149
32.	K. Räikkönen	41	29.101	2	59.242
33.	N. Heidfeld	41	29.018	2	59.008
34.	C. Albers	41	29.471	2	1:01.118
35.	J. Trulli	42	28.655	2	58.825
36.	H. Kovalainen	42	28.133	2	57.326
37.	F. Alonso	43	28.570	2	58.952
38.	R. Kubica	43	28.055	2	57.580
39.	L. Hamilton	44	28.717	2	1:00.461
40.	G. Fisichella	44	28.100	2	1:00.811
41.	R. Barrichello	46	28.879	2	59.651

•• Drive-through penalty: Liuzzi.
Drive-through penalty for having passed Schumacher under the safety car.

Race leader

Driver	Laps in the lead	Nbr of laps
F. Massa	1 > 21	21
K. Räikkönen	22 > 23	2
F. Massa	24 > 40	17
L. Hamilton	41 > 44	4
F. Massa	45 > 57	13

Driver	Nbr of laps	Kilometers
F. Massa	51	275,766 km
L. Hamilton	4	21,648 km
K. Räikkönen	2	10,824 km

Lap chart

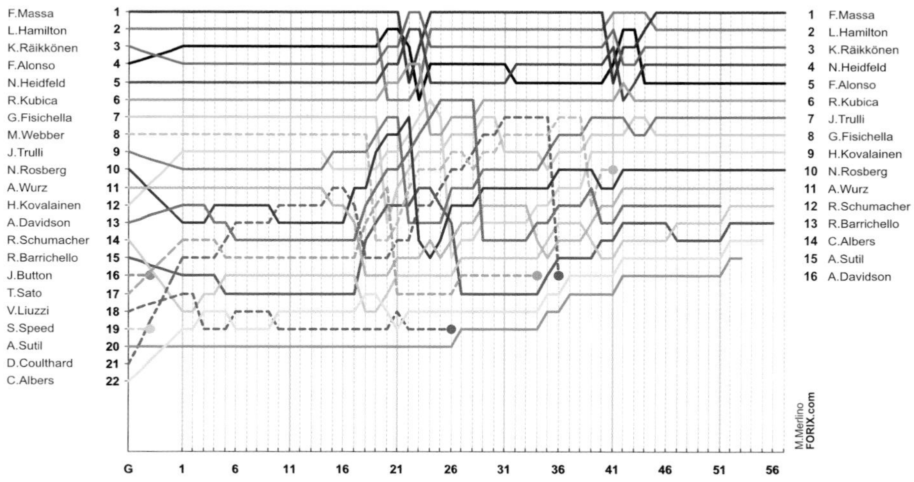
F.Massa
L.Hamilton
K.Räikkönen
F.Alonso
N.Heidfeld
R.Kubica
G.Fisichella
M.Webber
J.Trulli
N.Rosberg
A.Wurz
H.Kovalainen
A.Davidson
R.Schumacher
R.Barrichello
J.Button
T.Sato
V.Liuzzi
S.Speed
A.Sutil
D.Coulthard
C.Albers
G 1 6 11 16 21 26 31 36 41 46 51 56
1 F.Massa
2 L.Hamilton
3 K.Räikkönen
4 N.Heidfeld
5 F.Alonso
6 R.Kubica
7 J.Trulli
8 G.Fisichella
9 H.Kovalainen
10 N.Rosberg
11 A.Wurz
12 R.Schumacher
13 R.Barrichello
14 C.Albers
15 A.Sutil
16 A.Davidson
M.Merlino FORIX.com

Gaps on the lead board

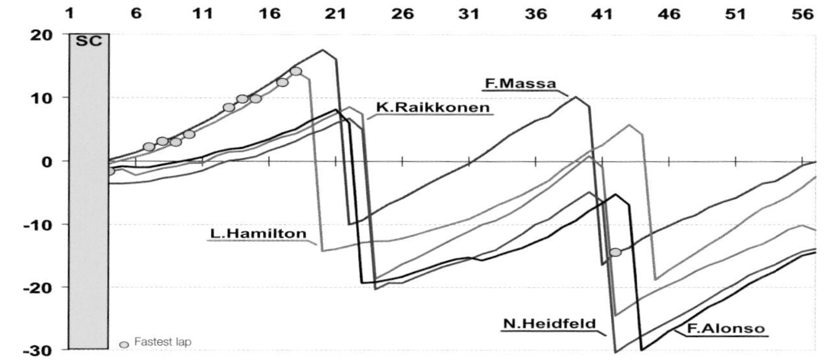
1 6 11 16 21 26 31 36 41 46 51 56
20
10
0
-10
-20
-30
SC
F.Massa
K.Raikkonen
L.Hamilton
N.Heidfeld
F.Alonso
Fastest lap

CHAMPIONSHIPS 3/17

Drivers

	Driver	Constructor	Wins	Points
1.	F. Alonso	McLaren Mercedes	1🏆	22
2.	K. Räikkönen	Ferrari	1🏆	22
3.	L. Hamilton	McLaren Mercedes		22
4.	F. Massa	Ferrari	1🏆	17
5.	N. Heidfeld	BMW		15
6.	G. Fisichella	Renault		8
7.	J. Trulli	Toyota		4
8.	R. Kubica	BMW		3
9.	N. Rosberg	Williams Toyota		2
10.	H. Kovalainen	Renault		1
11.	R. Schumacher	Toyota		1
12.	A. Wurz	Williams Toyota		0
13.	M. Webber	Red Bull Renault		0
14.	R. Barrichello	Honda		0
15.	T. Sato	Super Aguri Honda		0
16.	J. Button	Honda		0
17.	V. Liuzzi	STR Ferrari		0
18.	S. Speed	STR Ferrari		0
19.	C. Albers	Spyker Ferrari		0
20.	A. Sutil	Spyker Ferrari		0
21.	A. Davidson	Super Aguri Honda		0
	D. Coulthard	Red Bull Renault		-

Constructors

	Constructor	Wins	Points
1.	Vodafone McLaren Mercedes	1🏆	44
2.	Scuderia Ferrari Marlboro	2🏆	39
3.	BMW Sauber F1 Team		18
4.	ING Renault F1 Team		9
5.	Panasonic Toyota Racing		5
6.	AT&T Williams		2
7.	Red Bull Racing		0
8.	Honda Racing F1 Team		0
9.	Super Aguri F1 Team		0
10.	Scuderia Toro Rosso		0
11.	Etihad Aldar Spyker F1 Team		0

THE CIRCUIT

Name Bahrain International Circuit, Sakhir; Manama
Lenght 5412 m
Distance 57 tours, soit 308,238 km
Latitude 26°01'57.00"N
Longitude 50°30'37.55"E

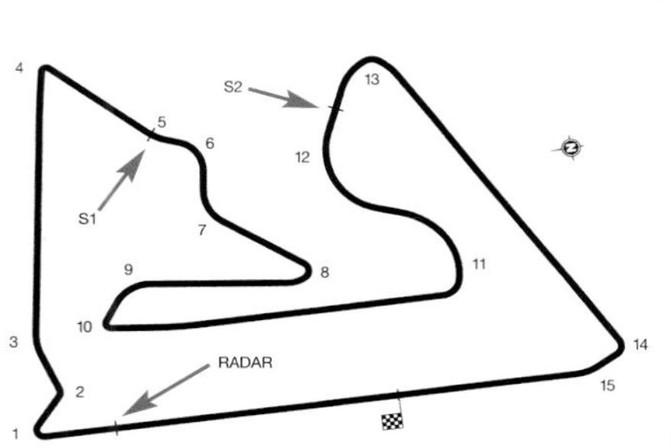
1
2
3
4
5
6
7
8
9
10
11
12
13
14
15
S1
S2
RADAR

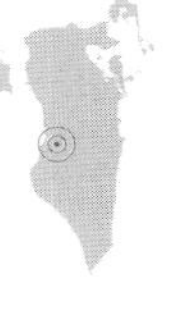

S1 au virage
S2 48m before corner
Radar 144m before corner

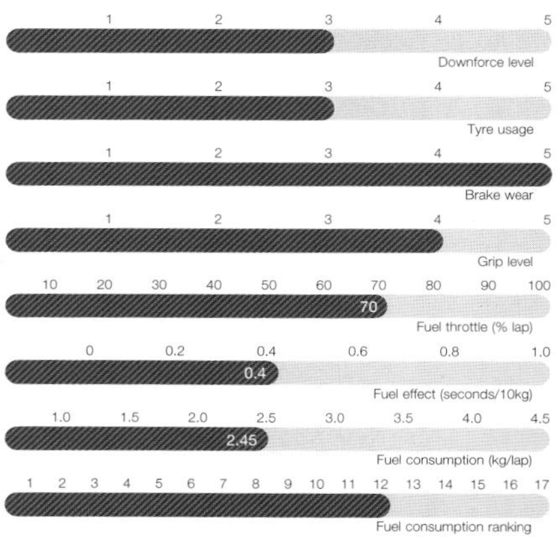
Downforce level
Tyre usage
Brake wear
Grip level
70
Fuel throttle (% lap)
0.4
Fuel effect (seconds/10kg)
2.45
Fuel consumption (kg/lap)
Fuel consumption ranking

FELIPE MASSA LEADS FROM START TO FINISH

While Ferrari continued to lead both the drivers' and constructors' championships, Ferrari seemed unbeatable at Barcelona. Starting from his third consecutive pole position, Felipe Massa dominated the race from lights to flag, cruising to the finish after surviving a skirmish with Fernando Alonso at the first corner and seeing his team mate Kimi Raikkonen retire.
In any case, Felipe Massa did not hesitate to take the lead as soon as Charlie Whiting started the race...

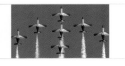

> Fernando Alonso saw pole position slip from his grasp, in front of a crowd that was entirely behind him.

Michael Schumacher is back

He is tanned, smiling and on top form as always. Michael Schumacher caused a stir in the Barcelona paddock on Thursday with his first appearance since retiring at the Brazilian Grand Prix last year. The German was there in his new role as a consultant for Ferrari, but he was not able to escape a press conference in the team's new motorhome. The conference revealed little about his new role within Scuderia Ferrari. *"Ferrari is doing incredibly well,"* he said. *"After Ross* (Brawn, the team's former technical director) *left over the winter, the re-structuring has been so successful that there's little room left for me ! But I'm very pleased to see how well the team is working now."*

As to his own future, Schumacher remained vague. *"I don't know exactly what I'd like to do,"* he said. *"If I knew it, I'd be doing it now ! For the moment, I'm just enjoying having some free time. It's so nice to get up in the morning without thinking of Formula 1 straight away, and without having your movements decided by someone else. Now, when the children are on holiday, we can think about where we want to go straight away without paying attention to anything else . You can imagine how good that feels !"*

But after 16 years in Formula 1, it was only natural that he would miss it. *"I miss going out with the team,"* he said. *"On Thursdays we used to play football together and then we would all go out to eat together. On Sundays, we often had a party together : it was a lot of fun. My fun is just a bit different now..."*

He still plays football though. *"Yes, I love it !"* he enthused. *"I play a lot with the Echichens team. It's also the only sport I play to keep fit. I don't do any more weight training."* Michael is still interested in Formula 1 as well, and he hasn't missed a single Grand Prix on television this year. *"It's a really exciting championship this year,"* he said. *"The competition is very close, which makes it a lot of fun."*

Yet Schumacher didn' have a lot more to say. While he didn't know what he might end up doing in the future, he knew for sure the job that wouldn't be doing: sporting director of Ferrari. *"That's completely out of the question,"* he stated categorically. "I really wouldn't want that job: I've got other ambitions. There's more to life than just F1...

Ferrari's new palace on wheels

On this point, Ferrari had put up a decided resistance. While its rivals pitched up at races with increasingly elaborate motorhomes, the Italian team was traditionally content with slightly older and more modest accommodation. Four years earlier, it had even bought an old double-deck motorhome that was formerly the property of the defunct Arrows team.

Jean Todt frequently used to say that he preferred to spend the team's money on the car rather than on the decoration. McLaren always had a different philosophy : in 1998 they were the first team with a motorhome over two floors.

In 2002 the team inaugurated its 'communications centre', which had little to do with a motorhome in the traditional sense of the word, as it no longer had an engine or wheels. Next to these plush facilities, Ferrari's hospitality cut a pallid figure. Not any more : a three-storey tower appeared in Barcelona for the first time, with a conference room and restaurant downstairs, offices and rooms for invited guests upstairs, and finally a panoramic terrace on the roof. Despite this finery, Ferrari reckoned their new facility to be quite modest. « We just wanted something quite efficient and economic, » explained Nigel Wolheim, one of the marketing people within the team.

> Remember him ? At Barcelona, Michael Schumacher visited a Grand Prix for the first time all year.

>> Ferrari's new three-storey motorhome.

Pole position - by just three-hundredths

It had been a while since we had seen such a close start to the World Championship. With Fernando Alonso, Kimi Raikkonen and Lewis Hamilton leading the series on 22 points, and Felipe Massa just behind on 17 points, a four-way fight was in store for the Spanish Grand Prix. This took place a whole month after the Bahrain Grand Prix - a long gap caused by the cancellation of the San Marino Grand Prix.

The previous week, on the Barcelona circuit, private testing had clearly shown to the superiority of Ferrari over their rivals - to the tune of seven-tenths of a second per lap. When it came to qualifying on Saturday though, this advantage had mysteriously disappeared. Felipe Massa only scored his third consecutive pole position by the skin of his teeth, or more specifically by three-hundredths of a second. *"It shows that our car is very competitive,"* said the Brazilian. *"My first lap wasn't great : I had to pass a backmarker and I must have made a few small mistakes, but the second lap was perfect. Having said all that, it was tight with the McLarens just behind us. I think it's going to be a very close race."* This was also Fernando Alonso's opinion. The Spaniard was disappointed to have just missed out on pole, but he thought he would be able to regain ground during the race. *"The important thing is to be on the first row,"* said the two-time World Champion. *"It proves that the car is working well. I actually think that we are quicker than the Ferraris here, but we are going to have to show that in competition. I reckon that everybody has got a lot closer actually : the BMW Saubers are not far off our times at all. It's good news for Formula 1 and for the public. I really enjoyed this qualifying session."*

Behind them, Kimi Raikkonen and Lewis Hamilton were ready to take advantage of any opportunities that came their way. It would be the fourth time in four Grands Prix that the McLarens would start from second and fourth - and things hadn't worked out too badly for them so far...

IN BRIEF

+ Scuderia Ferrari celebrated its 60th anniversary. Enzo Ferrari, who had been team manager of Alfa Romeo, decided to start his own team on May 11 1947. The team now holds most of Formula 1's records.

+ The news surprised the Barcelona paddock as there had not even been any rumours beforehand : Bernie Ecclestone had signed a six-year contract with the Spanish town of Valencia to host a Grand Prix on a street circuit - rather than on the well-known circuit just a few kilometres away from the city centre. *"It seems a strange idea to create a street circuit when there's a permanent one right next-door,"* said Fernando Alonso. *"Sometimes I really struggle to understand what goes through the heads of the people who are in charge of F1."*
The town of Valencia itself decided to finance this new Grand Prix, thanks to the revenue generated from the America's Cup. Nonetheless, the contract is conditional on the re-election of Valencia's mayor, Francisco Campos, in the elections next May 27. Spain's socialist sports minister declared that the contract was 'an insult to the Spanish people', as Bernie Ecclestone was trying to influence an election in which he had no right to vote.

< *"So how exactly do you get out of these seats?"* Kimi Raikkonen gets out of his Ferrari after qualifying. The Finn was third on the grid.

STARTING GRID

* J. TRULLI
cale lors de la première procédure de départ.
Starts from the pit lane.

 C. ALBERS 21 1:23.990
 M. WEBBER 19 1:23.398
 R. SCHUMACHER 17 1:22.666
 A. DAVIDSON 15
 T. SATO 13 1:22.115
 N. ROSBERG 11 1:21.968
 D. COULTHARD 9 1:22.749
 N. HEIDFELD 7 1:22.389
 R. KUBICA 5 1:22.253
 K. RÄIKKÖNEN 3 1:21.723
 F. MASSA 1 1:21.421 (205.819 km/h)

 S. SPEED 22 1:23.811
A. SUTIL 20
 A. WURZ 18 1:22.769
 V. LIUZZI 16
 J. BUTTON 14 1:22.120
R. BARRICHELLO 12 1:22.097
G. FISICHELLA 10 1:22.881
H. KOVALAINEN 8 1:22.568
 J. TRULLI* 6 1:22.324
L. HAMILTON 4 1:21.785
F. ALONSO 2 1:21.451

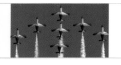

A big scare for Felipe Massa during his first fuel stop : when he took to the track again his engine cover caught fire, the result of some fuel splashing onto his car's hot bodywork. It was nothing serious, and Massa did not even notice. *"It was only a few drops,"* pointed out Mario Almondo, Ferrari's chief engineer.

Fernando Alonso accuses Felipe Massa: "It was really dangerous."

All the drivers on the front two rows knew that the start represented their best chance of making it past their rivals on such a twisty and tricky circuit. Fernando Alonso started from the dirty side of the track and followed Felipe Massa's Ferrari into the first corner, before ducking out to try and overtake him round the outside. It was a bold manœuvre that might have worked had Massa not resolutely held his line. The two cars touched and Alonso found himself in the gravel trap. *"I braked later than Felipe and I was half a car-length ahead of him,"* said the Spaniard. *"In these cases, the person who is in front stays there. Unfortunately, Felipe does not share the same opinion. I think that this type of accident is quite dangerous, because 99% of the time both parties end up going off. In any case the damage is to the rear of my car, which makes it pretty easy to tell who hit who..."*

With a damaged air deflector, the McLaren was just a shadow of its former self from that point on.

"We tried to compensate for the imbalance with some set-up changes during the fuel stops, butmy chances of victory had gone," said Fernando Alonso.

Felipe Massa, perhaps unsurprisingly, refused to take any of the blame for the accident. *"Whenever I make a mistake, I'm the first to own up to it,"* he said. *"But don't try to make out it was my fault here : I was on the inside of the corner, I held my line, and that was that".*

> The clash between Felipe Massa and Fernando Alonso put the Spaniard into the gravel trap at the first corner. Alonso regained the track just alongside his teammate Lewis Hamilton, who was clearly surprised by his antics (right)

> The Toro Rosso cars struggled to get up to the middle of the grid at the start of the season. This was down to a hastily modified chassis that had been revised to accommodate the Ferrari engine : a last-minute job that took place in January as the Faenza workforce was on holiday !

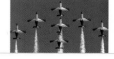

< It was Felipe Massa's second win on the trot, and the Brazilian seemed to have the upper hand over Kimi Raikkonen at Ferrari. Once more, the Finn was extremely unlucky…

Felipe Massa underlines Ferrari's advantage

The red alert had sounded during the week of testing that took place on the Circuit de Catalunya just before the Spanish Grand Prix. It was a week during which the Scuderia had crushed its rivals, stealing seven-tenths of a second per lap.

On Friday and Saturday in the build-up to the Grand Prix, this advantage had strangely vanished. But during the race on Sunday it was well and truly back…

Felipe Massa was able to calmly control the race from the front, sometimes setting lap times that were up to a second quicker than those of Lewis Hamilton, just behind him. Had he wanted to, the Brazilian could have finished the race nearly a minute up on his rivals.

So what had been going on, under the skin at Ferrari ? The Scuderia's technical director Luca Baldisseri explained : *"Once the official tests started, the surface offered a lot more grip than it did during private testing. We were a bit surprised by this, so it took some time to adapt ourselves. In race conditions, we were very pleased with our car's performance. Now we need to work on reliability, given what happened to Kimi. In the next few weeks, I'd say our focus is going to be 51% on reliability, and 49% on performance."*

McLaren however did not seem to be too worried by the prodigious pace of their key rivals. *"I think we're going to have a fantastic duel throughout the entire season,"* said team principal Ron Dennis. *"Felipe Massa was carrying a lighter fuel load than us during the race, which is why he seemed to be quicker. In actual fact, I think there's only a few hundredths of a second between us in terms of pure performance."*

The Monaco Grand Prix, two weeks later, would make for an interesting benchmarking exercise. Judging from the result of the Spanish Grand Prix though, it seemed as if Dennis and McLaren were just putting a brave face on things. McLaren continued to lead both championships -but it seemed to be still a long way off the pace of Ferrari.

< The Super Aguri team scored its very first point in Barcelona thanks to eighth place for Takuma Sato. The tiny Japanese outfit once more outperformed its big brother Honda, whose drivers again finished out of the points.

HEIKKI GETS IN FRONT

Throughout the first three Grands Prix of the season, Heikki Kovalainen was in the shadow of his teammate Giancarlo Fisichella. At Barcelona, the Finn qualified in front of him for the first time. Kovalainen finished seventh in the race whereas Fisichella was out of the points - and the die was cast for the rest of the season…

> Robert Kubica took a magnificent fourth place. *"I'm very happy, as it's the first race of the year that I've had no problems - and look at the result !"*

>> Lewis Hamilton took another second place finish - which allowed him to claim the exclusive lead of the World Championship.

SNAPSHOTS OF THE WEEKEND

+ Having started third on the grid, Kimi Raikkonen could have been on the podium had his Ferrari not given up the ghost on just the 10th lap, with a faulty alternator connection. *"It's a real shame, as Kimi started off with a strategy that would definitely have meant he finished in front of the McLarens,"* said Luca Baldisseri.

+ Another record for Lewis Hamilton : he became the youngest driver in the history of Formula 1 to lead the World Championship. Thanks to a second-place finish in Barcelona he racked up 30 championship points : two more than

Fernando Alonso. The Englishman also managed to finish on the podium for every one of his first four Grands Prix.
"The dream continues," he said simply.

+ There were 140,000 spectators present on Sunday at the Barcelona circuit - which has announced an extension of its contract until 2016 with Bernie Ecclestone, Formula 1's commercial rights-holder. Josep Lluis Carod-Rovira, the president of the circuit, modestly announced the next ambition : *"We want to become the best circuit in the world."*

> Fernando Alonso went to meet his devoted fans on Thursday. The more autographs he signed, the more people seemed to turn up. The session could have gone on for hours…

RESULTS

PRACTICE

	Date	Weather (AM)	Air temperature	Track temperature	Weather (PM)	Air temperature	Track temperature
	Friday May 11, 2007	○ Sunny	23-25°c	31-38°c	○ Sunny	25-26°c	45-48°c
	Saturday May 12, 2007	○ Sunny	25-26°c	32°c	○ Sunny	27-28°c	48°c

All the time trials

N° Driver	Nat.	N° Chassis- Engine (Nbr. GP)	Pos. Free 1 Laps Friday Tr. 10:00-11:30	Pos. Free 2 Laps Friday Tr. 14:00-15:30	Pos. Free 3 Laps Saturday Tr. 11:00-12:00	Pos. Q1 Laps Saturday Tr. 14:00-14:15	Pos. Q2 Laps Saturday Tr. 14:22-14:37	Pos. Q3 Nb. Saturday Tr. 14:45-15:00
1. Fernando Alonso	E	McLaren MP4-22 06 - Mercedes [2]	2. 1:22.268 21	1. 1:21.397 33	2. 1:21.312 13	3. 1:21.609 13	4. 1:20.797 25	2. 1:21.451 11
2. Lewis Hamilton	GB	McLaren MP4-22 05 - Mercedes [2]	1. 1:21.880 22	5. 1:22.188 37	1. 1:21.233 13	1. 1:21.713 3	3. 1:20.713 4	1. 1:21.785 11
3. Giancarlo Fisichella	I	Renault R27-04 [2]	15. 1:23.397 21	4. 1:22.048 31	11. 1:22.140 12	9. 1:22.064 6	10. 1:21.677 6	10. 1:22.881 11
4. Heikki Kovalainen	FIN	Renault R27-03 [2]	14. 1:23.322 24	3. 1:21.966 38	10. 1:22.067 18	5. 1:21.790 6	9. 1:21.623 6	8. 1:22.568 11
5. Felipe Massa	BR	Ferrari F2007 260 [2]	5. 1:22.565 15	1. 1:22.048 31	6. 1:21.659 14	2. 1:21.375 3	1. 1:20.597 12	3. 1:21.421 11
6. Kimi Räikkönen	FIN	Ferrari F2007 261 & 262 [2]	3. 1:22.291 19	6. 1:22.251 33	7. 1:21.829 15	6. 1:21.802 3	3. 1:20.741 13	3. 1:21.723 11
7. Jenson Button	GB	Honda RA107-04 [1]	10. 1:23.114 22	13. 1:22.808 39	17. 1:22.744 17	15. 1:22.503 6	14. 1:22.120 6	
8. Rubens Barrichello	BR	Honda RA107-02 [1]	18. 1:23.479 23	14. 1:22.926 40	13. 1:22.274 15	14. 1:22.502 6	12. 1:22.097 6	
9. Nick Heidfeld	D	BMW Sauber F1.07-05 [2]	12. 1:23.170 26	8. 1:22.543 40	4. 1:21.464 17	4. 1:21.625 4	5. 1:21.113 3	7. 1:22.389 11
10. Robert Kubica	PL	BMW Sauber F1.07-07 [2]	4. 1:22.446 21	11. 1:22.710 43	3. 1:21.364 17	7. 1:21.941 4	6. 1:21.381 6	5. 1:22.253 11
11. Ralf Schumacher	D	Toyota TF107/05 [2]	8. 1:22.843 23	17. 1:23.219 28	16. 1:22.570 21	17. 1:22.666 7		
12. Jarno Trulli	I	Toyota TF107/04 [2]	7. 1:22.740 28	18. 1:23.307 42	12. 1:22.174 25	13. 1:22.501 8		
14. David Coulthard	GB	Red Bull RB3 - Renault [2]	16. 1:23.428 21	12. 1:22.719 30	5. 1:21.556 12	12. 1:22.491 5	7. 1:21.488 6	9. 1:22.749 11
15. Mark Webber	AUS	Red Bull RB3 2 - Renault [2]	17. 1:23.444 21	9. 1:22.589 39	14. 1:22.759 13	19. 1:23.398 3		
16. Nico Rosberg	D	Williams FW29-05 - Toyota [2]	9. 1:23.048 28	7. 1:22.415 29	9. 1:21.943 17	8. 1:21.943 7	11. 1:21.968 6	
17. Alexander Wurz	AUT	Williams FW29-04 - Toyota [2]	11. 1:23.131 23	15. 1:22.950 30	19. 1:23.020 16	18. 1:22.769 7		
18. Vitantonio Liuzzi	I	Toro Rosso STR2-03 - Ferrari [2]	20. 1:24.104 24	16. 1:23.143 29	20. 1:23.367 8	16. 1:22.508 7	16.	
19. Scott Speed	USA	Toro Rosso STR2-04 - Ferrari [2]	21. 1:24.179 19	10. 1:22.617 35	12. 1:22.314 16	22. DNF 2		
20. Adrian Sutil	D	Spyker F8-VII/03 - Ferrari [2]	19. 1:23.584 25	21. 1:23.609 33	21. 1:23.584 22	20. 1:23.811 8		
21. Christian Albers	NL	Spyker F8-VII/02 & 01 - Ferrari [2]	22. 1:24.396 25	22. 1:23.736 30	22. 1:23.817 22	21. 1:23.990 8		
22. Takuma Sato	J	Super Aguri SA07-02 - Honda [1]	13. 1:23.316 22	19. 1:23.493 40	14. 1:22.295 11	10. 1:22.090 6	13. 1:22.115 3	
23. Anthony Davidson	GB	Super Aguri SA07-03 - Honda [1]	6. 1:22.665 21	20. 1:23.497 49	8. 1:21.845 15	11. 1:22.295 6	15. DNF 4	

Fastest lap overall
F. Massa 1:20.597 (207,923 km/h)

Maximum speed

N° Driver	S1 Qualifs	S1 Pos. Race	S2 Qualifs	S2 Pos. Race	Finish Qualifs	Finish Pos. Race	Radar Qualifs	Radar Pos. Race
1. F. Alonso	288,5	6 286,7 2	287,3 3	278,8 6	278,5 4	277,5 1	303,7 20	308,1 10
2. L. Hamilton	290,6	1 288,5 1	290,1 1	282,7 2	279,0 2	276,4 5	305,1 18	306,0 16
3. G. Fisichella	285,3	18 283,0 10	281,4 16	270,8 17	277,4 8	276,4 4	307,3 9	308,0 11
4. H. Kovalainen	285,4	17 283,4 8	279,5 17	277,9 8	276,4 16	276,2 6	307,8 7	307,4 12
5. F. Massa	288,6	5 285,4 5	286,7 4	283,2 1	278,4 5	276,8 3	308,7 6	306,2 14
6. K. Räikkönen	289,7	2 283,1 9	285,4 7	272,7 14	278,5 3	277,1 2	309,4 3	307,3 13
7. J. Button	283,9	20 280,9 14	283,5 13	274,8 13	276,0 17	274,6 11	305,1 19	308,6 9
8. R. Barrichello	287,0	13 280,6 15	284,0 10	276,0 12	277,4 9	275,9 7	309,1 5	309,9 3
9. N. Heidfeld	286,6	14 281,4 12	282,4 15	277,2 10	276,9 11	275,5 8	306,2 15	308,2 9
10. R. Kubica	286,3	15 284,2 6	282,6 14	280,9 5	276,4 14	274,2 13	306,8 12	308,3 8
11. R. Schumacher	288,6	4 285,7 4	283,8 12	281,3 4	275,2 18	273,3 15	307,6 8	304,0 19
12. J. Trulli	288,4	7 273,1 21	285,8 6	278,1 7	276,4 15	273,1 16	305,6 16	306,1 15
14. D. Coulthard	288,3	8 285,9 3	288,0 2	282,6 3	276,6 13	274,8 10	310,6 1	309,5 4
15. M. Webber	286,0	16 274,5 20	284,9 9	268,5 19	277,2 10	273,1 16	307,2 10	310,5 2
16. N. Rosberg	288,0	11 282,8 11	283,9 11	277,9 9	276,6 12	273,9 14	309,3 4	308,8 7
17. A. Wurz	288,8	3 246,6 22	279,3 18	220,1 22	277,0 10		306,8 11	292,9 22
18. V. Liuzzi	287,4	12 277,6 17	284,8 8	271,8 16	273,4 20	266,8 20	306,2 14	303,5 20
19. S. Speed	279,3	22 276,4 19	259,0 22	264,7 20	274,5 19	268,3 18	306,7 13	304,0 18
20. A. Sutil	282,5	21 278,2 16	269,6 21	263,5 21	271,0 21	266,8 21	302,8 21	299,9 21
21. C. Albers	284,5	19 277,4 18	272,0 20	269,1 18	270,4 22	267,7 19	301,9 22	305,4 17
22. T. Sato	288,3	9 283,7 7	286,1 5	276,5 11	279,4 1	274,5 12	310,0 2	309,0 5
23. A. Davidson	288,1	10 281,0 13	275,0 19	272,0 15	277,9 6	275,2 9	305,5 17	311,1 1

Best sector times

	S1		S2		S3		
Qualifs	S1 K. Räikkönen	22.550	S2 L. Hamilton	29.992	S3 F. Massa	27.788	= 1:20.330
Race	S1 F. Alonso	22.953	S2 F. Alonso	31.029	S3 H. Kovalainen	28.258	= 1:22.240

RACE

	Date	Weather	Air temperature	Track temperature	Humidity	Wind speed
	Sunday May 13, 2007 (14:00)	○ Sunny and warm	28-29°c	48-43°c	43-36%	2.7 m/s

Classification & retirements

Pos.	Driver	Constructor	Tyres	Laps	Time	Km/h
1.	F. Massa	Ferrari	MMH	65	1:31:36.230	198,102
2.	L. Hamilton	McLaren Mercedes	MMH	65	+ 6.790	197,857
3.	F. Alonso	McLaren Mercedes	MHM	65	+ 17.456	197,475
4.	R. Kubica	BMW	MMH	65	+ 31.615	196,949
5.	D. Coulthard	Red Bull Renault	MMH	65	+ 58.331	196,022
6.	N. Rosberg	Williams Toyota	MMH	65	+ 59.538	195,979
7.	H. Kovalainen	Renault	MMMH	65	+ 1:02.128	195,888
8.	T. Sato	Super Aguri Honda	MMH	64	1 tour	194,532
9.	G. Fisichella	Renault	MMH	64	1 tour	194,489
10.	R. Barrichello	Honda	MMH	64	1 tour	193,972
11.	A. Davidson	Super Aguri Honda	MMH	64	1 tour	193,613
12.	J. Button	Honda	MMMH	64	1 tour	192,656
13.	A. Sutil	Spyker Ferrari	MMH	63	2 tours	191,544
14.	C. Albers	Spyker Ferrari	MMH	63	2 tours	190,306

Driver	Constructor	Tyres	Laps	Reason
N. Heidfeld	BMW	MM	46	Gearbox problem
R. Schumacher	Toyota	MMM	44	Nosecone failure
V. Liuzzi	STR Ferrari	M	19	Hydraulic failure
S. Speed	STR Ferrari	H	9	Left-rear puncture due to lack of tyre pressure
K. Räikkönen	Ferrari	M	9	Electric problem, alternator connection
J. Trulli	Toyota	M	8	Fuel pressure proble,
M. Webber	Red Bull Renault	M	7	Broken transmission
A. Wurz	Williams Toyota	M	1	Chassis damage following collision with Schumacher

Tyres H: Hard & M: Medium

Fastest laps

	Driver	Time	Lap	Km/h
1.	F. Massa	1:22.680	14	202,685
2.	L. Hamilton	1:22.876	20	202,205
3.	F. Alonso	1:22.966	17	201,986
4.	H. Kovalainen	1:22.980	32	201,952
5.	R. Kubica	1:23.129	20	201,590
6.	K. Räikkönen	1:23.475	7	200,754
7.	N. Heidfeld	1:23.483	22	200,735
8.	D. Coulthard	1:23.524	18	200,636
9.	G. Fisichella	1:23.560	57	200,550
10.	N. Rosberg	1:23.693	60	200,231
11.	R. Schumacher	1:24.003	37	199,492
12.	T. Sato	1:24.110	23	199,239
13.	J. Button	1:24.186	64	199,059
14.	R. Barrichello	1:24.287	16	198,820
15.	A. Davidson	1:24.291	59	198,811
16.	A. Sutil	1:25.191	57	196,710
17.	V. Liuzzi	1:25.207	18	196,673
18.	C. Albers	1:25.260	61	196,551
19.	J. Trulli	1:26.094	4	194,647
20.	S. Speed	1:26.238	6	194,322
21.	M. Webber	1:26.323	4	194,131

Pit stops

	Driver	Lap	Duration	Stop	Total
1.	R. Schumacher	1	36.427	1	36.427
2.	R. Barrichello	18	27.927	1	27.927
3.	F. Massa	19	28.325	1	28.325
4.	F. Alonso	19	29.103	1	29.103
5.	H. Kovalainen	19	26.441	1	26.441
6.	D. Coulthard	20	26.652	1	26.652
7.	R. Kubica	21	27.467	1	27.467
8.	J. Button	21	27.420	1	27.420
9.	G. Fisichella	21	29.420	1	29.420
10.	L. Hamilton	22	27.531	1	27.531
11.	J. Button	22	38.845	2	1:06.265
12.	N. Rosberg	23	27.217	1	27.217
13.	A. Sutil	23	27.620	1	27.620
14.	N. Heidfeld	24	41.664	1	41.664
15.	T. Sato	24	28.084	1	28.084
16.	C. Albers	24	27.474	1	27.474
17.	N. Heidfeld	25	26.262	2	1:07.926
18.	A. Davidson	27	28.121	1	28.121
19.	R. Schumacher	27	26.964	2	1:03.391
20.	H. Kovalainen	30	26.202	2	52.643
21.	C. Albers	*33*	16.656	2	44.130

	Driver	Lap	Duration	Stop	Total
22.	G. Fisichella	40	25.498	2	54.918
23.	R. Barrichello	41	26.691	2	54.618
24.	F. Massa	42	27.403	2	55.728
25.	D. Coulthard	42	27.068	2	53.720
26.	H. Kovalainen	42	29.459	3	1:22.102
27.	N. Rosberg	43	27.367	2	54.584
28.	T. Sato	46	27.290	2	55.374
29.	L. Hamilton	47	25.655	2	53.186
30.	R. Kubica	47	25.726	2	53.193
31.	A. Sutil	46	31.719	2	59.339
32.	F. Alonso	48	25.834	2	54.937
33.	C. Albers	47	37.648	3	1:21.778
34.	J. Button	48	26.345	3	1:32.610
35.	A. Davidson	49	25.668	2	53.789
36.	G. Fisichella	58	23.904	3	1:18.822

** Drive-through penalty: Albers.
For ignoring blue flags

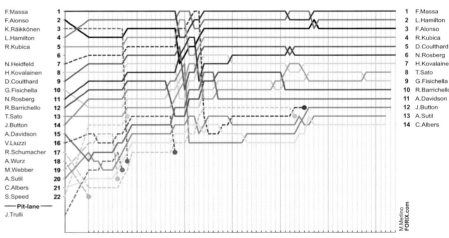

Race leader

Driver	Laps in the lead	Nbr of laps	Driver	Laps in the lead	Nbr of laps	Driver	Nbr of laps	Kilometers
F. Massa	1 > 19	19	F. Massa	25 > 42	18	F. Massa	55	255,899 km
L. Hamilton	20 > 22	3	L. Hamilton	43 > 47	5	L. Hamilton	8	37,240 km
N. Heidfeld	23 > 24	2	F. Massa	48 > 65	18	N. Heidfeld	2	9,310 km

Gaps on the lead board

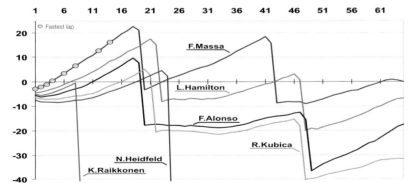

Lap chart

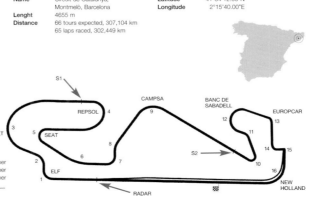

CHAMPIONSHIPS 4/17

Drivers

1.	L. Hamilton	McLaren Mercedes	30
2.	F. Alonso	McLaren Mercedes	1▼ 28
3.	F. Massa	Ferrari	2▼ 27
4.	K. Räikkönen	Ferrari	1▼ 22
5.	N. Heidfeld	BMW	15
6.	R. Kubica	BMW	8
7.	G. Fisichella	Renault	8
8.	N. Rosberg	Williams Toyota	5
9.	D. Coulthard	Red Bull Renault	4
10.	J. Trulli	Toyota	4
11.	H. Kovalainen	Renault	3
12.	T. Sato	Super Aguri Honda	1
13.	R. Schumacher	Toyota	1
14.	A. Wurz	Williams Toyota	0
15.	R. Barrichello	Honda	0
16.	M. Webber	Red Bull Renault	0
17.	A. Davidson	Super Aguri Honda	0
18.	J. Button	Honda	0
19.	A. Sutil	Spyker Ferrari	0
20.	C. Albers	Spyker Ferrari	0
21.	V. Liuzzi	STR Ferrari	0
22.	S. Speed	STR Ferrari	0

Constructors

1.	Vodafone McLaren Mercedes	1▼	58
2.	Scuderia Ferrari Marlboro	3▼	49
3.	BMW Sauber F1 Team		23
4.	ING Renault F1 Team		11
5.	AT&T Williams		5
6.	Panasonic Toyota Racing		5
7.	Red Bull Racing		4
8.	Super Aguri F1 Team		1
9.	Honda Racing F1 Team		0
10.	Etihad Aldar Spyker F1 Team		0
11.	Scuderia Toro Rosso		0

THE CIRCUIT

Name	Circuit de Catalunya; Montmeló, Barcelona	Latitude	41°34'12.00"N
Lenght	4655 m	Longitude	2°15'40.00"E
Distance	66 tours expected, 307,104 km		
	65 laps raced, 302,449 km		

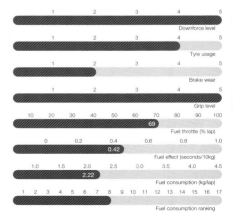

S1 60m before corner
S2 85m before corner
Radar 250m before corner

Downforce level
Tyre usage
Brake wear
Grip level — 69
Fuel throttle (% lap) — 0.42
Fuel effect (seconds/10kg) — 2.22
Fuel consumption (kg/lap)
Fuel consumption ranking

MCLAREN REGAINS
THE UPPER HAND

At Barcelona two weeks earlier, Felipe Massa seemed to be in a class of his own. At Monaco the opposite was the case, as the Brazilian finished more than a minute behind the winner, Fernando Alonso.

It was yet another striking u-turn to underline the fact that neither McLaren nor Ferrari would enjoy effortless domination this year.

When it came to the sinuous streets of Monaco though, nobody could trouble McLaren's silver arrows. Fernando Alonso started from pole and won the race, in front of his teammate Lewis Hamilton. The Englishman believed that he had a good strategy, until the team called him in for his pit stop slightly earlier than he would have wanted. It was the very first sign of schism between the two McLaren drivers...

> Will the roulette wheel come up with 2? No driver has ever won the Monaco Grand Prix in his first season of F1. That's no real surprise: Monaco is more tricky, narrow and bumpy than just about anywhere else. *"It's the ultimate challenge for any driver,"* says David Coulthard, himself a Monaco resident. *"On any given lap, from the first to the last, you can hit the barrier through just the tiniest mistake. And then it's all over."* This year, Lewis Hamilton was determined to break another record by making 2 the winning number on Monaco's famous roulette wheel.

McLaren the strong favourites

The rain that fell during the qualifying session looked like it might compromise his chances. But luckily for Fernando Alonso, only a few drops fell over Monaco and the racing line soon dried out. Alonso took full advantage in order to record his first pole position of the year, at a circuit where starting first is the key to winning.

Alonso won the Monaco Grand Prix in 2006, and was intent on repeating this exploit. *"I'm very happy,"* he said. *"Today was a bit unusual: we had the rain, traffic, tyres that we didn't change: you name it, it happened to us. As it turns out, the car seems to be just as good in the dry as it is in the rain, which is fortunate."*

Lewis Hamilton held fastest time throughout most of the session, before being knocked off in the dying seconds by his teammate. Starting from second place on the grid, he agreed he would not be doing anything desperate at the start. *"I'm not going to try anything desperate just to get past Fernando,"* he said. *"It's a long race and there will be other opportunities. On this circuit you need to be careful and sensible: it's not like anywhere else. McLaren*

Mark Webber destroyed a tyre and a wheel on Thursday morning. *"I barely kissed the guardrail: it's such a tricky corner,"* he said. He got back to the pits, where his mechanics also changed the Red Bull's gearbox as a precaution.
∨

have every possibility of a one-two here, so I just want to finish and get the points."

The situation at Ferrari was a lot less straightforward. The Scuderia had dominated the Spanish Grand Prix, but the twisty turns of Monaco suited the F2007 far less. To make matters worse, Kimi Raikkonen made a schoolboy error on Saturday by clipping the guardrail at the swimming pool complex. The

Finn broke his front suspension and dropped to 16th on the grid. Ironically, he stopped at exactly the same place as Michael Schumacher had in 2006 - but this time for a legitimate reason. *"There's nothing to say,"* commented the Finn laconically. *"After the impact I thought that the car was fine at first, but then at Rascasse it wouldn't turn in. You can't get away with any mistakes here..."*

The French GP states its case…with the help of salami

Eric Barbaroux, the director of the FFSA (the French motor sport federation), came to Barcelona in order to plead his case for the French Grand Prix, which had been threatened with the axe. *"We've got a contract until 2011, and this contract states clearly that the venue for the French Grand Prix will be Magny Cours,"* he explained. However, there's a clause relating to the standing and facilities - which basically means that Bernie can do what he wants. To stay at the right level for Formula 1 is a very relative thing. If tomorrow, as is the case for the Olympic Games, they ask us to build an international airport 20 kilometres from the circuit that's obviously going to be difficult.

Nonetheless, compared to modern autodromes like Sepang, Bahrain or Shanghai, there's no doubt that Magny Cours's facilities are old-fashioned. *"In 1991, we were considerably further ahead than the others,"* said Barbaroux. *"At the time, Magny Cours was the most advanced track of the season. But it's incredible how things have moved on and it's probably true that Magny Cours has not always kept the same pace. I don't think that we're of the same standard as the others at the moment, unfortunately."*

The ever-optimistic FFSA mounted a last-ditch attempt to get the French Grand Prix back at Monaco. On Thursday, there was a press conference - complete with tasting samples of local salami - to defend the race at Magny Cours. There were several convincing

arguments, and a press pack secured by a big plastic spiral on which the names of all the previous winners of the French Grand Prix had been written.

It was a persuasive tactic - but it fell on deaf ears as far as Bernie Ecclestone was concerned. On Thursday, Formula 1's powerbroker confirmed that the 2007 French Grand Prix would also be the last.

"I've spoken to the people from the FFSA" explained Bernie Ecclestone. *"And they agree that we should stop. Nobody wants to go to Magny Cours anymore. Contrary to what I was promised, there are no hotels, no airports, no historical interest, nothing. No reason to stay there at all."*

As it turned out, Ecclestone didn't even have to play his 'facilities' joker. "It's true that clause is there," he pointed out. *"But the biggest problem is that the French don't want to pay the agreed fee. Did they tell you that? That's the main reason why we're stopping everything. I've told the French that the only place that would interest me now would be Paris. That would be fantastic: put it on, and I'll sign a 99-year contract. And as Paris didn't get the Olympic Games, it would be a good way to make up for it. We'll try and get the idea off the ground: it would be good for France. I would be absolutely delighted to be able to put the French Grand Prix back on the calendar, given its long history."*

The only thing to hope for now is a miracle? But if the FFSA's salami did not work, what other weapons do they have up their sleeve?

STARTING GRID

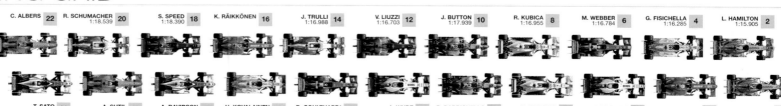

* D. COULTHARD was relegated for blocking KOVALAINEN in his fast lap.

C. ALBERS 22	R. SCHUMACHER 20	S. SPEED 18	K. RÄIKKÖNEN 16	J. TRULLI 14	V. LIUZZI 12	J. BUTTON 10	R. KUBICA 8	M. WEBBER 6	G. FISICHELLA 4	L. HAMILTON 2
	1:18.539	1:18.390	1:18.988	1:16.703	1:16.703	1:17.939	1:16.955	1:16.784	1:16.285	1:15.905

T. SATO 21	A. SUTIL 19	A. DAVIDSON 17	H. KOVALAINEN 15	D. COULTHARD* 13	A. WURZ 11	R. BARRICHELLO 9	N. HEIDFELD 7	N. ROSBERG 5	F. MASSA 3	F. ALONSO 1
1:18.554	1:18.418	1:18.250	1:17.125	1:16.319	1:16.662	1:17.498	1:16.832	1:16.439	1:15.967	1:15.726 (158.782 km/h)

Lewis could have won. Were the odds stacked against him?

Lewis Hamilton didn't stop adding to his own record : that of the number of consecutive podiums for a rookie F1 driver. So far, the Englishman had ended every race of his Grand Prix career tasting champagne.

But at Monaco, standing next to Prince Albert, a bit of disappointment could be seen on his face for the very first time. On Saturday young Lewis had qualified second, but just 18 hundredths behind Fernando Alonso and with a car that had 10 kilograms more fuel. That was the equivalent of about five more laps, or three-tenths of a second.

Make the fuel adjustment, and it seemed that the Englishman was faster than his Spanish teammate. He hoped to make use of that: by starting with more fuel he would stop six laps after his teammate. In those six crucial laps, with a light car, he would have an opportunity to take the lead. Or so the theory went.

Except that McLaren called him in three laps early. It seemed almost as if McLaren did not actually want him to win the race. *"I'll be delighted to hear the*

explanation from my engineers," was all that Hamilton would say curtly after the race.

McLaren's boss, Ron Dennis, rushed to the defence of his team as always. *"There has and never will be team orders at McLaren,"* he stated pointedly. *"However, if I didn't try and avoid an accident between my two cars, I would be seen as an idiot. I don't give orders to my drivers, I manage my team."*

The interpretation of this semantic exercise is best left to the individual. But Hamilton's camp believed that the team had just deprived him of his first win. Looking at it a bit closer though, this doesn't appear to be the case. Straight after his fuel stop, Fernando Alonso's lap time was 1m15.462s, where as Hamilton was lapping at 1m15.372s. Those meagre nine-hundredths of a second wouldn't have allowed the young Englishman to get past his teammate.

Nonetheless, it was a newsworthy incident - and the following day the FIA decided to get involved as well (see page 120).

Ferrari's fall from grace

At Barcelona two weeks earlier, Felipe Massa seemed to be untouchable. He had won the Spanish Grand Prix with such ease that the World Championship already seemed destined for Ferrari. How then, after such a dominant display in Spain, did Ferrari come to finish more than a minute behind in Monaco? For the prestigious Scuderia, it was a bitter pill to swallow.

Ferrari felt the tide beginning to turn on Thursday, the first day of practice before the Grand Prix. From the first few laps, it was clear that the McLarens were going to be the cars to beat. By the end of the first practice session, Felipe Massa was already a second behind the McLarens.

By the time qualifying came on Saturday, the gap had been brought down to just a few tenths of a second. But to finish at the front in Monaco you have to qualify at the front. This was made painfully obvious to Felipe Massa - who had set pole position at the three previous Grands Prix - after he finished more than a minute behind the winner. For Massa, it was a big and nasty surprise after his demolition of the opposition in Spain.

After the race on Sunday, Felipe Massa did everything he could to analyse this downturn in form. *"I don't really know what happened,"* he said. *"Maybe it's just down to the peculiarities of this track. Generally speaking we've been very happy with the performance of the car, apart from on this circuit. Something unexpected has clearly occurred, because we were not even as fast as the Renaults. We need to put our finger on the problem as soon as possible in order to stop it from happening again…"*

Jean Todt, at the helm of the Scuderia, tried to downplay the problem. *"We all know that Monaco is a unique circuit,"* he pointed out. *"Here the cars behave very differently to the way that they do anywhere else, and in particular they behave differently to the way they do in Montreal, the next Grand Prix. We're not at all happy here and we have to recognise that our rivals were better than us. Nonetheless, not by much though. We finished a long way back, but that was because we asked Felipe to slow down in order to be sure of third place. There was no point in being tucked up behind the McLarens."* Todt showed no signs of concern about the rest of the season either. *"Generally speaking, we're feeling confident,"* he said. *"We believe that we can win the World Championship. Having said that, our rivals are very strong and we cannot afford to relax for a minute."*

His optimism however did little to hide the concern as the Ferrari team packed up to return to Maranello. The problems in Monaco were completely unknown, and more worryingly Ferrari had absolutely no clue as to their cause. It was only later in the season that the issue would come to light : after Ferrari made some hurried changes to the floor of their F2007 following the Australian Grand Prix, the car constantly struggled on circuits with imperfect surfaces.

<
To finish first in Monaco you have to start first - and be quick off the lights! It was no problem for the first four drivers on the grid: Alonso, Hamilton, Massa and Fisichella, who started - and finished - in that order. There were no surprises out front at the legendary Monegasque circuit.

<
Fernando waving, Lewis with a wedged smile: Monaco was the end of the entente cordiale between the two McLaren drivers.

One point that is worth a championship: the world champion to be Kimi Raikkonen had a dismal weekend in Monaco, qualifying 16th on Saturday after a small impact with a guard rail and finishing eighth in the race to score a solitary point. At that point, he was 15 points behind Fernando Alonso. « So what? » said Jean Todt. « There are still 12 races to go, so 15 points is nothing. »
Only at the end of the year could Kimi reflect that the hard-earned point at Monaco, after fighting his way back up the field, was what won him the World Championship…
v <

A jungle of cars and wheels at the first corner. By some miracle, there were no accidents this year…
v

MONEGASQUE SCENERY

All the photographers say that the Monaco Grand Prix is their favourite, their paradise, and the circuit that reminds them why they chose this profession. When the sun is shining, as it was on Thursday, the Principality forms a unique backdrop for the best of Formula 1 design.

^
"Take that!" Lewis Hamilton was pleased to have finished once more on the podium. Even if he would have preferred it to be the top step…

«The FIA versus McLaren». Round 1

The whole affair caused a frenzy amongst the British media. On the Monday after the Monaco Grand Prix, the FIA decided to open an inquest to determine whether or not McLaren had violated article 151c of the sporting code. This innocent little article was the focus of much attention later in the year as well, and it forbids any action that could: «prejudice competition or motorsport in general.»

It's a vague wording, open to all sorts of interpretations. One of the things it apparently outlaws - amongst many others - is team orders. Once the investigation was confirmed, Ron Dennis probably started to regret his decision to actively manage the outcome of the Monaco Grand Prix. *"All I did was make sure that we won,"* he said at the time. *"You mustn't confuse strategy and orders. A strategy allows a team to win a Grand Prix. Orders, by contrast, are there to manipulate the result. In our history, we've hardly ever manipulated anything. The last time was in 1998".*

This, incidentally, was done to correct a mistake: the team asked David Coulthard to let Mika Hakkinen past, as the Finn had been called into the pits by accident and consequently lost the race lead.

After Monaco the FIA said that they would decide whether or not to punish McLaren in the coming days, following the analysis of evidence such as radio conversations between the team and drivers, as well as personal interviews with the people involved.

Whatever conclusions the FIA drew, it would seem unlikely that McLaren had substantially changed the outcome of the race by asking their drivers not to attack each other - which would also be a logical enough request. Fernando Alonso undoubtedly had a little left in reserve had he been forced to defend from his team-mate.

Thankfully reason prevailed in the end: the FIA decided that they did not have enough evidence to prove any wrongdoing on the part of McLaren.

SNAPSHOTS OF THE WEEKEND

+ As was the case in 2006, Red Bull's motorhome - the famous 'Energy Station' - was installed on a 26 by 55 metre floating island in Monaco's harbour, complete with a bar, disco and swimming pool! It was then towed into place in order to accommodate the team, its guests and the press. The 'Energy Station' can host up to 800 people at a time, with 11 chefs and 14 waiters to look after them.

+ New colours: Ferrari changed the look of their cars completely for the Monaco weekend, discarding the legendary rosso corsa red paintwork in favour of a metallic red that would give the cars better visibility on television.

+ Diamonds are forever: some small diamonds were incorporated into the helmets of the two McLaren drivers, Fernando Alonso and Lewis Hamilton. It was an initiative from Steinmetz, one of the team's partners, who did the same thing in 2006 and nearly caused a riot when one of the diamonds flew off in an accident.

+ To celebrate the 20th anniversary of Ayrton Senna's first victory at Monaco (on 31 May 1987) the Ayrton Senna foundation organised a series of commemorative events from

May 19-27. An exhibition about the Brazilian's six Monaco victories was held in the Fairmont Hotel, right in the middle of the circuit. An auction of memorabilia was also organised in aid of the foundation, which looks after disadvantaged children in Brazil.

+ On Saturday morning, Renault's chief executive Carlos Ghosn came to Monaco to talk about the team's start to the 2007 season. While Giancarlo Fisichella and Heikki Kovalainen had been a long way off the podium so far - the team was only fourth in the manufacturers' standings - Ghosn remained optimistic. *"I still think we will win the World Championship this year"* was one of his more memorable quotations: the product of either incurable optimism or a serious lack of knowledge about Formula 1. The French team would finish the season with just one trip to the podium - a lucky second place at the Japanese Grand Prix.

+ There were only three retirements at the end of the Grand Prix: the attrition rate in Monaco is normally a lot higher. Only two drivers hit the armco during the race: Vitantonio Liuzzi and Adrian Sutil, both at the Hotel de Paris.

>
«Don't I know you?» Michael Schumacher and Mika Hakkinen, old rivals from the late 1990s, bumped into each other in the Monaco paddock. A few months later, Hakkinen announced his definitive retirement from motorsport (having raced in the German DTM Touring Car championship until the end of 2007).

>
Giancarlo Fisichella qualified and finished fourth around the twisty streets of Monaco. He wasn't to know it, but this would be his best result of the year.

>>
At Monaco, you can be soothed to sleep by the roar of F1 engines…provided you remember your earplugs!

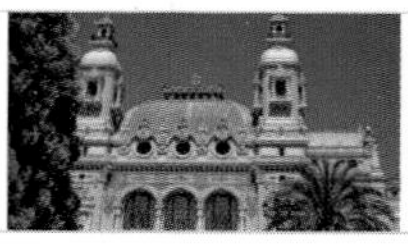

PRACTICE

Date	Weather (AM)	Air temperature	Track temperature	Weather (PM)	Air temperature	Track temperature
Thursday May 24, 2007	Sunny	26-29°c	33-41°c	Sunny	26-28°c	41-42°c
Saturday May 26, 2007	Rain	24-23°c	27-25°c	Overcast, drizzle during Q3	26-25°c	31-28°c

All the time trials

N° Driver	Nat.	N° Chassis- Engine [Nbr. GP]	Pos. Free 1 jeudi 10:00-11:30	Laps Tr.	Pos. Free 2 jeudi 14:00-15:30	Laps Tr.	Pos. Free 3 Saturday 11:00-12:00	Laps Tr.	Pos. Q1 Saturday 14:00-14:15	Laps Tr.	Pos. Q2 Saturday 14:22-14:37	Laps Tr.	Pos. Q3 Saturday 14:45-15:00	Nb. Tr.
1. Fernando Alonso	E	McLaren MP4-22 06 - Mercedes [1]	1. 1:16.973	33	1. 1:15.940	40	6. 1:37.020	16	2. 1:16.059	8	1. 1:15.431	3	1. **1:15.726**	11
2. Lewis Hamilton	GB	McLaren MP4-22 05 - Mercedes [1]	2. 1:17.601	14	3. 1:16.296	19	3. 1:36.767	15	1. 1:15.685	6	2. 1:15.479	4	2. **1:15.905**	12
3. Giancarlo Fisichella	I	Renault R27-05 [1]	4. 1:17.758	27	5. 1:16.753	41	4. 1:36.784	16	12. 1:17.596	7	6. 1:16.054	6	4. **1:16.285**	11
4. Heikki Kovalainen	FIN	Renault R27-03 [1]	16. 1:19.321	27	17. 1:18.086	41	7. 1:37.214	15	15. 1:17.836	8	15. **1:17.125**	8		
5. Felipe Massa	BR	Ferrari F2007 260 [1]	8. 1:18.189	29	6. 1:16.784	37	12. 1:37.997	12	5. 1:16.786	8	5. 1:16.034	7	3. **1:15.967**	12
6. Kimi Räikkönen	FIN	Ferrari F2007 262 [1]	5. 1:17.918	28	2. 1:16.215	43	2. 1:36.739	13	3. 1:16.251	9	16. **DNF**	2		
7. Jenson Button	GB	Honda RA107-04 [2]	17. 1:19.332	27	12. 1:17.457	45	9. 1:37.442	12	9. 1:17.297	10	11. 1:16.457	6	10. **1:17.939**	12
8. Rubens Barrichello	BR	Honda RA107-02 [2]	10. 1:18.676	22	11. 1:17.449	40	10. 1:37.463	14	8. 1:17.244	10	10. 1:16.454	6	9. **1:17.498**	11
9. Nick Heidfeld	D	BMW Sauber F1.07-05 [1]	3. 1:17.616	31	14. 1:17.486	43	18. 1:38.899	18	10. 1:17.385	5	4. 1:15.733	7	7. **1:16.832**	12
10. Robert Kubica	PL	BMW Sauber F1.07-07 [1]	9. 1:18.675	28	7. 1:16.848	48	16. 1:38.463	13	11. 1:17.584	5	3. 1:15.576	7	8. **1:16.955**	12
11. Ralf Schumacher	D	Toyota TF107/05 [1]	20. 1:19.799	25	20. 1:18.662	38	20. 1:40.677	17	20. **1:18.539**	8				
12. Jarno Trulli	I	Toyota TF107/04 [1]	19. 1:19.496	22	4. 1:16.354	39	22. 1:43.417	22	13. 1:17.686	8	14. **1:16.988**	6		
14. David Coulthard	GB	Red Bull RB3 3 - Renault [2]	13. 1:19.095	16	10. 1:17.414	16	15. 1:38.302	6	7. 1:17.204	9	11.(8.) **1:16.319**	7		
15. Mark Webber	AUS	Red Bull RB3 2 - Renault [1]	6. 1:17.956	19	9. 1:17.292	16	11. 1:37.732	13	14. 1:17.816	7	9. 1:16.420	6	6. **1:16.784**	12
16. Nico Rosberg	D	Williams FW29-05 - Toyota [1]	7. 1:18.074	27	8. 1:16.852	34	8. 1:37.388	15	6. 1:16.870	9	7. 1:16.100	3	5. **1:16.439**	12
17. Alexander Wurz	AUT	Williams FW29-04 - Toyota [1]	11. 1:18.869	29	15. 1:17.516	34	17. 1:38.876	14	16. 1:17.874	9	12. **1:16.662**	7		
18. Vitantonio Liuzzi	I	Toro Rosso STR2-03 - Ferrari [1]	15. 1:19.285	24	16. 1:17.898	42	21. 1:41.108	8	4. 1:16.720	11	13. **1:16.703**	6		
19. Scott Speed	USA	Toro Rosso STR2-04 - Ferrari [1]	12. 1:18.967	27	18. 1:18.233	40	5. 1:36.954	15	18. **1:18.390**	7				
20. Adrian Sutil	D	Spyker F8-VII/03 - Ferrari [1]	21. 1:21.634	19	22. 1:19.358	29	1. 1:36.612	12	19. **1:18.418**	8				
21. Christijan Albers	NL	Spyker F8-VII/02 & 01 - Ferrari [1]	22. 1:23.235	5	21. 1:18.820	35	19. 1:38.935	14	22. **DNF**	3				
22. Takuma Sato	J	Super Aguri SA07-04 - Honda [2]	14. 1:19.203	27	13. 1:17.459	47	13. 1:38.121	14	21. **1:18.554**	10				
23. Anthony Davidson	GB	Super Aguri SA07-03 - Honda [2]	18. 1:19.337	22	19. 1:18.328	25	14. 1:38.180	17	17. **1:18.250**	7				

Coulthard, initiallement classé 8e en Q2, n'est pas autorisé à prendre part à la Q3 pour avoir gêné Kovalainen dans son tour rapide.

Fastest lap overall

F. Alonso 1:15.431 (159,403 km/h)

Maximum speed

N° Driver	S1 Qualifs	Pos.	S1 Race	Pos.	S2 Qualifs	Pos.	S2 Race	Pos.	Finish Qualifs	Pos.	Finish Race	Pos.	Radar Qualifs	Pos.	Radar Race	Pos.
1. F. Alonso	209,3	8	213,0	1	228,1	2	227,2	3	261,9	1	262,8	1	289,2	1	288,9	2
2. L. Hamilton	209,0	9	211,6	2	226,4	6	229,3	1	261,2	3	262,3	2	288,4	2	289,0	1
3. G. Fisichella	214,4	1	211,2	3	226,7	3	227,8	2	259,1	6	258,8	8	286,1	5	286,0	3
4. H. Kovalainen	208,1	11	207,6	12	237,5	1	226,3	4	258,8	9	259,2	6	286,7	4	285,4	5
5. F. Massa	212,5	2	210,9	4	222,1	11	222,9	9	260,2	5	260,6	4	285,4	8	285,0	7
6. K. Räikkönen	207,5	13	204,2	15	226,5	5	220,9	11	260,9	4	261,8	3	285,6	7	284,8	8
7. J. Button	206,4	15	203,8	16	221,0	14	220,9	12	253,5	19	255,0	16	279,7	20	279,2	17
8. R. Barrichello	210,4	5	209,0	9	218,7	16	219,6	17	254,0	17	256,0	15	280,7	17	280,0	16
9. N. Heidfeld	210,2	6	210,7	6	226,3	7	220,3	15	261,8	2	259,4	5	286,0	6	285,9	4
10. R. Kubica	210,8	4	210,8	5	226,0	8	225,8	5	259,0	7	258,4	9	287,0	3	285,2	6
11. R. Schumacher	207,5	12	208,9	10	213,3	21	217,8	19	256,1	14	257,2	11	282,5	14	281,3	13
12. J. Trulli	209,4	7	209,3	8	226,6	4	218,7	18	255,6	15	257,0	12	283,4	12	280,6	15
14. D. Coulthard	206,8	14	203,8	17	221,9	12	219,7	16	258,2	10	258,9	7	281,8	16	281,6	12
15. M. Webber	202,6	19	197,0	21	221,0	15	210,9	21	258,8	8	258,1	10	281,9	15	281,1	14
16. N. Rosberg	211,3	3	209,8	7	225,8	9	223,3	8	257,0	12	257,0	13	285,4	9	283,0	9
17. A. Wurz	205,1	17	206,1	14	218,1	18	217,4	20	257,6	11	256,7	14	283,9	11	282,5	10
18. V. Liuzzi	208,9	10	166,1	22	223,7	10	188,1	22	256,4	13	249,3	22	285,1	10	270,7	22
19. S. Speed	205,5	16	208,2	11	221,5	13	225,8	6	253,9	18	253,9	18	283,3	13	282,1	11
20. A. Sutil	204,9	18	200,8	19	218,2	17	220,8	13	249,8	21	250,6	21	278,5	21	277,0	21
21. C. Albers	177,1	22	200,8	20	207,6	22	221,0	10	246,5	22	251,3	20	274,4	22	277,4	20
22. T. Sato	202,0	20	207,1	13	216,7	19	223,6	7	254,7	16	254,1	17	280,2	18	279,2	18
23. A. Davidson	195,1	21	203,4	18	216,6	20	220,7	14	252,6	20	253,5	19	279,8	19	277,8	19

Best sector times

Qualifs	**S1** F. Alonso	19.746	**S2** R. Kubica	37.211	**S3** L. Hamilton	18.210	= 1:15.167
Race	**S1** L. Hamilton	19.642	**S2** F. Alonso	37.099	**S3** F. Alonso	18.215	= 1:14.956

RACE

Date	Weather	Air temperature	Track temperature	Humidity	Wind speed
Sunday May 27, 2007 (14:00)	Sunny	23-26°c	34-41°c	54%	1.8 m/s

Classification & retirements

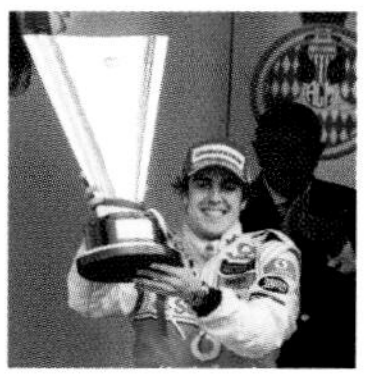

Pos.	Driver	Constructor	Tyres	Laps	Time	Km/h	
1.	F. Alonso	McLaren Mercedes	SSU	78	1:40:29.329	155,551	
2.	L. Hamilton	McLaren Mercedes	SSU	78	+ 4.095	155,446	
3.	F. Massa	Ferrari	SUU	78	+ 1:09.114	153,788	
4.	G. Fisichella	Renault	SSU	77	1 tour	153,263	
5.	R. Kubica	BMW	SU	77	1 tour	152,753	
6.	N. Heidfeld	BMW	US	77	1 tour	152,651	
7.	A. Wurz	Williams Toyota	SU	77	1 tour	152,480	
8.	K. Räikkönen	Ferrari	SU	77	1 tour	152,374	
9.	S. Speed	STR Ferrari	SU	77	1 tour	152,130	
10.	R. Barrichello	Honda	SSU	77	1 tour	152,101	
11.	J. Button	Honda	SSU	77	1 tour	152,077	
12.	N. Rosberg	Williams Toyota	SSU	77	1 tour	151,955	
13.	H. Kovalainen	Renault	SU	76	2 tours	151,630	Loss of engine power
14.	D. Coulthard	Red Bull Renault	SU	76	2 tours	151,255	
15.	J. Trulli	Toyota	SU	76	2 tours	150,610	
16.	R. Schumacher	Toyota	SU	76	2 tours	150,587	
17.	T. Sato	Super Aguri Honda	USU	76	2 tours	150,573	
18.	A. Davidson	Super Aguri Honda	SU	76	2 tours	150,559	
19.	C. Albers	Spyker Ferrari	USS	70	8 tours	148,644	Transmission failure

Driver	Constructor	Tyres	Laps	Reason
A. Sutil	Spyker Ferrari	SU	53	Went off and hit guardrail
M. Webber	Red Bull Renault	S	17	Broken gearbox due to engine misfire
V. Liuzzi	STR Ferrari	S	1	Right-rear puncture following collision with Coulthard, went off into guardrail.

Tyres S: Soft & U: Super Soft

Fastest laps

	Driver	Time	Lap	Km/h
1.	F. Alonso	1:15.284	44	159,715
2.	L. Hamilton	1:15.372	28	159,528
3.	R. Kubica	1:16.006	39	158,198
4.	F. Massa	1:16.183	47	157,830
5.	G. Fisichella	1:16.254	54	157,683
6.	K. Räikkönen	1:16.592	62	156,987
7.	A. Wurz	1:16.658	40	156,852
8.	D. Coulthard	1:16.786	75	156,591
9.	J. Button	1:16.802	40	156,558
10.	S. Speed	1:16.867	73	156,426
11.	N. Rosberg	1:16.991	70	156,174
12.	N. Heidfeld	1:17.041	30	156,072
13.	R. Barrichello	1:17.080	69	155,993
14.	H. Kovalainen	1:17.100	72	155,953
15.	T. Sato	1:17.183	74	155,785
16.	A. Davidson	1:17.223	63	155,704
17.	R. Schumacher	1:17.231	47	155,688
18.	J. Trulli	1:17.495	53	155,158
19.	A. Sutil	1:17.678	34	154,792
20.	C. Albers	1:17.689	70	154,770
21.	M. Webber	1:18.998	17	152,206

Pit stops

	Driver	Lap	Duration	Stop	Total
1.	G. Fisichella	23	29.057	1	29.057
2.	N. Rosberg	23	26.446	1	26.446
3.	T. Sato	24	28.747	1	28.747
4.	C. Albers	24	25.757	1	25.757
5.	F. Alonso	26	24.861	1	24.861
6.	F. Massa	26	25.872	1	25.872
7.	L. Hamilton	29	25.329	1	25.329
8.	N. Heidfeld	32	28.197	1	28.197
9.	A. Davidson	•36•	14.703	1	14.703
10.	R. Barrichello	37	24.726	1	24.726
11.	A. Davidson	37	28.595	2	43.298
12.	J. Button	41	24.998	1	24.998
13.	D. Coulthard	42	27.318	1	27.318
14.	A. Wurz	44	26.804	1	26.804
15.	H. Kovalainen	44	25.501	1	25.501
16.	A. Sutil	44	26.838	1	26.838
17.	R. Kubica	45	28.254	1	28.254
18.	S. Speed	45	26.479	1	26.479
19.	K. Räikkönen	47	25.002	1	25.002
20.	J. Trulli	47	25.228	1	25.228
21.	R. Schumacher	49	25.042	1	25.042
22.	F. Alonso	51	24.687	2	49.548
23.	L. Hamilton	53	23.297	2	48.626
24.	C. Albers	51	26.295	2	52.052
25.	F. Massa	55	28.150	2	54.022
26.	G. Fisichella	55	24.025	2	53.082
27.	T. Sato	57	23.948	2	52.695
28.	N. Rosberg	59	24.092	2	50.538
29.	R. Barrichello	60	24.010	2	48.736
30.	J. Button	61	24.936	2	49.934

•• Drive-through penalty: Davidson.
For ignoring blue flags

Race leader

Driver	Laps in the lead	Nbr of laps
F. Alonso	1 > 25	25
L. Hamilton	26 > 28	3
F. Alonso	29 > 50	22
L. Hamilton	51 > 52	2
F. Alonso	53 > 78	26

Driver	Nbr of laps	Kilometers
F. Alonso	73	243,820 km
L. Hamilton	5	16,700 km

Lap chart

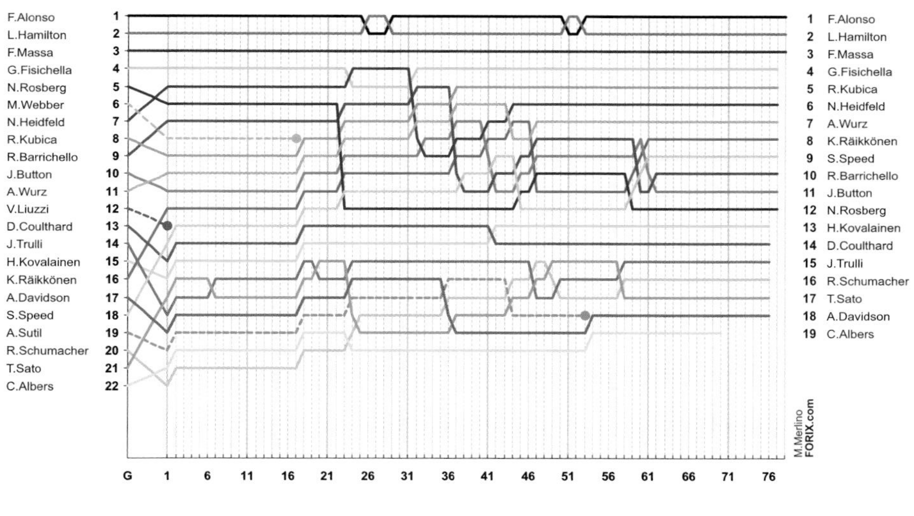
F.Alonso
L.Hamilton
F.Massa
G.Fisichella
N.Rosberg
M.Webber
N.Heidfeld
R.Kubica
R.Barrichello
J.Button
A.Wurz
V.Liuzzi
D.Coulthard
J.Trulli
H.Kovalainen
K.Räikkönen
A.Davidson
S.Speed
A.Sutil
R.Schumacher
T.Sato
C.Albers
1 2 3 4 5 6 7 8 9 10 11 12 13 14 15 16 17 18 19 20 21 22
G 1 6 11 16 21 26 31 36 41 46 51 56 61 66 71 76
1 F.Alonso
2 L.Hamilton
3 F.Massa
4 G.Fisichella
5 R.Kubica
6 N.Heidfeld
7 A.Wurz
8 K.Räikkönen
9 S.Speed
10 R.Barrichello
11 J.Button
12 N.Rosberg
13 H.Kovalainen
14 D.Coulthard
15 J.Trulli
16 R.Schumacher
17 T.Sato
18 A.Davidson
19 C.Albers
M.Merino FORIX.com

Gaps on the lead board

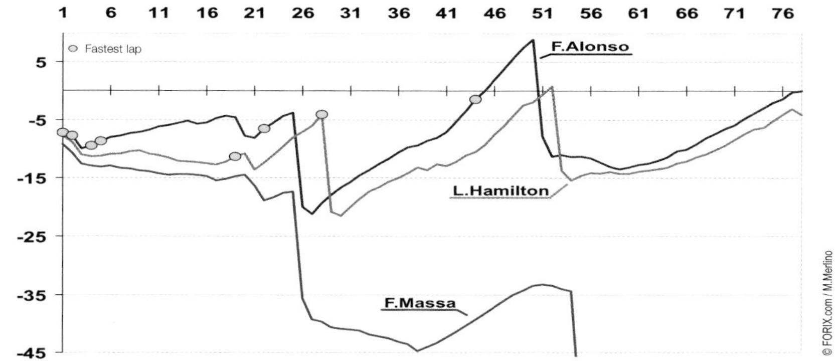
1 6 11 16 21 26 31 36 41 46 51 56 61 66 71 76
5
-5
-15
-25
-35
-45
Fastest lap
F.Alonso
L.Hamilton
F.Massa
© FORIX.com / M.Merino

CHAMPIONSHIPS 5/17

Drivers

1.	F. Alonso	McLaren Mercedes	2🏆	38
2.	L. Hamilton	McLaren Mercedes		38
3.	F. Massa	Ferrari	2🏆	33
4.	K. Räikkönen	Ferrari	1🏆	23
5.	N. Heidfeld	BMW		18
6.	G. Fisichella	Renault		13
7.	R. Kubica	BMW		12
8.	N. Rosberg	Williams Toyota		5
9.	D. Coulthard	Red Bull Renault		4
10.	J. Trulli	Toyota		4
11.	H. Kovalainen	Renault		3
12.	A. Wurz	Williams Toyota		2
13.	T. Sato	Super Aguri Honda		1
14.	R. Schumacher	Toyota		1
15.	S. Speed	STR Ferrari		0
16.	R. Barrichello	Honda		0
17.	M. Webber	Red Bull Renault		0
18.	J. Button	Honda		0
19.	A. Davidson	Super Aguri Honda		0
20.	A. Sutil	Spyker Ferrari		0
21.	C. Albers	Spyker Ferrari		0
22.	V. Liuzzi	STR Ferrari		0

Constructors

1.	Vodafone McLaren Mercedes	2🏆	76
2.	Scuderia Ferrari Marlboro	3🏆	56
3.	BMW Sauber F1 Team		30
4.	ING Renault F1 Team		16
5.	AT&T Williams		7
6.	Panasonic Toyota Racing		5
7.	Red Bull Racing		4
8.	Super Aguri F1 Team		1
9.	Scuderia Toro Rosso		0
10.	Honda Racing F1 Team		0
11.	Etihad Aldar Spyker F1 Team		0

THE CIRCUIT

Name Circuit de Monaco; Monte-Carlo
Lenght 3340 m
Distance 78 tours, soit 260,520 km
Latitude 43°44'06.45"N
Longitude 7°25'16.45"E

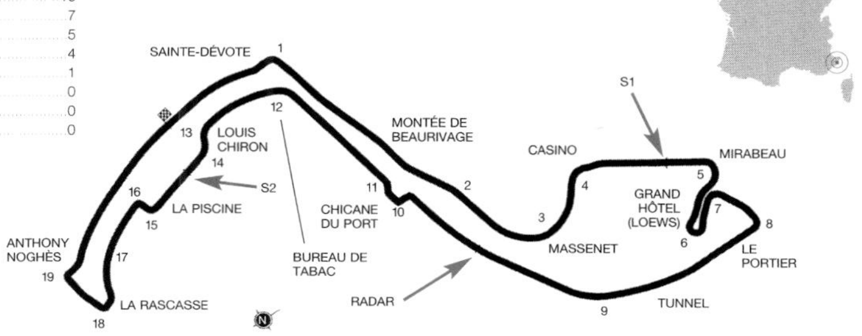
SAINTE-DÉVOTE
1
12
13
LOUIS CHIRON
14
S2
16
LA PISCINE
15
17
ANTHONY NOGHÈS
19
18
LA RASCASSE
BUREAU DE TABAC
CHICANE DU PORT
11
10
MONTÉE DE BEAURIVAGE
2
3
RADAR
CASINO
4
MASSENET
S1
MIRABEAU
5
GRAND HÔTEL (LOEWS)
6
7
8
LE PORTIER
9
TUNNEL

S1 70m before corner
S2 80m before corner
Radar 145m before corner

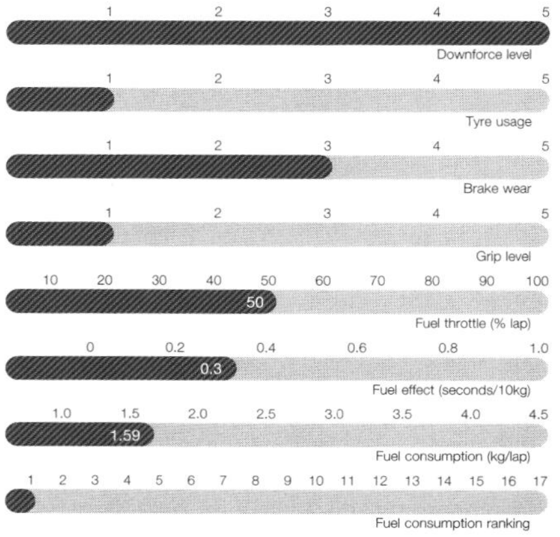
1 2 3 4 5
Downforce level
1 2 3 4 5
Tyre usage
1 2 3 4 5
Brake wear
1 2 3 4 5
Grip level
10 20 30 40 50 60 70 80 90 100
50
Fuel throttle (% lap)
0 0.2 0.4 0.6 0.8 1.0
0.3
Fuel effect (seconds/10kg)
1.0 1.5 2.0 2.5 3.0 3.5 4.0 4.5
1.59
Fuel consumption (kg/lap)
1 2 3 4 5 6 7 8 9 10 11 12 13 14 15 16 17
Fuel consumption ranking

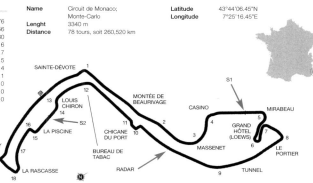

A CRAZY GRAND PRIX, A NEW WINNER... AND A MIRACLE.

What a Grand Prix!
Four stoppages behind the safety car, an incredible number of accidents and a new winner: Lewis Hamilton. The Briton managed to keep his cool despite all the obstacles against him, and remained doggedly determined to seal his first victory, even behind the safety car. Behind him, the biggest fright of the year came from Robert Kubica's terrifying accident, from which he emerged unscathed despite an impact of more than 300kph.

> Lewis Hamilton on the limit in Montreal. Pole position would be his reward.

Lewis Hamilton's first pole

Lewis Hamilton was unknown three months ago, but by the time he arrived in Canada he was already a star. At 22 years old, he already graced the cover of all the best magazines. And in the city of Montreal, it seemed that his photograph peered out from all the shop windows. On Saturday, the young McLaren driver wrote another chapter in his personal history by claiming the first pole position of his career, in only his sixth Grand Prix, and on only his first visit to the Gilles Villeneuve circuit.

There was a lot for him to be happy about. *"It's a fantastic day, a fantastic weekend, and the team has done a great job,"* he enthused on Saturday. Then he delivered a more measured version for the press conference. *"The car was easy to drive, the tyres were perfect, but I still had to dig extremely deep: I gave it everything in order to set fastest time. It's not easy when you have a two-time World Champion right behind you."*

This two-time World Champion (his team mate Fernando Alonso) could equally have taken pole position had he not made a mistake at the hairpin at the far end of the circuit. Up to that point the Spaniard had been quicker than his teammate, according to the sector times at least.

"Unfortunately, I came out of the hairpin a bit wide and I lost about three-tenths of a second," he said. *"I knew it was all over then, so I backed off."*

With pole position in his pocket, Lewis Hamilton could now think of victory. *"Starting from pole position will be a new experience for me,"* added the young Englishman. *"The most important thing will be to get through the first corner in front; then I have to stay there. It's going to be a long race so we'll just have to see."*

We did indeed see, exactly as Hamilton predicted, the following day. Alonso had finally met his match.

> Tsutomu Tomita experienced his last Grand Prix at the helm of the Toyota team. The popular team boss was being called back to Japan to take on a new role, but he had a good send off first from all the members of the squad.

A BMW in front of the Ferraris - which are booed by the public.

It was the surprise of the qualifying session: Nick Heidfeld managed to put his BMW Sauber third on the grid, just behind the two Ferraris. *"It's fantastic,"* said the diminutive German. *"Our car is getting better and better all the time and this circuit suits us particularly well. The Saubers have always gone very well here."*

Montreal has always been home to many Ferrari fans. This is partly down to a thriving Italian expat population, and also down to the legacy of Gilles Villeneuve, who drove all his Grands Prix (apart from one) at the wheel of a Ferrari. But the loyal fans were bitterly disappointed by a poor performance from the red cars, contrary to the high expectations. At the end of qualifying, as the Ferraris were heading back to their pit garage, they were whistled by a contemptuous crowd. Not that it worried the drivers. *"I'm not very happy with qualifying, but I think that our strategy and race pace is excellent,"* concluded Kimi Raikkonen.

STARTING GRID

Row	Driver	Time	Pos
	C. ALBERS*	1:19.196	21
	A. WURZ	1:18.089	19
	A. DAVIDSON	1:17.542	17
	J. BUTTON	1:17.541	15
	R. BARRICHELLO	1:17.116	13
	T. SATO	1:16.743	11
	G. FISICHELLA	1:17.229	9
	N. ROSBERG	1:16.919	7
	F. MASSA	1:16.570	5
	N. HEIDFELD	1:16.266	3
	L. HAMILTON	1:15.707 (207.373 km/h)	1

Driver	Time	Pos
H. KOVALAINEN	1:17.806	22
A. SUTIL	1:18.536	20
R. SCHUMACHER	1:17.634	18
S. SPEED	1:17.571	16
D. COULTHARD	1:17.304	14
V. LIUZZI	1:16.760	12
J. TRULLI	1:17.747	10
R. KUBICA	1:16.993	8
M. WEBBER	1:16.913	6
K. RÄIKKÖNEN	1:16.411	4
F. ALONSO	1:16.163	2

Lewis Hamilton survives a mad race

On the Saturday before the Canadian Grand Prix, many of the drivers complained about the Montreal circuit's configuration, and in particular the concrete walls that surround the circuit. This made the track relatively dangerous, so they said, as it prevented the emergency services from reaching any incident promptly. They were not to know how prophetic their words would be. Sunday's race would be a succession of surprises, accidents, and safety car periods. Lewis Hamilton and Nick Heidfeld, who were first and second out of the first corner, were virtually the only people to navigate their way through the 70 laps without any major problems.

At the start Hamilton managed to hold off Nick Heidfeld, but his McLaren team mate Alonso - who was trying to go round the outside - was forced to take to the grass at the first corner and found himself behind the BMW Sauber. From that point on, the

Spaniard could not keep up with Hamilton, and eventually wound up a modest seventh after going off the road several times. One to forget.

It was only after the first fuel stops that the race really started to become chaotic, with an accident for the Spyker driver Adrian Sutil on lap 22, followed by the biggest scare of the race: Robert Kubica's crash on lap 27 (see page 128). There was another accident for the remaining Spyker of Christijan Albers on lap 48, and finally Vitantonio Liuzzi made contact with the infamous 'wall of champions' at the last chicane on lap 54. All of these unforeseen dramas contributed to a busy day for the Mercedes safety car.

"I'm on another planet!"

Lewis Hamilton came away from Canada with a first win, a first pole position and the lead of the World Championship: what more could he ask for? *"Yes, it's incredible - I feel like I'm on a different planet,"* he said, stepping out of the car. *"So far everything is going really well in this whole adventure, and I really feel like I need to pinch myself virtually every day. To begin with there was my first test in the car, then there was my first Grand Prix, my first podium, my first pole and now my first win today. It's mad. I really don't know what's happening anymore!"*

Every driver says that the first GP win is something that feels very special - particularly at the exact moment of crossing the chequered flag. *"At that point, I was just screaming inside my helmet,"* said Hamilton. *"I wanted to stop the car there*

Through it all, Lewis Hamilton somehow managed to stay calm and crucially he remembered to keep up his tyre pressures - which was always tricky at slow speeds behind the safety car. But it was an essential skill that allowed him to overcome the problems and never lose the Grand Prix lead.

The hard-fought win also propelled the young Englishman into the championship lead, with an eight-point advantage over his teammate: a comfortable lead. This led to an intriguing possibility for the first time - which would have seemed preposterous just three months earlier. What if Lewis Hamilton were to win the World Championship in his first season of F1?

and then, right on the line just to hug everyone in the team. It was an incredible feeling. The last laps were terrifyingly long, and I seemed to be driving slower and slower. The challenge was just to try not to make any mistakes: at the same time my steering seemed to be pulling to the left."

So after crossing this historic threshold, what will be the next objective? He considers the question carefully. *"Well... the biggest dream would obviously be to win the World Championship,"* he says coolly. *"But I have to be realistic; things are not always going to go my way. Everything has been going astonishingly well for the moment, but I'm going to have to face up to some hard times as well. I hope they won't happen too often, but it's inevitable that at some point they will."*

^
'A glass of champagne, Sir?' Lewis Hamilton's pleasure on the podium was unbounded, having literally leapt from his car moments beforehand.

<
Nick Heidfeld finished second. It was his best result of the season, but his joy was tempered somewhat by the accident that befell his team mate Robert Kubica. « For me, the most important thing is knowing that Robert is fine ». The good news is that I could have still finished second even without the safety car periods and without the penalty for Fernando (Alonso). » Heidfeld has always been the optimistic type…

<
A third-placed finish for Alexander Wurz. He was able to take advantage of the numerous incidents that characterised the Grand Prix to place his Williams-Toyota on the podium for the first time in 2007.

LEWIS'S WEEKEND

The Canadian Grand Prix was all about just one man :
Lewis Hamilton. He set pole position, won the race and led
the championship : a perfect weekend for the young
Englishman at Montreal.

Kubica unharmed: a miracle on lap 27

Formula 1's biggest accident in recent years took place on lap 27 of the Canadian Grand Prix. In the midst of a fight with Jarno Trulli, Robert Kubica's BMW Sauber got away from him just before the braking zone for the hairpin, at a point where the cars are travelling at more than 300kph.

Kubica took off on the grass at the edge of the track and hit the concrete wall full on, without having slowed down at all. It was a sickening impact : the BMW Sauber disintegrated, was catapulted back onto the track, and finally came to rest next to the wall opposite. By some miracle, the survival cell round the cockpit withstood the colossal forces.

The Pole was extricated from his car - completely stunned but alive - and promptly taken to hospital. Mario Thiessen, the BMW Sauber team principal, hurried straight to Kubica's bedside after celebrating second place for their other car, driven by Nick Heidfeld.

"Can I race at Indianapolis?"

Formula 1 drivers operate on a different logic to the rest of us. Robert Kubica's first question in hospital was : *"Can I still race at Indianapolis ?"*

Apart from a brief 20-second blackout after the initial impact, the Pole remained entirely conscious from the time that the first marshals came to his aid, and throughout his helicopter transfer to Montreal's Sacre Cœur hospital. There, doctors could only find a small head injury and a twisted ankle. Nonetheless, the medical staff decided to keep him in for observation

until Monday morning as a precaution. The lucky Pole was also given the green light to race at Indianapolis just a week later, subject to passing a local medical before the Grand Prix.

At the circuit, the doctors on duty had feared the worst. *"Looking at the accident on the TV screens, I really thought that he was dead,"* said Dr Ronald Denis, the head of trauma at Sacre Cœur hospital, who was working at the circuit during the Canadian Grand Prix and one of the first people at the scene of the crash. *"Then he started talking to us straight away. I honestly wasn't expecting him to have got off so lightly."*

Twenty years ago, a similar accident would undoubtedly have had extremely dire consequences. *"With a crash like that in my day, I would have killed myself twice over,"* said Niki Lauda, a two-time World Champion who was watching at Montreal. *"The first time when I hit the wall, and the second time when I broke my neck."* Robert Kubica owes his life to the increasingly stringent safety regulations introduced by the FIA.

Towards the end of the 1980s the first monocoque chassis appeared, constructed entirely out of composite materials based on carbon fibre. These extremely strong chassis absorbed large impacts without deforming: at breaking point they would explode into millions of tiny fragments rather than bending. The FIA then introduced crash tests for each chassis: a major step forward. The tests consisted of applying front and side impacts to the chassis to check that they were strong enough to withstand the majority of accidents. These tests have become increasingly severe with every season, which was once more the case this year, thankfully.

The arrival of the monocoques also allowed the FIA to introduce the concept of 'survival cells', of fixed dimensions, in which the driver sits. On the Sunday of Canada, the BMW Sauber's survival cell stood up to the enormous impacts perfectly - with only one small piece breaking off, immediately beneath Robert Kubica's feet. At the start of this decade, another major contribution to safety made its debut : the HANS device (which stands for Head And Neck Support). It's generally unloved by drivers, as some say that it impedes their movements. Equally, it keeps their heads still in the event of an accident. In Canada, it was this that saved Robert Kubica from any severe whiplash injury.

The FIA is on a mission to continue to enforce these measures and constantly improve safety into the future. But this does not stop sheer bad luck from striking occasionally. When Ayrton Senna died at Imola in 1994, his survival cell withstood the impact. The Brazilian would undoubtedly still be alive today, had a rogue front-right suspension arm not randomly penetrated his helmet.

Trulli out in the cold

Ralf Schumacher, who had started from 18th on the grid, capitalised on all the drama around him to suddenly find himself in a provisional third. It didn't last: he ended the race in eighth place, claiming the final point. His teammate Jarno Trulli had an even more adventurous race, visiting the pits on four separate occasions (including one time after running over the debris from Robert Kubica's accident). A bit later, Trulli made contact with Nico Rosberg's Williams - which caused the safety car to stay out for longer than it had intended, just as it was about to come in. Finally, the Italian went off on the first corner after changing his tyres for the final time. Unfortunately they were cold, and his Toyota simply refused to turn in. The story of his race.

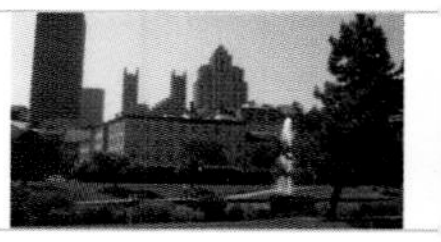

PRACTICE

Date	Weather (AM)	Air temperature	Track temperature	Weather (PM)	Air temperature	Track temperature
Friday June 8, 2007	Overcast	23-26°c	31-39°c	Sunny	29-31°c	46-49°c
Saturday June 9, 2007	Sunny	23-24°c	30-34°c	Sunny, some clouds	24-26°c	45-51°c

All the time trials

N° Driver	Nat.	N° Chassis- Engine [Nbr. GP]	Pos. Free 1 Friday 10:00-11:30	Laps Tr.	Pos. Free 2 Friday 14:00-15:30	Laps Tr.	Pos. Free 3 Saturday 10:00-11:00	Laps Tr.	Pos. Q1 Saturday 13:00-13:15	Laps Tr.	Pos. Q2 Saturday 13:22-13:37	Laps Tr.	Pos. Q3 Saturday 13:45-14:00	Nb. Tr.
1. Fernando Alonso	E	McLaren MP4-22 08 - Mercedes [2]	1. 1:17.759	17	1. 1:16.550	37	3. 1:16.465	9	2. 1:16.562	3	2. 1:15.522	3	2. **1:16.163**	12
2. Lewis Hamilton	GB	McLaren MP4-22 01 - Mercedes [2]	2. 1:17.967	20	3. 1:17.307	36	1. 1:16.071	12	3. 1:16.576	3	1. 1:15.486	3	1. **1:15.707**	12
3. Giancarlo Fisichella	I	Renault R27-02 & 05 [2]	6. 1:18.620	24	8. 1:18.130	40	11. 1:17.454	12	5. 1:16.805	6	7. 1:16.288	6	9. **1:17.229**	12
4. Heikki Kovalainen	FIN	Renault R27-06 & 03 [2] -> [1]	14. 1:18.997	26	22. 1:20.519	13	21. 1:18.758	10	19. **1:17.806**	6				
5. Felipe Massa	BR	Ferrari F2007 260 [2]	4. 1:18.167	21	2. 1:17.090	34	4. 1:16.666	13	4. 1:16.756	4	4. 1:16.138	3	5. **1:16.570**	12
6. Kimi Räikkönen	FIN	Ferrari F2007 262 [2]	3. 1:18.136	21	4. 1:17.515	37	2. 1:16.459	14	1. 1:16.468	6	9. 1:16.592	3	4. **1:16.411**	12
7. Jenson Button	GB	Honda RA107-04 [1]	13. 1:18.932	24	13. 1:18.474	36	12. 1:17.468	15	15. 1:17.522	6	15. **1:17.541**	6		
8. Rubens Barrichello	BR	Honda RA107-02 [1]	18. 1:19.937	18	7. 1:18.108	38	8. 1:17.329	16	7. 1:17.011	6	13. **1:17.116**	6		
9. Nick Heidfeld	D	BMW Sauber F1.07-05 [2]	7. 1:18.634	20	5. 1:17.827	42	19. 1:18.428	5	6. 1:17.006	5	3. 1:15.960	6	3. **1:16.266**	12
10. Robert Kubica	PL	BMW Sauber F1.07-07 [2]	22.	2	12. 1:18.399	29	13. 1:17.601	12	9. 1:17.267	7	8. 1:16.368	7	8. **1:16.993**	12
11. Ralf Schumacher	D	Toyota TF107/05 [2]	8. 1:18.652	32	19. 1:19.331	16	16. 1:17.748	13	18. **1:17.634**	8				
12. Jarno Trulli	I	Toyota TF107/06 [2]	12. 1:18.925	25	18. 1:18.895	16	14. 1:17.624	17	11. 1:17.324	8	10. 1:16.600	6	10. **1:17.747**	12
14. David Coulthard	GB	Red Bull RB3 3 - Renault [1]	9. 1:18.717	24	11. 1:18.316	40	9. 1:17.391	11	13. 1:17.436	7	14. **1:17.304**	8		
15. Mark Webber	AUS	Red Bull RB3 4 - Renault [2]	5. 1:18.301	21	9. 1:18.181	40	7. 1:17.071	11	10. 1:17.315	6	6. 1:16.257	6	6. **1:16.913**	11
16. Nico Rosberg	D	Williams FW29-05 - Toyota [2]			6. 1:17.992	25	6. 1:16.975	14	8. 1:17.016	6	5. 1:16.190	6	7. **1:16.919**	12
17. Alexander Wurz	AUT	Williams FW29-04 - Toyota [2]	15. 1:19.189	22	17. 1:18.871	25	20. 1:18.489	11	20. **1:18.089**	5				
18. Vitantonio Liuzzi	I	Toro Rosso STR2-03 - Ferrari [2]	19. 1:20.331	12	14. 1:18.493	33	17. 1:17.799	14	16. 1:17.541	6	12. **1:16.760**	7		
19. Scott Speed	USA	Toro Rosso STR2-04 - Ferrari [2]	16. 1:19.234	29	16. 1:18.602	37	15. 1:17.742	12	12. 1:17.433	6	16. **1:17.571**	7		
20. Adrian Sutil	D	Spyker F8-VII/03 - Ferrari [2]	21. 1:21.630	25	21. 1:19.662	25	18. 1:18.270	13	21. **1:18.536**	7				
21. Christijan Albers	NL	Spyker F8-VII/02 - Ferrari [2]	20. 1:21.251	17	20. 1:19.453	38	22. 1:18.933	13	22. **1:19.196**	7				
22. Takuma Sato	J	Super Aguri SA07-04 - Honda [1]	11. 1:18.898	20	10. 1:18.309	38	5. 1:16.864	12	14. 1:17.490	6	11. **1:16.743**	6		
23. Anthony Davidson	GB	Super Aguri SA07-03 - Honda [1]	10. 1:18.896	16	15. 1:18.545	35	10. 1:17.391	15	17. **1:17.542**	4				
38. Kazuki Nakajima	J	Williams FW29-03 - Toyota	17. 1:19.273	30										

Fastest lap overall
L. Hamilton 1:15.486 (207,980 km/h)

Maximum speed

N° Driver	S1 Qualifs	Pos.	S1 Race	Pos.	S2 Qualifs	Pos.	S2 Race	Pos.	Finish Qualifs	Pos.	Finish Race	Pos.	Radar Qualifs	Pos.	Radar Race	Pos.
1. F. Alonso	264,4	2	263,6	1	289,6	1	291,8	1	292,6	1	293,2	1	322,1	7	324,2	5
2. L. Hamilton	264,4	1	262,0	2	289,0	2	289,5	3	291,1	2	291,8	2	320,3	11	322,6	10
3. G. Fisichella	260,8	9	260,1	7	286,7	8	287,1	8	288,1	7	288,7	8	321,8	9	323,3	7
4. H. Kovalainen	262,3	6	260,8	5	287,8	4	290,5	2	289,2	5	290,4	4	324,1	2	327,8	1
5. F. Massa	261,6	7	260,8	4	287,6	5	288,1	5	290,0	3	289,6	5	323,7	4	323,3	6
6. K. Räikkönen	263,0	3	260,8	3	287,2	6	289,0	4	288,7	6	291,0	3	322,1	6	322,9	9
7. J. Button	259,1	13			281,6	20			284,3	19			316,1	17		
8. R. Barrichello	259,1	14	256,2	12	282,5	16	281,8	16	285,5	15	282,9	17	314,5	21	316,7	19
9. N. Heidfeld	263,0	4	260,2	6	286,8	7	286,1	11	289,9	4	287,4	10	324,2	1	322,0	12
10. R. Kubica	262,8	5	259,3	8	288,8	3	285,3	12	287,9	8	286,7	12	324,1	3	323,1	8
11. R. Schumacher	256,3	19	253,8	17	281,9	18	281,3	18	283,6	20	283,3	16	317,1	15	317,9	16
12. J. Trulli	258,1	17	253,9	16	281,6	19	281,3	17	284,4	18	281,5	18	314,5	22	315,5	21
14. D. Coulthard	260,2	10	254,1	15	285,8	9	287,8	7	287,4	10	287,5	9	322,1	5	324,5	4
15. M. Webber	259,8	11	258,2	10	285,6	10	287,8	6	287,6	9	289,6	6	321,2	10	324,6	3
16. N. Rosberg	260,9	8	259,3	9	285,4	11	286,3	9	286,7	12	288,8	7	320,0	14	325,3	2
17. A. Wurz	258,6	15	255,6	14	283,5	14	284,3	14	284,5	17	284,2	14	320,0	13	318,4	15
18. V. Liuzzi	256,7	18	253,0	19	283,0	15	283,7	15	286,6	13	284,4	13	322,0	8	321,7	13
19. S. Speed	256,1	20	249,8	21	282,3	17	279,0	21	284,5	16	280,9	21	320,1	12	322,1	11
20. A. Sutil	252,1	22	250,3	20	277,9	22	279,7	19	280,5	22	281,3	19	315,8	19	316,3	20
21. C. Albers	253,9	21	253,7	18	279,3	21	279,3	20	280,6	21	281,1	20	315,8	18	318,7	14
22. T. Sato	259,8	12	256,9	11	284,4	12	286,3	10	287,3	11	286,8	11	316,7	16	317,5	17
23. A. Davidson	258,2	16	255,8	13	284,0	13	285,0	13	286,2	14	284,1	15	315,5	20	317,2	18

Best sector times

Qualifs	**S1** F. Alonso	21.110	**S2** L. Hamilton	24.016	**S3** F. Alonso	30.255	= 1:15.381
Race	**S1** F. Alonso	21.324	**S2** F. Alonso	24.265	**S3** L. Hamilton	30.560	= 1:16.149

RACE

Date	Weather	Air temperature	Track temperature	Humidity	Wind speed
Sunday June 10, 2007 (13:00)	Sunny	27-29°c	49-53°c	54%	2.0 m/s

Classification & retirements

Pos.	Driver	Constructor	Tyres	Laps	Time	Km/h
1.	L. Hamilton	McLaren Mercedes	SSU	70	1:44:11.292	175,799
2.	N. Heidfeld	BMW	SSU	70	+ 4.343	175,677
3.	A. Wurz	Williams Toyota	SU	70	+ 5.325	175,649
4.	H. Kovalainen	Renault	SUS	70	+ 6.729	175,610
5.	K. Räikkönen	Ferrari	SSU	70	+ 13.007	175,434
6.	T. Sato	Super Aguri Honda	SSUS	70	+ 16.698	175,330
7.	F. Alonso	McLaren Mercedes	SSU	70	+ 21.936	175,184
8.	R. Schumacher	Toyota	SSU	70	+ 22.888	175,157
9.	M. Webber	Red Bull Renault	SSU	70	+ 22.960	175,155
10.	N. Rosberg	Williams Toyota	SSU	70	+ 23.984	175,127
11.	A. Davidson	Super Aguri Honda	SUS	70	+ 24.318	175,117
12.	R. Barrichello	Honda	SSU	70	+ 30.439	174,947

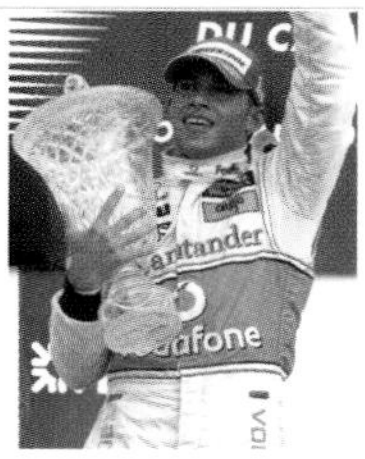

	Driver	Constructor	Tyres	Laps	Reason
	J. Trulli	Toyota	SSUS	58	Hits tyre wall at pit exit
	V. Liuzzi	STR Ferrari	SSUS	54	Hits concrete wall at last chicane
	C. Albers	Spyker Ferrari	SS	47	Loses front wing, brake failure
	D. Coulthard	Red Bull Renault	SSUS	36	Gearbox problem
	R. Kubica	BMW	SS	26	Crash
	A. Sutil	Spyker Ferrari	S	21	Hits concrete wall, turn 4
	S. Speed	STR Ferrari	S	8	Collision with Wurz
	J. Button	Honda	S	0	Gear selection problem
EX.	F. Massa	Ferrari	SS	51	Black flag. Exiting the pit lane when the pit exit lights were red
EX.	G. Fisichella	Renault	SSU	51	Black flag. Exiting the pit lane when the pit exit lights were red

Tyres S: Soft & U: Super Soft

Fastest laps

	Driver	Time	Lap	Km/h
1.	F. Alonso	1:16.367	46	205,580
2.	L. Hamilton	1:16.494	37	205,239
3.	N. Heidfeld	1:16.696	19	204,699
4.	F. Massa	1:16.849	22	204,291
5.	K. Räikkönen	1:16.861	21	204,259
6.	N. Rosberg	1:17.156	42	203,478
7.	G. Fisichella	1:17.411	22	202,808
8.	R. Kubica	1:17.529	19	202,499
9.	M. Webber	1:17.618	47	202,267
10.	R. Schumacher	1:17.910	38	201,509
11.	A. Wurz	1:17.947	67	201,413
12.	T. Sato	1:18.035	47	201,186
13.	H. Kovalainen	1:18.368	67	200,331
14.	R. Barrichello	1:18.543	62	199,885
15.	A. Davidson	1:18.780	36	199,284
16.	D. Coulthard	1:18.981	19	198,776
17.	J. Trulli	1:19.092	12	198,497
18.	C. Albers	1:19.254	21	198,092
19.	V. Liuzzi	1:19.375	9	197,790
20.	A. Sutil	1:19.452	20	197,598
21.	S. Speed	1:20.092	6	196,019

Pit stops

	Driver	Lap	Duration	Stop	Total
1.	N. Heidfeld	20	28.291	1	28.291
2.	L. Hamilton	22	29.642	1	29.642
3.	M. Webber	22	30.491	1	30.491
4.	F. Alonso	23	29.217	1	29.217
5.	N. Rosberg	23	29.112	1	29.112
6.	F. Massa	25	29.157	1	29.157
7.	K. Räikkönen	25	37.643	1	37.643
8.	G. Fisichella	25	28.361	1	28.361
9.	R. Kubica	25	34.776	1	34.776
10.	T. Sato	25	33.122	1	33.122
11.	J. Trulli	25	30.466	1	30.466
12.	V. Liuzzi	25	30.723	1	30.723
13.	C. Albers	25	30.381	1	30.381
14.	D. Coulthard	27	29.553	1	29.553
15.	H. Kovalainen	27	49.659	1	49.659
16.	J. Trulli	29	26.684	2	57.150
17.	R. Barrichello	30	28.480	1	28.480
18.	A. Wurz	30	32.921	1	32.921
19.	D. Coulthard	30	26.086	2	55.639
20.	V. Liuzzi	30	28.927	2	59.650
21.	J. Trulli	30	27.011	3	1:24.161
22.	D. Coulthard	31	28.012	3	1:23.651
23.	V. Liuzzi	32	27.998	3	1:27.648
24.	F. Alonso	•36•	30.591	2	59.808
25.	N. Rosberg	•36•	31.049	2	1:00.161
26.	A. Davidson	37	55.663	1	55.663
27.	A. Davidson	39	34.436	2	1:30.099
28.	R. Schumacher	40	27.623	1	27.623
29.	H. Kovalainen	44	30.466	2	1:20.125
30.	N. Heidfeld	47	28.901	2	57.192
31.	L. Hamilton	48	26.474	2	56.116
32.	G. Fisichella	48	28.346	2	56.707
33.	N. Rosberg	49	27.911	3	1:28.072
34.	T. Sato	50	45.674	2	1:18.796
35.	A. Davidson	51	25.834	3	1:55.933
36.	K. Räikkönen	53	27.411	2	1:05.054
37.	F. Alonso	53	26.911	3	1:26.719
38.	R. Schumacher	53	26.413	2	54.036
39.	T. Sato	53	28.194	3	1:46.990
40.	M. Webber	54	27.663	2	58.154
41.	J. Trulli	58	27.693	4	1:51.854
42.	R. Barrichello	63	27.460	2	55.940

•• Stop-go penalty (10 sec.): Alonso & Rosberg.
For pitting before the pit lane opening under safety car.

Race leader

Driver	Laps in the lead	Nbr of laps
L. Hamilton	1 > 21	21
F. Massa	22 > 24	3
L. Hamilton	25 > 70	46

Driver	Nbr of laps	Kilometers
L. Hamilton	67	292,187 km
F. Massa	3	13,083 km

Lap chart

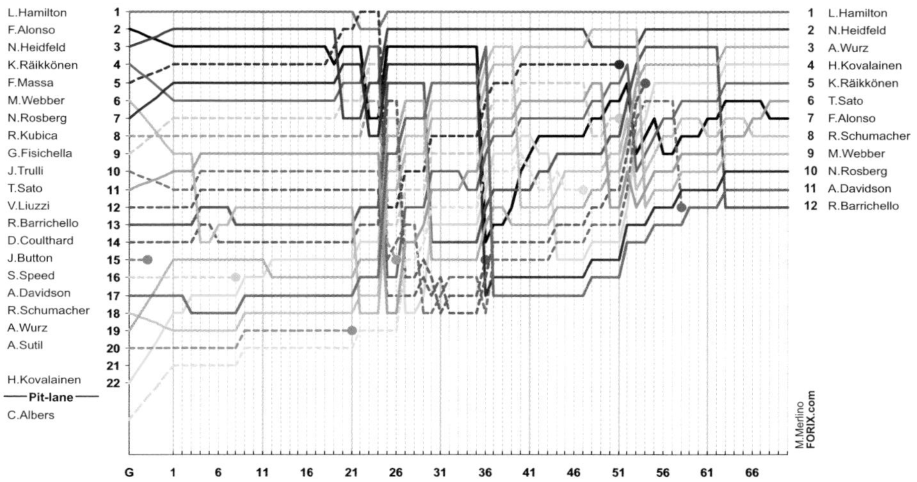
L.Hamilton
F.Alonso
N.Heidfeld
K.Räikkönen
F.Massa
M.Webber
N.Rosberg
R.Kubica
G.Fisichella
J.Trulli
T.Sato
V.Liuzzi
R.Barrichello
D.Coulthard
J.Button
S.Speed
A.Davidson
R.Schumacher
A.Wurz
A.Sutil
H.Kovalainen
Pit-lane
C.Albers
G
1
6
11
16
21
26
31
36
41
46
51
56
61
66
1 L.Hamilton
2 N.Heidfeld
3 A.Wurz
4 H.Kovalainen
5 K.Räikkönen
6 T.Sato
7 F.Alonso
8 R.Schumacher
9 M.Webber
10 N.Rosberg
11 A.Davidson
12 R.Barrichello
M.Merlino
FORIX.com

Gaps on the lead board

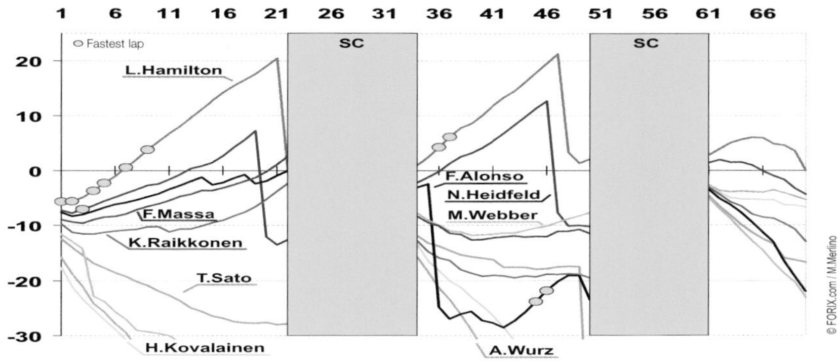
1
6
11
16
21
26
31
36
41
46
51
56
61
66
Fastest lap
SC
SC
20
10
0
-10
-20
-30
L.Hamilton
F.Massa
K.Raikkonen
T.Sato
H.Kovalainen
F.Alonso
N.Heidfeld
M.Webber
A.Wurz
© FORIX.com / M.Merlino

CHAMPIONSHIPS 6/17

Drivers

1.	L. Hamilton	McLaren Mercedes	1🏆	48
2.	F. Alonso	McLaren Mercedes	2🏆	40
3.	F. Massa	Ferrari	2🏆	33
4.	K. Räikkönen	Ferrari	1🏆	27
5.	N. Heidfeld	BMW		26
6.	G. Fisichella	Renault		13
7.	R. Kubica	BMW		12
8.	A. Wurz	Williams Toyota		8
9.	H. Kovalainen	Renault		8
10.	N. Rosberg	Williams Toyota		5
11.	D. Coulthard	Red Bull Renault		4
12.	T. Sato	Super Aguri Honda		4
13.	J. Trulli	Toyota		4
14.	R. Schumacher	Toyota		2
15.	M. Webber	Red Bull Renault		0
16.	S. Speed	STR Ferrari		0
17.	R. Barrichello	Honda		0
18.	A. Davidson	Super Aguri Honda		0
19.	J. Button	Honda		0
20.	A. Sutil	Spyker Ferrari		0
21.	C. Albers	Spyker Ferrari		0
22.	V. Liuzzi	STR Ferrari		0

Constructors

1.	Vodafone McLaren Mercedes	3🏆	88
2.	Scuderia Ferrari Marlboro	3🏆	60
3.	BMW Sauber F1 Team		38
4.	ING Renault F1 Team		21
5.	AT&T Williams		13
6.	Panasonic Toyota Racing		6
7.	Red Bull Racing		4
8.	Super Aguri F1 Team		4
9.	Scuderia Toro Rosso		0
10.	Honda Racing F1 Team		0
11.	Etihad Aldar Spyker F1 Team		0

THE CIRCUIT

Name	Circuit Gilles-Villeneuve; Ile Notre-Dame, Montréal	**Latitude**	45°30'00.00"N
Lenght	4361 m	**Longitude**	73°31'21.50"O
Distance	70 laps, 305,270 km		

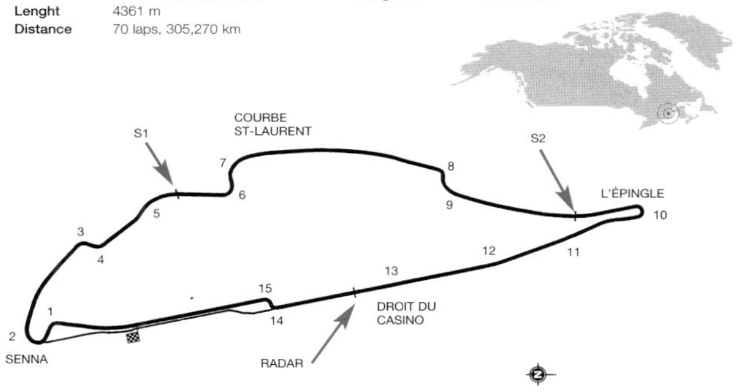
COURBE ST-LAURENT
S1
S2
L'ÉPINGLE
DROIT DU CASINO
RADAR
SENNA
1
2
3
4
5
6
7
8
9
10
11
12
13
14
15

S1 145m before corner
S2 190m before corner
Radar 255m before corner

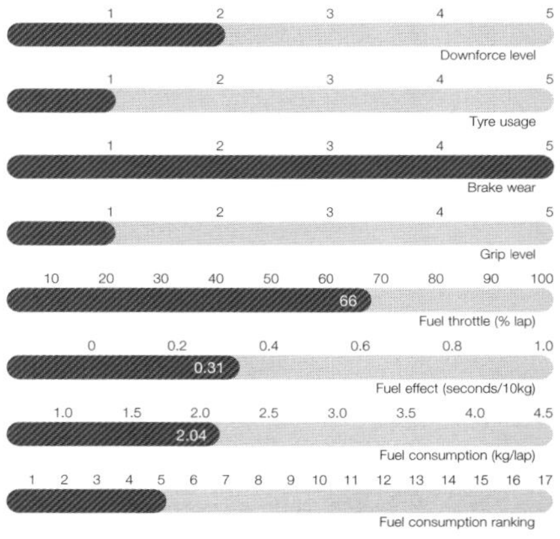
Downforce level
Tyre usage
Brake wear
Grip level
66
Fuel throttle (% lap)
0.31
Fuel effect (seconds/10kg)
2.04
Fuel consumption (kg/lap)
Fuel consumption ranking

LEWIS IS UNBEATABLE

The young Briton was impossible to beat at the United States. Despite his best efforts, his experience and a concerted attack, Hamilton's teammate Fernando Alonso could only manage second, in his wake. It was a stunning contest! Once more, McLaren dictated the pace and the two Ferraris finished behind - with third and fourth for Felipe Massa and Kimi Raikkonen respectively. Further back, Jarno Trulli finished sixth: his best result of the season.

After America, the championship fight seemed to be down to the two McLaren drivers. Kimi Raikkonen had dropped a lot of ground: in fact, at that point in the season, he was a full 26 points behind Lewis Hamilton.

Lewis Hamilton on the limit at the famous 'Speedway' corner on the Indianapolis banking. The young Briton set pole position on his first visit to the circuit, just as he had in Canada the previous weekend.

Second consecutive pole position for McLaren's super rookie

It was always a pleasure to meet Lewis Hamilton. While his more experienced colleagues often seemed quite blasé about the whole Formula 1 thing, Hamilton - for the time being, anyway - radiated enthusiasm every time he got out of the car.

His track record was simply stunning: there was no other word for it. Although it was only his first Formula 1 season, Lewis Hamilton was on the podium six times in six races - while leading the World Championship by an eight-point margin. One Grand Prix win and two pole positions were already behind him.

The McLaren driver was determined to forge onwards and upwards. At Indianapolis, Fernando Alonso set the fastest time in all the practice sessions - including the first two knockout phases of qualifying.

The Spaniard seemed set to grasp another pole position, but in actual fact it was his team mate who took the coveted first place on the grid: by just 169 thousandths of a second.

No wonder Lewis Hamilton was so demonstrably delighted afterwards. *"Up to this point in the weekend, I hadn't been able to find exactly the right set-up,"* said the Englishman. *"Then, on my final flying lap, I didn't have a brilliant second sector - and I knew that Fernando was very quick there. To be honest, I didn't think that I would be able to beat him this afternoon. So when my engineer told me that I was on pole I didn't believe it: I just screamed! It was so unexpected that I think it felt even better than Canada last week!"*

From that point, he felt confident of being able to convert his pole position into another win. *"The team has worked very hard to improve the car and I feel very confident,"* continued Hamilton. *"But the start will be tricky. It's never easy, as you have to be very careful but protect your position at the same time. I got a very bad start last week in Canada, and I need to do better here. Having said that, you never win a race at the first corner. It's important just to get round it, and then bring the car to the finish."*

Sebastian Vettel, BMW Sauber's third driver, replaced Robert Kubica in the race at the last minute. The young German rose to the occasion spectacularly, setting seventh-fastest time in qualifying - two places behind his team mate Nick Heidfeld.

Sebastian Vettel's big chance

In the end, it was 19 year-old Sebastian Vettel who replaced Robert Kubica for Indianapolis. The young German became BMW Sauber's third driver in August 2006, after Jacques Villeneuve was shown the door and the team's test driver at the time, Robert Kubica, became his permanent replacement from the Turkish Grand Prix onwards. This provided a vacancy in the test role, and was Vettel's first big chance.

Friday of the US Grand Prix was the first time that Vettel had even seen the Indianapolis circuit. It's never an easy circuit to master partly because of the famous 'banking'. This is a high-speed corner that exerts the highest aerodynamic loads on the car of the year. For the driver, this corner is actually quite simple: it's just a matter of burying the throttle. An idea of the extreme forces generated by this famous corner can be found in the fiasco that was the 2005 aAmerican Grand Prix, when Michelin's tyres were not actually capable of getting round it. So it was no real surprise when the circuit doctors decided that it was better for Robert Kubica to miss this race, following his huge accident in Canada a week earlier.

Vettel demonstrated his obvious talent by setting seventh-fastest time in qualifying. *"It was a very closely fought session,"* said Vettel on Saturday evening. *"With qualifying split into three phases, you've got three opportunities to have either a bad or a good lap. Now that this is behind me, I'm definitely going to sleep better."*

STARTING GRID

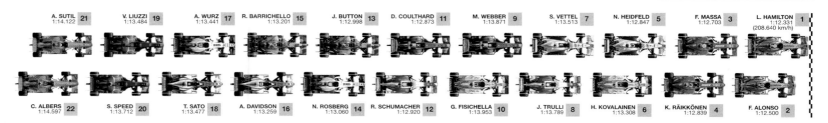

A. SUTIL 21	V. LIUZZI 19	A. WURZ 17	R. BARRICHELLO 15	J. BUTTON 13	D. COULTHARD 11	M. WEBBER 9	S. VETTEL 7	N. HEIDFELD 5	F. MASSA 3	L. HAMILTON 1
1:14.122	1:13.484	1:13.441	1:13.201	1:12.998	1:12.873	1:13.871	1:13.513	1:12.847	1:12.703	1:12.331 (208.640 km/h)

C. ALBERS 22	S. SPEED 20	T. SATO 18	A. DAVIDSON 16	N. ROSBERG 14	R. SCHUMACHER 12	G. FISICHELLA 10	J. TRULLI 8	H. KOVALAINEN 6	K. RÄIKKÖNEN 4	F. ALONSO 2
1:14.597	1:13.712	1:13.477	1:13.259	1:13.060	1:12.920	1:13.953	1:13.789	1:13.308	1:12.839	1:12.500

Lewis Hamilton head and shoulders over the others in Indianapolis

Finding the appropriate complimentary adjectives to describe Lewis Hamilton's performances was becoming more and more difficult. Following his first Grand Prix and first podium in Australia, the Englishman had inevitably taken his first win in Canada the weekend before the US Grand Prix. In America, his talent shone even brighter as he won the race and eclipsed his famous teammate Fernando Alonso.

At Montreal, Lewis Hamilton was 'helped' (although this is arguable) by four safety cat periods - which ruined Alonso's strategy before he even had the chance to put it into place. The unfortunate Spaniard ended up coming in for fuel when it was not actually allowed to do so - but otherwise he would have risked running out.

But in America, Lewis Hamilton had no need of third party help to claim the second Grand Prix win of his career. Having qualified on pole, he took the lead from the start of the race and didn't look back. He only surrendered the lead briefly during his fuel stops, making it pretty much a textbook win.

Fernando Alonso reluctantly had to settle for second place behind him. Only at one point during the 73-lap race was he ever really to have a serious go at his teammate, on lap 38.

Alonso had pulled up close enough to duck out of Hamilton's slipstream at the end of the straight and attempt a passing manœuvre. To no avail. A disappointed

Alonso explained: *"Everything was won and lost at the start today. If you start second, you're going to finish second. At this circuit, it's very difficult to follow another driver without losing downforce. I tried to keep up at the start, but my tyres started degrading so I was forced to back off. On the 38th lap, I saw Lewis make a mistake at turn nine. I knew that was my only real chance of the race, so I went for it. We were close, maybe just a centimetre or two away from each other, but it didn't work."* Now with a ten-point deficit to his rookie teammate, Alonso could not afford many more days like that.

The two best races of his career

When Lewis Hamilton arrived in north America ten days earlier, he didn't know either the Montreal circuit or Indy. Two weeks later, he got home with two Grand Prix wins in his pocket. *"I would never have dreamed of that 10 days ago: it's absolutely fantastic,"* he said. *"I'm coming to America for the first time, without even knowing the circuits, and I've managed to drive the two best races of my career. It's mad if you think about it. Everything's been a bit crazy actually: people have been really kind and the spectators here are amazingly enthusiastic."* Alonso was not so far from the young Briton at Indianapolis - finishing just two seconds behind him, and having even challenged for the lead at one point. Hamilton agreed that it had been a close run thing. *"Yes, Fernando kept the pressure on me throughout the race. I managed to pull out a small gap at the start of the race, but during the second stint my tyres were destroyed. Maybe I was pushing a bit too hard. When Fernando

tried to get past me, the back of my car had stepped out slightly just beforehand - so I knew that he would be trying to get me on the straight. I was a bit nervous, but I knew that if I braked hard he would stay behind me. From my perspective, it was a race that seemed to go on forever. I was just hoping that it was nearly all over when my engineer told me 'another 15 laps to go'. It wasn't what I wanted to hear, but I thought: 'OK - let's just go'. And we did."*

The Englishman has now extended his championship lead, another almighty achievement in the young career of Lewis Hamilton. *"When I started, I was hoping to do my best - no more and no less. I had hoped that maybe I could get onto the podium once this year. But now, of course, things are a bit different. I realise that I can be World Champion: that it's actually possible. It's important to stay realistic and I realise that it's far too soon to be thinking about that. But of course it's my goal."*

^
Victory! Lewis Hamilton receives a hero's welcome from his mechanics at the end of the race.

Legs that go on for miles: the Indianapolis grid girls are worth the trip alone. In the overall grid girl chart, they come a close second to Turkey (see pages 166 to 173).
< ∨

< First corner and the first accident, between Ralf Schumacher and David Coulthard. Rubens Barrichello has nowhere to go behind them. According to Ralf: « I braked normally but my tyres slightly locked up for some reason. David came round from the outside and then we touched. » The book of driver excuses is always an amusing one… For Coulthard it was all over: he broke an oil radiator and was forced into retirement.

> Fernando Alonso just in front of Felipe Massa. Both of them would finish on the podium, just behind Lewis Hamilton.

Fernando Alonso blames bad luck

It's never easy to work with the English. This is a fact that most businessmen know, but Fernando Alonso was to find out the hard way.

His move from Renault to McLaren meant going from a team he grew up in and was built around him to a team with its own individual philosophy, which was unused to his way of working. His teammate would be a young driver who had been a protege of McLaren since he was 13, as engrained in its culture as Alonso himself used to be.

When he signed his McLaren contract, in November 2005, Fernando Alonso had little idea of the thorn in his side that Lewis Hamilton would turn out to be. This was to complicate his task enormously. At McLaren, just as he was throughout the whole of England, Hamilton was held up as an idol. The win at Montreal

only reinforced the youngster' position. For his part, on Monday after the Canadian Grand Prix, Alonso told the Spanish radio station Cadena Ser : *"I don't really feel at ease in the team and it's been like that since my first day. I've got an English teammate in an English team so it's obviously going to be him having the support of most of the team. We all know that, and it's something that I understood from the very start. Having said that, I'm not complaining. I'm here to fight for the championship and that's what I'm going to do."* Alonso's declarations caused something of a fuss at McLaren. From the moment they arrived at Indianapolis on Thursday, Ron Dennis and his team were telling anybody who cared to listen that everyone at McLaren admired and respected their reigning World Champion Spaniard. Furthermore, McLaren was at

pains to point out, both drivers received absolutely equal treatment - just as had been the case in the days of the epic battles between Prost and Senna.

Lewis Hamilton claimed to be surprised by his teammate's sentiments. *"I think it's a bit bizarre if Fernando has said these things, because ever since he arrived in the team everybody has been entirely behind him. Maybe he thinks he's unfairly treated because he is Spanish and I am English, but if so I don't agree with him. We've become very close friends on a personal level, so it's quite hard to understand that sort of criticism."*

As the season went on, the face-off between Hamilton and Alonso would become increasingly intense. Alonso's disaffected comments were merely the first warning shot.

> Indianapolis, we love you. It was the last time that Formula 1 cars would race on the mythical American circuit, as the organisers have not reached a financial agreement with Bernie Ecclestone - which is a real shame.
> ∨

Circuit doctors stop Robert Kubica from racing

To see him in the paddock, smiling and insouciant, nobody would guess that Robert Kubica had been the victim of the most terrifying crash of the current era of Formula 1 just four days earlier. He walked without limping, cracked jokes with his team and friends, and seemed more laid-back than ever. *"I feel 100% fit,"* he said. *"There's absolutely nothing wrong with me. I don't have the slightest headache, and even that knock to my ankle has cleared up completely. It's as if the accident never happened !"*

While the world held its breath, watching the BMW Sauber slam into a concrete wall at Montreal, its drivers said that he felt nothing particularly special. *"I saw the accident on TV of course, but I had already seen it live !"* said Kubica. *"I was following Jarno and then the road

> There are several foreign fans at Indianapolis as well as Americans. The Brazilians turned out in droves to cheer on Felipe Massa.
> ∨

went slightly to the left. I thought that Jarno was going to follow the inside line, but instead he moved to the right. My front wing touched his rear wheel, I took off and then of course I couldn't steer any more. Then the car hit the wall and from that point it was just a question of waiting for the accident to be over. Once the car had stopped, I moved all my limbs around to check that everything was working, and everything was fine apart from a small pain in my ankle. They said to me in the hospital that I would be extremely stiff when I woke up the following morning, but when I got out of bed on Monday I felt fine. Not a single problem : no hint of stiffness at all. I know that I have been very lucky though, and that's all down to modern safety requirements. Ten years ago, it was impossible to survive

an accident like that."*

The Pole was determined to race at Indianapolis, partly to banish any demons that the accident may have raised. *"I think it's important to come back as quickly as possible after an accident like this one,"* he said. *"If I wasn't on 100% form, I wouldn't want to race anyway. I'm not the only person on the track, and I wouldn't want to cause a risk for anyone."*

Kubica was examined on Thursday by Dr Gary Hartstein, the FIA Medical Delegate, as by the leading doctor at the Indianapolis Motor Speedway medical centre. The two doctors decided that despite outward appearances, Robert Kubica wasn't quite ready to race in a GP again yet. So out went Kubica, onto a plane home, and in came Vettel.

135

UNITED STATES GRAND PRIX | THE 17 GRANDS PRIX

RESULTS

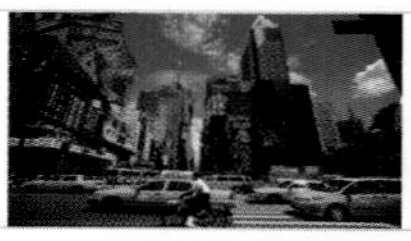

PRACTICE

Date	Weather (AM)	Air temperature	Track temperature	Weather (PM)	Air temperature	Track temperature
Friday June 15, 2007	Overcast but sunny	23-25°c	28-36°c	Sunny	29-32°c	43-54°c
Saturday June 16, 2007	Sunny	27-29°c	34-39°c	Sunny, some clouds	34-32°c	57-51°c

All the time trials

N° Driver	Nat.	N° Chassis- Engine [Nbr. GP]	Pos. Free 1 Friday 10:00-11:30	Laps Tr.	Pos. Free 2 Friday 14:00-15:30	Laps Tr.	Pos. Free 3 Saturday 10:00-11:00	Laps Tr.	Pos. Q1 Saturday 13:00-13:15	Laps Tr.	Pos. Q2 Saturday 13:22-13:37	Laps Tr.	Pos. Q3 Saturday 13:45-14:00	Nb. Tr.
1. Fernando Alonso	E	McLaren MP4-22 08 &06 - Mercedes [1]	1. 1:11.925	16	1. 1:12.156	35	1. 1:12.150	12	1. 1:12.416	3	1. 1:11.926	3	2. **1:12.500**	12
2. Lewis Hamilton	GB	McLaren MP4-22 01 - Mercedes [1]	3. 1:12.628	21	2. 1:12.309	34	3. 1:12.378	14	3. 1:12.563	3	2. 1:12.065	3	1. **1:12.331**	13
3. Giancarlo Fisichella	I	Renault R27-05 [1]	16. 1:14.000	19	15. 1:13.394	44	8. 1:12.710	20	11. 1:13.168	6	7. 1:12.603	6	10. **1:13.953**	12
4. Heikki Kovalainen	FIN	Renault R27-02 & 03 [2]	19. 1:14.189	18	8. 1:13.110	48	4. 1:12.574	21	8. 1:12.998	6	6. 1:12.599	6	6. **1:13.308**	12
5. Felipe Massa	BR	Ferrari F2007 260 [1]	7. 1:13.040	22	3. 1:12.435	36	7. 1:12.709	17	5. 1:12.731	5	4. 1:12.180	3	3. **1:12.703**	12
6. Kimi Räikkönen	FIN	Ferrari F2007 262 [1]	5. 1:12.966	21	4. 1:12.587	38	6. 1:12.692	16	6. 1:12.732	4	3. 1:12.111	6	4. **1:12.839**	12
7. Jenson Button	GB	Honda RA107-04 [2]	9. 1:13.597	23	10. 1:13.202	46	15. 1:13.318	20	14. 1:13.306	6	13. **1:12.998**	6		
8. Rubens Barrichello	BR	Honda RA107-02 [2]	18. 1:14.052	23	9. 1:13.144	40	18. 1:13.573	17	13. 1:13.203	6	15. **1:13.201**	6		
9. Nick Heidfeld	D	BMW Sauber F1.07-05 [1]	2. 1:12.391	24	5. 1:13.026	43	5. 1:12.646	24	2. 1:12.543	4	5. 1:12.188	3	5. **1:12.847**	13
10. Sebastian Vettel	D	BMW Sauber F1.07-03 & 07 [1]	4. 1:12.869	33	11. 1:13.217	50	2. 1:12.321	27	4. 1:12.711	6	8. 1:12.644	6	7. **1:13.513**	12
11. Ralf Schumacher	D	Toyota TF107/05 [1]	13. 1:13.819	27	20. 1:13.765	39	12. 1:13.061	23	7. 1:12.851	7	12. **1:12.920**	6		
12. Jarno Trulli	I	Toyota TF107/06 & 04 [1]	11. 1:13.777	32	17. 1:13.692	42	11. 1:13.057	23	12. 1:13.186	7	10. 1:12.828	7	8. **1:13.789**	12
14. David Coulthard	GB	Red Bull RB3 3 - Renault [2]	8. 1:13.159	22	6. 1:13.042	41	9. 1:12.940	17	15. 1:13.424	8	11. **1:12.873**	7		
15. Mark Webber	AUS	Red Bull RB3 4 - Renault [1]	10. 1:13.682	26	12. 1:13.263	21	14. 1:13.289	14	16. 1:13.425	7	9. 1:12.788	6	9. **1:13.871**	12
16. Nico Rosberg	D	Williams FW29-05 - Toyota [1]	6. 1:13.020	24	7. 1:13.057	35	10. 1:13.031	18	9. 1:13.128	6	14. **1:13.060**	6		
17. Alexander Wurz	AUT	Williams FW29-04 - Toyota [1]			16. 1:13.539	29	19. 1:13.626	18	17. **1:13.441**	6				
18. Vitantonio Liuzzi	I	Toro Rosso STR2-03 - Ferrari [1]	14. 1:13.907	28	13. 1:13.332	41	16. 1:13.415	23	19. **1:13.484**	7				
19. Scott Speed	USA	Toro Rosso STR2-04 - Ferrari [1]	15. 1:13.990	24	18. 1:13.712	34	20. 1:13.979	18	20. **1:13.712**	7				
20. Adrian Sutil	D	Spyker F8-VII/03 - Ferrari [1]	22. 1:14.810	27	22. 1:14.513	33	21. 1:14.142	24	21. **1:14.122**	6				
21. Christijan Albers	NL	Spyker F8-VII/02 - Ferrari [1]	21. 1:14.636	28	21. 1:14.225	30	22. 1:14.402	24	22. **1:14.597**	7				
22. Takuma Sato	J	Super Aguri SA07-04 - Honda [2]	17. 1:14.037	20	19. 1:13.753	46	17. 1:13.476	19	18. **1:13.477**	7				
23. Anthony Davidson	GB	Super Aguri SA07-03 & 02 - Honda [2]	20. 1:14.632	10	14. 1:13.364	46	13. 1:13.069	20	10. 1:13.164	7	16. **1:13.259**	6		
38. Kazuki Nakajima	J	Williams FW29-03 - Toyota	12. 1:13.786	27										

Fastest lap overall

F. Alonso 1:11.926 (209,815 km/h)

Maximum speed

N° Driver	S1 Qualifs	Pos.	S1 Race	Pos.	S2 Qualifs	Pos.	S2 Race	Pos.	Finish Qualifs	Pos.	Finish Race	Pos.	Radar Qualifs	Pos.	Radar Race	Pos.
1. F. Alonso	262,0	1	256,6	2	169,8	16	168,4	9	316,4	20	327,1	9	320,9	20	327,7	16
2. L. Hamilton	259,6	2	256,7	1	172,8	7	168,3	10	318,5	16	327,7	6	321,5	19	327,5	17
3. G. Fisichella	259,1	4	252,6	8	174,4	2	168,0	12	321,9	6	328,5	4	327,6	9	334,9	4
4. H. Kovalainen	258,3	6	254,1	6	174,8	1	169,4	3	325,6	2	327,6	7	331,3	3	334,6	5
5. F. Massa	258,0	7	256,4	3	171,5	10	169,2	4	319,6	13	325,6	14	326,7	11	333,5	7
6. K. Räikkönen	259,1	3	255,7	4	173,8	4	170,5	1	326,4	1	331,4	1	331,0	4	333,6	6
7. J. Button	254,7	18	246,5	17	170,2	11	168,4	8	316,9	18	325,8	13	321,6	18	330,9	11
8. R. Barrichello	257,9	9	107,5	21	170,1	13	111,9	21	320,9	9			327,6	8	300,3	20
9. N. Heidfeld	255,3	17	249,7	14	172,3	8	170,2	2	320,7	10	323,9	16	326,4	12	331,2	9
10. S. Vettel	258,0	8	250,5	13	172,8	6	168,6	7	319,5	14	323,0	17	321,8	17	330,8	13
11. R. Schumacher	256,1	15			173,8	3			319,5	15			327,6	7	291,2	21
12. J. Trulli	258,9	5	253,5	7	169,9	14	167,6	14	321,3	8	325,3	15	327,9	6	332,1	8
14. D. Coulthard	257,6	11	186,0	20	172,0	9	145,5	20	325,2	3			331,8	2	289,2	22
15. M. Webber	257,4	12	252,3	10	169,8	17	169,1	5	321,7	7	327,8	5	334,5	1	335,4	2
16. N. Rosberg	257,8	10	254,3	5	170,1	12	167,7	13	323,1	5	326,6	12	326,8	10	330,9	12
17. A. Wurz	256,8	13	252,4	9	173,7	5	168,2	11	320,0	12	326,6	11	323,9	14	331,0	10
18. V. Liuzzi	256,5	14	250,9	12	169,8	15	165,6	15	320,5	11	329,4	2	323,2	15	335,2	3
19. S. Speed	253,0	20	248,8	15	168,1	19	163,7	19	323,5	4	328,8	3	328,5	5	335,7	1
20. A. Sutil	251,3	22	246,9	16	167,1	22	164,6	17	317,5	17	322,6	18	323,9	13	329,4	15
21. C. Albers	251,7	21	246,1	18	167,3	20	164,8	16	316,5	19	326,7	10	322,2	16	329,6	14
22. T. Sato	254,3	19	241,2	19	168,8	18	164,5	18	313,9	21	319,9	19	318,4	21	324,7	19
23. A. Davidson	255,4	16	251,6	11	167,2	21	168,6	6	309,7	22	327,6	8	312,2	22	326,9	18

Best sector times

Qualifs	**S1** F. Alonso	22.117	**S2** F. Alonso	29.311	**S3** K. Räikkönen	20.274	= 1:11.702
Race	**S1** K. Räikkönen	22.509	**S2** L. Hamilton	29.434	**S3** K. Räikkönen	20.481	= 1:12.424

RACE

Date	Weather	Air temperature	Track temperature	Humidity	Wind speed
Sunday June 17, 2007 (13:00)	Sunny	34-36°c	57-58°c	35%	1.8 m/s

Classification & retirements

Pos.	Driver	Constructor	Tyres	Laps	Time	Km/h	
1.	L. Hamilton	McLaren Mercedes	SSM	73	1:31:09.965	201,401	
2.	F. Alonso	McLaren Mercedes	SSM	73	+ 1.518	201,345	
3.	F. Massa	Ferrari	SSM	73	+ 12.842	200,929	
4.	K. Räikkönen	Ferrari	MSS	73	+ 15.422	200,834	
5.	H. Kovalainen	Renault	SSM	73	+ 41.402	199,888	
6.	J. Trulli	Toyota	SSM	73	+ 1:06.703	198,974	
7.	M. Webber	Red Bull Renault	SSM	73	+ 1:07.331	198,952	
8.	S. Vettel	BMW	SSM	73	+ 1:07.783	198,936	
9.	G. Fisichella	Renault	SM	72	1 lap	197,403	
10.	A. Wurz	Williams Toyota	SM	72	1 lap	196,424	
11.	A. Davidson	Super Aguri Honda	MSS	72	1 lap	196,363	
12.	J. Button	Honda	SM	72	1 lap	196,015	
13.	S. Speed	STR Ferrari	SM	71	2 laps	195,619	
14.	A. Sutil	Spyker Ferrari	MSS	71	2 laps	195,546	
15.	C. Albers	Spyker Ferrari	MS	70	3 laps	192,887	
16.	N. Rosberg	Williams Toyota	SM	68	5 laps	198,896	Oil leak
17.	V. Liuzzi	STR Ferrari	MS	68	5 laps	195,415	Hydraulic pressure problem

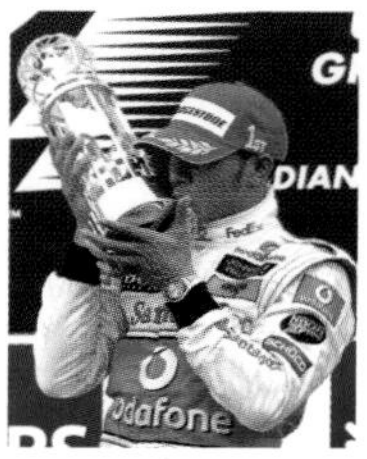

Driver	Constructor	Tyres	Laps	Reason
N. Heidfeld	BMW	SMM	55	Hydraulic leak
T. Sato	Super Aguri Honda	S	13	Spin
D. Coulthard	Red Bull Renault	S	0	Hit by Schumacher which caused a lot of damage
R. Schumacher	Toyota	S	0	Collision with Coulthard, front left suspension damaged
R. Barrichello	Honda	S	0	Hit by Schumacher, front suspension, wishbone and push rod broken

Tyres M: Medium & S: Soft

Fastest laps

	Driver	Time	Lap	Km/h
1.	K. Räikkönen	1:13.117	49	206,397
2.	L. Hamilton	1:13.222	20	206,101
3.	F. Alonso	1:13.257	21	206,003
4.	F. Massa	1:13.380	50	205,658
5.	N. Heidfeld	1:13.414	20	205,562
6.	S. Vettel	1:13.862	53	204,316
7.	H. Kovalainen	1:13.998	67	203,940
8.	M. Webber	1:14.004	57	203,924
9.	G. Fisichella	1:14.009	67	203,910
10.	J. Trulli	1:14.016	30	203,891
11.	N. Rosberg	1:14.066	34	203,753
12.	A. Davidson	1:14.066	55	203,753
13.	A. Wurz	1:14.486	41	202,604
14.	J. Button	1:14.703	42	202,015
15.	A. Sutil	1:14.858	49	201,597
16.	S. Speed	1:15.092	66	200,969
17.	V. Liuzzi	1:15.426	64	200,079
18.	C. Albers	1:15.902	65	198,824
19.	T. Sato	1:16.680	8	196,807

Pit stops

	Driver	Lap	Duration	Stop	Total
1.	L. Hamilton	21	27.210	1	27.210
2.	F. Massa	21	27.884	1	27.884
3.	N. Heidfeld	21	26.124	1	26.124
4.	F. Alonso	22	26.343	1	26.343
5.	K. Räikkönen	24	26.573	1	26.573
6.	S. Vettel	24	25.120	1	25.120
7.	H. Kovalainen	27	25.610	1	25.610
8.	A. Sutil	28	26.300	1	26.300
9.	M. Webber	30	26.446	1	26.446
10.	J. Trulli	31	26.339	1	26.339
11.	G. Fisichella	36	28.603	1	28.603
12.	S. Speed	36	28.492	1	28.492
13.	V. Liuzzi	37	37.649	1	37.649
14.	C. Albers	38	32.563	1	32.563
15.	N. Rosberg	40	31.752	1	31.752
16.	A. Davidson	41	25.298	1	25.298
17.	A. Wurz	43	27.556	1	27.556
18.	J. Button	43	34.015	1	34.015
19.	H. Kovalainen	47	26.615	2	52.225
20.	N. Heidfeld	48	25.450	2	51.574
21.	F. Alonso	50	24.986	2	51.329
22.	L. Hamilton	51	25.344	2	52.554
23.	K. Räikkönen	51	25.412	2	51.985
24.	A. Sutil	50	26.926	2	53.226
25.	S. Vettel	51	25.004	2	50.124
26.	F. Massa	52	25.626	2	53.510
27.	A. Davidson	53	25.331	2	50.629
28.	J. Trulli	56	24.351	2	50.690
29.	M. Webber	59	24.272	2	50.718

Race leader

Driver	Laps in the lead	Nbr of laps
L. Hamilton	1 > 20	20
F. Alonso	21	1
H. Kovalainen	22 > 26	5
L. Hamilton	27 > 50	24
F. Massa	51	1
L. Hamilton	52 > 73	22

Driver	Nbr of laps	Kilometers
L. Hamilton	66	276,672 km
H. Kovalainen	5	20,960 km
F. Alonso	1	4,192 km
F. Massa	1	4,192 km

Gaps on the lead board

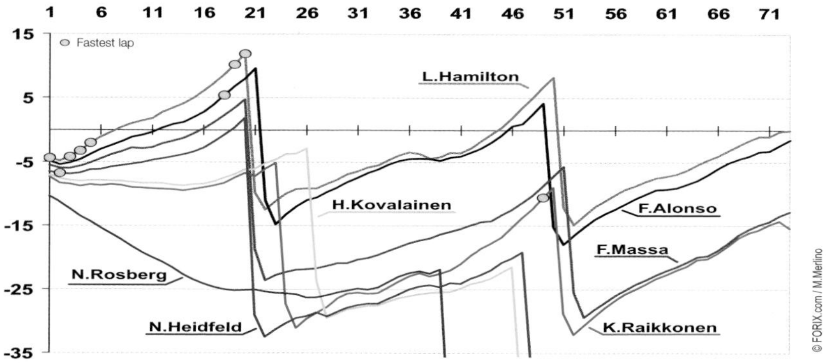
1
6
11
16
21
26
31
36
41
46
51
56
61
66
71
15
5
-5
-15
-25
-35
Fastest lap
L.Hamilton
H.Kovalainen
F.Alonso
F.Massa
N.Rosberg
N.Heidfeld
K.Raikkonen
© FORIX.com / M.Merlino

Lap chart

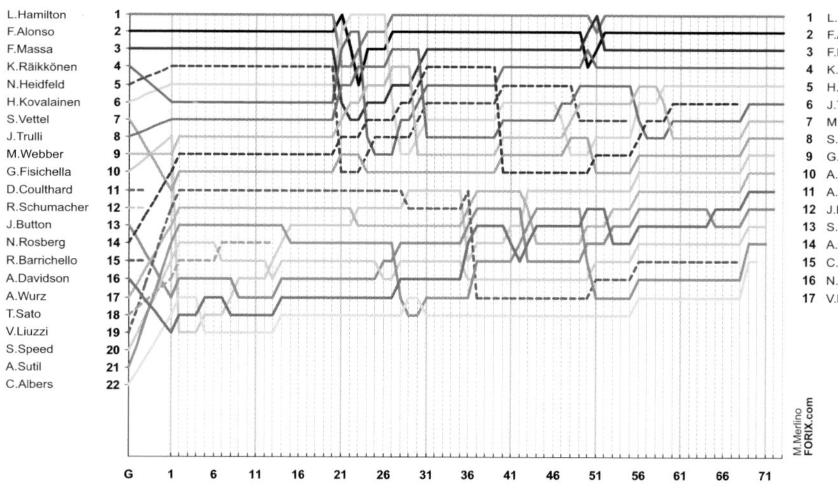
L.Hamilton 1
F.Alonso 2
F.Massa 3
K.Räikkönen 4
N.Heidfeld 5
H.Kovalainen 6
S.Vettel 7
J.Trulli 8
M.Webber 9
G.Fisichella 10
D.Coulthard 11
R.Schumacher 12
J.Button 13
N.Rosberg 14
R.Barrichello 15
A.Davidson 16
A.Wurz 17
T.Sato 18
V.Liuzzi 19
S.Speed 20
A.Sutil 21
C.Albers 22
G
1
6
11
16
21
26
31
36
41
46
51
56
61
66
71
1 L.Hamilton
2 F.Alonso
3 F.Massa
4 K.Räikkönen
5 H.Kovalainen
6 J.Trulli
7 M.Webber
8 S.Vettel
9 G.Fisichella
10 A.Wurz
11 A.Davidson
12 J.Button
13 S.Speed
14 A.Sutil
15 C.Albers
16 N.Rosberg
17 V.Liuzzi
M.Merlino
FORIX.com

CHAMPIONSHIPS 7/17

Drivers

1.	L. Hamilton	McLaren Mercedes	2🏆	58
2.	F. Alonso	McLaren Mercedes	2🏆	48
3.	F. Massa	Ferrari	2🏆	39
4.	K. Räikkönen	Ferrari	1🏆	32
5.	N. Heidfeld	BMW		26
6.	G. Fisichella	Renault		13
7.	R. Kubica	BMW		12
8.	H. Kovalainen	Renault		12
9.	A. Wurz	Williams Toyota		8
10.	J. Trulli	Toyota		7
11.	N. Rosberg	Williams Toyota		5
12.	D. Coulthard	Red Bull Renault		4
13.	T. Sato	Super Aguri Honda		4
14.	M. Webber	Red Bull Renault		2
15.	R. Schumacher	Toyota		2
16.	S. Vettel	BMW		1
17.	S. Speed	STR Ferrari		0
18.	R. Barrichello	Honda		0
19.	A. Davidson	Super Aguri Honda		0
20.	J. Button	Honda		0
21.	A. Sutil	Spyker Ferrari		0
22.	C. Albers	Spyker Ferrari		0
23.	V. Liuzzi	STR Ferrari		0

Constructors

1.	Vodafone McLaren Mercedes	4🏆	106
2.	Scuderia Ferrari Marlboro	3🏆	71
3.	BMW Sauber F1 Team		39
4.	ING Renault F1 Team		25
5.	AT&T Williams		13
6.	Panasonic Toyota Racing		9
7.	Red Bull Racing		6
8.	Super Aguri F1 Team		4
9.	Scuderia Toro Rosso		0
10.	Honda Racing F1 Team		0
11.	Etihad Aldar Spyker F1 Team		0

THE CIRCUIT

Name Indianapolis Motor Speedway; Indianapolis
Lenght 4192 m
Distance 73 laps, 306,016 km

Latitude 39°47'35.00"N
Longitude 86°14'20.00"O

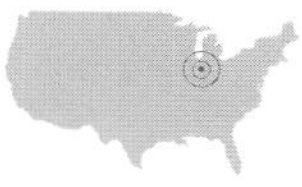

S1 50m before corner
S2 85m before corner
Radar 200m before corner

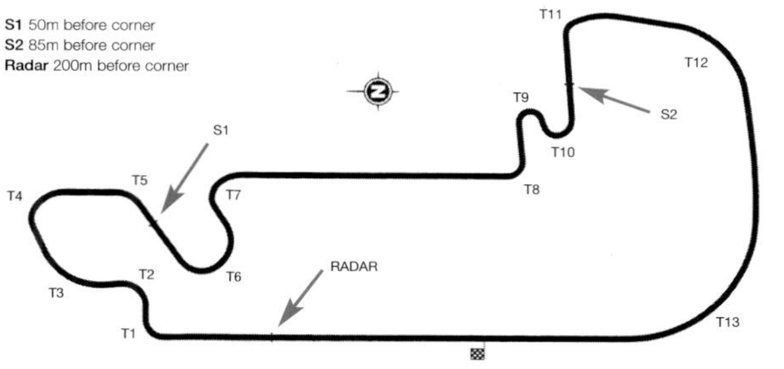
T1
T2
T3
T4
T5
T6
T7
T8
T9
T10
T11
T12
T13
S1
S2
RADAR

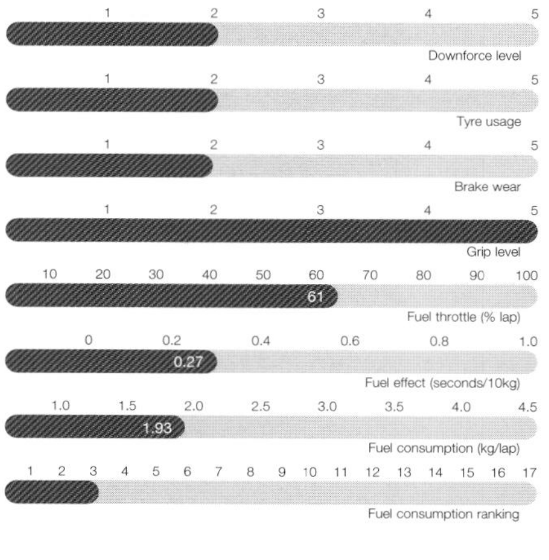
Downforce level
Tyre usage
Brake wear
Grip level
61
Fuel throttle (% lap)
0.27
Fuel effect (seconds/10kg)
1.93
Fuel consumption (kg/lap)
Fuel consumption ranking

PUTTING THE RED BACK INTO FORMULA 1

In Monaco, Canada and the United States McLaren had dominated the sport, and so the season seemingly promised to be theirs. This did not take into account the firepower of Ferrari, who were to set about overturning that position. At Magny-Cours, the Scuderia was unbeatable, from free practice right through to the chequered flag. It was this dominance that allowed them to get within 25 points of McLaren in the constructors' championship. It promised to be a very tight duel, played out upon the fast summer circuits.

> Fernando Alonso could only manage 10th on the grid, due to an unexpected gearbox problem. *"It came at just the wrong time,"* said the Spaniard. *"Now, I just have to hope that the forecasted rain finally arrives. I will be praying all night for this to happen. But everything is in the hands of fate now: there is little I can do."*

On the stroke of midday, Zinedine Zidane completed two laps of the Magny-Cours circuit in a Ferrari F50 road car driven by Michael Schumacher. On this occasion, their goal was to raise awareness of a new charity, the ICM (Brain and Spinal Cord Institute), which is set to open in 2009. *"I was quite cocky about it at first, but as we went round I became more and more apprehensive - which is something that Michael noticed,"* said the footballer.
>v

Robert Kubica got back behind the wheel of his BMW Sauber for the first time since his monster accident in the Canadian Grand Prix. He played himself back in gently on Friday with a 12th fastest time, but he was still in front of his teammate Nick Heidfeld. The German drove slowly in order not to aggravate a back injury that he had sustained during testing at Silverstone a week earlier.
v

Welcome back Felipe!

Ferrari had been impatiently awaiting the French Grand Prix for quite a while. After the trials encountered in Monaco, Montreal and Indianapolis, then after the wind tunnel breakdown that put the development of the 2007 Ferrari back by two weeks, the Italian team was hoping to regain the advantage on the quicker circuits - hopes that could well become concrete. *"Yes, we do seem to be back on top"*, confirmed Felipe Massa at Magny-Cours, after taking his fourth pole position of the season. *"It's really a great weekend, I'm happy that I've pushed myself to get pole again. The team has worked a great deal on the car, and you can really feel the difference: there is more grip and the car is responding better to changes."* It was the first pole for the Brazilian since the Spanish Grand Prix.
As for Lewis Hamilton, he could only manage to put his McLaren between the two Ferraris. *"OK, we can't always be at the front"*, said the Briton, playing it down. *"I had a car that could take pole, but I made a mistake at turn 15 on my last lap. But I still think that we are the quickest out there in race conditions."*, Lewis Hamilton hoped that it would be a positive race for him in the drivers' championship as his nearest rival, Fernando Alonso, had qualified only tenth on the grid.

IN BRIEF

+ *"I'm not coming to Magny-Cours,"* said Bernie Ecclestone laconically. *"I don't like funerals."* With these words, the fate of the French Grand Prix was sealed. Unfortunately for her, the new French Minister for Health and Sports - Roselyne Bachelot -had trekked all the way down to Magny-Cours to meet Ecclestone for further discussions…

+ Jean Todt didn't really want to talk about it on Friday, but the Scuderia fell victim to a wind tunnel breakdown that lasted for several days. This put the aerodynamic development programme back considerably, as the Maranello wind tunnel normally operates 24 hours a day with three teams of aerodynamicists taking turns to operate it.

Hamilton and Kubica focus on racing

The fact that this was the last French Grand Prix at Magny-Cours lent a rather sombre atmosphere to the paddock. Yet there were two people who were feeling distinctly upbeat: Robert Kubica and Lewis Hamilton. For the Polish driver, Friday's practice gave him the opportunity to get back into the cockpit of his car for the first time since his accident in Montreal. He had been given the all clear by the medics on the Thursday: *"In fact, at Indianapolis [where the doctors had not allowed him to drive], I felt really good. But the doctors decided that the risk was too great if I had another accident as bad as the first. That's why I haven't done any testing since either. Well, you can imagine that I couldn't wait to get back in the car...."*

For Lewis Hamilton, the winner of both the Canadian and American Grands Prix, the waiting was almost as bad, but for other reasons: since returning from Indianapolis, the 22 year old Briton was in a living hell in England. So much so that he was thinking of relocating to Monaco or Switzerland: *"The most surprising thing of all wasn't the two wins"*, he explains. *"On the track, I know what to expect. On the other hand, elsewhere, I never know how people are going to react. A few weeks ago nobody recognised me on the street, then all of a sudden the whole world knows who I am. I can never go out quietly now. To get out of the house, I have to hide myself in the boot of my dad's car. To be honest, it's not very funny. It's just a very bizarre situation...."*

STARTING GRID

Pos	Driver	Time
22	T. SATO*	1:16.244
20	C. ALBERS	1:17.826
18	A. WURZ	1:16.241
16	D. COULTHARD	1:15.806
14	M. WEBBER	1:15.806
12	J. BUTTON	1:15.584
10	F. ALONSO	1:15.935
8	J. TRULLI	1:15.935
6	H. KOVALAINEN	1:15.826
4	R. KUBICA	1:15.493
2	L. HAMILTON	1:15.104

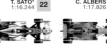

Pos	Driver	Time
21	A. SUTIL*	1:17.915
19	A. DAVIDSON	1:16.366
17	V. LIUZZI	1:16.142
15	S. SPEED	1:16.049
13	R. BARRICHELLO	1:15.761
11	R. SCHUMACHER	1:15.534
9	N. ROSBERG	1:16.328
7	N. HEIDFELD	1:15.900
5	G. FISICHELLA	1:15.674
3	K. RÄIKKÖNEN	1:15.257
1	F. MASSA	1:15.034 (211.632 km/h)

Ferrari's one-two at Magny-Cours re-ignites the championship

A pole position on Saturday followed by a one-two on Sunday: who would have bet on that sort of result for Ferrari, after the Italian team's dire performances in Monaco, Montreal and Indianapolis? In France though, the two red cars did not leave the front for a single moment, confirming their domination that started from the first free practice session on Friday.

So how exactly did the Scuderia manage to turn around a situation that seemed quite desperate at first?

Sporting Director Stefano Domenicali explained: *"We've worked very hard on every little detail that could give us a performance gain. We've gone over everything with a fine toothcomb to find those few extra tenths wherever we can: aerodynamics, engine and set-up."* The job was hindered somewhat by the wind tunnel breakdown that crippled the Scuderia for the best part of two weeks.

"It certainly wasn't convenient, but we worked wherever we could in every single other area," added Domenicali. *"At Indianapolis we didn't have a bad pace but the start was a disaster. We understood from that the importance of starting from the front, without any traffic to get in the way. Here, we had the best chassis-engine-tyre package but I have to say that our drivers were absolutely brilliant as well. Throughout the first 45 laps of the race, they were setting lap times that we wouldn't have dared to hope for."*

Nonetheless, the inner circle at Ferrari did not believe that this progress was enough. Chris Dyer, Kimi Raikkonen's engineer, said: *"It might look like we've taken a big step ahead of our rivals, but the championship is still very long. The truth is that sometimes we are going to be behind and sometimes we are going to be ahead. I just hope that we can continue to fight like this all the way to the end."*

Stefano Domenicali added: *"We're going to bring some new parts to Silverstone. From now on, we have to be very aggressive. We need to attack and not let the smallest opportunity pass us by. It's under those circumstances that we can be the best."*

Confident Kimi

Kimi Raikkonen won the French Grand Prix resoundingly, but two-thirds of the race was led by his teammate Felipe Massa. *"I missed out on pole on Saturday but I knew that things would be a lot better during the race,"* said an insouciant Raikkonen. *"Obviously things would have been slightly easier for me had I started from the front, because that's what it all depends on. Luckily, my start was fine. From that point on, all I had to do was make sure I stayed close to Felipe."*

The Finn's welcome victory marked the end of a painful dry spell for him. « It's not been easy and these last few weeks have been tough to deal with. We've identified the major problems for a while now, we've worked hard on them, and the results are beginning to show.

The whole process took a bit longer than I expected but I think that we are finally getting there. We're back where we belong now. The car is very good, but it's not perfect yet. We can definitely make it quicker.

∧
The start. The weather is grey but dry at Magny-Cours and Felipe Massa fires his Ferrari off the line, closely followed by his teammate.

Kimi Raikkonen finds something to smile about again. The Finn's season started well with a victory in Australia, but the barren spell afterwards was hard for him to stomach. Salvation came with his victory in France.
<

The first corner and it's already all over for Vitantonio Liuzzi. *"I was pushed from behind,"* complained the Italian. *"I think it was by Davidson as when I got back on the track we collided again."*
v<

Kimi Raikkonen was in front of Lewis Hamilton for the best part of the race.
v

> Magny-Cours was a race to forget for Fernando Alonso. He qualified 10th on the grid, finished seventh, and scored just two points. Looking back at it, this was a race that could have cost him the championship. *"I did what I could, but starting from 10th with a fuel strategy geared around the top three places was always going to be tough. After each stop, I found myself back behind the people I had just passed. I fought hard and took a few risks, but because it's the title at stake I obviously have to… "*

Will Flavio Briatore quit Formula 1?

Renault was a shadow of its former itself. The blue and yellow cars devoured all the four titles - drivers and constructors - in 2005 and 2006, but had been nowhere near a podium by the time they arrived at Magny-Cours. Renault would only take one podium finish throughout the year and that was only by chance, at a rainy Japanese Grand Prix. In terms of pure performance, Renault was surpassed by not only McLaren and Ferrari but also by BMW Sauber and even Red Bull on occasions - which used exactly the same engine.

Such a decline was hard to swallow for a big manufacturer like Renault, which was not used to being beaten by its main rivals such as Fiat (with Ferrari), Mercedes (with McLaren) and BMW.

At the start of the season, the Renault management led by Flavio Briatore stated that they aimed to win another world title. It was a misplaced optimism that went all the way to the very top. At Monaco - when it was more than clear that any chance of a title was long gone - Renault supremo Carlos Ghosn visited in person to deliver the message that Renault's chances

in the championship were still alive. With that comment he demonstrated a serious misunderstanding of the business of Formula 1. He also took the time to point out that the cost of Formula 1 wasn't justified if the team wasn't winning. Unsurprisingly, this caused some concern. The meagre results scored so far certainly didn't point to the justification that Ghosn had in mind.

The team's new title sponsor, Dutch bank ING, was nonetheless aware that it had sealed its deal under somewhat false pretences. At the time the sponsorship agreement was reached, in 2006, Renault had just claimed the world title for the second consecutive and was marketing itself as a top team. This is what ING believed they were getting. But as the boss of ING candidly explained: *"At the moment, the investment we have made is not really being justified by the results."* Flavio Briatore, Renault's team principal, viewed what was going on with a strangely detached air. The Italian is naturally loquacious, with a propensity for telling stories. On this occasion though, he was largely silent.

On Friday he was asked to take part in the official FIA press conference, where he was asked about his team's lack of competitiveness this year. He merely embarked on a vague technical answer, centred on the fact that the team concentrated too long on the 2006 championship and started the development of the 2007 car too late. He added that the car had also lost its engine advantage, because of new rules that limited maximum revs to 19,000 rpm. As far as drivers were concerned, he pointed out that the loss of Fernando Alonso and the appointment of Heikki Kovalainen - in his first year of F1 - to succeed him had hardly helped things either. Aged 57 now, Flavio was probably also thinking that it was about time he went and enjoyed the sunshine over his Sardinian property - the 'Billionaire Club'. Two years earlier, when Carlos Ghosn took over the reins at Renault, the Italian had said that he would leave at the end of 2005 - before suddenly postponing his departure. This time, he seemed quite determined to leave the sinking ship. Renault's results were almost indifferent to him. Briatore's successor will face a tough task in restoring the team to its former glory.

> Nick Heidfeld with Willy Rampf, Sauber's technical director. The German finished fifth and continued to add to his points total, which already stood at 30.

>> Mark Webber leads David Coulthard. The two Red Bulls drove in tandem for most of the race, but could only manage 12th and 13th places some way down the field.

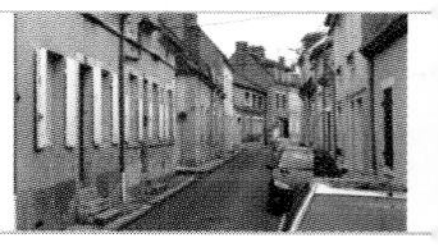

PRACTICE

Date	Weather (AM)	Air temperature	Track temperature	Weather (PM)	Air temperature	Track temperature
Friday June 29, 2007	Cloudy	17-19°c	22-26°c	Cloudy	19-22°c	26-28°c
Saturday June 30, 2007	Sunny	20-21°c	28-29°c	Sunny	24-25°c	43-45°c

All the time trials

N° Driver	Nat.	N° Chassis- Engine [Nbr. GP]	Pos. Free 1 Friday 10:00-11:30	Laps Tr.	Pos. Free 2 Friday 14:00-15:30	Laps Tr.	Pos. Free 3 Saturday 11:00-12:00	Laps Tr.	Pos. Q1 Saturday 14:00-14:15	Laps Tr.	Pos. Q2 Saturday 14:22-14:37	Laps Tr.	Pos. Q3 Saturday 14:45-15:00	Nb. Tr.
1. Fernando Alonso	E	McLaren MP4-22 06 - Mercedes [2]	3. 1:16.154	19	8. 1:16.049	32	8. 1:15.742	4	4. 1:15.322	3	5. 1:15.084	3	10. **DNS**	1
2. Lewis Hamilton	GB	McLaren MP4-22 04 - Mercedes [2]	6. 1:16.277	20	4. 1:15.780	36	1. 1:14.843	8	1. 1:14.805	3	1. 1:14.795	3	2. **1:15.104**	12
3. Giancarlo Fisichella	I	Renault R27-02 & 05 [2]	18. 1:17.226	20	11. 1:16.205	43	5. 1:15.489	20	12. 1:16.047	7	7. 1:15.227	6	5. **1:15.674**	12
4. Heikki Kovalainen	FIN	Renault R27-03 [1]	19. 1:17.348	21	17. 1:16.735	40	4. 1:15.404	19	5. 1:15.524	7	8. 1:15.272	6	6. **1:15.826**	12
5. Felipe Massa	BR	Ferrari F2007 260 [2]	2. 1:15.447	22	1. 1:15.453	38	2. 1:14.906	16	3. 1:15.303	3	2. 1:14.822	3	1. **1:15.034**	12
6. Kimi Räikkönen	FIN	Ferrari F2007 262 [2]	1. 1:15.382	22	2. 1:15.488	28	3. 1:15.276	15	2. 1:14.872	3	3. 1:14.828	3	3. **1:15.257**	13
7. Jenson Button	GB	Honda RA107-04 [1]	14. 1:17.047	24	15. 1:16.395	43	12. 1:15.902	16	14. 1:16.113	6	12. **1:15.584**	6		
8. Rubens Barrichello	BR	Honda RA107-02 [1]	13. 1:16.990	25	18. 1:16.950	47	16. 1:16.102	19	16. 1:16.140	6	13. **1:15.761**	6		
9. Nick Heidfeld	D	BMW Sauber F1.07-05 [2]	7. 1:16.338	25	19. 1:16.968	18	15. 1:16.060	18	9. 1:15.783	4	6. 1:15.149	7	7. **1:15.900**	12
10. Robert Kubica	PL	BMW Sauber F1.07-03 & 07 [2]	9. 1:16.441	19	12. 1:16.236	42	6. 1:15.535	20	8. 1:15.778	7	4. 1:15.066	3	4. **1:15.493**	12
11. Ralf Schumacher	D	Toyota TF107/05 [2]	17. 1:17.168	26	10. 1:16.184	41	14. 1:15.944	22	7. 1:15.760	6	11. **1:15.534**	6		
12. Jarno Trulli	I	Toyota TF107/06 [2]	10. 1:16.603	26	14. 1:16.285	46	9. 1:15.801	19	15. 1:16.118	5	10. 1:15.379	6	8. **1:15.935**	12
14. David Coulthard	GB	Red Bull RB3 3 - Renault [1]	5. 1:16.268	24	6. 1:15.958	36	10. 1:15.802	15	10. 1:15.915	7	16. **DNF**	2		
15. Mark Webber	AUS	Red Bull RB3 4 - Renault [2]	20. 1:17.435	26	16. 1:16.562	17	20. 1:16.573	14	6. 1:15.746	6	14. **1:15.806**	5		
16. Nico Rosberg	D	Williams FW29-05 - Toyota [1]	4. 1:16.214	24	7. 1:16.003	39	7. 1:15.735	18	13. 1:16.092	7	9. 1:15.331	6	9. **1:16.328**	12
17. Alexander Wurz	AUT	Williams FW29-04 - Toyota [2]	8. 1:16.407	23	13. 1:16.260	38	17. 1:16.104	16	18. **1:16.241**	7				
18. Vitantonio Liuzzi	I	Toro Rosso STR2-03 - Ferrari [1]	11. 1:16.895	32	5. 1:15.952	40	11. 1:15.872	22	17. **1:16.142**	6				
19. Scott Speed	USA	Toro Rosso STR2-04 - Ferrari [2]	15. 1:17.103	33	3. 1:15.773	21	18. 1:16.161	18	11. 1:15.980	6	15. **1:16.049**	6		
20. Adrian Sutil	D	Spyker F8-VII/03 & 04 - Ferrari [2]	22. 1:18.419	15	21. 1:18.213	32	21. 1:17.517	21	22. **1:17.915**	5				
21. Christijan Albers	NL	Spyker F8-VII/01 - Ferrari [2]	21. 1:18.178	28	22. 1:18.708	9	22. 1:17.705	23	21. **1:17.826**	6				
22. Takuma Sato	J	Super Aguri SA07-04 - Honda [1]	12. 1:16.967	22	20. 1:17.165	49	19. 1:16.221	18	19. **1:16.244**	6				
23. Anthony Davidson	GB	Super Aguri SA07-03 - Honda [1]	16. 1:17.166	26	9. 1:16.162	25	13. 1:15.925	20	20. **1:16.366**	5				

Fastest lap overall
L. Hamilton 1:14.795 (212,308 km/h)

Maximum speed

N° Driver	S1 Qualifs	Pos.	S1 Race	Pos.	S2 Qualifs	Pos.	S2 Race	Pos.	Finish Qualifs	Pos.	Finish Race	Pos.	Radar Qualifs	Pos.	Radar Race	Pos.
1. F. Alonso	302,3	5	306,4	3	275,8	7	284,6	1	167,1	2	161,8	6	303,7	4	304,3	3
2. L. Hamilton	299,5	14	303,9	9	276,9	4	278,6	5	166,5	5	158,4	15	300,0	14	302,4	7
3. G. Fisichella	299,7	13	302,1	15	275,7	8	276,3	10	166,1	6	162,0	5	301,5	11	301,6	9
4. H. Kovalainen	302,6	4	302,6	11	276,3	5	278,1	7	166,7	3	160,0	11	301,9	9	300,5	15
5. F. Massa	303,7	2	304,1	8	277,6	1	280,0	2	168,6	1	164,6	1	304,1	3	305,4	2
6. K. Räikkönen	301,7	8	304,7	6	277,0	3	278,7	4	165,3	9	164,0	2	302,3	7	304,1	5
7. J. Button	301,0	9	305,7	4	274,4	13	276,7	9	163,1	15	159,6	12	299,9	18	302,2	8
8. R. Barrichello	302,0	6	305,1	5	276,3	6	275,3	12	165,3	7	161,7	7	302,1	8	301,0	11
9. N. Heidfeld	297,4	19	300,1	17	272,5	20	274,0	17	165,0	11	162,4	4	300,0	15	300,5	14
10. R. Kubica	302,9	3	303,7	10	274,8	11	275,2	14	166,5	4	163,0	3	305,0	2	301,4	10
11. R. Schumacher	299,0	17	304,6	7	274,4	12	278,4	6	160,6	20	157,2	18	300,0	16	302,6	6
12. J. Trulli	300,5	10	302,5	12	274,4	14	139,2	21	162,7	16			302,6	6	275,2	20
14. D. Coulthard	300,0	12	302,2	13	275,3	9	275,7	11	164,2	13	159,3	14	301,4	12	300,8	13
15. M. Webber	300,4	11	302,1	14	273,9	15	275,2	13	161,7	17	160,9	9	301,9	10	300,5	16
16. N. Rosberg	304,5	1	306,5	2	277,5	2	277,3	8	165,2	10	160,2	10	305,6	1	306,7	1
17. A. Wurz	301,7	7	308,3	1	273,8	18	280,0	3	165,3	8	157,8	16	302,9	5	304,3	4
18. V. Liuzzi	296,5	20			272,5	19			161,7	18			300,0	13		
19. S. Speed	298,6	18	300,0	18	273,9	17	274,3	16	160,7	19	157,8	17	299,9	17	300,8	12
20. A. Sutil	291,8	22	295,8	19	266,9	21	271,4	18	159,9	21	161,0	8	295,1	22	295,7	19
21. C. Albers	292,6	21	295,6	20	266,2	22	269,3	19	158,6	22	159,3	13	295,2	21	296,2	18
22. T. Sato	299,2	16	301,9	16	273,9	16	275,0	15	164,3	12	156,8	19	299,7	19	299,1	17
23. A. Davidson	299,2	15	268,3	21	275,2	10	262,5	20	163,4	14			299,1	20	200,4	21

Best sector times

Qualifs	**S1** F. Massa	21.747	**S2** L. Hamilton	28.645	**S3** K. Räikkönen	24.164	= 1:14.556
Race	**S1** F. Massa	21.908	**S2** G. Fisichella	29.174	**S3** L. Hamilton	24.743	= 1:15.825

RACE

Date	Weather	Air temperature	Track temperature	Humidity	Wind speed
Sunday July 1st, 2007 (14:00)	Cloudy	24-25°c	37-42°c	60%	1.5 m/s

Classification & retirements

Pos.	Driver	Constructor	Tyres	Laps	Time	Km/h
1.	K. Räikkönen	Ferrari	MMS	70	1:30:54.200	203,679
2.	F. Massa	Ferrari	MMS	70	+ 2.414	203,589
3.	L. Hamilton	McLaren Mercedes	MMMS	70	+ 32.153	202,485
4.	R. Kubica	BMW	MMS	70	+ 41.727	202,133
5.	N. Heidfeld	BMW	MMS	70	+ 48.801	201,873
6.	G. Fisichella	Renault	MMS	70	+ 52.210	201,748
7.	F. Alonso	McLaren Mercedes	SMM	70	+ 56.516	201,590
8.	J. Button	Honda	MMS	70	+ 58.885	201,504
9.	N. Rosberg	Williams Toyota	MMS	70	+ 1:08.505	201,153
10.	R. Schumacher	Toyota	MMS	69	1 lap	200,584
11.	R. Barrichello	Honda	MMS	69	1 lap	199,778
12.	M. Webber	Red Bull Renault	MMS	69	1 lap	199,701
13.	D. Coulthard	Red Bull Renault	MMS	69	1 lap	199,547
14.	A. Wurz	Williams Toyota	MMS	69	1 lap	199,372
15.	H. Kovalainen	Renault	MMMS	69	1 lap	198,527
16.	T. Sato	Super Aguri Honda	SMM	68	2 laps	197,365
17.	A. Sutil	Spyker Ferrari (T-car)	SSM	68	2 laps	196,403

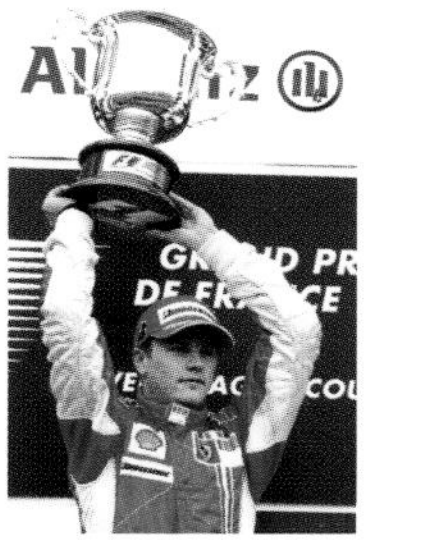

Driver	Constructor	Tyres	Laps	Reason
S. Speed	STR Ferrari	MMS	55	Gearbox failure
C. Albers	Spyker Ferrari	SS	28	Pulled away from his pit stop with the fuel hose still connected to the car
A. Davidson	Super Aguri Honda	M	1	Collision with Liuzzi
J. Trulli	Toyota	M	1	Hit Kovalainen, suspension broken
V. Liuzzi	STR Ferrari	M	0	Hit by Davidson… spin, collision with the Super Aguri

Tyres M: Medium & S: Soft

Fastest laps

	Driver	Time	Lap	Km/h
1.	F. Massa	1:16.099	42	208,670
2.	K. Räikkönen	1:16.207	20	208,374
3.	F. Alonso	1:16.495	36	207,590
4.	L. Hamilton	1:16.587	39	207,340
5.	G. Fisichella	1:16.703	70	207,027
6.	J. Button	1:16.770	70	206,846
7.	N. Heidfeld	1:16.875	70	206,563
8.	R. Schumacher	1:16.966	68	206,319
9.	N. Rosberg	1:17.011	69	206,199
10.	R. Kubica	1:17.153	44	205,819
11.	H. Kovalainen	1:17.206	69	205,678
12.	R. Barrichello	1:17.220	68	205,641
13.	A. Wurz	1:17.240	69	205,587
14.	M. Webber	1:17.249	69	205,563
15.	D. Coulthard	1:17.447	68	205,038
16.	T. Sato	1:17.796	39	204,118
17.	S. Speed	1:17.934	51	203,757
18.	A. Sutil	1:18.091	27	203,347
19.	C. Albers	1:18.955	27	201,122

Pit stops

	Driver	Lap	Duration	Stop	Total
1.	H. Kovalainen	1	24.761	1	24.761
2.	L. Hamilton	16	23.960	1	23.960
3.	F. Alonso	16	24.525	1	24.525
4.	T. Sato	18	35.119	1	35.119
5.	F. Massa	19	24.904	1	24.904
6.	R. Kubica	19	24.480	1	24.480
7.	G. Fisichella	19	26.012	1	26.012
8.	N. Rosberg	20	25.171	1	25.171
9.	K. Räikkönen	22	24.308	1	24.308
10.	N. Heidfeld	22	24.616	1	24.616
11.	H. Kovalainen	26	24.908	2	49.669
12.	R. Schumacher	27	24.608	1	24.608
13.	A. Wurz	28	24.225	1	24.225
14.	A. Sutil	28	26.675	1	26.675
15.	C. Albers	28	33.274	1	33.274
16.	M. Webber	30	24.189	1	24.189
17.	S. Speed	30	25.388	1	25.388
18.	J. Button	32	23.239	1	23.239
19.	D. Coulthard	32	24.488	1	24.488
20.	R. Barrichello	33	23.328	1	23.328
21.	A. Sutil	•34•	14.635	2	41.310
22.	L. Hamilton	37	22.822	2	46.782
23.	F. Alonso	37	26.998	2	51.523
24.	T. Sato	40	27.309	2	1:02.428
25.	F. Massa	43	25.412	2	50.316
26.	R. Kubica	45	24.221	2	48.701
27.	K. Räikkönen	46	24.145	2	48.453
28.	N. Rosberg	46	25.021	2	50.192
29.	M. Webber	46	23.888	2	48.077
30.	N. Heidfeld	47	23.889	2	48.505
31.	A. Sutil	46	25.342	3	1:06.652
32.	D. Coulthard	48	23.750	2	48.238
33.	G. Fisichella	50	22.862	2	48.874
34.	J. Button	50	23.781	2	47.020
35.	A. Wurz	50	25.812	2	50.037
36.	L. Hamilton	51	22.788	3	1:09.570
37.	R. Barrichello	51	22.869	2	46.197
38.	R. Schumacher	52	22.783	2	47.391
39.	S. Speed	52	23.584	2	48.972
40.	H. Kovalainen	54	22.684	3	1:12.353

•• Drive-through penalty: Sutil. Speeding in pit lane.

Race leader

Driver	Laps in the lead	Nbr of laps
F. Massa	1 > 19	19
K. Räikkönen	20 > 22	3
F. Massa	23 > 43	21
K. Räikkönen	44 > 70	27

Driver	Nbr of laps	Kilometers
F. Massa	40	176,256 km
K. Räikkönen	30	132,330 km

Gaps on the lead board

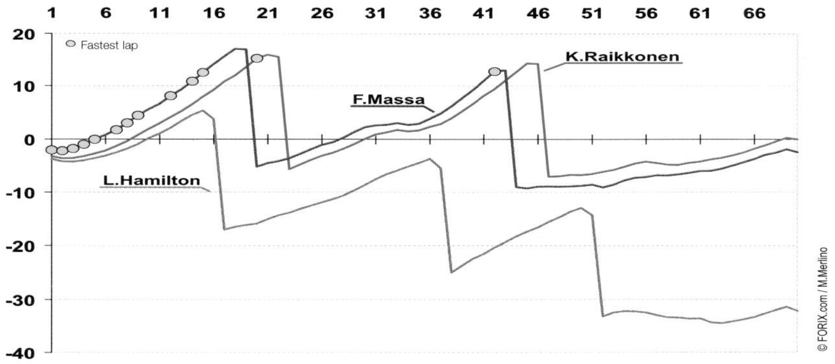
1 6 11 16 21 26 31 36 41 46 51 56 61 66
20 10 0 -10 -20 -30 -40
Fastest lap
K.Raikkonen
F.Massa
L.Hamilton
© FORIX.com / M.Merlino

Lap chart

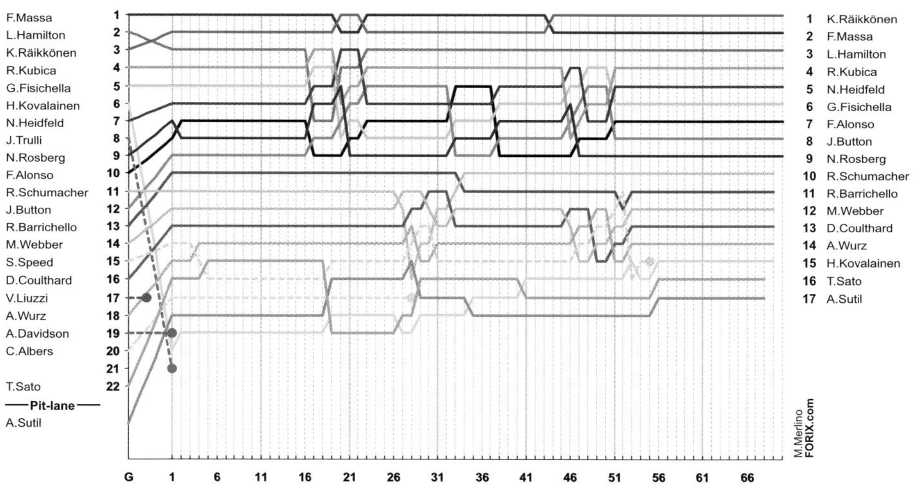
F.Massa
L.Hamilton
K.Räikkönen
R.Kubica
G.Fisichella
H.Kovalainen
N.Heidfeld
J.Trulli
N.Rosberg
F.Alonso
R.Schumacher
J.Button
R.Barrichello
M.Webber
S.Speed
D.Coulthard
V.Liuzzi
A.Wurz
A.Davidson
C.Albers
T.Sato
Pit-lane
A.Sutil
G 1 6 11 16 21 26 31 36 41 46 51 56 61 66
1 K.Räikkönen
2 F.Massa
3 L.Hamilton
4 R.Kubica
5 N.Heidfeld
6 G.Fisichella
7 F.Alonso
8 J.Button
9 N.Rosberg
10 R.Schumacher
11 R.Barrichello
12 M.Webber
13 D.Coulthard
14 A.Wurz
15 H.Kovalainen
16 T.Sato
17 A.Sutil
M.Merlino FORIX.com

CHAMPIONSHIPS 8/17

Drivers

1.	L. Hamilton	McLaren Mercedes	2🏆	64
2.	F. Alonso	McLaren Mercedes	2🏆	50
3.	F. Massa	Ferrari	2🏆	47
4.	K. Räikkönen	Ferrari	2🏆	42
5.	N. Heidfeld	BMW		30
6.	R. Kubica	BMW		17
7.	G. Fisichella	Renault		16
8.	H. Kovalainen	Renault		12
9.	A. Wurz	Williams Toyota		8
10.	J. Trulli	Toyota		7
11.	N. Rosberg	Williams Toyota		5
12.	D. Coulthard	Red Bull Renault		4
13.	T. Sato	Super Aguri Honda		4
14.	M. Webber	Red Bull Renault		2
15.	R. Schumacher	Toyota		2
16.	J. Button	Honda		1
17.	S. Vettel	BMW		1
18.	S. Speed	STR Ferrari		0
19.	R. Barrichello	Honda		0
20.	A. Davidson	Super Aguri Honda		0
21.	A. Sutil	Spyker Ferrari		0
22.	C. Albers	Spyker Ferrari		0
23.	V. Liuzzi	STR Ferrari		0

Constructors

1.	Vodafone McLaren Mercedes	4🏆	114
2.	Scuderia Ferrari Marlboro	4🏆	89
3.	BMW Sauber F1 Team		48
4.	ING Renault F1 Team		28
5.	AT&T Williams		13
6.	Panasonic Toyota Racing		9
7.	Red Bull Racing		6
8.	Super Aguri F1 Team		4
9.	Honda Racing F1 Team		1
10.	Scuderia Toro Rosso		0
11.	Etihad Aldar Spyker F1 Team		0

THE CIRCUIT

Name Circuit de Nevers Magny-Cours; Magny-Cours
Lenght 4411 m
Distance 70 laps, 308,586 km
Latitude 46°51'50.70"N
Longitude 3°09'48.50"E

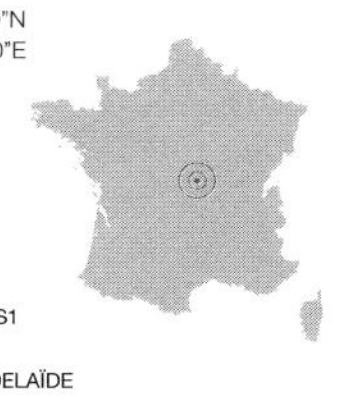

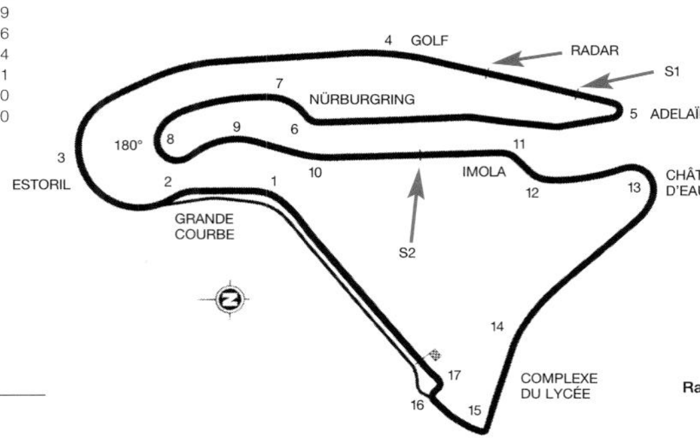
4 GOLF
RADAR
S1
7
NÜRBURGRING
5 ADELAÏDE
180°
8
9
6
11
3
ESTORIL
2
1
10
IMOLA
12
13
CHÂTEAU D'EAU
GRANDE COURBE
S2
14
17
16
15
COMPLEXE DU LYCÉE

S1 230m before corner
S2 135m before corner
Radar 110m before corner

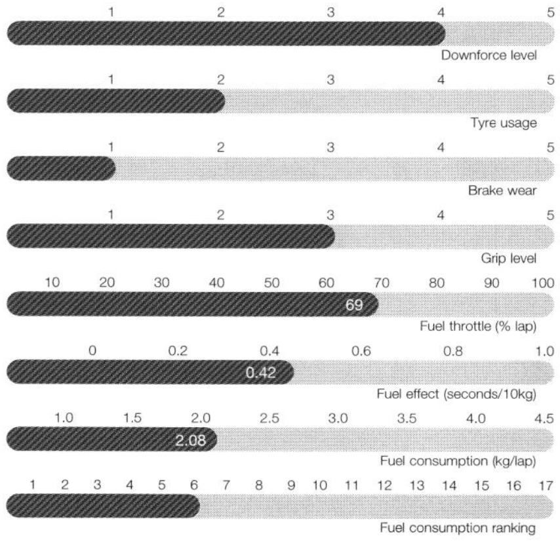
Downforce level
Tyre usage
Brake wear
Grip level
69
Fuel throttle (% lap)
0.42
Fuel effect (seconds/10kg)
2.08
Fuel consumption (kg/lap)
Fuel consumption ranking

KIMI-TASTIC!

Lewis Hamilton led the field away, but the McLarens were powerless in the face of the red tornado known as Kimi Raikkonen. Once more, on a quick circuit like Silverstone, the Ferraris proved to be impossible to beat. Felipe Massa would undoubtedly have been on the podium as well, had he not suffered a bizarre problem on the starting grid.

McLaren claimed that tyres made the difference in Britain. But in actual fact, they were far more concerned about events that were taking place away from the racetrack. The British Grand Prix was when the whole 'spygate' saga erupted - which would irreversibly change the whole look of the season.

> Lewis Hamilton salutes the crowd after claiming pole position on his home territory. On Saturday, 78,000 people turned up to watch qualifying: more than had come to the actual race in 2006.

Lewis excites Silverstone

There were no surprises on Saturday morning. While the traffic flow around Silverstone is generally peaceful ever since a new bypass was constructed, the morning of qualifying provoked a traffic jam that extended all the way to Northampton more than 20 kilometres away. Many people were still trapped in their cars by the time qualifying got underway at 2pm; their progress impeded by other cars that had been abandoned in the middle of the road as their owners tried to get to the circuit on foot. Lewis-mania had hit England big time, and the entire country was getting behind its new hero. The newspapers printed page after page about him, day after day. The public's thirst for information about him was hard to slake. It was an outpouring of national motor racing pride that eclipsed even the heyday of Mansell mania. When Hamilton claimed pole position for his home Grand Prix, there was what can only be described as an explosion of joy as he crossed the start-finish line. Up until that point, Lewis had kept his adoring fans in suspense. Judging from the first practice sessions on Friday morning, he seemed incapable of matching the Ferraris on pace. When qualifying came round on Saturday, he was the last driver to bolt on new tyres and go for an all-out qualifying lap. By the time he crossed the line to set pole, the session had been over for nearly a minute.

"When the team got on the radio to tell me I was quickest, I just screamed into my helmet!" said Hamilton. "I could actually hear the crowd cheering over the noise

of the engine, but I reckon I was screaming even louder! This is not something I've ever experienced before. I drive around the circuit and see all the flags with my name on them; wherever I look there are people cheering and waving. This gives me a lot of energy, and pushes me to go even faster. On my last flying lap I knew that I was fourth up to that point and that I had to do better. I promised myself that I would take the first corner flat-out in seventh. I didn't quite do it - but I almost did! All the way through that lap I was absolutely on the limit."

A total of 78,000 spectators turned out for qualifying on Saturday - which was more than had attended the actual race in 2006! The hospitality suites for corporate guests hosted more than 4000 people - as opposed to the 600 or so who turned up at Magny-Cours the previous weekend. And everybody was talking about HamiltonSilverstone was the young Briton's third pole position, having previously bagged the top sport in Canada and the United States. On both those occasions, he had gone on to win the race. The British public were asking for no less.

> Sixth on the grid for Ralf Schumacher was his best starting position of the season so far.
v

McLaren raises the standard

Even stretching the imagination (and the definition) to its utmost, it would be hard to call McLaren's paddock facility a mere 'motorhome'. With three floors, four meeting rooms, 28 offices, nine giant plasma screens and cutting-edge architecture, McLaren's structure has more in common with a luxury hotel than the trailer units that the teams used

as motorhomes right up until the 1990s. McLaren have led the way in motorhome design since 2002, when it introduced its 'communications centre'. This was a semi-permanent structure, which had nothing to do with the conventional motorhomes that were dragged across Europe by lorries.

At Silverstone McLaren raised the bar even higher by introducing the 'brand centre', financed equally by Vodafone, McLaren and Mercedes. The cost of it has never been revealed, but rumours suggest that it was something in the region of 30 million Euros. It's a lot of money, but the team believed that it was worth it for the number of meetings that the structure is able to host. The 'brand centre' is a lavish structure, featuring a lot of bespoke smoked glass. It eclipses the 'Ferrari tower' that was introduced in May last year and even the Red Bull 'energy station' - which is nonetheless a lot bigger (33 metres long as opposed to the 18 metres of the McLaren structure). It's not just about size though: the McLaren hospitality unit distinguishes itself by its quality.

To put it into context, the team needs just one lorry to transport the four racing cars that travel to each circuit, but 12 are needed to ferry the 'brand centre' around. It's not something that bothers team principal Ron Dennis. "Formula 1 is a sport that takes place between 2pm and 4pm on Sunday afternoons," he said, at a little ceremony to inaugurate the new facility on Thursday. "The rest of the time, it's business. The size of the centre just reflects our approach to racing." The narrow entrance to this monolith, which is constantly manned by security staff, hardly radiates a warm welcome or inspires friendship. Equally, that's not why McLaren go racing...

> McLaren's 'brand centre' was declared open on Thursday. For the British team, it was the calm before the storm...

STARTING GRID

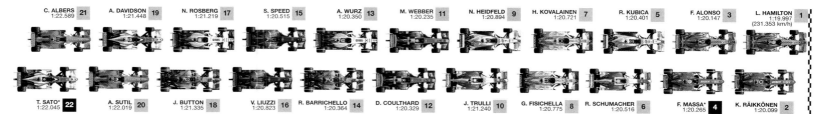

* T. SATO
starts from the pit lane.

F. MASSA
stalled at the first start.
Then starts from the pit lane.

Position	Driver	Time
21	C. ALBERS	1:22.589
19	A. DAVIDSON	1:21.448
17	N. ROSBERG	1:21.219
15	S. SPEED	1:20.515
13	A. WURZ	1:20.350
11	M. WEBBER	1:20.235
9	N. HEIDFELD	1:20.894
7	H. KOVALAINEN	1:20.721
5	R. KUBICA	1:20.401
3	F. ALONSO	1:20.147
1	L. HAMILTON	1:19.997 (231.353 km/h)
22	T. SATO*	1:22.045
20	A. SUTIL	1:22.019
18	J. BUTTON	1:21.335
16	V. LIUZZI	1:20.823
14	R. BARRICHELLO	1:20.364
12	D. COULTHARD	1:20.329
10	J. TRULLI	1:21.240
8	G. FISICHELLA	1:20.775
6	R. SCHUMACHER	1:20.516
4	F. MASSA*	1:20.265
2	K. RÄIKKÖNEN	1:20.099

Kimi Raikkonen gets stronger all the time

As the season went on, Kimi Raikkonen seemed to become progressively stronger. The week before, at Magny-Cours, he had given his rivals their first warning by setting fastest time in nearly all the free practice sessions.

He came to Britain riding the crest of this wave and looking for more success. Raikkonen qualified second, behind Lewis Hamilton, but he had to wait until the second round of fuel stops to take the lead. From that point on, nobody could stop him.

"When I saw Fernando (Alonso) stop for the first time and then set off more or less straight away, I knew that he had not taken on much fuel and that he would have to stop early again. All I had to do was stay in touch with him and wait to take the lead."

It was a strategy that he not only made sound simple, but also that he executed perfectly. The result propelled him right back into the championship fight. After winning the first race of the season in Australia, the Finn struggled slightly to fit into the very different culture that is Ferrari. By the mid-point of the year, these difficulties were very definitely behind him. *"The car is a lot better now,"* he said. *"Everything is a lot easier for me now generally. Having said that, there is still a long way to go in this championship and anything can happen."* Prophetic words...

Felipe Massa would certainly have joined his teammate on the Silverstone podium, had he not stalled on the grid after the warm-up lap.

"It's a real shame, as my car was fantastic today," said the Brazilian. *"When I came back onto the grid I warmed up my tyres as usual but then the engine stopped for reasons that we still don't know now."* Felipe Massa was forced to start from the pit lane but staged a fantastic fightback drive, climbing from last to second in the space of just 19 laps. In the

end he finished fifth, just behind Robert Kubica's BMW Sauber.

Massa's problems meant that the Scuderia was not quite able to repeat its one-two of Magny-Cours, but the gauntlet had been thrown down. Ferrari was the big favourite for all of the quick circuits from now on.

IN BRIEF

+ There were 85,000 spectators at Silverstone on race day, and most of them were Lewis Hamilton fans. That's the maximum number of people that the circuit can accommodate. The headline on the Sunday Express - a best-selling British newspaper - even shouted «Win for England, Lewis!» Ultimately though, it was all to end in disappointment.

+ *"They've known what they have to do for five or six years now. So if they don't do it, they won't be there in 2010,"* said Bernie Ecclestone, when he was asked about the future of the British Grand Prix at Silverstone.

+ The Red Bull team announced that Coulthard's contract had been extended by another year. The news came as something of a surprise, as rumours suggested that the Anglo-Austrian team wanted to launch the F1 career of one of the many young drivers that they have under contract.

+ Renault celebrated the 30th anniversary of its first GP at Silverstone. The French team embarked on its F1 adventure in 1977 at the British track, with a revolutionary turbo-charged car featuring radial tyres driven by Jean-Pierre Jabouille. Thirty years later, the team boasted eight constructors' titles, 113 victories and 154 pole positions.

∧
It was Kimi Raikkonen's third win of the season, which allowed him to close to within 18 points of Lewis Hamilton in the championship.

The celebrities flocked to the Grand Prix: Honda invited Mr and Mrs David Beckham, who visited t he paddock on Saturday. They practically caused a riot.
<∨

The start: Lewis Hamilton made an excellent getaway from pole position, before being held back by tyre problems.
∨

Lewis Hamilton beaten by Fernando Alonso

Having come to Britain after winning the last two races, and despite taking pole position, Lewis Hamilton was never really in a position to fight for victory at his home Grand Prix.

It was an unexpected situation, but a philosophical Hamilton commented: *"I fought to the end, without ever giving up, in case there was an incident in front or I could use the backmarkers to my advantage. But it's true that third place was not the result I was hoping for. Having said that, to finish my first British Grand Prix on the podium after the difficulties I had during my final two stints is really not a bad result at all. You've got to keep looking on the positive side."*

The problems were caused, according to Hamilton, by his tyres. *"Everything was fine with my first set of tyres, even*

though I had a lot of pressure from Kimi," said the McLaren driver. *"But my second set off tyres started to wear from more or less the moment that I left the pit lane. I hoped that they would stabilise, but actually they got worse. I tried to keep in contact, but Kimi and Fernando were able to go quicker than me and there was nothing I could do to keep up. It's my fault: I made a mistake by choosing a different rear suspension set-up to Fernando and this gave me problems during the race. It's a good lesson for me and I won't be making the same mistake again."*

The effect was to make Hamilton's championship position somewhat less comfortable. *"I just need to keep progressing and not make any more mistakes,"* he said. *"But I'm still at a very early point in my career - I'm learning all the time."*

THE MAGIC OF SILVERSTONE

Even though some of the facilities are no longer state of the art, the Silverstone circuit maintains the charm that has always distinguished it. Its fans, campsites and miles of green grass all reflect the passion and history of motorsport.

Meanwhile, back at Maranello...

^
Three more points for
Nick Heidfeld (top) while
Fernando Alonso took
another two points off his
title rival and team mate
by finishing second
(below). The Spaniard
said : *"We didn't have the
pace of the Ferraris today
so second place was the
best that I could do."*

Nigel Mansell got back
behind the wheel of a
modern Formula 1 car at
Silverstone, as part of
BMW Sauber's 'pit lane
park' exhibition. Looking
at the amount of tyre
smoke, 'Nige' certainly
hasn't lost his touch. Or
his heavy right foot !
>V

Lewis Hamilton fans were
everywhere at
Silverstone, and
often in an
unsubtle way...
V

The conversation in the Silverstone paddock revolved around the spy scandal, from Wednesday all the way to Sunday night. It was quite clear that this remarkable story, which had broken on the Tuesday before the race, risked reducing the on-track efforts of Lewis Hamilton and Fernando Alonso to nothing.

On Tuesday, Scuderia Ferrari filed a complaint to the High Court in London, having heard that some of their confidential documents had fallen into the hands of McLaren. On the same day hundreds of Ferrari plans were found at the home of McLaren designer Mike Coughlan, as a result of a search warrant issued by the British judges. Coughlan was immediately suspended from his duties. In a panic, McLaren issued a press release (still on the same day) categorically stating that an internal enquiry had revealed that none of Ferrari's intellectual property was to be found on the current MP4-22 and inviting the FIA to go over the car and see for themselves.

720 confidential pages

On Wednesday, it emerged that the leak came on April 28. Ferrari had been informed that their confidential information was in circulation by an employee of a photocopying shop in Woking, not far from McLaren's headquarters. The person had warned Ferrari when a customer came into the shop asking for a 720-page book to be photocopied, which carried the famous Prancing Horse logo : the emblem of the Scuderia.
The book described certain elements of the F2007's suspension, as well as some details about the team structure, plus some telemetry data. Another part described how best to set up the car according to the unique demands of each individual circuit. The photocopy shop employee phoned Maranello as soon as he spotted the following message of the book : *"Confidential. If you find this document, please telephone +39 536 949 111"* (the number of Ferrari's main switchboard). That one phone call sparked the whole story off. It turned out that the customer wanting the photocopies was none other than Mike Coughlan -the designer of the MP4-22- and the

information was supplied by Nigel Stepney, who was in charge of Ferrari's test team. It was a role that Stepney never liked, as it took him away from the Grands Prix. Later on Wednesday, Ferrari confirmed that Stepney had been sacked with immediate effect. On the 28 April, near the port in Barcelona, Nigel Stepney was seen having a drink with Mike Coughlan in a bar. Ferrari's confidential document was almost certainly handed over then.

A tearful Ron Dennis defends McLaren

On Thursday, McLaren boss Ron Dennis fought tooth and nail to defend his team against accusations that it had made use of Ferrari's intellectual property. While inaugurating the new McLaren motorhome (or 'brand centre'), he briefly touched upon the saga. *"I am McLaren : I live and breathe McLaren,"* he said, visibly upset. *"I can assure you that nothing untoward goes on in this team."* As he said this, he shed a tear - his first tears in more than 25 years of F1.
On Friday, Honda boss Nick Fry confirmed that Nigel Stepney and Mike Coughlan had come to see him in June, looking for work with the team. This was a revelation that at least explained the motivation behind Stepney and Coughlan's actions : they were after a new job.
This is what Ron Dennis believed - or wanted to believe - anyway. *"These mens' motives were extremely simple,"* he said. *"The whole thing will blow over by itself very soon. As soon as I heard what was going on, I immediately phoned Jean Todt (the boss of Ferrari) and Max Mosley (the president of the FIA) so that we could collaborate better to resolve the situation. An hour later, I suggested that I would supply the FIA with all our internal documents in order to prove that we had not benefited from any intellectual property belonging to any other team."*

Max Mosley talks of severe punishments

On Saturday, the whole scandal ratcheted itself up a gear. Max Mosley was visiting the Silverstone paddock, and he was keen to tell people just how seriously he was taking

the whole spygate affair. According to him, a punishment was likely even if it was demonstrably shown that the MP4-22 did not benefit from Ferrari's secrets. *"If it is proved that McLaren had knowledge of information that came from Ferrari, we will hand out severe punishments,"* he said. *"Those punishments might not be limited to taking away points from the team. We might also take away points from the drivers."*
Suddenly it seemed that all the points scored by Lewis Hamilton and Fernando Alonso so far this year could have been in vain, as it was undoubtedly true that some sort of Ferrari dossier had certainly landed on Mike Coughlan's desk.
Mosley was not in the mood for clemency. *"Legally, Ron Dennis is responsible for the actions of all his employees,"* said the FIA President (who is also a qualified lawyer). *"This could become quite a serious matter, as these days just a simple bit of information about fuel stop strategies could benefit a rival."* Ferrari was also eager to point out that McLaren seemed to have enjoyed a remarkable upturn in performance since that infamous 28 April...

Sabotage and white powder

According to Max Mosley, the FIA would conclude its investigation in two or three weeks. On Sunday Jean Todt pointed out that Ferrari had filed an initial lawsuit against Nigel Stepney in June with an Italian court in Modena, for 'sabotage'. Ferrari's former employee was accused of having sabotaged the cars of Kimi Raikkonen and Felipe Massa shortly before the Monaco Grand Prix by putting 'white powder' into their fuel tanks.
At the time, Nigel Stepney was actively seeking work with other teams, which might explain his quixotic behaviour. Ferrari also accused Stepney of having given the famous dossier to Mike Coughlan. This matter was being dealt with London's High Court, following another lawsuit filed by the Italian team.
There were two separate incidents being investigated, with Nigel Stepney the common denominator in both. He was contacted by phone and robustly denied any wrongdoing whatsoever.

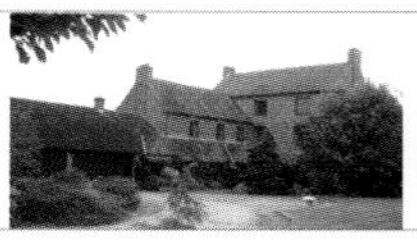

PRACTICE

Date	Weather (AM)	Air temperature	Track temperature	Weather (PM)	Air temperature	Track temperature
Friday July 6, 2007	Cloudy and windy	16-18°c	19-22°c	Cloudy, light rain	17°c	20-21°c
Saturday July 7, 2007	Scattered clouds	18-19°c	23-27°c	Scattered clouds	21°c	31-32°c

All the time trials

N° Driver	Nat.	N° Chassis- Engine [Nbr. GP]	Pos. Free 1 Friday 10:00-11:30	Laps Tr.	Pos. Free 2 Friday 14:00-15:30	Laps Tr.	Pos. Free 3 Saturday 10:00-11:00	Laps Tr.	Pos. Q1 Saturday 13:00-13:15	Laps Tr.	Pos. Q2 Saturday 13:22-13:37	Laps Tr.	Pos. Q3 Saturday 13:45-14:00	Nb. Tr.
1. Fernando Alonso	E	McLaren MP4-22 06 - Mercedes [1]	4. 1:21.675	21	6. 1:21.616	35	2. 1:19.920	12	1. 1:19.330	3	1. 1:19.152	3	3. **1:20.147**	12
2. Lewis Hamilton	GB	McLaren MP4-22 04 - Mercedes [1]	1. 1:21.100	24	4. 1:21.381	39	4. 1:20.344	12	4. 1:19.885	4	3. 1:19.400	3	1. **1:19.997**	12
3. Giancarlo Fisichella	I	Renault R27-02 & 05 [1]	14. 1:23.179	21	12. 1:22.257	39	11. 1:20.983	19	12. 1:20.842	7	6. 1:20.042	6	8. **1:20.775**	11
4. Heikki Kovalainen	FIN	Renault R27-03 [2]	13. 1:23.099	25	11. 1:22.189	42	8. 1:20.882	17	8. 1:20.570	7	8. 1:20.077	6	7. **1:20.721**	11
5. Felipe Massa	BR	Ferrari F2007 260 [1]	3. 1:21.285	26	2. 1:21.138	30	3. 1:19.969	17	3. 1:19.790	3	4. 1:19.421	3	4. **1:20.265**	12
6. Kimi Räikkönen	FIN	Ferrari F2007 262 [1]	2. 1:21.211	26	1. 1:20.639	35	1. 1:19.751	17	2. 1:19.753	4	2. 1:19.252	3	2. **1:20.099**	11
7. Jenson Button	GB	Honda RA107-05 [2]	15. 1:23.517	17			19. 1:21.583	24	18. **1:21.335**	6				
8. Rubens Barrichello	BR	Honda RA107-04 [2]	10. 1:22.956	27	17. 1:22.511	39	14. 1:21.140	22	16. 1:21.169	6	14. **1:20.364**	6		
9. Nick Heidfeld	D	BMW Sauber F1.07-05 [1]	7. 1:22.176	13	15. 1:22.486	34	9. 1:20.882	19	7. 1:20.534	3	10. 1:20.178	3	9. **1:20.894**	11
10. Robert Kubica	PL	BMW Sauber F1.07-03 & 07 [1]	6. 1:22.107	25	13. 1:22.372	41	16. 1:21.156	17	5. 1:20.294	8	7. 1:20.054	3	5. **1:20.401**	11
11. Ralf Schumacher	D	Toyota TF107/05 [1]	9. 1:22.878	21	3. 1:21.381	34	6. 1:20.770	21	6. 1:20.513	6	5. 1:19.860	6	6. **1:20.516**	11
12. Jarno Trulli	I	Toyota TF107/06 [1]	11. 1:23.030	26	5. 1:21.467	35	17. 1:21.321	18	13. 1:21.150	7	9. 1:20.133	6	10. **1:21.240**	11
14. David Coulthard	GB	Red Bull RB3 3 - Renault [2]	18. 1:23.618	15	14. 1:22.428	23	18. 1:21.343	16	14. 1:21.154	7	12. **1:20.329**	7		
15. Mark Webber	AUS	Red Bull RB3 4 - Renault [1]	17. 1:23.564	21	9. 1:22.137	31	12. 1:21.002	16	9. 1:20.583	6	11. **1:20.235**	6		
16. Nico Rosberg	D	Williams FW29-05 - Toyota [2]	5. 1:22.006	24	7. 1:21.619	40	5. 1:20.666	17	17. **1:21.219**	6				
17. Alexander Wurz	AUT	Williams FW29-03 - Toyota [1]	8. 1:22.216	23	8. 1:21.650	37	15. 1:21.148	17	10. 1:20.830	9	13. **1:20.350**	6		
18. Vitantonio Liuzzi	I	Toro Rosso STR2-03 - Ferrari [2]	21. 1:24.154	23	20. 1:23.105	35	7. 1:20.876	21	15. 1:21.160	7	16. **1:20.823**	8		
19. Scott Speed	USA	Toro Rosso STR2-04 - Ferrari [1]	19. 1:23.854	20	19. 1:22.840	42	13. 1:21.039	19	11. 1:20.834	6	15. **1:20.515**	6		
20. Adrian Sutil	D	Spyker F8-VII/03 - Ferrari [2]	20. 1:23.954	25	22. 1:23.720	30	22. 1:22.180	24	20. **1:22.019**	8				
21. Christijan Albers	NL	Spyker F8-VII/04 - Ferrari [1]	22. 1:24.172	30	21. 1:23.113	35	21. 1:22.101	23	22. **1:22.589**	6				
22. Takuma Sato	J	Super Aguri SA07-04 - Honda [2]	16. 1:23.548	18	16. 1:22.487	38	20. 1:21.745	23	21. **1:22.045**	6				
23. Anthony Davidson	GB	Super Aguri SA07-03 & 02 - Honda [1]	12. 1:23.037	24	10. 1:22.143	40	10. 1:20.915	23	19. **1:21.448**	5				
34. Christian Klien	AUT	Honda RA107-04			18. 1:22.833	45								

Fastest lap overall
F. Alonso 1:19.152 (233,823 km/h)

Maximum speed

N° Driver	S1 Qualifs	Pos.	S1 Race	Pos.	S2 Qualifs	Pos.	S2 Race	Pos.	Finish Qualifs	Pos.	Finish Race	Pos.	Radar Qualifs	Pos.	Radar Race	Pos.
1. F. Alonso	300,2	1	302,2	4	269,3	10	268,4	3	289,8	3	289,2	3	298,4	1	299,8	1
2. L. Hamilton	295,9	9	297,6	14	274,1	1	271,0	1	289,6	4	287,1	8	296,4	7	298,2	4
3. G. Fisichella	297,6	4	300,7	6	271,9	3	267,7	5	288,9	7	287,6	5	296,0	10	297,1	6
4. H. Kovalainen	299,3	2	299,6	8	263,1	17	253,6	22	289,0	6	287,3	7	297,4	4	296,0	8
5. F. Massa	297,2	5	304,2	1	269,5	9	267,8	4	289,0	5	291,4	1	297,1	5	299,3	2
6. K. Räikkönen	298,5	3	304,2	2	266,9	12	264,0	8	290,9	1	290,6	2	298,0	2	298,5	3
7. J. Button	292,8	19	293,7	20	255,6	22	258,0	18	285,4	19	282,7	20	294,4	13	293,0	14
8. R. Barrichello	294,3	15	296,4	15	263,4	16	254,5	21	286,6	13	283,2	19	293,6	15	290,9	20
9. N. Heidfeld	292,8	20	294,7	18	270,2	5	267,3	6	287,3	12	284,5	12	296,1	9	293,8	13
10. R. Kubica	295,8	10	295,7	17	269,5	8	263,4	9	286,5	14	284,3	14	296,9	6	293,8	12
11. R. Schumacher	293,3	17	293,2	21	267,1	11	265,8	7	284,6	20	284,8	11	290,7	20	291,9	18
12. J. Trulli	292,9	18	294,0	19	269,6	7	261,4	13	285,8	16	283,7	17	293,0	17	291,9	19
14. D. Coulthard	295,1	13	298,5	11	263,9	15	262,7	12	288,1	8	285,7	10	295,5	12	295,8	9
15. M. Webber	296,7	6	298,0	12	269,8	6	258,2	17	289,9	2	283,8	16	295,6	11	292,8	15
16. N. Rosberg	294,3	14	303,2	3	265,1	13	262,7	11	285,8	17	288,2	4	291,8	19	296,4	7
17. A. Wurz	295,3	11	300,7	5	272,6	2	270,2	2	287,5	9	287,6	6	296,2	8	297,4	5
18. V. Liuzzi	296,7	8	299,0	10	270,5	4	262,7	10	287,4	11	286,8	9	297,6	3	294,0	11
19. S. Speed	296,7	7	299,0	9	264,6	14	261,3	14	287,5	10	283,9	15	294,1	14	294,0	10
20. A. Sutil	289,3	22	288,0	22	258,9	20	255,9	20	280,3	22	275,7	22	288,5	21	285,1	22
21. C. Albers	289,6	21	295,7	16	255,8	21	256,8	19	281,1	21	279,6	21	287,8	22	288,4	21
22. T. Sato	293,7	16	298,0	13	259,7	19	260,4	15	285,4	18	284,4	13	293,6	16	292,4	16
23. A. Davidson	295,1	12	299,9	7	261,6	18	259,8	16	286,3	15	283,3	18	292,1	18	292,3	17

Best sector times

	S1		S2		S3		
Qualifs	**S1** F. Alonso	25.298	**S2** K. Räikkönen	33.890	**S3** F. Alonso	19.697	= 1:18.885
Race	**S1** K. Räikkönen	25.514	**S2** K. Räikkönen	34.471	**S3** K. Räikkönen	20.398	= 1:20.383

RACE

Date	Weather	Air temperature	Track temperature	Humidity	Wind speed
Sunday July 8, 2007 (13:00)	Sunny, scattered clouds	21-23°c	37-45°c	40%	0.9 m/s

Classification & retirements

Pos.	Driver	Constructor	Tyres	Laps	Time	Km/h	
1.	K. Räikkönen	Ferrari	MMH	59	1:21:43.074	222,629	
2.	F. Alonso	McLaren Mercedes	HMH	59	+ 2.459	222,518	
3.	L. Hamilton	McLaren Mercedes	HHM	59	+ 39.373	220,856	
4.	R. Kubica	BMW	HHM	59	+ 53.319	220,234	
5.	F. Massa	Ferrari	MMH	59	+ 54.063	220,201	
6.	N. Heidfeld	BMW	HHM	59	+ 56.336	220,100	
7.	H. Kovalainen	Renault	HHM	58	1 lap	218,652	
8.	G. Fisichella	Renault	HHM	58	1 lap	218,441	
9.	R. Barrichello	Honda	MH	58	1 lap	217,158	
10.	J. Button	Honda	MH	58	1 lap	216,874	
11.	D. Coulthard	Red Bull Renault	HHM	58	1 lap	216,846	
12.	N. Rosberg	Williams Toyota	MMH	58	1 lap	216,790	
13.	A. Wurz	Williams Toyota	MMH	58	1 lap	216,576	
14.	T. Sato	Super Aguri Honda	HMM	57	2 laps	214,440	
15.	C. Albers	Spyker Ferrari	HMM	57	2 laps	213,637	
16.	V. Liuzzi	STR Ferrari	HHM	53	6 laps	215,316	Gearbox failure

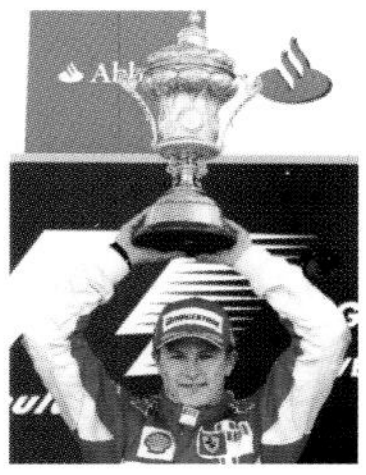

Driver	Constructor	Tyres	Laps	Reason
J. Trulli	Toyota	HHM	43	Handling, called back by his team
A. Davidson	Super Aguri Honda	HM	35	Floor hitting the track, called back by his team
S. Speed	STR Ferrari	HH	29	Collision with Wurz, front left suspension broken
R. Schumacher	Toyota	HM	22	Wheel fixation problem at the front left
A. Sutil	Spyker Ferrari	H	16	Engine failure
M. Webber	Red Bull Renault	H	8	Differential failure which caused the hydraulic system to fail

Tyres H: Hard & M: Medium

Fastest laps

	Driver	Time	Lap	Km/h
1.	K. Räikkönen	1:20.638	17	229,514
2.	F. Massa	1:20.858	17	228,890
3.	F. Alonso	1:21.117	35	228,159
4.	L. Hamilton	1:21.675	11	226,600
5.	N. Heidfeld	1:21.991	17	225,727
6.	R. Kubica	1:22.105	14	225,413
7.	G. Fisichella	1:22.136	13	225,328
8.	R. Schumacher	1:22.510	12	224,307
9.	H. Kovalainen	1:22.552	11	224,193
10.	A. Wurz	1:22.693	57	223,810
11.	N. Rosberg	1:22.896	49	223,262
12.	D. Coulthard	1:23.118	40	222,666
13.	R. Barrichello	1:23.387	28	221,948
14.	T. Sato	1:23.413	42	221,879
15.	S. Speed	1:23.570	19	221,462
16.	J. Button	1:23.581	29	221,433
17.	V. Liuzzi	1:23.628	46	221,308
18.	J. Trulli	1:23.708	17	221,097
19.	M. Webber	1:23.767	6	220,941
20.	A. Davidson	1:24.144	26	219,951
21.	C. Albers	1:24.390	56	219,310
22.	A. Sutil	1:25.015	16	217,698

Pit stops

	Driver	Lap	Duration	Stop	Total
1.	H. Kovalainen	15	28.384	1	28.384
2.	N. Rosberg	15	27.098	1	27.098
3.	L. Hamilton	16	26.170	1	26.170
4.	R. Kubica	16	26.036	1	26.036
5.	G. Fisichella	16	27.030	1	27.030
6.	R. Schumacher	16	26.541	1	26.541
7.	K. Räikkönen	18	26.975	1	26.975
8.	J. Trulli	18	25.951	1	25.951
9.	N. Heidfeld	19	25.752	1	25.752
10.	F. Alonso	20	24.065	1	24.065
11.	F. Massa	20	27.006	1	27.006
12.	C. Albers	23	25.962	1	25.962
13.	V. Liuzzi	24	26.680	1	26.680
14.	S. Speed	25	26.096	1	26.096
15.	D. Coulthard	26	25.702	1	25.702
16.	A. Wurz	26	24.992	1	24.992
17.	T. Sato	28	25.575	1	25.575
18.	A. Davidson	30	9:04.703	1	9:04.703
19.	R. Barrichello	31	28.200	1	28.200
20.	J. Button	33	27.371	1	27.371
21.	J. Trulli	33	26.095	2	52.046
22.	G. Fisichella	35	26.064	2	53.094
23.	F. Alonso	37	25.923	2	49.988
24.	H. Kovalainen	37	25.738	2	54.122
25.	L. Hamilton	38	25.557	2	51.727
26.	N. Rosberg	38	24.829	2	51.927
27.	R. Kubica	40	24.919	2	50.955
28.	C. Albers	39	26.705	2	52.667
29.	N. Heidfeld	42	25.230	2	50.982
30.	K. Räikkönen	43	24.181	2	51.156
31.	A. Wurz	42	24.705	2	49.697
32.	F. Massa	45	24.454	2	51.460
33.	V. Liuzzi	44	24.458	2	51.138
34.	D. Coulthard	45	25.178	2	50.880
35.	T. Sato	45	25.258	2	50.833

Race leader

Driver	Laps in the lead	Nbr of laps
L. Hamilton	1 > 15	15
K. Räikkönen	16 > 17	2
F. Alonso	18 > 37	20
K. Räikkönen	38 > 59	22

Driver	Nbr of laps	Kilometers
K. Räikkönen	24	123,384 km
F. Alonso	20	102,820 km
L. Hamilton	15	77,010 km

Gaps on the lead board

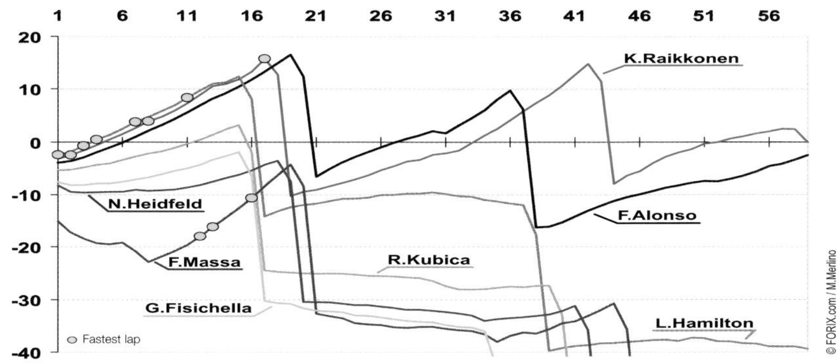
1 6 11 16 21 26 31 36 41 46 51 56
20
10
0
-10
-20
-30
-40
K.Raikkonen
N.Heidfeld
F.Alonso
F.Massa
R.Kubica
G.Fisichella
L.Hamilton
Fastest lap
© FORIX.com / M.Merlino

Lap chart

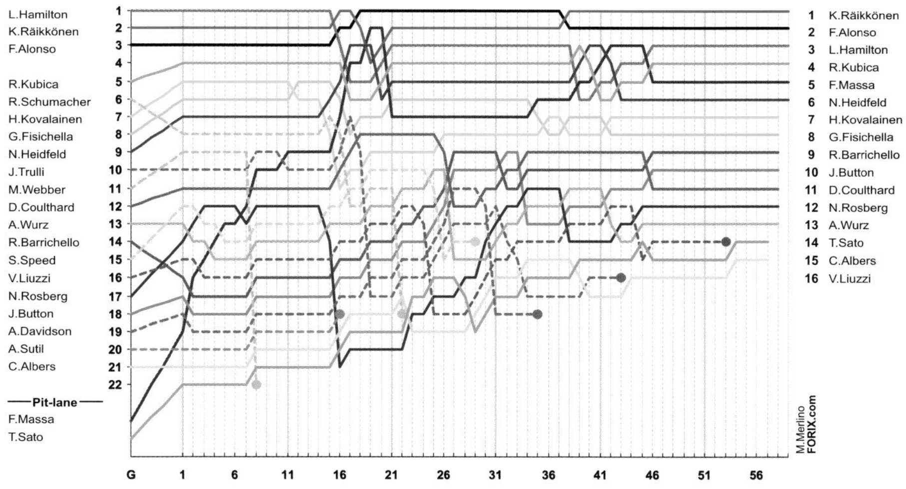
L.Hamilton
K.Räikkönen
F.Alonso
R.Kubica
R.Schumacher
H.Kovalainen
G.Fisichella
N.Heidfeld
J.Trulli
M.Webber
D.Coulthard
A.Wurz
R.Barrichello
S.Speed
V.Liuzzi
N.Rosberg
J.Button
A.Davidson
A.Sutil
C.Albers
Pit-lane
F.Massa
T.Sato
1 K.Räikkönen
2 F.Alonso
3 L.Hamilton
4 R.Kubica
5 F.Massa
6 N.Heidfeld
7 H.Kovalainen
8 G.Fisichella
9 R.Barrichello
10 J.Button
11 D.Coulthard
12 N.Rosberg
13 A.Wurz
14 T.Sato
15 C.Albers
16 V.Liuzzi
G 1 6 11 16 21 26 31 36 41 46 51 56
M.Merlino FORIX.com

CHAMPIONSHIPS 9/17

Drivers

	Driver	Team	Wins	Points
1.	L. Hamilton	McLaren Mercedes	2🏆	70
2.	F. Alonso	McLaren Mercedes	2🏆	58
3.	K. Räikkönen	Ferrari	3🏆	52
4.	F. Massa	Ferrari	2🏆	51
5.	N. Heidfeld	BMW		33
6.	R. Kubica	BMW		22
7.	G. Fisichella	Renault		17
8.	H. Kovalainen	Renault		14
9.	A. Wurz	Williams Toyota		8
10.	J. Trulli	Toyota		7
11.	N. Rosberg	Williams Toyota		5
12.	D. Coulthard	Red Bull Renault		4
13.	T. Sato	Super Aguri Honda		4
14.	M. Webber	Red Bull Renault		2
15.	R. Schumacher	Toyota		2
16.	J. Button	Honda		1
17.	S. Vettel	BMW		1
18.	R. Barrichello	Honda		0
19.	S. Speed	STR Ferrari		0
20.	A. Davidson	Super Aguri Honda		0
21.	A. Sutil	Spyker Ferrari		0
22.	C. Albers	Spyker Ferrari		0
23.	V. Liuzzi	STR Ferrari		0

Constructors

	Constructor	Wins	Points
1.	Vodafone McLaren Mercedes	4🏆	128
2.	Scuderia Ferrari Marlboro	5🏆	103
3.	BMW Sauber F1 Team		56
4.	ING Renault F1 Team		31
5.	AT&T Williams		13
6.	Panasonic Toyota Racing		9
7.	Red Bull Racing		6
8.	Super Aguri F1 Team		4
9.	Honda Racing F1 Team		1
10.	Scuderia Toro Rosso		0
11.	Etihad Aldar Spyker F1 Team		0

S1 400m before corner
S2 100m before corner
Radar 100m before corner

THE CIRCUIT

Name Silverstone Circuit; Silverstone
Lenght 5141 m
Distance 60 tours expected, 308,355 km
59 tours raced, 303,214 km
Latitude 52°04'43.70"N
Longitude 1°00'55.60"O

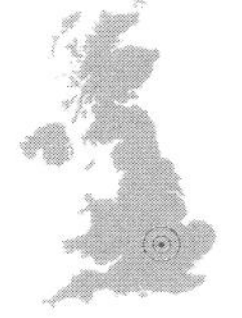

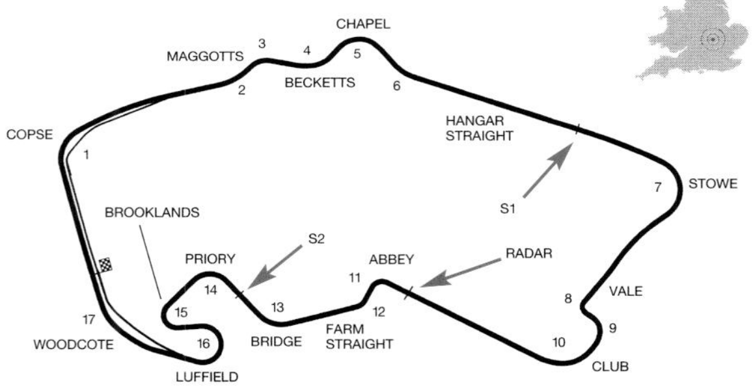
CHAPEL
MAGGOTTS
BECKETTS
COPSE
HANGAR STRAIGHT
STOWE
BROOKLANDS
S1
S2
PRIORY
ABBEY
RADAR
VALE
WOODCOTE
LUFFIELD
BRIDGE
FARM STRAIGHT
CLUB
1 2 3 4 5 6 7 8 9 10 11 12 13 14 15 16 17

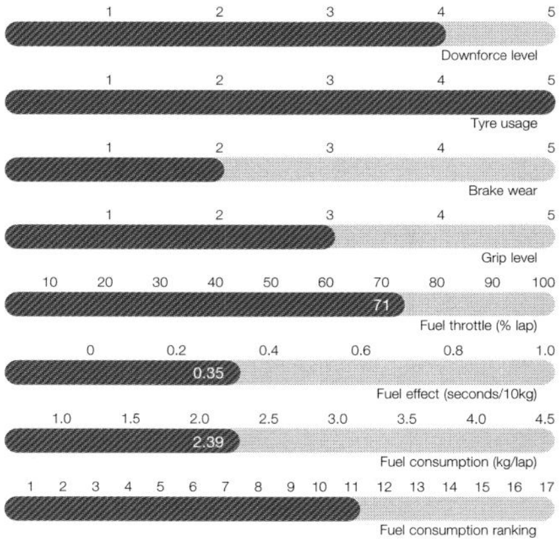
Downforce level
Tyre usage
Brake wear
Grip level
71
Fuel throttle (% lap)
0.35
Fuel effect (seconds/10kg)
2.39
Fuel consumption (kg/lap)
Fuel consumption ranking

All results: © 2007 Formula One Administration Ltd, 6 Princes Gate, London, SW7 1QJ, England

A CRAZY RACE

A massive storm broke over the Nurburgring circuit shortly after the start. In just a few seconds, six cars slid off the road - including four at the very first corner. The race was stopped until conditions improved, before yet another rainstorm at the end of the Grand Prix allowed Fernando Alonso to win from Felipe Massa. McLaren's World Champion needed every ounce of his skill to seal the victory despite the appalling conditions.
For Alonso, this race was crucial from a championship point of view as neither Lewis Hamilton nor Fernando Alonso managed to score any points. Both of them fell foul of the now infamous gravel trap at the first corner.

> Lewis Hamilton remained fully conscious during his accident, but he was taken to Koblenz hospital on a stretcher to be on the safe side.

A fright at the Nurburgring

Lewis Hamilton was the victim of an extremely nasty surprise during qualifying at the Nurburgring. Having made a pit stop to bolt some new tyres onto his McLaren MP4-22, Hamilton found himself behind the Ferrari of Felipe Massa on the circuit. The young Englishman decided to slow down in order to allow Massa to pull ahead and find some clear space for his own hot lap.

So far, so good - but then it went horribly wrong. During his flying lap, his front-right tyre seemingly exploded in the middle of turn eight: a long left-hander taken at about 260kph. The Briton tried to keep his car under control but it was an impossible task: the McLaren slammed into the tyre wall at more or less unabated speed.

It was a big impact, burying the car halfway into the tyre wall. A minute later, Hamilton climbed out of the car unaided before lying down on the gravel, completely winded, to try and get his breath back.

He was taken to the circuit medical centre by ambulance, before being airlifted to the Bundeswehr hospital in Koblenz for a brain scan. Less than three hours after the accident, Lewis Hamilton was back at the circuit as if nothing had happened. Luckily for him, there was no bruising and no pain: yet more living testimony to the admirable strength of modern Formula 1 cars. Ron Dennis, McLaren's team boss, confirmed: "*Lewis has no injuries, and he is very hopeful of taking part in the European Grand Prix.*" At the same time on Saturday afternoon, Hamilton himself was taking part in several technical debriefs with his engineers. There was no doubt that he meant business.

McLaren had several theories as to the cause of the accident. "*Our telemetry shows that the front-right tyre deflated more or less instantly,*" said Ron Dennis. "*It seems that the nuts holding the wheel onto the car were not properly secured, undoubtedly because of a problem with one of our airguns.*"

A winning team! Adrian Sutil (left) and his Spyker team mate for the weekend, Markus Winkelhock. Markus is the nephew of the sadly missed Manfred Winkelhock, who contested 47 Grands Prix between 1982 and 1985.
∨

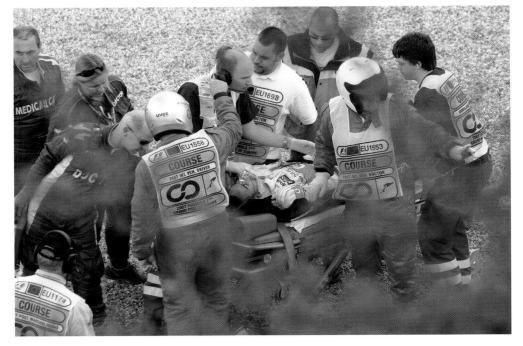

The play in the front-right wheel would have caused the tyre to puncture at turn eight, where the car is running with maximum downforce. Lewis still needed approval from the FIA medical delegate on Sunday morning before being allowed to race, but this turned into a mere formality.

He would start from an unaccustomed 10th place on the grid, because he had not been able to take part in the third phase of qualifying. This meant that he had a mountain to climb before the race even started. As it turned out, he would be playing catch-up from much further behind.

Kimi takes advantage of Fernando's mistake.

Kimi Raikkonen is not by nature a particularly outgoing person. Whether he wins or loses, his demeanour is largely unchanged. Only the words change.

On Saturday, after he claimed his first pole position since Australia, the Finn's joy - if it was there - remained characteristically well hidden. "*Things are going better than they were a few weeks ago,*" said the Finn. "*But this is still only pole position. It doesn't make a huge amount of difference as you can still win the race starting from the back. I'm still not certain that we've got the upper hand over McLaren.*"

His rationale was understandable. Fernando Alonso had qualified alongside him, dropping just three-tenths of a second to the flying Finn despite making a costly mistake. "*I had a big moment,*" said the reigning World Champion. "*The back of the car got away from me at turn five. I touched the grass and for 50 or 60 metres I was a passenger. Luckily, the car then got back onto the track in time for turn seven. It was really just a happy coincidence. At the time I was sure that I had lost a lot of time, so I*

tried to carry on just to be sure of fifth or six place on the grid. I was very surprised when I found out that I was second. It seems that I only lost a few tenths after all..." Without which, the Spaniard could have claimed pole position.

Even though he had won the last two Grands Prix, Kimi Raikkonen did not start as a particular favourite. It's fair to say though that he was helped by Lewis Hamilton's lowly grid position, diminishing the Englishman's chances of another victory.

"*This is not really the way I would like to take points away from Lewis,*" said a philosophical Raikkonen. "*But at the end of the day, what has happened to him is just part of racing. Accidents can happen sometimes, and sometimes it's your fault and sometimes it's the fault of something else. It's how the sport goes. Something similar could just as easily happen to me.*"

The truth was though that Lewis Hamilton would struggle to maintain his incredible run of podiums, with nine top three places in as many Grands Prix. So far...

> Kimi Raikkonen found himself on pole position for the first time since the Australian Grand Prix.

STARTING GRID

* M. WINKELHOCK starts from the pit lane.

| A. SUTIL 21 1:34.500 | V. LIUZZI 19 1:33.148 | J. BUTTON 17 1:32.983 | A. DAVIDSON 15 1:32.451 | G. FISICHELLA 13 1:32.010 | N. ROSBERG 11 1:31.978 | R. SCHUMACHER 9 1:32.570 | H. KOVALAINEN 7 1:32.478 | R. KUBICA 5 1:32.123 | F. MASSA 3 1:31.778 | K. RÄIKKÖNEN 1 1:31.450 (202.655 km/h) |

| M. WINKELHOCK 22 1:35.940 | D. COULTHARD 20 1:33.151 | S. SPEED 18 1:33.038 | T. SATO 16 1:32.838 | R. BARRICHELLO 14 1:32.221 | A. WURZ 12 1:31.996 | L. HAMILTON 10 1:33.833 | J. TRULLI 8 1:32.501 | M. WEBBER 6 1:32.476 | N. HEIDFELD 4 1:31.840 | F. ALONSO 2 1:31.741 |

Alonso, like a duck to water.

To win at the Nurburgring, it was first necessary to survive the carnage of the opening three laps. Then it was necessary to hang onto this German terror ride all the way to the finish, while remembering to overtake Felipe Massa during the second downpour - who at one point had quite a comfortable lead.

Fernando Alonso managed to calmly overcome all these obstacles to win his third Grand Prix of the season. It was a crucial victory that allowed him to close to within just two tiny points of Lewis Hamilton in the World Championship. In the tricky conditions of the Nurburgring, Alonso's talent and experience shone through ¬- giving the Spaniard a much-needed advantage over his young British teammate. These are just some of the problems he had to deal with during the course of a chaotic weekend:

1. The storm
The first drops of heavy rain began to fall on the Nurburgring just as the start was taking place. The first person to react was the young Markus Winkelhock (or rather Colin Kolles, the Spyker team boss, who called his driver back into the pits). At the end of the warm-up lap the German switched onto full wet tyres, while the rest of the field struggled with their intermediates. One by one they all had to pit for wets - and Winkelhock moved up the field to take the lead on lap two of his very first Grand Prix! After the race was stopped, he found himself in pole position for the re-start. But in the dry, he was quickly overhauled by quicker rivals before retiring on lap 14.

2. Excuses, excuses
Felipe Massa was in the race lead for most of it: 20 laps from the end he had more than a seven-second cushion over Fernando Alonso. But when the rain began to fall for the second time, the Brazilian lost ground on his new set of rain tyres. He explained: *"I'm not exactly sure what happened, but the tyres that I had at the end of the race were vibrating very strongly and I could not hold Fernando off."* Nonetheless, the Ferrari driver defended robustly - to the point that the two cars fighting for the lead actually touched twice. This time though, it was the Spanish World Champion who triumphed.

3. The end of a series
For Lewis Hamilton, the European Grand Prix is where his remarkable run of nine consecutive podiums came to an

end. The Englishman finished the 10th Grand Prix of his career in ninth place: out of the points after a chaotic afternoon. He went off into the gravel trap on lap three but managed to keep his engine running while a crane arrived to put him back on the circuit. He got going again, but was now a lap down on the leaders. This meant that he would re-start from 17th and last place on the grid. On lap six, he stopped to switch to dry tyres but it was a big mistake: the track was still too wet and he ended up going off again.

4. Bad luck strikes again
The Nurburgring circuit has never been kind to Kimi Raikkonen. It was here that the Finn once had to retire two laps from a certain victory, when his front wheel broke. This year, he was able to match Fernando Alonso's pace and even set competitive lap times in the rain - but then he was forced to retire on lap 35. *"I was sure I could win,"* said the disappointed Ferrari driver. His car's hydraulic system thought otherwise. *"I had a hydraulic problem that was getting worse and worse so I was forced to retire,"* explained Raikkonen. So that was that.

5. The surprise
The several twists and turns of the race allowed Mark Webber to score his first podium for Red Bull. *"It's a big relief, but you have to judge each situation on its individual merits,"* said the Australian. *"Nobody wants*

excuses; we just have to take the results as they are. You can't say that it's down to this or that. Today, we weren't really quick enough to be on the podium - but we've managed it as we were in the right place at the right time."

6. The obstacle
On lap 47 Giancarlo Fisichella's Renault lost a wheel covering, which somehow found its way onto the racing line in the middle of the straight. Felipe Massa only just managed to avoid it...

Fernando Alonso: *"I loved that race!"*

Fernando Alonso was even happier than usual on the podium (as the photo opposite attests), as if this were somehow a special victory. *"No: I wouldn't say that it was special, but it was certainly important,"* he said. *"It means that I'm back in the championship fight, and of course it has been very tough in the conditions. The first three laps were unbelievable: it was just about impossible to drive. Afterwards, on the dry, the Ferrari was a little bit quicker than us. But I thought it was a great race: I love it when the conditions are changeable."*

In terms of set-up, the McLaren was poorly prepared for wet conditions. *"We weren't expecting rain,"* added Alonso. *"But of course every car is different in different conditions. There*

are so many parameters - such as chassis, suspension and engine - that affect the overall feeling. All these details seemed to have worked in our favour during the rain: our car is naturally well suited to these conditions. Having said that, it wasn't at all easy to get past Felipe. Only the racing line was dry, and we touched twice. At the time I was angry, and I had a few words to say to him when we got out of the car."

In fact, he accused Massa of having blocked him deliberately and the two men traded insults while they were weighed before going onto the podium. Later on, Alonso had mellowed considerably. *"I'm sorry for what I said, because at the end of the day these things are all just racing incidents - they happen."*

The Spaniard had closed to within two points of Lewis Hamilton's series lead, but he confirmed that he would not be changing his approach to the races. *"The championship is still very long: there are seven Grands Prix still to go. Anything can happen, and every race is unpredictable. The Ferraris were very quick here, but Kimi Raikkonen is heading home empty-handed. I wouldn't bet money on any of the drivers because every single race this year has been entirely unpredictable. I'm just going to concentrate on doing my best at every race."*

HIGH-SPEED OFF

On Saturday afternoon, Lewis Hamilton went off the road in the middle of the qualifying session and hit the tyre wall at more than 200kph. Hamilton was uninjured, but he was taken to hospital for a precautionary check-up.

Spygate: the FIA lets off McLaren

> It's important to know how to be in the right place at the right time: Mark Webber profited from the chaos of this fragmented Grand Prix to score a podium finish. *"I stayed out on intermediate rain tyres for a long time, which put me ahead of most of my rivals,"* explained Webber. *"It's fair to say that I wasn't too upset when Kimi was forced to retire as well."*

"I've never slept as little as I have over these past three days." When he uttered those memorable words at Silverstone, Ron Dennis was not to know that the worst was still to come.

The basic problem revolved around a 780-page report that somehow landed on the desk of McLaren designer Mike Coughlan. Afterwards a new element came to light: at the beginning of March Nigel Stepney had also sent an e-mail to Mike Coughlan detailing how the Ferrari F2007's new flat floor worked.

That is how McLaren were able to appeal the Ferrari floor at the first race of the season in Australia, causing the FIA to clarify the regulations with immediate effect. Consequently, Ferrari had to change their car hurriedly before the Malaysian Grand Prix - with disastrous consequences. Not only that, but the clarification seriously hindered the competitiveness of the Ferrari for several weeks.

Having seen Stepney's e-mail, the FIA summoned McLaren to appear in front of the World Council on the Thursday following the European Grand Prix. The team was now in serious danger of seeing all their hard-earned points from the season taken away.

But when he emerged from the FIA's headquarters at the Place de la Concorde in Paris on 26 July 2007, Ron Dennis felt nothing but big relief. *"These have been the most difficult 24 days of my career,"* he commented. After several hours of deliberation, the FIA judges concluded that McLaren had indeed been in possession of confidential documents belonging to Ferrari, which violated article 151c of the sporting code. This article outlaws: `all fraudulent activities or acts prejudicial to the general interest of motor sport.'

Nonetheless, the judges decided not to apply any penalties to the guilty parties because "there was not sufficient proof to demonstrate that this information had been used in a way to manipulate the Formula 1 World Championship."

The FIA reserved the right to summon McLaren back before the World Council should any new evidence emerge in the future to suggest that the team had used the information fraudulently. If found guilty, McLaren were warned that they could face exclusion not just from the 2007 World Championship but also from the 2008 series.

While Ron Dennis was more than satisfied with the outcome of the 26 July meeting, saying that he just wanted now to concentrate on *"a championship that is down to us to win,"* Ferrari were bitterly disappointed. The team statement said: *"Ferrari notes that McLaren has been found guilty by the FIA. Consequently, it is incomprehensible that a fundamental breach of the principles of sport has not therefore been punished. This decision is damaging to the sport."*

The Italian team added that it would continue to pursue its civil actions in Italy and England against Nigel Stepney and Mike Coughlan respectively. Ironically their biggest help would eventually come from Fernando Alonso himself, who would become the unexpected catalyst for another meeting of the FIA's appeal tribunal...

> Alexander Wurz brought his Williams-Toyota home in a magnificent fourth place. *"It was very difficult, and the hardest part was just to keep a cool head and know when it was safe to push,"* said the Austrian. *"Under these sorts of circumstances, it's very easy to get carried away by an excess of enthusiasm and make a mistake."* Wurz finished just two-tenths of a second off Mark Webber and a podium place. He concluded: *"Sure, it's frustrating to finish so close to the podium, but under the circumstances I am very happy with today…"*

SNAPSHOTS OF THE WEEKEND

> Scott Speed was also one of the first corner victims, aquaplaning straight on into the gravel trap when the storm was at its worst. When the American got back to the pits, Toro Rosso team manager Franz Tost asked him why he had gone off. This led to a full and frank exchange of views after Speed asked Tost why the team had been so slow to change to wet tyres. The situation then degenerated into a somewhat undignified fistfight. Speed was fired with immediate effect, to make way for Sebastian Vettel from the Hungarian Grand Prix onwards. >

+ Felipe Massa wore a black stripe on the back of his helmet throughout the weekend. *"It's a symbol of mourning after the recent aeroplane crash at São Paulo,"* he explained. *"It's a very difficult time for my country."*

+ On Thursday night, the French Motor Sport Federation (FFSA) published an incomprehensible press release that basically said that they had decided not decide anything about the French GP next year. The Federation was waiting for assurances that its financial losses (the 2007 French Grand Prix resulted in a deficit of several million Euros) would be covered by the local government, which benefits from the economic impact of a Grand Prix.

+ Indianapolis Motor Speedway announced that it had not reached an agreement with Bernie Ecclestone to host a Grand Prix in 2008. The problem was a financial one: Indianapolis could not afford to run the Grand Prix with its own funds and asked Ecclestone for a reduced tariff. Formula 1's ringmaster refused point blank, arguing that many other circuits managed to host a Grand Prix successfully, despite the sums of money involved.

+ The loss of the United States Grand Prix was bad news for F1's big constructors such as Mercedes, Honda, BMW and Toyota. The previous week, Honda team principal Nick Fry had said that it was «crucial» for the Japanese marque to have one, two or even three Grands Prix in America. *"We're very disappointed that there will be no United States Grand Prix,"* he said. *"We'll do everything in our power to get it back for 2009. The United States is a very important market for Honda."*

At the same time, Honda announced that it had extended the contracts of Jenson Button and Rubens Barrichello for another year.

+ «Bild» is Germany's best-known paper - with a print run of three million copies. Most of the content centres around half-naked women, gossip and especially scandal. The sports section follows the same logic. On Saturday, Bild came up with its own formula to predict that Lewis Hamilton had an 80.7% chance of becoming World Champion in 2007. The formula was loosely based on the history of F1 and the number of points already gained by the Englishman.

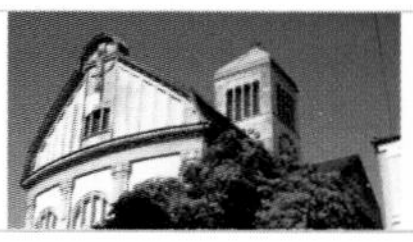

PRACTICE

Date	Weather (AM)	Air temperature	Track temperature	Weather (PM)	Air temperature	Track temperature
Friday July 20, 2007	Cloudy	19-21°c	23-25°c	Sunny, some clouds	20-21°c	23-26°c
Saturday July 21, 2007	Sunny	19-21°c	27-31°c	Cloudy	22-21°c	37-32°c

All the time trials

N° Driver	Nat.	N° Chassis- Engine [Nbr. GP]	Pos.	Free 1 Friday 10:00-11:30	Laps Tr.	Pos.	Free 2 Friday 14:00-15:30	Laps Tr.	Pos.	Free 3 Saturday 11:00-12:00	Laps Tr.	Pos.	Q1 Saturday 14:00-14:15	Laps Tr.	Pos.	Q2 Saturday 14:22-14:37	Laps Tr.	Pos.	Q3 Saturday 14:45-15:00	Nb. Tr.
1. Fernando Alonso	E	McLaren MP4-22 06 - Mercedes [2]	3.	1:32.932	27	4.	1:33.637	30	3.	1:32.039	11	1.	1:31.074	3	2.	1:30.983	3	2.	**1:31.741**	10
2. Lewis Hamilton	GB	McLaren MP4-22 01 & 05 - Mercedes [2]	1.	1:32.515	26	2.	1:33.478	28	2.	1:31.627	12	4.	1:31.587	3	3.	1:31.185	3	10.	**1:33.833**	6
3. Giancarlo Fisichella	I	Renault R27-05 [2]	19.	1:35.077	22	15.	1:34.431	28	16.	1:33.214	17	9.	1:32.378	7	13.	**1:32.010**	6			
4. Heikki Kovalainen	FIN	Renault R27-02 & 03 [1]	18.	1:34.921	21	16.	1:34.446	25	18.	1:33.484	13	12.	1:32.594	7	8.	1:31.783	6	7.	**1:32.478**	10
5. Felipe Massa	BR	Ferrari F2007 260 [2]	6.	1:33.605	24	3.	1:33.590	27	5.	1:32.217	18	2.	1:31.447	3	1.	1:30.912	3	3.	**1:31.778**	10
6. Kimi Räikkönen	FIN	Ferrari F2007 262 [2]	2.	1:32.751	24	1.	1:33.339	28	1.	1:31.396	18	3.	1:31.522	3	4.	1:31.237	3	1.	**1:31.450**	10
7. Jenson Button	GB	Honda RA107-04 [1]	8.	1:33.936	28	8.	1:33.880	36	12.	1:32.869	18	17.	**1:32.983**	6						
8. Rubens Barrichello	BR	Honda RA107-05 [1]	10.	1:34.142	25	14.	1:34.411	26	17.	1:33.229	19	14.	1:32.674	6	14.	**1:32.221**	6			
9. Nick Heidfeld	D	BMW Sauber F1.07-05 [2]	4.	1:32.975	35	9.	1:34.146	22	7.	1:32.581	20	5.	1:31.889	5	6.	1:31.652	5	4.	**1:31.840**	10
10. Robert Kubica	PL	BMW Sauber F1.07-03 [2]	5.	1:33.205	34	10.	1:34.221	19	4.	1:32.039	18	6.	1:31.961	4	5.	1:31.444	6	5.	**1:32.123**	10
11. Ralf Schumacher	D	Toyota TF107/05 [2]	7.	1:33.825	32	5.	1:33.668	18	10.	1:32.788	21	11.	1:32.446	6	9.	1:31.843	6	9.	**1:32.570**	10
12. Jarno Trulli	I	Toyota TF107/04 [2]	11.	1:34.152	34	6.	1:33.746	22	13.	1:32.936	20	10.	1:32.381	7	10.	1:31.859	5	8.	**1:32.501**	10
14. David Coulthard	GB	Red Bull RB3 3 - Renault [1]	9.	1:34.062	25	17.	1:34.504	19	9.	1:32.679	18	20.	**1:33.151**	6						
15. Mark Webber	AUS	Red Bull RB3 4 - Renault [2]	15.	1:34.683	22	11.	1:34.235	29	8.	1:32.632	16	13.	1:32.629	6	7.	1:31.661	6	6.	**1:32.476**	10
16. Nico Rosberg	D	Williams FW29-05 - Toyota [1]	13.	1:34.563	32	7.	1:33.845	24	6.	1:32.344	16	7.	1:32.117	7	11.	**1:31.978**	6			
17. Alexander Wurz	AUT	Williams FW29-03 - Toyota [2]	12.	1:34.345	32	12.	1:34.264	21	15.	1:33.154	16	8.	1:32.173	6	12.	**1:31.996**	6			
18. Vitantonio Liuzzi	I	Toro Rosso STR2-03 - Ferrari [1]	17.	1:34.907	31	20.	1:35.653	24	11.	1:32.841	20	19.	**1:33.148**	6						
19. Scott Speed	USA	Toro Rosso STR2-04 - Ferrari [2]	20.	1:35.643	15	19.	1:35.320	26	14.	1:32.974	14	18.	**1:33.038**	6						
20. Adrian Sutil	D	Spyker F8-VII/03 - Ferrari [1]	21.	1:36.340	22	21.	1:36.527	25	21.	1:34.423	20	21.	**1:34.500**	9						
21. Markus Winkelhock	D	Spyker F8-VII/04 - Ferrari [2]	22.	1:37.116	30	22.	1:37.319	19	22.	1:36.090	19	22.	**1:35.940**	6						
22. Takuma Sato	J	Super Aguri SA07-04 & 02 - Honda [1]	16.	1:34.708	36	13.	1:34.357	26	20.	1:33.945	19	15.	1:32.678	6	16.	**1:32.838**	5			
23. Anthony Davidson	GB	Super Aguri SA07-03 - Honda [1]	14.	1:34.567	30	18.	1:34.554	26	19.	1:33.792	20	16.	1:32.793	6	15.	**1:32.451**	6			

Fastest lap overall

F. Massa 1:30.912 (203,854 km/h)

Maximum speed

N° Driver	S1 Qualifs	Pos.	S1 Race	Pos.	S2 Qualifs	Pos.	S2 Race	Pos.	Finish Qualifs	Pos.	Finish Race	Pos.	Radar Qualifs	Pos.	Radar Race	Pos.
1. F. Alonso	269,5	2	264,1	7	233,7	1	228,0	2	251,1	1	244,3	6	299,6	2	303,4	1
2. L. Hamilton	268,0	6	266,0	1	229,6	7	225,5	5	250,1	3	244,7	4	298,5	7	303,4	2
3. G. Fisichella	266,1	15	265,1	6	231,3	4	223,0	12	246,4	15	243,2	8	295,5	20	299,0	10
4. H. Kovalainen	267,5	8	265,2	5	230,3	6	226,9	3	247,4	8	245,0	3	298,0	9	299,1	9
5. F. Massa	270,1	1	265,8	2	233,0	3	230,5	1	248,8	5	246,6	1	299,5	3	302,2	4
6. K. Räikkönen	268,1	5	265,4	3	233,2	2	225,4	6	248,6	6	244,5	5	299,6	1	300,1	7
7. J. Button	265,1	17	249,4	17	226,1	20	189,8	18	245,7	16	228,7	17	296,0	16	286,4	17
8. R. Barrichello	267,3	9	258,0	15	227,9	14	223,1	11	246,5	14	240,2	14	297,5	11	298,1	13
9. N. Heidfeld	267,0	11	265,4	4	230,9	5	225,0	7	247,1	11	246,4	2	299,0	5	302,6	3
10. R. Kubica	265,1	18	260,6	11	226,4	19	222,2	13	246,7	13	242,5	9	295,9	17	298,9	12
11. R. Schumacher	265,0	19	258,6	14	227,6	15	221,0	15	244,8	20	241,1	13	296,2	14	299,0	11
12. J. Trulli	265,3	16	260,3	13	226,9	17	223,1	10	245,0	19	240,1	15	295,8	19	297,6	15
14. D. Coulthard	267,2	10	262,5	8	227,1	16	224,5	8	247,1	12	241,4	12	297,4	12	297,9	14
15. M. Webber	266,6	12	261,5	9	229,4	10	225,7	4	247,8	7	242,0	11	296,1	15	300,4	5
16. N. Rosberg	268,7	3	213,1	21	228,1	13	160,7	22	249,4	4	228,2	18	298,6	6	263,2	20
17. A. Wurz	267,9	7	261,3	10	229,4	9	224,0	9	250,5	2	244,1	7	298,0	8	300,2	6
18. V. Liuzzi	266,4	14	237,6	19	229,4	8	172,9	20	245,4	18			297,9	10	243,6	22
19. S. Speed	264,6	20	204,1	22	228,2	12	165,8	21	245,5	17	223,7	20	296,4	13	252,9	21
20. A. Sutil	260,2	21	227,1	20	220,1	20	178,9	19	240,0	21	221,0	21	291,4	21	269,6	19
21. M. Winkelhock	257,5	22	245,3	18	216,9	22	206,7	17	238,4	22	226,8	19	286,8	22	283,0	18
22. T. Sato	268,2	4	257,6	16	228,9	11	217,5	16	247,2	10	238,5	16	299,0	4	296,5	16
23. A. Davidson	266,6	13	260,5	12	226,6	18	221,8	14	247,3	9	242,0	10	295,8	18	299,7	8

Best sector times

Qualifs	**S1** F. Massa	29.736	**S2** F. Alonso	37.761	**S3** M. Webber	22.239	= 1:29.736
Race	**S1** F. Massa	30.703	**S2** F. Massa	38.376	**S3** F. Alonso	23.741	= 1:32.820

RACE

Date	Weather	Air temperature	Track temperature	Humidity	Wind speed
Sunday, July 22, 2007 (14:00)	Rain then sunny then light rain	16-19°c	19-26°c	81-52%	2.3-5.4 m/s

Classification & retirements

Pos.	Driver	Constructor	Tyres (Départ 1 & 2)		Laps	Time	Km/h
1.	F. Alonso	McLaren Mercedes	MW	WMMW	60	2:06:26.358	146,566
2.	F. Massa	Ferrari	MW	WMMW	60	+ 8.155	146,409
3.	M. Webber	Red Bull Renault	MW	WMMW	60	+ 1:05.674	145,308
4.	A. Wurz	Williams Toyota	ME	WMMW	60	+ 1:05.937	145,303
5.	D. Coulthard	Red Bull Renault	MW	WMMW	60	+ 1:13.656	145,157
6.	N. Heidfeld	BMW	MWE	EMMW	60	+ 1:20.298	145,031
7.	R. Kubica	BMW	ME	WMMW	60	+ 1:22.415	144,991
8.	H. Kovalainen	Renault	MW	WMMW	59	1 lap	143,913
9.	L. Hamilton	McLaren Mercedes	MW	WMMW	59	1 lap	143,883
10.	G. Fisichella	Renault	MW	WMMW	59	1 lap	143,869
11.	R. Barrichello	Honda	MWE	WMMW	59	1 lap	143,086
12.	A. Davidson	Super Aguri Honda	MWE	EWMME	59	1 lap	142,496
13.	J. Trulli	Toyota	MWE	WMMW	59	1 lap	142,420

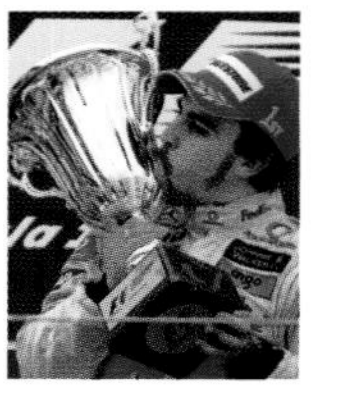

Driver	Constructor	Tyres (Départ 1 & 2)		Laps	Reason
K. Räikkönen	Ferrari	MW	WM	34	Hydraulic problem
T. Sato	Super Aguri Honda	MWE	WM	19	Hydraulic system problem
R. Schumacher	Toyota	MWE	WM	18	Hit by Heidfeld and tapped into a spin
M. Winkelhock	Spyker Ferrari	WE	EM	13	Hydraulic problem
J. Button	Honda	MW		2	Aquaplaned off at first corner
A. Sutil	Spyker Ferrari	MW		2	Aquaplaned off at first corne
N. Rosberg	Williams Toyota	MW		2	Aquaplaned off at first corne
S. Speed	STR Ferrari	MW		2	Aquaplaned off at first corne
V. Liuzzi	STR Ferrari	MWE		2	Aquaplaned off at first corne

Tyres M: Medium & S: Soft // E: Extreme Wet & W: Wet

Fastest laps

	Driver	Time	Lap	Km/h
1.	F. Massa	1:32.853	34	199,592
2.	F. Alonso	1:33.231	35	198,783
3.	L. Hamilton	1:33.401	29	198,421
4.	K. Räikkönen	1:33.904	32	197,359
5.	A. Wurz	1:34.235	33	196,665
6.	D. Coulthard	1:34.316	48	196,496
7.	N. Heidfeld	1:34.354	49	196,417
8.	M. Webber	1:34.449	29	196,220
9.	R. Kubica	1:34.451	49	196,216
10.	J. Trulli	1:34.496	29	196,122
11.	H. Kovalainen	1:34.603	48	195,900
12.	G. Fisichella	1:34.893	48	195,302
13.	A. Davidson	1:35.282	46	194,504
14.	R. Barrichello	1:35.632	37	193,792
15.	R. Schumacher	1:36.195	18	192,658
16.	T. Sato	1:37.401	18	190,273
17.	M. Winkelhock	1:42.783	13	180,309
18.	J. Button	2:20.041	2	132,338
19.	A. Sutil	2:25.798	2	127,112
20.	N. Rosberg	2:50.950	2	108,410
21.	S. Speed	3:01.900	2	101,884
22.	V. Liuzzi	3:22.300	2	91,610

Pit stops

	Driver	Lap	Duration	Stop	Total
1.	F. Massa	1	30.701	1	30.701
2.	F. Alonso	1	30.431	1	30.431
3.	M. Webber	1	28.644	1	28.644
4.	J. Button	1	28.309	1	28.309
5.	H. Kovalainen	1	35.046	1	35.046
6.	S. Speed	1	1:03.138	1	1:03.138
7.	V. Liuzzi	1	1:13.592	1	1:13.592
8.	A. Davidson	1	55.816	1	55.816
9.	R. Schumacher	1	50.049	1	50.049
10.	N. Rosberg	1	52.917	1	52.917
11.	D. Coulthard	1	29.482	1	29.482
12.	L. Hamilton	1	31.974	1	31.974
13.	R. Barrichello	1	29.515	1	29.515
14.	A. Sutil	1	31.285	1	31.285
15.	N. Heidfeld	1	35.136	1	35.136
16.	K. Räikkönen	2	28.332	1	28.332
17.	T. Sato	2	28.555	1	28.555
18.	A. Wurz	2	29.143	1	29.143
19.	J. Trulli	2	30.310	1	30.310
20.	G. Fisichella	2	30.048	1	30.048
21.	R. Kubica	2	32.959	1	32.959
22.	V. Liuzzi	2	27.751	2	1:41.343
23.	M. Winkelhock	3	27.487	1	27.487
24.	R. Barrichello	3	29.884	2	59.399
25.	R. Schumacher	3	30.789	2	1:20.838
26.	T. Sato	3	29.661	2	58.216
27.	J. Trulli	3	44.752	2	1:15.062
28.	N. Heidfeld	3	28.594	2	1:03.730
29.	A. Davidson	3	30.447	2	1:26.263
30.	N. Heidfeld	5	27.994	3	1:31.724
31.	J. Trulli	6	26.919	3	1:41.981
32.	A. Davidson	6	42.478	3	2:08.741
33.	L. Hamilton	6	28.796	2	1:00.770
34.	K. Räikkönen	11	25.955	2	54.287
35.	A. Wurz	11	26.502	2	55.645
36.	A. Davidson	11	28.277	4	2:37.018
37.	M. Winkelhock	11	33.738	2	1:01.225
38.	F. Massa	12	25.652	2	56.353
39.	F. Alonso	12	27.550	2	57.981
40.	M. Webber	12	26.472	2	55.116
41.	H. Kovalainen	12	26.822	2	1:01.868
42.	G. Fisichella	12	31.263	2	1:01.311
43.	R. Schumacher	12	26.347	3	1:47.185
44.	R. Kubica	12	25.669	2	58.628
45.	R. Barrichello	12	26.626	3	1:26.025
46.	T. Sato	12	26.483	3	1:24.699
47.	J. Trulli	12	44.688	4	2:26.669
48.	D. Coulthard	13	25.841	2	55.323
49.	N. Heidfeld	13	24.705	4	1:56.429
50.	H. Kovalainen	27	27.288	3	1:29.156
51.	G. Fisichella	30	30.003	3	1:31.314
52.	J. Trulli	34	27.943	5	2:54.612
53.	L. Hamilton	34	28.847	3	1:29.617
54.	F. Alonso	37	27.448	3	1:25.429
55.	A. Wurz	37	28.495	3	1:24.140
56.	N. Heidfeld	37	27.416	5	2:23.845
57.	F. Massa	38	28.422	3	1:24.775
58.	A. Davidson	38	29.311	5	3:06.329
59.	R. Kubica	39	27.995	3	1:26.623
60.	R. Barrichello	39	27.514	4	1:53.539
61.	M. Webber	41	27.435	3	1:22.551
62.	D. Coulthard	43	27.702	3	1:23.025
63.	H. Kovalainen	49	26.181	4	1:55.337
64.	A. Davidson	51	25.678	6	3:32.007
65.	D. Coulthard	52	25.324	4	1:48.349
66.	R. Kubica	52	25.190	4	1:51.813
67.	F. Massa	53	26.470	4	1:51.245
68.	G. Fisichella	52	26.950	4	1:58.264
69.	F. Alonso	53	25.997	4	1:51.426
70.	R. Barrichello	52	26.124	5	2:19.663
71.	M. Webber	53	25.816	4	1:48.367
72.	A. Wurz	53	26.630	4	1:50.770
73.	N. Heidfeld	53	25.545	6	2:49:390
74.	J. Trulli	53	26.316	6	3:20.928
75.	L. Hamilton	54	27.191	4	1:56.808

Race leader

Driver	Laps in the lead	Nbr of laps
K. Räikkönen	1	1
M. Winkelhock	2 > 7	6
F. Massa	8 > 12	5
D. Coulthard	13	1
F. Massa	14 > 55	42
F. Alonso	56 > 60	5

Driver	Nbr of laps	Kilometers
F. Massa	47	241,956 km
M. Winkelhock	6	30,888 km
F. Alonso	5	25,740 km
D. Coulthard	1	5,148 km
K. Räikkönen	1	5,131 km

Gaps on the lead board

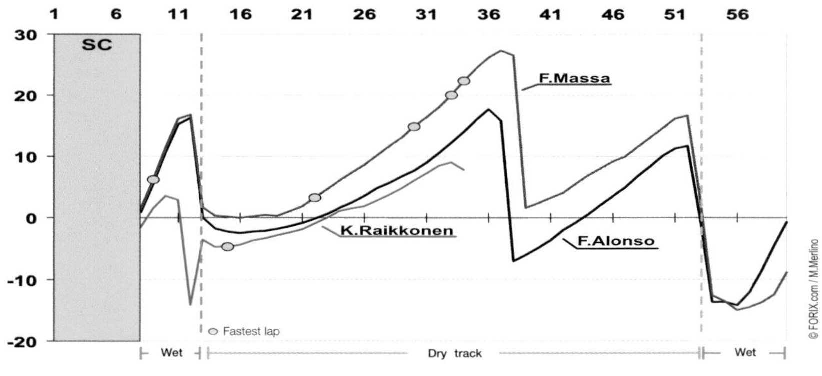

Lap chart

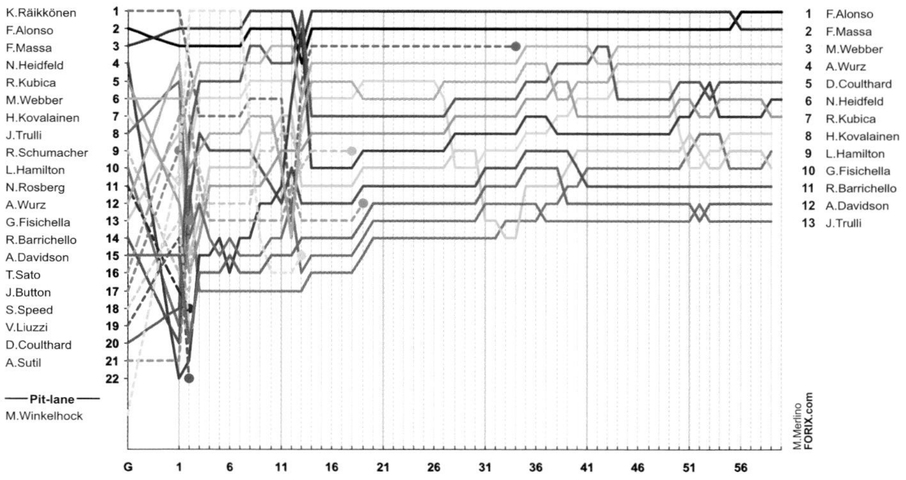

CHAMPIONSHIPS 10/17

Drivers

	Driver	Team	Wins	Points
1.	L. Hamilton	McLaren Mercedes	2	70
2.	F. Alonso	McLaren Mercedes	3	68
3.	F. Massa	Ferrari	2	59
4.	K. Räikkönen	Ferrari	3	52
5.	N. Heidfeld	BMW		36
6.	R. Kubica	BMW		24
7.	G. Fisichella	Renault		17
8.	H. Kovalainen	Renault		15
9.	A. Wurz	Williams Toyota		13
10.	M. Webber	Red Bull Renault		8
11.	D. Coulthard	Red Bull Renault		8
12.	J. Trulli	Toyota		7
13.	N. Rosberg	Williams Toyota		5
14.	T. Sato	Super Aguri Honda		4
15.	R. Schumacher	Toyota		2
16.	J. Button	Honda		1
17.	S. Vettel	BMW		1
18.	R. Barrichello	Honda		0
19.	S. Speed	STR Ferrari		0
20.	A. Davidson	Super Aguri Honda		0
21.	A. Sutil	Spyker Ferrari		0
22.	C. Albers	Spyker Ferrari		0
23.	V. Liuzzi	STR Ferrari		0
	M. Winkelhock	Spyker Ferrari		-

Constructors

	Team	Wins	Points
1.	Vodafone McLaren Mercedes	5	138
2.	Scuderia Ferrari Marlboro	5	111
3.	BMW Sauber F1 Team		61
4.	ING Renault F1 Team		32
5.	AT&T Williams		18
6.	Red Bull Racing		16
7.	Panasonic Toyota Racing		9
8.	Super Aguri F1 Team		4
9.	Honda Racing F1 Team		1
10.	Scuderia Toro Rosso		0
11.	Etihad Aldar Spyker F1 Team		0

THE CIRCUIT

Name	Nürburgring; Nürburg	**Latitude**	50°20'07.70"N
Lenght	5148 m	**Longitude**	6°56'51.70"E
Distance	60 laps, 308,863 km		

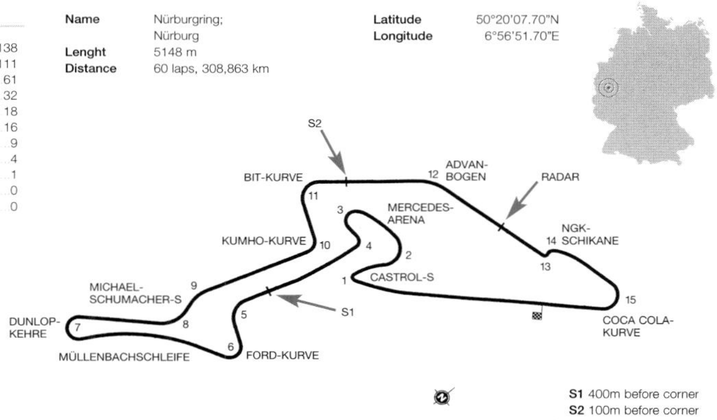

S1 400m before corner
S2 100m before corner
Radar 100m before corner

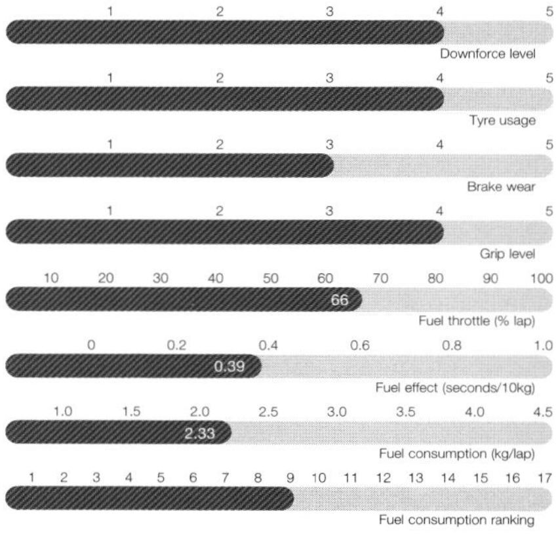

THE BIG FALL-OUT

Up until this race, Fernando Alonso and Lewis Hamilton still managed to get on reasonably well, even though Alonso had not been willing to share his set-up information with Hamilton for several weeks now.

But in Budapest, the argument that had been simmering just below the surface finally boiled over. During qualifying, Lewis Hamilton disobeyed his team in order to disadvantage Fernando Alonso, while the Spaniard managed to hold up Hamilton in the pit lane to prevent him from completing a final qualifying lap.

It emerged later that the Hungarian Grand Prix was also when Fernando Alonso decided to betray his team and supply the FIA with e-mails proving that McLaren had known about the Ferrari dossier for quite some time. It was really at this race when relations between the Spaniard and his team became untenable, making it a practical certainty that he would not drive for McLaren in 2008. In fact, he was already looking elsewhere.

On track, Lewis Hamilton won the race. But that was virtually a sideshow…

> Having already replaced Robert Kubica at BMW-Sauber for the United States Grand Prix, Sebastian Vettel made his real F1 debut at Budapest. The young German took over Scott Speed's drive - who had been acrimoniously fired by team bosses Franz Tost and Gerhard Berger.

Fastest time for Alonso, followed by a penalty for 'stealing' pole position

The qualifying session had just two minutes left to run when the two McLarens made a pit stop as planned, to bolt on their final sets of new tyres. Fernando Alonso came in first, followed by Lewis Hamilton.

When he received the signal that he was clear to go however, Fernando Alonso didn't move at all for a good ten seconds. Throughout that time, Lewis Hamilton was forced to sit and wait behind him before he too could change onto new tyres and take to the track again for his final qualifying lap.

Once the Briton had finally got going, it was ever so slightly too late. In the meantime, Fernando Alonso had just enough time to get round the circuit and embark on a final flying lap. That lap would earn him pole position. Lewis Hamilton never got the chance. By the time he had

got round the circuit and was ready to begin his flyer, the session was over. He had to stick with his previous best time, which was still good enough for second place.

An hour and a half later, McLaren tried to explain what had just happened. Team principal Ron Dennis stated: *"We approach qualifying in a very precise way. Everything is mapped out beforehand, but it was Lewis who overturned the plan by not letting Fernando past as we had agreed at the beginning of the session. Lewis and Fernando are two excellent drivers, but they're going through a very tense duel for the championship and under those circumstances it's not very easy to tell them what they should do on the track..."*

Anthony Hamilton, Lewis's father, was not buying that explanation. He stormed off to see the race organisers and

managed to convince the stewards to summon Ron Dennis, the two drivers and their engineers, in order to find out whether or not Fernando Alonso was guilty of unsporting behaviour.

At 23:55 on Saturday night, the race stewards decided to inflict a penalty of five grid positions on Alonso. They too were not buying his story - which he had waited in the pit lane because he was asking which type of tyres had gone on the car. Not only that, but they were also very unhappy with McLaren's version of events. In order to punish the team, they decided that McLaren would not be scoring any constructor points in Budapest.

The gloves were now off between Alonso and Hamilton. It was officially war. Even in the heyday of the Prost-Senna rivalry, tensions at McLaren had never run this high.

> Sakon Yamamoto made his debut for the Spyker team. On Thursday, he was allowed to practice some fuel stops.

>> Nico Rosberg put in a magnificent qualifying performance, with his best grid position of the year in fifth place. *"We've found some settings that seem to suit the car well,"* he commented.

STARTING GRID

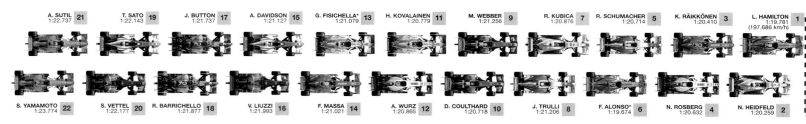

* F. ALONSO
was relegated of 5 pos. for deliberately blocking HAMILTON in pit lane.

G. FISICHELLA
was relegated of 5 pos. YAMAMOTO in his fast lap (article 31.7).

	Top row										
A. SUTIL 21 1:22.737	T. SATO 19 1:22.143	J. BUTTON 17 1:21.737	A. DAVIDSON 15 1:21.127	G. FISICHELLA* 13 1:21.079	H. KOVALAINEN 11 1:20.779	M. WEBBER 9 1:21.256	R. KUBICA 7 1:20.876	R. SCHUMACHER 5 1:20.714	K. RÄIKKÖNEN 3 1:20.410	L. HAMILTON 1 1:19.781 (197.686 km/h)

| S. YAMAMOTO 22 1:23.774 | S. VETTEL 20 1:22.177 | R. BARRICHELLO 18 1:21.877 | V. LIUZZI 16 1:21.993 | F. MASSA 14 1:21.021 | A. WURZ 12 1:20.865 | D. COULTHARD 10 1:20.718 | J. TRULLI 8 1:21.206 | F. ALONSO* 6 1:19.674 | N. ROSBERG 4 1:20.632 | N. HEIDFELD 2 1:20.259 |

< They're off! Lewis Hamilton makes a perfect start, while behind him Kimi Raikkonen gets the better off Nick Heidfeld. Hamilton would lead from start to finish, including throughout all the fuel stops.

Lewis Hamilton apologises and wins

Lewis Hamilton was hauled up before his bosses on race morning and forced to apologise for the problems he had sparked off the evening before (see page 164). A few hours later though he won the Hungarian Grand Prix, doing well to soak up the pressure from Kimi Raikkonen, while Fernando Alonso was fourth. Despite the fact that McLaren had to deal with a civil war, the team showed astonishing strength in depth to rise above it all and seal the race win.

The bizarre situation prompted Ron Dennis to make a statement after the race. *"We've got long-term contracts with both of our drivers, and our firm intention is to treat them both with absolute equality. It's very difficult to manage two personalities like Lewis and Fernando but that is my job. I have to make the decisions that are in the best interests of the team."* And that, of course, is more or less how the trouble started...

Kimi Raikkonen's Ferrari finished the race less than a second behind the winner, even though the tight and twisty Budapest circuit theoretically did not really suit the F2007. *"I think we're very competitive,"* said the Finn. *"Here we had to fight very hard, but I think that things should be better for us in Turkey."*

Lewis Hamilton's point of view

-Why did you not let your team mate past at the beginning of qualifying on Saturday, as your team had asked you to do?
LH: When the team asked me to let Fernando past during qualifying, it seemed to me that Kimi Raikkonen was a bit too close to him and so this would be risky. So I accelerated, but Fernando did not follow me. Then when the team asked me again to let him past I couldn't, as he was too far behind. Having said that, it's true that I didn't obey my boss even though he repeated his instructions and I feel very bad about that. It's hard to stay concentrated under those circumstances. I'm wondering if the team hates me now...
- The incident means that McLaren aren't allowed to score points in Hungary now. That can't have made you very popular...
LH : Obviously Ron (Dennis) is very angry. I've asked him to forgive me and I promised him it will never happen again. I still don't understand what Fernando was doing when he blocked me in the pits though. There's no excuse for that. Now he doesn't even want to talk to me but that's his problem. I just want to win the World Championship...

Fernando Alonso's point of view

- What do you think about the penalty you were given on Saturday night ?
FA : I don't understand it. I find this punishment unfair, and I don't see how it is based on any of the rules. That sort of penalty has never been applied before until now. We need to be very careful, because if the stewards are going to start punishing people for spending time in the pits then anything could happen. Having said that, I just need to accept what has happened now and keep looking forwards. There's no point in complaining.
- You've finished fourth, which has at least limited the damage...
FA : I actually think that I could have won the GP if I had started from the front. The potential was there. I had a very good rhythm but I was stuck first behind Ralf Schumacher and then behind Nick Heidfeld. It's just impossible to overtake on this circuit. I thought for a long time that I would finish sixth or seventh, so I'm happy with fourth.
- What is your relationship with Lewis Hamilton like now ?
FA : I'm just going to do my job, that's all. This is the first time that Lewis has not done what he was told to do, so we'll see where that takes him. I'm disappointed by the team as things are not happening in the way that I thought they would. But I can still win the championship : I'm only seven points behind. If I don't win, it will be my fault.

Lewis Hamilton is happy and it shows ! He gains five points over Fernando Alonso with the victory to take his advantage over the Spaniard to seven points, and his margin over Kimi Raikkonen to 20 points !
∨ <

The winner of the day goes walkabout, protected by a team mechanic.
∨

LOOKING ON THE BRIGHT SIDE

Fernando Alonso set fastest time in qualifying, but was forced to start from fifth on the grid following a penalty. Not even this, apparently, could dampen the Spaniard's high spirits.

One day in hell

> Saturday afternoon : Ron Dennis and Fernando Alonso head off to see the Hungarian Grand Prix stewards - in visibly different moods.

In Budapest, it was as if the entire paddock revolved around McLaren. Even though Kimi Raikkonen finished second in Budapest, hot on the heels of the winner, nobody was really paying much attention to the action on the circuit.

Instead, the real action in Hungary took place behind the scenes. News of Fernando Alonso's penalty was made public on Saturday night, just five minutes before midnight. Most people had already gone back to their hotels and did not find out until they returned to the circuit on Sunday morning.

It was the beginning of an elaborate daylong ballet, with the giant McLaren hospitality unit as a backdrop. This is how the drama unfolded :

10:05 Fernando Alonso's father, accompanied by Alonso's manager Luis Garcia Abad, leave the McLaren motorhome to go to Renault. They have a meeting scheduled with Flavio Briatore, no doubt to discuss the ways in which Alonso could return to drive for his former employer.

10:25 Lewis Hamilton is summoned to Ron Dennis's office on the third floor of the McLaren brand centre. Also present at the meeting - where Hamilton was asked to explain his actions on Saturday - were Martin Whitmarsh and John Neale. The youngster apologises for what he did and promises that it will never happen again.

17:10 The race is finally over and Ron Dennis draws his conclusions from what has been a black weekend. McLaren has been unable to score points and consequently the gap over Ferrari is now down to just 19 points. *"We're part of a team,"* says Dennis. *"We need to fully discuss everything that has happened internally before the Turkish Grand Prix. But being in a team is also like being in a family. It's a way of life that only works if everyone is pulling in the same direction. There is no room for mavericks."* That last remark was addressed directly to Fernando Alonso, his father and his manager, all of whom seemed to be considering their options elsewhere.

A new twist to the spy scandal

When Ron Dennis emerged from the FIA World Council meeting on the Thursday after the European Grand Prix, looking physically drained, he declared that enough time had been wasted and that now *"we have a championship to get on and win."*

Unfortunately for him, he had to wait for several more weeks to learn of McLaren's fate and invest several more hours of his precious time. In theory there was no appeal against the FIA's judgment of July 26, as it came from the highest sporting authority. Nonetheless Ferrari had continued to cry foul since the judgement was announced, citing the fact that the World Council was seemingly not interested in even looking at its evidence - which naturally portrayed the Scuderia as an aggrieved victim.

In Italy, the FIA's decision caused nothing less than a scandal, sparking off an unprecedented campaign in the media to highlight McLaren's guilt. This was not without some basis, as the World Council did indeed recognise that McLaren had violated the sporting code. In their opinion though, there was not sufficient proof to warrant a punishment. The Italian media retaliated by saying that any recognised breach should lead to a punishment - which had always been the case so far in the history of the sport.

On the Tuesday before the Hungarian Grand Prix, the president of the Italian Automobile Club's sporting commission, Luigi Macaluso, wrote a confidential letter to Max Mosley asking the FIA president to use his discretionary powers to put the matter before the FIA appeal court. This would give Ferrari the opportunity to get its arguments heard. Max Mosley then did two things that were somewhat surprising : firstly he made the letter public, and secondly he agreed to do what it suggested. Suddenly, the whole spy scandal would be opened up again at a new hearing in Paris. And suddenly, the threat that seemed to have gone away - the annulment of manufacturers' and drivers' points scored by McLaren in 2007 and even 2008 - hung once more over the heads of Lewis Hamilton and Fernando Alonso.

Ron Dennis fights back with five pages

As soon as the race had finished, the fans invaded the track for riotous celebrations under the podium.
∨

Max Mosley's decision to re-open the spy scandal between McLaren and Ferrari at an FIA appeal court (see above) was obviously a thorn in the side of the British team.

Suddenly, McLaren's carefully-formulated arguments to present its point of view to the FIA World Council on July 26 were back to square one. Contrary to his usual policy of silence though, Ron Dennis decided to tell all in a five-page press release issued on Wednesday August 1. From this, we learnt that everything had started back in March when Nigel Stepney, who was responsible for Ferrari's test team, informed McLaren designer Mike Coughlan about two elements of the Ferrari F2007 that he believed to be illegal : the rear wing design and the flat floor attachments. Coughlan mentioned these items to Ron Dennis, who in turn pointed these infractions out to the FIA.

Consequently, the FIA decided to ban Ferrari's flat floor after Australia. *"What it means is that our rivals won the Australian Grand Prix with an illegal car,"* said Ron Dennis. *"In the interests of the sport, we didn't appeal against this. But had not Mr Stepney brought the Ferrari's floor to our attention, I think it would be fair to assume that Ferrari would have continued to run an illegal car."* Dennis clearly felt that Ferrari were actively cheating.

Later on, Dennis would give his word that nobody at McLaren knew about the 780-page dossier given by Stepney to Coughlan - who apparently showed just a few pages of it to two other McLaren employees.

Unsurprisingly Ron Dennis also went on to say that he did not quite understand why the whole matter had to go up before the FIA appeal court again at the end of August, when Ferrari - contrary to what the Italian team maintained - had received every possible opportunity to put forward written and spoken evidence at the original hearing.

"It's been a fantastic World Championship so far," added Dennis. *"It would be a tragedy if the action of two employees of Ferrari and McLaren - who acted entirely on their own account - succeeded in ruining the season."*

But the McLaren team boss was as much on the attack as he was on the defensive. *"Ferrari's press releases, the organised leaks to the Italian press and these latest events have seriously damaged Formula 1 as well as McLaren,"* he said, hinting that Ferrari had also violated article 151c of the sporting code : exactly the charge laid against McLaren.

"The World Championship should be fought out on the track, not in the courtrooms or newspaper columns," Dennis concluded.

Ferrari : an emphatic denial

Ferrari reacted to the accusations of cheating made by Ron Dennis in his letter to the Italian Automobile Club (see above) with a very short press release the following morning. The team stated « emphatically » that Ron Dennis's letter contained « very serious and untrue » allegations.

Ferrari also pointed out that its car had been fully scrutineered following the victory in Australia, and found to be perfectly legal.

The Scuderia added that it would consider its position further once the appeal court judgment was known.

> Lewis Hamilton's eventful weekend ended with a victory : his third of the season after winning in Canada and the USA.

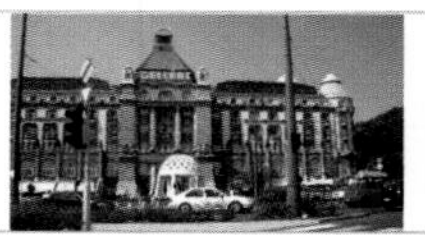

PRACTICE

Date	Weather (AM)	Air temperature	Track temperature	Weather (PM)	Air temperature	Track temperature
Friday August 3, 2007	Sunny	27-29°c	36-42°c	Cloudy then rainy	31-29°c	44-36°c
Saturday August 4, 2007	Some clouds	24-25°c	29-34°c	Sunny	26°c	31-39°c

All the time trials

N° Driver	Nat.	N° Chassis- Engine [Nbr. GP]	Pos. Free 1 Friday 10:00-11:30	Laps Tr.	Pos. Free 2 Friday 14:00-15:30	Laps Tr.	Pos. Free 3 Saturday 11:00-12:00	Laps Tr.	Pos. Q1 Saturday 14:00-14:15	Laps Tr.	Pos. Q2 Saturday 14:22-14:37	Laps Tr.	Pos. Q3 Saturday 14:45-15:00	Nb. Tr.
1. Fernando Alonso	E	McLaren MP4-22 06 - Mercedes [1]	4. 1:22.585	18	1. 1:20.919	29	2. 1:20.414	11	5. 1:20.425	3	2. 1:19.661	3	1. **1:19.674**	11
2. Lewis Hamilton	GB	McLaren MP4-22 05 - Mercedes [1]	5. 1:22.654	19	3. 1:21.338	32	3. 1:20.461	11	1. 1:19.570	3	1. 1:19.301	3	2. **1:19.781**	11
3. Giancarlo Fisichella	I	Renault R27-02 & 05 [1]	17. 1:24.920	19	8. 1:21.698	36	17. 1:22.131	22	15. 1:21.645	7	9. 1:20.590	6	8. **1:21.079**	12
4. Heikki Kovalainen	FIN	Renault R27-03 [2]	15. 1:24.733	18	2. 1:21.283	39	13. 1:21.666	22	2. 1:20.285	6	12. **1:20.779**	6		
5. Felipe Massa	BR	Ferrari F2007 260 [1]	2. 1:22.519	18	7. 1:21.620	29	1. 1:20.183	15	4. 1:20.408	3	14. **1:21.021**	6		
6. Kimi Räikkönen	FIN	Ferrari F2007 262 [1]	3. 1:22.540	21	6. 1:21.589	29	5. 1:20.741	15	6. 1:20.435	4	4. 1:20.107	3	4. **1:20.410**	12
7. Jenson Button	GB	Honda RA107-04 [2]	8. 1:23.294	20	16. 1:22.550	47	18. 1:22.202	23	17. **1:21.737**	6				
8. Rubens Barrichello	BR	Honda RA107-05 [2]	9. 1:23.601	20	18. 1:22.727	29	20. 1:22.596	18	18. **1:21.877**	6				
9. Nick Heidfeld	D	BMW Sauber F1.07-05 [1]	6. 1:22.891	24	5. 1:21.517	37	4. 1:20.565	18	10. 1:20.751	5	6. 1:20.322	6	3. **1:20.259**	11
10. Robert Kubica	PL	BMW Sauber F1.07-03 [1]	1. 1:22.390	25	10. 1:21.906	37	12. 1:21.652	18	3. 1:20.366	6	10. 1:20.703	6	7. **1:20.876**	11
11. Ralf Schumacher	D	Toyota TF107/05 [1]	10. 1:23.802	27	11. 1:21.912	29	8. 1:20.933	21	7. 1:20.449	7	8. 1:20.455	6	6. **1:20.714**	11
12. Jarno Trulli	I	Toyota TF107/06 [1]	12. 1:24.318	30	9. 1:21.857	35	7. 1:20.878	22	8. 1:20.481	6	3. 1:19.951	3	9. **1:21.206**	11
14. David Coulthard	GB	Red Bull RB3 3 - Renault [2]	14. 1:24.474	17	14. 1:22.483	33	14. 1:21.752	15	14. 1:21.291	6	11. **1:20.718**	6		
15. Mark Webber	AUS	Red Bull RB3 4 - Renault [1]	20. 1:25.584	14	13. 1:22.325	28	9. 1:21.220	13	11. 1:20.794	6	7. 1:20.439	5	10. **1:21.256**	11
16. Nico Rosberg	D	Williams FW29-05 - Toyota [2]	7. 1:22.983	19	4. 1:21.485	40	6. 1:20.868	16	9. 1:20.547	6	5. 1:20.188	5	5. **1:20.632**	11
17. Alexander Wurz	AUT	Williams FW29-03 - Toyota [1]	13. 1:24.321	12	12. 1:21.987	35	10. 1:21.323	15	13. 1:21.243	9	13. **1:20.865**	9		
18. Vitantonio Liuzzi	I	Toro Rosso STR2-03 - Ferrari [2]	18. 1:24.976	20	19. 1:23.136	42	16. 1:21.909	21	16. 1:21.730	9	16. **1:21.993**	7		
19. Sebastian Vettel	D	Toro Rosso STR2-04 - Ferrari [1]	16. 1:24.905	26	20. 1:23.148	39	19. 1:22.394	20	20. **1:22.177**	7				
20. Adrian Sutil	D	Spyker F8-VII/03 - Ferrari [2]	21. 1:26.332	29	21. 1:23.673	34	21. 1:23.560	22	21. **1:22.737**	9				
21. Sakon Yamamoto	J	Spyker F8-VII/04 - Ferrari [1]	22. 1:28.118	30	22. 1:26.307	29	22. 1:24.062	24	22. **1:23.774**	7				
22. Takuma Sato	J	Super Aguri SA07-02 - Honda [2]	19. 1:25.307	13	17. 1:22.556	42	15. 1:21.839	18	19. **1:22.143**	6				
23. Anthony Davidson	GB	Super Aguri SA07-03 - Honda [2]	11. 1:24.102	13	15. 1:22.510	41	11. 1:21.501	20	12. 1:21.018	6	15. **1:21.127**	6		

Fastest lap overall

L. Hamilton 1:19.301 (198,882 km/h)

Maximum speed

N° Driver	S1 Qualifs	Pos.	S1 Race	Pos.	S2 Qualifs	Pos.	S2 Race	Pos.	Finish Qualifs	Pos.	Finish Race	Pos.	Radar Qualifs	Pos.	Radar Race	Pos.
1. F. Alonso	286,3	1	290,5	1	246,0	1	246,9	2	252,4	2	254,0	1	289,4	1	299,7	1
2. L. Hamilton	286,0	2	287,8	2	245,8	2	247,7	1	252,8	1	253,1	3	288,3	2	296,0	2
3. G. Fisichella	283,9	5	284,9	7	245,1	4	241,8	11	248,9	11	249,5	6	286,3	5	292,7	5
4. H. Kovalainen	283,0	8	285,0	6	245,0	5	242,2	10	249,4	8	249,1	10	285,6	6	291,2	12
5. F. Massa	285,0	4	286,0	4	245,0	6	244,2	5	249,1	9	253,0	4	282,8	15	292,2	6
6. K. Räikkönen	285,9	3	287,6	3	244,6	7	245,7	3	250,4	3	253,4	2	288,0	4	295,1	3
7. J. Button	276,6	20	279,7	20	238,4	18	236,3	20	245,8	19	245,3	20	278,4	21	286,9	20
8. R. Barrichello	278,7	19	280,4	18	237,3	19	239,1	15	243,9	20	246,0	19	278,9	20	288,0	17
9. N. Heidfeld	282,5	12	283,3	14	245,7	3	244,5	4	249,0	10	249,1	9	283,1	13	290,8	15
10. R. Kubica	282,6	11	282,5	15	243,7	8	243,4	8	247,1	16	249,2	8	283,6	12	291,0	14
11. R. Schumacher	283,1	6	283,3	13	242,3	15	243,1	9	248,6	13	248,9	11	283,0	14	291,7	8
12. J. Trulli	280,5	16	281,6	17	243,2	10	237,7	19	250,0	4	247,9	14	282,5	16	291,4	11
14. D. Coulthard	283,0	9	286,0	5	242,7	14	238,6	17	248,3	14	248,6	12	283,9	10	291,6	10
15. M. Webber	283,0	7	284,3	8	242,7	13	243,4	7	249,6	6	248,2	13	284,2	8	293,3	4
16. N. Rosberg	281,9	14	283,8	11	242,9	12	244,1	6	249,7	5	249,3	7	283,7	11	291,1	13
17. A. Wurz	282,2	13	284,0	10	241,2	17	238,5	18	249,5	7	249,7	5	285,1	7	291,7	9
18. V. Liuzzi	282,7	10	284,2	9	241,5	16	238,9	16	248,7	12	246,6	16	288,3	3	292,2	7
19. S. Vettel	281,3	15	281,6	16	236,4	20	239,2	14	248,3	15	246,3	18	284,0	9	290,6	16
20. A. Sutil	272,9	22	275,0	21	236,3	21	236,3	21	239,7	21	244,0	21	274,6	22	284,0	21
21. S. Yamamoto	274,7	21	272,4	22	233,6	22	220,8	22	238,8	22	235,6	22	279,3	19	278,8	22
22. T. Sato	278,9	18	283,6	12	243,4	9	241,6	12	246,2	18	247,4	15	280,8	17	287,6	18
23. A. Davidson	280,0	17	279,9	19	243,1	11	239,3	13	246,7	17	246,5	17	280,3	18	287,0	19

Best sector times

Qualifs	**S1** L. Hamilton	28.397	**S2** L. Hamilton	28.390	**S3** L. Hamilton	22.424	= 1:19.211
Race	**S1** L. Hamilton	28.708	**S2** L. Hamilton	28.690	**S3** K. Räikkönen	22.313	= 1:19.711

RACE

Date	Weather	Air temperature	Track temperature	Humidity	Wind speed
Sunday August 5, 2007 (14:00)	Sunny	28°c	43-34°c	39%	3.2-1.6 m/s

Classification & retirements

Pos.	Driver	Constructor	Tyres	Laps	Time	Km/h
1.	L. Hamilton	McLaren Mercedes	SSU	70	1:35:52.991	191,897
2.	K. Räikkönen	Ferrari	SSU	70	+ 0.715	191,874
3.	N. Heidfeld	BMW	SSSU	70	+ 43.129	190,469
4.	F. Alonso	McLaren Mercedes	SSU	70	+ 44.858	190,413
5.	R. Kubica	BMW	SSSU	70	+ 47.616	190,322
6.	R. Schumacher	Toyota	SSU	70	+ 50.669	190,222
7.	N. Rosberg	Williams Toyota	SSSU	70	+ 59.139	189,945
8.	H. Kovalainen	Renault	UUS	70	+ 1:08.104	189,652
9.	M. Webber	Red Bull Renault	SSSU	70	+ 1:16.331	189,385
10.	J. Trulli	Toyota	SSU	69	1 lap	188,582
11.	D. Coulthard	Red Bull Renault	SSU	69	1 lap	188,530
12.	G. Fisichella	Renault	USS	69	1 lap	188,338
13.	F. Massa	Ferrari	SUU	69	1 lap	188,317
14.	A. Wurz	Williams Toyota	SSU	69	1 lap	188,299
15.	T. Sato	Super Aguri Honda	SSU	69	1 lap	187,832
16.	S. Vettel	STR Ferrari	SSU	69	1 lap	186,829
17.	A. Sutil	Spyker Ferrari	SSU	68	2 laps	185,261
18.	R. Barrichello	Honda	USS	68	2 laps	185,144

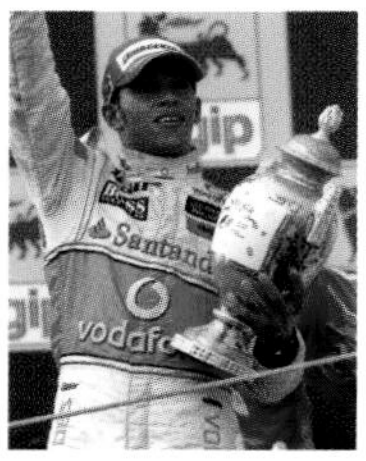

Driver	Constructor	Tyres	Laps	Reason
V. Liuzzi	STR Ferrari	SS	42	Lost power due to electrical problem
A. Davidson	Super Aguri Honda	SS	41	Contact with Fisichella, front-right suspension damage and spin
J. Button	Honda	SS	35	Throttle sensor problem, engine stalled
S. Yamamoto	Spyker Ferrari	S	4	Went off

Tyres S: Soft & U: Super Soft

Fastest laps

	Driver	Time	Lap	Km/h
1.	K. Räikkönen	1:20.047	70	197,029
2.	L. Hamilton	1:20.171	13	196,724
3.	F. Alonso	1:20.324	49	196,349
4.	R. Kubica	1:20.419	40	196,117
5.	N. Heidfeld	1:20.582	16	195,721
6.	N. Rosberg	1:20.672	68	195,502
7.	M. Webber	1:20.915	63	194,915
8.	H. Kovalainen	1:20.935	69	194,867
9.	R. Schumacher	1:20.961	69	194,804
10.	T. Sato	1:20.980	66	194,759
11.	F. Massa	1:20.981	37	194,756
12.	J. Trulli	1:21.253	48	194,104
13.	A. Wurz	1:21.264	49	194,078
14.	D. Coulthard	1:21.553	67	193,390
15.	G. Fisichella	1:21.695	66	193,054
16.	S. Vettel	1:21.915	65	192,536
17.	R. Barrichello	1:22.004	34	192,327
18.	A. Davidson	1:22.166	39	191,948
19.	A. Sutil	1:22.263	67	191,721
20.	V. Liuzzi	1:22.410	35	191,379
21.	J. Button	1:22.906	25	190,234
22.	S. Yamamoto	1:26.741	4	181,824

Pit stops

	Driver	Lap	Duration	Stop	Total
1.	N. Heidfeld	17	23.787	1	23.787
2.	N. Rosberg	17	22.792	1	22.792
3.	F. Alonso	17	26.116	1	26.116
4.	R. Barrichello	17	22.799	1	22.799
5.	R. Schumacher	18	25.405	1	25.405
6.	L. Hamilton	19	25.951	1	25.951
7.	K. Räikkönen	19	24.833	1	24.833
8.	R. Kubica	19	23.358	1	23.358
9.	G. Fisichella	19	23.754	1	23.754
10.	M. Webber	20	23.463	1	23.463
11.	J. Trulli	20	25.655	1	25.655
12.	V. Liuzzi	20	24.135	1	24.135
13.	D. Coulthard	26	24.950	1	24.950
14.	H. Kovalainen	27	23.566	1	23.566
15.	A. Sutil	27	24.205	1	24.205
16.	A. Wurz	29	24.458	1	24.458
17.	A. Davidson	30	24.674	1	24.674
18.	J. Button	30	24.789	1	24.789
19.	S. Vettel	31	24.068	1	24.068
20.	N. Rosberg	32	23.622	2	46.414
21.	T. Sato	32	24.304	1	24.304
22.	F. Massa	35	22.618	1	22.618
23.	R. Barrichello	35	27.962	2	50.761
24.	M. Webber	40	22.882	2	46.345
25.	N. Heidfeld	41	22.182	2	45.969
26.	G. Fisichella	41	26.351	2	50.105
27.	R. Kubica	42	21.566	2	44.924
28.	D. Coulthard	43	23.024	2	47.974
29.	K. Räikkönen	46	24.180	2	49.013
30.	A. Sutil	45	24.486	2	48.694
31.	R. Schumacher	48	24.247	2	49.652
32.	H. Kovalainen	49	24.112	2	47.678
33.	L. Hamilton	50	24.079	2	50.030
34.	S. Vettel	49	24.259	2	48.327
35.	F. Alonso	50	23.184	2	49.300
36.	F. Massa	50	23.195	2	45.813
37.	J. Trulli	51	24.328	2	49.983
38.	A. Wurz	51	24.372	2	48.830
39.	N. Heidfeld	54	22.023	3	1:07.992
40.	N. Rosberg	55	23.331	3	1:09.745
41.	T. Sato	55	22.396	2	46.700
42.	R. Kubica	56	21.833	3	1:06.757
43.	M. Webber	58	21.444	3	1:07.789

Race leader

Driver	Laps in the lead	Nbr of laps	Driver	√Nbr of laps	Kilometers
L. Hamilton	1 > 70	70	L. Hamilton	70	306,663 km

Lap chart

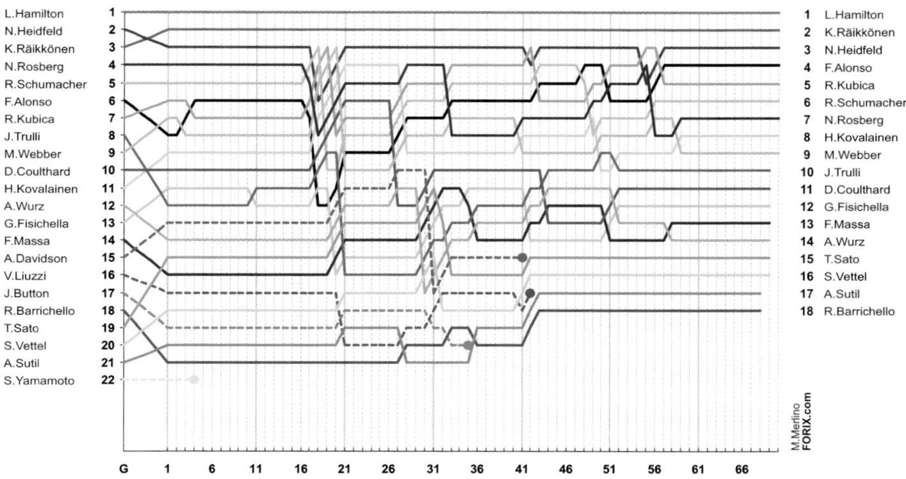
L.Hamilton 1
N.Heidfeld 2
K.Räikkönen 3
N.Rosberg 4
R.Schumacher 5
F.Alonso 6
R.Kubica 7
J.Trulli 8
M.Webber 9
D.Coulthard 10
H.Kovalainen 11
A.Wurz 12
G.Fisichella 13
F.Massa 14
A.Davidson 15
V.Liuzzi 16
J.Button 17
R.Barrichello 18
T.Sato 19
S.Vettel 20
A.Sutil 21
S.Yamamoto 22
G 1 6 11 16 21 26 31 36 41 46 51 56 61 66
1 L.Hamilton
2 K.Räikkönen
3 N.Heidfeld
4 F.Alonso
5 R.Kubica
6 R.Schumacher
7 N.Rosberg
8 H.Kovalainen
9 M.Webber
10 J.Trulli
11 D.Coulthard
12 G.Fisichella
13 F.Massa
14 A.Wurz
15 T.Sato
16 S.Vettel
17 A.Sutil
18 R.Barrichello
M.Merlino
FORIX.com

Gaps on the lead board

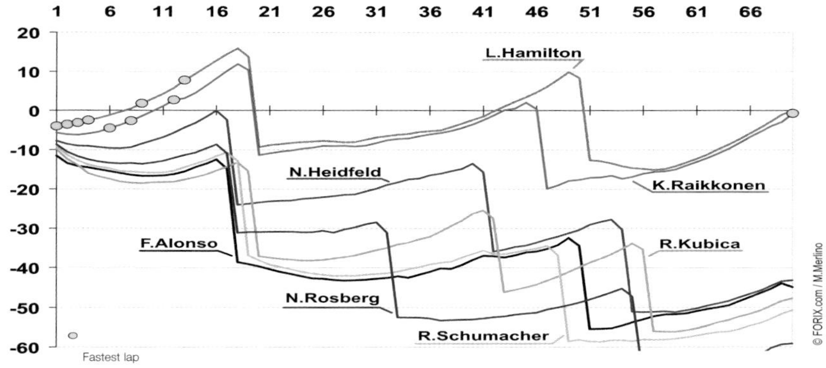
1 6 11 16 21 26 31 36 41 46 51 56 61 66
20
10
0
-10
-20
-30
-40
-50
-60
L.Hamilton
N.Heidfeld
K.Raikkonen
F.Alonso
R.Kubica
N.Rosberg
R.Schumacher
Fastest lap
© FORIX.com / M.Merlino

CHAMPIONSHIPS 11/17

Drivers

	Driver	Constructor	Wins	Points
1.	L. Hamilton	McLaren Mercedes	3	80
2.	F. Alonso	McLaren Mercedes	3	73
3.	K. Räikkönen	Ferrari	3	60
4.	F. Massa	Ferrari	2	59
5.	N. Heidfeld	BMW		42
6.	R. Kubica	BMW		28
7.	G. Fisichella	Renault		17
8.	H. Kovalainen	Renault		16
9.	A. Wurz	Williams Toyota		13
10.	M. Webber	Red Bull Renault		8
11.	D. Coulthard	Red Bull Renault		8
12.	N. Rosberg	Williams Toyota		7
13.	J. Trulli	Toyota		7
14.	R. Schumacher	Toyota		5
15.	T. Sato	Super Aguri Honda		4
16.	J. Button	Honda		1
17.	S. Vettel	BMW 1 /// STR Ferrari 0		1
18.	R. Barrichello	Honda		0
19.	S. Speed	STR Ferrari		0
20.	A. Davidson	Super Aguri Honda		0
21.	A. Sutil	Spyker Ferrari		0
22.	C. Albers	Spyker Ferrari		0
23.	V. Liuzzi	STR Ferrari		0
	M. Winkelhock	Spyker Ferrari		-
	S. Yamamoto	Spyker Ferrari		-

Constructors

	Constructor	Wins	Points
1.	Vodafone McLaren Mercedes	6	[153]138
2.	Scuderia Ferrari Marlboro	5	119
3.	BMW Sauber F1 Team		71
4.	ING Renault F1 Team		33
5.	AT&T Williams		20
6.	Red Bull Racing		16
7.	Panasonic Toyota Racing		12
8.	Super Aguri F1 Team		4
9.	Honda Racing F1 Team		1
10.	Scuderia Toro Rosso		0
11.	Etihad Aldar Spyker F1 Team		0

THE CIRCUIT

Name	Hungaroring; Budapest	**Latitude**	47°34'43.10"N
Lenght	4381 m	**Longitude**	19°14'55.00"E
Distance	70 laps, 306,663 km		

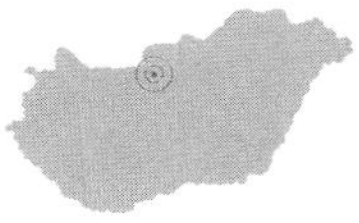

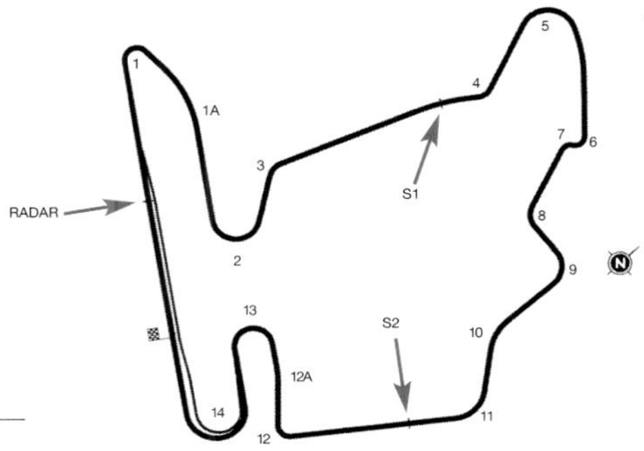
1
1A
2
3
4
5
6
7
8
9
10
11
12
12A
13
14
S1
S2
RADAR

S1 95m before corner
S2 255m before corner
Radar 310m before corner

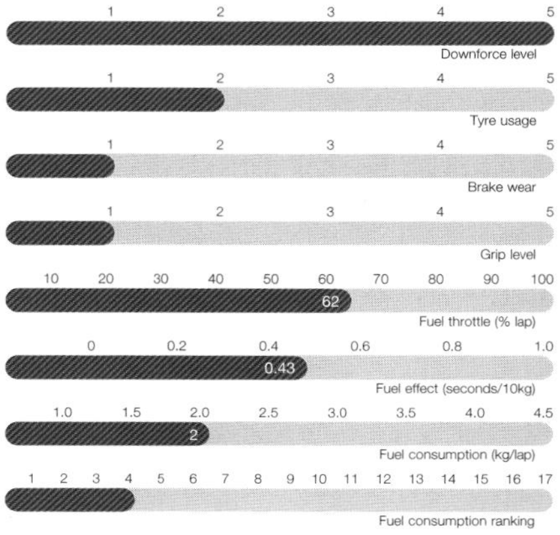
Downforce level
Tyre usage
Brake wear
Grip level
62
Fuel throttle (% lap)
0.43
Fuel effect (seconds/10kg)
2
Fuel consumption (kg/lap)
Fuel consumption ranking

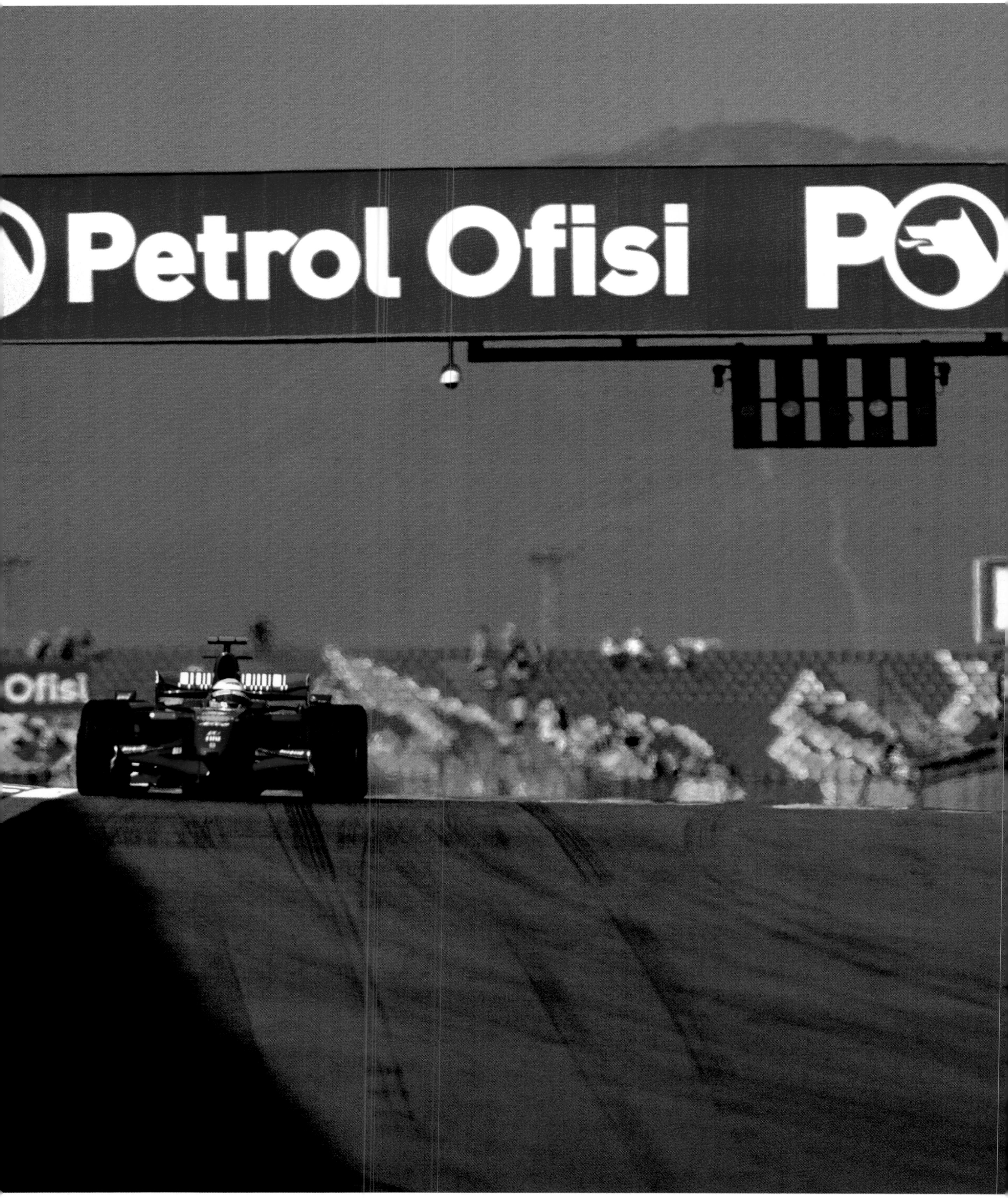
Petrol Ofisi
Ofisi

FELIPE'S LAST STAND

Felipe Massa had not won a Grand Prix since France, and he seemed to be losing ground compared to his teammate Kimi Raikkonen. At Istanbul the diminutive Brazilian had one final push, finishing in front of Raikkonen for the final time of the season. From here on, the story would be quite different.
Behind the two Ferraris, Lewis Hamilton was set for a podium finish until a puncture cost him two places - and ultimately the World Championship. At the end of the season, those two lost points would have given him the title.

> Felipe Massa, Lewis Hamilton and Giancarlo Fisichella leave the pit lane. Massa and Hamilton would make the front row of the grid, while Fisichella would qualify in the top 10 for the final time of the season.

Felipe Massa in pole position

Ferrari knew only too well that with just six Grands Prix left to the end of the season, they could not afford to lose any more ground to the McLarens. The Scuderia hoped to resume their winning ways at the Istanbul Park circuit. With Felipe Massa on pole and Kimi Raikkonen third on the grid, the early signs were good.

For the Brazilian, pole position came at exactly the right time after a demoralising Hungarian Grand Prix where he had trailed home in a miserable 13th place. *"I won here last year and I hope to do the same again his year,"* said Massa. *"I hope I've already shown that when everything is working well, I can be very quick."*

Kimi Raikkonen, back in third, felt a bit disappointed to have missed out on pole position. *"Looking on the bright side, I would rather be third than second,"* he said. *"On this circuit, it's much better to be on the clean side of the track."*

Lewis Hamilton, who was second on the grid, qualified just 44 thousandths of a second slower than Massa. Even though he would be starting from the dirty side of the track, the young Englishman had high hopes of victory.

The previous year, Hamilton had driven the best race of his GP2 career on the same track. On

that occasion he spun at the start of the race and dropped to the tail of the field, but he then fought back to finish an incredible second.

"The car is fantastic," he said on the subject of his McLaren MP4-22. *"The team has worked incredibly hard in three-week gap : it seems that nobody has really been on holiday !
I only just missed pole because I went slightly wide at the final corner, but I'm sure I'll be able to fight for the victory during the race."*

Another win would make Hamilton the firm title favourite. But on Saturday night in Istanbul, he still had a very long way to go.

High noon at McLaren

> Istanbul is well known for its lively markets, or 'bazaars'. A lot of these markets specialise in jewels, clothes and spices.
> >

> Friday morning. David Coulthard's Red Bull catches fire leaving the pit lane, due to a fuel leak that would force the team's mechanics to change the Renault engine during the lunch break.
> ᵛ

By now, relations between Fernando Alonso and Lewis Hamilton had irretrievably broken down. The saga started at Monaco, when the McLaren team called Hamilton into the pits earlier than he would have liked. This cost him the victory - and looking back at it, also the World Championship title.

After Monaco, the atmosphere between McLaren's drivers became more and more tense. From the British Grand Prix onwards, Fernando Alonso decided that he would not be sharing any set-up information with his teammate. At that point they were no longer talking to each other. Then came the Hungarian Grand Prix, where Alonso deliberately blocked his teammate during qualifying while team boss Ron Dennis exchanged copious insults with

Hamilton over the radio... During the three-week gap that followed the tempestuous Hungarian weekend, everybody had time to reflect on events.

On the Thursday of the Turkish Grand Prix, McLaren summoned their drivers to a hotel in Istanbul. Ron Dennis spoke to them individually, before forcing them to meet each other and make up.

"We had a meeting with Ron and Fernando," explained Lewis Hamilton. *"We decided to just forget about everything that had happened before and start again with a clean sheet of paper. I said sorry, Fernando said sorry and Ron said sorry and we decided to draw a line under everything and start again. Ron assured us that we are both treated equally. Now we've got a*

championship to get on with, which myself and Fernando are both desperate to win."

According to Hamilton, the press were constantly fanning the flames of the argument with his teammate. *"In England, all the papers write that I'm at war with Fernando,"* he said. *"That's not true. We're rivals on the track, that's all. If I win it's good for the team, and if he wins it's good for the team. End of story. Myself and Fernando are not the world's greatest friends but we get on well enough. Just yesterday we were playing on the Playstation together. Hungary was a difficult time for everyone, but that won't happen again. We've all learned from our mistakes."*

It seemed that the hatchet was buried...until the next time.

STARTING GRID

R. BARRICHELLO* 22 1:28.188	S. YAMAMOTO 20 1:31.479	S. VETTEL 18 1:29.408	R. SCHUMACHER 16 1:28.809	A. WURZ 14 1:28.390	M. WEBBER 12 1:28.013	G. FISICHELLA 10 1:29.322	N. ROSBERG 8 1:28.501	N. HEIDFELD 6 1:28.037	F. ALONSO 4 1:27.574	L. HAMILTON 2 1:27.373

J. BUTTON* 21 1:28.220	A. SUTIL 19 1:29.861	T. SATO 17 1:28.953	V. LIUZZI 15 1:28.798	D. COULTHARD 13 1:28.100	A. DAVIDSON 11 1:28.002	J. TRULLI 9 1:28.740	H. KOVALAINEN 7 1:28.491	R. KUBICA 5 1:27.722	K. RÄIKKÖNEN 3 1:27.546	F. MASSA 1 1:27.329 (220.050 km/h)

Ferrari energised by one-two

Each of the four championship protagonists had now won three races each : a sign of how close and well balanced the 2007 series was between Ferrari and McLaren. Lewis Hamilton, Fernando Alonso, Felipe Massa and Kimi Raikkonen were all on three victories after Istanbul. Who would blink first ?

Having lost out to the McLarens at Budapest, Ferrari regained the upper hand at Istanbul with an undisputed one-two. Their closest rival from McLaren, Lewis Hamilton, fell victim to a puncture 15 laps from the end - and that only reinforced the Scuderia's dominance in Turkey.

On Sunday afternoon, Ferrari's team principal Jean Todt could not mask the enormous smile on his face. After struggling through several tough weeks, Todt was now convinced that Ferrari could fight for the title. *"I have to say that this was a really pleasing and satisfying weekend,"* said the Frenchman. *"We knew that our car would be quick this weekend. So we were able to start from the front and stay there. Often, when you start from the front like this, everything just goes according to plan without incident and thankfully that was the case again today."*

Todt was also at pains to emphasise the harmony of day-to-day life at Ferrari - in contrast to the bitter rivalries that were eating up McLaren. *"Both our drivers want to win the championship and they are both extremely talented,"* said Jean Todt. *"They are separated by just one point at the moment, which goes to show how closely-matched they are.*

Lap 43 : Just when he is about to stop for fuel, Lewis Hamilton's front-right tyre delaminates during the 'S' curves after the straight. The Englishman is forced to complete an entire lap with the damaged wheel before diving into the pits. Along with that strip of rubber, Lewis's 2007 drivers' championship went flying as well : the two points lost would have made the difference.

We give them exactly the same equipment and the same level of support. All of us at Ferrari are determined to everything we can in order to go all the way and win the title."

Todt was cautiously optimistic that Ferrari would put in a strong showing at Monza as well. *"We know that Monza requires a very specialised set-up, particularly in terms of aerodynamics,"* he added. The Frenchman also took the opportunity to point out that rumours of his imminent retirement had been greatly exaggerated. *"Some people have been saying that I might stop at the end of the season,"* he continued. *"I'm sorry to disappoint them but I'm staying. I still love this team, and I get just as much pleasure out of every victory now as I always did. I think I'll be here for another 10 or 15 years !"*

Lewis Hamilton upbeat despite losing points

Lewis Hamilton was all set to finish on the final step of the podium in Turkey, two places ahead of his teammate Fernando Alonso. Then he picked up a puncture on lap 43 and dropped down to fifth place. McLaren's young superstar said : *"Things were going quite well up to that point. We had a good pace. I think that we were probably about as quick as the Ferraris, but every time I got close to them, I lost downforce. Suddenly, I saw some bits of rubber flying off my front-right tyre and then it just exploded. I couldn't slow down quickly enough, the wheel locked up and I felt the car wanting to swap ends.*

It was all a bit tricky, but luckily I finally managed to get the car back to the pits without losing too much time."
The offending tyre was soon changed, along with the other three wheels, but the McLaren pit crew left the front wing alone. *"I was surprised by that : I honestly thought that they would change it,"* said Hamilton. *"I was sure that it had been damaged by the flailing tyre. Maybe they thought that swapping it would cost too much time, but I wish they had changed it as I had massive understeer for the rest of the race. The car just wouldn't turn in, so I had no chance of catching Nick Heidfeld in front of me."*

At the end of the Turkish Grand Prix, the Englishman had a five-point championship advantage over Fernando Alonso, 15 points over Felipe Massa and 16 over Kimi Raikkonen.

"It's normal to expect to have one or two small problems over the course of the season," said Hamilton. *"But I'm really not worried : I won three weeks ago in Hungary and there are five Grands Prix left this year. I've still got something of a lead in the championship, and I'm more convinced than ever that we can do it. Don't worry about me : nothing's lost yet !"*

First corner : Jarno Trulli is hit from behind by Giancarlo Fisichella, the Toyota snaps sideways, and Trulli loses the benefit of his hard-fought ninth place on the grid.
∨ <

The winner of the day goes walkabout, protected by one of the team's mechanics.
∨

QUOTES

+ *"I wanted the truth to come out. I wanted it for Ferrari, for F1 and for me. The truth must be known and believe me - it will be !"* Jean Todt, Sunday night, to justify his reasons for lodging the appeal against McLaren in the spy scandal. The appeal would be heard by the FIA appeal court in Paris on September 13.

+ *"Alonso is behaving like a spoilt child looking for excuses for his mistakes. He'd be better off putting his foot down on the track rather than making excuses off it."* Niki Lauda, on Fernando Alonso's account of why Lewis Hamilton was quicker than him.

+ *"It's true enough that Lewis has a lot of fans in our team. He's been part of the family for a long time."* Ron Dennis, on the internal allegiances of the McLaren team. It had by now split into two camps : Lewis Hamilton fans and Fernando Alonso fans. The first group was considerably bigger than the second.

THE DOG DAYS OF SUMMER

Having put in some giant-killing performances at the start of the year - notably a famous sixth place in Montreal - Super Aguri slipped into anonymity during the summer months. Takuma Sato could only manage 18th place in Istanbul.

^
Kimi Raikkonen kept a reasonably low profile in Turkey, but he came away with eight points that helped make him a World Champion two months later.

^
Heikki Kovalainen takes a somewhat unconventional line. The Finn finished sixth after a solid and consistent race.

>
On Wednesday night Fernando Alonso took part in a friendly football match. The following day he did not participate in the traditional Thursday press conference, officially because he was «resting»…

>
Istanbul port at daybreak, with its famous minarets in shadow.

Technical rules : the FIA versus the world.

Whether you call it Istanbul, Constantinople or Byzantium, the Turkish metropolis breathes thousands of years of history from every street corner. Its towering minarets offer a breathtaking view of the Bosphorus, that mythical river that forms the border between Europe and Asia.

Nonetheless, the history and culture of this territory where empires have been built and then fallen left most of the Formula 1 team bosses cold. They met near the Bosphorus on Friday morning not to contemplate the majestic view, but to debate the future technical rules of Formula 1. There was a lot to talk about. In 2008 the cars will not look very different, as the aerodynamic regulations will be largely unaltered, but they will hide several innovations under the skin.

For 2008 the FIA has decided to introduce a standard engine ECU (Electronic Control Unit). This will be the only way to end the era of traction control definitively, as the teams have always managed to find a way round every previous attempt to ban traction control.

In 2006 the FIA put out an offer to tender, in order to find a supplier to make the new ECUs.

Ironically the tender was won by Microsoft in association with McLaren Electronic Systems, a subsidiary of the Formula 1 team also based in Woking.

This means that even Ferrari will be to a small extent powered by McLaren next year. In theory, this will work fine as long as the British firm ensures scrupulous equality in the manufacture of every unit.

In practice, many people are very unhappy about it. Gilles Simon, responsible for engines at Ferrari said : *"We've got some big problems with the McLaren unit. We've tested the system but it doesn't work well and switches itself off occasionally - sometimes at full speed. That's very dangerous and we refuse to take any risks with the safety of our drivers."*

At BMW-Sauber the problems were even more fundamental. When equipped with the McLaren system, the car simply refused to start. Team principal Mario Thiessen related : *"We've explained these problems to the FIA. All the teams need to get together and sign a petition to ask for the postponement of the introduction of a standard ECU, but so far nobody is listening to us."*

This is partly because some teams are in favour of the idea. There's McLaren, of course, but also Honda. *"It's not going to be easy to manage, but a standard ECU will at least slow the cars down,"* said team boss Nick Fry. *"At the end of the day, that's precisely what the FIA is aiming to do."*

While the ECU problem formed the crux of the debate, the engineers were even more vehemently opposed to another revolutionary item on the FIA's wish list : the KERS system (which stands for Kinetic Energy Recovery System). This is cutting-edge technology designed to harness the energy expended during braking, and the prospect of its introduction in 2009 is causing several sleepless nights amongst leading engineers (Rob Whyte, in charge of Renault's engine division, makes his views clear on pages 5 and 56). No agreement could be found on this subject either, and Max Mosley has indicated that he is not willing to compromise.

It's easy to see why the teams need to urgently unite if they are to stand a chance of convincing the FIA to change its stance. It's also clear to see why they had no time to take in the charms of the Bosphorus…

SNAPSHOTS OF THE WEEKEND

+ Rumour had it that Flavio Briatore wanted to concentrate on running his exclusive nightclub in Sardinia, or the London-based Queen's Park Rangers football team that he was planning to buy. All untrue. At Istanbul, the Italian declared that he was 100% committed to the Renault Formula 1 team and that he hoped to help them back to the top again next year. *"Everything else I do is just for fun,"* he added.

+ The Sepang circuit, on the outskirts of Kuala Lumpur, announced that it had extended its contract with F1's commercial rights-holder Bernie Ecclestone until 2015.

+ There's no point in asking who was the darling of the McLaren team. While Fernando Alonso had three quiet weeks of holiday on his own, Hamilton spent his vacation off St Tropez on a yacht belonging to Mansour Ojjeh : McLaren's co-owner. Hamilton was even snapped by the paparazzi with Ojjeh's daughter - an indication that he was hardly hiding himself away..

+ Renault decided to put a stop to development of the disappointing 2007 car in order to concentrate on the new 2008 car from August onwards, and have a chance of a better season next year. For Ferrari, the division of labour was not so clear-cut. As Aldo Costa explained : *"We're a bit torn. On the one hand, we're fighting for the 2007 title and we need to keep working on our current car. On the other hand, it would be high time we worked on our 2008 car, as we plan to launch it in January…"*

+ According to Fernando Alonso, he would be happy to stay at McLaren in 2008 ! Or so he claimed at Istanbul. After Hungary he said he no longer felt comfortable in the team, but by the time the Turkish Grand Prix came round he had changed his story. *"When it comes down to it, I have no choice,"* he said. *"There are not so many options available and I have a McLaren contract for next year. As long as the team keeps giving me a car capable of winning, then I'm not going to change…"*

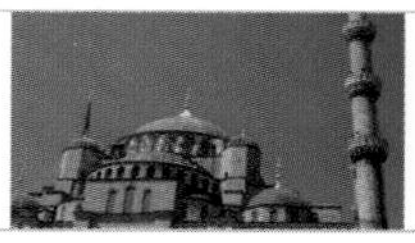

PRACTICE

Date	Weather (AM)	Air temperature	Track temperature	Weather (PM)	Air temperature	Track temperature
Friday August 24, 2007	Sunny	32-35°c	42-51°c	Sunny	34-36°c	47-55°c
Saturday August 25, 2007	Sunny	31-35°c	42-48°c	Sunny	35°c	44-52°c

All the time trials

N° Driver	Nat.	N° Chassis- Engine [Nbr. GP]	Pos. Free 1 Friday 10:00-11:30	Laps Tr.	Pos. Free 2 Friday 14:00-15:30	Laps Tr.	Pos. Free 3 Saturday 11:00-12:00	Laps Tr.	Pos. Q1 Saturday 14:00-14:15	Laps Tr.	Pos. Q2 Saturday 14:22-14:37	Laps Tr.	Pos. Q3 Saturday 14:45-15:00	Nb. Tr.
1. Fernando Alonso	E	McLaren MP4-22 06 - Mercedes [2]	3. 1:29.222	20	6. 1:28.947	24	4. 1:27.743	13	2. 1:27.328	3	1. 1:26.841	3	4. **1:27.574**	11
2. Lewis Hamilton	GB	McLaren MP4-22 01 - Mercedes [2]	4. 1:29.261	10	1. 1:28.469	28	1. 1:27.325	12	4. 1:27.513	3	3. 1:26.936	3	2. **1:27.373**	11
3. Giancarlo Fisichella	I	Renault R27-05 [2]	8. 1:29.541	19	12. 1:29.456	28	8. 1:28.261	20	10. 1:28.313	7	10. 1:27.880	6	10. **1:29.322**	11
4. Heikki Kovalainen	FIN	Renault R27-02 & 03 [1]	5. 1:29.346	19	8. 1:29.025	28	10. 1:28.364	17	7. 1:28.127	7	8. 1:27.784	6	7. **1:28.491**	11
5. Felipe Massa	BR	Ferrari F2007 263 [2]	2. 1:28.391	20	5. 1:28.884	25	2. 1:27.366	15	3. 1:27.488	4	4. 1:27.039	3	1. **1:27.329**	11
6. Kimi Räikkönen	FIN	Ferrari F2007 262 [2]	1. 1:27.988	22	2. 1:28.762	21	3. 1:27.506	16	1. 1:27.294	4	2. 1:26.902	3	3. **1:27.546**	11
7. Jenson Button	GB	Honda RA107-04 [1] -> [1]	14. 1:30.483	17	14. 1:29.945	26	15. 1:28.548	16	13. 1:28.373	6	15. **1:28.220**	6		
8. Rubens Barrichello	BR	Honda RA107-05 [1] -> [1]	15. 1:30.580	25	15. 1:30.055	31	16. 1:28.715	18	16. 1:28.792	6	14. **1:28.188**	6		
9. Nick Heidfeld	D	BMW Sauber F1.07-08 [2]	9. 1:29.641	20	13. 1:29.792	30	6. 1:28.184	18	6. 1:28.099	3	5. 1:27.253	3	6. **1:28.037**	11
10. Robert Kubica	PL	BMW Sauber F1.07-03 [2]	11. 1:29.710	23	10. 1:29.368	31	7. 1:28.224	21	5. 1:27.997	3	6. 1:27.253	3	5. **1:27.722**	11
11. Ralf Schumacher	D	Toyota TF107/05 [2]	7. 1:29.414	24	3. 1:28.773	23	13. 1:28.481	20	18. **1:28.809**	7				
12. Jarno Trulli	I	Toyota TF107/04 [2]	10. 1:29.685	26	4. 1:28.874	28	14. 1:28.520	21	11. 1:28.318	7	9. 1:27.801	6	9. **1:28.740**	11
14. David Coulthard	GB	Red Bull RB3 5 - Renault [1]	13. 1:30.398	23	11. 1:29.435	12	12. 1:28.448	14	14. 1:28.395	6	13. **1:28.100**	6		
15. Mark Webber	AUS	Red Bull RB3 4 - Renault [2]	19. 1:30.917	22	17. 1:30.315	25	9. 1:28.337	15	15. 1:28.500	6	12. **1:28.013**	6		
16. Nico Rosberg	D	Williams FW29-05 - Toyota [1]	6. 1:29.403	23	7. 1:28.995	27	5. 1:28.056	16	8. 1:28.275	3	7. 1:27.750	6	8. **1:28.501**	11
17. Alexander Wurz	AUT	Williams FW29-03 - Toyota [2]	18. 1:30.876	12	9. 1:29.093	27	11. 1:28.413	16	12. 1:28.360	6	16. **1:28.390**	8		
18. Vitantonio Liuzzi	I	Toro Rosso STR2-03 - Ferrari [1]	16. 1:30.612	21	19. 1:30.702	24	18. 1:28.937	20	17. **1:28.798**	9				
19. Sebastian Vettel	D	Toro Rosso STR2-04 - Ferrari [2]	20. 1:31.383	22	20. 1:30.801	16	19. 1:29.408	19	20. **1:29.408**	6				
20. Adrian Sutil	D	Spyker F8-VII/01 - Ferrari [1]	21. 1:31.445	31	21. 1:31.153	32	21. 1:30.044	22	21. **1:29.861**	9				
21. Sakon Yamamoto	J	Spyker F8-VII/02 - Ferrari [2]	22. 1:32.270	35	22. 1:31.175	32	22. 1:30.712	21	22. **1:31.479**	7				
22. Takuma Sato	J	Super Aguri SA07-02 - Honda [1]	17. 1:30.624	15	16. 1:30.104	27	20. 1:29.436	14	19. **1:28.953**	8				
23. Anthony Davidson	GB	Super Aguri SA07-03 - Honda [1]	12. 1:30.384	17	18. 1:30.530	24	17. 1:28.755	16	9. 1:28.304	6	11. **1:28.002**	6		

Fastest lap overall
F. Alonso 1:26.841 (221,287 km/h)

Maximum speed

N° Driver	S1 Qualifs	Pos.	S1 Race	Pos.	S2 Qualifs	Pos.	S2 Race	Pos.	Finish Qualifs	Pos.	Finish Race	Pos.	Radar Qualifs	Pos.	Radar Race	Pos.
1. F. Alonso	288,9	1	284,2	2	295,6	2	295,8	1	245,0	1	242,4	3	323,9	1	319,9	2
2. L. Hamilton	287,4	2	285,0	1	296,3	1	294,3	2	244,2	3	242,5	2	322,0	2	320,2	1
3. G. Fisichella	284,0	9	282,0	7	291,8	7	289,8	9	241,5	6	240,0	7	319,7	6	314,9	11
4. H. Kovalainen	284,6	7	282,8	5	292,3	5	291,1	6	242,2	5	241,3	5	319,9	5	316,6	4
5. F. Massa	284,8	6	283,0	4	292,2	6	291,1	5	242,9	4	241,7	4	319,5	7	316,1	8
6. K. Räikkönen	284,6	8	284,2	3	292,9	4	293,6	3	244,5	2	243,4	1	319,1	11	317,1	3
7. J. Button	282,2	17	280,3	11	290,3	17	289,6	11	239,3	16	238,7	12	316,3	17	314,4	12
8. R. Barrichello	282,4	14	277,7	17	290,4	14	289,0	14	239,6	13	238,9	10	316,8	16	313,2	16
9. N. Heidfeld	285,1	3	280,6	10	291,1	12	289,8	10	238,5	19	238,2	14	319,3	10	313,4	15
10. R. Kubica	284,9	5	280,2	12	290,3	16	289,3	13	241,2	8	238,8	11	320,1	4	316,2	6
11. R. Schumacher	282,9	12	279,2	14	291,4	10	289,6	12	239,5	14	239,0	8	318,7	12	314,2	13
12. J. Trulli	282,5	13	282,5	6	290,5	13	289,9	8	239,7	11	238,9	9	321,3	3	316,1	7
14. D. Coulthard	282,2	16	278,0	16	290,3	15	287,2	17	239,7	12	237,3	15	313,2	20	310,3	20
15. M. Webber	282,0	18	276,1	21	289,9	18	283,7	22	238,6	18	234,5	19	313,3	19	311,6	17
16. N. Rosberg	283,4	10	281,1	9	293,6	3	292,0	4	241,2	9	238,7	13	319,3	9	316,1	9
17. A. Wurz	282,3	15	281,2	8	291,4	11	291,0	7	241,5	7	240,7	6	319,4	8	316,3	5
18. V. Liuzzi	281,1	19	277,7	18	286,9	19	287,0	18	239,4	15	236,1	18	316,9	14	310,5	19
19. S. Vettel	279,9	20	276,4	20	285,4	22	283,9	21	235,8	20	233,8	20	315,9	18	308,1	22
20. A. Sutil	279,5	21	277,6	19	286,3	20	286,7	19	234,4	21	233,4	21	312,0	22	310,0	21
21. S. Yamamoto	277,7	22	275,7	22	286,2	21	284,8	20	233,7	22	232,8	22	312,2	21	311,4	18
22. T. Sato	283,0	11	278,4	15	291,5	8	288,7	16	238,9	17	237,2	16	317,1	13	313,7	14
23. A. Davidson	284,9	4	280,1	13	291,4	9	288,9	15	240,4	10	236,7	17	316,9	15	315,7	10

Best sector times

Qualifs	**S1** K. Räikkönen	32.076	**S2** F. Alonso	30.633	**S3** K. Räikkönen	24.033	= 1:26.742
Race	**S1** K. Räikkönen	32.330	**S2** L. Hamilton	30.678	**S3** K. Räikkönen	24.191	= 1:27.199

RACE

Date	Weather	Air temperature	Track temperature	Humidity	Wind speed
Sunday August 26, 2007 (15:00)	Sunny	34-37°c	48-51°c	26%	1.6 m/s

Classification & retirements

Pos.	Driver	Constructor	Tyres	Laps	Time	Km/h	
1.	F. Massa	Ferrari	MMH	58	1:26.42.161	214,108	
2.	K. Räikkönen	Ferrari	MMH	58	+ 2.275	214,014	
3.	F. Alonso	McLaren Mercedes	HHM	58	+ 26.181	213,036	
4.	N. Heidfeld	BMW	HHM	58	+ 39.674	212,487	
5.	L. Hamilton	McLaren Mercedes	HHM	58	+ 45.085	212,268	
6.	H. Kovalainen	Renault	HHM	58	+ 46.169	212,224	
7.	N. Rosberg	Williams Toyota	HHM	58	+ 55.778	211,836	
8.	R. Kubica	BMW	MHM	58	+ 56.707	211,799	
9.	G. Fisichella	Renault	HHM	58	+ 59.491	211,687	
10.	D. Coulthard	Red Bull Renault	MMH	58	+ 1:11.009	211,225	
11.	A. Wurz	Williams Toyota	HHM	58	+ 1:19.628	210,880	
12.	R. Schumacher	Toyota	HM	57	1 lap	210,389	
13.	J. Button	Honda	HHM	57	1 lap	209,838	
14.	A. Davidson	Super Aguri Honda	HMM	57	1 lap	209,608	
15.	V. Liuzzi	STR Ferrari	MMH	57	1 lap	209,228	
16.	J. Trulli	Toyota	HHM	57	1 lap	209,207	
17.	R. Barrichello	Honda	HMM	57	1 lap	209,166	
18.	T. Sato	Super Aguri Honda	HM	57	1 lap	208,250	
19.	S. Vettel	STR Ferrari	HMM	57	1 lap	207,819	
20.	S. Yamamoto	Spyker Ferrari	MMH	56	2 laps	204,128	
21.	A. Sutil	Spyker Ferrari	MMH	53	5 laps	197,852	Fuel pressure problem

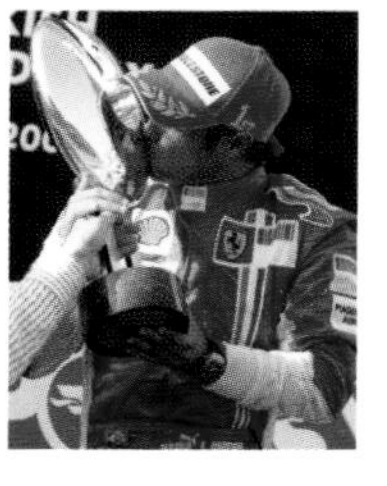

Driver	Constructor	Tyres	Laps	Reason
M. Webber	Red Bull Renault	M	9	Differential problem causing a hydraulic malfunction

Tyres H: Hard & M: Medium

Fastest laps

	Driver	Time	Lap	Km/h
1.	K. Räikkönen	1:27.295	57	220,136
2.	F. Massa	1:27.922	18	218,566
3.	L. Hamilton	1:27.963	17	218,464
4.	F. Alonso	1:28.070	39	218,199
5.	N. Heidfeld	1:28.319	39	217,583
6.	N. Rosberg	1:28.536	37	217,050
7.	H. Kovalainen	1:28.603	20	216,886
8.	A. Wurz	1:28.737	55	216,559
9.	G. Fisichella	1:28.793	56	216,422
10.	J. Button	1:28.873	34	216,227
11.	R. Kubica	1:28.918	11	216,118
12.	R. Schumacher	1:28.924	55	216,103
13.	D. Coulthard	1:29.068	54	215,754
14.	J. Trulli	1:29.459	39	214,811
15.	R. Barrichello	1:29.513	35	214,681
16.	V. Liuzzi	1:29.563	56	214,561
17.	A. Davidson	1:29.658	38	214,334
18.	T. Sato	1:29.916	56	213,719
19.	S. Vettel	1:29.983	39	213,560
20.	A. Sutil	1:30.617	52	212,066
21.	M. Webber	1:30.808	4	211,620
22.	S. Yamamoto	1:30.951	21	211,287

Pit stops

	Driver	Lap	Duration	Stop	Total
1.	R. Kubica	12	28.993	1	28.993
2.	N. Heidfeld	17	28.993	1	28.993
3.	N. Rosberg	17	29.085	1	29.085
4.	D. Coulthard	17	29.665	1	29.665
5.	K. Räikkönen	18	29.075	1	29.075
6.	F. Alonso	18	29.495	1	29.495
7.	A. Wurz	18	30.246	1	30.246
8.	F. Massa	19	29.150	1	29.150
9.	L. Hamilton	20	29.570	1	29.570
10.	J. Trulli	20	29.158	1	29.158
11.	H. Kovalainen	21	28.436	1	28.436
12.	A. Sutil	21	3:45.816	1	3:45.816
13.	G. Fisichella	22	28.603	1	28.603
14.	J. Button	22	27.358	1	27.358
15.	S. Yamamoto	22	38.357	1	38.357
16.	R. Barrichello	23	27.499	1	27.499
17.	V. Liuzzi	24	27.885	1	27.885
18.	A. Davidson	26	26.625	1	26.625
19.	S. Vettel	28	43.362	1	43.362
20.	R. Schumacher	32	29.712	1	29.712
21.	T. Sato	32	29.513	1	29.513
22.	J. Button	35	29.428	2	56.786
23.	A. Sutil	33	30.169	2	4:15.985
24.	R. Barrichello	36	27.859	2	55.358
25.	R. Kubica	37	28.164	2	57.157
26.	S. Yamamoto	36	29.144	2	1:07.501
27.	V. Liuzzi	37	28.262	2	56.147
28.	N. Rosberg	39	27.713	2	56.798
29.	K. Räikkönen	41	27.006	2	56.081
30.	N. Heidfeld	41	27.411	2	56.404
31.	F. Massa	42	27.164	2	56.314
32.	H. Kovalainen	42	27.034	2	55.470
33.	D. Coulthard	42	26.821	2	56.486
34.	A. Davidson	42	28.906	2	55.531
35.	F. Alonso	43	26.802	2	56.297
36.	L. Hamilton	43	31.079	2	1:00.649
37.	G. Fisichella	43	30.215	2	58.818
38.	S. Vettel	43	27.010	2	1:10.372
39.	A. Wurz	44	26.120	2	56.366
40.	J. Trulli	44	26.906	2	56.064

Race leader

Driver	Laps in the lead	Nbr of laps
F. Massa	1 > 19	19
L. Hamilton	20	1
H. Kovalainen	21	1
F. Massa	22 > 42	21
F. Alonso	43	1
F. Massa	44 > 58	15

Driver	Nbr of laps	Kilometers
F. Massa	55	293,382 km
L. Hamilton	1	5,338 km
H. Kovalainen	1	5,338 km
F. Alonso	1	5,338 km

Lap chart

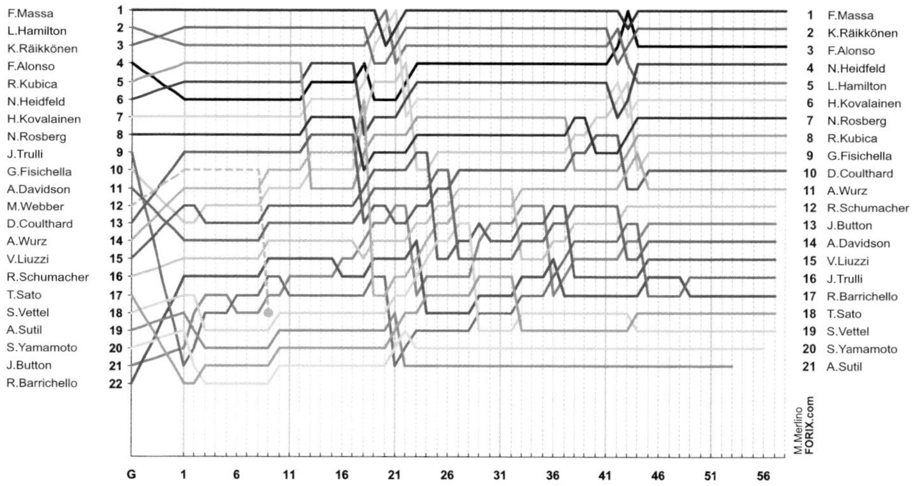
F.Massa 1
L.Hamilton 2
K.Räikkönen 3
F.Alonso 4
R.Kubica 5
N.Heidfeld 6
H.Kovalainen 7
N.Rosberg 8
J.Trulli 9
G.Fisichella 10
A.Davidson 11
M.Webber 12
D.Coulthard 13
A.Wurz 14
V.Liuzzi 15
R.Schumacher 16
T.Sato 17
S.Vettel 18
A.Sutil 19
S.Yamamoto 20
J.Button 21
R.Barrichello 22
G 1 6 11 16 21 26 31 36 41 46 51 56
1 F.Massa
2 K.Räikkönen
3 F.Alonso
4 N.Heidfeld
5 L.Hamilton
6 H.Kovalainen
7 N.Rosberg
8 R.Kubica
9 G.Fisichella
10 D.Coulthard
11 A.Wurz
12 R.Schumacher
13 J.Button
14 A.Davidson
15 V.Liuzzi
16 J.Trulli
17 R.Barrichello
18 T.Sato
19 S.Vettel
20 S.Yamamoto
21 A.Sutil
M.Merlino FORIX.com

Gaps on the lead board

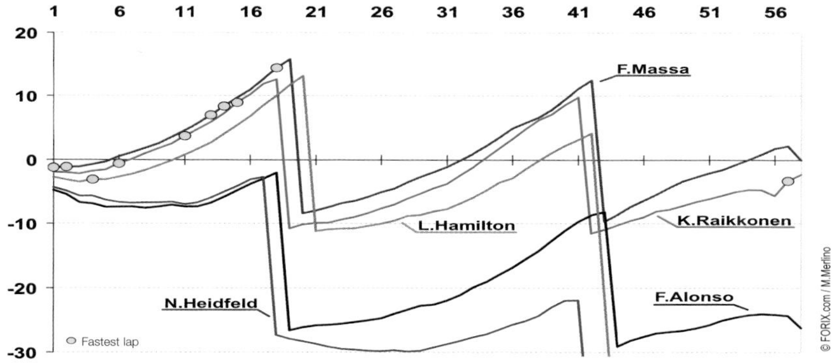
1 6 11 16 21 26 31 36 41 46 51 56
20
10
0
-10
-20
-30
F.Massa
L.Hamilton
K.Raikkonen
N.Heidfeld
F.Alonso
Fastest lap
© FORIX.com / M.Merlino

CHAMPIONSHIPS 12/17

Drivers

1.	L. Hamilton	McLaren Mercedes	3🏆	84
2.	F. Alonso	McLaren Mercedes	3🏆	79
3.	F. Massa	Ferrari	3🏆	69
4.	K. Räikkönen	Ferrari	3🏆	68
5.	N. Heidfeld	BMW		47
6.	R. Kubica	BMW		29
7.	H. Kovalainen	Renault		19
8.	G. Fisichella	Renault		17
9.	A. Wurz	Williams Toyota		13
10.	N. Rosberg	Williams Toyota		9
11.	M. Webber	Red Bull Renault		8
12.	D. Coulthard	Red Bull Renault		8
13.	J. Trulli	Toyota		7
14.	R. Schumacher	Toyota		5
15.	T. Sato	Super Aguri Honda		4
16.	J. Button	Honda		1
17.	S. Vettel	BMW 1 /// STR Ferrari 0		1
18.	R. Barrichello	Honda		0
19.	S. Speed	STR Ferrari		0
20.	A. Davidson	Super Aguri Honda		0
21.	A. Sutil	Spyker Ferrari		0
22.	C. Albers	Spyker Ferrari		0
23.	V. Liuzzi	STR Ferrari		0
24.	S. Yamamoto	Spyker Ferrari		0
	M. Winkelhock	Spyker Ferrari		-

Constructors

1.	Vodafone McLaren Mercedes	6🏆	163 148
2.	Scuderia Ferrari Marlboro	6🏆	137
3.	BMW Sauber F1 Team		77
4.	ING Renault F1 Team		36
5.	AT&T Williams		22
6.	Red Bull Racing		16
7.	Panasonic Toyota Racing		12
8.	Super Aguri F1 Team		4
9.	Honda Racing F1 Team		1
10.	Scuderia Toro Rosso		0
11.	Etihad Aldar Spyker F1 Team		0

THE CIRCUIT

Name Istanbul Speed Park; Istanbul
Lenght 5338 m
Distance 58 laps, 309,396 km
Latitude 40°57'07.80"N
Longitude 29°24'22.00"E

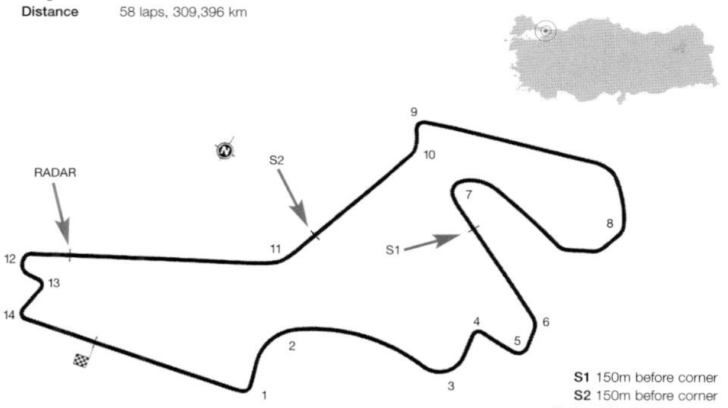
RADAR
S2
S1
1
2
3
4
5
6
7
8
9
10
11
12
13
14

S1 150m before corner
S2 150m before corner
Radar 170m before corner

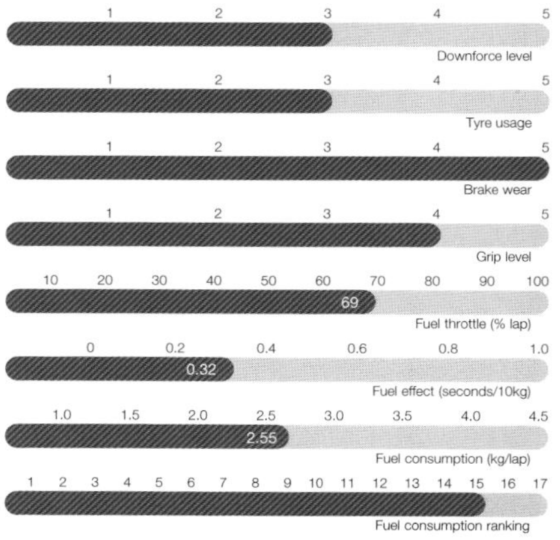
Downforce level
Tyre usage
Brake wear
Grip level
Fuel throttle (% lap)
69
Fuel effect (seconds/10kg)
0.32
Fuel consumption (kg/lap)
2.55
Fuel consumption ranking

MCLAREN SPOILS THE PARTY - BUT FINDS ITSELF IN A SPIN

After Ferrari's dominant performance in Turkey, McLaren got its revenge in Monza, blowing away the competition with a one-two finish. Within the British team, though, all was not well and the atmosphere had corroded further. Following the emergence of new evidence in the spy affair, the team had received a new summons from the FIA. Furthermore, it appeared that the new evidence had been revealed by none other than Fernando Alonso! In such stormy times, it was something of a miracle to see the two McLaren drivers put in such an impressive performance, with Ferrari powerless to respond.

> The illusion of teamwork was still alive and well between the two McLaren drivers, in parc ferme after qualifying.

Fernando takes his revenge

Fernando Alonso was truly alone. Isolated within his own team, where many considered him to be a traitor (see page 180); fighting not only against the two Ferrari drivers, chasing him in the championship, but also his team-mate Lewis Hamilton; the Spaniard had the world against him, with no idea what the future held.

Although he held a McLaren contract for 2008, he seemed to desire nothing more than a return to Renault. This, however, depended on whether or not his current employer would release him. While he waited for news, the Spaniard had decided to fight. On Saturday in Monza, he claimed his first pole position since the Monaco Grand Prix.

For the race, his plan was to lead from lights to flag. *"In Turkey, I had a lucky break which helped me close the gap to Lewis in the championship* (Hamilton had suffered a tyre failure). *Over the past two weeks since, I have thought about the situation and re-focused. I am approaching each of the last five races as if they were the championship decider: for me, it is as if the Italian Grand Prix was the Brazilian, and the title is being decided here. I am hoping to take five wins."*

At Ferrari, they endured a difficult weekend at their home circuit. On Saturday morning, Kimi Raikkonen suffered a violent accident under braking for the Ascari chicane, further proof of how tricky the car was to drive. *"It's true that the car isn't easy,"* admitted Felipe Massa, who would start from third on the grid.

"The balance isn't great, and we are struggling over the kerbs... Hopefully we can be competitive in the race, but McLaren will be hard to beat."

Having been untouchable two weeks earlier in Turkey, Ferrari were now struggling to live up to the tifosi's expectations on home turf. In reality, they needed a miracle.

> Martini embellished the Monza paddock with several models, who did everything they could to fade discreetly into the background…

STARTING GRID

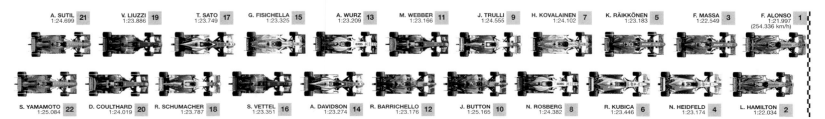

A. SUTIL 21	V. LIUZZI 19	T. SATO 17	G. FISICHELLA 15	A. WURZ 13	M. WEBBER 11	J. TRULLI 9	H. KOVALAINEN 7	K. RÄIKKÖNEN 5	F. MASSA 3	F. ALONSO 1
1:24.699	1:23.886	1:23.749	1:23.325	1:23.209	1:23.166	1:24.555	1:24.102	1:23.183	1:22.549	1:21.997 (254.336 km/h)

S. YAMAMOTO 22	D. COULTHARD 20	R. SCHUMACHER 18	S. VETTEL 16	A. DAVIDSON 14	R. BARRICHELLO 12	J. BUTTON 10	N. ROSBERG 8	R. KUBICA 6	N. HEIDFELD 4	L. HAMILTON 2
1:25.084	1:24.019	1:23.787	1:23.351	1:23.274	1:23.176	1:25.165	1:24.382	1:23.446	1:23.174	1:22.034

One-two for McLaren: the calm before the storm, forecast for Thursday in Paris

Following the Turkish Grand Prix two weeks earlier, the situation had clarified itself. On certain circuits, McLaren were unbeatable, but on others the pendulum swung decisively towards Ferrari. The British cars were most at ease among slow corners, long straights and chicanes while the Italian cars excelled in the high-speed curves.

Within the Scuderia, nobody was particularly surprised to see McLaren dominate at Monza: *"We expected to struggle here,"* admitted Kimi Raikkonen, who finished third. *"This isn't the type of circuit that suits our car. The car wasn't too bad, we just didn't have the speed..."* The reason for this was the chassis architecture: Ferrari's designers chose to lengthen the wheelbase (the space between the front and rear axles) for 2007, putting them at the opposite extreme from McLaren.

This gave the Ferraris more downforce and grip in the fast corners, but they struggled on twistier circuits. And there was also the 'floor factor': the underbody of the F2007 underwent urgent modifications ahead of the Malaysian Grand Prix, and since then, the car had struggled on bumpy surfaces and over the kerbs.

They needed a billiard-smooth track to really shine. At Monza, the two Silver Arrows were on another planet, and within the team, Lewis Hamilton never managed to get on terms with

Fernando Alonso. The young Briton drove a great race, producing a dramatic overtaking manoeuvre on Kimi Raikkonen, but he was a few tenths shy of his teammate all weekend.

It seemed that Alonso's talent and experience were still sufficient to overcome the three-point gap separating him from Hamilton. As for Ferrari, while the final circuits of the year were expected to favour them (aside from Fuji), the Italian team was going to struggle to make up a

23-point deficit to its British rival. Unless, of course, the FIA World Motor Sport Council, due to convene the following Thursday in Paris, was to penalise McLaren and offer the Scuderia the championship on a plate.

Well aware of what was at stake in the days to come, McLaren team principal Ron Dennis was moved to tears at Monza, when his cars took their fourth one-two finish of he season, in his rivals' back yard.

Alonso: "I wasn't happy with my performance in Turkey"

After Alonso led for 48 of the 53 laps, it looked like the Spaniard had enjoyed an easy afternoon.

"You know, it's never easy in Formula 1," he responded. *"You can never completely relax, because the race is never completely under control. Having said that, everything went as planned apart from the safety car period. We expected that Kimi would only make one stop, so we needed to build a good gap before we pitted, and we managed to do it in spite of the safety car period..."*

The win took Alonso to within just three points of Lewis Hamilton. With only four races to go, the battle for the title was well and truly on: *"I am behind him, so I can't afford to let any chance slip away. I am approaching every race*

the same way, trying to do the best possible job. Sometimes it works, sometimes not. In Turkey, two weeks ago, I wasn't happy with my performance, even though I took two more points out of Lewis. I knew I had to do better here. If I am going to win the title, I need to concentrate better, to drive faster, to qualify better, etc... Here, I gave everything I had."

However, it remained to be seen how the balance of power between Ferrari and McLaren would shift in the final races: *"We have seen that the advantage can swing very quickly from one team to another,"* concluded Alonso. *"I can't predict anything for the final races. At Spa, we need to see how the car performs in Friday practice before we know where we stand."*

THE CHOSEN ONE

Lewis Hamilton finished the Italian Grand Prix in second position. The Briton was powerless in the face of Alonso's superiority in Monza, and settled for second in the Spaniard's wheel-tracks.

> Lap 8: after shadowing the Williams from the start of the race, Jenson Button finally managed to pass Nico Rosberg at the end of the straight. In 2007, though, Honda couldn't do right for doing wrong, and the Briton ultimately finished two positions behind the German. Nevertheless, he scored points for just the second time of the season, taking eighth place and the final point.

Jlt may not have seemed like much, but all things are relative. Trulli hauled his Toyota to ninth position in qualifying, while teammate Ralf Schumacher languished in eighteenth. However, the Italian went backwards in the race and could only managed 11th: *"I made a bad start, lost three positions, and that ruined my race."*

>v

Felipe Massa was forced to retire after just 11 laps. After a strong start, he was running in third position ahead of teammate Kimi Raikkonen when an unidentified rear suspension failure occurred on lap 9. *"At first, I thought it was a puncture, so I pitted to change tyres - but that didn't improve the situation. The car was undriveable, and I had to retire. It's very disappointing, but these things happen in racing."*

v

The traitor went by the name of Fernando

Let's just say they have history... The mutual antipathy between McLaren boss Ron Dennis and FIA President Max Mosley can be traced back to the moment when Dennis attempted to establish a parallel championship to Formula 1, a venture entitled the GPMA (Grand Prix Manufacturers Association) intended to appeal to the sport's major manufacturers. At the time, the goals were purely financial: Ron Dennis was seeking, on behalf of the teams, a greater percentage of the television rights money than he and others had agreed to when signing the new Concorde Agreement in 1997.

Initially, it appeared that Dennis' gamble had succeeded, until Bernie Ecclestone, the sport's commercial rights holder, succeeding in luring away first Ferrari and then Renault. What followed was the implosion of the GPMA, and Dennis' project lay in tatters. Max Mosley nonetheless harboured something of resentment towards the McLaren team principal, and was probably waiting patiently for the opportunity that would allow him to settle an old score.

That opportunity came in the form of the so-called spying affair between Ferrari and McLaren. Ever since the scandal had broken in July, Ron Dennis had insisted that only chief designer Mike Coughlan was aware of the confidential information passed to him by a disillusioned Ferrari employee.

Dennis was insistent: in his version of events, nobody at McLaren knew of the existence of this information. Citing insufficient proof, the FIA World Motor Sport Council had on 26 July acquitted the team.

In the week before the Italian Grand Prix, however, an unidentified informant had made the FIA aware that others at McLaren knew of this confidential information, and that the team's test driver Pedro de la Rosa had discussed Ferrari set-up information in an email exchange with Fernando Alonso.

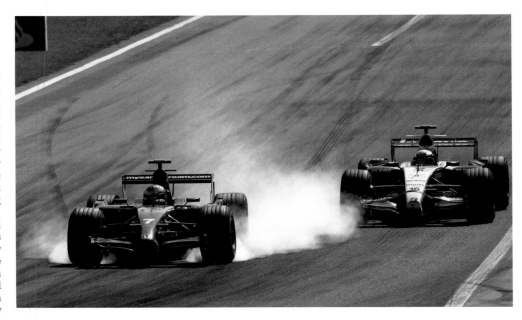

Max Mosley consequently forced McLaren drivers Alonso, Hamilton and de la Rosa to reveal what they knew of the affair, threatening them with the loss of their licences, but promising immunity if they cooperated.

Their answers constituted the 'new evidence' that persuaded the FIA to reconvene the WMSC. After Ron Dennis had clearly (although perhaps unwittingly) lied, it was impossible to see how the team could escape serious punishment.

The air at Monza buzzed with gossip and rumour, notably that Alonso himself had revealed the existence of the emails to the FIA, in the hop of breaking his 2008 contract with McLaren. Indeed, the Spaniard had just one thing on his mind: leaving the British team. But whatever other consequences this had, the Italian Grand Prix was proof that it hadn't affected his performances.

The FIA collects $50,000

"It never rains, it pours", and deluge was aimed squarely at McLaren as it set up its equipment in the Monza paddock. Another matter was hanging over the team, in addition to the 'new evidence' in the spy affair with Ferrari.

This second affair came to light on Thursday at the Italian Grand Prix, during scrutineering - the process during which race officials assess legality of the competitors before the event.

They realised that McLaren during the Hungarian Grand Prix in early August, McLaren had raced with a lightweight gearbox that had not undergone the mandatory crash test required for 'significant' changes to the structures that are impact tested at the start of the season.

In the team's opinion, the changes made for Budapest did not meet these criteria, but the Stewards decided otherwise after several hours' debate: *"It was the view of the FIA that the changes made to the original gearbox were 'significant',"* they stated, fining McLaren $50,000 for their troubles.

It was but a drop in the ocean of the team's estimated $440 million annual budget... and nothing alongside what was in store for them the following Thursday at the WMSC.

SNAPSHOTS OF THE WEEKEND

+ 349.6 km/h: this was the top speed recorded in qualifying, a mark set by the BMW Sauber of Nick Heidfeld. At the other end of the table, Jenson Button was the slowest man through the speed trap, at a 'mere' 338 km/h!

+ FOM (Formula One Management), holder of the F1 commercial rights, announced during the weekend that an agreement had been reached between Mount Fuji (owned by Toyota) and Suzuka (belong to Honda) to alternate the Japanese Grand Prix from 2009 onwards.

+ McLaren confirmed it had received a number of summonses from the Italian authorities concerning the on-going spy affair with

Ferrari. Nobody had been officially charged at this point. Nevertheless, McLaren issued a release that said *"we strongly suspect that the nature and timing of this wholly unnecessary contact, just before the start of qualifying, was to disrupt our preparation for this important session."*

+ David Coulthard's second lap crash at the Curva Grande brought out the safety car for six laps. *"I touched the back of Fisichella's car in the middle of the first chicane and broke my front wing,"* explained the Scot. *"When I accelerated, the downforce pushed the wing underneath the front of the car and broke the steering. I went straight off the track and into the tyres, that was the end of the weekend."*

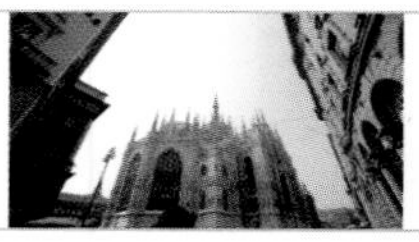

PRACTICE

Date	Weather (AM)	Air temperature	Track temperature	Weather (PM)	Air temperature	Track temperature
Friday September 7, 2007	Sunny	18-22°c	25-29°c	Sunny	26-27°c	36-38°c
Saturday September 8, 2007	Sunny	25°c	30-28°c	Sunny	28°c	36-32°c

All the time trials

N° Driver	Nat.	N° Chassis- Engine [Nbr. GP]	Pos. Free 1 Friday 10:00-11:30	Laps Tr.	Pos. Free 2 Friday 14:00-15:30	Laps Tr.	Pos. Free 3 Saturday 11:00-12:00	Laps Tr.	Pos. Q1 Saturday 14:00-14:15	Laps Tr.	Pos. Q2 Saturday 14:22-14:37	Laps Tr.	Pos. Q3 Saturday 14:45-15:00	Nb. Tr.
1. Fernando Alonso	E	McLaren MP4-22 06 - Mercedes [1]	4. 1:22.840	12	1. 1:22.386	30	1. 1:22.054	10	1. 1:21.718	3	1. 1:21.356	3	1. **1:21.997**	11
2. Lewis Hamilton	GB	McLaren MP4-22 01 - Mercedes [1]	3. 1:22.618	18	2. 1:23.209	33	2. 1:22.200	11	2. 1:21.956	3	2. 1:21.746	3	2. **1:22.034**	11
3. Giancarlo Fisichella	I	Renault R27-02 & 05 [1]	7. 1:23.671	22	3. 1:23.584	38	14. 1:23.877	12	10. 1:23.559	7	15. **1:23.325**	6		
4. Heikki Kovalainen	FIN	Renault R27-03 [2]	11. 1:24.076	21	9. 1:23.848	32	9. 1:23.672	12	9. 1:23.505	7	10. 1:23.134	6	7. **1:24.102**	11
5. Felipe Massa	BR	Ferrari F2007 263 [1]	2. 1:22.590	17	6. 1:23.722	27	3. 1:22.615	11	3. 1:22.309	3	3. 1:21.993	3	3. **1:22.549**	11
6. Kimi Räikkönen	FIN	Ferrari F2007 262 [1]	1. 1:22.446	20	8. 1:23.833	12	20. 1:24.442	3	4. 1:22.673	7	4. 1:22.369	3	5. **1:23.183**	11
7. Jenson Button	GB	Honda RA107-04 [2]	6. 1:23.668	21	13. 1:24.137	36	11. 1:23.803	15	13. 1:23.639	6	8. 1:23.021	6	10. **1:25.165**	11
8. Rubens Barrichello	BR	Honda RA107-05 [2]	12. 1:24.564	19	15. 1:24.462	40	12. 1:23.830	14	8. 1:23.474	7	12. **1:23.176**	6		
9. Nick Heidfeld	D	BMW Sauber F1.07-08 [1]	9. 1:23.886	17	7. 1:23.821	38	4. 1:22.855	15	6. 1:23.107	4	6. 1:22.466	3	4. **1:23.174**	11
10. Robert Kubica	PL	BMW Sauber F1.07-03 [1]	8. 1:23.703	22	4. 1:23.599	44	5. 1:23.287	14	5. 1:23.088	4	5. 1:22.400	3	6. **1:23.446**	11
11. Ralf Schumacher	D	Toyota TF107/05 [1]	15. 1:24.660	20	12. 1:23.922	29	18. 1:24.167	13	18. **1:23.787**	7				
12. Jarno Trulli	I	Toyota TF107/04 & 06 [1]	10. 1:23.965	29	11. 1:23.919	39	8. 1:23.672	16	15. 1:23.724	7	9. 1:23.107	6	9. **1:24.555**	11
14. David Coulthard	GB	Red Bull RB3 5 - Renault [2]	18. 1:24.810	19	16. 1:24.605	31	17. 1:24.055	12	20. **1:24.019**	6				
15. Mark Webber	AUS	Red Bull RB3 4 - Renault [1]	14. 1:24.595	22	14. 1:24.328	31	10. 1:23.708	13	11. 1:23.575	7	11. **1:23.166**	6		
16. Nico Rosberg	D	Williams FW29-05 - Toyota [2]	5. 1:23.472	21	5. 1:23.679	33	6. 1:23.454	13	7. 1:23.333	7	7. 1:22.748	6	8. **1:24.382**	11
17. Alexander Wurz	AUT	Williams FW29-03 - Toyota [1]	16. 1:24.689	29	10. 1:23.881	32	7. 1:23.596	15	16. 1:23.739	5	13. **1:23.209**	6		
18. Vitantonio Liuzzi	I	Toro Rosso STR2-03 - Ferrari [2]	22. 1:25.762	25	20. 1:25.567	26	19. 1:24.208	15	19. **1:23.886**	6				
19. Sebastian Vettel	D	Toro Rosso STR2-04 - Ferrari [1]	20. 1:25.439	25	18. 1:25.459	36	13. 1:23.853	14	12. 1:23.578	8	16. **1:23.351**	7		
20. Adrian Sutil	D	Spyker F8-VII/03 B-spec - Ferrari [2]	19. 1:25.130	24	19. 1:25.531	24	22. 1:24.943	18	21. **1:24.699**	10				
21. Sakon Yamamoto	J	Spyker F8-VII/04 B-spec - Ferrari [1]	21. 1:25.448	25	21. 1:25.863	40	21. 1:24.736	17	22. **1:25.084**	8				
22. Takuma Sato	J	Super Aguri SA07-02 - Honda [2]	13. 1:24.587	15	17. 1:25.328	27	16. 1:24.022	16	17. **1:23.749**	5				
23. Anthony Davidson	GB	Super Aguri SA07-03 - Honda [2]	17. 1:24.694	17	22. 1:26.021	6	15. 1:23.942	12	14. 1:23.646	6	14. **1:23.274**	6		

Fastest lap overall
F. Alonso 1:21.356 (256,340 km/h)

Maximum speed

N° Driver	S1 Qualifs	Pos.	S1 Race	Pos.	S2 Qualifs	Pos.	S2 Race	Pos.	Finish Qualifs	Pos.	Finish Race	Pos.	Radar Qualifs	Pos.	Radar Race	Pos.
1. F. Alonso	331,5	6	335,8	2	336,3	4	340,5	1	318,6	2	318,4	2	346,7	6	350,5	2
2. L. Hamilton	333,5	3	334,8	3	338,4	1	338,5	2	319,2	1	319,5	1	345,0	9	350,3	3
3. G. Fisichella	332,7	4	332,3	6	336,0	5	335,0	8	315,3	7	316,9	4	347,3	4	347,7	7
4. H. Kovalainen	330,6	8	329,6	15	332,1	12	333,8	11	314,1	9	312,7	10	347,1	5	347,6	8
5. F. Massa	333,7	2	339,1	1	337,9	3	337,9	4	317,7	4	316,0	5	346,2	7	345,7	11
6. K. Räikkönen	333,8	1	333,5	5	338,0	2	338,1	3	318,0	3	314,6	7	346,0	8	346,4	9
7. J. Button	325,3	19	328,4	19	329,2	18	328,8	21	310,7	19	310,5	18	338,0	22	341,6	20
8. R. Barrichello	327,2	16	329,0	18	329,3	17	331,3	17	309,5	20	311,0	13	338,6	19	341,2	22
9. N. Heidfeld	331,3	7	333,5	4	334,9	6	335,9	5	317,3	5	316,9	3	349,6	1	349,5	4
10. R. Kubica	330,5	9	331,5	8	333,7	7	335,6	6	316,6	6	315,6	6	348,8	2	351,7	1
11. R. Schumacher	327,3	15	331,5	9	329,0	20	335,4	7	313,4	12	314,3	9	340,8	14	348,8	6
12. J. Trulli	332,2	5	331,0	10	331,0	13	334,7	9	315,0	8	314,5	8	347,7	3	349,5	5
14. D. Coulthard	326,3	18	325,3	20	329,4	15	323,5	22	311,4	17	307,3	22	340,0	17	343,8	16
15. M. Webber	327,8	12	329,2	16	329,6	14	330,8	18	312,3	16	310,6	17	340,5	15	344,8	13
16. N. Rosberg	327,4	14	329,8	14	329,3	16	330,0	19	313,8	10	312,5	11	340,1	16	345,6	12
17. A. Wurz	324,7	21	325,2	21	326,2	22	329,9	20	313,5	11	311,1	12	338,5	20	341,5	21
18. V. Liuzzi	327,0	17	329,1	17	332,1	11	332,8	14	310,9	18	308,6	21	342,2	11	344,2	14
19. S. Vettel	329,9	10	332,1	7	332,6	8	333,6	12	312,7	14	310,7	16	344,7	10	345,9	10
20. A. Sutil	324,6	22	325,0	22	327,8	21	332,8	15	308,5	21	309,4	20	338,3	21	343,5	17
21. S. Yamamoto	325,2	20	330,1	11	329,1	19	332,9	13	308,4	22	310,8	14	340,0	18	344,0	15
22. T. Sato	327,7	13	329,9	13	332,1	10	333,8	10	312,4	15	309,6	19	341,3	13	343,1	18
23. A. Davidson	329,3	11	330,0	12	332,5	9	332,5	16	312,8	13	310,8	15	341,4	12	342,4	19

Best sector times

Qualifs	**S1** F. Alonso	26.605	**S2** L. Hamilton	27.709	**S3** F. Alonso	26.949	= 1:21.263
Race	**S1** L. Hamilton	26.799	**S2** F. Alonso	28.021	**S3** F. Alonso	27.592	= 1:22.412

RACE

Date	Weather	Air temperature	Track temperature	Humidity	Wind speed
Sunday September 9, 2007 (14:00)	Sunny	26-28°c	34-38°c	41%	1.6 m/s

Classification & retirements

Pos.	Driver	Constructor	Tyres	Laps	Time	Km/h
1.	F. Alonso	McLaren Mercedes	MMS	53	1:18:37.806	234,047
2.	L. Hamilton	McLaren Mercedes	MMS	53	+ 6.062	233,747
3.	K. Räikkönen	Ferrari	SM	53	+ 27.325	232,699
4.	N. Heidfeld	BMW	MMS	53	+ 56.562	231,274
5.	R. Kubica	BMW	MMS	53	+ 1:00.558	231,081
6.	N. Rosberg	Williams Toyota	MS	53	+ 1:05.810	230,827
7.	H. Kovalainen	Renault	MMS	53	+ 1:06.751	230,782
8.	J. Button	Honda	MS	53	+ 1:12.168	230,521
9.	M. Webber	Red Bull Renault	MS	53	+ 1:15.879	230,343
10.	R. Barrichello	Honda	MS	53	1 lap	230,291
11.	J. Trulli	Toyota	MS	53	1 lap	230,253
12.	G. Fisichella	Renault	MS	52	1 lap	229,546
13.	A. Wurz	Williams Toyota	MS	52	1 lap	229,240
14.	A. Davidson	Super Aguri Honda	MS	52	1 lap	229,066
15.	R. Schumacher	Toyota	MS	52	1 lap	228,995
16.	T. Sato	Super Aguri Honda	MS	52	1 lap	228,888
17.	V. Liuzzi	STR Ferrari	MS	52	1 lap	228,583
18.	S. Vettel	STR Ferrari	MMS	52	1 lap	228,328
19.	A. Sutil	Spyker Ferrari	SMS	52	1 lap	226,211
20.	S. Yamamoto	Spyker Ferrari	SSM	52	1 lap	225,662

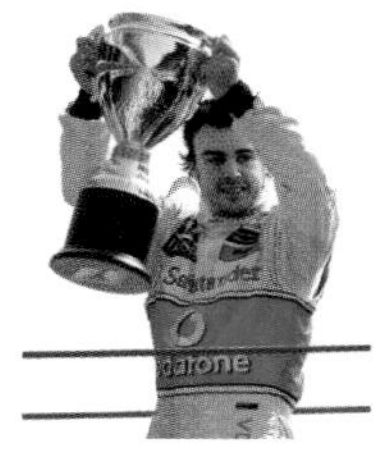

Driver	Constructor	Tyres	Laps	Reason
F. Massa	Ferrari	MM	10	Rear damper failure
D. Coulthard	Red Bull Renault	S	1	Contact with Fisichella, front wing gets stuck under car and breaks steering, car goes straight on and hits tyre wall

Tyres M: Medium & S: Soft

Fastest laps

	Driver	Time	Lap	Km/h
1.	F. Alonso	1:22.871	15	251,653
2.	L. Hamilton	1:22.936	17	251,456
3.	K. Räikkönen	1:23.370	21	250,147
4.	N. Heidfeld	1:23.681	19	249,217
5.	R. Kubica	1:23.908	22	248,543
6.	F. Massa	1:23.971	8	248,357
7.	H. Kovalainen	1:24.226	53	247,605
8.	N. Rosberg	1:24.472	52	246,884
9.	J. Button	1:24.532	32	246,708
10.	J. Trulli	1:24.622	49	246,446
11.	T. Sato	1:24.669	49	246,309
12.	R. Barrichello	1:24.767	52	246,024
13.	M. Webber	1:24.824	46	245,859
14.	G. Fisichella	1:24.849	32	245,787
15.	R. Schumacher	1:24.951	49	245,492
16.	A. Wurz	1:25.000	42	245,350
17.	A. Davidson	1:25.116	46	245,016
18.	S. Vettel	1:25.313	47	244,450
19.	V. Liuzzi	1:25.373	45	244,278
20.	A. Sutil	1:25.377	30	244,267
21.	S. Yamamoto	1:25.478	34	243,978

Pit stops

	Driver	Lap	Duration	Stop	Total
1.	S. Vettel	1	32.765	1	32.765
2.	F. Massa	9	33.363	1	33.363
3.	L. Hamilton	18	29.868	1	29.868
4.	F. Alonso	20	30.805	1	30.805
5.	S. Yamamoto	20	29.014	1	29.014
6.	N. Heidfeld	21	28.630	1	28.630
7.	H. Kovalainen	21	29.693	1	29.693
8.	A. Sutil	21	30.290	1	30.290
9.	R. Kubica	23	38.641	1	38.641
10.	K. Räikkönen	25	32.678	1	32.678
11.	N. Rosberg	30	30.717	1	30.717
12.	J. Trulli	30	31.041	1	31.041
13.	R. Schumacher	31	29.498	1	29.498
14.	S. Vettel	31	30.749	2	1:03.244
15.	V. Liuzzi	32	30.054	1	30.054
16.	J. Button	33	30.094	1	30.094
17.	G. Fisichella	33	29.757	1	29.757
18.	M. Webber	34	29.504	1	29.504
19.	R. Barrichello	34	29.772	1	29.772
20.	T. Sato	34	29.853	1	29.853
21.	A. Davidson	35	29.582	1	29.582
22.	S. Yamamoto	35	30.424	2	59.438
23.	A. Wurz	37	31.563	1	31.563
24.	A. Sutil	37	29.987	2	1:00.277
25.	N. Heidfeld	39	27.517	2	56.147
26.	L. Hamilton	40	27.428	2	57.296
27.	H. Kovalainen	41	27.459	2	57.152
28.	F. Alonso	43	27.245	2	58.050
29.	R. Kubica	43	27.388	2	1:06.029

Race leader

Driver	Laps in the lead	Nbr of laps
F. Alonso	1 > 20	20
K. Räikkönen	21 > 25	5
F. Alonso	26 > 53	28

Driver	Nbr of laps	Kilometers
F. Alonso	48	277,755 km
K. Räikkönen	5	28,965 km

Gaps on the lead board

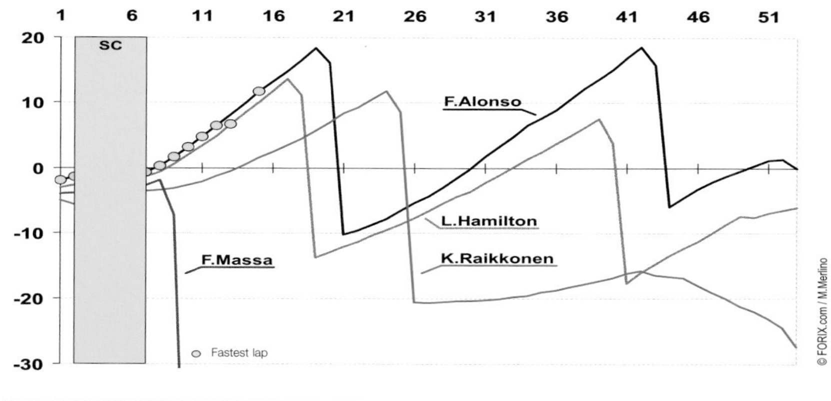
1 6 11 16 21 26 31 36 41 46 51
20
10
0
-10
-20
-30
SC
F.Alonso
L.Hamilton
K.Raikkonen
F.Massa
Fastest lap

Lap chart

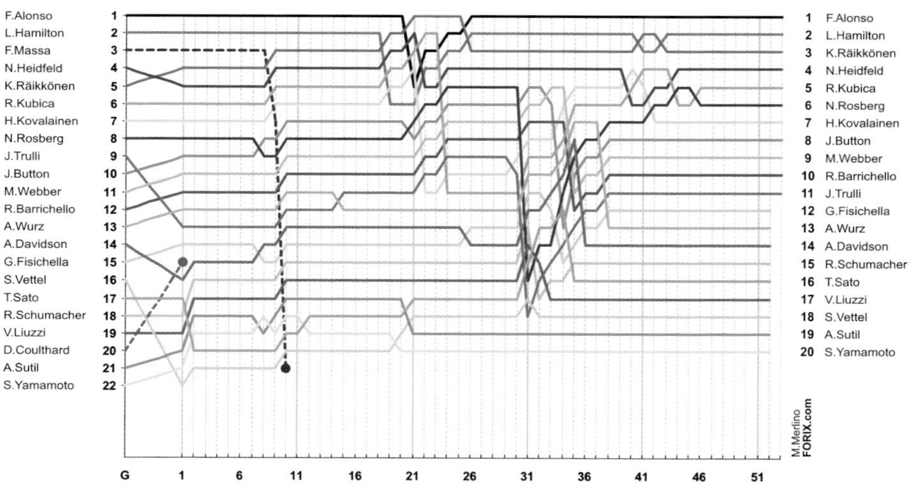
F.Alonso 1
L.Hamilton 2
F.Massa 3
N.Heidfeld 4
K.Räikkönen 5
R.Kubica 6
H.Kovalainen 7
N.Rosberg 8
J.Trulli 9
J.Button 10
M.Webber 11
R.Barrichello 12
A.Wurz 13
A.Davidson 14
G.Fisichella 15
S.Vettel 16
T.Sato 17
R.Schumacher 18
V.Liuzzi 19
D.Coulthard 20
A.Sutil 21
S.Yamamoto 22
1 F.Alonso
2 L.Hamilton
3 K.Räikkönen
4 N.Heidfeld
5 R.Kubica
6 N.Rosberg
7 H.Kovalainen
8 J.Button
9 M.Webber
10 R.Barrichello
11 J.Trulli
12 G.Fisichella
13 A.Wurz
14 A.Davidson
15 R.Schumacher
16 T.Sato
17 V.Liuzzi
18 S.Vettel
19 A.Sutil
20 S.Yamamoto
G 1 6 11 16 21 26 31 36 41 46 51
M.Merlino
FORIX.com

© FORIX.com / M.Merlino

CHAMPIONSHIPS 13/17

Drivers

	Driver	Constructor	Wins	Points
1.	L. Hamilton	McLaren Mercedes	3	92
2.	F. Alonso	McLaren Mercedes	4	89
3.	K. Räikkönen	Ferrari	3	74
4.	F. Massa	Ferrari	3	69
5.	N. Heidfeld	BMW		52
6.	R. Kubica	BMW		33
7.	H. Kovalainen	Renault		21
8.	G. Fisichella	Renault		17
9.	A. Wurz	Williams Toyota		13
10.	N. Rosberg	Williams Toyota		12
11.	M. Webber	Red Bull Renault		8
12.	D. Coulthard	Red Bull Renault		8
13.	J. Trulli	Toyota		7
14.	R. Schumacher	Toyota		5
15.	T. Sato	Super Aguri Honda		4
16.	J. Button	Honda		2
17.	S. Vettel	BMW 1 /// STR Ferrari 0		1
18.	R. Barrichello	Honda		0
19.	S. Speed	STR Ferrari		0
20.	A. Davidson	Super Aguri Honda		0
21.	A. Sutil	Spyker Ferrari		0
22.	C. Albers	Spyker Ferrari		0
23.	V. Liuzzi	STR Ferrari		0
24.	S. Yamamoto	Spyker Ferrari		0
	M. Winkelhock	Spyker Ferrari		-

Constructors

	Constructor	Wins	Points
1.	Vodafone McLaren Mercedes	7	[181] 166
2.	Scuderia Ferrari Marlboro	6	143
3.	BMW Sauber F1 Team		86
4.	ING Renault F1 Team		38
5.	AT&T Williams		25
6.	Red Bull Racing		16
7.	Panasonic Toyota Racing		12
8.	Super Aguri F1 Team		4
9.	Honda Racing F1 Team		2
10.	Scuderia Toro Rosso		0
11.	Etihad Aldar Spyker F1 Team		0

THE CIRCUIT

Name Autodromo Nazionale Monza; Monza
Lenght 5793 m
Distance 53 laps, 306,720 km

Latitude 45°37'08.20"N
Longitude 9°16'52.15"E

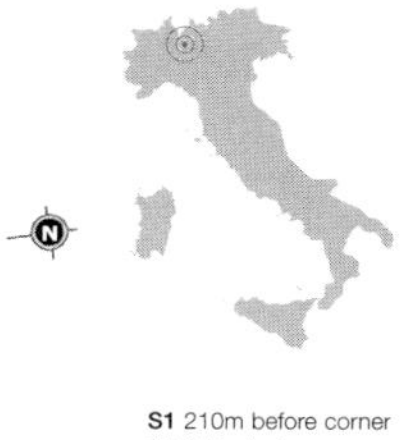

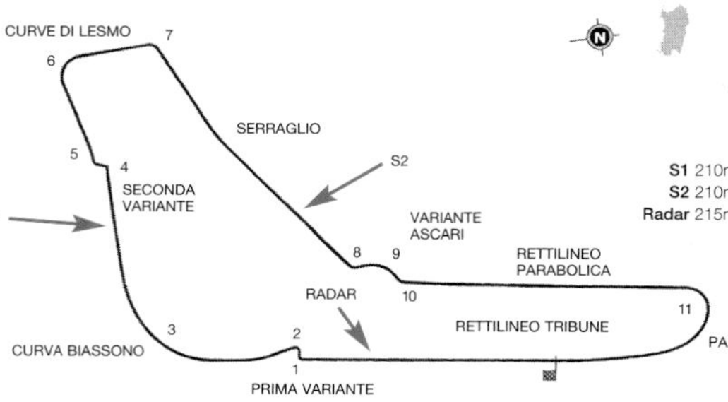
CURVE DI LESMO
SERRAGLIO
SECONDA VARIANTE
VARIANTE ASCARI
RETTILINEO PARABOLICA
RADAR
RETTILINEO TRIBUNE
PARABOLICA
CURVA BIASSONO
PRIMA VARIANTE
S1
S2
1 2 3 4 5 6 7 8 9 10 11

S1 210m before corner
S2 210m before corner
Radar 215m before corner

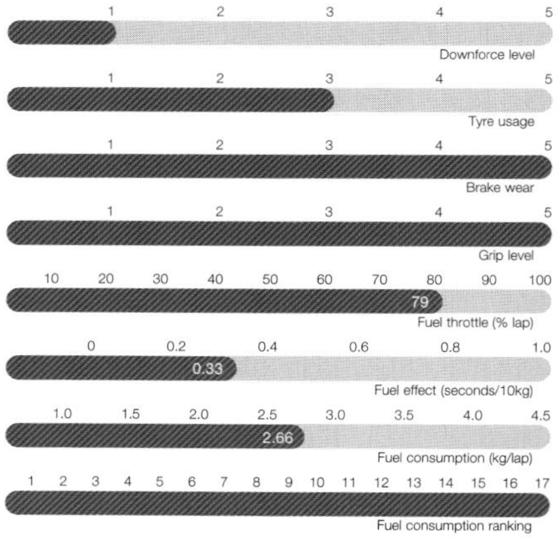
1 2 3 4 5
Downforce level
1 2 3 4 5
Tyre usage
1 2 3 4 5
Brake wear
1 2 3 4 5
Grip level
10 20 30 40 50 60 70 80 90 100
79
Fuel throttle (% lap)
0 0.2 0.4 0.6 0.8 1.0
0.33
Fuel effect (seconds/10kg)
1.0 1.5 2.0 2.5 3.0 3.5 4.0 4.5
2.66
Fuel consumption (kg/lap)
1 2 3 4 5 6 7 8 9 10 11 12 13 14 15 16 17
Fuel consumption ranking

AFTER THE SCANDAL, VICTORY

History will record that Kimi Raikkonen won the Belgian Grand Prix at Spa-Francorchamps, after a memorably dull race in which the top four qualifiers went on to finish in the top four positions.

However, the action off the track was anything but tedious. On the Thursday before the race, the FIA World Council met in Paris to consider the 'spygate' scandal between McLaren and Ferrari for the second and final time.

In the light of the evidence that was furnished at the first hearing, which took place on 26 July, the World Council decided this time to exclude McLaren from the 2007 constructors' championship and to fine the team a record 100 million dollars.

Naturally, this astonishing turn of events dominated conversation in the paddock at Spa. Kimi Raikkonen's win - and his stealthy progress up the drivers' championship table - almost passed unnoticed. The Finn left Belgium with a 13-point gap to the series leader Lewis Hamilton, while Fernando Alonso finished third to close to within just two points of his team mate.

> Saturday. After a brief round of handshakes, Ron Dennis and Max Mosley go their separate ways on the steps of the McLaren motorhome. Their opinion of each other seems quite clear…

A fine of 100 million dollars and 166 points

Paris, Place de la Concorde, Thursday 13 September. In the FIA's sumptuous headquarters at number 8 Place de la Concorde, a battle was raging. McLaren was in front of the FIA World Council, answering charges of industrial espionage against Ferrari.

At 11: 30, Lewis Hamilton was the first to leave the building. Fernando Alonso was not present, as he had submitted his evidence in writing.

Half an hour later, McLaren team principal Ron Dennis emerged dressed in a black suit, together with the team's co-owner Mansour Ojjeh and McLaren's third driver Pedro de la Rosa. They hurried off to join Lewis Hamilton at the restaurant of the nearby Hotel Crillon.

Two hours later, they returned to the fray. The representatives of Ferrari were more discreet, using a secret entrance to the building. Finally, judgement was handed down in the evening.

For McLaren, it was bad news: the team was found guilty of having violated article 151c of the sporting code, which is all about bringing the sport into disrepute. Consequently, the team was fined 100 million dollars and stripped of all its constructor points (which so far had amounted to 166 points: 23 points more than Ferrari). Not only that, but McLaren was comprehensively thrown out of this year's constructors' championship.

However, it was allowed to deduct from the fine all the bonuses given for each point scored. For a team that wins the World Championship, those bonuses add up to about 50 million dollars. The fine was hardly going to break McLaren's budget, but nonetheless it blew a big hole in the team's balance sheets.

The drivers, however, weren't punished. FIA President Max Mosley had promised them immunity provided they collaborated fully with the World Council hearing. The FIA also decided to go over the 2008 McLaren with a fine toothcomb. If they happened to find any elements of the design 'borrowed' from Ferrari, then they reserved the right to impose further sanctions.

Punishing the McLaren team while sparing the drivers represented a half measure. Either the British team did not have access to Ferrari's confidential information or it did. If it did not, then it was entirely innocent and the case should have dropped. If it did, however, then the team was well and truly guilty of cheating and deserved its punishment: even though it was unprecedented. In which case, the drivers would have profited from the situation as well, and also deserved to be punished.

By choosing a middle way, the FIA was clearly trying to avoid an even bigger scandal. With McLaren stripped of its points, Ferrari was comfortably constructors' champion. Not that anybody pays particular attention to the manufacturers' title, which is only really there so that one of the big car companies can put a laurel wreath on their advertising posters at the end of the year…

The drivers' championship, however, is where it's at. The whole of England was behind the country's new idol Lewis Hamilton, while Fernando Alonso enjoyed the same fervent support in Spain.

To touch the drivers' championship risked antagonising the general public all over the world. So the FIA chose a somewhat half-hearted punishment, which only really affected the ego of the McLaren management - plus one or to of their ample purse strings…

> Max Mosley had several questions to answer in the paddock at Spa. Going for a quick wander around on Saturday was probably not such a good idea.

Ron Dennis undecided as to whether or not to appeal

The FIA's decision on Thursday night rocked McLaren to the core. Ron Dennis, leaving the Place de la Concorde, said that he was mystified. *"All the evidence furnished by our drivers, engineers and team members have clearly demonstrated that we did not use any information from Ferrari to our advantage."* Unsurprisingly he did not elaborate on the fact that he had perhaps unwittingly lied for several weeks, stating that nobody from McLaren was aware of any information coming from Ferrari when several of the testimonies seemed to suggest otherwise.

He also went onto to suggest that any information received had not been used to the benefit of McLaren. *"Our group of engineers, consisting of more than 140 people, have all testified that they have not received the slight bit of information about Ferrari,"* added Dennis. *"Our three drivers have also explained that they have not given the slightest bit of information about Ferrari to the team, contrary to what the press has assumed. The most important thing though is that we are going to race this weekend, next year and for the coming years. We've got the best car and the best drivers and we fully intend to win the World Championship."*

Crime and punishment

At first sight, the penalty inflicted on the FIA by McLaren seemed harsh. However, it was justified by the detailed text of Thursday's judgement that was published on Friday by the FIA. The transcript makes it quite clear that McLaren designer Mike Coughlan received several pieces of information from Nigel Stepney. McLaren, like everybody else, knew that to be in receipt of that information was a grave violation of the sporting code.

This explains why Ron Dennis was so anxious to play down the whole story from the very beginning. During the British Grand Prix in July, Dennis swore that nobody other than Mike Coughlan had access to Ferrari's secrets. He was even in tears, making his words seem sincere.

It was a good bit of acting. Once the transcript was released on Friday, it was clear that all the McLaren management and driver had knowledge of the dossier for some time. As the following illustrates:
• E-mail of 21 March between Pedro de la Rosa, the team's third driver, and Mike Coughlan: *"Hi Mike,*

can you let me know the weight distribution of the Ferrari? That's important for us because we can test it in the simulator." Coughlan was asked to send the data required, to the precision of two decimal points.
• E-mail of 25 March between Pedro de la Rosa and Fernando Alonso, describing a special gas that Ferrari uses to inflate its tyres, which stops them from overheating. *"We have to try it,"* concludes the McLaren third driver.
• E-mail of 12 April between Pedro de la Rosa and Mike Coughlan: *"Can you explain to me how the Ferrari braking system works? Can the drivers adjust it from the cockpit?"* In his reply, Coughlan explains that McLaren is working on «an identical system.»
• Despite Ron Dennis's claims, the leaks are not just limited to the infamous 780-page dossier. Nigel Stepney and Mike Coughlan had a full-time flow of information: between 11 March and 3 July 2007, they exchanged 288 text messages, 35 phone calls and several e-mails.

• The e-mail exchanges also described Ferrari's fuel strategy, specifying exactly on which laps the cars would stop at every Grand Prix.
This was crucial information, which undoubtedly allowed McLaren to come up with policies to foil Ferrari.
Pedro de la Rosa insisted on Thursday that at his request McLaren never tested the Ferrari weight distribution on their simulator, and that the team never tested the special gas for the tyres.
The judges were somewhat dubious : how could a mere test driver divert or even influence the development programme formulated by the team's engineers?
But these lies were not the crux of the case. At the heart of the matter was the fact that McLaren had profited from Ferrari's leaked information, and that this information could have led to some of the seven victories racked up by the team over the course of the season. Bearing all that in mind, the punishment seemed to fit the crime.

Mosley: *"We were too lenient!"*

FIA President Max Mosley was present at Spa over the weekend, where he described the FIA World Council's decision on Thursday as being «too lenient.»
He elaborated: *"You have to consider what exactly 100 million dollars means for these people. It's less than the difference between McLaren's budget and that of Williams or Renault. All this fine does is reduce their budget to the level of that of a less*

wealthy team. It's certainly not disproportionate: in fact I would call it quite a modest fine. In fact, McLaren was extremely lucky not to have simply been excluded for the next two years. We nearly said that they have polluted this 2007 Championship, and that they have probably polluted the 2008 Championship as well, through their knowledge of the inner workings of Ferrari. In a few years' time,

when history judges this episode, we will probably be reproached for not having done enough."
Max Mosley was probably right: Ron Dennis said on Friday night that he would pay the fine without touching the race team budget. *"We will just have to find the 100 million from other income streams,"* he said. Just to wind up Max Mosley and the FIA a little more...

Closed shop. The McLaren team garage was locked up all day on Thursday, while the team management was answering the 'spygate' case in Paris.

∨

McLaren's punishment: the reactions

• *"The partnership between Mercedes and McLaren hasn't been called into question. This affair has no negative repercussions on the image of Mercedes whatsoever. With all our wins this year, it has been a very good season for us."* Norbert Haug, Mercedes competitions director.
• *"As soon as I found out that that there was some new evidence against us on the morning of the Hungarian Grand Prix, I personally alerted the FIA straight away."* Ron Dennis, confirming that it was him who started the chain of events leading to Thursday's World Council hearing in Paris.
• *"If we were forced to pay a fine like that it's very simple: we'd go bust."* Gerhard Berger, co-owner of the Toro Rosso team.
• *"I really had to work hard to get McLaren off the hook at the World Council meeting and persuade the judges to go down the route of a fine. We came within a hair's breadth of seeing the team thrown out for the next two seasons."* Bernie Ecclestone, the sport's commercial rights-holder, who was at the FIA World Council meeting on Thursday.
• *"If you haven't got 100 million dollars and nobody's willing to lend them to you then you have to close down."* Mario Thiessen, team principal of BMW Sauber - which is now second in the 2007 World Championship.

> Kimi Raikkonen took his third pole position of the season, and his first since the European Grand Prix. The paddock was so intent on the drama at McLaren that few people paid much attention to what was happening on the track.

> Smiles in the paddock. If it were like this in Belgium all the time, hundreds of mechanics and journalists would not hesitate to move here.

> Some of the new paddock facilities were as impressive as they were impractical.

Ferrari back in front

With all the controversy surrounding the opinions of Ron Dennis and his dealings with the FIA (see page 184), Saturday's action on the circuit was almost relegated to a sideshow.

That was a pity, as some interest lay in the fact that the two Ferraris managed to monopolise the front row of the grid for the first time all season. Kimi Raikkonen, who led Felipe Massa, said: *"I felt that there was something a bit strange at the rear of the car but the mechanics didn't find anything, so I pushed hard again. It wasn't perfect, but the car was quick enough for pole. Now we've just got to make it work during the race."*

Felipe Massa, in the second Ferrari, was second by just 17 thousandths of a second after losing a tiny bit of time under braking for the final chicane. *"My lap was perfect,"* said the Brazilian. *"I was a little bit optimistic at the final chicane though. My rear tyres locked up, and it was here that I must have lost those fractions of seconds that I needed to claim pole."*

Behind them the two McLarens locked out the second row, with Fernando Alonso having lost time because of a spin that flat-spotted his tyres. *"Without that, I would have been on pole,"* claimed the Spaniard.

Kimi Raikkonen was 15 points behind Fernando Alonso and 18 points behind Lewis Hamilton in the championship. With only four Grands Prix left to run, he couldn't afford to waste any more time.

STARTING GRID

G. FISICHELLA* 22 1:46.603	A. DAVIDSON* 20 1:48.199	T. SATO 18 1:47.980	S. VETTEL 16 1:47.581	R. KUBICA* 14 1:46.996	J. BUTTON 12 1:46.955	R. SCHUMACHER 10 1:46.618	J. TRULLI 8 1:47.798	N. HEIDFELD 6 1:47.409	L. HAMILTON 4 1:46.406	F. MASSA 2 1:46.011
S. YAMAMOTO 21 1:49.577	A. SUTIL 19 1:48.044	R. BARRICHELLO 17 1:47.954	A. WURZ 15 1:47.394	V. LIUZZI 13 1:47.115	D. COULTHARD 11 1:46.800	H. KOVALAINEN 9 1:48.505	M. WEBBER 7 1:47.524	N. ROSBERG 5 1:47.334	F. ALONSO 3 1:46.091	K. RÄIKKÖNEN 1 1:45.994 (237.885 km/h)

Ferraris unbeatable at Spa

Rarely has a season been so varied in the history of Formula 1. Since the start of the summer, things had gone either Ferrari's or McLaren's way at every race - with the pendulum swinging one way or another. The two teams hardly ever experienced a race that was completely open, where the win could have gone either way.

At Monaco, Montreal, Indianapolis, Budapest and Monza, the Silver Arrows were absolutely untouchable. At Magny-Cours, Silverstone, Istanbul and Spa nobody could get on top of the Ferraris.

The red cars dominated the Belgian Grand Prix, in stark contrast to the poor showing that they had displayed in Monza just a week earlier. It was as if Kimi Raikkonen and Felipe Massa were driving completely different cars. Even Ferrari struggled to explain the dramatic turnaround in their fortunes. "It's to do with the flat floor," explained the technical director of a rival team. "Ever since Ferrari were forced to modify it in a hurry, following McLaren's complaint after the Australian Grand Prix, they've been forced to run with very hard suspension. Of course that only works on very smooth tracks like this that don't require much in the way of suspension travel."

His analysis is borne out by the list of circuits where Ferrari have struggled: Monza, with its big kerbs that both Raikkonen and Massa said they struggled to negotiate, Monaco, with its bumpy streets, Montreal, with its frost-damaged asphalt, and Hungary, with its track built by the tanks of the Hungarian army.

On newer tracks by contrast - or those that had been recently resurfaced - the Ferraris reigned supreme. "It's true that we've lacked grip in places like Monaco, Monza or Indianapolis," said Ferrari team principal Jean Todt. "We're also not quick enough over bumps and kerbs. That's something we will be working on for 2008. Generally speaking though, our biggest problem this year has been that we are not reliable enough."

There was no point even in discussing the 'flat floor' theory with Ferrari: that would be giving away too much information. If it was true though, the thesis suggested that Ferrari would be equally difficult to beat in Japan and China: two brand new circuits that would suit the Scuderia's purposes perfectly.

Jean Todt hopes for McLaren appeal

At 7pm on Sunday night, before speaking to all the journalists, Jean Todt asked for a minute's silence to be observed in memory of Colin McRae the former World Rally Champion killed in a helicopter crash on Saturday night together with his young son and two friends.

Afterwards, the Frenchman delivered his opinion on the McLaren saga for the first time all weekend. "To be honest, I think that the punishment is too light. If you look closely at the whole sorry saga it's easy to see that the sentence was too lenient, even though we will of course respect it. The most important thing is that the guilty parties have finally been punished, which was not the case after the first World Council meeting on 26 July." The Ferrari boss went on to say that he hoped McLaren would appeal against the decision. "We really hope that McLaren will decide to appeal. Because if they do, then I think we will see a rather different result. It's a personal feeling, but let's say that I reckon the FIA have taken several factors into account when making their decision. They've tried to balance out the interests of the championship rather than looking at the case on its own. That's why I'm not going to talk about the drivers' championship situation today. Let's see first if McLaren decides to appeal." The deadline for appeal would expire the following Wednesday…

The FIA also required McLaren to submit their 2008 car for inspection, in order to determine whether or not it incorporated any of Ferrari's intellectual property. This was another subject upon which Jean Todt was reticent. "I don't want to talk about 2008," he said. "In any case, the interest of the team is the most important thing. There are also some civil cases pending: we have filed a lawsuit against an individual in Italy [their

former employee Nigel Stepney] and there is a case in England (against former McLaren designer Mike Coughlan) as well. These two cases have nothing to do with the FIA; they are down to individual judges. All these things aren't very good for Formula 1: it's a bit like drugs in cycling."

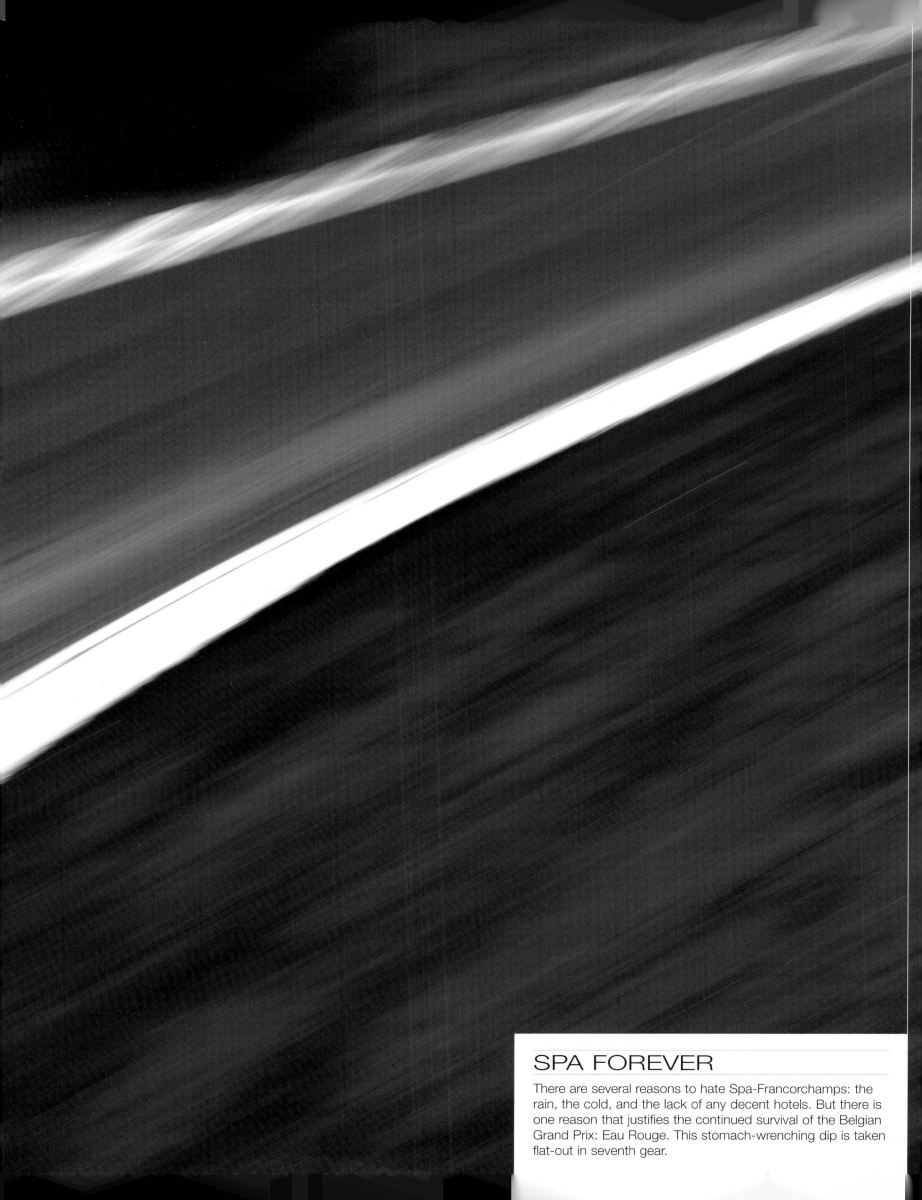

SPA FOREVER

There are several reasons to hate Spa-Francorchamps: the rain, the cold, and the lack of any decent hotels. But there is one reason that justifies the continued survival of the Belgian Grand Prix: Eau Rouge. This stomach-wrenching dip is taken flat-out in seventh gear.

Fernando was the trator

> Lewis Hamilton gets crossed up under braking for La Source. The Englishman could not do much about his teammate in front of him, and settled for fourth. In fact, the first four places on the grid at Spa were also the first four places at the finish.

Ron Dennis invited several journalists to the McLaren motorhome on Saturday morning in order to hear his version of the e-mail dialogue between Pedro de la Rosa and Fernando Alonso: an escapade that cost McLaren all of its constructor points and 100 million dollars. Dennis revealed that it was actually Fernando Alonso who caused his team's downfall. At the Hungarian Grand Prix Alonso lost his pole position after the event stewards penalised him five grid places for blocking Lewis Hamilton in the pitlane, and the Spaniard was on a knife-edge.

On that Sunday morning, Alonso asked to leave the team at the end of the season - even though his contract ran to the end of 2008. After Dennis refused to let him go, Alonso threatened to tell the FIA what he knew about the 'spygate' scandal. *"Fernando had breakfast with me that morning in Budapest,"* Dennis related. *"He was angry, for all sorts of reasons. He told me that he was in possession of some e-mails that could harm the team and that those e-mails came from one of our engineers. I told him that he should show them to the FIA. As soon as he had gone, I called Max Mosley (the president of the FIA) to explain to him what had just happened. Half an hour later, Fernando's manager came up to me to apologise on behalf of Fernando. But it was too late."* Max Mosley confirmed this version of events. *"Ron called me to tell me about his discussion with Alonso, but he said that there was nothing special contained within the e-mails in question. To start with I believed him - after all, I've known him for 40 years and I trust him. But then I received a report from the Italian police stating that more than 300 text messages had passed between Mike Coughlan and Nigel Stepney. I thought that there must be more to it: nobody sends that many messages without good reason. So I asked the McLaren drivers to show us the famous e-mails."*

It was Fernando Alonso's threat to Ron Dennis at Budapest that had opened up the whole can of worms. It also led to a glacial atmosphere between Alonso and theengineers. *"I'm not worried,"* said the two-time World Champion. *"I'm sure that the team will do everything it can to give me a competitive car."*

This may not necessarily have been the case, given that since Thursday McLaren were no longer scoring points and fighting for the constructors' championship. Was there any advantage to be gained in helping their wayward Spaniard?

> Nico Rosberg starred once more in the Belgian Grand Prix. The young German started sixth and finished sixth, scoring points for the fourth consecutive time. *"I'm very happy, as I've shown what I'm capable of with a good car,"* he said.

SNAPSHOTS OF THE WEEKEND

+ It was no longer a secret: Fernando Alonso, embittered by what he saw as favouritism towards Lewis Hamilton, wanted nothing more than to steal the championship from under his young team mate's nose and quit McLaren. Up until Spa, his two-year contract prevented him from doing so. The judgment of the FIA World Council seemed to throw him a lifeline. Like all contracts, there was a clause in his McLaren deal that allowed the Spaniard to leave in the case of a major deficiency within the team. The spy scandal did the job. A source within Renault said that it was « 99% sure » that Alonso would be back with them in 2008.

+ After Kimi Raikkonen won the Belgian Grand Prix, Ferrari's president Luca di Montezemolo declared: *"I would like to dedicate this win to all those fans who believe in sporting values, and to a gentleman in Britain who let us know that an individual from a rival team had come into his shop wanting to photocopy several pages of technical information relating to our car. Without that man's actions, one of the most shocking stories in the history of motorsport would never have come to light."* This impressive speech was delivered from his home in Italy.

+ With yet another one-two, Ferrari sealed the constructors' championship. Its only heoretical rival, BMW Sauber, scored just four points on Sunday meaning that Ferrari could not be caught. Nonetheless, Ferrari refused to celebrate their title in the paddock as they were waiting to see if McLaren would appeal the FIA's decision. In any case, a riotous party would have seemed somewhat inappropriate in the funereal atmosphere of the Spa paddock.

> Sebastian Vettel qualified 17th but had to retire after eight laps for an unusual reason: his Toro Rosso no longer wanted to turn right Left-handers were no problem, but the young German found himself struggling to turn right more and more as the race went on…

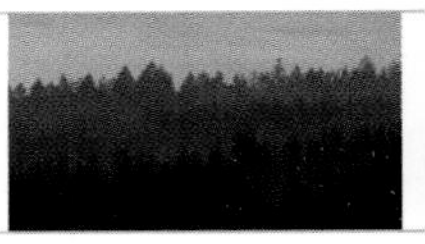

PRACTICE

Date	Weather (AM)	Air temperature	Track temperature	Weather (PM)	Air temperature	Track temperature
Friday September 14, 2007	Sunny	13-17°c	16-23°c	Scattered clouds	19-20°c	30-35°c
Saturday September 15, 2007	Sunny	16-17°c	20-21°c	Cloudy	17-18°c	27-28°c

All the time trials

N° Driver	Nat.	N° Chassis- Engine [Nbr. GP]	Pos. Free 1 Friday 10:00-11:30	Laps Tr.	Pos. Free 2 Friday 14:00-15:30	Laps Tr.	Pos. Free 3 Saturday 11:00-12:00	Laps Tr.	Pos. Q1 Saturday 14:00-14:15	Laps Tr.	Pos. Q2 Saturday 14:22-14:37	Laps Tr.	Pos. Q3 Saturday 14:45-15:00	Nb. Tr.
1. Fernando Alonso	E	McLaren MP4-22 06 - Mercedes [2]	3. 1:47.994	17	1. 1:46.654	29	3. 1:46.507	10	1. 1:46.058	3	4. 1:45.442	3	3. **1:46.091**	9
2. Lewis Hamilton	GB	McLaren MP4-22 01 - Mercedes [2]	2. 1:47.881	19	2. 1:46.765	29	4. 1:46.782	14	4. 1:46.437	3	2. 1:45.132	3	4. **1:46.406**	9
3. Giancarlo Fisichella	I	Renault R27-05 [2] -> [1]	11. 1:49.380	25	7. 1:48.086	30	11. 1:47.564	16	11. 1:47.143	7	11. **1:46.603**	6		
4. Heikki Kovalainen	FIN	Renault R27-03 [1]	9. 1:49.138	22	10. 1:48.567	38	5. 1:47.065	13	8. 1:46.971	7	7. 1:46.240	5	10. **1:48.505**	9
5. Felipe Massa	BR	Ferrari F2007 263 [2]	22.	2	3. 1:46.953	27	2. 1:46.388	17	2. 1:46.060	3	3. 1:45.173	3	2. **1:46.011**	9
6. Kimi Räikkönen	FIN	Ferrari F2007 262 [2]	1. 1:47.339	16	4. 1:47.166	26	1. 146.137	17	3. 1:46.242	3	1. 1:45.070	3	1. **1:45.994**	9
7. Jenson Button	GB	Honda RA107-04 [1]	10. 1:49.330	22	14. 1:48.919	29	12. 1:47.767	18	14. 1:47.474	6	14. **1:46.955**	6		
8. Rubens Barrichello	BR	Honda RA107-05 [1]	15. 1:50.264	22	15. 1:49.364	31	19. 1:48.528	16	18. **1:47.954**	6				
9. Nick Heidfeld	D	BMW Sauber F1.07-08 [2]	4. 1:48.052	20	11. 1:48.606	36	8. 1:47.359	16	6. 1:46.923	3	6. 1:45.994	6	7. **1:47.409**	9
10. Robert Kubica	PL	BMW Sauber F1.07-03 [2] -> [1]	6. 1:48.605	20	9. 1:48.279	37	22.	2	5. 1:46.707	7	5. 1:45.885	6	5. **1:46.996**	9
11. Ralf Schumacher	D	Toyota TF107/05 [2]	12. 1:49.548	21	6. 1:47.946	34	9. 1:47.454	19	12. 1:47.300	6	12. **1:46.618**	5		
12. Jarno Trulli	I	Toyota TF107/04 [2]	8. 1:48.994	19	5. 1:47.491	33	6. 1:47.218	11	10. 1:47.143	6	10. 1:46.480	6	9. **1:47.798**	9
14. David Coulthard	GB	Red Bull RB3 3 - Renault [1]	14. 1:49.931	19	13. 1:48.883	17	13. 1:47.806	10	13. 1:47.340	6	13. **1:46.800**	6		
15. Mark Webber	AUS	Red Bull RB3 4 - Renault [2]	13. 1:49.894	23	8. 1:48.271	29	10. 1:47.527	15	9. 1:47.084	6	8. 1:46.426	5	8. **1:47.524**	9
16. Nico Rosberg	D	Williams FW29-05 - Toyota [1]	5. 1:48.372	18	12. 1:48.840	32	7. 1:47.251	16	7. 1:46.950	6	9. 1:46.469	6	6. **1:47.334**	9
17. Alexander Wurz	AUT	Williams FW29-03 - Toyota [2]	7. 1:48.920	20	16. 1:49.393	28	15. 1:47.902	16	15. 1:47.522	6	16. **1:47.394**	6		
18. Vitantonio Liuzzi	I	Toro Rosso STR2-03 - Ferrari [1]	20. 1:51.628	12	22. 1:50.865	9	17. 1:48.163	21	16. 1:47.576	6	15. **1:47.115**	6		
19. Sebastian Vettel	D	Toro Rosso STR2-04 - Ferrari [2]	16. 1:50.482	27	18. 1:49.720	34	14. 1:47.838	19	17. **1:47.581**	6				
20. Adrian Sutil	D	Spyker F8-VII/03 B-spec - Ferrari [1]	19. 1:50.768	22	20. 1:50.399	24	18. 1:48.348	18	20. **1:48.044**	8				
21. Sakon Yamamoto	J	Spyker F8-VII/04 B-spec - Ferrari [2]	21. 1:52.379	21	17. 1:49.697	32	21. 1:49.179	14	22. **1:49.577**	5				
22. Takuma Sato	J	Super Aguri SA07-02 - Honda [1]	17. 1:50.640	16	19. 1:50.168	23	16. 1:48.129	16	19. **1:47.980**	6				
23. Anthony Davidson	GB	Super Aguri SA07-03 - Honda [1]	18. 1:50.648	20	21. 1:50.542	24	20. 1:48.955	16	21. **1:48.199**	6				

Fastest lap overall
K. Räikkönen 1:45.070 (259,977 km/h)

Maximum speed

N° Driver	S1 Qualifs	Pos.	S1 Race	Pos.	S2 Qualifs	Pos.	S2 Race	Pos.	Finish Qualifs	Pos.	Finish Race	Pos.	Radar Qualifs	Pos.	Radar Race	Pos.
1. F. Alonso	324,8	7	324,9	7	204,3	6	204,2	1	227,2	4	220,0	1	311,1	8	310,7	3
2. L. Hamilton	323,8	9	324,6	8	205,4	4	200,2	6	227,5	2	219,6	3	310,2	11	310,1	4
3. G. Fisichella	324,1	8	320,0	21	205,9	3	141,2	22	224,1	15			311,0	9	279,7	22
4. H. Kovalainen	323,7	10	322,9	10	203,5	12	197,1	10	227,7	1	218,2	8	314,6	1	307,8	9
5. F. Massa	329,9	2	329,0	2	207,9	1	202,4	2	226,9	7	218,9	5	311,5	6	311,6	2
6. K. Räikkönen	330,7	1	330,3	1	203,9	8	201,4	4	227,3	3	219,9	2	314,5	2	313,5	1
7. J. Button	319,7	21	322,0	14	203,9	9	193,4	19	226,7	8	218,9	6	308,9	15	305,7	14
8. R. Barrichello	320,3	18	319,8	22	202,3	13	195,1	13	224,6	14	217,7	9	308,8	16	304,6	15
9. N. Heidfeld	325,8	3	325,4	5	204,5	5	202,1	3	226,1	10	219,0	4	311,2	7	309,5	5
10. R. Kubica	324,8	5	326,5	3	206,8	2	200,9	5	225,2	11	218,2	7	311,7	5	309,5	6
11. R. Schumacher	321,1	15	321,3	17	195,0	22	195,7	11	225,0	12	216,1	15	305,2	20	304,6	16
12. J. Trulli	325,1	4	325,1	6	197,1	20	194,6	14	223,7	16	216,7	11	307,6	18	304,2	19
14. D. Coulthard	320,1	20	320,0	20	203,6	10	193,4	18	224,8	13	216,3	13	311,7	4	307,1	11
15. M. Webber	322,5	13	322,3	12	203,6	11	197,1	9	226,2	9	216,3	14	312,6	3	307,0	12
16. N. Rosberg	322,0	14	320,8	19	204,2	7	198,2	7	227,0	6	216,4	12	309,3	14	303,7	20
17. A. Wurz	318,1	22	321,1	18	201,7	14	194,5	15	227,1	5	214,3	19	305,1	21	304,4	17
18. V. Liuzzi	323,1	11	322,9	11	200,7	15	197,5	8	222,8	18	214,4	18	309,8	13	306,5	13
19. S. Vettel	322,5	12	322,3	13	200,1	16	192,4	21	222,4	19	210,4	21	310,2	10	304,3	18
20. A. Sutil	324,8	6	325,9	4	199,1	19	193,2	20	221,9	20	214,7	16	309,9	12	307,8	8
21. S. Yamamoto	320,8	16	323,3	9	195,5	21	193,8	16	218,1	22	213,8	20	304,9	22	307,3	10
22. T. Sato	320,4	17	321,9	15	199,3	18	195,1	12	223,6	17	216,8	10	308,3	17	308,1	7
23. A. Davidson	320,1	19	321,7	16	199,8	17	193,8	17	220,9	21	214,5	17	306,7	19	303,7	21

Best sector times

Qualifs	**S1** F. Massa	30.484	**S2** L. Hamilton	45.724	**S3** K. Räikkönen	28.616	= 1:44.824
Race	**S1** F. Massa	31.166	**S2** F. Alonso	47.283	**S3** F. Massa	28.564	= 1:47.013

RACE

Date	Weather	Air temperature	Track temperature	Humidity	Wind speed
Sunday September 16, 2007 (14:00)	Scattered clouds	21-22°c	34-37°c	54-51%	1.8 m/s

Classification & retirements

Pos.	Driver	Constructor	Tyres	Laps	Time	Km/h
1.	K. Räikkönen	Ferrari	MMS	44	1:20:39.066	229,174
2.	F. Massa	Ferrari	MMS	44	+ 4.695	228,952
3.	F. Alonso	McLaren Mercedes	MMS	44	+ 14.343	228,497
4.	L. Hamilton	McLaren Mercedes	MMS	44	+ 23.615	228,061
5.	N. Heidfeld	BMW	MMS	44	+ 51.879	226,743
6.	N. Rosberg	Williams Toyota	MMS	44	+ 1:16.876	225,590
7.	M. Webber	Red Bull Renault	MMS	44	+ 1:20.639	225,418
8.	H. Kovalainen	Renault	MS	44	+ 1:25.106	225,213
9.	R. Kubica	BMW	MMS	44	+ 1:25.661	225,188
10.	R. Schumacher	Toyota	MS	44	+ 1:28.574	225,055
11.	J. Trulli	Toyota	MSS	44	+ 1:43.653	224,368
12.	V. Liuzzi	STR Ferrari	MS	43	1 lap	222,923
13.	R. Barrichello	Honda	MS	43	1 lap	222,412
14.	A. Sutil	Spyker Ferrari	SSM	43	1 lap	222,304
15.	T. Sato	Super Aguri Honda	MSS	43	1 lap	222,275
16.	A. Davidson	Super Aguri Honda	MS	43	1 lap	221,012
17.	S. Yamamoto	Spyker Ferrari	SMM	43	1 lap	220,332

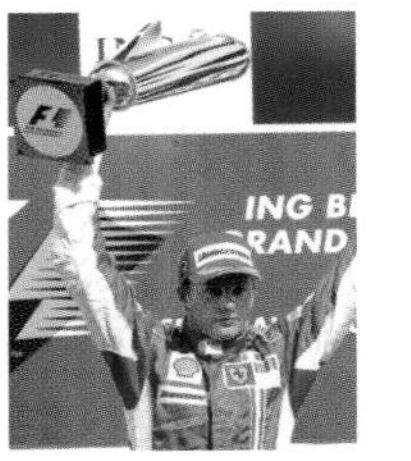
ING B
RAND

Driver	Constructor	Tyres	Laps	Reason
J. Button	Honda	MS	36	Clutch and steering problems due to a hydraulic malfunction
A. Wurz	Williams Toyota	MSM	34	Fuel pressure problem
D. Coulthard	Red Bull Renault	MS	29	Throttle problem steering problems due to a hydraulic malfunction
S. Vettel	STR Ferrari	MM	8	Steering problem
G. Fisichella	Renault	M	1	Brakes probl., went off. Front-left suspension rod broken

Tyres M: Medium & S: Soft

Fastest laps

	Driver	Time	Lap	Km/h
1.	F. Massa	1:48.036	34	233,388
2.	K. Räikkönen	1:48.095	12	233,261
3.	F. Alonso	1:48.182	44	233,073
4.	L. Hamilton	1:48.215	41	233,002
5.	N. Heidfeld	1:48.663	33	232,042
6.	R. Kubica	1:48.894	32	231,549
7.	J. Trulli	1:48.990	43	231,345
8.	H. Kovalainen	1:49.600	21	230,058
9.	N. Rosberg	1:49.769	29	229,704
10.	R. Schumacher	1:50.022	43	229,175
11.	M. Webber	1:50.049	12	229,119
12.	R. Barrichello	1:50.678	43	227,817
13.	V. Liuzzi	1:50.730	40	227,710
14.	T. Sato	1:50.886	32	227,390
15.	A. Sutil	1:50.902	29	227,357
16.	J. Button	1:51.141	22	226,868
17.	D. Coulthard	1:51.156	24	226,837
18.	A. Wurz	1:51.270	18	226,605
19.	A. Davidson	1:51.391	43	226,359
20.	S. Yamamoto	1:51.648	30	225,838
21.	S. Vettel	1:52.724	4	223,682

Pit stops

	Driver	Lap	Duration	Stop	Total
1.	S. Vettel	1	26.953	1	26.953
2.	N. Rosberg	14	27.656	1	27.656
3.	M. Webber	14	28.064	1	28.064
4.	J. Trulli	14	27.496	1	27.496
5.	K. Räikkönen	15	29.203	1	29.203
6.	F. Alonso	15	29.380	1	29.380
7.	R. Kubica	15	28.107	1	28.107
8.	F. Massa	16	28.612	1	28.612
9.	L. Hamilton	16	29.378	1	29.378
10.	A. Sutil	16	27.819	1	27.819
11.	S. Yamamoto	17	29.074	1	29.074
12.	N. Heidfeld	18	27.288	1	27.288
13.	R. Schumacher	20	29.947	1	29.947
14.	T. Sato	21	26.608	1	26.608
15.	A. Wurz	21	30.167	1	30.167
16.	H. Kovalainen	22	31.109	1	31.109
17.	J. Button	24	29.268	1	29.268
18.	V. Liuzzi	24	32.463	1	32.463
19.	D. Coulthard	25	28.676	1	28.676
20.	A. Davidson	25	28.871	1	28.871
21.	R. Barrichello	26	28.746	1	28.746
22.	N. Rosberg	30	27.642	2	55.298
23.	K. Räikkönen	31	26.719	2	55.922
24.	A. Sutil	30	27.716	2	55.535
25.	M. Webber	31	26.479	2	54.543
26.	J. Trulli	31	26.764	2	54.260
27.	F. Massa	32	26.203	2	54.815
28.	S. Yamamoto	31	27.674	2	56.748
29.	F. Alonso	33	25.612	2	54.992
30.	A. Wurz	32	25.655	2	55.822
31.	R. Kubica	33	25.818	2	53.925
32.	T. Sato	33	25.777	2	52.385
33.	N. Heidfeld	34	26.276	2	53.564
34.	L. Hamilton	37	26.032	2	55.410

Race leader

Driver	Laps in the lead	Nbr of laps
K. Räikkönen	1 > 15	15
F. Massa	16	1
K. Räikkönen	17 > 31	15
F. Massa	32	1
K. Räikkönen	33 > 44	12

Driver	Nbr of laps	Kilometers
K. Räikkönen	42	294,045 km
F. Massa	2	14,008 km

Lap chart

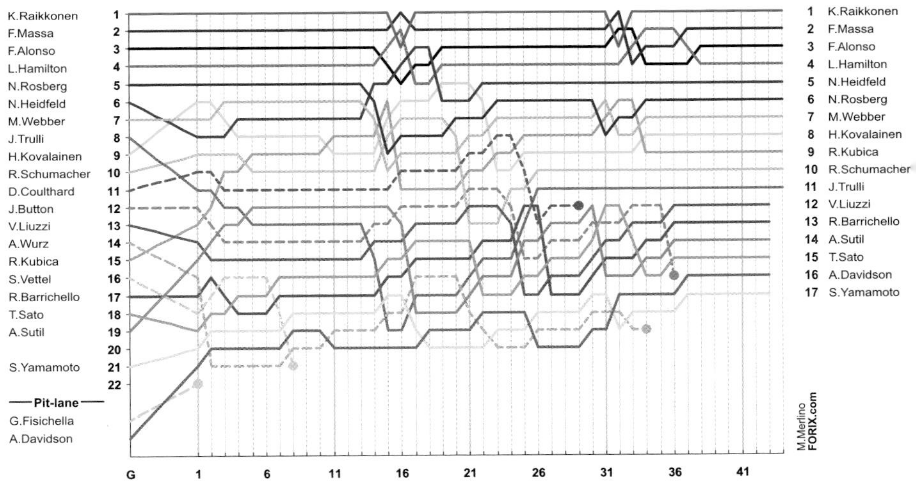
K.Raikkonen 1
F.Massa 2
F.Alonso 3
L.Hamilton 4
N.Rosberg 5
N.Heidfeld 6
M.Webber 7
J.Trulli 8
H.Kovalainen 9
R.Schumacher 10
D.Coulthard 11
J.Button 12
V.Liuzzi 13
A.Wurz 14
R.Kubica 15
S.Vettel 16
R.Barrichello 17
T.Sato 18
A.Sutil 19
20
S.Yamamoto 21
22
Pit-lane
G.Fisichella
A.Davidson
G 1 6 11 16 21 26 31 36 41
1 K.Raikkonen
2 F.Massa
3 F.Alonso
4 L.Hamilton
5 N.Heidfeld
6 N.Rosberg
7 M.Webber
8 H.Kovalainen
9 R.Kubica
10 R.Schumacher
11 J.Trulli
12 V.Liuzzi
13 R.Barrichello
14 A.Sutil
15 T.Sato
16 A.Davidson
17 S.Yamamoto
M.Merlino
FORIX.com

Gaps on the lead board

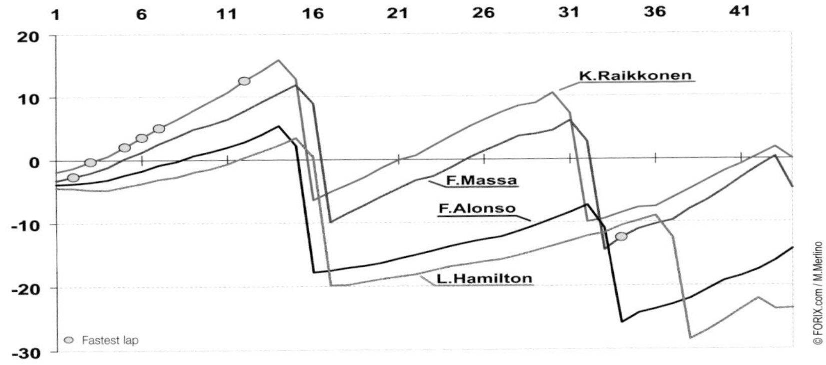
1 6 11 16 21 26 31 36 41
20
10
0
-10
-20
-30
K.Raikkonen
F.Massa
F.Alonso
L.Hamilton
Fastest lap
© FORIX.com / M.Merlino

CHAMPIONSHIPS 14/17

Drivers

1.	L. Hamilton	McLaren Mercedes	3🏆	97
2.	F. Alonso	McLaren Mercedes	4🏆	95
3.	K. Räikkönen	Ferrari	4🏆	84
4.	F. Massa	Ferrari	3🏆	77
5.	N. Heidfeld	BMW		56
6.	R. Kubica	BMW		33
7.	H. Kovalainen	Renault		22
8.	G. Fisichella	Renault		17
9.	N. Rosberg	Williams Toyota		15
10.	A. Wurz	Williams Toyota		13
11.	M. Webber	Red Bull Renault		10
12.	D. Coulthard	Red Bull Renault		8
13.	J. Trulli	Toyota		7
14.	R. Schumacher	Toyota		5
15.	T. Sato	Super Aguri Honda		4
16.	J. Button	Honda		2
17.	S. Vettel	BMW 1 /// STR Ferrari 0		1
18.	R. Barrichello	Honda		0
19.	S. Speed	STR Ferrari		0
20.	A. Davidson	Super Aguri Honda		0
21.	V. Liuzzi	STR Ferrari		0
22.	A. Sutil	Spyker Ferrari		0
23.	C. Albers	Spyker Ferrari		0
24.	S. Yamamoto	Spyker Ferrari		0
	M. Winkelhock	Spyker Ferrari		-

Constructors

1.	**Scuderia Ferrari Marlboro**	7🏆	161
2.	BMW Sauber F1 Team		90
3.	ING Renault F1 Team		39
4.	AT&T Williams		28
5.	Red Bull Racing		18
6.	Panasonic Toyota Racing		12
7.	Super Aguri F1 Team		4
8.	Honda Racing F1 Team		2
9.	Scuderia Toro Rosso		0
10.	Etihad Aldar Spyker F1 Team		0
11.	Vodafone McLaren Mercedes	7🏆	177

THE CIRCUIT

Name	Circuit de Spa-Francorchamps; Spa	**Latitude**	50°26'40.00"N
Lenght	7004 m	**Longitude**	5°57'53.00"E
Distance	44 laps, 308,053 km		

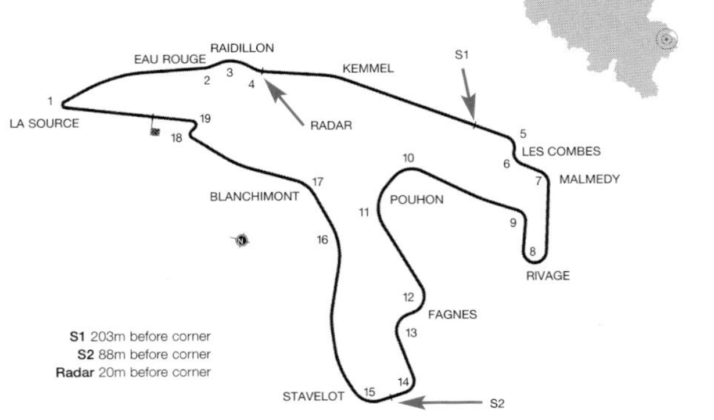
RAIDILLON
EAU ROUGE
KEMMEL
S1
LA SOURCE
RADAR
LES COMBES
MALMEDY
BLANCHIMONT
POUHON
RIVAGE
FAGNES
STAVELOT
S2

S1 203m before corner
S2 88m before corner
Radar 20m before corner

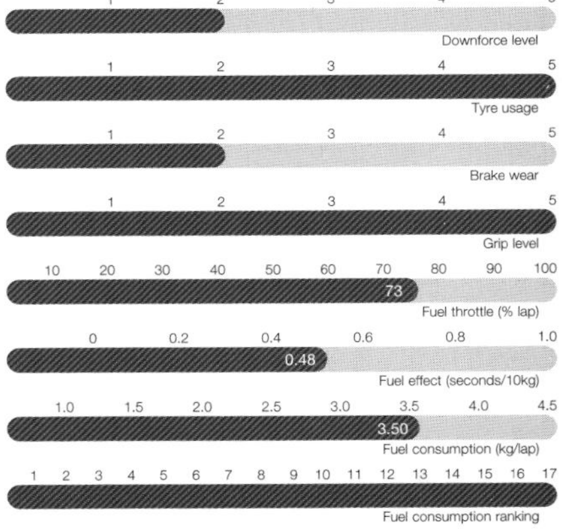
Downforce level
Tyre usage
Brake wear
Grip level
73
Fuel throttle (% lap)
0.48
Fuel effect (seconds/10kg)
3.50
Fuel consumption (kg/lap)
Fuel consumption ranking

CARNAGE
AT MOUNT FUJI

After a fine day on Friday, the weather around Mount Fuji became atrocious from Saturday morning onwards.

The race was not spared the horrific conditions: before the start the drivers had to accept the stark fact that the medical helicopter could not fly, which meant that anybody involved in a serious accident would have to be taken to hospital by road.

The start took place behind the safety car, which stayed out for a full 19 laps. Nobody knew quite why though, as the conditions on lap 20 were no better or worse than before. Under these tricky circumstances Lewis Hamilton took advantage of his pole position to make a clean getaway, while chaos reigned behind him. There was a multitude of spins, accidents and pile-ups (such as Alexander Wurz's adventure in the photo, who just managed to avoid the Ferrari of Felipe Massa). Hamilton took a huge step forward in the championship, as his closest rival Fernando Alonso crashed out of the event.

> Lewis Hamilton had not claimed pole position since the British Grand Prix at the beginning of July. In the wet conditions of Japan, Hamilton finally got the upper hand over his teammate Fernando Alonso again - but only by seven hundredths of a second.

Lewis Hamilton understands why Alonso was quickest...

Lewis Hamilton may have held a consistent lead in the drivers' championship, but Fernando Alonso was eating into his advantage point by point following the Hungarian Grand Prix. When they touched down in Japan, Hamilton was just two points ahead of his team mate with only three races left to go.

The Englishman was determined not to concede any more ground. The drivers used Friday to get used to the all-new Mount Fuji circuit, which was characterised by the longest straight of the season at nearly a kilometre and a half in length. It was the sort of feature that should provide a number of overtaking opportunities throughout the race. *"It's long enough for you to drink a cup of tea while you're on it,"* was Lewis Hamilton's description.

Behind his levity, the young Englishman meant business: he set the fastest time on Friday in front of his team mate Fernando Alonso, which had not happened for a little while.

"Last week, I did a lot of work with my engineers in order to understand where I was losing time compared to Fernando," said Hamilton. *"Now I've found out. I had chosen some set-ups that were completely different to his for the recent Grands Prix and that was a mistake. This is such a complex car that it does not work as well if the set-up isn't perfect. Now I'm not going to go in the same direction that I went before and I'm sure I can get back on top again."*

Naturally, the events of the previous weeks

(McLaren's exclusion from the constructors' championship and the record 100 million dollar fine) had hardly made Alonso flavour of the month at McLaren, as it was the Spaniard's actions that had directly led to the extraordinary penalty. *"Fernando has not been very loyal to the team,"* confirmed Lewis Hamilton. *"At the start of the season I was the rookie while he was the double world champion. But I think the team has realised everybody's real personality now, and they know whom they need to support. Fernando is not the person who I thought he was, but that's life..."*

Alonso was becoming increasingly isolated within McLaren, and he faced a tough and lonely job all the way to the end of the season.

> Giancarlo Fisichella pushes hard on the Japanese circuit. He would be 10th on the starting grid.

>> The famous Mount Fuji is 3776 metres high. It can be seen from Tokyo on a clear day, but Japan's most celebrated volcano was only spotted briefly on Friday morning during the Grand Prix on account of the terrible weather all weekend. On Saturday morning the third free practice session was cancelled (after only three drivers went out for three laps) while the medical helicopter was grounded by fog (below).

STARTING GRID

* N. ROSBERG penalty for an engine exchange (-10 pos).

V. LIUZZI starts from the pit lane.

Pos	Driver	Time
21	T. SATO	1:28.792
19	A. DAVIDSON	1:27.564
17	R. BARRICHELLO	1:27.323
15	R. SCHUMACHER	
13	J. TRULLI	1:26.253
11	H. KOVALAINEN	1:26.232
9	R. KUBICA	1:27.225
7	M. WEBBER	1:26.914
5	N. HEIDFELD	1:26.505
3	K. RÄIKKÖNEN	1:25.516
1	L. HAMILTON	1:25.368 (192.423 km/h)

Pos	Driver	Time
22	S. YAMAMOTO	1:29.668
20	A. SUTIL	1:28.628
18	A. WURZ	1:27.454
16	N. ROSBERG*	1:26.728
14	V. LIUZZI*	1:26.948
12	D. COULTHARD	1:26.247
10	G. FISICHELLA	1:26.033
8	S. VETTEL	1:26.973
6	J. BUTTON	1:26.913
4	F. MASSA	1:25.765
2	F. ALONSO	1:25.438

Lewis on the verge of greatness

After the Japanese Grand Prix, it seemed that nothing and nobody could stop Lewis Hamilton from becoming the youngest World Champion in history. Hamilton came away from the race with a 12-point championship lead over Fernando Alonso and a 17-point margin over Raikkonen. It was almost a whitewash: the World Championship was practically in his pocket.

By making a mistake at Mount Fuji when it mattered most, Alonso had virtually kissed goodbye to his chances of claiming a third consecutive title. His mistake was easy to make: conditions were appalling and he was by no means the only person to go off.

Despite Lewis Hamilton's comparative inexperience in the rain, he made no mistakes at all and triumphed. All around him though the race turned into a proper crash-fest, thankfully with no injuries.

Races like these can often throw up some unpredictable results - and it wasn't just Hamilton celebrating when the chequered flag fell. The champagne flowed at Renault as well: Heikki Kovalainen had just finished second, scoring Renault's first podium in a miserable season.

The Finn said: *"This year has been one of ups and downs. But I believe that we truly deserve this podium. Towards the end, it was getting very tough for me to keep Kimi [Raikkonen] behind: he was a gaining a second per lap. I couldn't see him as my mirrors were all fogged up but I was determined to win the battle."*

At Shanghai the following Sunday, Lewis Hamilton could claim the World Championship if he simply finished in front of his teammate.

Ferrari let down by the post

At 12:35 on Sunday, race control sent an e-mail to all the teams informing them that if the race started behind the safety car, it would be mandatory for all the cars to use full wet tyres. All the teams complied apart from Ferrari - which received the e-mail at 13:37, seven minutes after the race start! The Scuderia called its drivers in to change tyres, which they were about to do anyway as conditions were becoming so extreme. Ferrari had the option to lodge a complaint about the e-mail service but team principal Jean Todt chose not to, *"in the interests of the sport."* In any case, the damage was done. In future the FIA resolved that any urgent messages of this nature would be delivered the old fashioned way, by hand, as well as by e-mail.

The duel of the year

The most extraordinary duel of the year, if not the decade, took place on the final lap of the Japanese Grand Prix between Felipe Massa and Robert Kubica. Their fight for sixth place in the end went to the Brazilian. The two drivers swapped positions several times in just half a lap, in scenes

<
Lap 20: the Grand Prix really gets underway. The weather conditions forced the race organisers to start the Grand Prix behind the safety car. It was expected to come in straight away, but remained out until the 19th lap.

<
Lewis Hamilton's joy in parc ferme, after two hours of racing, is perfectly understandable.

reminiscent of the classic duel between Rene Arnoux and Gilles Villeneuve at Dijon in 1979.

Jean Todt denies everything

The Ferrari team principal categorically denied rumours linking Fernando Alonso to Ferrari in 2008. *"We've got contracts with both our current drivers next year and we're very pleased with them,"* he said.

Sick note for Webber

Mark Webber was on course to finish second before Sebastian Vettel punted him off while the pack was queued up behind the safety car. Sebastian was found to be guilty of causing an avoidable accident and was docked 10 grid places for the next Grand Prix in China. In any case, it wasn't Mark Webber's day. He had been ill with food poisoning all night and vomited into his helmet.

Lewis Hamilton stays focussed

A two-hour race in heavy rain, punctuated by several safety car periods: Lewis Hamilton had no easy task in the long shadow of Mount Fuji. *"It was a nightmare,"* he said. *"This was the longest and certainly the most difficult race of my career. It felt like it went on forever,* *and I couldn't see a thing. Some drops of water had actually come inside my visor, and I just had to guess where the track went. The wing mirrors were completely misted over, so they were useless as well. When Kubica pushed me, I didn't even see him coming. He caught me by surprise and so I spun. As the race went on the rain came down even harder. The amount of aquaplaning was incredible. You can imagine how pleased I was to get to the finish with the car in one piece!"*

Hamilton secured himself a solid advantage in the championship points table, putting the title within his reach. *"It's not done yet, absolutely anything can happen,"* he said prophetically.

"But I can't deny that I'm thinking about it, of course. I'm going to be flat-out at the Chinese Grand Prix, hoping to do my best. For the moment, I just have to stay concentrated. Next Sunday, when there will be just one race left to go, is the time to start thinking seriously about the championship. I don't know what more to say really. I can hardly believe that we're in this situation now. I remember taking my first pole, my first win and then after that I said to myself 'stop dreaming son, it's going to be all over soon. Yet now, here we are talking about the championship. It's simply incredible."

<
There were incidents and accidents of all sorts at Mount Fuji.
Lap 28: Sebastian Vettel has a go at Fernando Alonso - are we seeing things?
The two cars touch and the McLaren spins, while the Toro Rosso continues and even leads the race on the following lap.

HARD TIMES

Fernando Alonso's mission had been to finish just behind Lewis Hamilton and avoid losing too much ground in the championship, when he had a big accident on lap 42. His car hit the concrete wall before bouncing back onto the circuit minus several pieces. *"I approached turn five as usual, braked, and then the car just got away from me. Unfortunately, the wall is very close to the track at that part of the circuit."*

Welcome to Fuji-San

Japanese corporations are often huge businesses with several different interests, and the large motor manufacturers are no exceptions to the rule. The Suzuka circuit and theme park that has hosted the Japanese Grand Prix for the last 20 years belongs to Honda, but the Mount Fuji circuit is part of the empire of their key rivals, Toyota. The two companies have waged an enduring war to host the Japanese Grand Prix. Like many things in Japan, it is primarily a question of honour. The fact that a team owns a circuit does not give it any particular technical advantage there - although Toyota has had previous experience of the Fuji circuit over the last two years.

Now Fuji (and Toyota) has won the right to host the Japanese Grand Prix for the next five years, although for some mysterious reason they have agreed to alternate the venue of the race with Suzuka starting from 2009. In the meantime the F1 circus found itself in the middle of nowhere, about four hours from Tokyo, on the slopes of Fuji-San: a 3776 metre high volcano that has earned the respect of al of Japan. Scenic as it was, nobody really had the opportunity to admire one of Japan's most famous natural landmarks. Apart from Friday morning, the weather cast a wet and foggy veil over the region throughout the weekend.

It brought back sombre memories for those who were at Fuji in 1976, which was the first year that the Japanese Grand Prix took place on the circuit. On that occasion the rain was so heavy that the drivers actually went on strike to stop the race taking place. It finally got going after the weather died down slightly, just before evening fell. But Niki Lauda, who was fighting for the championship, wanted no part of it. He chose to retire and handed his championship crown over to James Hunt. One year later, just before the 1977 Japanese Grand Prix, the circuit was judged to be too dangerous and closed down. Salvation came in the form of German architect Hermann Tilke (who created the modern circuits at Shanghai and Bahrain). Tilke entirely re-designed the Mount Fuji circuit in 2003 - and four years after his work was completed it hosted its first Grand Prix, despite the fact that few people had heard of it. *"I know nothing about this track at all,"* confirmed Lewis Hamilton. *"I've not even tried to play it on my Playstation!"* This does not matter though, as a good driver will always go well on a new circuit after just a few kilometres. Those who needed a bit more time had to pick their moment carefully, as the only dry free practice session was on Friday morning.

Fernando Alonso alone in the world

Mount Fuji paddock, Saturday, 17:00. Night has already fallen in Japan, while the low clouds cast menacing shapes across the gloom.

In the McLaren motorhome, there is not the carefree and jolly atmosphere before the traditional press conference that would be expected of a team that has just seen its two cars qualify on the front row.

In fact, the tension was palpable at McLaren from the verystart of the weekend. Fernando Alonso found himself increasingly isolated in a team that was unwilling to forgive him for being the epicentre of the storm created by the 13 September FIA hearing in Paris.

The Spaniard has grown tired of wearing his black and silver corporate uniform but he is stuck in it until the end of 2009. That's not his only problem: since the Belgian Grand Prix Alonso has also been at war with his team mate Lewis Hamilton, who has accused him of dangerous driving and betraying the team.

The icing on the cake is that his boss, Ron Dennis, has no longer been talking to him since about a month. Yet this still did not stop the team prinicipal from trying to pour oil on troubled waters - at least from the outside. *"We've got two drivers both fighting extremely hard for the championship,"* he stated. *"There are some tensions between them sure, and so? What do you expect?"*

Hamilton, for one, was sick of hearing about the whole situation. *"Let's not talk about this anymore and let's just concentrate on the end of the season. We've still got some Grands Prix to win. If the line-up's going to change, let's talk about it after Brazil."*

It was just a throwaway line that suggested Fernando Alonso may be freed from his McLaren contract at the end of the year after all, and could be at liberty to look for another drive. Nonetheless, he too had a title to try and win in the meantime, and the Spaniard insisted to anybody who cared to listen that he was sure that the two McLarens would be identical right up to the end of the year.

That lay at the root of his problems. Logic would dictate otherwise: who would the team be more likely to favour out of a young Briton who has been a disciple of McLaren for 10 years and shakes every mechanic by the hand after every race, or a Spaniard seen as a traitor who is desperate to leave? The answer is not a difficult one to work out.

But if McLaren wanted to do something to tip the balance in Hamilton's favour then it would have to do so extremely discreetly. The team knew that the FIA would be policing fair play assiduously right up to the end of the season. *"But it's very easy to slow a car down with anyone noticing,"* said an engineer from a rival team. *"Take away a few horsepower and nobody is any the wiser. It's certainly not the sort of thing that could ever be proved."*

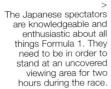

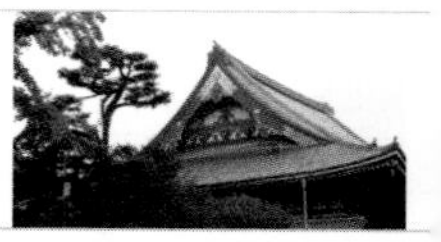

PRACTICE

Date	Weather (AM)	Air temperature	Track temperature	Weather (PM)	Air temperature	Track temperature
Friday September 28, 2007	Cloudy	26-27°c	43-50°c	Cloudy	26-27°c	46-48°c
Saturday September 29, 2007	Rain and fog	15°c	21°c	Fog, wet track	14-15°c	20°c

All the time trials

N° Driver	Nat.	N° Chassis- Engine [Nbr GP]	Pos. Free 1 Friday 10:00-11:30	Laps	Pos. Free 2 Friday 14:00-15:30	Laps	Pos. Free 3 Saturday 11:00-12:00	Laps	Pos. Q1 Saturday 14:00-14:15	Laps	Pos. Q2 Saturday 14:22-14:37	Laps	Pos. Q3 Saturday 14:45-15:00	Laps
1. Fernando Alonso	E	McLaren MP4-22 06 - Mercedes [1]	3. 1:19.667	27	2. 1:18.948	34		2	2. 1:25.379	6	2. 1:24.806	10	2. **1:25.438**	11
2. Lewis Hamilton	GB	McLaren MP4-22 05 - Mercedes [1]	4. 1:19.807	24	1. 1:18.734	38		1	4. 1:25.489	10	1. 1:24.753	9	1. **1:25.368**	11
3. Giancarlo Fisichella	I	Renault R27-05 & 02 [1]	16. 1:20.851	23	7. 1:19.926	39		1	13. 1:26.909	7	11. **1:26.033**	10		
4. Heikki Kovalainen	FIN	Renault R27-03 [2]	12. 1:20.718	27	6. 1:19.789	40		1	15. 1:27.223	7	12. **1:26.232**	10		
5. Felipe Massa	BR	Ferrari F2007 263 [1]	2. 1:19.498	27	3. 1:19.483	36		1	1. 1:25.359	8	4. 1:25.049	10	4. **1:25.765**	11
6. Kimi Räikkönen	FIN	Ferrari F2007 262 [1]	1. 1:19.119	26	5. 1:19.714	29		1	3. 1:25.390	10	3. 1:24.988	8	3. **1:25.516**	11
7. Jenson Button	GB	Honda RA107-04 [1]	19. 1:21.541	22	14. 1:20.336	44		2	10. 1:26.614	10	6. 1:25.454	10	7. **1:26.913**	11
8. Rubens Barrichello	BR	Honda RA107-05 & 02 [2]	11. 1:20.686	24	17. 1:20.889	33		2	17. **1:27.323**	10				
9. Nick Heidfeld	D	BMW Sauber F1.07-08 [1]	13. 1:20.728	26	15. 1:20.462	36		1	6. 1:25.971	10	5. 1:25.248	9	5. **1:26.505**	11
10. Robert Kubica	PL	BMW Sauber F1.07-03 [2]	6. 1:20.297	26	10. 1:20.069	45		1	8. 1:26.300	11	7. 1:25.530	11	10. **1:27.225**	11
11. Ralf Schumacher	D	Toyota TF107/05 [1]	15. 1:20.828	28	9. 1:19.969	40		2	14. **1:27.191**	10	16.			
12. Jarno Trulli	I	Toyota TF107/04 [1]	8. 1:20.483	32	4. 1:19.711	35	3. 1:36.150	3	11. 1:26.711	11	14. **1:26.253**	10		
14. David Coulthard	GB	Red Bull RB3 3 - Renault [1]	21. 1:22.436	18	8. 1:19.949	33		1	12. 1:26.904	11	13. **1:26.247**	10		
15. Mark Webber	AUS	Red Bull RB3 4 - Renault [1]	18. 1:21.437	18	11. 1:20.069	35		1	5. 1:25.970	10	8. 1:25.535	8	8. **1:26.914**	11
16. Nico Rosberg	D	Williams FW29-05 - Toyota [2] -> [1]	5. 1:20.058	26	13. 1:20.270	43	2. 1:34.758	3	9. 1:26.579	11	9. 1:25.816	11	6. **1:26.728**	11
17. Alexander Wurz	AUT	Williams FW29-03 - Toyota [1]	7. 1:20.411	24	12. 1:20.233	37	1. 1:32.746	3	18. **1:27.454**	10				
18. Vitantonio Liuzzi	I	Toro Rosso STR2-03 - Ferrari [2]	14. 1:20.808	29	18. 1:20.985	44		1	16. 1:27.234	11	15. **1:26.948**	11		
19. Sebastian Vettel	D	Toro Rosso STR2-04 - Ferrari [1]	20. 1:21.854	18	19. 1:20.997	38		1	7. 1:26.025	11	10. 1:25.909	11	9. **1:26.973**	11
20. Adrian Sutil	D	Spyker F8-VII/03 B-spec - Ferrari [2]	9. 1:20.516	29	16. 1:20.736	37		1	20. **1:28.628**	10				
21. Sakon Yamamoto	J	Spyker F8-VII/04 B-spec - Ferrari [1]	22. 1:22.902	17	21. 1:21.305	38		1	22. **1:29.668**	10				
22. Takuma Sato	J	Super Aguri SA07-02 - Honda [2]	17. 1:21.186	15	22. 1:21.352	34		2	21. **1:28.792**	10				
23. Anthony Davidson	GB	Super Aguri SA07-03 - Honda [2]	10. 1:20.601	22	20. 1:21.007	34		2	19. **1:27.564**	10				

Fastest lap overall
L. Hamilton 1:24.753 (193,819 km/h)

Maximum speed

N° Driver	S1 Qualifs	Pos.	S1 Race	Pos.	S2 Qualifs	Pos.	S2 Race	Pos.	Finish Qualifs	Pos.	Finish Race	Pos.	Radar Qualifs	Pos.	Radar Race	Pos.
1. F. Alonso	217,0	1	206,8	2	174,7	6	165,0	12	300,0	9	295,5	11	305,8	15	303,7	11
2. L. Hamilton	213,8	3	201,0	10	170,5	16	169,8	3	305,0	1	297,6	7	308,3	11	300,3	14
3. G. Fisichella	212,8	5	200,0	12	174,1	8	166,4	9	301,0	4	297,6	8	313,9	1	310,2	2
4. H. Kovalainen	210,8	11	204,0	4	175,4	4	164,9	13	300,7	5	297,2	9	313,1	2	308,1	6
5. F. Massa	214,1	2	200,9	11	172,3	11	161,9	18	302,7	2	303,0	1	313,1	3	308,3	5
6. K. Räikkönen	212,4	7	205,8	3	173,2	9	162,5	16	301,9	3	299,0	5	312,7	4	308,4	3
7. J. Button	212,7	6	195,1	16	174,1	7	163,9	14	295,8	16	291,5	17	305,1	17	301,4	12
8. R. Barrichello	204,0	19	193,6	18	172,2	12	165,9	10	292,8	20	290,7	18	301,2	19	301,4	13
9. N. Heidfeld	211,3	9	192,8	19	177,9	2	167,9	5	296,5	14	300,4	3	307,1	13	305,5	9
10. R. Kubica	210,6	12	204,0	5	174,8	5	167,7	6	297,8	12	295,7	10	308,7	10	307,0	7
11. R. Schumacher	210,9	10	199,9	13	166,5	21	159,6	21	296,4	15	292,6	13	307,7	12	299,8	17
12. J. Trulli	206,7	16	189,3	21	167,1	19	160,3	20	293,5	17	289,8	20	305,1	16	299,8	18
14. D. Coulthard	209,3	13	201,8	7	178,1	1	168,9	4	299,0	11	299,3	4	309,5	7	308,3	4
15. M. Webber	209,1	14	207,7	1	169,5	17	162,6	15	300,0	8	294,5	12	309,3	8	306,5	8
16. N. Rosberg	213,6	4	201,5	8	169,2	18	162,0	17	299,4	10	301,7	2	310,7	6	304,9	10
17. A. Wurz	208,4	15	169,5	22	170,6	15	141,2	22	297,1	13	248,0	22	306,8	14	184,6	22
18. V. Liuzzi	204,0	18	201,2	9	172,6	10	165,2	11	300,2	7	292,2	16	311,6	5	300,2	15
19. S. Vettel	212,4	8	203,6	6	177,0	3	170,4	2	300,5	6	298,2	6	309,1	9	310,5	1
20. A. Sutil	199,0	21	196,3	15	171,8	13	167,1	8	287,3	22	292,3	15	295,9	22	298,3	20
21. S. Yamamoto	199,7	20	196,5	14	171,0	14	167,1	7	293,3	19	284,7	21	297,8	21	294,7	21
22. T. Sato	197,6	22	190,6	20	165,4	22	160,9	19	293,4	18	290,2	19	301,3	18	299,1	19
23. A. Davidson	204,8	17	194,6	17	166,7	20	182,1	1	292,3	21	292,4	14	300,3	20	300,0	16

Best sector times

Qualifs	**S1** L. Hamilton	23.160	**S2** L. Hamilton	31.275	**S3** F. Alonso	30.054	= 1:24.489
Race	**S1** L. Hamilton	24.024	**S2** F. Alonso	32.333	**S3** N. Heidfeld	31.250	= 1:27.607

RACE

Date	Weather	Air temperature	Track temperature	Humidity	Wind speed
Sunday September 30, 2007 (13:30)	Rain and fog	15-17°c	20-22°c	95%	0.8 m/s

Classification & retirements

Pos.	Driver	Constructor	Tyres	Laps	Time	Km/h	
1.	L. Hamilton	McLaren Mercedes	EE	67	2:00:34.579	151,978	
2.	H. Kovalainen	Renault	EE	67	+ 8.377	151,802	
3.	K. Räikkönen	Ferrari	WEEE	67	+ 9.478	151,779	
4.	D. Coulthard	Red Bull Renault	EE	67	+ 20.297	151,552	
5.	G. Fisichella	Renault	EE	67	+ 38.864	151,166	
6.	F. Massa	Ferrari	WEEEE	67	+ 49.042	150,954	
7.	R. Kubica	BMW	EEE	67	+ 49.285	150,949	
8.	A. Sutil	Spyker Ferrari	EE	67	+ 1:00.129	150,725	
9.	V. Liuzzi	STR Ferrari	EEE	67	+ *1:20.622	150,818	*55.622+25.0 penalty
10.	R. Barrichello	Honda	EEE	67	+ 1:28.342	150,144	
11.	J. Button	Honda	EE	66	1 lap	149,992	Collision with Sato, suspension
12.	S. Yamamoto	Spyker Ferrari	EEE	66	1 lap	149,302	
13.	J. Trulli	Toyota	EEE	66	1 lap	149,050	
14.	N. Heidfeld	BMW	EE	65	2 laps	150,268	Ignition problem
15.	T. Sato	Super Aguri Honda	EEEE	65	2 laps	147,704	Crash with Button

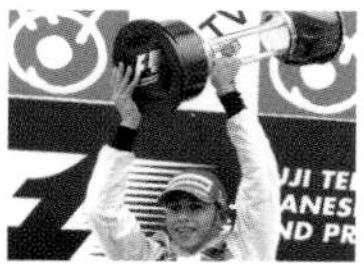

Driver	Constructor	Tyres	Laps	Reason
R. Schumacher	Toyota	EEEE	55	Electrical problem, slow puncture
A. Davidson	Super Aguri Honda	EE	54	Broken throttle sensor
N. Rosberg	Williams Toyota	EEE	49	Electrical problem affecting traction control and gearshift
S. Vettel	STR Ferrari	EE	46	Caught out by the slow speed of Hamilton behind the safety car, hits Webber
M. Webber	Red Bull Renault	EE	45	Hit by Vettel
F. Alonso	McLaren Mercedes	EE	41	Aquaplanes and spins, hitting the wall
A. Wurz	Williams Toyota	EE	19	Hit from behind, hits Massa

Tyres E: Extreme Wet & W: Wet

Fastest laps

	Driver	Time	Lap	Km/h
1.	L. Hamilton	1:28.193	27	186,259
2.	F. Alonso	1:28.511	25	185,590
3.	M. Webber	1:28.940	30	184,695
4.	R. Kubica	1:29.021	32	184,527
5.	S. Vettel	1:29.057	31	184,452
6.	N. Heidfeld	1:29.084	28	184,396
7.	F. Massa	1:29.588	32	183,359
8.	K. Räikkönen	1:29.619	29	183,295
9.	H. Kovalainen	1:29.655	34	183,222
10.	N. Rosberg	1:29.926	27	182,670
11.	D. Coulthard	1:30.086	56	182,345
12.	G. Fisichella	1:30.387	33	181,738
13.	V. Liuzzi	1:30.653	35	181,205
14.	R. Schumacher	1:30.865	33	180,782
15.	R. Barrichello	1:31.060	57	180,395
16.	T. Sato	1:31.507	54	179,514
17.	A. Davidson	1:31.803	27	178,935
18.	A. Sutil	1:31.891	54	178,763
19.	J. Button	1:31.951	58	178,647
20.	S. Yamamoto	1:32.130	33	178,300
21.	J. Trulli	1:32.414	55	177,752
22.	A. Wurz	2:05.636	19	130,749

Pit stops

	Driver	Lap	Duration	Stop	Total
1.	F. Massa	2	33.588	1	33.588
2.	K. Räikkönen	3	34.105	1	34.105
3.	V. Liuzzi	10	34.516	1	34.516
4.	S. Yamamoto	13	38.944	1	38.944
5.	K. Räikkönen	14	32.031	2	1:06.136
6.	F. Massa	15	34.520	2	1:08.108
7.	A. Wurz	16	35.403	1	35.403
8.	R. Barrichello	18	34.843	1	34.843
9.	T. Sato	18	35.025	1	35.025
10.	J. Trulli	18	36.262	1	36.262
11.	F. Massa	•20•	23.769	3	1:31.877
12.	T. Sato	22	51.419	2	1:26.444
13.	J. Button	23	38.945	1	38.945
14.	F. Alonso	27	38.483	1	38.483
15.	L. Hamilton	28	38.286	1	38.286
16.	R. Schumacher	28	34.683	1	34.683
17.	S. Vettel	32	37.388	1	37.388
18.	N. Heidfeld	35	37.076	1	37.076
19.	M. Webber	36	36.213	1	36.213
20.	R. Kubica	36	38.947	1	38.947
21.	A. Davidson	37	38.155	1	38.155
22.	H. Kovalainen	39	35.845	1	38.845
23.	D. Coulthard	39	34.403	1	34.403
24.	K. Räikkönen	40	40.000	3	1:46.136
25.	N. Rosberg	40	35.510	1	35.510
26.	R. Kubica	•40•	23.893	2	1:02.840
27.	G. Fisichella	41	35.295	1	35.295
28.	V. Liuzzi	44	34.873	2	1:09.389
29.	A. Sutil	44	36.663	1	36.663
30.	T. Sato	43	34.754	3	2:01.198
31.	R. Schumacher	48	34.916	2	1:09.599
32.	N. Rosberg	49	34.198	2	1:09.708
33.	R. Schumacher	53	14:35.538	3	15:45.137
34.	S. Yamamoto	57	34.678	2	1:13.622
35.	F. Massa	58	32.499	4	2:04.376
36.	R. Barrichello	60	30.873	2	1:05.716
37.	J. Trulli	60	34.598	2	1:10.860

•• Drive-through penalty:
> Massa. Drive-through penalty for having passed under the safety car.
> Kubica.For having caused a collision with Hamilton

Race leader

Driver	Laps in the lead	Nbr of laps
L. Hamilton	1 > 28	28
S. Vettel	29 > 31	3
M. Webber	32 > 36	5
H. Kovalainen	37 > 39	3
G. Fisichella	40	1
L. Hamilton	41 > 67	27

Driver	Nbr of laps	Kilometers
L. Hamilton	55	250,660 km
M. Webber	5	22,815 km
S. Vettel	3	13,689 km
H. Kovalainen	3	13,689 km
G. Fisichella	1	4,563 km

Gaps on the lead board

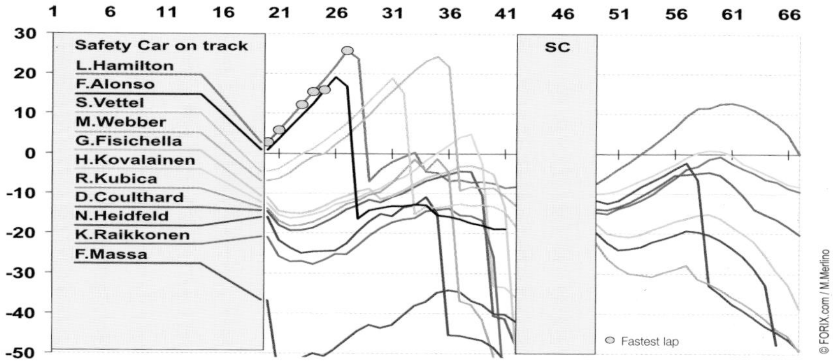
1 6 11 16 21 26 31 36 41 46 51 56 61 66
30 20 10 0 -10 -20 -30 -40 -50
Safety Car on track
L.Hamilton
F.Alonso
S.Vettel
M.Webber
G.Fisichella
H.Kovalainen
R.Kubica
D.Coulthard
N.Heidfeld
K.Raikkonen
F.Massa
SC
Fastest lap
© FORIX.com / M.Merlino

Lap chart

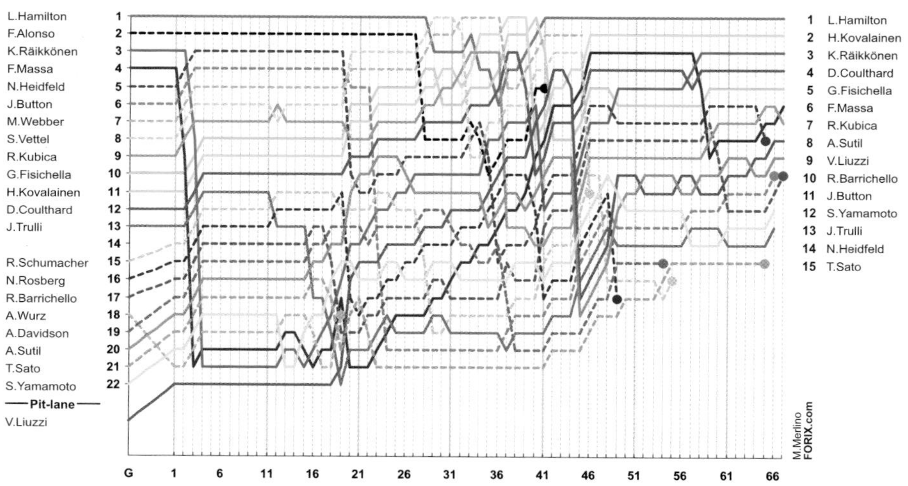
L.Hamilton 1
F.Alonso 2
K.Räikkönen 3
F.Massa 4
N.Heidfeld 5
J.Button 6
M.Webber 7
S.Vettel 8
R.Kubica 9
G.Fisichella 10
H.Kovalainen 11
D.Coulthard 12
J.Trulli 13
14
R.Schumacher 15
N.Rosberg 16
R.Barrichello 17
A.Wurz 18
A.Davidson 19
A.Sutil 20
T.Sato 21
S.Yamamoto 22
Pit-lane
V.Liuzzi
G 1 6 11 16 21 26 31 36 41 46 51 56 61 66
1 L.Hamilton
2 H.Kovalainen
3 K.Räikkönen
4 D.Coulthard
5 G.Fisichella
6 F.Massa
7 R.Kubica
8 A.Sutil
9 V.Liuzzi
10 R.Barrichello
11 J.Button
12 S.Yamamoto
13 J.Trulli
14 N.Heidfeld
15 T.Sato
M.Merlino
FORIX.com

CHAMPIONSHIPS 15/17

Drivers

1.	L. Hamilton	McLaren Mercedes	4🏆	107
2.	F. Alonso	McLaren Mercedes	4🏆	95
3.	K. Räikkönen	Ferrari	4🏆	90
4.	F. Massa	Ferrari	3🏆	80
5.	N. Heidfeld	BMW		56
6.	R. Kubica	BMW		35
7.	H. Kovalainen	Renault		30
8.	G. Fisichella	Renault		21
9.	N. Rosberg	Williams Toyota		15
10.	A. Wurz	Williams Toyota		13
11.	D. Coulthard	Red Bull Renault		13
12.	M. Webber	Red Bull Renault		10
13.	J. Trulli	Toyota		7
14.	R. Schumacher	Toyota		5
15.	T. Sato	Super Aguri Honda		4
16.	J. Button	Honda		2
17.	A. Sutil	Spyker Ferrari		1
18.	S. Vettel	BMW 1 /// STR Ferrari 0		1
19.	R. Barrichello	Honda		0
20.	V. Liuzzi	STR Ferrari		0
21.	S. Speed	STR Ferrari		0
22.	A. Davidson	Super Aguri Honda		0
23.	S. Yamamoto	Spyker Ferrari		0
24.	C. Albers	Spyker Ferrari		0
	M. Winkelhock	Spyker Ferrari		-

Constructors

1.	**Scuderia Ferrari Marlboro**	7🏆	170
2.	BMW Sauber F1 Team		92
3.	ING Renault F1 Team		51
4.	AT&T Williams		28
5.	Red Bull Racing		23
6.	Panasonic Toyota Racing		12
7.	Super Aguri F1 Team		4
8.	Honda Racing F1 Team		2
9.	Etihad Aldar Spyker F1 Team		1
10.	Scuderia Toro Rosso		0
11.	Vodafone McLaren Mercedes	8🏆	*187

THE CIRCUIT

Name Fuji Speedway; Mont Fuji
Lenght 4563 m
Distance 67 laps, 305,416 km
Latitude 35°22'23.00"N
Longitude 138°55'41.30"E

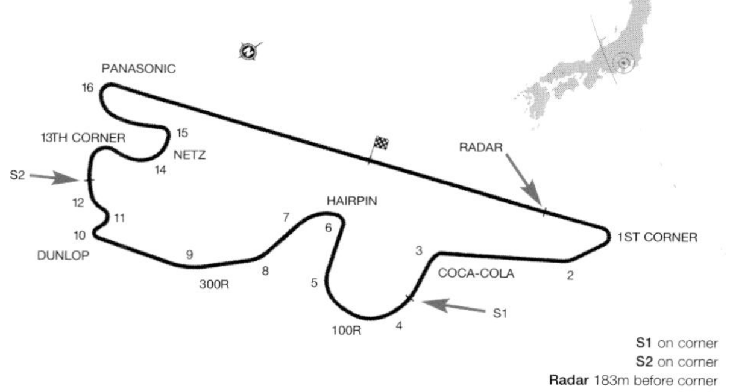
PANASONIC
16
15
13TH CORNER
NETZ
14
S2
12
11
10
DUNLOP
9
300R
8
7
6
HAIRPIN
5
100R
4
3
COCA-COLA
2
1ST CORNER
RADAR
S1

S1 on corner
S2 on corner
Radar 183m before corner

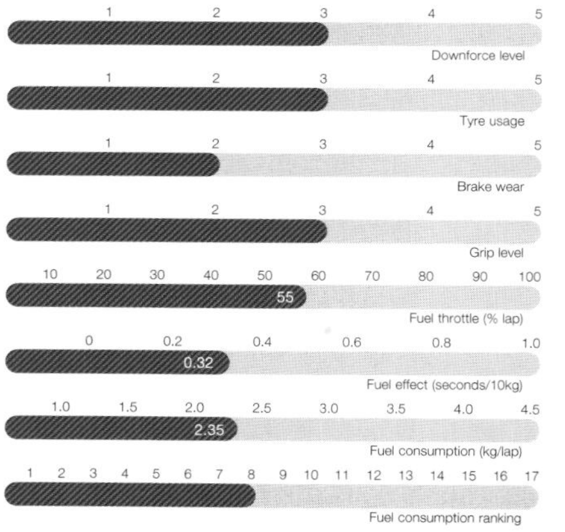
1 2 3 4 5
Downforce level
1 2 3 4 5
Tyre usage
1 2 3 4 5
Brake wear
1 2 3 4 5
Grip level
10 20 30 40 50 60 70 80 90 100
55
Fuel throttle (% lap)
0 0.2 0.4 0.6 0.8 1.0
0.32
Fuel effect (seconds/10kg)
1.0 1.5 2.0 2.5 3.0 3.5 4.0 4.5
2.35
Fuel consumption (kg/lap)
1 2 3 4 5 6 7 8 9 10 11 12 13 14 15 16 17
Fuel consumption ranking

THE SUSPENSE CONTINUES, AFTER LEWIS FAILS AND KIMI WINS

In the end, the fairly tale was too good to be true. Lewis Hamilton so far had not retired from a single Grand Prix, nor made a mistake, nor been the victim of any mechanical failures. His charmed run of luck came to end in Shanghai when he became stuck in a gravel trap on the way into the pits. It was a driving error but also a mistake on the part of McLaren, which had insisted on Hamilton staying out until the rain stopped despite the fact that his tyres were seriously worn.

It was hard to understand how a team as experienced as McLaren could make such an amateur mistake, particularly given that Lewis Hamilton had enough of a margin in the championship not to have to take any big risks. Just scoring a few points would have been enough.

By pushing their luck and trying to win, the team took a huge risk. The price they paid was enormous, as Lewis Hamilton saw his title chances fade as a result of this monumental gaffe.

As the proverb says, the higher you fly, the further you fall. Lewis had plenty of time to reflect on that before Brazil...

Pole position, despite being caught on camera...

Lewis Hamilton was determined to claim his first world title over the weekend and took his sixth pole position of the season in China. This would in theory be an enormous advantage if the expected rain fell, Typhoon Krosa was expected over Shanghai on Sunday.

The Spyker team was upbeat after the news of their takeover by the partnership of Vijay Mallia and Michiel Moll. Just after the end of the season the team was re-named Force India, having been Jordan and Midland in the past.

First of all, a flashback to the 46th lap of the Japanese Grand Prix. The race had been neutralised behind the safety car following Fernando Alonso's accident. Lewis Hamilton, following behind the AMG Mercedes safety car, was dictating the pace. Suddenly the Toro Rosso of Sebastian Vettel, in third, hits the back of Mark Webber's Red Bull just in front of him. Both are out. The same evening, the Japanese stewards decide to penalise Vettel for causing an avoidable accident. Consequently he will drop 10 places on the grid in Shanghai.

On Thursday before the Chinese Grand Prix Toro Rosso co-owner Franz Tost went to see the Chinese Grand Prix stewards to show them a video posted on the 'you tube' internet site by a spectator sitting in a grandstand opposite the Webber-Vettel incident.

The film showed that Lewis Hamilton had deliberately slowed down in order to put off the people behind him: a classic trick used under the safety car regime in order to destabilise the opposition, which has been banned since 2000.

As soon as he braked, the young Briton forced Mark Webber to brake sharply as well. Sebastian Vettel, blinded by the spray in front of him, could not avoid running into Webber. *"I asked the race organisers to cancel Sebastian's penalty,"* said Franz Tost. *"As the film clearly shows, it is completely unfair."* The Chinese stewards took the incident extremely seriously and decided to gather all the people involved together. On Thursday, Mark Webber did not have many kind words to say about Lewis Hamilton.

"Lewis did a terrible job," stormed Webber. *"We actually spoke about this before the race. He promised that he would drive by the book behind the safety car and in actual fact he did the complete opposite. I'm not going to forget that."*

Now it was Lewis Hamilton who risked the penalty for causing an avoidable accident. Even Lewis himself was convinced that he would pick up a penalty on Friday. The possibilities seemed to range from dropping some places on the grid to having his victory in Japan annulled. In his defence, Hamilton said that when the collision took place he was trying to warm up his brakes in preparation for the safety car's return to the pits and that he had deliberately moved away from the racing line in order to do this. A mistake that could also be perhaps put down to his lack of experience in the wet.

Finally, on Friday night it emerged that Lewis Hamilton had been entirely exonerated. The FIA representatives said: *"All the drivers explained that conditions under the safety car were worse than they had ever seen before. Consequently, under these exceptional circumstances, it seemed inappropriate to punish a driver for a mistake that would have earned a penalty under normal conditions."*

Given the situation, Sebastian Vettel's penalty was also cancelled and instead turned into a reprimand.

STARTING GRID

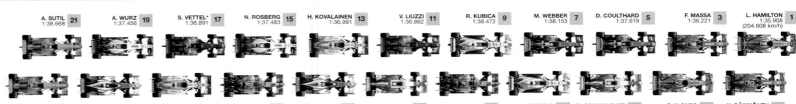

* S. VETTEL was relegated of 5 pos. for blocking KOVALAINEN. (Article 31.7)

A. SUTIL 21	A. WURZ 19	S. VETTEL* 17	N. ROSBERG 15	H. KOVALAINEN 13	V. LIUZZI 11	R. KUBICA 9	M. WEBBER 7	D. COULTHARD 5	F. MASSA 3	L. HAMILTON 1
1:38.668	1:37.456	1:36.891	1:37.483	1:36.991	1:36.862	1:38.472	1:38.153	1:37.619	1:36.221	1:35.908 (204.608 km/h)

S. YAMAMOTO 22	T. SATO 20	G. FISICHELLA 18	R. BARRICHELLO 16	A. DAVIDSON 14	J. TRULLI 12	J. BUTTON 10	N. HEIDFELD 8	R. SCHUMACHER 6	F. ALONSO 4	K. RÄIKKÖNEN 2
1:39.336	1:38.218	1:37.290	1:37.251	1:37.247	1:36.959	1:39.285	1:38.455	1:38.013	1:36.576	1:36.044

<
For the second consecutive Grand Prix, the action gets underway in the rain. Once more, Lewis Hamilton gets the jump on his rivals.

Faux pas from Hamilton and McLaren means title goes to Sao Paulo

What an action-packed race! Typhoon Krosa eventually decided to stay in Taiwan over the weekend and instead there were just a few showers that made their presence felt during the Grand Prix.

Nonetheless, these were enough to change the complexion of the race - particularly given that the first few drops fell while the cars were still lining up on the grid. All the drivers set off on intermediate tyres, led by a Lewis Hamilton who was clearly intent on winning the World Championship that same evening. Nonetheless, he would have to wait until Brazil. The rain quickly stopped and a dry line emerged, causing the rain tyres to degrade. Race control announced that another shower was expected in the next few minutes, and consequently many of the drivers chose to stay out on the by now quite badly worn intermediates. Felipe Massa was the first to stop and change onto dry tyres, on lap 26. It was a good call: Lewis Hamilton stayed out too long and was passed by Kimi Raikkonen. Far worse was to come: the Englishman went off the road on a corner at less than 60kph on his way into the pits and became beached in a gravel trap. *"I'm completely gutted,"* said Hamilton, as soon as he returned to his pit garage. *"I've not made the smallest mistake at all this year, and look what happens now. I actually tried to be really careful, which is why I didn't resist Kimi when he came past me. Everything was going fine until this stupid mistake..."*

With his key rival off the scene, Kimi Raikkonen could cruise to victory in front of Fernando Alonso. Having scored 10 and eight championship points respectively to Hamilton's zero, the two men had made a giant leap forward in the championship - although Hamilton still remained the favourite.

Raikkonen commented: *"The Brazilian Grand Prix should be an interesting one but I've got no idea what will happen. I'm just going to try and do what I did today and win the race. The rest isn't down to me but you never know - we could have a nice surprise. We just have to try and believe it."* Fernando Alonso intended to adopt a similar strategy. *"Taking four points off Lewis in Interlagos won't be easy,"* said the Spaniard. *"If the race goes as normal, with no rain or anything like that I'd say it was virtually impossible."* The Chinese Grand Prix was a timely reminder that every race can end in the unexpected. The final race of the season at Sao Paulo would be tense in the extreme...

Lewis Hamilton's right-rear tyre was worn down to the canvas. No wonder he struggled to keep his McLaren on a wet road...
< V

Bernie Ecclestone declared that he would prefer Hamilton to be champion as *"Kimi doesn't talk enough to be interesting."* His comments left the iceman cold. *"I really don't care what people think of me,"* he replied. In the meantime, Raikkonen got on with the serious business of winning his fifth Grand Prix of the year.
V

The pursuit of a world title...

• At the start, Lewis Hamilton took advantage of his pole position to claim the lead and pull out a gap over Kimi Raikkonen. Up to lap 15 he was potentially world champion.

• Lewis Hamilton makes his first stop on lap 15 and drops to fourth behind Fernando Alonso. Nonetheless, he is still potentially world champion.

• After Kimi Raikkonen stops on lap 19, Lewis Hamilton is back in the lead until lap 28. So far, everything is on course for him to become world champion.

• From lap 26 onwards, Lewis Hamilton starts to lose ground. He laps in 1m43s on lap 25, then 1m46s on the next lap followed by a 1m50s and 1m55s. It's clear that something is badly wrong on the number 2 McLaren, but all is far from lost.

• On lap 29, Lewis Hamilton is passed by Kimi Raikkonen. He is still losing time but stays out for two more laps. By finishing second, he would still be world champion.

• On lap 31 - five laps after he first hit tyre trouble - he comes into the pits for new rubber. It's too late. He arrives slightly too fast and slides off into the gravel trap. Powerless and furious he gestures for the marshals to push him - but they don't, as it is not allowed. He retires, knowing that he has it all to do in Brazil.

<
The two BMW Saubers put in another solid race. Nick Heidfeld was seventh at the finish but he felt disappointed. *"I think we could have been fourth here today,"* said the German. The team hung on for too long before changing his tyres (on lap 28). He bolted on another set of wets, but as the circuit rapidly dried he was forced to go back in for slicks on lap 32.

> Young Sebastian Vettel put in some surprising performances towards the end of the season : the week previously, in Japan, he could have been third had it not been for a collision with Mark Webber. In Shanghai he was fourth, the best result of the season for the Toro Rosso team. *"It's a fantastic day for the team,"* said the young German. *"I did however make a mistake : I went onto dry tyres at the exact moment when it started raining again. It was fine, I just dealt with it…"*
v

There were some fierce battles wherever you looked during the Chinese Grand Prix. The two Renaults found themselves locked in a big scrap with Nico Rosberg at round about lap 15.
v

Ferrari also feels the heat

After the draconian penalty handed to McLaren on September 13 - the loss of all its constructors' points plus a 100 million dollar fine - the spy scandal involving Ferrari and McLaren finally seemed to be over.

At least this is what everyone thought - until a letter arrived just before the Chinese Grand Prix. It was addressed to Max Mosley, as well as Ron Dennis and Jean Todt, and it was from Nigel Stepney: Ferrari's traitor.

Curiously, Stepney's evidence had never been heard by the FIA either in July or September. It was as if he had vanished into thin air. Stepney had always maintained to his close friends that he was in possession of another dossier, detailing every single bit of cheating carried out by Ferrari over the last 10 years. Did that have anything to do with it ?

In his letter, he explained that Ferrari - through his own dealings with Mike Coughlan - equally had knowledge of McLaren's secrets. *"I knew on exactly which lap they were going to come in for fuel,"* he wrote. *"I was aware of their weight distribution and several other technical aspects of the car, which I told other engineers at Ferrari about."* His conclusion was the Ferrari too «should lose all its points.»

Jean Todt refused to dignify these allegations with an answer. *"Mr Stepney and myself are not dealing at the same level,"* he retorted. *"He behaved in an inappropriate fashion, and we are going after him through the Italian courts. I think that he has lost his mind. There is no way we are going to give any credit to somebody who is apparently capable of putting powder in the fuel tanks of his own team's cars."*

SNAPSHOTS OF THE WEEKEND

+ Lewis Hamilton was not even World Champion yet, but seven books about him were due to come out in England. One of the publishing houses had shelled out two million British pounds for his official autobiography, 'My Story', which was due to come out just after the end of the season. It was useful pocket money for a driver who was paid less than a million dollars when he started the 2007 season.

+ Bernie Ecclestone and Flavio Briatore were not in Shanghai for the Chinese Grand Prix. A friend of the pair commented : *"They're busy in London with some more important problems."* Ecclestone and Briatore had invested in the London-based football team Queens Park Rangers, which seemed to be bringing more problems than satisfactions.

+ Fernando Alonso was asked on Thursday whether or not he believed that McLaren would favour Lewis Hamilton by subtly 'sabotaging' his own car, maybe by altering the tyre pressures. His answer

was evasive. *"That's a difficult question…I won't answer that."* On Friday it was clear that Ron Dennis had taken great offence to Alonso's reply, which was interpreted by most as a thinly veiled 'yes'. Dennis said : *"At McLaren we've always believed in fair play. I don't understand how anyone who knows our way of working could reply in such a way."*

+ Frank Williams confirmed that Alexander Wurz was retiring with immediate effect after the Chinese Grand Prix and that Kazuki Nakajima (the son of former F1 driver Satoru Nakajima) would replace him in Brazil. Nico Rosberg, the son of former World Champion Keke Rosberg, would be retained in 2008.

+ Ralf Schumacher announced that he would no longer be a Toyota driver in 2008, but that he wished to continue his Formula 1 career. He did not elaborate further…

> Nanjing Road, around which Shanghai's history was built. It used to be lined with small shops, but now it has become one of the most bright and colourful pedestrian zones in the world.

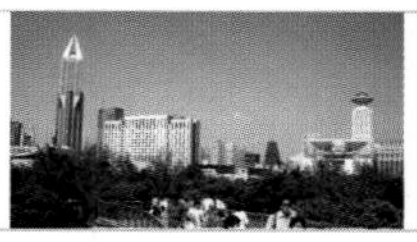

PRACTICE

Date	Weather (AM)	Air temperature	Track temperature	Weather (PM)	Air temperature	Track temperature
Friday October 5, 2007	Scattered clouds	28-30°c	38-44°c	Sunny	30-31°c	41-46°c
Saturday October 6, 2007	Sunny	28-29°c	42°c	Scattered clouds	30°c	43-46°c

All the time trials

N° Driver	Nat.	N° Chassis- Engine [Nbr. GP]	Pos. Free 1 Friday 10:00-11:30	Laps	Pos. Free 2 Friday 14:00-15:30	Laps	Pos. Free 3 Saturday 11:00-12:00	Laps	Pos. Q1 Saturday 14:00-14:15	Laps	Pos. Q2 Saturday 14:22-14:37	Laps	Pos. Q3 Saturday 14:45-15:00	Laps
1. Fernando Alonso	E	McLaren MP4-22 03 - Mercedes [1]	2. 1:37.108	18	2. 1:36.613	28	2. 1:36.126	13	4. 1:35.809	3	3. 1:35.845	3	4. **1:36.576**	10
2. Lewis Hamilton	GB	McLaren MP4-22 05 - Mercedes [2]	4. 1:37.210	20	4. 1:36.876	33	3. 1:36.227	14	3. 1:35.798	3	4. 1:35.898	3	1. **1:35.908**	10
3. Giancarlo Fisichella	I	Renault R27-02 [2]	8. 1:38.217	16	10. 1:37.970	32	17. 1:37.791	17	18. **1:37.290**	7				
4. Heikki Kovalainen	FIN	Renault R27-03 [1]	11. 1:38.551	17	11. 1:38.062	21	8. 1:37.106	14	16. 1:37.225	6	14. **1:36.991**	6		
5. Felipe Massa	BR	Ferrari F2007 263 [2]	3. 1:37.128	21	3. 1:36.630	29	4. 1:36.405	14	2. 1:35.792	3	2. 1:35.796	3	3. **1:36.221**	10
6. Kimi Räikkönen	FIN	Ferrari F2007 262 [2]	1. 1:37.024	24	1. 1:36.607	31	1. 1:36.100	15	1. 1:35.692	4	1. 1:35.381	3	2. **1:36.044**	10
7. Jenson Button	GB	Honda RA107-04 [1]	14. 1:38.942	18	12. 1:38.205	41	13. 1:37.564	19	10. 1:37.092	6	10. 1:36.771	6	10. **1:39.285**	10
8. Rubens Barrichello	BR	Honda RA107-05 & 02 [1]	15. 1:38.945	22	13. 1:38.304	40	18. 1:37.920	20	17. **1:37.251**	6				
9. Nick Heidfeld	D	BMW Sauber F1.07-08 [1]	10. 1:38.445	13	15. 1:38.388	16	9. 1:37.176	18	6. 1:36.737	5	6. 1:36.217	6	8. **1:38.455**	10
10. Robert Kubica	PL	BMW Sauber F1.07-03 [1]	6. 1:38.055	23	14. 1:38.879	39	7. 1:37.024	23	5. 1:36.309	4	5. 1:36.116	6	9. **1:38.472**	10
11. Ralf Schumacher	D	Toyota TF107/05 [2]	12. 1:38.661	23	7. 1:37.524	32	5. 1:36.959	18	11. 1:37.135	7	9. 1:36.709	6	6. **1:38.013**	10
12. Jarno Trulli	I	Toyota TF107/04 [2]	7. 1:38.208	30	5. 1:37.151	36	14. 1:37.679	20	15. 1:37.209	7	13. **1:36.959**	6		
14. David Coulthard	GB	Red Bull RB3 3 - Renault [2]	13. 1:38.700	25	8. 1:37.617	27	6. 1:36.964	13	7. 1:36.930	6	7. 1:36.252	6	5. **1:37.619**	10
15. Mark Webber	AUS	Red Bull RB3 4 - Renault [2]	18. 1:39.535	23	6. 1:37.450	34	10. 1:37.315	13	13. 1:37.199	6	8. 1:36.602	6	7. **1:38.153**	10
16. Nico Rosberg	D	Williams FW29-05 - Toyota [2]	5. 1:37.707	23	9. 1:37.646	36	11. 1:37.323	16	12. 1:37.144	7	16. **1:37.483**	6		
17. Alexander Wurz	AUT	Williams FW29-03 - Toyota [2]			16. 1:38.531	32	19. 1:37.926	16	19. **1:37.456**	6				
18. Vitantonio Liuzzi	I	Toro Rosso STR2-03 - Ferrari [2]	17. 1:39.497	22	18. 1:39.065	36	12. 1:37.463	18	9. 1:37.047	6	11. **1:36.862**	6		
19. Sebastian Vettel	D	Toro Rosso STR2-04 - Ferrari [2]	20. 1:39.898	24	21. 1:39.404	34	16. 1:37.759	19	8. 1:37.006	6	12. **1:36.891**	6		
20. Adrian Sutil	D	Spyker F8-VII/03 B-spec - Ferrari [1]	22. 1:40.149	26	19. 1:39.224	37	21. 1:38.868	20	21. **1:38.668**	8				
21. Sakon Yamamoto	J	Spyker F8-VII/04 B-spec - Ferrari [2]	21. 1:40.126	27	22. 1:40.051	38	22. 1:39.517	21	22. **1:39.336**	7				
22. Takuma Sato	J	Super Aguri SA07-02 - Honda [1]	16. 1:39.238	23	20. 1:39.360	37	20. 1:38.577	16	20. **1:38.218**	6				
23. Anthony Davidson	GB	Super Aguri SA07-03 - Honda [1]	19. 1:39.539	20	17. 1:38.975	38	15. 1:37.732	15	14. 1:37.203	6	15. **1:37.247**	6		
38. Kazuki Nakajima	J	Williams FW29-03 - Toyota	9. 1:38.270	30										

Fastest lap overall
K. Räikkönen 1:35.381 (205,739 km/h)

Maximum speed

N° Driver	S1 Qualifs	Pos.	S1 Race	Pos.	S2 Qualifs	Pos.	S2 Race	Pos.	Finish Qualifs	Pos.	Finish Race	Pos.	Radar Qualifs	Pos.	Radar Race	Pos.
1. F. Alonso	285,5	2	281,6	2	279,5	1	275,1	2	264,5	1	260,7	1	312,4	3	313,5	1
2. L. Hamilton	286,0	1	277,4	8	278,5	3	268,5	11	263,1	2	255,7	5	311,0	4	306,0	11
3. G. Fisichella	280,0	10	278,7	5	273,7	11	269,8	7	258,0	14	255,3	8	307,5	9	308,7	7
4. H. Kovalainen	280,7	6	278,0	7	274,6	6	270,8	5	260,1	6	255,3	7	308,2	5	309,0	6
5. F. Massa	284,2	4	281,7	1	278,8	2	275,5	1	261,8	3	259,6	2	313,6	2	312,1	3
6. K. Räikkönen	285,1	3	280,5	3	278,4	4	273,6	3	261,5	4	258,1	3	314,7	1	312,5	2
7. J. Button	279,7	14	275,3	15	272,1	18	269,5	9	259,0	9	254,1	12	305,1	17	305,6	13
8. R. Barrichello	278,6	17	270,7	20	272,3	16	264,3	19	258,6	10	249,8	20	306,4	12	301,0	19
9. N. Heidfeld	280,5	7	278,4	6	274,3	8	270,0	6	259,9	7	256,0	4	303,8	19	310,3	4
10. R. Kubica	280,9	5	275,3	14	274,8	5	269,7	8	260,8	5	253,5	15	305,5	14	302,7	16
11. R. Schumacher	280,3	8	276,9	9	272,9	14	265,4	18	258,2	12	253,9	14	307,6	7	306,4	10
12. J. Trulli	279,9	12	275,8	10	272,7	15	265,8	17	258,1	13	252,0	17	306,9	11	301,2	18
14. D. Coulthard	280,2	9	275,7	11	274,5	7	268,3	13	259,1	8	254,3	10	307,8	6	306,0	12
15. M. Webber	279,8	13	275,5	13	273,9	10	268,2	14	257,8	15	254,3	11	306,9	10	307,1	8
16. N. Rosberg	278,7	16	274,5	17	272,1	17	268,0	15	257,8	16	254,7	9	307,6	8	310,0	5
17. A. Wurz	278,4	18	280,1	4	271,3	19	271,0	4	257,4	17	255,5	6	305,4	15	306,8	9
18. V. Liuzzi	278,2	19	275,2	16	273,4	13	269,4	10	257,4	18	254,0	13	305,2	16	304,8	15
19. S. Vettel	280,0	11	275,5	12	273,4	12	268,5	12	257,2	19	252,3	16	305,5	13	305,5	14
20. A. Sutil	274,8	20	263,3	22	268,2	21	255,1	22	253,4	22	242,3	21	301,6	21	296,2	21
21. S. Yamamoto	273,6	22	270,9	19	266,5	22	263,4	20	253,6	21	250,8	19	302,2	20	298,9	20
22. T. Sato	274,8	21	271,6	18	268,7	20	266,1	16	255,9	20	251,3	18	297,6	22	295,4	22
23. A. Davidson	279,7	15	264,9	21	274,1	9	255,1	21	258,4	11	240,5	22	304,1	18	301,6	17

Best sector times

Qualifs	**S1** K. Räikkönen	25.146	**S2** K. Räikkönen	28.093	**S3** F. Massa	42.124	= 1:35.363
Race	**S1** F. Alonso	25.880	**S2** F. Massa	28.835	**S3** F. Massa	42.714	= 1:37.429

RACE

Date	Weather	Air temperature	Track temperature	Humidity	Wind speed
Sunday October 7, 2007 (14:00)	Overcast, intermittent rain	30-29°c	33-30°c	82%	2.5 m/s

Classification & retirements

Pos.	Driver	Constructor	Tyres	Laps	Time	Km/h
1.	K. Räikkönen	Ferrari	WWM	56	1:37:58.395	186,826
2.	F. Alonso	McLaren Mercedes	WWH	56	+ 9.806	186,514
3.	F. Massa	Ferrari	WWM	56	+ 12.891	186,417
4.	S. Vettel	STR Ferrari	WM	56	+ 53.509	185,140
5.	J. Button	Honda	WMM	56	+ 1:08.666	184,668
6.	V. Liuzzi	STR Ferrari	WWM	56	+ 1:13.673	184,513
7.	N. Heidfeld	BMW	WWH	56	+ 1:14.224	184,496
8.	D. Coulthard	Red Bull Renault	WWM	56	+ 1:20.750	184,294
9.	H. Kovalainen	Renault	WM	56	+ 1:21.186	184,281
10.	M. Webber	Red Bull Renault	WHWH	56	+ 1:24.685	184,172
11.	G. Fisichella	Renault	WMM	56	+ 1:26.683	184,111
12.	A. Wurz	Williams Toyota	WMM	55	1 lap	183,345
13.	J. Trulli	Toyota	WM	55	1 lap	182,817
14.	T. Sato	Super Aguri Honda	WM	55	1 lap	182,193
15.	R. Barrichello	Honda	WMWM	55	1 lap	180,567
16.	N. Rosberg	Williams Toyota	WMWM	54	2 laps	179,346
17.	S. Yamamoto	Spyker Ferrari	EWMWM	53	3 laps	174,576

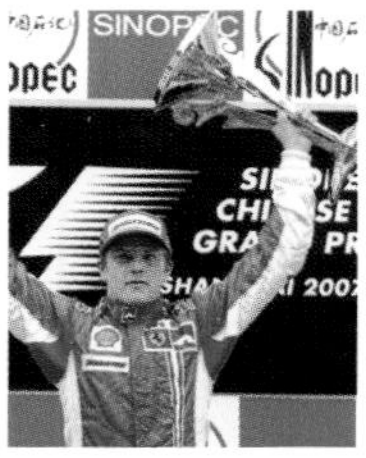

Driver	Constructor	Tyres	Laps	Reason
R. Kubica	BMW	WH	33	Hydraulic leak affecting steering and gearshift
L. Hamilton	McLaren Mercedes	WW	30	Went off, car stuck in gravel trap at pit lane entry
R. Schumacher	Toyota	WM	25	Spin, stall
A. Sutil	Spyker Ferrari	EWM	24	Went off into guardrail
A. Davidson	Super Aguri Honda	WW	11	Rear brakes too badly damaged following collision with Barrichello

Tyres H: Hard & M: Medium // E: Extreme Wet & W: Wet

Fastest laps

	Driver	Time	Lap	Km/h
1.	F. Massa	1:37.454	56	201,362
2.	F. Alonso	1:37.991	54	200,259
3.	K. Räikkönen	1:38.285	52	199,660
4.	G. Fisichella	1:38.900	39	198,418
5.	J. Button	1:38.913	39	198,392
6.	N. Rosberg	1:39.223	54	197,752
7.	N. Heidfeld	1:39.325	55	197,569
8.	H. Kovalainen	1:39.331	52	197,557
9.	M. Webber	1:39.371	55	197,478
10.	D. Coulthard	1:39.640	55	196,945
11.	V. Liuzzi	1:39.654	53	196,917
12.	A. Wurz	1:39.743	54	196,741
13.	S. Vettel	1:39.890	52	196,452
14.	J. Trulli	1:39.911	55	196,410
15.	T. Sato	1:40.126	54	195,989
16.	R. Barrichello	1:40.516	55	195,228
17.	S. Yamamoto	1:40.764	52	194,748
18.	R. Kubica	1:40.926	32	194,435
19.	L. Hamilton	1:43.131	22	190,278
20.	R. Schumacher	1:44.062	25	188,576
21.	A. Sutil	1:47.603	22	182,370
22.	A. Davidson	1:51.765	9	175,579

Pit stops

	Driver	Lap	Duration	Stop	Total
1.	A. Sutil	6	27.782	1	27.782
2.	S. Yamamoto	7	28.711	1	28.711
3.	A. Davidson	11	32.689	1	32.689
4.	L. Hamilton	15	27.290	1	27.290
5.	F. Massa	17	27.465	1	27.465
6.	F. Alonso	18	27.810	1	27.810
7.	K. Räikkönen	19	27.644	1	27.644
8.	D. Coulthard	19	27.556	1	27.556
9.	V. Liuzzi	19	26.508	1	26.508
10.	A. Wurz	22	28.990	1	28.990
11.	M. Webber	23	27.287	1	27.287
12.	R. Schumacher	23	32.481	1	32.481
13.	H. Kovalainen	24	29.540	1	29.540
14.	J. Button	24	27.728	1	27.728
15.	R. Kubica	25	26.805	1	26.805
16.	J. Trulli	25	29.071	1	29.071
17.	N. Rosberg	25	31.037	1	31.037
18.	G. Fisichella	25	26.535	1	26.535
19.	R. Barrichello	25	29.815	1	29.815
20.	A. Sutil	24	29.113	2	56.895
21.	T. Sato	25	31.392	1	31.392
22.	S. Yamamoto	24	54.949	2	1:23.660
23.	F. Massa	26	28.643	2	56.108
24.	S. Vettel	26	32.182	1	32.182
25.	D. Coulthard	26	27.522	2	55.078
26.	R. Barrichello	26	34.047	2	1:03.862
27.	M. Webber	27	26.469	2	53.756
28.	N. Heidfeld	28	30.377	1	30.377
29.	S. Yamamoto	26	27.838	3	1:51.498
30.	N. Rosberg	28	30.559	2	1:01.596
31.	V. Liuzzi	31	29.436	2	55.944
32.	M. Webber	31	27.199	3	1:20.955
33.	K. Räikkönen	32	28.543	2	56.187
34.	F. Alonso	32	29.267	2	57.077
35.	R. Barrichello	31	26.822	3	1:30.684
36.	N. Heidfeld	32	29.351	2	59.728
37.	N. Rosberg	31	27.257	3	1:28.853
38.	S. Yamamoto	30	28.624	4	2:20.122
39.	A. Wurz	37	27.117	2	56.107
40.	J. Button	42	26.716	2	54.444
41.	G. Fisichella	45	25.693	2	52.228

Race leader

Driver	Laps in the lead	Nbr of laps
L. Hamilton	1 > 15	15
K. Räikkönen	16 > 19	4
L. Hamilton	20 > 28	9
K. Räikkönen	29 > 32	4
R. Kubica	33	1
K. Räikkönen	34 > 56	23

Driver	Nbr of laps	Kilometers
K. Räikkönen	31	168,981 km
L. Hamilton	24	130,634 km
R. Kubica	1	5,451 km

Gaps on the lead board

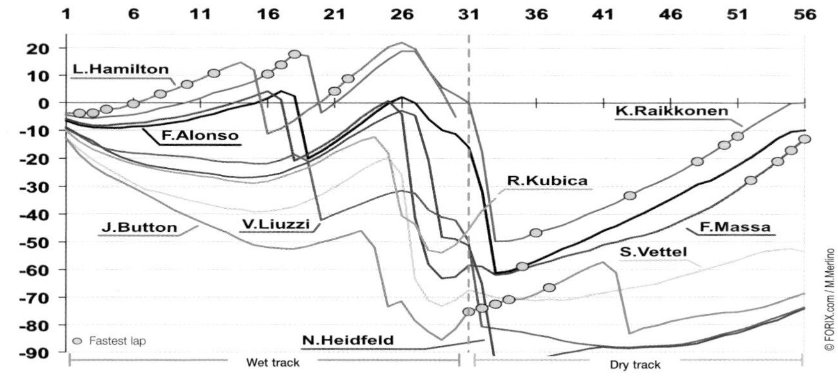

Lap chart

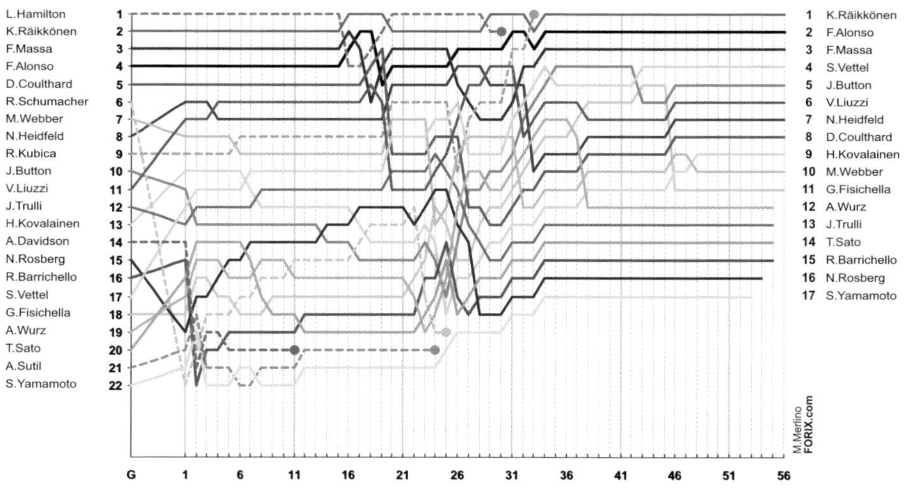

CHAMPIONSHIPS 16/17

Drivers

	Driver	Constructor	Wins	Points
1.	L. Hamilton	McLaren Mercedes	4	107
2.	F. Alonso	McLaren Mercedes	4	103
3.	K. Räikkönen	Ferrari	5	100
4.	F. Massa	Ferrari	3	86
5.	N. Heidfeld	BMW		58
6.	R. Kubica	BMW		35
7.	H. Kovalainen	Renault		30
8.	G. Fisichella	Renault		21
9.	N. Rosberg	Williams Toyota		15
10.	D. Coulthard	Red Bull Renault		14
11.	A. Wurz	Williams Toyota		13
12.	M. Webber	Red Bull Renault		10
13.	J. Trulli	Toyota		7
14.	S. Vettel	BMW 1 /// STR Ferrari 5		6
15.	J. Button	Honda		6
16.	R. Schumacher	Toyota		5
17.	T. Sato	Super Aguri Honda		4
18.	V. Liuzzi	STR Ferrari		3
19.	A. Sutil	Spyker Ferrari		1
20.	R. Barrichello	Honda		0
21.	S. Speed	STR Ferrari		0
22.	A. Davidson	Super Aguri Honda		0
23.	S. Yamamoto	Spyker Ferrari		0
24.	C. Albers	Spyker Ferrari		0
	M. Winkelhock	Spyker Ferrari		-

Constructors

	Constructor	Wins	Points
1.	**Scuderia Ferrari Marlboro**	8	186
2.	BMW Sauber F1 Team		94
3.	ING Renault F1 Team		51
4.	AT&T Williams		28
5.	Red Bull Racing		24
6.	Panasonic Toyota Racing		12
7.	Scuderia Toro Rosso		8
8.	Honda Racing F1 Team		6
9.	Super Aguri F1 Team		4
10.	Etihad Aldar Spyker F1 Team		1
11.	Vodafone McLaren Mercedes	8	195

THE CIRCUIT

Name Shanghai International Circuit; Shanghai
Lenght 5451 m
Distance 56 laps, 305,066 km
Latitude 31°20'13.90"N
Longitude 121°13'11.70"E

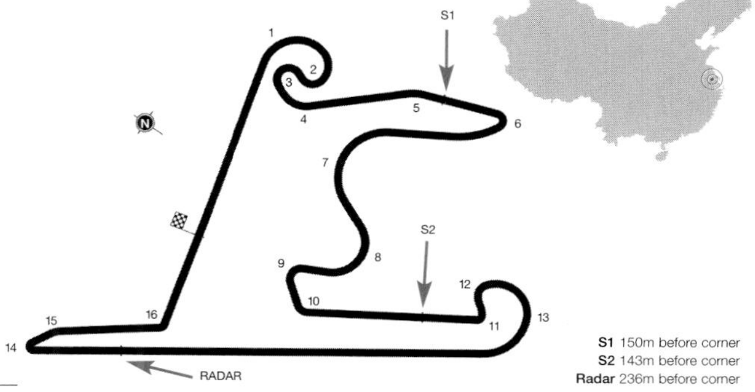

S1 150m before corner
S2 143m before corner
Radar 236m before corner

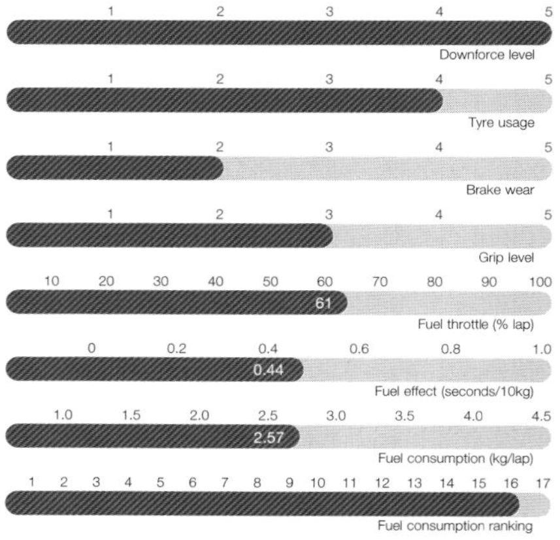

AN INCREDIBLE STORY AND A SUPERB CHAMPION

He didn't have a realistic chance of challenging, but he achieved the impossible: Kimi Raikkonen clinched the 2007 Formula 1 world driver's championship. It was the end of an incredible story.

To reach his goal, the Finn had to win the Brazilian Grand Prix, but he also had to hope that his rivals encountered problems. He wasn't disappointed: after an excursion off the track on the first lap, Lewis Hamilton had a gearbox problem before stopping in the pits three times, compared to the two stops of his adversaries. The Briton couldn't quite handle the pressure, while his car encountered its first technical problems of the season. All in all, it was particularly bad timing...

High tension at McLaren: big brother is watching…

It was the race of his life. Lewis Hamilton, at 22 years of age, was the best placed of the three candidates to pull off his first world title at the end of the Brazilian Grand Prix.

With a four point advantage over his closest rival (his team mate Fernando Alonso), the Briton was still the firm favourite for this last round of the Formula 1 world championship.

Fernando Alonso had only one possible strategy this weekend: to win. He needed to win with Lewis Hamilton finishing lower than third in order to take his third consecutive world championship.

To achieve this, Fernando Alonso was mainly going to have to fight a battle against his own team. So the atmosphere was even tenser at McLaren than usual. Following suspicions aroused by the Spaniard at the Chinese Grand Prix two weeks earlier, when he hinted that his team had altered his tyre pressures to

make his car less competitive, the FIA had appointed an observer especially for McLaren. This person would remain in the McLaren garage constantly, to ensure complete equality of treatment between the two drivers.

Predictably the presence of "big brother" under their feet hardly amused the McLaren engineers and mechanics. At the Chinese Grand Prix moreover, Ron Dennis said that his team's main rival wasn't Kimi Raikkonen, but actually Fernando Alonso himself. So the atmosphere was heavy at the heart of the English team. « I was very surprised to hear this from Ron », commented the Spanish driver when he arrived at the Interlagos circuit on Thursday. "But one often says anything in the heat of moment after a race. Me too: I sometimes say things that I don't really mean."

The FIA observer didn't totally reassure Fernando Alonso : "To be honest, we don't need that," he said.

"I'm not really in favour of having a representative of the FIA in the garage, but what can I do ?"

The situation was so delicate at this point that the McLaren PR team explained to the Spaniard that it was best for him not to make any more statements in public at all.

During a heavily policed interview on Thursday, Alonso revisited his thoughts on Shanghai : "There I felt something strange during qualifying," he explained. "We then noticed that the tyre pressures were too high. This sort of problem can happen sometimes, it's just a coincidence..." Alonso was doing a reasonably good job of convincing the outside world that all was well within McLaren. He even said that he wanted to stay on in 2008. No surprise really : the two-time World Champion was not about to do anything that would compromise his chances of winning on Sunday.

> Red Bull family portrait. This was taken on Thursday, with the two race drivers and the 18 year-old Sebastian Buemi. In qualifying, Mark Webber was fifth and David Coulthard was ninth : the strongest showing from the British-based team all year.

A Swiss driver in F1

The Swiss driver Sebastian Buemi officially became a Formula 1 driver after the Brazilian Grand Prix. Having tested the Red Bull three times during the summer at Jerez, the Swiss was named as the third driver alongside David Coulthard and Mark Webber. He would have already played his part in Japan and China, had he not been obliged to honour his commitments in Formula 3 - where he finished second in the European championship. The third driver plays a vital role in a Formula 1 team, standing in for the race drivers in the event of any problem or injury - often at the last minute. So he has to be ready at a moment's notice and know the car inside out. "I go to all the team's technical meetings," commented Sebastian Buemi. "It's really very interesting. There's a lot to take in, but I'm taking it a bit at a time. As I'm only starting out I don't say anything but I just listen, except when the engineers ask for my opinion." Even though nothing is yet confirmed, the 2008 season is looking good for the young Swiss. If everything goes to plan, he'll compete on the entire GP2 championship, and do a lot of testing for Red Bull in F1 as well.

IN BRIEF

+ An error by the McLaren team (one of many) meant that Lewis Hamilton used two different sets of wet tyres during Friday morning's practice, which was affected by wet weather. The rules only allow one set to be used during each session on Friday (article 25.3 of the sporting regulations), so Lewis Hamilton was hit with a $15,000 dollar fine - the same penalty handed to Jenson Button and Takuma Sato. During the day, there was even talk of putting the Briton at the back of the grid.

+ Fernando Alonso did not want to stay a day longer at McLaren than he had to. He signed a letter of intent with Renault for the 2008 to 2010 seasons, but his contract with McLaren until the end of 2009 meant that he had two conflicting commitments. All concerned refused to comment before the end of the season.

+ There is no United States Grand Prix in 2008, but the BMW team is making a trip there all the same. From 7-10 January, one of their F1 cars will be exhibited at a Las Vegas computer show. The Hinwil team is going at the request of its sponsors Intel and Dell.

+ The Prodrive team, which was planning to enter F1 in 2008 using McLaren customer cars, seemed to have thrown in the towel. McLaren effectively decided that it was now too late to reach an agreement for 2008, while Williams launched a Court action designed to prevent teams from using chassis bought from another team.

+ Rumour had it that Jean Todt, the boss of the Ferrari team, was attending his last Grand Prix in Sao Paulo. The story went that Ferrari president Luca di Montezemolo had a disagreement with Todt over the idea of employing Fernando Alonso, and that Todt would consequently be given other responsibilities. Jean Todt is also looking to buy the Grand Sambuc circuit, close to Aix-en-Provence - a 600 hectare site for sale for 10 million euros.

+ The Red Bulls appeared to become increasingly competitive towards the end of the season. Mark Webber qualified fifth, his best grid position of the year.

STARTING GRID

* A. SUTIL starts from the pit lane.	S. YAMAMOTO 22 1:15.487	A. DAVIDSON 20 1:14.596	T. SATO 18 1:14.098	J. BUTTON 16 1:13.469	V. LIUZZI 14 1:13.251	G. FISICHELLA 12 1:12.968	N. ROSBERG 10 1:13.477	J. TRULLI 8 1:13.195	N. HEIDFELD 6 1:13.081	F. ALONSO 4 1:12.356	L. HAMILTON 2 1:12.082

| A. SUTIL* 21 1:15.217 | K. NAKAJIMA 19 1:14.417 | H. KOVALAINEN 17 1:14.078 | R. SCHUMACHER 15 1:13.315 | S. VETTEL 13 1:13.058 | R. BARRICHELLO 11 1:12.932 | D. COULTHARD 9 1:13.272 | R. KUBICA 7 1:13.129 | M. WEBBER 5 1:12.928 | K. RÄIKKÖNEN 3 1:12.322 | F. MASSA 1 1:11.931 (215.656 km/h) |

Lewis stares history in the face on the first row

Nothing was yet decided, that was sure enough. But by claiming a spot on the front row of the grid for Sunday's race, Lewis Hamilton had taken a big step towards claiming his first world title.
Felipe had seemingly done everything to take pole for his home race, including running with a very light fuel load. Hamilton, however, would have the advantage of starting beside him and in front of his two championship rivals. Kimi Raikkonen

was third on the grid, while Fernando Alonso was fourth.
This time, it seemed that Hamilton had learnt his lesson from Shanghai the hard way. He would not try to win at all costs : instead he would happily settle for any position that allowed him to become the youngest World Champion in the history of Formula 1. The Englishman said : *"It was quite a tense qualifying session but the car has been*

fantastic and I've got a very good feeling on this circuit. Now I know exactly what I need to do in order to win the championship and that will do nicely : I'm not going all-out to win the race."
Fernando Alonso was bitterly disappointed after qualifying. He knew that his only chance of becoming World Champion was through winning the race. By starting behind Lewis Hamilton, he would have to overtake his team mate as the first major task. *"I obviously would have preferred to be on the front row,"* he said. *"We made some changes to the car, and those didn't work out quite how I had hoped. I didn't feel particularly comfortable with it."* The Spaniard was now just relying on the vagaries of the race to deliver him a third world title. Kimi Raikkonen, the third championship protagonist, started from third place on the grid but had an ace up his sleeve. He knew that he could rely on the support of his team mate in pole position, who was ready to help in any way that he could. With a seven-point deficit to Hamilton, Raikkonen was in any case the outsider. *"Pole would have been better, but I was actually held up a bit on my quickest qualifying lap,"* said the Finn, referring to the previous day when Lewis Hamilton had emerged from the pits in front of him. *"That's a pity but there's no point in making a fuss about it. I still think I've got some chances left."* Looking at the grid, it seemed that all Lewis Hamilton needed to do was keep his nose clean for 71 laps in order to become World Champion.

Hamilton urged to remain dignified

How do you control a 22 year-old youngster who has just won the World Championship in his first year of Formula 1 ? This was a problem that the FIA were clearly worried about. On Friday they asked McLaren to ensure that Lewis Hamilton would behave in a dignified manner on the podium on Sunday, whatever happened. *"It's just a question of following protocols,"* commented McLaren boss Ron Dennis.
Lewis Hamilton found the FIA's concern quite amusing. Up until he took the chequered flag in Brazil, he would remain focussed on the race and nothing else. *"I'd obviously love to win the Grand Prix,"* said the Englishman. *"But sometimes it's better just to concentrate on the points. I'm going to be inspired by what Fernando [Alonso] did for the last two years, and by what Michael [Schumacher] did before him. I'm going to take their example and try to copy it. Above all, my plan is to stay on the track this time !"*
Hamilton's mistake in Shanghai two weeks earlier - when he went off into a gravel trap at a mere 50kph - still haunted the young Englishman. *"First of all, I*

thought that the mistake would have ruined my confidence and made me a bit too cautious here in Brazil," he said. *"But that's not the case at all ; in fact it's taken a bit of pressure off me. I actually think that experience has made me stronger. I can't quite explain why, but I view China as a positive experience now. I feel relaxed and confident."*
Nonetheless Hamilton was completely unfamiliar with the Interlagos circuit, having driven on it for the first time on Friday. *"That's a fair point but I've driven it on the PlayStation with my brother before !"* said Hamilton. *"I know where the corners are. In actual fact, I didn't even bother driving it on the McLaren simulator : I don't think that would have achieved very much."*
As it happened Lewis Hamilton set fastest time on the first day of practice on Friday, on a drying track after some rain in the morning. The young Briton's weekend had got off to a good start.

>
The last start of the year.
Felipe Massa takes the
lead, while Kimi
Raikkonen dives to the
outside in order to follow
him. At this point, Lewis
Hamilton is just about
staying ahead of
Fernando Alonso.

Kimi Raikkonen wins the Grand Prix and the title. Breathtaking stuff.

Incredible, mesmerising and memorable : there are hardly enough adjectives to describe the grand finale of the 2007 Formula 1 season.

During the 71 laps of the Brazilian Grand Prix, the destiny of the title changed hands five times between the three drivers fighting for glory : Lewis Hamilton, Fernando Alonso et Kimi Raikkonen. Finally it was the driver who came into the race with the smallest chance who carted off the spoils, beating the two McLaren drivers by just one point. No World Championship has ever been so close amongst the three leading drivers. By taking the lead 21 laps from the finish and hanging onto it all the way to the chequered flag, Kimi Raikkonen did everything he could to seal the title. But he still couldn't have done it without some mistakes from Lewis Hamilton. The Englishman understandably struggled to resist the titanic pressure he was under.

Having got boxed behind Kimi Raikkonen at the start, the Englishman made an ill-advised passing manœuvre to get past Fernando Alonso - who had taken advantage of the situation to make a move on his team mate.

That first mistake may have been of no consequence, had Hamilton not experienced a gearbox problem on the eighth lap. *"The car suddenly found itself in neutral for no reason,"* said Hamilton. *"I had to re-boot the system, which means re-start the gearbox management software."* This is quite easy to do from the

cockpit of the McLaren but it takes time and so Hamilton dropped to 18th.

From that point on, Hamilton was faced with a race against time to climb back up the leaderboard. The frantic rush took its toll on his tyres, as he was forced to make three stops to change them. He finished seventh, scoring two points, and ended up second in the championship : just one point behind Kimi Raikkonen.

After the race, Hamilton reflected : *"It's naturally disappointing to stumble at the final hurdle having led for most of the season. But it's still only my first season in Formula 1 and I have to say that it's been phenomenal. There's still plenty of time ahead for me to fulfil my dream of becoming Formula 1 World Championship."*

A few hours later, Hamilton could be found in a Sao Paulo night club, pretending to be a DJ with members of his team. He seemed already to have consigned the Brazilian Grand Prix to history.

Instead, it was Kimi Raikkonen fulfilling his dream. The Finn could hardly believe it : in a rare moment of emotion at the end of the race he punched the air with both fists on his slowing down lap. By Raikkonen's standards, this was an unprecedented outpouring of joy.

Kimi Raikkonen may not be particularly demonstrative but he is extremely popular. The fact that he drives for Ferrari undoubtedly helps. Formula 1 was preparing to celebrate its new

champion when the news came through from the FIA technical delegate shortly after the race that the BMW Sauber and Williams cars will not in full compliance with the rules (see page 214). This meant that if these cars were disqualified, Lewis Hamilton would make up three places. He would therefore score five points rather than two, and become World Champion ! This Formula 1 season had more twists and turns than any best-selling thriller.

>
After his gearbox
problem, Lewis Hamilton
didn't give up. He tried to
pick off all the cars
one by one.
From top to bottom :
• Lap 1, eighth behind
Mark Webber, the two
BMWs and Jarno Trulli
(whom he passes),
• Lap 13, 16th behind
Anthony Davidson and
Ralf Schumacher,
• Lap 15, 12th behind
Kazuki Nakajima,
• Lap 28, 13th and
attacking Rubens
Barrichello

>
"Good luck my son!"
Anthony Hamilton's final
words to his son Lewis
on the grid. There was an
electric tension in the air
before the cars got
underway.

<
Party time ?
Kimi Raikkonen let his hair down slightly after winning his first World Championship. But it was hardly a riot. During the press conference, the Finn remained his usual monosyllabic and muted self.

> For once in his career, chance was on Kimi Raikkonen's side. Going into the final two Grands Prix of the season, he was 17 points behind Lewis Hamilton : practically a hopeless situation. The Finn did everything in his power to win those two races, but he also needed Lewis Hamilton to come away with very little. And it was there that fate intervened.

Kimi Raikkonen:
"The title isn't going to change my life"

The Brazilian Grand Prix was action-packed from start to finish. Felipe Massa, who started from pole, was clearly not going to stand in Kimi Raikkonen's way, so it all came down to whether or not Lewis Hamilton would score enough points to claim the title. This kept Raikkonen in suspense all the way to the chequered flag. *"I only realised that I was World Champion when I crossed the finish line,"* he said. *"I just tried to stay concentrated all the way to the end. At the start I saw Hamilton going off in my mirrors and then I thought that maybe I had a chance. But I also knew that he could come back up, or that other people in front of him might retire. So I just waited. It felt like a very long wait !"*

Most drivers find it hard to describe what winning the World Championship feels like : particularly if it is for the first time. Kimi Raikkonen is no exception to the rule, having chased Formula 1's ultimate goal for seven years now.

"I've had some difficult times in my career but this title is what I have always wanted," he said. *"This season has not been so easy either. We had some reliability problems but we have managed to get it all back in the end. The whole team never lost faith. When I crossed the line it was quite hard for me to realise what was happening. We came from so far behind that it was difficult to believe that we had actually arrived at where we wanted to be !"*

The Brazilian Grand Prix made exciting television, but it was considerably calmer from inside the cockpit of the number six Ferrari. *"It was not a stressful race at all, me and Felipe (Massa) were just driving along normally. We could have gone a lot quicker if we needed to, but it was important to look after the cars."*

For Kimi Raikkonen, Lewis Hamilton's problems were a golden opportunity. *"I don't believe in good luck or bad luck,"* said the Finn. *"If you have bad luck, it's because you've not worked hard enough to avoid mistakes. But if you want to talk about luck, or opportunities then sure - I will take whatever comes my way !"*

The title may have been a long time coming, but it is unlikely to change Raikkonen's life. He will always be his own man. *"The title's going to change nothing at all,"* he said. *"Maybe there will be more people who will be interested in me and write shit about me, but I really don't care. They can do what they want."*

In strength as well as in adversity, the iceman remains the master of his emotions.

The enthusiastic public at Interlagos was not disappointed : they witnessed a splendid race in magnificent sunshine. So what if local hero Felipe Massa had to surrender his chances to Kimi Raikkonen ?

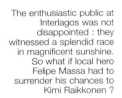

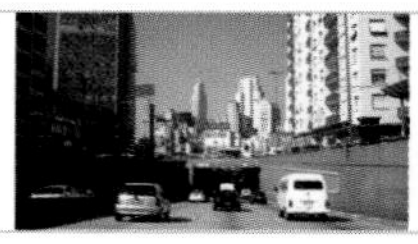

PRACTICE

Date	Weather (AM)	Air temperature	Track temperature	Weather (PM)	Air temperature	Track temperature
Friday October 19, 2007	Rain	16-19°c	23-26°c	Cloudy, wet	18-19°c	19-21°c
Saturday October 20, 2007	Sunny	25-27°c	36-42°c	Sunny	30-33°c	49-54°c

All the time trials

N° Driver	Nat.	N° Chassis- Engine [Nbr. GP]	Pos. Free 1 Friday 10:00-11:30	Laps	Pos. Free 2 Friday 14:00-15:30	Laps	Pos. Free 3 Saturday 11:00-12:00	Laps	Pos. Q1 Saturday 14:00-14:15	Laps	Pos. Q2 Saturday 14:22-14:37	Laps	Pos. Q3 Saturday 14:45-15:00	Laps
1. Fernando Alonso	E	McLaren MP4-22 03 - Mercedes [2]	21.	1	2. 1:12.889	28	8. 1:12.594	12	2. 1:12.895	6	4. 1:12.637	3	4. **1:12.356**	13
2. Lewis Hamilton	GB	McLaren MP4-22 05 - Mercedes [1]	5. 1:21.121	10	1. 1:12.767	27	2. 1:11.934	18	4. 1:13.033	3	2. 1:12.296	3	2. **1:12.082**	13
3. Giancarlo Fisichella	I	Renault R27-02 & 05 [1]	22.	2	5. 1:13.549	22	12. 1:12.913	20	10. 1:13.482	6	12. **1:12.968**	6		
4. Heikki Kovalainen	FIN	Renault R27-03 [2]	3. 1:20.829	19	12. 1:13.879	28	15. 1:13.090	20	17. **1:14.078**	7				
5. Felipe Massa	BR	Ferrari F2007 263 [1]	2. 1:20.062	10	3. 1:13.075	30	1. 1:11.810	22	1. 1:12.303	4	3. 1:12.374	3	1. **1:11.931**	13
6. Kimi Räikkönen	FIN	Ferrari F2007 262 [1]	1. 1:19.580	9	4. 1:13.112	30	3. 1:11.942	21	3. 1:13.016	4	1. 1:12.161	3	3. **1:12.322**	13
7. Jenson Button	GB	Honda RA107-04 [2]	12. 1:22.477	22	14. 1:14.095	44	13. 1:13.015	22	16. 1:14.054	6	16. **1:13.469**	6		
8. Rubens Barrichello	BR	Honda RA107-02 [2]	11. 1:22.434	23	13. 1:13.892	45	6. 1:12.478	24	12. 1:13.661	6	11. **1:12.932**	6		
9. Nick Heidfeld	D	BMW Sauber F1.07-08 [2]	19.	1	10. 1:13.785	44	7. 1:12.579	25	9. 1:13.472	6	10. 1:12.888	6	6. **1:13.081**	12
10. Robert Kubica	PL	BMW Sauber F1.07-03 [1]	20.	1	6. 1:13.587	34	20. 1:13.525	14	6. 1:13.085	7	5. 1:12.641	3	7. **1:13.129**	13
11. Ralf Schumacher	D	Toyota TF107/05 [1]	6. 1:21.243	22	11. 1:13.829	29	14. 1:13.046	23	14. 1:13.767	6	15. **1:13.315**	6		
12. Jarno Trulli	I	Toyota TF107/04 & 03 [1]	9. 1:22.104	26	16. 1:14.179	25	5. 1:12.461	23	8. 1:13.470	7	8. 1:12.832	6	8. **1:13.195**	12
14. David Coulthard	GB	Red Bull RB3 3 & 5 - Renault [1]	13. 1:22.667	16	9. 1:13.706	30	16. 1:13.117	12	7. 1:13.264	6	9. 1:12.846	6	9. **1:13.272**	12
15. Mark Webber	AUS	Red Bull RB3 4 - Renault [1]	8. 1:22.104	12	20. 1:14.543	35	4. 1:12.446	14	5. 1:13.081	6	6. 1:12.683	6	5. **1:12.928**	12
16. Nico Rosberg	D	Williams FW29-05 - Toyota [1]	4. 1:21.064	14	7. 1:13.655	33	10. 1:12.823	20	13. 1:13.707	6	7. 1:12.752	6	10. **1:13.477**	12
17. Kazuki Nakajima	J	Williams FW29-03 - Toyota [1]	16. 1:23.261	26	8. 1:13.664	38	19. 1:13.474	17	19. **1:14.417**	6				
18. Vitantonio Liuzzi	I	Toro Rosso STR2-03 - Ferrari [1]	10. 1:22.250	17	15. 1:14.152	33	11. 1:12.893	20	11. 1:13.607	6	14. **1:13.251**	6		
19. Sebastian Vettel	D	Toro Rosso STR2-04 - Ferrari [1]	7. 1:21.598	22	17. 1:14.409	37	9. 1:12.767	18	15. 1:13.853	6	13. **1:13.058**	6		
20. Adrian Sutil	D	Spyker F8-VII/03 B-spec - Ferrari [2]	15. 1:23.248	30	21. 1:15.095	35	21. 1:13.684	21	21. **1:15.217**	3				
21. Sakon Yamamoto	J	Spyker F8-VII/04 B-spec - Ferrari [1]	18. 1:24.366	25	22. 1:15.715	32	22. 1:13.872	21	22. **1:15.487**	6				
22. Takuma Sato	J	Super Aguri SA07-02 - Honda [2]	14. 1:22.929	19	18. 1:14.431	27	18. 1:13.331	16	18. **1:14.098**	6				
23. Anthony Davidson	GB	Super Aguri SA07-03 - Honda [2]	17. 1:23.551	20	19. 1:14.477	31	17. 1:13.299	16	20. **1:14.596**	6				

Fastest lap overall

F. Massa 1:11.931 (215,656 km/h)

Maximum speed

N° Driver	S1 Qualifs	Pos.	S1 Race	Pos.	S2 Qualifs	Pos.	S2 Race	Pos.	Finish Qualifs	Pos.	Finish Race	Pos.	Radar Qualifs	Pos.	Radar Race	Pos.
1. F. Alonso	309,7	3	309,1	2	261,3	3	259,7	2	317,0	1	315,3	4	317,4	1	316,7	2
2. L. Hamilton	306,7	4	311,0	1	260,9	4	258,8	4	314,3	3	317,4	1	317,1	2	317,5	1
3. G. Fisichella	306,0	6	291,3	22	259,7	7	230,0	21	312,3	6	314,1	9	315,0	5	311,7	12
4. H. Kovalainen	305,7	7	303,7	8	258,3	13	253,1	15	311,2	9	311,4	12	311,1	13	310,7	16
5. F. Massa	310,8	1	306,9	5	263,6	1	258,9	3	313,9	4	314,2	8	316,7	3	316,4	3
6. K. Räikkönen	310,1	2	307,8	3	262,2	2	260,4	1	315,4	2	315,3	5	316,4	4	315,9	5
7. J. Button	299,6	20	301,2	20	258,4	12	254,1	12	306,5	18	306,2	22	305,9	22	306,1	21
8. R. Barrichello	299,2	21	299,7	21	257,5	15	251,6	20	305,6	20	307,5	21	306,4	21	307,4	19
9. N. Heidfeld	300,3	17	301,5	19	258,8	9	256,8	10	312,5	5	309,5	16	313,7	8	312,6	11
10. R. Kubica	306,2	5	305,9	6	259,1	8	257,4	7	309,8	11	314,4	7	313,1	9	315,8	6
11. R. Schumacher	301,6	14	301,5	18	260,8	5	258,8	5	307,6	16	311,2	13	310,7	14	311,3	13
12. J. Trulli	301,5	15	303,2	12	258,5	10	256,8	9	305,6	19	308,4	19	309,7	16	310,7	15
14. D. Coulthard	302,6	11	307,5	4	260,2	6	255,6	11	307,7	15	308,5	18	308,4	18	308,3	18
15. M. Webber	305,2	8	302,8	13	258,4	11	253,9	13	310,4	10	309,2	17	311,7	11	311,1	14
16. N. Rosberg	302,6	12	303,2	11	257,8	14	257,0	8	311,7	7	316,1	2	314,9	6	316,0	4
17. K. Nakajima	296,9	22	303,3	10	254,8	18	257,8	6	306,9	17	314,6	6	311,5	12	315,1	8
18. V. Liuzzi	303,2	10	301,7	16	256,7	16	252,9	16	311,4	8	312,7	10	313,8	7	313,0	10
19. S. Vettel	302,0	13	301,5	17	256,5	17	253,5	14	308,4	13	312,2	11	313,1	10	313,3	9
20. A. Sutil	301,2	16	305,2	7	251,8	21	252,2	17	302,5	22	315,6	3	307,6	20	315,6	7
21. S. Yamamoto	300,1	18	303,3	9	251,3	22	221,6	22	304,5	21	309,7	15	309,4	17	274,9	22
22. T. Sato	303,6	9	302,0	14	254,6	19	252,2	18	309,1	12	307,5	20	309,8	15	306,2	20
23. A. Davidson	299,7	19	302,0	15	252,5	20	252,0	19	308,0	14	310,8	14	307,7	19	308,5	17

Best sector times

Qualifs	**S1** F. Massa	18.287	**S2** L. Hamilton	36.405	**S3** F. Massa	17.031	= 1:11.723
Race	**S1** F. Massa	18.511	**S2** L. Hamilton	36.609	**S3** K. Räikkönen	16.990	= 1:12.110

RACE

Date	Weather	Air temperature	Track temperature	Humidity	Wind speed
Sunday October 21, 2007 (14:00)	Sunny	36-38°c	60-61°c	27%	2.1 m/s

Classification & retirements

Pos.	Driver	Constructor	Tyres	Laps	Time	Km/h
1.	K. Räikkönen	Ferrari	SSU	71	1:28:15.270	207,972
2.	F. Massa	Ferrari	SSU	71	+ 1.493	207,914
3.	F. Alonso	McLaren Mercedes	SSU	71	+ 57.019	205,757
4.	N. Rosberg	Williams Toyota	SSU	71	+ 1:02.848	205,533
5.	R. Kubica	BMW	SSSU	71	+ 1:10.957	205,222
6.	N. Heidfeld	BMW	SSU	71	+ 1:11.317	205,209
7.	L. Hamilton	McLaren Mercedes	SUSS	70	1 lap	204,885
8.	J. Trulli	Toyota	SSSU	70	1 lap	204,446
9.	D. Coulthard	Red Bull Renault	SSU	70	1 lap	203,523
10.	K. Nakajima	Williams Toyota	SSU	70	1 lap	203,478
11.	R. Schumacher	Toyota	SSU	70	1 lap	203,393
12.	T. Sato	Super Aguri Honda	SUU	69	2 laps	201,013
13.	V. Liuzzi	STR Ferrari	SSSU	69	2 laps	199,309
14.	A. Davidson	Super Aguri Honda	SSUS	68	3 laps	196,963

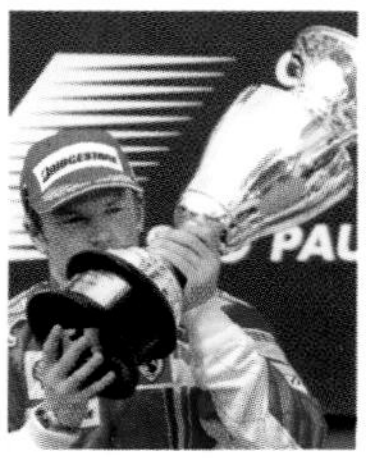

Driver	Constructor	Tyres	Laps	Reason
A. Sutil	Spyker Ferrari	SSSSSU	43	Brake pressure problem
R. Barrichello	Honda	SSS	40	Engine failure
H. Kovalainen	Renault	US	35	Went off following technical problem
S. Vettel	STR Ferrari	SS	34	Hydraulic problem affecting gearshift and steering
J. Button	Honda	S	20	Overheating engine
M. Webber	Red Bull Renault	S	14	Transmission problem, no drive between engine and gearbox
S. Yamamoto	Spyker Ferrari	SS	2	Could not avoid Fisichella and hits him violently from behind
G. Fisichella	Renault	S	2	Hit by Yamamoto getting back onto the track

Tyres S: Soft & U: Super Soft

Fastest laps

	Driver	Time	Lap	Km/h
1.	K. Räikkönen	1:12.445	66	214,126
2.	L. Hamilton	1:12.506	58	213,946
3.	F. Massa	1:12.584	71	213,716
4.	R. Kubica	1:12.686	61	213,416
5.	K. Nakajima	1:13.116	69	212,161
6.	F. Alonso	1:13.150	59	212,062
7.	N. Rosberg	1:13.159	56	212,036
8.	J. Trulli	1:13.361	68	211,452
9.	R. Schumacher	1:13.368	65	211,432
10.	N. Heidfeld	1:13.452	53	211,190
11.	V. Liuzzi	1:13.643	56	210,643
12.	J. Button	1:14.039	20	209,516
13.	D. Coulthard	1:14.195	22	209,076
14.	A. Davidson	1:14.329	64	208,699
15.	M. Webber	1:14.398	13	208,505
16.	S. Vettel	1:14.423	18	208,435
17.	R. Barrichello	1:14.742	32	207,545
18.	H. Kovalainen	1:14.891	31	207,133
19.	T. Sato	1:14.914	39	207,069
20.	A. Sutil	1:15.202	13	206,276
21.	S. Yamamoto	1:50.404	2	140,505
22.	G. Fisichella	2:02.680	2	126,446

Pit stops

	Driver	Lap	Duration	Stop	Total
1.	V. Liuzzi	1	34.899	1	34.899
2.	H. Kovalainen	1	34.164	1	34.164
3.	R. Barrichello	•9•	17.362	1	17.362
4.	R. Kubica	19	27.933	1	27.933
5.	F. Massa	20	29.333	1	29.333
6.	K. Räikkönen	21	29.163	1	29.163
7.	F. Alonso	22	28.964	1	28.964
8.	J. Trulli	22	26.528	1	26.528
9.	S. Vettel	22	28.329	1	28.329
10.	L. Hamilton	22	26.753	1	26.753
11.	A. Davidson	22	28.718	1	28.718
12.	A. Sutil	22	26.873	1	26.873
13.	N. Rosberg	23	29.534	1	29.534
14.	D. Coulthard	23	27.421	1	27.421
15.	N. Heidfeld	25	27.047	1	27.047
16.	T. Sato	25	29.890	1	29.890
17.	A. Davidson	24	42.189	2	1:10.907
18.	A. Sutil	26	2:49.325	2	3:16.198
19.	A. Sutil	27	3:10.813	3	6:27.011
20.	R. Barrichello	30	27.154	2	44.516
21.	V. Liuzzi	30	33.743	2	1:08.642
22.	K. Nakajima	31	34.201	1	34.201
23.	R. Schumacher	33	34.708	1	34.708
24.	A. Sutil	•29•	33.207	4	7:00.218
25.	L. Hamilton	36	26.468	2	53.221
26.	R. Kubica	38	25.569	2	53.502
27.	D. Coulthard	42	28.376	2	55.797
28.	J. Trulli	43	26.261	2	52.789
29.	A. Sutil	38	32.288	5	7:32.506
30.	T. Sato	44	28.700	2	58.590
31.	F. Massa	50	26.974	2	56.307
32.	A. Davidson	48	28.565	3	1:39.472
33.	N. Heidfeld	51	26.507	2	53.554
34.	F. Alonso	52	26.469	2	55.433
35.	K. Räikkönen	53	26.166	2	55.329
36.	N. Rosberg	54	28.398	2	57.932
37.	V. Liuzzi	54	27.482	3	1:36.124
38.	L. Hamilton	56	25.261	3	1:18.482
39.	R. Kubica	58	25.220	3	1:18.722
40.	K. Nakajima	61	28.706	2	1:02.907
41.	R. Schumacher	61	27.982	2	1:02.690
42.	J. Trulli	63	25.879	3	1:18.668

•• Drive-through penalty:
> Barrichello. Jump start.
> Sutil. For having caused a collision with Davidson.

Race leader

Driver	Laps in the lead	Nbr of laps
F. Massa	1 > 19	19
K. Räikkönen	20 > 21	2
F. Alonso	22	1

Driver	Laps in the lead	Nbr of laps
F. Massa	23 > 49	27
K. Räikkönen	50 > 71	22

Driver	Nbr of laps	Kilometers
F. Massa	46	198,184 km
K. Räikkönen	24	103,416 km
F. Alonso	1	4,309 km

Gaps on the lead board

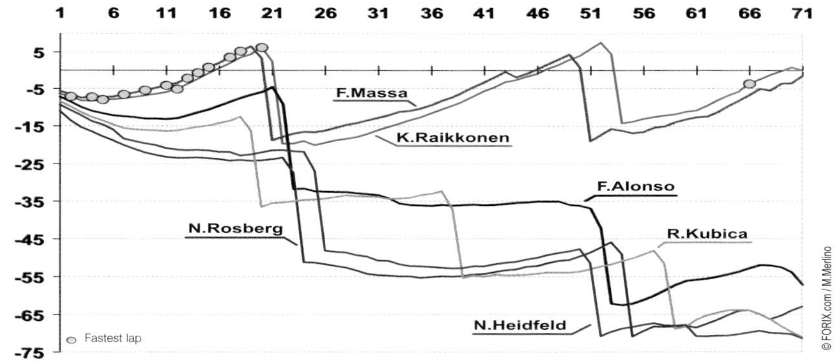
1
6
11
16
21
26
31
36
41
46
51
56
61
66
71
5
-5
-15
-25
-35
-45
-55
-65
-75
F.Massa
K.Raikkonen
F.Alonso
N.Rosberg
R.Kubica
N.Heidfeld
Fastest lap
© FORIX.com / M.Merlino

Lap chart

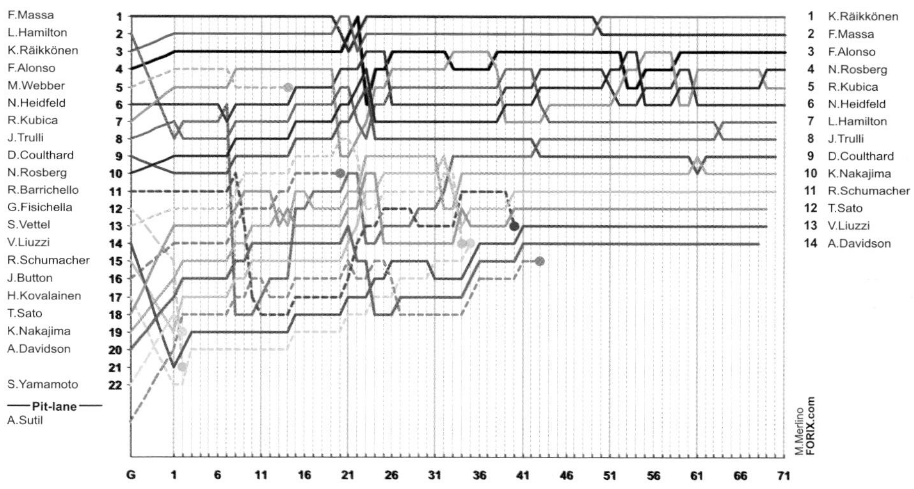
F.Massa
L.Hamilton
K.Räikkönen
F.Alonso
M.Webber
N.Heidfeld
R.Kubica
J.Trulli
D.Coulthard
N.Rosberg
R.Barrichello
G.Fisichella
S.Vettel
V.Liuzzi
R.Schumacher
J.Button
H.Kovalainen
T.Sato
K.Nakajima
A.Davidson
S.Yamamoto
Pit-lane
A.Sutil
1 K.Räikkönen
2 F.Massa
3 F.Alonso
4 N.Rosberg
5 R.Kubica
6 N.Heidfeld
7 L.Hamilton
8 J.Trulli
9 D.Coulthard
10 K.Nakajima
11 R.Schumacher
12 T.Sato
13 V.Liuzzi
14 A.Davidson
G
M.Merlino
FORIX.com

CHAMPIONSHIPS 17/17

Drivers

	Driver	Team	Wins	Points
1.	**K. Räikkönen**	Ferrari	6	110
2.	L. Hamilton	McLaren Mercedes	4	109
3.	F. Alonso	McLaren Mercedes	4	109
4.	F. Massa	Ferrari	3	94
5.	N. Heidfeld	BMW		61
6.	R. Kubica	BMW		39
7.	H. Kovalainen	Renault		30
8.	G. Fisichella	Renault		21
9.	N. Rosberg	Williams Toyota		20
10.	D. Coulthard	Red Bull Renault		14
11.	A. Wurz	Williams Toyota		13
12.	M. Webber	Red Bull Renault		10
13.	J. Trulli	Toyota		8
14.	S. Vettel	BMW 1 /// STR Ferrari 5		6
15.	J. Button	Honda		6
16.	R. Schumacher	Toyota		5
17.	T. Sato	Super Aguri Honda		4
18.	V. Liuzzi	STR Ferrari		3
19.	A. Sutil	Spyker Ferrari		1
20.	R. Barrichello	Honda		0
21.	S. Speed	STR Ferrari		0
22.	K. Nakajima	Williams Toyota		0
23.	A. Davidson	Super Aguri Honda		0
24.	S. Yamamoto	Spyker Ferrari		0
25.	C. Albers	Spyker Ferrari		0
	M. Winkelhock	Spyker Ferrari		-

Constructors

	Team	Wins	Points
1.	**Scuderia Ferrari Marlboro**	9	204
2.	BMW Sauber F1 Team		101
3.	ING Renault F1 Team		51
4.	AT&T Williams		33
5.	Red Bull Racing		24
6.	Panasonic Toyota Racing		13
7.	Scuderia Toro Rosso		8
8.	Honda Racing F1 Team		6
9.	Super Aguri F1 Team		4
10.	Etihad Aldar Spyker F1 Team		1
11.	Vodafone McLaren Mercedes	8	*203

THE CIRCUIT

Name Autódromo José Carlos Pace; São Paulo
Lenght 4309 m
Distance 71 laps, 305,909 km
Latitude 23°42'13.20"S
Longitude 46°42'00.30"O

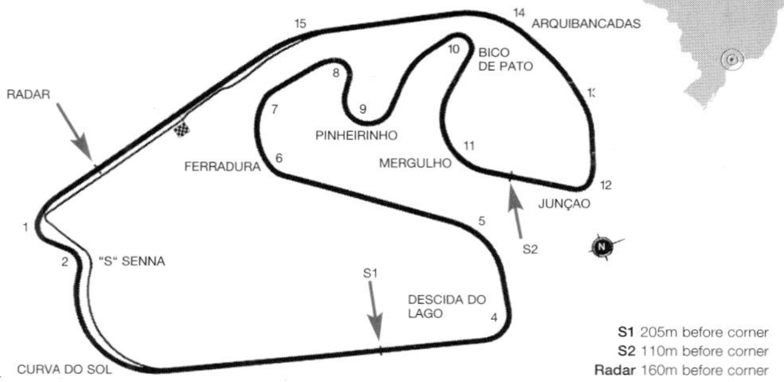
RADAR
1
2
"S" SENNA
CURVA DO SOL
S1
DESCIDA DO LAGO
4
5
6
FERRADURA
7
8
9
PINHEIRINHO
10
BICO DE PATO
11
MERGULHO
12
JUNÇAO
S2
14
ARQUIBANCADAS
15
N

S1 205m before corner
S2 110m before corner
Radar 160m before corner

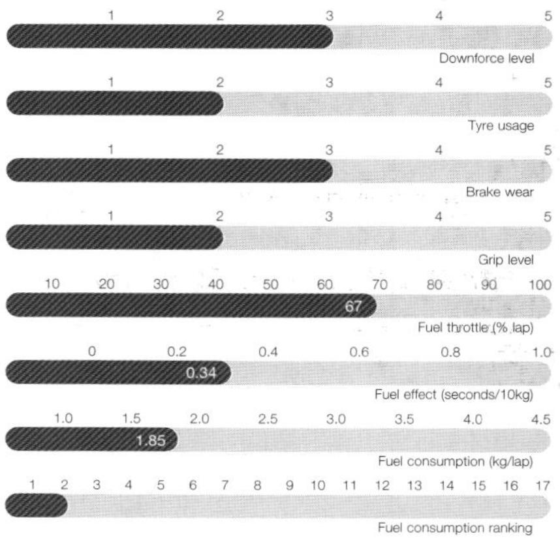
Downforce level
Tyre usage
Brake wear
Grip level
67
Fuel throttle (% lap)
0.34
Fuel effect (seconds/10kg)
1.85
Fuel consumption (kg/lap)
Fuel consumption ranking

^
Champion at last!
A month after the
Brazilian Grand Prix, Kimi
Raikkonen could finally
celebrate his first World
Championship title.

Kimi Raikkonen's world title finally confirmed on November 16

After the celebrations, a cold shower. At exactly the same time that many of the Ferrari team members were posing for a celebratory photo in the garage at Interlagos following Kimi Raikkonen's title victory, the Brazilian Grand Prix stewards were examining a report from FIA technical delegate Jo Bauer.

In it, Bauer stated that the fuel temperatures of the Williams and BMW Sauber cars during the race were more than 10 degrees below the ambient temperature - which infringes article 6.5.5 of the technical rules.

Several fuel temperatures of between 23 and 25 degrees centigrade were recorded on those two cars during the pit stops, while according to the timing screens the ambient temperature in Brazil was 37 degrees.

This infringement was of vital importance: if the BMW Sauber and the Williams did not conform to the rules, then they had to be disqualified. This would mean that Lewis Hamilton would climb three places up the grid, finish fourth, score five points instead of two, and depose Kimi Raikkonen as World Champion. At 21:35 local time on Sunday, about six hours after the race had finished, the stewards decided not to penalise the two teams. Their conclusion was that the measurements taken could not be judged to be precise enough to warrant a punishment.

It was a sensible enough conclusion. For a start, Jo Bauer did not actually take the temperature of the fuel on board the car (this would be impossible) but instead from the fuel reservoir in the pits. Furthermore, the measurement was taken using a thermometer that was not homologated by the FIA - so its accuracy was doubtful.

The other problem was that there were important differences between the ambient temperature readings supplied by FOM (Formula One Management, which organises the official timing) and Meteo France, the FIA's official weather service

Article 6.5.5. does not state where the ambient temperature reading should be taken from, so the Brazilian Grand Prix stewards decided to give Williams and BMW Sauber the benefit of the doubt by not applying any penalty.

Kimi Raikkonen was therefore confirmed as champion - for just under an hour at least. At 22:30, within the strict hour's deadline, McLaren announced that it would be appealing against the stewards' decision.

The matter would therefore be put in front of the FIA Appeal Court in Paris on 16 November: nearly four weeks after the Brazilian Grand Prix.

It seemed as if the championship was over, without anybody being entirely sure who had completely won it. That would have to wait for the FIA's judgement.

During the following few days after the Grand Prix, Max Mosley often repeated that he would be extremely surprised if the title were to change hands in a courtroom.

Without waiting for the outcome, the Scuderia held their World Championship celebration back at Maranello. A fine time was had by all.

And yet... if the World Council had decided to exclude the Williams and the BMW Sauber from the Brazilian Grand Prix and then decided to promote the cars behind (which they are not obliged to do) Lewis Hamilton would indeed have become World Champion in a Paris courtroom.

Of course, the conspiracy theorists believed that it was all a big scandal and cover-up (see Fernando Alonso's comments opposite). But actually, it would

have been a bigger scandal to allow cars not in full compliance with the technical rules to keep their places. Formula 1 has only one immutable rule: any car not complying with the technical rules is out with no negotiations, fines or compromises. It's a system that has worked well.

Most of the time, the teams accept this to be the case without question. In 2004, Ralf Schumacher lost second place at the Canadian Grand Prix because the air scoops on the brakes of his Williams were a few millimetres over the prescribed limit. He took the penalty on the chin.

At any other Grand Prix towards the beginning of the season the matter would have ended with the disqualification of the cars in question - and it's unlikely that anything more would have been said about it. By chance, this happened at a time when the World Championship was depending on it. But that was still no reason to treat this case any differently - merely because it would determine whether or not the title would go to a Finn or an Englishman. Wasn't it?

>
Jarno Trulli has a Toyota
contract up until the end
of the 2008 season. Ralf
Schumacher announced
his departure from the
Japanese team and will
be replaced by another
German: Timo Glock, the
winner of the 2007 GP2
Championship.

Alonso cries foul

It was only a matter of time: as soon as the season was over, Fernando Alonso had no reason to hold back about what he really thought about life at McLaren. On Sunday night of the Brazilian Grand Prix, Alonso told the Spanish radio station "Cadena Ser" that it would be a farce if McLaren's appeal against the stewards' decision succeeded. *"It would be a massive farce, and we've had enough of those already this season,"* he said. *"If that happened, it would bury Formula 1."*

There was fury at Ferrari as well. The same evening, Jean Todt was quietly hosting a press conference to explain his team's joy at the world title. Then somebody whispered in his ear that the conformity of the BMW Sauber and the Williams had been called into question.

The Frenchman alerted Ferrari's President Luca di Montezemolo, who was back in Italy, straight away. The story has it that di Montezemolo flew into a rage and was straight on the phone to FIA President Max Mosley, telling him that if Kimi Raikkonen were stripped of his title then Ferrari would withdraw from Formula 1. It was an old threat that di Montezemolo had used several times before, but it always worked. Max Mosley knew it as much as anyone else: Formula 1 without Ferrari was inconceivable.

The following day, Luca di Montezemolo was relaxed and confident on Italian television. He described the McLaren appeal as "useless stress" and maintained that he was certain Ferrari had won the title. As he pointed out, even if the BMW Sauber and the Williams lost their places, it did not necessarily mean that Hamilton would gain any.

Why chill the fuel?

Back in the days when fuel tanks were limited, in the 1980s, the teams used to regularly refrigerate the fuel in order to reduce its volume. This would allow them to get more into the tank and hopefully last the race. The fuel would warm up and expand as the race went on, allowing the cars to have nearly a full tank for some distance.

In 2007 the size of the fuel tank is no longer limited, but refrigeration of the fuel allows a team to get more fuel in the tank during the pit stops (as the flow is limited to 12.1 litres a second. As a litre is just a measure of volume, it's possible to put more petrol in if it occupies less volume - although a few degrees here or there makes very little difference.

However if the fuel is at less than 30 degrees centigrade it becomes much more combustible: which is the really important point as far as the teams are concerned. This explains why they bother to refrigerate it.

On Saturday the meteorologists had predicted temperatures in the region of 30 degrees for Sunday. This figure was what the teams had in mind when they programmed their fuel rigs for Sunday - hence the readings of 23 to 25 degrees that were discovered. In actual fact, the race was run at an unexpectedly warm 37 degrees, which led to BMW Sauber and Williams exceeding the 10-degree discrepancy that was allowed.

^
Make no mistake: they're not at war but equally there's little love lost between Kimi Raikkonen and Lewis Hamilton. Even if they shared a podium several times throughout 2007.

Deals between friends

The decision that Kimi Raikkonen would keep his title, which came late in the evening on Friday 16 November, took too long to have been entirely honest and straightforward. The Appeal Court had been sitting since the previous morning in London (a late change from the scheduled venue, Paris, due to transport strikes in France).

Judging from the arguments employed by the lawyers on both sides on Thursday, it seemed that Kimi Raikkonen ran a very real risk of losing his title. McLaren's lawyer, Ian Mill, described several examples of historical precedents where cars that did not conform to the rules had been disqualified and those behind all moved up a place. In the meantime, the best that Ferrari's lawyer could do was to say that it would be "unfair" to deprive Kimi Raikkonen of his title a month after he had already celebrated it.

In the end, a change of champion would have benefited nobody. Lewis Hamilton went on the record to say that he did not want to win the title that way, while McLaren risked becoming unpopular if they made their driver world champion through a court hearing. The team's managing director, Martin Whitmarsh, was at pains to point out that his team was not looking to gain the world title out of the case. Bernie Ecclestone thought that the sport would lose credibility, while Luca di Montezemolo re-iterated his threat to withdraw Ferrari from Formula 1 if Kimi Raikkonen was deprived of a championship that has already been celebrated. The fall-out would have been huge, and it was best avoided at all costs. The fundamental issues could have been dealt with in five minutes. The fact that it took a whole two days underlined just how much negotiating went on behind the scenes to arrive at this elegant solution between friends.

Nobody was really fooled. But the most important thing was that the 2007 Formula 1 World Champion was finally confirmed, and that a line could at last be drawn under a season that has occasionally been just a little bit too exciting. Now it is all merely history.

<
Kimi Raikkonen had to wait until 16 November to see his title confirmed. Ferrari didn't bother: they were already celebrating a title that had eluded them for the past two seasons.

A recap of the 2007 season

Driver	Nat.	Team	Pts	1 AUS 18/03	2 MAL 08/04	3 BAH 15/04	4 SPA 13/05	5 MON 27/05	6 CAN 10/06	7 USA 17/06	8 FRA 01/07	9 GB 08/07	10 EUR 22/07	11 HUN 05/08	12 TUR 26/08	13 ITA 09/09	14 BEL 16/09	15 JAP 30/09	16 CHI 07/10	17 BRA 21/10	Poles	Wins	FL	Pod.	GP led	Laps led	Km led
1. Kimi RÄIKKÖNEN	FIN	Ferrari	110	10^1	6^3	6^3	NC	1^8	4^5	5^4	10^1	10^1	NC	8^2	8^2	6^3	10^1	6^3	10^1	10^1	3	6	6	12	10	212	1 148,375
2. Lewis HAMILTON	GB	McLaren Mercedes	109	6^3	8^2	8^2	8^2	8^2	10^1	10^1	6^3	6^3	9	10^1	4^5	8^2	5^4	10^1	NC	2^7	6	4	2	12	12	321	1 447,050
3. Fernando ALONSO	E	McLaren Mercedes	109	8^2	10^1	4^5	6^3	10^1	2^7	8^2	2^7	8^2	10^1	5^4	6^3	10^1	6^3	NC	8^2	6^3	2	4	3	12	9	203	962,816
4. Felipe MASSA	BR	Ferrari	94	3^6	4^5	10^1	10^1	6^3	DG	6^3	8^2	4^5	8^2	1	10^1	NC	8^2	3^6	8^2	3^6	6	3	6	10	9	300	1 472,726
5. Nick HEIDFELD	D	BMW	61	5^4	5^4	5^4	NC	3^6	8^2	NC	4^5	3^6	3^6	6^3	5^4	5^4	4^5	NC	2^7	3^6	-	-	-	3	1	1	14,853
6. Robert KUBICA	PL	BMW	39	NC	18	3^6	5^4	4^5	NC		5^4	5^4	2^7	4^5	1^8	4^5	9	2^7	NC	4^5	-	-	-	-	1	1	5,451
7. Heikki KOVALAINEN	FIN	Renault	30	10	1^8	9	2^7	13	5^4	4^5	15	2^7	1^8	1^8	3^6	2^7	1^8	8^2	9	NC	-	-	-	1	3	9	39,987
8. Giancarlo FISICHELLA	I	Renault	21	4^5	3^6	1^8	9	5^4	DQ	9	3^6	1^8	10	12	9	12	NC	4^5	11	NC	-	-	-	-	1	1	4,563
9. Nico ROSBERG	D	Williams Toyota	20	2^7	NC	NC	3^6	12	10	16	9	12	2^7	2^7	3^6	3^6	NC	16	5^4		-	-	-	-	-	-	-
10. David COULTHARD	GB	Red Bull Renault	14	NC	5^4	NC	4^5	14	NC		13	11	4^5	11	NC	11	5^4	1^8	NC		-	-	-	-	1	1	5,148
11. Alexander WURZ	A	Williams Toyota	13	NC	9	11	NC	2^7	6^3		10	14	5^4	14	11	13	NC	12			-	-	1	-	-	-	-
12. Mark WEBBER	AUS	Red Bull Renault	10	13	10	NC	NC	9		2^7	12	NC	6^3	9	NC	9	2^7	NC	NC		-	-	-	1	1	5	22,815
13. Jarno TRULLI	I	Toyota	8	9	2^7	2^7	NC	15	NC	3^6	NC	NC	13	10	16	11	13	13	1^8		-	-	-	-	-	-	-
14. Sebastian VETTEL	D	BMW /// STR Ferrari	6							1^8			16	19	18	NC	5^4	NC			-	-	-	-	1	3	13,689
15. Jenson BUTTON	GB	Honda	6	15	12	NC	12	11	NC	12	1^8	10	NC	NC	13	1^8	NC	11	4^5	NC	-	-	-	-	-	-	-
16. Ralf SCHUMACHER	D	Toyota	5	1^8	15	12	NC	16	1^8	NC	10	NC	3^6	12	15	10	NC	NC	11		-	-	-	-	-	-	-
17. Takuma SATO	J	Super Aguri Honda	4	12	13	NC	1^8	17	3^6	NC	16	16	NC	15	16	15	15	15	14		-	-	-	-	-	-	-
18. Vitantonio LIUZZI	I	STR Ferrari	3	14	17	NC	NC	NC	NC	17	NC	16	NC	15	17	12	9	3^6	13		-	-	-	-	-	-	-
19. Adrian SUTIL	D	Spyker Ferrari	1	17	NC	15	13	NC	NC	14	17	NC	NG	17	21	19	14	1^8	NC	NC	-	-	-	-	-	-	-
20. Rubens BARRICHELLO	BR	Honda	0	11	11	13	10	10	NC	NC	9	11	18	17	10	13	10	15	NC		-	-	-	-	-	-	-
21. Scott SPEED	USA	STR Ferrari	0	NC	14	NC	NC	NC	NC	13	NC	NC	NC								-	-	-	-	-	-	-
22. Kazuki NAKAJIMA	J	Williams Toyota	0																10		-	-	-	-	-	-	-
23. Anthony DAVIDSON	GB	Super Aguri Honda	0	16	16	16	11	18	11	11	16			NC	14	14	16	NC	NC	14	-	-	-	-	-	-	-
24. Sakon YAMAMOTO	J	Spyker Ferrari	0											NC	20	20	17	12	17		-	-	-	-	-	-	-
25. Christijan ALBERS	NL	Spyker Ferrari	0	NC	NC	14	14	19	NC	15	NC	15									-	-	-	-	-	-	-
Markus WINKELHOCK	D	Spyker Ferrari	-										NC								-	-	-	-	1	6	30,888

Constructor	Nat.		Pts	1	2	3	4	5	6	7	8	9	10	11	12	13	14	15	16	17	Poles	Wins	FL	Pod.	GP led	Laps led	Km led
1. Ferrari	I		204	13	10	16	10	7	4	11	18	14	8	8	18	6	18	9	16	18	9	9	12	22	14	512	2 621,101
2. BMW	D		101	5	5	8	5	7	8	1	9	8	5	10	6	9	4	2	2	7	-	-	-	2	3	4	20,304
3. Renault	F		51	4	4	1	2	5	5	4	3	3	1	1	3	2	1	12			-	-	-	1	3	10	44,550
4. Williams-Toyota	GB		33	2			3	2	6				5	2	2	3	3		5		-	-	1	-	-	-	-
5. Red Bull-Renault	A		24				4		2		10			2	5	1					-	-	-	1	2	6	27,963
6. Toyota	J		13	1	2	2			1	3			3				1				-	-	-	-	-	-	-
7. STR-Ferrari	I		8														8				-	-	-	-	1	3	13,689
8. Honda	J		6						1						1		4				-	-	-	-	-	-	-
9. Super Aguri-Honda	J		4			1		3													-	-	-	-	-	-	-
10. Spyker-Ferrari	NL		1														1				-	-	-	-	1	6	30,888
11. McLaren-Mercedes	GB	(218 203 points)	0	14	18	12	14	18	12	18	8	14	10	15 0	10	18	11	10	8	8	8	8	5	24	15	524	2 409,866

Family picture of the World Championship.
From left to right: Vitantonio Liuzzi, Scott Speed, Takuma Sato, Anthony Davidson, Christijan Albers, Adrian Sutil, Nico Rosberg & Alexander Wurz.
In the middle: Jarno Trulli, Ralf Schumacher, Mark Webber, David Coulthard, Nick Heidfeld & Robert Kubica.
Sitting: Jenson Button, Rubens Barrichello, Felipe Massa, Kimi Räikkönen, Fernando Alonso, Lewis Hamilton, Giancarlo Fisichella & Heikki Kovalainen.

Number of kms and laps raced in 2007

	Maximum 5168,361 km	Maximum 1065 laps	GP finished	GP classified	GP raced
1. F. Alonso	5049,723	1039	16	16	17
2. L. Hamilton	5017,178	1037	16	16	17
3. N. Heidfeld	4991,994	1025	14	15	17
4. H. Kovalainen	4986,554	1023	15	16	17
5. F. Massa	4832,022	1002	15	15	17
6. K. Räikkönen	4767,493	982	15	15	17
7. N. Rosberg	4664,395	965	13	14	17
8. R. Barrichello	4663,258	948	15	15	17
9. T. Sato	4494,301	923	13	14	17
10. G. Fisichella	4454,359	927	14	14	17
11. J. Trulli	4422,906	902	13	13	17
12. R. Kubica	4419,539	901	13	13	16
13. A. Davidson	4208,597	865	12	12	17
14. A. Wurz	4184,317	854	12	12	16
15. R. Schumacher	4091,631	840	11	11	17
16. D. Coulthard	4005,311	834	10	10	17
17. J. Button	3789,068	778	10	11	17
18. M. Webber	3728,573	749	10	10	17
19. V. Liuzzi	3640,260	721	8	10	17
20. A. Sutil	3639,014	753	9	10	17
21. S. Vettel	1930,327	395	5	5	8
22. C. Albers	1830,847	407	4	5	9
23. S. Yamamoto	1516,367	276	5	5	7
24. S. Speed	1486,502	334	3	3	10
25. K. Nakajima	301,600	70	1	1	1
26. M. Winkelhock	66,907	13	0	0	1

	Maximum 10336,722	Max. 2130			
1. McLaren Mercedes	10066,901	2076	32	32	34
2. BMW	9717,549	1999	28	29	34
3. Ferrari	9599,515	1984	30	30	34
4. Renault	9440,913	1950	29	30	34
5. Williams Toyota	9150,312	1889	26	27	34
6. Super Aguri Honda	8702,898	1788	25	26	34
7. Toyota	8514,537	1742	24	24	34
8. Honda	8452,326	1726	25	26	34
9. Red Bull Renault	7733,884	1583	20	20	34
10. Spyker Ferrari	7053,135	1449	18	20	34
11. STR Ferrari	6751,073	1377	15	17	34

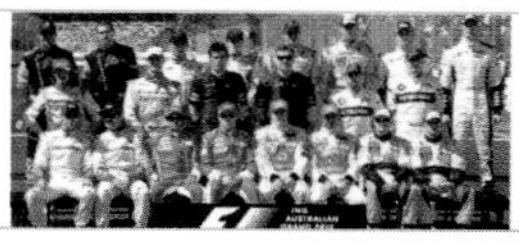

Drivers: GP raced

PATRESE Riccardo	256	STUCK Hans Joachim	74	VILLORESI Luigi	31
BARRICHELLO Rubens	250	BRAMBILLA Vittorio	74	NILSSON Gunnar	31
SCHUMACHER Michael	249	NAKAJIMA Satoru	74	De ADAMICH Andrea	30
COULTHARD David	228	GUGELMIN Mauricio	74	REVSON Peter	30
BERGER Gerhard	210	CLARK Jim	72	GETHIN Peter	30
De CESARIS Andrea	208	PACE Carlos	72	MANZON Robert	28
PIQUET Nelson	204	De La ROSA Pedro	72	BEUTTLER Mike	28
ALESI Jean	201	PIRONI Didier	70	BERNOLDI Enrique	28
PROST Alain	199	MODENA Stefano	70	Da MATTA Cristiano	28
ALBORETO Michele	194	GIACOMELLI Bruno	69	SPEED Scott	28
FISICHELLA Giancarlo	194	WURZ Alexander	69	TAYLOR Trevor	27
MANSELL Nigel	187	VILLENEUVE Gilles	67	COURAGE Piers	27
TRULLI Jarno	181	MORBIDELLI Gianni	67	ROSSET Ricardo	27
SCHUMACHER Ralf	180	MOSS Stirling	66	GONZALEZ Jose-Froilan	26
LAFFITE Jacques	176	FABI Teo	64	Von TRIPS Wolfgang	26
HILL Graham	175	SUZUKI Aguri	64	GODIN de BEAUFORT Carel	26
LAUDA Niki	171	LEHTO JJ	62	PEREZ-SALA Luis	26
BOUTSEN Thierry	163	BLUNDELL Mark	61	MAGGS Tony	25
VILLENEUVE Jacques	163	RINDT Jochen	60	ANDERSON Bob	25
SENNA Ayrton	161	COMAS Erik	59	KEEGAN Rupert	25
HERBERT Johnny	161	MERZARIO Arturo	57	ROTHENGATTER Huub	25
HAKKINEN Mika	161	PESCAROLO Henri	56	MAGNUSSEN Jan	25
BRUNDLE Martin	158	CAFFI Alex	56	SALAZAR Eliseo	24
PANIS Olivier	158	SCHELL Harry	55	BRABHAM David	24
FRENTZEN Heinz-Harald	156	RODRIGUEZ Pedro	54	MARQUES Tarso	24
WATSON John	152	BEHRA Jean	53	CLAES Johnny	23
ARNOUX René	149	STOMMELEN Rolf	53	MUSSO Luigi	23
REUTEMANN Carlos	146	STREIFF Philippe	53	BOESEL Raul	23
WARWICK Derek	146	GINTHER Richie	52	LAMMERS Jan	23
IRVINE Eddie	146	FANGIO Juan-Manuel	51	DALMAS Yannick	23
FITTIPALDI Emerson	144	IRELAND Innes	50	De GRAFFENRIED Emmanuel	22
BUTTON Jenson	135	HAILWOOD Mike	50	WISELL Reine	22
JARIER Jean-Pierre	134	OLIVER Jackie	49	KUBICA Robert	22
REGAZZONI Clay	132	JABOUILLE Jean-Pierre	49	BAGHETTI Giancarlo	21
CHEEVER Eddie	132	DALY Derek	49	GUERRERO Roberto	21
HEIDFELD Nick	132	LARINI Nicola	49	MAZZACANE Gaston	21
ANDRETTI Mario	128	BADOER Luca	49	BELLOF Stefan	20
BRABHAM Jack	123	HILL Phil	47	MONTERMINI Andrea	20
PETERSON Ronnie	123	WINKELHOCK Manfred	47	BAUMGARTNER Zsolt	20
RAIKKONEN Kimi	121	GACHOT Bertrand	47	PIZZONIA Antonio	20
MARTINI Pierluigi	118	SALVADORI Roy	46	DAVIDSON Anthony	20
JONES Alan	116	CEVERT François	46	BIRA Prince	19
HILL Damon	115	KLIEN Christian	46	ERTL Harald	19
ICKX Jacky	114	ALBERS Christijan	46	HENTON Brian	19
ROSBERG Keke	114	HAWTHORN Mike	45	HESNAULT François	19
TAMBAY Patrick	114	BERNARD Eric	45	KARTHIKEYAN Narain	19
HULME Denny	112	BANDINI Lorenzo	42	TARUFFI Piero	18
SCHECKTER Jody	112	PRYCE Tom	42	SCHECKTER Ian	18
SURTEES John	111	MORENO Roberto	42	SERRA Chico	18
SALO Mika	110	REBAQUE Hector	41	CECOTTO Johnny	18
ALLIOT Philippe	109	GROUILLARD Olivier	41	INOUE Taki	18
De ANGELIS Elio	108	WENDLINGER Karl	41	BRUNI Gimmi	18
VERSTAPPEN Jos	107	ZANARDI Alessandro	41	MIERES Roberto	17
MASS Jochen	105	FITTIPALDI Christian	40	HERRMANN Hans	17
ALONSO Fernando	104	LIUZZI Vitantonio	39	BIANCHI Lucien	17
BONNIER Jo	103	ROSIER Louis	38	GALLI Nanni	17
WEBBER Mark	103	BROOKS Tony	38	CAMPOS Adrian	17
STEWART Jackie	99	GREGORY Masten	38	HAMILTON Lewis	17
McLAREN Bruce	98	TARQUINI Gabriele	38	KOVALAINEN Heikki	17
DINIZ Pedro	98	PIRRO Emanuele	37	SUTIL Adrian	17
SIFFERT Jo	96	ZONTA Ricardo	37	ALLISON Cliff	16
AMON Chris	96	MONTEIRO Tiago	37	ATTWOOD Dick	16
DEPAILLER Patrick	95	SPENCE Mike	36	TUERO Esteban	16
KATAYAMA Ukyo	95	BALDI Mauro	36	McNISH Allan	16
MONTOYA Juan-Pablo	94	DANNER Christian	36	WILSON Justin	16
CAPELLI Ivan	93	GENE Marc	36	BONETTO Felice	15
HUNT James	92	GANLEY Howden	35	CHIRON Louis	15
MASSA Felipe	87	FITTIPALDI Wilson	35	WHARTON Ken	15
GURNEY Dan	86	ROSBERG Nico	35	BURGESS Ian	15
SATO Takuma	86	SCHENKEN Tim	34	SULLIVAN Danny	15
BELTOISE Jean-Pierre	85	LUNGER Brett	34	DUMFRIES Johnny	15
PALMER Jonathan	83	FARINA Giuseppe	33	BURTI Luciano	15
SURER Marc	82	NAKANO Shinji	33	…	
TRINTIGNANT Maurice	81	ASCARI Alberto	32	YAMAMOTO Sakon	14
JOHANSSON Stefan	79	COLLINS Peter	32	VETTEL Sebastian	8
GHINZANI Piercarlo	76	LAMY Pedro	32	WINKELHOCK Markus	1
NANNINI Alessandro	76	TAKAGI Tora	32	NAKAJIMA Kazuki	1

Drivers: GP in the lead

SCHUMACHER Michael	141	ALBORETO Michele	10	WARD Rodger	2
SENNA Ayrton	86	TRULLI Jarno	10	IRELAND Innes	2
PROST Alain	84	GONZALEZ Jose-Froilan	9	REVSON Peter	2
COULTHARD David	61	TAMBAY Patrick	9	MASS Jochen	2
PIQUET Nelson	58	GINTHER Richie	8	De CESARIS Andrea	2
MANSELL Nigel	55	IRVINE Eddie	8	JOHANSSON Stefan	2
STEWART Jackie	51	COLLINS Peter	7	WARWICK Derek	2
HAKKINEN Mika	48	BEHRA Jean	7	CAPELLI Ivan	2
ALONSO Fernando	48	BANDINI Lorenzo	7	SALO Mika	2
HILL Damon	45	RODRIGUEZ Pedro	7	KUBICA Robert	2
BARRICHELLO Rubens	44	AMON Chris	7	HOLLAND Bill	1
RAIKKONEN Kimi	44	PACE Carlos	7	ROSE Mauri	1
CLARK Jim	43	JABOUILLE Jean-Pierre	7	SOMMER Raymond	1
LAUDA Niki	41	BROOKS Tony	6	DAVIES Jimmy	1
FANGIO Juan-Manuel	38	DEPAILLER Patrick	6	GREEN Cecil	1
BERGER Gerhard	33	RATHMANN Jim	5	WALLARD Lee	1
HILL Graham	32	McLAREN Bruce	5	VILLORESI Luigi	1
MONTOYA Juan-Pablo	32	SIFFERT Jo	5	BONETTO Felice	1
MOSS Stirling	31	CEVERT François	5	TARUFFI Piero	1
PATRESE Riccardo	29	BOUTSEN Thierry	5	AGABASHIAN Fred	1
BRABHAM Jack	28	VUKOVICH Bill	4	DAYWALT Jimmy	1
PETERSON Ronnie	28	McGRATH Jack	4	MIERES Roberto	1
ARNOUX René	25	BONNIER Jo	4	SWEIKERT Bob	1
HUNT James	24	Von TRIPS Wolfgang	4	MENDITEGUY Carlos	1
JONES Alan	24	BELTOISE Jean-Pierre	4	LEWIS-EVANS Stuart	1
SCHECKTER Jody	23	BRAMBILLA Vittorio	4	BETTENHAUSEN Tony	1
ANDRETTI Mario	22	De ANGELIS Elio	4	AMICK George	1
ASCARI Alberto	21	HERBERT Johnny	4	BOYD Johnny	1
SCHUMACHER Ralf	21	WEBBER Mark	4	GENDEBIEN Olivier	1
REGAZZONI Clay	20	FAGIOLI Luigi	3	BAGHETTI Giancarlo	1
ROSBERG Keke	20	KLING Karl	3	TAYLOR Trevor	1
VILLENEUVE Jacques	20	SCHELL Harry	3	MAIRESSE Willy	1
ICKX Jacky	19	CASTELLOTTI Eugenio	3	SCARFIOTTI Ludovico	1
REUTEMANN Carlos	19	HANKS Sam	3	PARKES Mike	1
ALESI Jean	19	MUSSO Luigi	3	LOVE John	1
FITTIPALDI Emerson	18	TRINTIGNANT Maurice	3	SERVOZ-GAVIN Johnny	1
VILLENEUVE Gilles	18	BRYAN Jimmy	3	COURAGE Piers	1
SURTEES John	17	RUTTMAN Troy	3	GETHIN Peter	1
HULME Denny	17	THOMSON Johnny	3	HAILWOOD Mike	1
GURNEY Dan	16	OLIVER Jackie	3	STOMMELEN Rolf	1
FARINA Giuseppe	14	JARIER Jean-Pierre	3	PRYCE Tom	1
LAFFITE Jacques	14	NANNINI Alessandro	3	NILSSON Gunnar	1
FISICHELLA Giancarlo	14	HEIDFELD Nick	3	STUCK Hans Joachim	1
MASSA Felipe	14	KOVALAINEN Heikki	3	GIACOMELLI Bruno	1
FRENTZEN Heinz-Harald	13	CROSS Art	2	MARTINI Pierluigi	1
BUTTON Jenson	13	FREELAND Don	2	PANIS Olivier	1
HAWTHORN Mike	12	PARSONS Johnnie	2	Da MATTA Cristiano	1
RINDT Jochen	12	O'CONNOR Pat	2	SATO Takuma	1
HAMILTON Lewis	12	RUSSO Paul	2	PIZZONIA Antonio	1
HILL Phil	10	FLAHERTY Pat	2	WINKELHOCK Markus	1
PIRONI Didier	10	GREGORY Masten	2	VETTEL Sebastian	1
WATSON John	10	SACHS Eddie	2		

Drivers: laps in the lead

SCHUMACHER Michael	5108	GURNEY Dan	203	SACHS Eddie	22
SENNA Ayrton	2931	AMBAY Patrick	195	CASTELLOTTI Eugenio	21
PROST Alain	2683	WARD Rodger	188	NILSSON Gunnar	21
MANSELL Nigel	2091	AMON Chris	183	NANNINI Alessandro	21
CLARK Jim	1940	JABOUILLE Jean-Pierre	179	DAVIES Jimmy	18
STEWART Jackie	1921	HILL Phil	172	KLING Karl	18
PIQUET Nelson	1600	WALLARD Lee	165	BOYD Johnny	18
8LAUDA Niki	1592	DEPAILLER Patrick	164	AMICK George	18
HAKKINEN Mika	1488	BOUTSEN Thierry	164	Da MATTA Cristiano	17
HILL Damon	1358	IRVINE Eddie	157	WARWICK Derek	16
FANGIO Juan-Manuel	1347	Von TRIPS Wolfgang	156	PANIS Olivier	16
MOSS Stirling	1181	FRENTZEN Heinz-Harald	150	ROSE Mauri	15
ALONSO Fernando	1159	RATHMANN Jim	147	SCHELL Harry	15
HILL Graham	1101	TRULLI Jarno	147	STUCK Hans Joachim	14
ASCARI Alberto	927	BANDINI Lorenzo	143	GREGORY Masten	13
COULTHARD David	896	HANKS Sam	140	LOVE John	13
RAIKKONEN Kimi	850	BONNIER Jo	139	WEBBER Mark	10
BRABHAM Jack	825	FLAHERTY Pat	138	KOVALAINEN Heikki	9
ANDRETTI Mario	798	BROOKS Tony	133	HOLLAND Bill	8
BERGER Gerhard	748	PARSONS Johnnie	131	FAGIOLI Luigi	8
BARRICHELLO Rubens	722	CEVERT François	129	DAYWALT Jimmy	8
PETERSON Ronnie	707	COLLINS Peter	127	STOMMELEN Rolf	8
SCHECKTER Jody	675	GINTHER Richie	116	FREELAND Don	7
HUNT James	666	BEHRA Jean	107	BAGHETTI Giancarlo	7
REUTEMANN Carlos	649	BUTTON Jenson	104	PARKES Mike	7
VILLENEUVE Jacques	633	BELTOISE Jean-Pierre	101	MUSSO Luigi	6
MONTOYA Juan-Pablo	605	SIFFERT Jo	99	WINKELHOCK Markus	6
JONES Alan	589	SWEIKERT Bob	86	KUBICA Robert	6
PATRESE Riccardo	565	RODRIGUEZ Pedro	86	SOMMER Raymond	5
VILLENEUVE Gilles	534	JARIER Jean-Pierre	79	GREEN Cecil	5
ICKX Jacky	529	TRINTIGNANT Maurice	78	LEWIS-EVANS Stuart	5
ROSBERG Keke	512	McGRATH Jack	71	HAILWOOD Mike	5
ARNOUX René	507	REVSON Peter	63	MASS Jochen	5
VUKOVICH Bill	485	RUTTMAN Troy	59	LARINI Nicola	5
FITTIPALDI Emerson	478	THOMSON Johnny	55	MIERES Roberto	4
MASSA Felipe	456	SCARFIOTTI Ludovico	55	TAYLOR Trevor	4
HULME Denny	435	PACE Carlos	50	HEIDFELD Nick	4
SCHUMACHER Ralf	401	TARUFFI Piero	46	GENDEBIEN Olivier	3
RINDT Jochen	387	O'CONNOR Pat	46	MAIRESSE Willy	3
REGAZZONI Clay	360	CAPELLI Ivan	46	SERVOZ-GAVIN Johnny	3
FARINA Giuseppe	336	HERBERT Johnny	44	GETHIN Peter	3
HAMILTON Lewis	321	IRELAND Innes	43	JOHANSSON Stefan	3
SURTEES John	308	McLAREN Bruce	41	VETTEL Sebastian	3
PIRONI Didier	295	MENDITEGUY Carlos	39	VILLORESI Luigi	2
WATSON John	287	OLIVER Jackie	36	COURAGE Piers	2
LAFFITE Jacques	283	RUSSO Paul	35	PRYCE Tom	2
GONZALEZ Jose-Froilan	272	CROSS Art	32	SALO Mika	2
ALESI Jean	265	BRAMBILLA Vittorio	32	SATO Takuma	2
HAWTHORN Mike	225	De CESARIS Andrea	32	BONETTO Felice	1
ALBORETO Michele	218	GIACOMELLI Bruno	31	AGABASHIAN Fred	1
BRYAN Jimmy	216	De ANGELIS Elio	28	MARTINI Pierluigi	1
FISICHELLA Giancarlo	210	BETTENHAUSEN Tony	24	PIZZONIA Antonio	1

Drivers: points

SCHUMACHER Michael	1369	JABOUILLE Jean-Pierre	21
PROST Alain	798,5	HANKS Sam	20
SENNA Ayrton	614	COURAGE Piers	20
COULTHARD David	527	CASTELLOTTI Eugenio	19,5
BARRICHELLO Rubens	519	VUKOVICH Bill	19
ALONSO Fernando	490	SALVADORI Roy	19
PIQUET Nelson	485,5	PRYCE Tom	19
MANSELL Nigel	482	ROSIER Louis	18
RAIKKONEN Kimi	456	BRYAN Jimmy	18
LAUDA Niki	420,5	GENDEBIEN Olivier	18
HAKKINEN Mika	420	MARTINI Pierluigi	18
BERGER Gerhard	385	BONETTO Felice	17,5
STEWART Jackie	360	KLING Karl	17
HILL Damon	360	SCARFIOTTI Ludovico	17
SCHUMACHER Ralf	329	SURER Marc	17
REUTEMANN Carlos	310	MODENA Stefano	17
MONTOYA Juan-Pablo	307	VERSTAPPEN Jos	17
HILL Graham	289	MANZON Robert	16
FITTIPALDI Emerson	281	LEWIS-EVANS Stuart	16
PATRESE Riccardo	281	NAKAJIMA Satoru	16
FANGIO Juan-Manuel	277,64	BRAMBILLA Vittorio	15,5
CLARK Jim	274	DALY Derek	15
FISICHELLA Giancarlo	267	MORENO Roberto	15
BRABHAM Jack	261	WARD Rodger	14
SCHECKTER Jody	255	PARKES Mike	14
HULME Denny	248	BAGHETTI Giancarlo	14
ALESI Jean	241	STOMMELEN Rolf	14
VILLENEUVE Jacques	235	PALMER Jonathan	14
BUTTON Jenson	229	GIACOMELLI Bruno	14
LAFFITE Jacques	228	WENDLINGER Karl	14
REGAZZONI Clay	212	KLIEN Christian	14
PETERSON Ronnie	206	MIERES Roberto	13
JONES Alan	206	WISELL Reine	13
MASSA Felipe	201	OLIVER Jackie	13
McLAREN Bruce	196,5	REBAQUE Hector	13
IRVINE Eddie	191	Da MATTA Cristiano	13
MOSS Stirling	186,64	PARSONS Johnnie	12
ALBORETO Michele	186,5	ARUNDELL Peter	12
TRULLI Jarno	183	PESCAROLO Henri	12
ICKX Jacky	181	FITTIPALDI Christian	12
ARNOUX René	181	FRERE Paul	11
SURTEES John	180	BETTENHAUSEN Tony	11
ANDRETTI Mario	180	ALLISON Cliff	11
HUNT James	179	ATTWOOD Dick	11
FRENTZEN Heinz-Harald	174	GETHIN Peter	11
WATSON John	169	MERZARIO Arturo	11
ROSBERG Keke	159,5	STREIFF Philippe	11
DEPAILLER Patrick	141	FISCHER Rudi	10
ASCARI Alberto	140,14	THOMSON Johnny	10
HEIDFELD Nick	140	HERRMANN Hans	10
GURNEY Dan	133	GANLEY Howden	10
BOUTSEN Thierry	132	GUGELMIN Mauricio	10
HAWTHORN Mike	127,64	LEHTO JJ	10
FARINA Giuseppe	127,33	BERNARD Eric	10
De ANGELIS Elio	122	DINIZ Pedro	10
RINDT Jochen	109	RUTTMAN Troy	9,5
HAMILTON Lewis	109	WALLARD Lee	9
GINTHER Richie	107	PARNELL Reg	9
VILLENEUVE Gilles	107	McGRATH Jack	9
TAMBAY Patrick	103	De GRAFFENRIED Emmanuel	9
PIRONI Didier	101	MENDITEGUY Carlos	9
HILL Phil	98	SERVOZ-GAVIN Johnny	9
BRUNDLE Martin	98	RUSSO Paul	8,5
HERBERT Johnny	98	MORBIDELLI Gianni	8,5
CEVERT François	89	MARIMON Onofre	8,14
JOHANSSON Stefan	88	NAZARUK Mike	8
AMON Chris	83	CROSS Art	8
WEBBER Mark	79	BIRA Prince	8
GONZALEZ Jose-Froilan	77,64	SWEIKERT Bob	8
BELTOISE Jean-Pierre	77	FLAHERTY Pat	8
PANIS Olivier	76	ANDERSON Bob	8
BROOKS Tony	75	TAYLOR Trevor	8
TRINTIGNANT Maurice	72,33	ELFORD Vic	8
RODRIGUEZ Pedro	71	REDMAN Brian	8
MASS Jochen	71	DONOHUE Mark	8
WARWICK Derek	71	SUZUKI Aguri	8
CHEEVER Eddie	70	PIZZONIA Antonio	8
SIFFERT Jo	68	MAIRESSE Willy	7
NANNINI Alessandro	65	SCHENKEN Tim	7
REVSON Peter	61	ANDRETTI Michael	7
De CESARIS Andrea	59	ALLIOT Philippe	7
BANDINI Lorenzo	58	COMAS Erik	7
PACE Carlos	58	LARINI Nicola	7
Von TRIPS Wolfgang	56	MONTEIRO Tiago	7
BEHRA Jean	51,14	CARTER Duane	6,5
VILLORESI Luigi	49	HOLLAND Bill	6
COLLINS Peter	47	AMICK George	6
IRELAND Innes	47	GODIA-SALES Chico	6
WURZ Alexander	45	GOLDSMITH Paul	6
KUBICA Robert	45	BIANCHI Lucien	6
MUSSO Luigi	44	LOVE John	6
SATO Takuma	44	De ADAMICH Andrea	6
TARUFFI Piero	41	CAFFI Alex	6
BONNIER Jo	39	VETTEL Sebastian	6
SALO Mika	33	GIRAUD-CABANTOUS Yves	5
FAGIOLI Luigi	32	PERDISA Cesare	5
SCHELL Harry	32	LINDEN Andy	5
BLUNDELL Mark	32	FLOCKHART Ron	5
JARIER Jean-Pierre	31,5	FAIRMAN Jack	5
NILSSON Gunnar	31	FOLLMER George	5
CAPELLI Ivan	31	BALDI Mauro	5
KOVALAINEN Heikki	30	GACHOT Bertrand	5
RATHMANN Jim	29	KATAYAMA Ukyo	5
HAILWOOD Mike	29	GENE Marc	5
STUCK Hans Joachim	29	KARTHIKEYAN Narain	5
De la ROSA Pedro	29	LIUZZI Vitantonio	5
SPENCE Mike	27	…	
MAGGS Tony	26	ALBERS Christijan	4
ROSBERG Nico	24	SUTIL Adrian	1
FABI Teo	23		
GREGORY Masten	21		

Drivers: podiums

SCHUMACHER Michael	154	BRABHAM Jack	31	ROSBERG Keke	17	BANDINI Lorenzo	8
PROST Alain	106	MONTOYA Juan-Pablo	30	MASSA Felipe	17	REVSON Peter	8
SENNA Ayrton	80	REGAZZONI Clay	28	HILL Phil	16	BELTOISE Jean-Pierre	8
BARRICHELLO Rubens	61	McLAREN Bruce	27	GONZALEZ Jose-Froilan	15	MASS Jochen	8
COULTHARD David	61	SCHUMACHER Ralf	27	BOUTSEN Thierry	15	MUSSO Luigi	7
PIQUET Nelson	60	PETERSON Ronnie	26	BUTTON Jenson	15	RODRIGUEZ Pedro	7
MANSELL Nigel	59	IRVINE Eddie	26	GINTHER Richie	14	HERBERT Johnny	7
LAUDA Niki	54	ICKX Jacky	25	RINDT Jochen	13	TRULLI Jarno	7
HAKKINEN Mika	51	MOSS Stirling	24	CEVERT François	13	HEIDFELD Nick	7
ALONSO Fernando	49	SURTEES John	24	VILLENEUVE Gilles	13	FAGIOLI Luigi	6
BERGER Gerhard	48	JONES Alan	24	PIRONI Didier	13	Von TRIPS Wolfgang	6
RAIKKONEN Kimi	48	HUNT James	23	JOHANSSON Stefan	12	SIFFERT Jo	6
REUTEMANN Carlos	45	ALBORETO Michele	23	HAMILTON Lewis	12	PACE Carlos	6
STEWART Jackie	43	VILLENEUVE Jacques	23	AMON Chris	11	TARUFFI Piero	5
HILL Damon	42	ARNOUX René	22	TAMBAY Patrick	11	De CESARIS Andrea	5
PATRESE Riccardo	37	FARINA Giuseppe	20	TRINTIGNANT Maurice	10	PANIS Olivier	5
HILL Graham	36	WATSON John	20	BROOKS Tony	10	…	
FANGIO Juan-Manuel	35	GURNEY Dan	19	BEHRA Jean	9	WURZ Alexander	3
FITTIPALDI Emerson	35	DEPAILLER Patrick	19	COLLINS Peter	9	WEBBER Mark	2
HULME Denny	33	ANDRETTI Mario	19	De ANGELIS Elio	9	PARNELL Reg	1
SCHECKTER Jody	33	HAWTHORN Mike	18	CHEEVER Eddie	9	SATO Takuma	1
CLARK Jim	32	FRENTZEN Heinz-Harald	18	NANNINI Alessandro	9	KUBICA Robert	1
LAFFITE Jacques	32	FISICHELLA Giancarlo	18	BRUNDLE Martin	9	KOVALAINEN Heikki	1
ALESI Jean	32	ASCARI Alberto	17	VILLORESI Luigi	8		

Drivers: pole positions

SCHUMACHER Michael	68	PATRESE Riccardo	8	ALBORETO Michele	2
SENNA Ayrton	65	LAFFITE Jacques	7	ALESI Jean	2
CLARK Jim	33	HILL Phil	6	FRENTZEN Heinz-Harald	2
PROST Alain	33	FITTIPALDI Emerson	6	FAULKNER Walt	1
MANSELL Nigel	32	JABOUILLE Jean-Pierre	6	NALON Duke	1
FANGIO Juan-Manuel	29	JONES Alan	6	AGABASHIAN Fred	1
HAKKINEN Mika	26	REUTEMANN Carlos	6	VUKOVICH Bill	1
LAUDA Niki	24	SCHUMACHER Ralf	6	McGRATH Jack	1
PIQUET Nelson	24	HAMILTON Lewis	6	HOYT Jerry	1
HILL Damon	20	FARINA Giuseppe	5	CASTELLOTTI Eugenio	1
ANDRETTI Mario	18	AMON Chris	5	FLAHERTY Pat	1
ARNOUX René	18	REGAZZONI Clay	5	O'CONNOR Pat	1
STEWART Jackie	17	TAMBAY Patrick	5	RATHMANN Dick	1
ALONSO Fernando	17	ROSBERG Keke	5	THOMSON Johnny	1
MOSS Stirling	16	HAWTHORN Mike	4	BONNIER Jo	1
ASCARI Alberto	14	PIRONI Didier	4	SACHS Eddie	1
HUNT James	14	GONZALEZ Jose-Froilan	3	Von TRIPS Wolfgang	1
PETERSON Ronnie	14	BROOKS Tony	3	BANDINI Lorenzo	1
RAIKKONEN Kimi	14	GURNEY Dan	3	PARKES Mike	1
HILL Graham	13	JARIER Jean-Pierre	3	REVSON Peter	1
BRABHAM Jack	13	CHECKTER Jody	3	HULME Denny	1
ICKX Jacky	13	De ANGELIS Elio	3	DEPAILLER Patrick	1
VILLENEUVE Jacques	13	FABI Teo	3	PACE Carlos	1
BARRICHELLO Rubens	13	TRULLI Jarno	3	BRAMBILLA Vittorio	1
MONTOYA Juan-Pablo	13	FISICHELLA Giancarlo	3	PRYCE Tom	1
BERGER Gerhard	12	BUTTON Jenson	3	GIACOMELLI Bruno	1
COULTHARD David	12	LEWIS-EVANS Stuart	2	De CESARIS Andrea	1
RINDT Jochen	10	SIFFERT Jo	2	BOUTSEN Thierry	1
MASSA Felipe	9	WATSON John	2	HEIDFELD Nick	1
SURTEES John	8	VILLENEUVE Gilles	2		

Drivers: fastest laps

SCHUMACHER Michael	76	HILL Phil	6	VILLORESI Luigi	1
PROST Alain	41	GURNEY Dan	6	McGRATH Jack	1
MANSELL Nigel	30	FITTIPALDI Emerson	6	HERRMANN Hans	1
CLARK Jim	28	REUTEMANN Carlos	6	MARIMON Onofre	1
HAKKINEN Mika	25	LAFFITE Jacques	6	BEHRA Jean	1
RAIKKONEN Kimi	25	FRENTZEN Heinz-Harald	6	KLING Karl	1
LAUDA Niki	24	FARINA Giuseppe	5	MIERES Roberto	1
FANGIO Juan-Manuel	23	PACE Carlos	5	RUSSO Paul	1
PIQUET Nelson	23	SCHECKTER Jody	5	MUSSO Luigi	1
BERGER Gerhard	21	PIRONI Didier	5	BETTENHAUSEN Tony	1
MOSS Stirling	19	WATSON John	5	THOMSON Johnny	1
SENNA Ayrton	19	ALBORETO Michele	5	TRINTIGNANT Maurice	1
HILL Damon	19	SIFFERT Jo	4	IRELAND Innes	1
COULTHARD David	18	BELTOISE Jean-Pierre	4	BAGHETTI Giancarlo	1
STEWART Jackie	15	DEPAILLER Patrick	4	SCARFIOTTI Ludovico	1
REGAZZONI Clay	15	ALESI Jean	4	ATTWOOD Dick	1
BARRICHELLO Rubens	15	VUKOVICH Bill	3	RODRIGUEZ Pedro	1
ICKX Jacky	14	BROOKS Tony	3	OLIVER Jackie	1
JONES Alan	13	McLAREN Bruce	3	PESCAROLO Henri	1
PATRESE Riccardo	13	GINTHER Richie	3	HAILWOOD Mike	1
ASCARI Alberto	12	RINDT Jochen	3	BRAMBILLA Vittorio	1
BRABHAM Jack	12	AMON Chris	3	HASEMI Masahiro	1
ARNOUX René	12	JARIER Jean-Pierre	3	NILSSON Gunnar	1
MONTOYA Juan-Pablo	12	ROSBERG Keke	3	SURER Marc	1
SURTEES John	11	RATHMANN Jim	2	HENTON Brian	1
ALONSO Fernando	11	BANDINI Lorenzo	2	De CESARIS Andrea	1
HILL Graham	10	CEVERT François	2	PALMER Jonathan	1
ANDRETTI Mario	10	MASS Jochen	2	GUGELMIN Mauricio	1
HULME Denny	9	TAMBAY Patrick	2	NAKAJIMA Satoru	1
PETERSON Ronnie	9	WARWICK Derek	2	BOUTSEN Thierry	1
VILLENEUVE Jacques	9	FABI Teo	2	GACHOT Bertrand	1
HUNT James	8	NANNINI Alessandro	2	MORENO Roberto	1
VILLENEUVE Gilles	8	FISICHELLA Giancarlo	2	WURZ Alexander	1
SCHUMACHER Ralf	8	HAMILTON Lewis	2	IRVINE Eddie	1
MASSA Felipe	8	PARSONS Johnnie	1	DE LA ROSA Pedro	1
GONZALEZ Jose-Froilan	6	WALLARD Lee	1	ROSBERG Nico	1
HAWTHORN Mike	6	TARUFFI Piero	1		

Number of Constructors' Championship

(since 1958)

15 titles
Ferrari 1961-1964
1975-1976-1977-1979-1982-
1983-1999-2000-2001-2002-
2003-2004-2007

9 titles
Williams 1980-1981-1986-
1987-1992-1993-1994-1996-
1997

8 titles
McLaren 1974
1984-1985-1988-1989
1990-1991-1998

7 titles
Lotus 1963-1965-1968
1970-1972-1973-1978

2 titles
Cooper 1959-1960
Brabham 1966-1967
Renault 2005-2006

1 title
Vanwall 1958
BRM 1962
Matra 1969
Tyrrell 1971
Benetton 1995

Constructors: victories

Ferrari	201	Alfa Romeo	10	Wolf	3
McLaren	156	Mercedes	9	Honda	3
Williams	113	Maserati	9	Epperly	2
Lotus	79	Vanwall	9	Kuzma	1
Brabham	35	Matra	9	Porsche	1
Renault	33	Ligier	9	Eagle	1
Benetton	27	Kurtis Kraft	5	Hesketh	1
Tyrrell	23	Jordan	4	Penske	1
BRM	17	Watson	3	Shadow	1
Cooper	16	March	3	Stewart	1

Constructors: pole positions

Ferrari	195	Ligier	9	Honda	2
McLaren	133	Mercedes	8	Stevens	1
Williams	125	Vanwall	7	Lesovsky	1
Lotus	107	Kurtis	6	Ewing	1
Renault	50	March	5	Lola	1
Brabham	39	Matra	4	Porsche	1
Benetton	15	Shadow	3	Wolf	1
Tyrrell	14	Lancia	2	Arrows	1
Alfa Romeo	12	Watson	2	Toleman	1
Cooper	11	Jordan	2	Stewart	1
BRM	11	B·A·R	2		
Maserati	10	Toyota	2		

Constructors: Grands Prix

Ferrari	758	RAM	28	Emeryson	4
McLaren	630	Eagle	25	Martini	4
Williams	511	Spirit	23	Deidt	3
Lotus	491	Forti	23	Pawl	3
Tyrrell	430	Pacific	22	Moore	3
Brabham	394	Simtek	21	Dunn	3
Minardi	340	Rial	20	Gilby	3
Ligier	326	Fondmetal	19	Token	3
Arrows	291	Midland	18	LEC	3
Benetton	260	Connaught	17	RAM March	3
Jordan	250	Spyker	17	Marchese	2
Renault	227	Parnelli	16	Sherman	2
Sauber	215	Onyx	16	Aston	2
BRM	197	Venturi	16	BMW	2
March	197	Simca Gordini	14	Nichels	2
Lola	149	HWM	14	Pankratz	2
Osella	132	Eurobrun	14	Ewing	2
Cooper	128	Talbot Lago	13	Christensen	2
Surtees	118	BRP	13	Scarab	2
B·A·R	117	Coloni	13	Alfa Special	2
Alfa Romeo	110	Mercedes	12	Bellasi	2
Shadow	104	Kurtis Kraft	12	Kojima	2
Toyota	104	Kuzma	10	Olson	1
Ensign	99	De Tomaso	10	Langley	1
Footwork	91	Tecno	10	Rae	1
ATS	89	Hill	10	Wetteroth	1
Jaguar	85	Merzario	10	Snowberger	1
Prost	83	Lesovsky	9	Adams	1
Dallara	78	Watson	9	Hall	1
Copersucar	71	Eifelland March	8	Del Roy	1
Maserati	70	ERA	7	Turner	1
Honda	70	Phillips	7	EMW	1
Matra	60	Veritas	6	Klenk	1
Toleman	57	Stevens	6	Bugatti	1
Zakspeed	53	A-T-S	6	Elder	1
Red Bull	53	Trojan	6	Sutton	1
Hesketh	52	Boro	6	Tec Mec	1
Stewart	49	Lamborghini	6	Meskowski	1
Wolf	47	Alta	5	Ferguson	1
AGS	47	Epperly	5	ENB	1
Penske	40	Aston Martin	5	Stebro	1
BMW Sauber	35	JBW	5	Shannon	1
Toro Rosso	35	Scirocco	5	Protos	1
Super Aguri	35	LDS	5	Politoys	1
Theodore	34	Maserati Milano	4	Connew	1
Gordini	33	Frazer Nash	4	Amon	1
Fittipaldi	32	OSCA	4	Lyncar	1
Larrousse	32	AFM	4	Rebaque	1
Porsche	31	Bromme	4	Monteverdi	1
Iso-Marlboro	30	Schroeder	4	Andrea Moda	1
Leyton House	30	Lancia	4		
Vanwall	28	Trevis	4		

Constructors: fastest laps

Ferrari	205	Matra	12	Toleman	2
Williams	134	Mercedes	9	Jordan	2
McLaren	129	Ligier	9	Gordini	1
Lotus	71	Kurtis Kraft	7	Lancia	1
Brabham	41	March	7	Lesovsky	1
Benetton	36	Vanwall	6	Watson	1
Renault	27	Surtees	3	Hesketh	1
Tyrrell	20	Epperly	2	Parnelli	1
Maserati	15	Eagle	2	Kojima	1
BRM	15	Honda	2	Ensign	1
Cooper	14	Shadow	2	Toyota	1
Alfa Romeo	14	Wolf	2		

Constructeurs: points

Ferrari	3851,5	Wolf	79	Fittipaldi	12
McLaren	3159,5	Red Bull	74	BRP	11
Williams	2539,5	Shadow	67,5	Toro Rosso	9
Lotus	1368	Vanwall	57	Leyton House	8
Renault	976	Surtees	53	ATS	7
Brabham	864	Alfa Romeo	50	Maserati	6
Benetton	851,5	Jaguar	49	Iso-Marlboro	6
Tyrrell	621	Porsche	48	Parnelli	6
BRM	433	Hesketh	48	Rial	6
Ligier	388	Stewart	47	Onyx	6
Cooper	342	Lola	43	Osella	5
Jordan	291	Minardi	38	Larrousse	5
BAR	227	Prost	35	Super Aguri	4
Sauber	195	Copersucar	32	Hill	3
March	173,5	Toleman	26	Theodore	2
Matra	163	Footwork	25	Zakspeed	2
Toyota	163	Penske	23	AGS	2
Arrows	142	Ensign	19	Tecno	1
Honda	140	Eagle	17	Venturi	1
BMW Sauber	137	Dallara	15	Spyker	1

Constructors: 1-2

Ferrari	76	Mercedes	5	Renault	2
McLaren	44	BRM	5	Benetton	2
Williams	33	Alfa Romeo	4	Maserati	1
Lotus	8	Kurtis Kraft	2	Ligier	1
Brabham	8	Epperly	2	Jordan	1
Tyrrell	8	Watson	2		
Cooper	6	Matra	2		

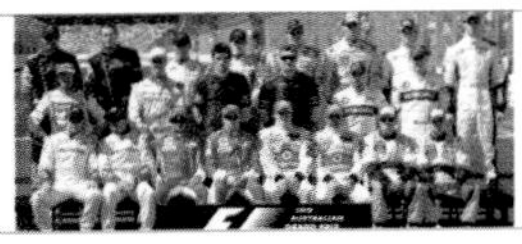

	GB	MC	INDY 500	CH	B	F	I	D	E	NL	RA	PESCARA	P	MA	USA	ZA	MEX
1950	Farina Alfa Romeo	Fangio Alfa Romeo	Parsons Kurtis Kraft Offenhauser	Farina Alfa Romeo	Fangio Alfa Romeo	Fangio Alfa Romeo	Farina Alfa Romeo										
1951	Gonzalez Ferrari		Wallard Kurtis Kraft Offenhauser	Fangio Alfa Romeo	Farina Alfa Romeo	Fagioli/Fangio Alfa Romeo	Ascari Ferrari	Ascari Ferrari	Fangio Alfa Romeo								
1952	Ascari Ferrari		Ruttman Kuzma Offenhauser	Taruffi Ferrari	Ascari Ferrari	Ascari Ferrari	Ascari Ferrari	Ascari Ferrari		Ascari Ferrari							
1953	Ascari Ferrari		Vukovich Kurtis Kraft Offenhauser	Ascari Ferrari	Ascari Ferrari	Hawthorn Ferrari	Fangio Maserati	Farina Ferrari		Ascari Ferrari	Ascari Ferrari						
1954	Gonzalez Ferrari		Vukovich Kurtis Kraft Offenhauser	Fangio Mercedes	Fangio Maserati	Fangio Mercedes	Fangio Mercedes	Fangio Mercedes	Hawthorn Ferrari		Fangio Maserati						
1955	Moss Mercedes	Trintignant Ferrari	Sweikert Kurtis Kraft Offenhauser		Fangio Mercedes		Fangio Mercedes			Fangio Mercedes	Fangio Mercedes						
1956	Fangio Ferrari	Moss Maserati	Flaherty Watson Offenhauser		Collins Ferrari	Collins Ferrari	Moss Maserati	Fangio Ferrari			Musso/Fangio Ferrari						
1957	Brooks / Moss Vanwall	Fangio Maserati	Hanks Epperly Offenhauser			Fangio Maserati	Moss Vanwall	Fangio Maserati			Fangio Maserati	Moss Vanwall					
1958	Collins Ferrari	Trintignant Cooper-Climax	Bryan Epperly Offenhauser		Brooks Vanwall	Hawthorn Ferrari	Brooks Vanwall	Brooks Vanwall		Moss Vanwall	Moss Cooper-Climax		Moss Vanwall	Moss Vanwall			
1959	Brabham Cooper-Climax	Brabham Cooper-Climax	Ward Watson Offenhauser			Brooks Ferrari	Moss Cooper-Climax	Brooks Ferrari		Bonnier BRM			Moss Cooper-Climax		McLaren Cooper-Climax		
1960	Brabham Cooper-Climax	Moss Lotus-Climax	Rathmann Watson Offenhauser		Brabham Cooper-Climax	Brabham Cooper-Climax	P. Hill Ferrari			Brabham Cooper-Climax	McLaren Cooper-Climax		Brabham Cooper-Climax		Moss Lotus-Climax		
1961	Von Trips Ferrari	Moss Lotus-Climax			Hill Ferrari	Baghetti Ferrari	P. Hill Ferrari	Moss Lotus-Climax		Von Trips Ferrari					Ireland Lotus-Climax		
1962	Clark Lotus-Climax	McLaren Cooper-Climax			Clark Lotus-Climax	Gurney Porsche	G. Hill BRM	G. Hill BRM		G. Hill BRM					Clark Lotus-Climax	G. Hill BRM	
1963	Clark Lotus-Climax	G. Hill BRM			Clark Lotus-Climax	Clark Lotus-Climax	Clark Lotus-Climax	Surtees Ferrari		Clark Lotus-Climax					G. Hill BRM	Clark Lotus-Climax	Clark Lotus-Climax
1964	Clark Lotus-Climax	G. Hill BRM			Clark Lotus-Climax	Gurney Brabham-Climax	Surtees Ferrari	Surtees Ferrari		Clark Lotus-Climax					G. Hill BRM		Gurney Brabham-Climax
1965	Clark Lotus-Climax	G. Hill BRM			Clark Lotus-Climax	Clark Lotus-Climax	Stewart BRM	Clark Lotus-Climax		Clark Lotus-Climax					G. Hill BRM	Clark Lotus-Climax	Ginther Honda
1966	Brabham Brabham-Repco	Stewart BRM			Surtees Ferrari	Brabham Brabham-Repco	Scarfiotti Ferrari	Brabham Brabham-Repco		Brabham Brabham-Repco					Clark Lotus-BRM		Surtees Cooper-Maserati
1967	Clark Lotus-Ford	Hulme Brabham-Repco			Gurney Eagle-Weslake	Brabham Brabham-Repco	Surtees Honda	Hulme Brabham-Repco		Clark Lotus-Ford					Clark Lotus-Ford	Rodriguez Cooper-Maserati	Clark Lotus-Ford
1968	Siffert Lotus-Ford	G. Hill Lotus-Ford			McLaren McLaren-Ford	Ickx Ferrari	Hulme McLaren-Ford	Stewart Matra-Ford	G. Hill Lotus-Ford	Stewart Matra-Ford					Stewart Matra-Ford	Clark Lotus-Ford	G. Hill Lotus-Ford
1969	Stewart Matra-Ford	G. Hill Lotus-Ford				Stewart Matra-Ford	Stewart Matra-Ford	Ickx Brabham-Ford	Stewart Matra-Ford	Stewart Matra-Ford					Rindt Lotus-Ford	Stewart Matra-Ford	Hulme McLaren-Ford
1970	Rindt Lotus-Ford	Rindt Lotus-Ford			Rodriguez BRM	Rindt Lotus-Ford	Regazzoni Ferrari	Rindt Lotus-Ford	Stewart March-Ford	Rindt Lotus-Ford					E. Fittipaldi Lotus-Ford	Brabham Brabham-Ford	Ickx Ferrari
1971	Stewart Tyrrell-Ford	Stewart Tyrrell-Ford				Stewart Tyrrell-Ford	Gethin BRM	Stewart Tyrrell-Ford	Stewart Tyrrell-Ford	Ickx Ferrari					Cevert Tyrrell-Ford	Andretti Ferrari	
1972	E. Fittipaldi Lotus-Ford	Beltoise BRM			E. Fittipaldi Lotus-Ford	Stewart Tyrrell-Ford	E. Fittipaldi Lotus-Ford	Ickx Ferrari	E. Fittipaldi Lotus-Ford		Stewart Tyrrell-Ford				Stewart Tyrrell-Ford	Hulme McLaren-Ford	
1973	Revson McLaren-Ford	Stewart Tyrrell-Ford			Stewart Tyrrell-Ford	Peterson Lotus-Ford	Peterson Lotus-Ford	Stewart Tyrrell-Ford	E. Fittipaldi Lotus-Ford	Stewart Tyrrell-Ford	E. Fittipaldi Lotus-Ford				Peterson Lotus-Ford	Stewart Tyrrell-Ford	
1974	Scheckter Tyrrell-Ford	Peterson Lotus-Ford			E. Fittipaldi McLaren-Ford	Peterson Lotus-Ford	Peterson Lotus-Ford	Regazzoni Ferrari	Lauda Ferrari	Lauda Ferrari	Hulme McLaren-Ford				Reutemann Brabham-Ford	Reutemann Brabham-Ford	
1975	E. Fittipaldi McLaren-Ford	Lauda Ferrari			Lauda Ferrari	Lauda Ferrari	Regazzoni Ferrari	Reutemann Brabham-Ford	Mass McLaren-Ford	Hunt Hesketh-Ford	E. Fittipaldi McLaren-Ford				Lauda Ferrari	Scheckter Tyrrell-Ford	
1976	Lauda Ferrari	Lauda Ferrari			Lauda Ferrari	Hunt McLaren-Ford	Peterson March-Ford	Hunt McLaren-Honda	Hunt McLaren-Ford	Hunt McLaren-Ford						Lauda Ferrari	
1977	Hunt McLaren-Ford	Scheckter Wolf-Ford			Nilsson Lotus-Ford	M. Andretti Lotus-Ford	M. Andretti Lotus-Ford	Lauda Ferrari	M. Andretti Lotus-Ford	Lauda Ferrari	Scheckter Wolf-Ford					Lauda Ferrari	
1978	Reutemann Ferrari	Depailler Tyrrell-Ford			M. Andretti Lotus-Ford	M. Andretti Lotus-Ford	Lauda Brabham- Alfa Romeo	M. Andretti Lotus-Ford	M. Andretti Lotus-Ford	M. Andretti Lotus-Ford	M. Andretti Lotus-Ford					Peterson Lotus-Ford	
1979	Regazzoni Williams-Ford	Scheckter Ferrari			Scheckter Ferrari	Jabouille Renault	Scheckter Ferrari	Jones Williams-Ford	Depailler Ligier-Ford	Jones Williams-Ford	Laffite Ligier-Ford					G. Villeneuve Ferrari	
1980	Jones Williams-Ford	Reutemann Williams-Ford			Pironi Ligier-Ford	Jones Williams-Ford	Piquet Brabham-Ford	Laffite Ligier-Ford		Piquet Brabham-Ford	Jones Williams-Ford					Arnoux Renault	
1981	Watson McLaren-Ford	G. Villeneuve Ferrari			Reutemann Williams-Ford	Prost Renault	Prost Renault	Piquet Brabham-Ford	G. Villeneuve Ferrari	Prost Renault	Piquet Brabham-Ford						
1982	Lauda McLaren-Ford	Patrese Brabham-Ford		K. Rosberg Williams-Ford	Watson McLaren-Ford	Arnoux Renault	Arnoux Renault	Tambay Ferrari		Pironi Ferrari						Prost Renault	
1983	Prost Renault	K. Rosberg Williams-Ford			Prost Renault	Prost Renault	Piquet Brabham-BMW	Arnoux Ferrari		Arnoux Ferrari						Patrese Brabham-BMW	
1984	Lauda McLaren- TAG Porsche	Prost McLaren- TAG Porsche			Alboreto Ferrari	Lauda McLaren- TAG Porsche	Lauda McLaren- TAG Porsche	Prost McLaren- TAG Porsche		Prost McLaren- TAG Porsche			Prost McLaren- TAG Porsche		K. Rosberg Williams-Honda	Lauda McLaren- TAG Porsche	
1985	Prost McLaren- TAG Porsche	Prost McLaren- TAG Porsche			Senna Lotus-Renault	Piquet Brabham-BMW	Prost McLaren- TAG Porsche	Alboreto Ferrari		Lauda McLaren- TAG Porsche			Senna Lotus-Renault		K. Rosberg Williams-Honda	Mansell Williams-Honda	
1986	Mansell Williams-Honda	Prost McLaren- TAG Porsche			Mansell Williams-Honda	Mansell Williams-Honda	Piquet Williams-Honda	Piquet Williams-Honda	Senna Lotus-Renault				Mansell Williams-Honda		Senna Lotus-Renault		Berger Benetton-BMW
1987	Mansell Williams-Honda	Senna Lotus-Honda			Prost McLaren- TAG Porsche	Mansell Williams-Honda	Piquet Williams-Honda	Piquet Williams-Honda	Mansell Williams-Honda				Prost McLaren- TAG Porsche		Senna Lotus-Honda		Mansell Williams-Honda
1988	Senna McLaren-Honda	Prost McLaren-Honda			Senna McLaren-Honda	Prost McLaren-Honda	Berger Ferrari	Senna McLaren-Honda	Prost McLaren-Honda				Prost McLaren-Honda		Senna McLaren-Honda		Prost McLaren-Honda
1989	Prost McLaren-Honda	Senna McLaren-Honda			Senna McLaren-Honda	Prost McLaren-Honda	Prost McLaren-Honda	Senna McLaren-Honda	Senna McLaren-Honda				Berger Ferrari		Prost Ferrari		Senna McLaren-Honda
1990	Prost Ferrari	Senna McLaren-Honda			Senna McLaren-Honda	Prost Ferrari	Senna McLaren-Honda	Senna McLaren-Honda	Prost Ferrari				Mansell Ferrari		Senna McLaren-Honda		Prost Ferrari
1991	Mansell Williams-Renault	Senna McLaren-Honda			Senna McLaren-Honda	Mansell Williams-Renault	Mansell Williams-Renault	Mansell Williams-Renault	Mansell Williams-Renault				Patrese Williams-Renault		Senna McLaren-Honda		Patrese Williams-Renault
1992	Mansell Williams-Renault	Senna McLaren-Honda			M. Schumacher Benetton-Ford	Mansell Williams-Renault	Senna McLaren-Honda	Mansell Williams-Renault	Mansell Williams-Renault				Mansell Williams-Renault			Mansell Williams-Renault	Mansell Williams-Renault
1993	Prost Williams-Renault	Senna McLaren-Ford			D. Hill Williams-Renault	Prost Williams-Renault	D. Hill Williams-Renault	Prost Williams-Renault	Prost Williams-Renault				M. Schumacher Benetton-Ford			Prost Williams-Renault	
1994	D. Hill Williams-Renault	M. Schumacher Benetton-Ford			D. Hill Williams-Renault	M. Schumacher Benetton-Ford	D. Hill Williams-Renault	Berger Ferrari	D. Hill Williams-Renault				D. Hill Williams-Renault				
1995	Herbert Benetton-Renault	M. Schumacher Benetton-Renault			M. Schumacher Benetton-Renault	M. Schumacher Benetton-Renault	Herbert Benetton-Renault	M. Schumacher Benetton-Renault	M. Schumacher Benetton-Renault		D. Hill Williams-Renault		Coulthard Williams-Renault				
1996	J. Villeneuve Williams-Renault	Panis Ligier- Mugen Honda			M. Schumacher Ferrari	D. Hill Williams-Renault	M. Schumacher Ferrari	D. Hill Williams-Renault	M. Schumacher Ferrari		D. Hill Williams-Renault		J. Villeneuve Williams-Renault				
1997	J. Villeneuve Williams-Renault	M. Schumacher Ferrari			M. Schumacher Ferrari	M. Schumacher Ferrari	Coulthard McLaren-Mercedes	Berger Benetton-Renault	J. Villeneuve Williams-Renault		J. Villeneuve Williams-Renault						
1998	M. Schumacher Ferrari	Häkkinen McLaren-Mercedes			D. Hill Jordan- Mugen Honda	M. Schumacher Ferrari	M. Schumacher Ferrari	Häkkinen McLaren-Mercedes	Häkkinen McLaren-Mercedes		M. Schumacher Ferrari						
1999	Coulthard McLaren-Mercedes	M. Schumacher Ferrari			Coulthard McLaren-Mercedes	Frentzen Jordan Mugen Honda	Frentzen Jordan Mugen Honda	Irvine Ferrari	Häkkinen McLaren-Mercedes								
2000	Coulthard McLaren-Mercedes	Coulthard McLaren-Mercedes			Häkkinen McLaren-Mercedes	Coulthard McLaren-Mercedes	M. Schumacher Ferrari	Barrichello Ferrari	Häkkinen McLaren-Mercedes						M. Schumacher Ferrari		
2001	Häkkinen McLaren-Mercedes	M. Schumacher Ferrari			M. Schumacher Ferrari	M. Schumacher Ferrari	Montoya Williams-BMW	R. Schumacher Williams-BMW	M. Schumacher Ferrari						Häkkinen McLaren-Mercedes		
2002	M. Schumacher Ferrari	Coulthard McLaren-Mercedes			M. Schumacher Ferrari	M. Schumacher Ferrari	Barrichello Ferrari	M. Schumacher Ferrari	M. Schumacher Ferrari						Barrichello Ferrari		
2003	Barrichello Ferrari	Montoya Williams-BMW				R. Schumacher Williams-BMW	M. Schumacher Ferrari	Montoya Williams-BMW	M. Schumacher Ferrari						M. Schumacher Ferrari		
2004	M. Schumacher Ferrari	Trulli Renault			Räikkönen McLaren-Mercedes	M. Schumacher Ferrari	Barrichello Ferrari	M. Schumacher Ferrari	M. Schumacher Ferrari						M. Schumacher Ferrari		
2005	Montoya McLaren-Mercedes	Räikkönen McLaren-Mercedes			Räikkönen McLaren-Mercedes	Alonso Renault	Montoya McLaren-Mercedes	Alonso Renault	Räikkönen McLaren-Mercedes						M. Schumacher Ferrari		
2006	Alonso Renault	Alonso Renault				M. Schumacher Ferrari	M. Schumacher Ferrari	M. Schumacher Ferrari	Alonso Renault						M. Schumacher Ferrari		
2007	Räikkönen Ferrari	Alonso McLaren-Mercedes			Räikkönen Ferrari	Räikkönen Ferrari	Alonso McLaren-Mercedes		Massa Ferrari						Hamilton McLaren-Mercedes		

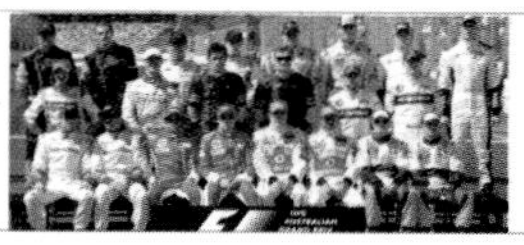

Drivers: victories

SCHUMACHER Michael	91	HAWTHORN Mike	3
PROST Alain	51	COLLINS Peter	3
SENNA Ayrton	41	HILL Phil	3
MANSELL Nigel	31	PIRONI Didier	3
STEWART Jackie	27	BOUTSEN Thierry	3
CLARK Jim	25	FRENTZEN Heinz-Harald	3
LAUDA Niki	25	HERBERT Johnny	3
FANGIO Juan-Manuel	24	FISICHELLA Giancarlo	3
PIQUET Nelson	23	VUKOVICH Bill	2
HILL Damon	22	GONZALEZ Jose-Froilan	2
HAKKINEN Mika	20	TRINTIGNANT Maurice	2
ALONSO Fernando	19	Von TRIPS Wolfgang	2
MOSS Stirling	16	RODRIGUEZ Pedro	2
RAIKKONEN Kimi	15	SIFFERT Jo	2
HILL Graham	14	REVSON Peter	2
BRABHAM Jack	14	DEPAILLER Patrick	2
FITTIPALDI Emerson	14	JABOUILLE Jean-Pierre	2
ASCARI Alberto	13	TAMBAY Patrick	2
COULTHARD David	13	De ANGELIS Elio	2
ANDRETTI Mario	12	PARSONS Johnnie	1
REUTEMANN Carlos	12	WALLARD Lee	1
JONES Alan	12	FAGIOLI Luigi	1
VILLENEUVE Jacques	11	TARUFFI Piero	1
HUNT James	10	RUTTMAN Troy	1
PETERSON Ronnie	10	SWEIKERT Bob	1
SCHECKTER Jody	10	MUSSO Luigi	1
BERGER Gerhard	10	FLAHERTY Pat	1
BARRICHELLO Rubens	9	HANKS Sam	1
ICKX Jacky	8	BRYAN Jimmy	1
HULME Denny	8	WARD Rodger	1
ARNOUX René	7	BONNIER Jo	1
MONTOYA Juan-Pablo	7	RATHMANN Jim	1
BROOKS Tony	6	BAGHETTI Giancarlo	1
SURTEES John	6	IRELAND Innes	1
RINDT Jochen	6	BANDINI Lorenzo	1
VILLENEUVE Gilles	6	GINTHER Richie	1
LAFFITE Jacques	6	SCARFIOTTI Ludovico	1
PATRESE Riccardo	6	GETHIN Peter	1
SCHUMACHER Ralf	6	CEVERT François	1
FARINA Giuseppe	5	BELTOISE Jean-Pierre	1
REGAZZONI Clay	5	PACE Carlos	1
WATSON John	5	MASS Jochen	1
ALBORETO Michele	5	BRAMBILLA Vittorio	1
ROSBERG Keke	5	NILSSON Gunnar	1
MASSA Felipe	5	NANNINI Alessandro	1
GURNEY Dan	4	ALESI Jean	1
McLAREN Bruce	4	PANIS Olivier	1
IRVINE Eddie	4	TRULLI Jarno	1
HAMILTON Lewis	4	BUTTON Jenson	1

The 58 World Champions

Year	Driver	Nationality	Team	GP	Poles	Victories	Fastest laps
1950	Giuseppe Farina	I	Alfa Romeo	7	2	3	3
1951	Juan Manuel Fangio	RA	Alfa Romeo	8	4	3	5
1952	Alberto Ascari	I	Ferrari	8	5	6	5
1953	Alberto Ascari	I	Ferrari	9	6	5	4
1954	Juan Manuel Fangio	RA	Mercedes/Maserati	9	5	6	3
1955	Juan Manuel Fangio	RA	Mercedes	7	3	4	3
1956	Juan Manuel Fangio	RA	Lancia/Ferrari	8	5	3	3
1957	Juan Manuel Fangio	RA	Maserati	8	4	4	2
1958	Mike Hawthorn	GB	Ferrari	11	4	1	5
1959	Jack Brabham	AUS	Cooper Climax	9	1	2	1
1960	Jack Brabham	AUS	Cooper Climax	10	3	5	3
1961	Phil Hill	USA	Ferrari	8	5	2	2
1962	Graham Hill	GB	BRM	9	1	4	3
1963	Jim Clark	GB	Lotus Climax	10	7	7	6
1964	John Surtees	GB	Ferrari	10	2	2	2
1965	Jim Clark	GB	Lotus Climax	10	6	6	6
1966	Jack Brabham	AUS	Brabham Repco	9	3	4	1
1967	Denny Hulme	NZ	Brabham Repco	11	0	2	2
1968	Graham Hill	GB	Lotus Ford	12	2	3	0
1969	Jackie Stewart	GB	Matra Ford	11	2	6	5
1970	Jochen Rindt	A	Lotus Ford	13	3	5	1
1971	Jackie Stewart	GB	Tyrrell Ford	11	6	6	3
1972	Emerson Fittipaldi	BR	Lotus Ford	12	3	5	0
1973	Jackie Stewart	GB	Tyrrell Ford	15	3	5	1
1974	Emerson Fittipaldi	BR	McLaren Ford	15	2	3	0
1975	Niki Lauda	A	Ferrari	14	9	5	2
1976	James Hunt	GB	McLaren Ford	16	8	6	2
1977	Niki Lauda	A	Ferrari	17	2	3	3
1978	Mario Andretti	USA	Lotus Ford	16	8	6	3
1979	Jody Scheckter	ZA	Ferrari	15	1	3	1
1980	Alan Jones	AUS	Williams Ford	14	3	5	5
1981	Nelson Piquet	BR	Brabham Ford	15	4	3	1
1982	Keke Rosberg	FIN	Williams Ford	16	1	1	0
1983	Nelson Piquet	BR	Brabham BMW Turbo	15	1	3	4
1984	Niki Lauda	A	McLaren TAG Porsche Turbo	16	0	5	5
1985	Alain Prost	F	McLaren TAG Porsche Turbo	16	2	5	5
1986	Alain Prost	F	McLaren TAG Porsche Turbo	16	1	4	2
1987	Nelson Piquet	BR	Williams Honda Turbo	16	4	3	4
1988	Ayrton Senna	BR	McLaren Honda Turbo	16	13	8	3
1989	Alain Prost	F	McLaren Honda	16	2	4	5
1990	Ayrton Senna	BR	McLaren Honda	16	10	6	2
1991	Ayrton Senna	BR	McLaren Honda	16	8	7	2
1992	Nigel Mansell	GB	Williams Renault	16	14	9	8
1993	Alain Prost	F	Williams Renault	16	13	7	6
1994	Michael Schumacher	D	Benetton Ford	14	6	8	9
1995	Michael Schumacher	D	Benetton Renault	17	4	9	7
1996	Damon Hill	GB	Williams Renault	16	9	8	5
1997	Jacques Villeneuve	CDN	Williams Renault	17	10	7	3
1998	Mika Häkkinen	FIN	McLaren Mercedes	16	9	8	6
1999	Mika Häkkinen	FIN	McLaren Mercedes	16	11	5	6
2000	Michael Schumacher	D	Ferrari	17	9	9	2
2001	Michael Schumacher	D	Ferrari	17	11	9	3
2002	Michael Schumacher	D	Ferrari	17	7	11	7
2003	Michael Schumacher	D	Ferrari	16	5	6	5
2004	Michael Schumacher	D	Ferrari	18	8	13	10
2005	Fernando Alonso	E	Renault	19	6	7	2
2006	Fernando Alonso	E	Renault	18	6	7	5
2007	Kimi Räikkönen	FIN	Ferrari	17	3	6	6

A	CDN	BR	S	USA-W (Long Beach)	USA-E	J	RSM	LAS VEGAS	EUR	AUS	H	PACIFIC	L	MAL	BRN	PRC	TR	
																		1950
																		1951
																		1952
																		1953
																		1954
																		1955
																		1956
																		1957
																		1958
																		1959
																		1960
																		1961
																		1962
																		1963
Bandini Ferrari																		1964
																		1965
																		1966
	Brabham Brabham-Repco																	1967
	Hulme McLaren-Ford																	1968
	Ickx Brabham-Ford																	1969
Ickx Ferrari	Ickx Ferrari																	1970
Siffert BRM	Stewart Tyrrell-Ford																	1971
E. Fittipaldi Lotus-Ford	Stewart Tyrrell-Ford																	1972
Peterson Lotus-Ford	Revson McLaren-Ford	E. Fittipaldi Lotus-Ford	Hulme McLaren-Ford															1973
Reutemann Brabham-Ford	E. Fittipaldi McLaren-Ford	E. Fittipaldi McLaren-Ford	Scheckter Tyrrell-Ford															1974
Brambilla March-Ford		Pace Brabham-Ford	Lauda Ferrari															1975
Watson Penske-Ford	Hunt McLaren-Ford	Lauda Ferrari	Scheckter Tyrrell-Ford	Regazzoni Ferrari	Hunt McLaren-Ford	M. Andretti Lotus-Ford												1976
Jones Shadow-Ford	Scheckter Wolf-Ford	Reutemann Ferrari	Laffite Ligier-Matra	Andretti Lotus-Ford	Hunt McLaren-Ford	Hunt McLaren-Ford												1977
Peterson Lotus-Ford	G. Villeneuve Ferrari	Reutemann Ferrari	Lauda Brabham- Alfa Romeo	Reutemann Ferrari	Reutemann Ferrari													1978
Jones Williams-Ford	Jones Williams-Ford	Laffite Ligier-Ford		G. Villeneuve Ferrari	G. Villeneuve Ferrari													1979
Jabouille Renault	Jones Williams-Ford	Arnoux Renault		Piquet Brabham-Ford	Jones Williams-Ford													1980
Laffite Ligier-Matra	Laffite Ligier-Matra	Reutemann Williams-Ford		Jones Williams-Ford			Piquet Brabham-Ford	Jones Williams-Ford										1981
De Angelis Lotus-Ford	Piquet Brabham-BMW	Prost Renault		Lauda McLaren-Ford	Watson McLaren-Ford		Pironi Ferrari	Alboreto Tyrrell-Ford										1982
Prost Renault	Arnoux Ferrari	Piquet Brabham-BMW		Watson McLaren-Ford	Alboreto Tyrrell-Ford		Tambay Ferrari		Piquet Brabham-BMW									1983
Lauda McLaren- TAG Porsche	Piquet Brabham-BMW	Prost McLaren- TAG Porsche			Piquet Brabham-BMW		Prost McLaren- TAG Porsche		Prost McLaren- TAG Porsche									1984
Prost McLaren- TAG Porsche	Alboreto Ferrari	Prost McLaren- TAG Porsche					De Angelis Lotus-Renault		Mansell Williams-Honda	K. Rosberg Williams-Honda								1985
Prost McLaren- TAG Porsche	Mansell Williams-Honda	Piquet Williams-Honda					Prost McLaren- TAG Porsche			Prost McLaren- TAG Porsche	Piquet Williams-Honda							1986
Mansell Williams-Honda		Prost McLaren- TAG Porsche				Berger Ferrari	Mansell Williams-Honda			Berger Ferrari	Piquet Williams-Honda							1987
	Senna McLaren-Honda	Prost McLaren-Honda				Senna McLaren-Honda	Senna McLaren-Honda			Prost McLaren-Honda	Senna McLaren-Honda							1988
	Boutsen Williams-Renault	Mansell Ferrari				Nannini Benetton-Ford	Senna McLaren-Honda			Boutsen Williams-Renault	Mansell Ferrari							1989
	Senna McLaren-Honda	Prost Ferrari				Piquet Benetton-Ford	Patrese Williams-Renault			Piquet Benetton-Ford	Boutsen Williams-Renault							1990
	Piquet Benetton-Ford	Senna McLaren-Honda				Berger McLaren-Honda	Senna McLaren-Honda			Senna McLaren-Honda	Senna McLaren-Honda							1991
	Berger McLaren-Honda	Mansell Williams-Renault				Mansell Williams-Renault	Mansell Williams-Renault			Berger McLaren-Honda	Senna McLaren-Honda							1992
	Prost Williams-Renault	Senna McLaren-Ford				Senna McLaren-Ford	Prost Williams-Renault		Senna McLaren-Ford	Senna McLaren-Ford	D. Hill Williams-Renault							1993
	M. Schumacher Benetton-Ford	M. Schumacher Benetton-Ford				D. Hill Williams-Renault	M. Schumacher Benetton-Ford		M. Schumacher Benetton-Ford	Mansell Williams-Renault	M. Schumacher Benetton-Ford	M. Schumacher Benetton-Ford						1994
	Alesi Ferrari	M. Schumacher Benetton-Renault				M. Schumacher Benetton-Renault	D.Hill Williams-Renault		M. Schumacher Benetton-Renault	D. Hill Williams-Renault	D. Hill Williams-Renault	M. Schumacher Benetton-Renault						1995
	D. Hill Williams-Renault	D. Hill Williams-Renault				D. Hill Williams-Renault	D. Hill Williams-Renault		J. Villeneuve Williams-Renault	D. Hill Williams-Renault	J. Villeneuve Williams-Renault							1996
J. Villeneuve Williams-Renault	M. Schumacher Ferrari	J. Villeneuve Williams-Renault				M. Schumacher Ferrari	Frentzen Williams-Renault		Häkkinen McLaren-Mercedes	Coulthard McLaren-Mercedes	J. Villeneuve Williams-Renault		J. Villeneuve Williams-Renault					1997
Häkkinen McLaren-Mercedes	M. Schumacher Ferrari	Häkkinen McLaren-Mercedes				Häkkinen McLaren-Mercedes	Coulthard McLaren-Mercedes			Häkkinen McLaren-Mercedes	M. Schumacher Ferrari		Häkkinen McLaren-Mercedes					1998
Irvine Ferrari	Häkkinen McLaren-Mercedes	Häkkinen McLaren-Mercedes				Häkkinen McLaren-Mercedes	M. Schumacher Ferrari		Herbert Stewart-Ford	Irvine Ferrari	Häkkinen McLaren-Mercedes			Irvine Ferrari				1999
Häkkinen McLaren-Mercedes	M. Schumacher Ferrari	M. Schumacher Ferrari				M. Schumacher Ferrari	M. Schumacher Ferrari		M. Schumacher Ferrari	M. Schumacher Ferrari	Häkkinen McLaren-Mercedes			M. Schumacher Ferrari				2000
Coulthard McLaren-Mercedes	R. Schumacher Williams-BMW	Coulthard McLaren-Mercedes				M. Schumacher Ferrari	R. Schumacher Williams-BMW		M. Schumacher Ferrari	M. Schumacher Ferrari	M. Schumacher Ferrari			M. Schumacher Ferrari				2001
M. Schumacher Ferrari	M. Schumacher Ferrari	M. Schumacher Ferrari				M. Schumacher Ferrari	M. Schumacher Ferrari		Barrichello Ferrari	M. Schumacher Ferrari	Barrichello Ferrari			M. Schumacher Ferrari				2002
M. Schumacher Ferrari	M. Schumacher Ferrari	Fisichella Jordan-Ford				Barrichello Ferrari	M. Schumacher Ferrari		R. Schumacher Williams-BMW	Coulthard McLaren-Mercedes	Alonso Renault			Räikkönen McLaren-Mercedes				2003
	M. Schumacher Ferrari	Montoya Williams-BMW				M. Schumacher Ferrari	M. Schumacher Ferrari		M. Schumacher Ferrari	M. Schumacher Ferrari	M. Schumacher Ferrari			M. Schumacher Ferrari	M. Schumacher Ferrari	Barrichello Ferrari		2004
	Räikkönen McLaren-Mercedes	Montoya McLaren-Mercedes				Räikkönen McLaren-Mercedes	Alonso Renault		Alonso Renault	Fisichella Renault	Räikkönen McLaren-Mercedes			Alonso Renault	Alonso Renault	Alonso Renault	Räikkönen McLaren-Mercedes	2005
	Alonso Renault	Massa Ferrari				Alonso Renault	M. Schumacher Ferrari		M. Schumacher Ferrari	Alonso Renault	Button Honda			Fisichella Renault	Alonso Renault	M. Schumacher Ferrari	Massa Ferrari	2006
	Hamilton McLaren-Mercedes	Räikkönen Ferrari				Hamilton McLaren-Mercedes			Alonso McLaren-Mercedes	Räikkönen Ferrari	Hamilton McLaren-Mercedes			Alonso McLaren-Mercedes	Massa Ferrari	Räikkönen Ferrari	Massa Ferrari	2007

The FIA will organise the FIA Formula One World Championship (the Championship) which is the property of the FIA and comprises two titles of World Champion, one for drivers and one for constructors. It consists of the Formula One Grand Prix races which are included in the Formula One calendar and in respect of which the ASNs and organisers have signed the organisation agreement provided for in the 1998 Concorde Agreement (Events). All the participating parties (FIA, ASNs, organisers, competitors and circuits) undertake to apply as well as observe the rules governing the Championship and must hold FIA Super Licences which are issued to drivers, competitors, officials, organisers and circuits.

REGULATIONS

1. The final text of these Sporting Regulations shall be the English version which will be used should any dispute arise as to their interpretation. Headings in this document are for ease of reference only and do not form part of these Sporting Regulations.
2.These Sporting Regulations were first published on 30 October 2006 and came into force on 1 January 2007. They were subsequently amended on 13 July 2007 with the unanimous agreement of all competing teams and replace all previous FIA Formula One World Championship Sporting Regulations

GENERAL UNDERTAKING

3. All drivers, competitors and officials participating in the Championship undertake, on behalf of themselves, their employees and agents, to observe all the provisions as supplemented or amended of the International Sporting Code (the Code), the Formula One Technical Regulations (the Technical Regulations) and the present Sporting Regulations together with all the provisions of the 1998 Concorde Agreement (the Agreement) of which they have had due notice.
4. The Championship is governed by the Agreement and its schedules.
5. Any special national regulations must be submitted to the FIA with the original application for inclusion of an Event on the international calendar. Only with the approval of the FIA can such special regulations come into force for an Event. The FIA will ensure that all applicant competitors are informed of such special regulations before entries close under Article 13.1.

GENERAL CONDITIONS

6. It is the competitor's responsibility to ensure that all persons concerned by his entry observe all the requirements of the Agreement, the Code, the Technical Regulations and the Sporting Regulations. If a competitor is unable to be present in person at the Event he must nominate his representative in writing. The person having charge of an entered car during any part of an Event is responsible jointly and severally with the competitor for ensuring that the requirements are observed.
7. Competitors must ensure that their cars comply with the conditions of eligibility and safety throughout practice and the race.
8. The presentation of a car for scrutineering will be deemed an implicit statement of conformity.
9. All persons concerned in any way with an entered car or present in any other capacity whatsoever in the paddock, pit lane, or track must wear an appropriate pass at all times.

LICENCES

10. All drivers, competitors and officials participating in the Championship must hold a FIA Super Licence. Applications for Super Licences must be made to the FIA through the applicant's ASN. The driver's name will remain on the list for Super Licences for one year.

CHAMPIONSHIP EVENTS

11. Events are reserved for Formula One cars as defined in the Technical Regulations.
12. Each Event will have the status of an international restricted competition.
13. The distance of all races, from the start signal referred to in Article 38.11 to the chequered flag, shall be equal to the least number of complete laps which exceed a distance of 305 km (Monaco 260km). However, should two hours elapse before the scheduled race distance is completed, the leader will be shown the chequered flag when he crosses the control line (the Line) at the end of the lap during which the two hour period ended. However, should the race be suspended (see Article 41) the length of the suspension will be added to this period.
The Line is a single line which crosses both the track and the pit lane.
14. The maximum number of Events in the Championship is 17, the minimum is 8.
15. The final list of Events is published by the FIA before 1st January each year.
16. An Event which is cancelled with less than three months written notice to the FIA will not be considered for inclusion in the following year's Championship unless the FIA judges the cancellation to have been due to force majeure.
17. An Event may be cancelled if fewer than 12 cars are available for it.

WORLD CHAMPIONSHIP

18. The Formula One World Championship driver's title will be awarded to the driver who has scored the highest number of points, taking into consideration all the results obtained during the Events which have actually taken place.
19. The title of Formula One World Champion Constructor will be awarded to the make which has scored the highest number of points, results from both cars being taken into account.
20. The constructor of an engine or rolling chassis is the person (including any corporate or unincorporated body) which owns the intellectual property rights to such engine or chassis. The make of an engine or chassis is the name attributed to it by its constructor. If the make of the chassis is not the same as that of the engine, the title will be awarded to the former which shall always precede the latter in the name of the car.
21. Points for both titles will be awarded at each Event according to the following scale: 1st: 10 points,
2nd: 8 points, 3rd: 6 points, 4th: 5 points, 5th: 4 points, 6th: 3 points, 7th: 2 points, 8th: 1 point
22. If a race is suspended under Article 41, and cannot be resumed, no points will be awarded if the leader has completed less than two laps, half points will be awarded if the leader has completed more than two laps but less than 75% of the original race distance and full points will be awarded if the leader has completed more than 75% of the original race distance.
23. The drivers finishing first, second and third in the Championship must be present at the annual FIA Prize Giving ceremony.

DEAD HEAT

24. Prizes and points awarded for all the positions of competitors who tie, will be added together and shared equally.
25. If two or more constructors or drivers finish the season with the same number of points, the higher place in the Championship (in either case) shall be awarded to:
a) the holder of the greatest number of first places,
b) if the number of first places is the same, the holder of the greatest number of second places,
c) if the number of second places is the same, the holder of the greatest number of third places and so on until a winner emerges.
d) if this procedure fails to produce a result, the FIA will nominate the winner according to such criteria as it thinks fit.

COMPETITORS APPLICATIONS

41. Applications to compete in the Championship may be submitted to the FIA at any time between 1 March two years prior to the Championship in which the applicant wishes to compete and 15 November immediately preceding such Championship, on an entry form as set out in Appendix 2 hereto accompanied by the entry fee provided for in the Agreement, together with the deposit provided for in Article 13.4 where applicable. Applications from teams not already competing in the Championship will only be considered where a place is available, taking into account all the teams who are entitled to compete under the Agreement. Entry forms will be made available by FIA who will notify the applicant of the result of the application within thirty days of its receipt. Successful applicants are automatically entered in all Events of the Championship and will be the only competitors at Events.
42. Applications shall include:
a) confirmation that the applicant has read and understood the Agreement (including its schedules), the Code, the Technical Regulations and the Sporting Regulations and agrees, on its own behalf and on behalf of everyone associated with its participation in the Championship, to observe them,
b) the name of the team (which must include the name of the chassis),
c) the make of the competing car,
d) the make of the engine,
e) the names of the drivers. A driver may be nominated subsequent to the application upon payment of a fee fixed by the FIA,
f) an undertaking by the applicant to participate in every Event with the number of cars and drivers entered.
g) an undertaking that the car does not make use of any component, system, software or device which has been (or might reasonably be suspected to have been) designed, supplied or constructed by or with the help of anyone who has been involved on behalf of the FIA with checking Formula One electronic systems during the 24 months immediately preceding the application.
43. A competitor may change the make and/or type of engine at any time during the Championship. All points scored with an engine of different make to that which was first entered in the Championship will count (and will be aggregated) for the assessment of Benefits, however such points will not count towards (nor be aggregated for) the FIA Formula One Constructors Championship.
44. With the exception of those whose cars have scored points in the Championship of the previous year, applicants must supply information about the size of their company, their financial position and their ability to meet their prescribed obligations. Any applicant which did not take part in the Championship for the previous year must also deposit US$48,000,000 (forty-eight million United States dollars) with the FIA when submitting its application. This sum will be returned to it forthwith if its application is refused or in twelve equal monthly instalments (including interest) commencing immediately after the first Event in which it competes, provided it has met and continues to meet all the requirements of the Agreement and its schedules. If the applicant fails to appear for the Championship for which it has entered, its deposit will be forfeit save only that the applicant may delay its participation by one year, in which case US$12,000,000 (twelve million United States dollars) will be forfeit and the balance repaid as set out above.
45. All applications will be studied by the FIA which will publish the list of cars and drivers accepted together with their race numbers on 1 December (or the following Monday if 1 December falls on a weekend), having first notified unsuccessful applicants as set out in Article 13.1.
46. No more than 24 cars will be admitted to the Championship, two being entered by each competitor.
47. If in the opinion of the Formula One Commission a competitor fails to operate his team in a manner compatible with the standards of the Championship or in any way brings the Championship into disrepute, the FIA may exclude such competitor from the Championship forthwith.

PASSES

48. No pass may be issued except in accordance with the Agreement. A pass may be used only by the person and for the purpose for which it was issued.

INSTRUCTIONS AND COMMUNICATIONS TO COMPETITORS

49. In exceptional circumstances, the stewards or race director may give instructions to competitors by means of special circulars in accordance with the Code. These circulars will be distributed to all competitors who must acknowledge receipt.
50. All classifications and results of practice and the race, as well as all decisions issued by the officials, will be posted on the official notice board.
51. Any decision or communication concerning a particular competitor should be given to him within twenty five minutes of such decision, and receipt must be acknowledged.

INCIDENTS

52. "Incident" means any occurrence or series of occurrences involving one or more drivers, or any action by any driver, which is reported to the stewards by the race director (or noted by the stewards and referred to the race director for investigation) which :
- necessitated the stopping of a race under Article 41;
- constituted a breach of these Sporting Regulations or the Code;
- caused a false start by one or more cars;
- caused a collision;
- forced a driver off the track;
- illegitimately prevented a legitimate overtaking manoeuvre by a driver;
- illegitimately impeded another driver during overtaking.

Unless it was completely clear that a driver was in breach of any of the above, any incidents involving more than one car will normally be investigated after the race.
53. a) It shall be at the discretion of the stewards to decide, upon a report or a request by the race director, if a driver or drivers involved in an incident shall be penalised.
b) If an incident is under investigation by the stewards a message informing all teams which driver or drivers are involved will be displayed on the timing monitors.
Provided that such a message is displayed no later than five minutes after the race has finished the driver or drivers concerned may not leave the circuit without the consent of the stewards.
54. The stewards may impose any one of three penalties on any driver involved in an Incident:
a) A drive-through penalty. The driver must enter the pit lane and re-join the race without stopping;
b) A ten second time penalty. The driver must enter the pit lane, stop at his pit for at least ten seconds and then re-join the race.
c) a drop of ten grid positions at the driver's next Event.
However, should either of the penalties under a) and b) above be imposed during the last five laps, or after the end of a race, Article 16.4b) below will not apply and 25 seconds will be added to the elapsed race time of the driver concerned.
55. Should the stewards decide to impose either of the penalties under Article 16.3a) or b), the following procedure will be followed :
a) The stewards will give written notification of the penalty which has been imposed to an official of the team concerned and will ensure that this information is also displayed on the timing monitors.
b) From the time the stewards' decision is notified on the timing monitors the relevant driver may cover no more than three complete laps before entering the pit lane and, in the case of a penalty under Article 16.3b), proceeding to his garage where he shall remain for the period of the time penalty.
However, unless the driver was already in the pit entry for the purpose of serving his penalty, he may not carry out the penalty after the Safety Car has been deployed. Any laps carried out behind the Safety Car will be added to the three lap maximum.
Whilst a car is stationary in the pit lane as a result of incurring a time penalty it may not be worked on. However, if the engine stops it may be started after the time penalty period has elapsed.
c) When the time penalty period has elapsed the driver may rejoin the race.
d) Any breach or failure to comply with Articles 55b) or 55c) may result in the car being excluded.

PROTESTS

56. Protests shall be made in accordance with the Code and accompanied by a fee of 2000 US Dollars.

SANCTIONS

57. The stewards may inflict the penalties specifically set out in these Sporting Regulations in addition to or instead of any other penalties available to them under the Code.

CHANGES OF DRIVER

58. a) During a season, each team will be permitted to use four drivers (excluding any third driver taking part in either of the free practice sessions on the first day of practice). Changes may be made at any time before the start of the qualifying practice session provided any change proposed after 16.00 on the day of scrutineering receives the consent of the stewards.
Additional changes for reasons of force majeure will be considered separately.
Any new driver may score points in the Championship.
b) b) In addition to the above Ueach teamU will be permitted to run additional drivers during P1 and P2 provided:
- the stewards are informed which cars and drivers each team intends to use in each session before the end of initial scrutineering, changes after this time may only be made with the consent of the stewards;
- no more than two drivers are used in any one session ;
- they are in possession of a Super Licence.

c) If one of the team's nominated drivers is unable to drive at some stage after the end of initial scrutineering, and the stewards consent to a change of driver, the replacement driver must use the engine and tyres which were allocated to the original driver (see Articles 25.3 and 28.4).

DRIVING

CAR LIVERY

60. The provisions of the Code relating to national colours shall not apply to the Championship.
Both cars entered by a competitor must be presented in substantially the same livery at each Event, any change to this livery during a Championship season may only be made with the agreement of the Formula One Commission.
In order that the cars of each team may be easily distinguished from one another whilst they are on the track, the on board cameras located above the principle roll structure of the first car must be predominantly fluorescent red and the second car fluorescent yellow.
61. Each car will carry the race number of its driver (or his replacement) as published by the FIA at the beginning of the season. This number must be clearly visible from the front of the car.
62. The name or the emblem of the make of the car must appear on the front of the nose of the car and in either case be at least 25mm in its largest dimension. The name of the driver must appear on the external bodywork and be clearly legible.

TESTING

63. a) No testing is permitted at sites which are not currently approved for use by Formula 1 cars. In order to ensure that venue licence conditions are respected at all times during testing, Competitors are required to inform the FIA of their test schedule in order that an observer may be appointed if deemed necessary.
b) During all Formula One testing :
- red flag procedures must be respected ;
- no other type of vehicle is permitted on the track ;
- every reasonable effort should be made to ensure that the recommendations concerning emergency services detailed in Article 16 of Appendix H to the Code are followed.

c) If, after an incident, the Medical Warning Light signals that threshold forces have been exceeded the driver must present himself for examination in the circuit medical centre without delay.

PIT LANE

64. a) For the avoidance of doubt and for description purposes, the pit lane shall be divided into two lanes. The lane closest to the pit wall is designated the "fast lane", and the lane closest to the garages is designated the "inner lane". Other than when cars are at the end of the pit lane under Article 38.3, the inner lane is the only area where any work can be carried out on a car.
b) The FIA will designate an area in the pit lane where each team may work and one place where pit stops may be carried out.
c) Unless a car is pushed from the grid at any time during the start procedure, cars may only be driven from the team's designated garage area to the end of the pit lane.
d) Any driver intending to start the race from the pit lane may not drive his car from his team's designated garage area until the 15 minute signal has been given and must stop in a line in the fast lane.
Under these circumstances working in the fast lane will be permitted but any such work is restricted to :
- starting the engine and any directly associated preparation;
- the fitting or removal of cooling and heating devices ;
- changing wheels.

When cars are permitted to leave the pit lane they must do so in the order they arrived at the end of the pit lane unless another car is unduly delayed. At all times drivers must follow the directions of the marshals.
e) Other than drying, sweeping or any tyre rubber left when cars leave their pit stop position, Competitors may not attempt to enhance the grip of the surface in the pit lane unless a problem has been clearly identified and a solution agreed UtoU by the FIA safety delegate.
f) Competitors must not paint lines on any part of the pit lane.
g) Other than under Ud)U above no equipment may be left in the fast lane.
h) Team personnel are only allowed in the pit lane immediately before they are required to work on a car and must withdraw as soon as the work is complete.

SCRUTINEERING

65. Between 10.00 and 16.00 three days before the race (four days in Monaco) initial scrutineering of all cars will take place in the garage assigned to each team.
66. Unless a waiver is granted by the stewards, competitors who do not keep to these time limits will not be allowed to take part in the Event.
67. No car may take part in the Event until it has been passed by the scrutineers.
68. The scrutineers may:
a) check the eligibility of a car or of a competitor at any time during an Event,
b) require a car to be dismantled by the competitor to make sure that the conditions of eligibility or conformity are fully satisfied,
c) require a competitor to pay the reasonable expenses which exercise of the powers mentioned in this Article may entail,
d) require a competitor to supply them with such parts or samples as they may deem necessary.
69. Any car which, after being passed by the scrutineers, is dismantled or modified in a way which might affect its safety or call into question its eligibility, or which is involved in an accident with similar consequences, must be re-presented for scrutineering approval.
70. The race director or the clerk of the course may require that any car involved in an accident be stopped and checked.
71. Checks and scrutineering shall be carried out by duly appointed officials who shall also be responsible for the operation of the parc fermé and who alone are authorised to give instructions to the competitors.
72. The stewards will publish the findings of the scrutineers each time cars are checked during the Event. These results will not include any specific figure except when a car is found to be in breach of the Technical Regulations.

SUPPLY OF TYRES IN THE CHAMPIONSHIP AND TYRE LIMITATION DURING THE EVENT

73. Supply of tyres:
a) Any tyre company wishing to supply tyres to Formula One teams must notify the FIA of its intention to do so no later than 1 January preceding the year during which such tyres will be supplied.
Any tyre company wishing to cease the supply of tyres to Formula One Teams must notify the FIA of its intention to do so no later than 1 January of the year preceding that in which such tyres were to be supplied.
b) No tyre may be used in the Championship unless the company supplying such tyre accepts and adheres to the following conditions :
- one tyre supplier present in the Championship: this company must equip 100% of the entered teams on ordinary commercial terms and make available identical quantities and specifications of tyres to all teams during a calendar year;
- two tyre suppliers present: each of them must, if called upon to do so, be prepared to equip up to 60% of the entered teams on ordinary commercial terms;
- three or more tyre suppliers present: each of them must, if called upon to do so, be prepared to equip up to 40% of the entered teams on ordinary commercial terms;
- each tyre supplier must undertake to provide no more than two specifications of dry-weather tyre to each team at each Event, each of which must be of one homogenous compound and visibly distinguishable from one another when a car is on the track. Any modification or treatment, other than heating, carried out to a tyre or tyres will be considered a change of specification ;
- each tyre supplier must undertake to provide no more than two specifications of dry-weather tyre to each team at each Event, each of which must be of one homogenous compound. Any modification or treatment, other than heating, carried out to a tyre or tyres will be considered a change of specification ;
- each tyre supplier must undertake to provide no more than one specification of wet-weather tyre at each Event which must be of one homogenous compound ;
- each tyre supplier must undertake to provide no more than one specification of extreme-weather tyre at each Event which must be of one homogenous compound ;
- if, in the interests of maintaining current levels of circuit safety, the FIA deems it necessary to reduce tyre grip, it shall introduce such rules as the tyre suppliers may advise or, in the absence of advice which achieves the FIA's objectives, specify the maximum permissible contact areas for front and rear tyres.

74. Type of tyres :
a) All dry-weather tyres must incorporate circumferential grooves square to the wheel axis and around the entire circumference of the contact surface of each tyre.
b) Each front dry-weather tyre, when new, must incorporate 4 grooves which are :
- arranged symmetrically about the centre of the tyre tread ;
- at least 14mm wide at the contact surface and which taper uniformly to a minimum of 10mm at the lower surface;
- at least 2.5mm deep across the whole lower surface ;
- 50mm (+/- 1.0mm) between centres.

Furthermore, the tread width of the front tyres must not exceed 270mm.
c) Each rear dry-weather tyre, when new, must incorporate 4 grooves which are:
- arranged symmetrically about the centre of the tyre tread ;
- at least 14mm wide at the contact surface and which taper uniformly to a minimum of 10mm at the lower surface ;
- at least 2.5mm deep across the whole lower surface ;
- 50mm (+/- 1.0mm) between centres.

The measurements referred to in b) and c) above will be taken when the tyre is fitted to a wheel and inflated to 1.4 bar.
d) A wet-weather tyre is one which has been designed for use on a wet or damp track.
All wet-weather tyres must, when new, have a contact area which does not exceed 280cm2 when fitted to the front of the car and 440cm2 when fitted to the rear. Contact areas will be measured over any square section of the tyre which is normal to and symmetrical about the tyre centre line and which measures 200mm x 200mm when fitted to the front of the car and 250mm x 250mm when fitted to the rear. For the purposes of establishing conformity, void areas which are less than 2.5mm in depth will be deemed to be contact areas.
Prior to use at an Event, each tyre manufacturer must provide the technical delegate with a full scale drawing of each type of wet-weather tyre intended for use.
e) An extreme-weather tyre is one which has been designed for use on a wet track.
All extreme-weather tyres must, when new, have a contact area which does not exceed 240cm2 when fitted to the front of the car and 375cm2 when fitted to the rear. Contact areas will be measured over any square section of the tyre which is normal to and symmetrical about the tyre centre line and which measures 200mm x 200mm when fitted to the front of the car and 250mm x 250mm when fitted to the rear. For the purposes of establishing conformity, void areas which are less than 5.0mm in depth will be deemed to be contact areas.
Prior to use at an Event, each tyre manufacturer must provide the technical delegate with a full scale drawing of each type of extreme-weather tyre intended for use.
f) Tyre specifications will be determined by the FIA no later than 1 September of the previous season. Once determined in this way, the specification of the tyres will not be changed during the Championship season without the agreement of the Formula One Commission.
75. Quantity of tyres:
During the Event no driver may use more than fourteen sets of dry-weather tyres, four sets of wet-weather tyres and three sets of extreme-weather tyres.
No driver may use more than two sets of each specification of dry-weather tyre during P1 and P2.
No driver may use more than one set of wet and one set of extreme-weather tyres during P1 and P2.
A set of tyres will be deemed to comprise two front and two rear tyres all of which must be of the same specification.
76. Control of tyres :
a) The outer sidewall of all tyres which are to be used at an Event must be marked with a unique identification.
b) Other than in cases of force majeure (accepted as such by the stewards of the meeting), all tyres intended for use at an Event must be presented to the FIA technical delegate for allocation prior to the end of initial scrutineering.
c) At any time during an Event, and at his absolute discretion, the FIA technical delegate may select alternative dry-weather tyres to be used by any team or driver from among the relevant stock of tyres which such team's designated supplier has present at the Event.
d) A competitor wishing to replace one unused tyre by another identical unused one must present both tyres to the FIA technical delegate.
e) The use of tyres without appropriate identification may result in deletion of the relevant driver's qualifying time or exclusion from the race.
f) The only permitted type of tyre heating devices are blankets which use resistive heating elements.
77. Use of tyres :
a) Each team will be allocated eight sets of dry-weather tyres, four of each specification, for use during P1 and P2. These are the only dry-weather tyres which may be used during these sessions and must be returned to the tyre supplier before the start of P3.
b) Each driver will be allocated ten further sets of dry-weather tyres, five of each specification, for use during the remainder of the Event. However, one set of each specification must be returned to the tyre supplier before the start of the qualifying practice session and may not be used during the remainder of the Event.
c) Prior to the start of the qualifying practice session wet and extreme-weather tyres may only be used after the track has been declared wet by the race director, following which extreme, wet or dry-weather tyres may be used for the remainder of the session.
d) Unless he has used wet or extreme-weather tyres during the race, each driver must use at least one set of each specification of dry-weather tyres during the race.
78. Wear of tyres :
The Championship will be contested on grooved tyres. The FIA reserve the right to introduce at any time a method of measuring remaining groove depth if performance appears to be enhanced by high wear or by the use of tyres which are worn so that the grooves are no longer visible.

WEIGHING

79. a) During the qualifying practice session cars will be weighed as follows:
1) the FIA will install weighing equipment in the first pit garage (the FIA garage) which will be used for the weighing procedure;
2) all cars which complete a flying lap will undergo the weighing procedure ;
3) the driver will proceed directly to the FIA garage and stop his engine ;
4) the car will then be weighed with driver (and without driver if necessary) and the result given to the driver in writing ;
5) if the car is unable to reach the FIA garage under its own power it will be placed under the exclusive control of the marshals who will take the car to be weighed;
6) a car or driver may not leave the FIA garage without the consent of the FIA technical delegate;
7) if a car stops on the circuit and the driver leaves the car, he must go to the FIA garage immediately on his return to the pit lane in order for his weight to be established.
b) After the race every classifed car will be weighed. If a driver wishes to leave his car before it is weighed he must ask the technical delegate to weigh him in order that this weight may be added to that of the car.
c) The relevant car may be excluded should its weight be less than that specified in Article 4.1 of the Technical Regulations when weighed under a) or b) above, save where the deficiency in weight results from the accidental loss of a component of the car.
d) No substance may be added to, placed on, or removed from a car after it has been selected for weighing or has finished the race or during the weighing procedure. (Except by a scrutineer when acting in his official capacity).
e) No oneother than scrutineers and officials may enter or remain in the FIA garage without the the specific permission of the FIA technical delegate.
80. In the event of any breach of these provisions for the weighing of cars the stewards may drop the driver such number of grid positions as they consider appropriate or exclude him from the race.

GENERAL CAR REQUIREMENTS

81. Electromagnetic radiation between 2.0 and 2.7GHz is forbidden save with the written consent of the FIA.
82. Accident data recording :
a) Each car must be fitted with an FIA accident data recorder during each Event and during all tests which are attended by more than one team. Teams must use their best endeavours to ensure that the recorder is in working order at all times. The only purpose of these units is to monitor, record or control one or more of the following :
- data relevant to an accident or incident ;
- a deceleration warning light on board the car ;
- a lap trigger ;
- the driver input signal used to initiate the propulsion of the car at the start of a race.

b) At any time following an accident or incident competitors must make the data recorder available and accessible to the FIA.
A representative of the team concerned may be present when data relevant to an accident or incident is being uploaded from the recorder. A copy of the data will be made available to the team.
c) Any conclusions as to the cause of an accident, or any data relevant to an accident, may only be published in the form of a report which has been agreed between the team concerned and the FIA.
83. During the entire Event, no screen, cover or other obstruction which in any way obscures any part of a car will be allowed at any time in the paddock, garages, pit lane or grid, unless it is clear any such covers are needed solely for mechanical reasons, which could, for example, include protecting against fire.
In addition to the above the following are specifically not permitted :
- engine, gearbox or radiator covers whilst engines are being changed or moved around the garage ;
- covers over spare wings when they are on a stand in the pit lane not being used ;
- parts such as (but not limited to) spare floors, fuel rigs or tool trolleys may not be used as an obstruction.

The following are permitted :
- covers which are placed over damaged cars or components;
- a transparent tool tray, no more than 50mm deep, placed on top of the rear wing ;
- warming or heat retaining covers for the engine and gearbox on the grid ;
- a rear wing cover designed specifically to protect a mechanic starting the car from fire ;
- tyre heating blankets ;
- covers over the tyre manufacturer's code numbers (not the FIA bar code numbers) ;
- a cover over the car in the parc ferme overnight ;
- a cover over the car in the pit lane or grid if it is raining.

SPARE CARS AND ENGINES

84. Subject to the requirements of Article 87, a competitor may use several cars for practice and the race provided that :
a) he has no more than three cars available for use at any one time ;
b) he uses no more than two cars for each practice session (other than when a third driver is used under Article 58). A car will be deemed to have been used once the timing transponder has shown that it has left the pit lane ;
c) they are all of the same make and were entered in the Championship by the same competitor,
d) they have been scrutineered in accordance with these Sporting Regulations,
e)each car carries its driver's race number.
85. Any driver who decides to use another race car or a spare car following the qualifying practice session, must start the race from the pit lane following the procedures detailed in Article 136. Under these circumstances no restrictions on fuel load will be applied.
86. No change of car is permitted after the start of the race.
A change of car will be deemed to have taken place once a driver is seated in his new car and such change may only take place in the team's designated garage area.
87. For the purposes of this Article only, an Event will be deemed to comprise P3, the qualifying practice session and the race.
a) Each driver may use no more than one engine for two consecutive Events in which his team competes. Should a driver use a replacement engine before the end of the qualifying practice session he will drop ten places on the starting grid at that Event and an additional ten places each time a further engine is used.
Unless the driver fails to finish the race (see below) the engine fitted to the car at the end of the Event must remain in it until the end of the next Event. Any driver who failed to finish the race at the first of the two Events for reasons which the technical delegate accepts as being beyond the control of the team or driver, may start the second with a different engine without a penalty being incurred.
An engine will be deemed to have been used once the car's timing transponder has shown that it has left the pit lane.
b) If a driver is replaced after the first of a two Event period, having finished the first Event, the replacement driver must use the engine which was used for the first Event.
c) Should a driver use a replacement engine after the qualifying practice session, he will be required to start the relevant race from the back of the starting grid in accordance with Article 36.2c).
d) After consultation with the relevant engine supplier the FIA will attach seals to each engine in order to ensure that no significant moving parts can be rebuilt or replaced.
Following the first of the two Events, and within two hours of the end of the post race parc fermé, exhaust blanking plates (with one 10mm diameter inspection hole per cylinder) and further seals will be applied in order to ensure that the engine cannot be run until the second Event. These seals will be removed at 09.00 on the day of initial scrutineering at the second Event.
e) Other than the straightforward replacement of one engine unit with another, a change will also be deemed to have taken place if any of the FIA seals are damaged or removed from the original engine after it has been used for the first time.
Only engines which have been homologated by the FIA in accordance with Appendix 4 may be used at an Event during the 2007, 2008, 2009 and 2010 seasons.

REFUELLING

88. a) Refuelling is only permitted in the team's designated garage area or the FIA garage.
b) Fuel may not be added to nor removed from any car eligible to take part in Q3 during that period. Fuel used during Q3 may be replaced immediately after the cars are released from parc ferme on the day of the race, this will be carried out in grid order.
c) Other than a fuel breather and an external fuel pressurising device for starting the engine (in which case only fuel on board the car may be used for running the engine), no connection may be made to the fuel system of any car eligible to take part in Q3 during that period.
d) Other than a fuel breather and an external fuel pressurising device for starting the engine (in which case only fuel on board the car may be used for running the engine), or when race fuel is being added, no connection may be made to the fuel system of any car between the end of qualifying practice and the start of the race.
e) If a race is suspended refuelling is forbidden unless a car is already in the pit entry or pit lane when the signal to stop is given.
89. The driver may remain in his car throughout refuelling but, unless an FIA approved race refuelling system is used, the engine must be stopped.
Race refuelling systems may only be used in the pit lane but may not be used during, or immediately after, any free practice session. Whilst being used during the qualifying practice session or the race all team personnel working on the car must wear clothing which will protect all parts of their body from fire. Each competitor must ensure that an assistant equipped with a suitable fire extinguisher of adequate capacity is beside the car throughout all refuelling operations.

GENERAL SAFETY

90. Official instructions will be given to drivers by means of the signals laid out in the Code. Competitors must not use flags similar to these.
91. Drivers are strictly forbidden to drive their car in the opposite direction to the race unless this is absolutely necessary in order to move the car from a dangerous position.
92. Any driver intending to leave the track should signal his intention to do so in good time making sure that he can do this without danger.
93. a) During practice and the race, drivers may use only the track and must at all times observe the provisions of the Code relating to driving behaviour on circuits.
b) Other than by driving on the track, Competitors are not permitted to attempt to alter the grip of any part of the track surface.
94. A driver who abandons a car must leave it in neutral or with the clutch disengaged and with the steering wheel in place.
95. The organiser must make at least two fire extinguishers of 5kg capacity available to each competitor and ensure that they work properly.
96. Save as specifically authorised by the Code or these Sporting Regulations, no one except the driver may touch a stopped car unless it is in the paddock, the team's designated garage area, the pit lane or on the starting grid.

97. At no time may a car be reversed in the pit lane under its own power.
98. During the period commencing 15 minutes prior to and ending 5 minutes after every practice session and the period between the commencement of the formation lap which immediately precedes the race and the time when the last car enters the parc fermé, no one is allowed on the track, the pit entry or the pit exit with the exception of :
a) marshals or other authorised personnel in the execution of their duty ;
b) drivers when driving or on foot, having first received permission to do so from a marshal ;
c) team personnel when either pushing a car or clearing equipment from the grid after all cars able to do so have left the grid on the formation lap;
d) team personnel when assisting marshals to remove a car from the grid after the start of the race.
99. During a race, the engine may only be started with the starter except :
a) in the pit lane or the team's designated garage area where the use of an external starting device is allowed, or ;
b) under Article 142(b).
100. Drivers taking part in practice and the race must always wear the clothes, helmets and head and neck supports specified in the Code.
101. A speed limit of 60km/h will be imposed in the pit lane during all free practice sessions, this will be raised to 80km/h for the remainder of the Event. However, this limit may be amended by the Permanent Bureau of the Formula One Commission following a recommendation from the FIA F1 safety delegate.
Except in the race, any driver who exceeds the limit will be fined 200 for each km/h above the limit (this may be increased in the case of a second offence in the same Championship season).
During the race, the stewards may impose either of the penalties under Article 16.3a) or b) on any driver who exceeds the limit.
102. If a driver has serious mechanical difficulties during practice or the race he must leave the track as soon as it is safe to do so.
103. The car's rear light must be illuminated at all times when it is running on wet-weather tyres. It shall be at the discretion of the race director to decide if a driver should be stopped because his rear light is not working. Should a car be stopped in this way it may re-join when the fault has been remedied.
104. Only six team members per participating car (all of whom shall have been issued with and wearing special identification) are allowed in the signalling area during practice and the race. People under 16 years of age are not allowed in the pit lane.
105. Animals, except those which may have been expressly authorised by the FIA for use by security services, are forbidden on the track, in the pit lane, in the paddock or in any spectator area.
106. The race director, the clerk of the course or the FIA medical delegate can require a driver to have a medical examination at any time during an Event.
If, after an incident, the Medical Warning Light signals that threshold forces have been exceeded the driver must present himself for examination in the circuit medical centre without delay.

PRACTICE SESSIONS
107. Save where these Sporting Regulations require otherwise, pit lane and track discipline and safety measures will be the same for all practice sessions as for the race.
108. No driver may start in the race without taking part in at least one practice session on the second day of practice.
109. During all practices there will be a green and a red light at the end of the pit lane. Cars may only leave the pit lane when the green light is on. Additionally, a blue flag and/or a flashing blue light will be shown at the pit exit to warn drivers leaving the pits if cars are approaching on the track.
110. Unless written permission has been given by the FIA to do otherwise, the circuit may only be used for purposes other than the Event after the last practice session on each day of practice and on the day of the race no less than one hour before the pit lane is opened to allow cars to cover a reconnaissance lap.
111. The interval between the fourth free practice session and the qualifying practice session may never be less than two hours.
112. In the event of a driving infringement during any practice session the Stewards may Udrop the driver such number of grid positions as they consider appropriate. Unless it is completely clear that a driver committed a driving infringement any such incident will normally be investigated after the relevant session, anyU Upenalty imposed shall not be subject to appeal.
Where appropriate, regard will also be given to the provisions of Article 18.1.
Any driver taking part in any practice session who, in the opinion of the stewards, stops unnecessarily on the circuit or unnecessarily impedes another driver shall be subject to the penalties referred to in Article 31.6.
113. The clerk of the course may interrupt practice as often and for as long as he thinks necessary to clear the track or to allow the recovery of a car. However, only during qualifying practice will the session be extended as a result.
Should one or more sessions be thus interrupted, no protest can be accepted as to the possible effects of the interruption on the qualification of drivers admitted to start.

FREE PRACTICE
114. Free practice sessions will take place :
a) The day after initial scrutineering from 10.00 to 11.30 (P1) and from 14.00 to 15.30 (P2).
b) The day before the race from 11.00 to 12.00 (P3).

QUALIFYING PRACTICE
115. The qualifying practice session will take place on the day before the race from 14.00 to 15.00.
The session will be run as follows :
a) From 14.00 to 14.15 (Q1) all cars will be permitted on the track and at the end of this period the slowest five cars will be prohibited from taking any further part in the session.
Lap times achieved by the fifteen remaining cars will then be deleted.
b) From 14.22 to 14.37 (Q2) the fifteen remaining cars will be permitted on the track and at the end of this period the slowest five cars will be prohibited from taking any further part in the session.
Lap times achieved by the ten remaining cars will then be deleted.
c) From 14.45 to 15.00 (Q3) the ten remaining cars will be permitted on the track.
The above procedure is based upon a Championship entry of 20 cars. If 22 are entered six cars will be excluded after Q1 and Q2 and, if 24 are entered, six cars will be excluded after Q1 and Q2 leaving 12 cars eligible for Q3.
116. a) Any driver whose car stops on the circuit during the qualifying session will not be permitted to take any further part in the session. Any car which stops on the circuit during the qualifying session, and which is returned to the pits before the end of the session, will be held in parc ferme until the end of the session.
b) If, in the opinion of the stewards, a driver deliberately stops on the circuit or impedes another driver in any way during the qualifying practice session his times will be cancelled.

POST QUALIFYING PARC FERMÉ
117. Each car will be deemed to be in parc fermé from the time at which it leaves the pit lane for the first time during qualifying practice until the green lights are illuminated at the start of the formation lap which immediately precedes the start of the race.
Between these times, other than when cars are returned to the parc fermé overnight, the following work may be carried out :
- engines may be started ;
- subject to the requirements of Article 88 fuel may be added or removed and a fuel breather fitted ;
- wheels and tyres may be removed, changed or rebalanced and tyre pressures checked ;
- spark plugs may be removed in order to carry out an internal engine inspection and cylinder compression checks ;
- heating or cooling devices may be fitted ;
- a jump battery may be connected and on board electrical units may be freely accessed via a physical connection to the car ;
- the main electrical battery and radio batteries may be changed ;
- the brake system may be bled ;
- engine oil may be drained ;
- compressed gases may be drained or added ;
- fluids used for replenishment must conform to the same specification as the original fluid. Fluids with a specific gravity less than 1.1 may be drained and / or replenished, however, no replenishment may take place less than one hour and 30 minutes before the start of the formation lap unless specific approval has been given by the FIA. In order to ensure that fluids are not being used as ballast the FIA reserves the right to weigh cars which took part in Q3 at random during the one hour period commencing one hour and 30 minutes before the start of the formation lap. When a car is weighed in this way, and taking into account any fuel added under Article 88(b), its weight must be within 3kg of its weight at the completion of its final qualifying run, if not, fluids other than fuel may be replenished or drained under FIA supervision ;
- the aerodynamic set up of the front wing may be adjusted using the existing parts. No parts may be added, removed or replaced ;
- if the FIA technical delegate is satisfied that changes in climatic conditions necessitate alterations to the specification of a car, changes may be made to the air ducts around the front and rear brakes and radiator ducts. These changes may be made at any time after the message "CHANGE IN CLIMATIC CONDITIONS" is shown on the timing monitors, from this point the choice of brake cooling and radiator ducts is free.
- bodywork (excluding radiators) may be removed and / or cleaned ;
- cosmetic changes may be made to the bodywork and tape may be added ;
- any part of the car may be cleaned ;
- on board cameras, timing transponders and any associated equipment may be removed, refitted or checked ;
- any work required by the FIA technical delegate ;
- changes to improve the drivers comfort. In this context anything other than addition or removal of padding (or similar material) and adjustment of mirrors, seat belts and pedals may only be carried out with the specific permission of the FIA technical delegate ;
- repair of genuine accident damage ;
- any parts which are removed from the car in order to carry out any work specifically permitted above,
or any parts removed to carry out essential safety checks, must remain close to it and, at all times, be visible to the scrutineer assigned to the relevant car.
Any work not listed above may only be undertaken with the approval of the FIA technical delegate following a written request from the team concerned. It must be clear that any replacement part a team wishes to fit is similar in mass, inertia and function to the original. Any parts removed will be retained by the FIA.
However, if a team wishes to change a part during the qualifying session and/or on the grid before the start of the race, this may be done without first seeking the permission of the technical delegate, provided it is reasonable for the relevant team to believe permission would be given if there was time to ask and the broken or damaged part remains in full view of the scrutineer assigned to the car at all times.
118. At the end of the qualifying practice at least six cars will be chosen at random to undergo further checks, once informed their car has been selected the team concerned must take the car to the parc fermé immediately.
At some time before 18.30 all cars used during the qualifying practice session (or which were intended for use but failed to leave the pit lane) must be taken to the parc fermé, where they will remain secure until the following day. Whilst cars are in the parc fermé they may be covered and fitted with devices to keep them warm, no team personnel will be permitted there unless specifically authorised by the FIA technical delegate.
At 08.30 on the day of the race, or at other times if the relevant Event timetable makes this necessary, teams will be permitted to take their cars back to their garages where, again, they will remain under parc fermé conditions until the green lights are illuminated at the start of the formation lap which immediately precedes the first start of the race.
If a competitor modifies any part on the car or makes changes to the set up of the suspension whilst the car is being held under parc fermé conditions the relevant driver must start the race from the pit lane and follow the procedures laid out in Article 38.3.
One scrutineer will be allocated to each car for the purpose of ensuring that no unauthorised work is carried out whilst cars are being held under parc fermé conditions.
A list of parts replaced with the specific agreement of the FIA technical delegate whilst cars áre being held under parc fermé conditions will be published and distributed to all teams prior to the race.
In order that the scrutineers may be completely satisfied that no alterations have been made to the suspension systems or aerodynamic configuration of the car (with the exception of the front wing) whilst in post-qualifying parc fermé, it must be clear from physical inspection that changes cannot be made without the use of tools.

PRESS CONFERENCES AND DRIVERS PARADE
126. The FIA press delegate will choose a maximum of five drivers who must attend a press conference in the media centre for a period of one hour at 15.00 on the day before first practice. At Events taking place in North or South America this press conference will take place at 11.00. These drivers' teams will be notified no less than 48 hours before the conference. In addition, a maximum of two team personalities may be chosen by the FIA press delegate to attend this press conference.
On the first day of practice, a minimum of three and a maximum of six drivers and/or team personalities, (other than those who attended the press conference on the previous day and subject to the consent of the team principal) will be chosen by ballot or rota by the FIA press delegate during the Event and must make themselves available to the media for a press conference in the media centre for a period of one hour at 16.00.
No driver may enter into a contract which restricts his right to talk to any representative of the media during an Event. It shall be the duty of each team to ensure that their drivers do not unreasonably refuse to speak to any representative of the media during the Event.
127. Immediately after the qualifying practice session the first three drivers in the session will be required to make themselves available for television interviews in the unilateral room and then attend a press conference in the media centre for a maximum period of 30 minutes.
128. One and a half hours before the race all drivers must attend a drivers parade, Competitors will be given details of the parade by the press delegate.

THE GRID
129. At the end of qualifying practice the times achieved by each driver will be officially published.
130. a) The grid will be drawn up as follows :
I. The last five positions will be occupied by the cars eliminated during Q1, the fastest in 16th position.
II. The next five positions will be occupied by the cars eliminated during Q2, the fastest in 11th position.
III. The top ten positions will be occupied by the cars which took part in Q3, the fastest from the position on the grid which was the pole position in the previous year or, on a new circuit, has been designated as such by the FIA safety delegate.
If two or more drivers set identical times during Q1, Q2 or Q3 priority will be given to the one who set it first.
If more than 20 cars are entered in the Championship appropriate amendments will be made to the above in accordance with Article 115.
b) If more than one driver fails to set a time during Q1, Q2 or Q3 they will be arranged in the following order :
I. any driver who attempted to set a qualifying time by starting a flying lap ;
II. any driver who failed to start a flying lap ;
III. any driver who failed to leave the pits during the period.
c) Once the grid has been established in accordance with a) and b) above, grid position penalties will be applied to the drivers in question in the order the offences were committed. If more than one driver incurs a penalty under Article 28.4a) preference will be given to the driver whose team first informed the technical delegate that an engine change will be carried out.
d) Any driver who incurs a penalty under Article 28.4c) will take precedence over any driver whose qualifying times have been deleted for any reason.
If more than one driver falls into a single category in b) or d) above they will be arranged on the grid in numerical order.
131. The starting grid will be published no less than four hours before the race. Any competitor whose car(s) is (are) unable to start for any reason whatsoever (or who has good reason to believe that their car(s) will not be ready to start) must inform the stewards accordingly at the earliest opportunity and, in any event, no later than one hour and fifteen minutes before the start of the race. If one or more cars are withdrawn the grid will be closed up accordingly. The final starting grid will be published one hour before the start of the race.
132. The grid will be in a staggered 1 x 1 formation and the rows on the grid will be separated by 16 metres.

MEETINGS
133. Meetings, chaired by the race director, will take place at 16.00 on the day before first practice and 17.00 on the first day of practice. The first must be attended by all team managers and the second by all drivers.
Should the race director consider another meeting necessary it will take place three hours before the race, Competitors will be informed no later than three hours after the end of the qualifying practice session. All drivers and team managers must attend.

STARTING PROCEDURE
134. 30 minutes before the start of the formation lap the cars will leave the pit lane to cover a reconnaissance lap. At the end of this lap they will stop on the grid in starting order with their engines stopped.
Should they wish to cover more than one reconnaissance lap, this must be done by driving down the pit lane at greatly reduced speed between each of the laps.
135. Any car which has not taken up its position on the grid by the time the five minute signal is shown will not be permitted to do so and must start from the pit lane in accordance with Article 136.
136. 17 minutes before the start of the formation lap, a warning signal will be given indicating that the end of the pit lane will be closed in two minutes.
15 minutes before the start of the formation lap the end of the pit lane will be closed and a second warning signal will be given. Any car which is still in the pit lane can start from the end of the pit lane provided it got there under its own power. If more than one car is affected they must line up in the order in which they reached the end of the pit lane. These cars may then join the race once the whole field has passed the end of the pit lane for the first time after the start.
137. The approach of the start will be announced by signals shown ten minutes, five minutes, three minutes, one minute and fifteen seconds before the start of the formation lap, each of which will be accompanied by an audible warning.
When the ten minute signal is shown, everybody except drivers, officials and team technical staff must leave the grid. When the three minute signal is shown all cars must have their wheels fitted, after this signal wheels may only be removed in the pit lane or on the grid during a race suspension.
Any car which does not have all its wheels fully fitted at the three minute signal must start the race from the back of the grid or the pit lane. Under these circumstances a marshal holding a yellow flag will prevent the car (or cars) from leaving the grid until all cars able to do so have left to start the formation lap.
When the one minute signal is shown, engines should be started and all team personnel must leave the grid by the time the 15 second signal is given taking all equipment with them. If any driver needs assistance after the 15 second signal he must raise his arm and, when the remainder of the cars able to do so have left the grid, marshals will be instructed to push the car into the pit lane. In this case, marshals with yellow flags will stand beside any car (or cars) concerned to warn drivers behind.
When the green lights are illuminated, the cars will begin the formation lap with the pole position driver leading.
When leaving the grid all drivers must proceed at a greatly reduced speed until clear of any team personnel standing beside the track. Marshals will be instructed to push any car (or cars) which remain on the grid into the pit lane by the fastest route immediately after cars able to do so have left the grid. Any driver being pushed from the grid may not attempt to start the car and must follow the instructions of the marshals.
During the formation lap practice starts are forbidden and the formation must be kept as tight as possible.
Overtaking during the formation lap is only permitted if a car is delayed when leaving its grid position and cars behind cannot avoid passing it without unduly delaying the remainder of the field. In this case, drivers may only overtake to re-establish the original starting order.
Any driver who is delayed leaving the grid may not overtake another moving car if he was stationary after the remainder of the cars had crossed the Line, and must start the race from the back of the grid. If more than one driver is affected, they must form up at the back of the grid in the order they left to complete the formation lap. If the Line is not situated in front of pole position, and for the purposes of this Article as well as 138 and 149(m), it will be deemed to be a white line one metre in front of pole position.
Either of the penalties under Article 54a) or b) will be imposed on any driver who, in the opinion of the Stewards, unnecessarily overtook another car during the formation lap.
138. Any driver who is unable to start the formation lap must raise his arm and, after the remainder of the cars have crossed the Line, of the cars have crossed the Line, the car will be pushed into the pit lane by the fastest route.
139. When the cars come back to the grid at the end of the formation lap, they will stop on their respective grid positions, keeping their engines running.
There will be a standing start, the signal being given by means of lights activated by the permanent starter.
Once all the cars have come to a halt the five second light will appear followed by the four, three, two and one second lights. At any time after the one second light appears, the race will be started by extinguishing all red lights.
140. Unless specifically authorised by the FIA, during the start of a race the pit wall must be kept free of all persons with the exception of officials and fire marshals.
141. Any car which is unable to maintain starting order during the entire formation lap or is moving when the one second light comes on must enter the pit lane and start from the end of the pit lane as specified in Article 136.
This will not apply to any car which is temporarily delayed during the lap and which is able to regain its position, without endangering itself or any other car, before the leading car has taken up its position on the grid.
142. If, after returning to the starting grid at the end of the formation lap a problem arises, the following procedures shall apply :
a) If a car develops a problem that could endanger the start the driver must immediately raise his hands above his head and the marshal responsible for that row must immediately wave a yellow flag. If the race director decides the start should be delayed the green lights will be illuminated two seconds after the abort lights are switched on, a board saying "EXTRA FORMATION LAP" will be displayed and all cars able to do so must complete a further formation lap whilst the car which developed the problem is moved into the pit lane.
Every time this happens the race will be shortened by one lap.
b) If any other problem arises, and if the race director decides the start should be delayed, the following procedures shall apply :
1) If the race has not been started, the abort lights will be switched on, a board saying "DELAYED START" will be displayed, all engines will be stopped and the new formation lap will start 5 minutes later with the race distance reduced by one lap. The next signal will be the three minute signal.
Every time this happens the race will be shortened by one lap.
2) If the race has been started the marshals alongside the grid will wave their yellow flags to inform the drivers that a car is stationary on the grid.
3) If, after the start, a car is immobilised on the starting grid, it shall be the duty of the marshals to push it into the pit lane by the fastest route. Any driver being pushed from the grid may not attempt to start the car.
4) Once the car is in the pit lane his mechanics may attempt to start it, if successful the driver may rejoin the race. The driver and mechanics must follow the instructions of the track marshals at all times during such a procedure.
143. Should Article 142 apply, the race will nevertheless count for the Championship no matter how often the procedure is repeated, or how much the race is shortened as a result.
144. Either of the penalties under Article 54a) or b) will be imposed for a false start judged using an FIA supplied transponder which must be fitted to the car as specified.
145. Only in the following cases will any variation in the start procedure be allowed:
a) If it starts to rain after the three minute signal but before the race is started and, in the opinion of the race director teams should be given the opportunity to change tyres, the abort lights will be shown on the Line and the starting procedure will begin again at the ten minute point. If necessary the procedure set out in Article 137 will be followed.
b) If the start of the race is imminent and, in the opinion of the race director, the volume of water on the track is such that it cannot be negotiated safely even on wet-weather tyres, the abort lights will be shown on the Line and information concerning the likely delay will be displayed on the timing monitors. Once the start time is known at least ten minutes warning will be given.
c) If the race is started behind the safety car, Article 149(m) will apply.
146. The stewards may use any video or electronic means to assist them in reaching a decision. The stewards may overrule judges of fact. A breach of the provisions of the Code or these Sporting Regulations relating to the starting procedure, may result in the exclusion of the car and driver concerned from the Event.

THE RACE
147. Team orders which interfere with a race result are prohibited.
148. During the race, drivers leaving the pit lane may only do so when the light at the end of the pit lane is green and on their own responsibility. A marshal with a blue flag and/or a flashing blue light, will also warn the driver if cars are approaching on the track.

SAFETY CAR
149. The FIA safety car will be driven by an experienced circuit driver. It will carry an FIA observer capable of recognising all the competing cars, who is in permanent radio contact with race control.
30 minutes before thestart of the formation lap the safety car will take up position at the front of the grid and remain there until the five minute signal is given. At this point (except under m) below) it will cover a whole lap of the circuit and enter the pit lane.
The safety car may be brought into operation to neutralise a race upon the order of the clerk of the course.
It will be used only if competitors or officials are in immediate physical danger but the circumstances are not such as to necessitate suspending the race.
When the order is given to deploy the safety car the message "SAFETY CAR DEPLOYED" will be displayed on the timing monitors and all marshal's posts will display waved yellow flags and "SC" boards for the duration of the intervention.
The safety car will start from the pit lane with its orange lights illuminated and will join the track regardless of where the race leader is.
From the time at which the "SAFETY CAR DEPLOYED" message is displayed no car may enter the pit lane for the purpose of refuelling until all cars on the track have formed up in a line behind the safety car and the message "PIT LANE OPEN" is shown on the timing monitors. A ten second time penalty (see Article 16.3b) will be imposed on any driver who enters the pit lane and whose car is refuelled before the second message is shown on the timing monitors. However, any car which was in the pit entry or pit lane when the safety car was deployed will not incur a penalty.
If it is deemed necessary for the safety car to use the pit lane (see 40.11 below) cars following it will not incur a penalty but may not stop in their designated garage areas for the purpose of refuelling until the message "PIT LANE OPEN" is shown on the timing monitors. A ten second time penalty will be imposed on any driver who stops in his designated garage area and whose car is refuelled before the second message is shown on the timing monitors.
Any car being driven unnecessarily slowly, erratically or which is deemed potentially dangerous to other drivers at any time whilst the safety car is deployed will be reported to the stewards. This will apply whether any such car is being driven on the track, the pit entry or the pit lane.
All competing cars must then form up in line behind the safety car no more than 5 car lengths apart and overtaking, with the following exceptions, is forbidden until the cars reach the Line after the safety car has returned to the pits. Overtaking will be permitted under the following circumstances :
- if a car is signalled to do so from the safety car ;
- under m) below ;
- any car entering the pits may pass another car or the safety car remaining on the track after it has crossed the first safety car line ;
- any car leaving the pits may be overtaken by another car on the track before it crosses the second safety car line ;
- when the safety car is returning to the pits it may be overtaken by cars on the track once it has crossed the first safety car line ;
- any car stopping in its designated garage area whilst the safety car is using the pit lane (see 40.11 below) may be overtaken ;
- if any car slows with an obvious problem.
When ordered to do so by the clerk of the course the observer in the car will use a green light to signal to any cars between it and the race leader that they should pass. These cars will continue at reduced speed and without overtaking until they reach the line of cars behind the safety car.
The safety car shall be used at least until the leader is behind it and all remaining cars are lined up behind him.
Once behind the safety car, the race leader must keep within 5 car lengths of it (except under j) below) and all remaining cars must keep the formation as tight as possible.
Subject to the requirements of 40.6 above, whilst the safety car is in operation, competing cars may enter the pit lane, but may only rejoin the track when the green light at the end of the pit lane is on. It will be on at all times except when the safety car and the line of cars following it are about to pass or are passing the pit exit. A car rejoining the track must proceed at reduced speed until it reaches the end of the line of cars behind the safety car.
Under certain circumstances the clerk of the course may ask the safety car to use the pit lane. In these cases, and provided it's orange lights remain illuminated, all cars must follow it into the pit lane without overtaking. Subject to the requirements of 40.6 above, any car entering the pit lane under these circumstances may stop at its designated garage area.
When the clerk of the course calls in the safety car, it must extinguish its orange lights, this will be the signal to the drivers that it will be entering the pit lane at the end of that lap.
At this point the first car in line behind the safety car may dictate the pace and, if necessary, fall more than five car lengths behind it.
As the safety car is approaching the pit entry the yellow flags and SC boards will be withdrawn and replaced by waved green flags with green lights at the Line. These will be displayed until the last car crosses the Line.
Each lap completed while the safety car is deployed will be counted as a race lap.
If the race ends whilst the safety car is deployed it will enter the pit lane at the end of the last lap and the cars will take the chequered flag as normal without overtaking.
m) In exceptional circumstances the race may be started behind the safety car. In this case, at any time before the one minute signal its orange lights will be turned on. This is the signal to the drivers that the race will be started behind the safety car. When the green lights are illuminated the safety car will leave the grid with all cars following in grid order no more than 5 car lengths apart. There will be no formation lap and race will start when the green lights are illuminated.
Overtaking, during the first lap only, is permitted if a car is delayed when leaving its grid position and cars behind cannot avoid passing it without unduly delaying the remainder of the field. In this case, drivers may only overtake to re-establish the original starting order.
Any driver who is delayed leaving the grid may not overtake another moving car if he was stationary after the remainder of the cars had crossed the Line, and must form up at the back of the line of cars behind the safety car. If more than one driver is affected, they must form up at the back of the field in the order they left the grid.
Either of the penalties under Article 54a) or b) will be imposed on any driver who, in the opinion of the Stewards, unnecessarily overtook another car during the first lap.

SUSPENDING A RACE
150. Should it become necessary to suspend the race because the circuit is blocked by an accident or because weather or other conditions make it dangerous to continue, the clerk of the course will order red flags to be shown at all marshal posts and the abort lights to be shown at the Line.
When the signal is given overtaking is forbidden, the pit exit will be closed and all cars must proceed slowly to the red flag line where they must stop in staggered formation.
If any cars are unable to return to the grid as a result of the track being blocked they will be brought back when the track is cleared and will be arranged in the order they occupied before the race was suspended. The order will be taken at the last point at which it was possible to determine the position of all cars. Any such cars will then be permitted to resume the race.
The Safety Car will then be driven to the front of the line of cars behind the red flag line.
Whilst the race is suspended :
- neither the race nor the timekeeping system will stop ;
- cars may be worked on once they have stopped behind the red flag line or entered the pits but any such work must not impede the resumption of the race ;
- refuelling is forbidden unless a car was already in the pit entry or pit lane when the signal to suspend the race was given ;
- only team members and officials will be permitted on the grid.
Cars may enter the pit lane when the race is suspended but a drive through penalty (see Article 54) will be imposed on any driver who enters the pit lane or whose car is pushed from the grid to the pit lane after the race has been suspended. Any car which was in the pit entry or pit lane when the race was suspended will not incur a penalty.
All cars in the pit lane will be permitted to leave the pits once the race has been resumed but any which were in the pit entry or pit lane when the race was suspended will be released before any others. Subject to the above, any car intending to resume the race from the pit exit may do so in the order they got there under their own power, unless another car was unduly delayed. Under these circumstances working in the fast lane will be permitted but any such work will be restricted to:
- starting the engine and any directly associated preparation ;
- the fitting or removal of cooling and heating devices ;
- changing wheels.
At all times drivers must follow the directions of the marshals.

RESUMING A RACE
151. The delay will be kept as short as possible and as soon as a resumption time is known teams will be informed via the timing monitors, in all cases at least ten minutes warning will be given.
Signals will be shown ten minutes, five minutes, three minutes, one minute and fifteen seconds before the resumption and each of these will be accompanied by an audible warning.
When the three minute signal is shown all cars must have their wheels fitted, after this signal wheels may only be removed in the pit lane or on the grid during a further race suspension. Any car which does not have all its wheels fully fitted at the three minute signal must start the race from the back of the grid or the pit lane. Under these circumstances a marshal holding a yellow flag will prevent the car (or cars) from leaving the grid until all cars able to do so have crossed the red flag line.
At some point after the three minute signal, which will be dependent upon the expected lap time, any cars between the red flag line and the leader, in addition to any lapped cars between cars on the lead lap, will be waved off to complete a further lap, without overtaking, and join the line of cars behind the safety car.
When the one minute signal is shown, engines should be started and all team personnel must leave the grid by the time the 15 second signal is given taking all equipment with them. If any driver needs assistance after the 15 second signal he must raise his arm and, when the remainder of the cars able to do so have left the grid, marshals will be instructed to push the car into the pit lane. In this case, marshals with yellow flags will stand beside any car (or cars) concerned to warn drivers behind.
The race will be resumed behind the safety car when the green lights are illuminated. The safety car will enter the pits after one lap unless :
- all cars are not yet in a line behind the safety car ;
- team personnel are still clearing the grid ;
- a further incident occurs necessitating another intervention.
When the green lights are illuminated the safety car will leave the grid with all cars following no more than 5 car lengths apart. Soon after the last car in line behind the safety car passes the end of the pit lane (including any cars which were waved off under 42.3 above) the pit exit light will be turned green, any car in the pit lane may then enter the track and join the line of cars behind the safety car.
Overtaking during the lap is permitted only if a car is delayed when leaving the red flag line and cars behind cannot avoid passing it without unduly delaying the remainder of the field. In this case, drivers may only overtake to re-establish the order before the race was suspended.
Any driver who is delayed leaving the red flag line may not overtake another moving car if he was stationary after the remainder of the cars had crossed the Line, and must form up at the back of the line of cars behind the safety car. If more than one driver is affected, they must form up at the back of the field in the order they left the grid.
Either of the penalties under Article 54a) or b) will be imposed on any driver who, in the opinion of the Stewards, unnecessarily overtook another car during the lap.
During this lap Articles 40.13, 40.14, 40.15 and 40.16 will apply.
If the race cannot be resumed the results will be taken at the end of the penultimate lap before the lap during which the signal to suspend the race was given.

FINISH
152. The end-of-race signal will be given at the Line as soon as the leading car has covered the full race distance in accordance with Article 5.3.
153. Should for any reason the end-of-race signal be given before the leading car completes the scheduled number of laps, or the prescribed time has been completed, the race will be deemed to have finished when the leading car last crossed the Line before the signal was given.
Should the end-of- race signal be delayed for any reason, the race will be deemed to have finished when it should have finished.
154. After receiving the end-of-race signal all cars must proceed on the circuit directly to the post race parc fermé without any unnecessary delay, without receiving any object whatsoever and without any assistance (except that of the marshals if necessary).
Any classified car which cannot reach the post race parc fermé under its own power will be placed under the exclusive control of the marshals who will take the car to the parc fermé.

POST RACE PARC FERME
155. Only those officials charged with supervision may enter the post race parc fermé. No intervention of any kind is allowed there unless authorised by such officials.
156. When the parc fermé is in use, parc fermé regulations will apply in the area between the Line and the parc fermé entrance.
157. The parc fermé shall be secured such that no unauthorised persons can gain access to it.

CLASSIFICATION
158. The car placed first will be the one having covered the scheduled distance in the shortest time, or, where appropriate, passed the Line in the lead at the end of two hours (or more if the race is suspended, see Article 5.3). All cars will be classified taking into account the number of complete laps they have covered, and for those which have completed the same number of laps, the order in which they crossed the Line.
159. Cars having covered less than 90% of the number of laps covered by the winner (rounded down to the nearest whole number of laps), will not be classified.
160. The official classification will be published after the race. It will be the only valid result subject to any amendments which may be made under the Code and these Sporting Regulations.

PODIUM CEREMONY
161. The drivers finishing the race in 1st, 2nd and 3rd positions and a representative of the winning constructor must attend the prize-giving ceremony on the podium and abide by the podium procedure set out in Appendix 3 (except Monaco); and immediately thereafter make themselves available for a period of one hour and 30 minutes for the purpose of television unilateral interviews and the press conference in the media centre.

Meaning of the flags

- White flag: service vehicule on track
- Blue flag: (immobile): a car is close behind you
  (waving): a car is about to overtake you
- Yellow flag: (immobile): overtaking is prohibited, danger
  (waving) immediate danger, slow down
- Red flag: (by marshals and the Clerk of the race): stopping of the race on the Line
- Green flag: end of danger, free track
- Yellow with red stripes flag: danger, slippery surface
- Black flag: (with car number): stop on the next lap
- Black with yellow circle flag: your car is in danger
- Black and white flag: non-sporting behaviour, warning
- Chequered flag: end of the race or the practice